Data-Driven Monetization Strategies for Economic Insights

Olga Ergunova
https://orcid.org/0009-0006-2267-8121
Peter the Great St. Petersburg Polytechnic University, Russia

Tawheed Nabi
Lovely Professional University, India

Pooja Kansra
https://orcid.org/0000-0003-2229-0662
Mittal School of Business, Lovely Professional University, India

Utkarsh Gupta
University of Connecticut, USA

IGI Global
Scientific Publishing
Publishing Tomorrow's Research Today

Vice President of Editorial	Melissa Wagner
Director of Acquisitions	Mikaela Felty
Director of Book Development	Jocelynn Hessler
Production Manager	Mike Brehm
Cover Design	Jose Rosado

Published in the United States of America by
IGI Global Scientific Publishing
701 East Chocolate Avenue
Hershey, PA, 17033, USA
Tel: 717-533-8845 | Fax: 717-533-7115
Website: https://www.igi-global.com E-mail: cust@igi-global.com

Library of Congress Cataloging-in-Publication Data

Names: Ergunova, Olga Titovna, 1980- editor
Title: Data-driven monetization strategies for economic insights / [edited by] Olga Titovna Ergunova, Tawheed Nabi, Pooja Kansra, Utkarsh Gupta.
Description: Hershey, PA : IGI Global Scientific Publishing, 2026. | Includes bibliographical references and index. | Summary: "This book aims to explore the broader implications of data-driven decision-making, emphasizing the role of economic insights in shaping business strategies, improving operational efficiency, and fostering innovation"-- Provided by publisher.
Identifiers: LCCN 2025021288 (print) | LCCN 2025021289 (ebook) | ISBN 9798337327723 hardcover | ISBN 9798337327730 paperback | ISBN 9798337327747 ebook
Subjects: LCSH: Decision making | Strategic planning | Big data--Economic aspects | Information technology--Management
Classification: LCC HD30.23 .D371595 2026 (print) | LCC HD30.23 (ebook) | DDC 658.4/03--dc23/eng/20260126
LC record available at https://lccn.loc.gov/2025021288
LC ebook record available at https://lccn.loc.gov/2025021289
British Cataloguing in Publication Data
A Cataloguing in Publication record for this book is available from the British Library.

Table of Contents

Detailed Table of Contents

This study investigates the function of data-driven marketing in providing tailored solutions to insurance consumers through the approach of predictive analysis. Availability of authentic consumer data helps insurance companies to understand patterns of consumer behaviour and risk profiles more accurately and tailor their marketing strategies. In this study, we examined the impact of factors of data-driven customized marketing on the overall effectiveness of customized insurance solutions. We collected primary data from 125 insurance customers who have bought an insurance policy in the last five years and who have been offered a new policy at least twice in the last year. It was found that the factors, namely Proactive Engagement, Customer satisfaction, Targeted communication, and Personalized products, affect the overall effectiveness of customized insurance solutions significantly.

In the present digital economy, data has become one of the most powerful economic assets reshaping how businesses create value, consumers experience services and governments design policy. This chapter takes a deep dive into strategically transforming raw and unstructured data into monetizable economic value. It explores deeply how organizations use different types of data through structured processes of collection, preservation, integration, and analysis to drive efficiency, innovation, and competitive advantage. By highlighting different data monetization models ranging from direct commercialization to insight-driven service enhancement, this chapter presents a roadmap for leveraging data in ways that go beyond operational

universality and strategic alignment, while revealing limitations in ethical compliance and direct commercialization. Case studies from companies like Walmart, JPMorgan Chase, and Amazon illustrate practical applications and scalability challenges. Recommendations include enhancing adaptability, addressing data quality, and incorporating ethical considerations.

India stands at a pivotal juncture in its economic development, with digital innovation and data analytics poised to be key drivers of inclusive and sustainable growth. This study explores the role of data-driven monetization strategies in promoting robust economic growth and investigates how technological infrastructure and policy interventions influence their success. Data is increasingly seen as a vital economic asset, "the new oil" capable of enhancing efficiencies and generating revenue across sectors, from agriculture and manufacturing to governance and services. Yet, India's progress in leveraging this asset remains modest due to regional disparities in digital infrastructure and fragmented policy frameworks. This research emphasises that the benefits of data monetization extend beyond technology, requiring supportive policy environments. Holistic efforts, such as investments in digital literacy, data protection, and innovation-friendly governance, are essential to ensure inclusive, nationwide participation.

Digital currencies such as cryptocurrencies and central bank digital currencies (CBDC.s) have transformed the financial transactions and economies across the globe. The monetization of such digital assets hinges on data driven strategies, with block-chain analytics, market trends, and economic indicators. This paper explores direct and indirect revenue models, focusing on trading, stacking, decentralized finance (DeFi), and block-chain analytics. Additionally, it examines regulatory and ethical challenges while presenting case studies of successful monetization strategies. The research highlights how businesses and investors can utilize big data and AI-driven insights to maximize profitability in the digital currency market. The study also explores emerging trends in digital currency adaption and discusses potential risks

Social media platforms are among the most effective tools for modern marketing. They help increase brand awareness and allow direct communication with consumers. This chapter discusses the steps needed to effectively manage social media marketing. It provides guidance for marketers aiming to achieve better results. The chapter highlights the importance of using data to create effective social media plans. It emphasizes selecting the right channels for target audiences and developing engaging content. Key topics include audience segmentation and defining audience personas. Understanding user behaviour and preferences is crucial for success. Real-life examples and case studies are included to show how to improve campaigns. The chapter also explores new trends and developments in social media marketing. It discusses how businesses can adapt to innovations in the digital environment. Whether you are new to marketing or experienced, this chapter helps you confidently navigate and succeed in social media marketing.

This chapter provides a thorough analysis of the gender pay gap persistent in India, which impedes inclusive economic growth along with social justice. It describes the gap, current statistical overview, and indicators, and examines the causes, including deep-rooted labor division, cultural & social norms, education, and uneven burden of unpaid domestic work, and workplace discrimination. At the lower levels of wage distribution, there is a vivid manifestation of the "sticky floor" effect, and it targets women, especially those who belong prominently to marginalized communities. In addition to the visible factors, the essential contributors are employment segregation, the lack of equity due to the unequal distribution of unpaid household care among women, and workplace discrimination. The chapter advocates for multi-dimensional policy response, aimed at interventions by targeting discrimination, to challenge deep-rooted gender norms, to establish equitable pay structures and open more flexible working opportunities, to create the truly thriving and equitable work culture in India.

The research aimes to develop an AI literacy assessment approach for university faculty members in Russia. Theoretical background formed the TPACK framework and theory of planned behavior. The research design included two stages. During the first stage we conducted an exploratory literature review to analyze existing frameworks for AI-literacy of non-experts in AI, which could be relevant for educational context. During the second stage, content analysis of universities' faculty personal plans and vacancies' announcements on hh.ru helped to derive a list of jobs to be done with a help of generative AI tools. The introduced scale consists of 6 groups of tasks, 4 in each: Teaching Activities, Research Activities, Organizational and Methodological Work, Educational and Methodological Work, Professional Development, Consulting Services. We developed a scoring scale to evaluate the level of AI literacy. The authors acknowledges contribution offered by AI Lab of the Center for Teaching Excellence in business education at GSOM SPBU.

In a promptly altering data-driven business scape, managing teams including data analysts, economists, and managers becomes a key factor in the success of organizations. This chapter of the monograph scrutinizes the primary aspects and superior practices of integrating these three professional squads in order to create highly effective teams capable of making informed decisions based on data analysis and economic forecasting. Effective cooperation between data analysts, economists,

Preface

In the digital age, data is often heralded as the new oil—an abundant resource with the potential to fuel innovation, drive strategy, and generate tangible economic value. Yet, just as crude oil must be refined to yield energy, data must be strategically analyzed and activated to unlock its true potential. As editors of *Data-Driven Monetization Strategies for Economic Insights*, we are pleased to present a volume that tackles this pressing challenge: transforming raw data into actionable, revenue-generating insights.

Today's organizations operate in a landscape defined by complexity, speed, and constant change. Businesses now have access to unprecedented volumes of data—from internal operations and customer interactions to external market signals. However, the real competitive advantage lies not in the mere possession of data but in the ability to extract economic insight from it. This book bridges the gap between data analytics and economic strategy, offering a comprehensive and practical guide to data monetization in a business context.

The chapters in this volume collectively offer a blend of strategic frameworks, analytical tools, and real-world case studies, equipping decision-makers with the knowledge needed to identify data assets, derive value from them, and convert that value into business outcomes. By integrating foundational economic principles with modern data science techniques, the book delivers both theoretical depth and practical relevance.

We structured this book to address some of the most urgent and frequently asked questions among today's business leaders:

- How can organizations identify and quantify the value of their data assets?
- Which tools and models best support the generation of economic insights?
- What strategies can firms adopt to monetize data—directly or indirectly?
- How can a data-first culture be built and aligned with long-term economic goals?

- What ethical boundaries must be respected as data becomes an increasingly monetizable asset?

This book is intended for a diverse audience. Mid-to-senior-level managers will find actionable strategies to enhance decision-making and operational efficiency. Entrepreneurs and startups can leverage these insights to build scalable, data-driven business models. Students and academics will gain a practical lens on how economic theories translate into real-world applications. And for data analysts and consultants, the book offers a broader understanding of how their work impacts business strategy and financial performance.

Ultimately, our aim is to empower organizations to move beyond data collection—to treat data as a strategic asset capable of driving innovation, informing strategy, and delivering measurable economic returns. We hope this book serves as both a guide and an inspiration for anyone seeking to lead in the emerging data economy.

ORGANIZATION OF THE BOOK

As editors of this comprehensive reference book, we are delighted to present a collection of cutting-edge research that explores the transformative power of data-driven strategies across diverse industries and contexts. Each chapter offers unique insights into how data, as a pivotal economic asset, reshapes business practices, policy frameworks, and societal outcomes. From personalized insurance solutions to digital currency monetization and sustainable finance, the studies compiled here provide both theoretical depth and practical applications for leveraging data to drive innovation, efficiency, and economic value. This preface offers an overview of the chapters, each contributing to our understanding of data's role in the modern digital economy.

Chapter 1: Role of Data-Driven Marketing in Providing Customised Solutions to Insurance Customers: A Predictive Analysis Approach

In this opening chapter, the authors explore how data-driven marketing revolutionizes the insurance industry by enabling tailored solutions for customers. Through predictive analysis, the study leverages authentic consumer data to uncover patterns in behavior and risk profiles, allowing insurers to craft targeted marketing strategies. Drawing on primary data from 125 insurance customers, the research identifies key factors—proactive engagement, customer satisfaction, targeted communication, and personalized products—that significantly enhance the effectiveness of customized insurance solutions. This chapter sets the stage for understanding how data empowers organizations to meet individual customer needs with precision.

Chapter 2: Data as an Asset: From Raw Information to Revenue

This chapter delves into the strategic transformation of raw data into a monetizable asset in today's digital economy. The authors outline how organizations harness structured processes for data collection, preservation, integration, and analysis to drive efficiency, innovation, and competitive advantage. By examining various monetization models, from direct commercialization to insight-driven service enhancements, the chapter provides a roadmap for organizations to unlock data's economic potential. It also addresses institutional challenges such as data ownership, governance, and regulatory compliance, emphasizing data's role as a valuable resource when managed effectively.

Chapter 3: Data-Driven Monetization Strategies for Economic Insights—Models, Tools, and Impact on Decision-Making

Focusing on data-driven monetization strategies, this chapter highlights their transformative impact on economic decision-making. The authors explore how organizations employ direct and indirect models to extract value from data, utilizing tools like business intelligence, predictive analytics, and artificial intelligence. The study underscores the importance of fostering a data-centric culture, bridging cross-functional expertise, and addressing ethical considerations around privacy and transparency. Through industry-specific case studies, the chapter illustrates how these strategies enhance profitability and enable resilient, informed decision-making.

Chapter 4: From Data Extraction to Economic Insights: A Holistic Approach to Monetization

This chapter proposes a comprehensive framework for data monetization, integrating automated tools such as machine learning (XGBoost, Prophet), web scraping (Scrapy, Airflow), and business intelligence platforms (Tableau, Power BI). Aligned with Balanced Scorecard perspectives, the model optimizes processes and enhances customer experiences while delivering measurable financial outcomes. Through comparative analysis with frameworks like DAMA DMBOK and case studies from companies like Walmart and Amazon, the authors highlight the model's strengths and limitations, offering recommendations to address ethical compliance and scalability challenges.

Chapter 5: Unlocking India's Economic Potential: Data-Driven Monetization Strategies for Sustainable Growth

Focusing on India's economic landscape, this chapter examines how data-driven monetization strategies can drive inclusive and sustainable growth. The authors explore how technological infrastructure and policy interventions shape the success of these strategies across sectors like agriculture, manufacturing, and governance. Despite India's potential, challenges such as regional disparities and fragmented policies hinder progress. The study advocates for holistic efforts, including investments in digital literacy and data protection, to ensure that data, often termed "the new oil," fosters nationwide economic participation.

Chapter 6: Strategic Perspectives on Digital Currency Monetization: Balancing Risk and Opportunity

This chapter investigates the monetization of digital currencies, such as cryptocurrencies and central bank digital currencies, through data-driven strategies. By leveraging blockchain analytics, market trends, and AI-driven insights, the authors explore revenue models like trading, staking, and decentralized finance (DeFi). Case studies highlight successful monetization approaches, while the chapter also addresses regulatory, ethical, and security challenges. This work provides a forward-looking perspective on how businesses and investors can maximize profitability in the evolving digital currency market.

Chapter 7: Digital Transformation in Banking—Enhancing Customer Experience Through Technological Innovation

This chapter examines the role of digital technologies, such as AI-powered chatbots, blockchain, and mobile banking apps, in transforming the banking sector. By enabling seamless access to services and personalized customer experiences, these innovations strengthen client relationships and loyalty. The authors highlight how digitalization not only enhances customer support but also drives the development of new financial products tailored to evolving consumer needs. This study bridges theoretical insights with practical implications for the banking industry's digital evolution.

Chapter 8: Leveraging Artificial Intelligence for Tax Monetization

Focusing on India's tax collection system, this chapter explores how artificial intelligence enhances compliance, efficiency, and revenue forecasting. By integrating AI-driven methods, the study demonstrates improvements in tax administration through well-maintained records and streamlined processes. The authors emphasize the potential of AI to create a robust, equitable tax system, offering insights for policymakers and future research. This chapter underscores the transformative role of AI in generating tax-related income.

Chapter 9: Navigating the Social Media Landscape: Strategies for Effective Marketing

This chapter provides a practical guide for marketers to harness social media platforms for effective brand communication. By emphasizing data-driven strategies, the authors highlight the importance of audience segmentation, persona development, and engaging content tailored to specific channels. Real-life case studies illustrate how businesses can optimize campaigns and adapt to emerging trends in the digital environment. This chapter equips both novice and experienced marketers with strategies to succeed in the dynamic world of social media marketing.

Chapter 10: Gender Pay Gap in India—Causes, Consequences, and Cures

Addressing a critical social and economic issue, this chapter analyzes the persistent gender pay gap in India, which hinders inclusive growth and social justice. The authors examine causes such as labor division, cultural norms, and workplace discrimination, with a focus on the "sticky floor" effect impacting marginalized women. Proposing a multi-dimensional policy response, the chapter advocates for interventions to challenge gender norms, establish equitable pay structures, and promote flexible work arrangements to foster a thriving, inclusive work culture.

Chapter 11: Exploring Operational and Strategic Issues in India-China Trade from Indian Stakeholders' Perspective

This chapter investigates challenges faced by Indian stakeholders in trade with China, based on a survey of 120 exporters and importers. The study identifies internal barriers like high import duties and inadequate infrastructure, alongside external challenges such as tariff barriers and price sensitivity. Recommendations include rationalizing tariffs, improving infrastructure, and enhancing manufacturing capabilities to align with initiatives like Make in India. This work offers stakeholder-driven insights to strengthen India's trade competitiveness.

Chapter 12: Predict and Prosper: Application of Advanced Machine Learning for FMCG Consumer Behavior Prediction

In the fast-moving consumer goods (FMCG) industry, this chapter explores how machine learning algorithms, including decision trees and deep learning models, predict consumer behavior. By integrating structured transactional data with unstructured sources like social media sentiment, the study develops holistic predictive models. The results demonstrate how predictive analytics enhances supply chain efficiency, reduces inefficiencies, and improves customer experiences, empowering FMCG companies to stay competitive.

Chapter 13: Generative AI Literacy of University Faculty Members in Russia

This chapter develops an AI literacy assessment framework for university faculty in Russia, grounded in the TPACK framework and theory of planned behavior. Through literature reviews and content analysis of faculty plans and job postings, the authors identify key tasks where generative AI tools can enhance teaching, research, and professional development. The proposed scoring scale offers a practical tool for evaluating AI literacy, contributing to educational innovation in business contexts.

Chapter 14: Teams' Management Derived from Data: Incentive Collaboration Between Data Analysts, Economists, and Managers

This chapter examines how effective collaboration between data analysts, economists, and managers drives organizational success in a data-driven business landscape. By analyzing the unique skills of each group, the authors propose strategies to foster an environment conducive to informed decision-making and innovation. The study addresses barriers to collaboration and offers practical solutions to enhance team performance and organizational outcomes.

Chapter 15: Higher Education Students' Engagement with Data-Driven Fintech for Sustainable Finance

Focusing on higher education students as future fintech users, this chapter explores how digital technologies like mobile banking, blockchain, and AI influence financial literacy and sustainability. Based on surveys, the study highlights students' exposure to fintech and its role in fostering financial inclusion, particularly for underserved populations. The findings underscore fintech's potential to drive sustainable finance among younger generations.

Chapter 16: User-Oriented Business Process Visualization to Close the Information Gap Between User and Company

This chapter addresses the information gap between organizations and end-users through business process visualization. By integrating user narratives into data visualizations, the study demonstrates improvements in employee performance, cost reduction, and user trust. The authors advocate for narrative-driven visualizations to enhance transparency, user satisfaction, and strategic economic outcomes.

Chapter 17: Hope, Nihilism, and Faith in the World of Professional Wrestling and Its Data-Driven Monetization

Exploring philosophical themes in the context of professional wrestling, this chapter examines how data-driven monetization intersects with concepts of humanity, hope, and nihilism. The authors analyze how data strategies enhance fan engagement and revenue generation in this unique industry, while reflecting on the broader societal implications of hope and disenchantment in a data-driven world.

We hope this collection inspires researchers, practitioners, and policymakers to harness data's potential for innovation, equity, and sustainable growth across diverse domains.

CONCLUSION

As editors of this reference book, we are immensely proud to present a collection that illuminates the profound impact of data-driven strategies across industries, economies, and societies. The chapters within this volume collectively underscore the transformative potential of data as a catalyst for innovation, efficiency, and equitable progress. From revolutionizing insurance and banking through personalized solutions to unlocking sustainable economic growth in India, the studies highlight how data empowers organizations to navigate complex challenges and seize new opportunities. The exploration of digital currencies, social media marketing, and AI-driven tax systems further demonstrates the versatility of data as a strategic asset, while critical analyses of issues like the gender pay gap and India-China trade remind us of the need for inclusive and ethical approaches. The philosophical reflections in the final chapter, set against the backdrop of professional wrestling, invite us to consider the broader human implications of a data-driven world. Together, these works provide a robust framework for researchers, practitioners, and policymakers to harness data's potential responsibly. We hope this book inspires continued exploration and application of data-driven insights to foster a future that is innovative, inclusive, and resilient.

Chapter 1
Role of Data-Driven Marketing in Providing Customised Solutions to Insurance Customers:
A Predictive Analysis Approach

Arun Mittal
https://orcid.org/0000-0003-0602-8066
Birla Institute of Technology, India

Nirmal Singh
https://orcid.org/0009-0006-5627-0511
Sri Guru Gobind Singh College of Commerce, Univesity of Delhi, India

Manmohan Chaudhry
K.R. Mangalam University, Gurgaon, India

Dimitrie Stoica
https://orcid.org/0000-0001-5495-7076
Dunarea de Jos University of Galati, Romania

ABSTRACT

This study investigates the function of data-driven marketing in providing tailored solutions to insurance consumers through the approach of predictive analysis. Availability of authentic consumer data helps insurance companies to understand patterns of consumer behaviour and risk profiles more accurately and tailor their marketing strategies. In this study, we examined the impact of factors of data-driven customized marketing on the overall effectiveness of customized insurance solutions.

DOI: 10.4018/979-8-3373-2772-3.ch001

We collected primary data from 125 insurance customers who have bought an insurance policy in the last five years and who have been offered a new policy at least twice in the last year. It was found that the factors, namely Proactive Engagement, Customer satisfaction, Targeted communication, and Personalized products, affect the overall effectiveness of customized insurance solutions significantly.

INTRODUCTION

In the modern era, it is seen that communication technologies have loopholes in strategies and lead to incomplete and ineffective processes. In the rapidly evolving world, effective communication can help in shaping the company's internal and external alterations. Study helps in understanding the challenges in changing people's mindsets and behaviors, and not just processes and structures, to make a larger impact. Insurance is considered the backbone of the nation's risk management system. As risk is an imperative part of our lives, insurance becomes a shield and a necessary element to be added by individuals. The insurers provide a plethora of products to consumers for protection and financial security. As an intermediary, insurance industry helps in maintaining the liquidity in the financial system and plays an active role in stabilizing the market during any fluctuations (Krishnamurthy et al., 2005). The insurance sector is experiencing new ideas for selling its products and connecting with customers in the long term. Disruptive technology like blockchain, Internet of Things (IoT), Artificial Intelligence, Chatbots, Telematics, Virtual Reality, Electronic word of mouth (E-WoM) etc. (Yadav et al., 2023; Kudeshia & Mittal, 2015), has become an integral part of the entire process of designing and selling insurance products. In the context of the conglomeration of the insurance industry and technology, several elements of technology have been explored that play a crucial role in the performance of the insurance sector. Technology can assist in attracting new consumers and retain old consumers, which facilitates increasing the premium base on an everyday basis. Additionally, technologies used in the insurance sector can help in the distribution of more data about current and potential consumers and project ways of reducing risk in this business (Mesut et al., 2023; Mittal et al., 2023; Ahmad et al., 2024). Insurance technology, or Insur-Tech, is changing the global horizon of the insurance industry (Chakravaram et al., 2021). Another important aspect of technological advancement is blockchain technology. There is a significant role of blockchain technology in the effect on several angles, like claim management, policy management, underwriting, prevention of fraud, and upcoming trends. The advantages of automation, clarity, and effectiveness in claim management are put in the limelight along with samples of fruitful implementation. The effect of blockchain technology in improving the process of underwriting and risk analysis via access to lucid data is clearly demonstrated. The benefits of clear and trustable records of policy, insurance of policy, policy insurance, and smart contracts enforcements have been well- explained in this study.

The insurance sector is one such sector that has a major financial impact due to its nature of service, hence it must help customers in creating various values. The insurance companies are expected to make efforts involved in marketing to attract and retain customers. This may be implemented through facilitating loyalty programs such as Customer Lifetime Value (CLV). Researchers have evaluated that marketers craft and evaluate the loyalty program of customers based on the lifetime value. As the world is experiencing a learning curve towards technology and its infusion in all sectors, insurance company makers are also trying to integrate technology that is user-friendly and can provide swift service for all activities related to the insurance sector.

Contemporary research indicates that customized solutions have great importance in the insurance sector, and data driven marketing can deliver such customized solutions by segmenting them judiciously and disseminating information or connecting with them with tailor-made solutions and communication strategies. The present study was conducted in the context of insurance customers to explore how data-driven customization has been successful in providing them the customized and relevant solutions from the insurance companies. Though there are many studies in the area, however, there is a lack of empirical studies conducted from the customers' viewpoint in the Indian context.

LITERATURE REVIEW

Intangible aspects of the insurance sector, along with the long-term programs that it provides, attract and retain more prime consumers. However, long-term yet tangible loyalty programs are suitable for consumers with intermittent regularity. The customers believe in immediate loyalty programs, while intangible loyalty programs are more attractive to prodigal customers. (Ebrahimi et al., 2023). Healthcare insurance premiums vary throughout the consumer categories. Particularly, it focuses on recognizing the factors that can affect the pricing of health insurance premiums and their importance in various customer customizations. With a utilization of a dataset from customer surveys, mixed with various models of machine learning, the research has filtered and predicted crucial elements for the premiums that are invested by multiple profiles of people, consisting of age groups, gender, health conditions, duration of policy, and the total members included in the policy, etc. After all, the usage of Artificial Intelligence is used to determine the price of insurance policies for individuals. The study shows how parameters like demographics and lifestyle affect the pricing of the insurance among the different segments of customers. It, in turn, helps buyers and decision makers select the most preferable option (Kapse et al., 2025). Literature has also stressed understanding the elements that drive end-users' usage of fintech services in the insurance sector. The trust factor of consumers plays an important role in shaping the sector's dynamics and creates practical implications for academicians, researchers, companies, and regulatory bodies related to the insurance sector. The researchers who work on such topics are consistently working towards creating nations that can work on the acceptance of fintech by consumers based on findings.

With the foundation laid, the insurance companies and regulatory bodies can help in standardizing strategies to facilitate the adoption of the financial technology services in this sector (Hassan et al., 2024). Along with the big technology's slowly growing portion of the financial services sector, Fintech is changing the dynamics of financial intermediation. It has made consumers' lives easy through the integration of fintech applications in their insurance processes and empowers them to handle multiple fiscal related activities like making payments, borrowing money, management of risks, and taking financial advice (Aloulou et al., 2023).

In comparison to the other sectors like tourism, education, and healthcare sectors, the satisfaction of consumers is slightly understudied in the insurance industry, despite its major size and volume of operations. The satisfaction obtained in the case of health insurance can be managed through the level of communication between service seekers and the providers (Arkorful et al., 2021). Based on the context, having consumer satisfaction can be portrayed with the happiness and satisfaction level of a customer who has purchased healthcare insurances and has availed services in a seamless manner (Rahman et al., 2014). Customer Satisfaction is illustrated by how well a product or service that was expected of people. If it surpasses the expectations, people feel satisfied; if not, then people are not satisfied (Abu-Salim et al., 2017).

Baranauskas (2021a) conducted a study in the Baltic region that consists of countries like Lithuania, Latvia, and Estonia, and is experiencing a steady shift towards the digital horizon. In the last three years. This research dives deep into knowing how digital platforms in the insurance sectors in the Baltic countries assist customization and intrusion of consumers. It was also found that with utilization of technology for personalized services and proves that the process is advantageous for both the insurers and customers, putting light on the digital transformation experienced by the region. Abdul-Rahman (2021) portrays how the insurance sector can easily segment and analyze their consumers in a better manner using better data analysis techniques. It has introduced two main methods – one where the customers are sorted into high-value, low-value, and disinterested categories. The method comprises of customer profiles classified into different decision trees. These results can help marketing teams to make customized approaches for separate customer groups. This, in turn, can provide more tailored insurance plans and services to the consumers. Non-life companies in the Baltic region are making a move towards technological and tailored solutions. Even though digitalization is all over the sector, true personalization and the presence of advanced digital apparatus have very limited access. It is seen that most of the companies use one-size-fits-all services and hesitate to customize. Therefore, the researcher concludes that the rise of digital is still slow compared to the requirements of the consumers (Baranauskas, 2021b).

Organizations should invest in building solid long-term connections based on notions of how much customers are valued and feel vulnerable. To attain this, businesses need to align their goals with loyalty programs and services. This study helps in better targeting and focusing on the ongoing relationships with the consumers and elevates its value from either side. The managers in this sector should see these activities as a continued commitment and not just as temporary activity (Wong et al., 2008). Tailoring the products in the insurance sector can help consumers choose services that fit their requirements and, in turn, provide utmost loyalty and satisfaction. The study put forward dual options for personalizing insurance and looked at how advice can make an impact on customer choices. It was seen that customers are seen to be choosing a premium insurance option when there's a default option shown, but their customization preferences are not affected by their acceptance of the default option. However, it makes the strongest impact when the default option is mixed with lucid and well-laborated advice (Grösch & Steul-Fischer, 2017). As there is a noticeable evolution in blockchain technology, the new framework showed that technology mixed with economic principles can help in providing effective and balanced systems. This study lays a foundation for upcoming research and real-time applications that can be a great game-changer in the modern health insurance industries (Shouri & Ramezani, 2025). Kapse et al. (2025) found that the best models for predicting insurance premiums are XG Boost and Gradient Boosting. The insurance industry's business strategy may be influenced by the knowledge gathered from these models. This may lead to better risk analysis, targeted client segmentation, and more efficient pricing strategies, all of which would eventually enhance business performance. The accuracy of premium estimates is also significantly impacted by several crucial criteria, including policy holding duration, number of members, age group, BMI, self, smoking habits, and heart disease, according to the detailed research. These important factors, which are obtained from a variety of prediction models, including Gradient Boosting and XG Boost, do provide vital information about how the insurance sector makes decisions.

OBJECTIVES

This study has mainly two objectives: firstly, to determine the various factors of data-driven marketing in providing customized solutions to insurance customers, and secondly, to examine the impact of effective data-driven marketing on insurance customers.

RESEARCH METHODOLOGY

Research Design

An exploratory cum descriptive research approach was followed in this study. We explored the extant literature to prepare the structured questionnaire for the collection of data. In the descriptive design, the goal of the research is to ascertain the relation among variables identified though literature and determined through "Exploratory Factor Analysis".

Sampling Method and Sample Size

Sample method: Judgement sampling with the following criteria:

a) Customers who have bought an insurance policy in the last five years.
b) Who has been offered and reviewed a new policy at least twice in the last year.

Sampling Unit: Customers with the judgement criteria mentioned.
Sample size: 125 insurance customers.

Statistical Techniques

Data has been reduced to extract the factors with "Exploratory Factor Analysis (EFA)" for further analysis. "Stepwise multiple regression" was applied to examine the Overall Effectiveness of Data-Driven Marketing for Providing Customized Solutions. The independent variable in the form of a factor is represented by the "Factor Score" obtained from the EFA process, and the dependent variable was measured through one statement (manifest variable) on a five-point interval scale.

Respondents Profile

Male respondents are 60.8% and 39.2% are female. Looking at the age, 34.4% are below 35 years of age, 41.6% are between 35 and 45 years of age, and 24.0% are above 45 years of age. With regards to their experience as insurance customers, 43.2% of the customers have been insurance customers for the last 5-10 years. 34.4% have this experience of 10-15 years, and 22.4% have experience as an insurance customer of over 15 years. 45.6% respondents were offered and reviewed the insurance policies twice in the last one year. 39.2% were offered and reviewed insurance policy three to five times, and lastly, only 15.2% were offered and reviewed insurance policy more than five times (Table 1).

Table 1. Respondents' details

"Variables"	"Participants"	"Percentage"
Gender		
Male	76	60.8
Female	49	39.2
Total	**125**	**100**
Ages in years		
Below 35	43	34.4
35 to 45	52	41.6
Above 45	30	24.0
Total	**125**	**100**
Experience as Insurance Customer		
5-10	54	43.2
10-15	43	34.4
Above 15	28	22.4
Total	**125**	**100**
No. of Times Insurance Policy Offered and Reviewed in Last one Year		
Twice	57	45.6
Three to Five Times	49	39.2
More than Five Times	19	15.2
Total	**125**	**100**

DATA ANALYSIS AND INTERPRETATION

"Exploratory Factor Analysis" was applied to determine the factors. To check the sample adequacy and further validity of factor analysis, Bartlett's Test was applied. The value of KMO is .789, which indicates that the sample is adequate and "Bartlett's Test is significant ($p<0.05$), which reflects that the items are adequately correlated with each other (Table 2).

KMO and Bartlett's Test

Table 2. Kaiser-Meyer-Olkin measure of sampling adequacy

"Kaiser-Meyer-Olkin Measure of Sampling Adequacy"		**.789**
"Bartlett's Test of Sphericity"	"Approx. Chi-Square"	1377.640
	Df	66
	Significance	.000

Table 3. Total variance explained

"Component"	"Initial Eigenvalues"			"Rotation Sums of Squared Loadings"		
	"Total"	"% Of Variance"	"Cumulative %"	"Total"	"% Of Variance"	"Cumulative %"
1.	4.863	40.524	40.524	2.748	22.902	22.902
2.	2.349	19.575	60.099	2.701	22.511	45.413
3.	2.025	16.873	76.972	2.617	21.805	67.217
4.	1.430	11.917	88.888	2.601	21.671	88.888
5.	.276	2.296	91.184			
6.	.257	2.138	93.323			
7.	.203	1.691	95.014			
8.	.169	1.406	96.420			
9.	.137	1.145	97.565			
10.	.120	1.002	98.567			
11.	.100	.830	99.397			
12.	.072	.603	100.000			

The four factors contribute towards explaining a total of 88.888% of the variance. Variance explained by Targeted communication is 22.902%, Customer satisfaction is

22.511%, Proactive Engagement is 21.805%, and Personalized products is 21.671%. (Table 3).

Table 4. Rotated component matrix

"S. No."	"Statements"	"Factor Loading"	"Factor Reliability"
	Targeted communication		**.952**
1	Personalized messaging through preferred channels	.949	
2	Timely reminders for renewals, premium payments, and policy upgrades	.943	
3	Enable insurers to provide lifecycle-based offers	.906	
	Customer satisfaction		**.943**
4	Clear, data-supported explanations of policy terms, premiums, and benefits	.931	
5	Data enables insurers to simplify the onboarding process	.925	
6	Data-driven services increase transparency amid customer and service provider	.909	
	Proactive Engagement		**.923**
7	Enables insurers to understand and engage with customers more effectively	.929	
8	Predictive analytics help insurers to identify life events	.915	
9	Data-driven marketing helps insurers anticipate customer needs	.893	
	Personalized products		**.925**
10	Data on lifestyle choices enables insurers to personalize plans	.919	
11	Allow insurer to offer flexible renewal and premium options	.904	
12	Helps in providing Profession-Specific Insurance	.868	

Factor "Targeted communication" includes the variables like Personalized messaging through preferred channels, Timely reminders for renewals, premium payments, and policy upgrades, and Enable insurers to provide lifecycle-based offers. The factor "Customer satisfaction" consists of variables like Clear, data-supported explanations of policy terms, premiums, and benefits. Data enables insurers to simplify the onboarding process, and Data-driven services increase transparency between customer and service provider. Factor "Proactive Engagement" includes the variables like enabling insurers to understand and engage with customers more effectively, Predictive analytics help insurers to identify life events, and Data-driven marketing helps insurers anticipate customer needs. Factor "Personalized products" includes the variables like Data on lifestyle choices, enabling insurers to personalize plans, allowing insurers to offer flexible renewal and premium options, and helps in providing Profession-Specific Insurance (Table 4).

Table 5. Reliability statistics

"Cronbach's Alpha"	**"N of Items"**
.865	12

The overall reliability is 0.865, which is more than the minimum threshold value of 0.7 (Table 5).

Table 6. Details of the dependent and independent variables

"Variables"	**"Type of the Variable"**	**"Denotation"**
Targeted communication	"IDV"	"β_1"
Customer satisfaction	"IDV"	"β_2"
Proactive Engagement	"IDV"	"β_3"
Personalized products	"IDV"	"β_4"
Effective data-driven marketing providing customised solutions	"DV"	"Y"
Constant		α

"Note: IDV- Independent Variable, DV – Dependent Variable"

"Multiple Regression Equation proposed:

Y = "α (Constant) + $\beta1$* (X1) + $\beta2$* (X2) + $\beta3$* (X3) + $\beta4$* (X4) + ϵ"

Y = Dependent Variable α = Constant or Intercept

$\beta1$ to $\beta4$ = Parameters to be estimated ϵ = Error Term or Residual"

Table 7. Model summary

"Model"	"R"	"R Square"	"Adjusted R Square"	"Std. Error of the Estimate"
1	.893[a]	.797	.795	.40065
2	.900[b]	.810	.807	.38905
3	.904[c]	.817	.812	.38369
4	.907[d]	.823	.817	.37845

a. Predictors: (Constant), Proactive Engagement
b. Predictors: (Constant), Proactive Engagement, and Customer satisfaction
c. Predictors: (Constant), Proactive Engagement, Customer satisfaction, and Targeted communication
d. Predictors: (Constant), Proactive Engagement, Customer satisfaction, Targeted communication, and Personalized products

The multiple correlation coefficient (MCC) of model 1 is .797, indicating approximately 80% of the variance of Targeted communication. The MCC of model 2 is .810 with 81% of the variance of the Targeted communication, and Customer satisfaction. The MCC of model 3 is .817 with 82% of the variance of the Targeted communication, Customer satisfaction, and Proactive Engagement. The MCC of model 4 is .823 with 82% of the variance of the Targeted communication, Customer satisfaction, Proactive Engagement, and Personalized products (Table 7). Model 4, "Sig." value of ANOVA shows that at least one IDV has significant impact on the DV (Table 8).

Table 8. ANOVA[a]

"Model"		"Sum of Squares"	"df"	"Mean Square"	"F"	"Sig."
1	"Regression"	77.456	1	77.456	482.526	.000[b]
	Residual	19.744	123	.161		
	Total	97.200	124			
2	Regression	78.734	2	39.367	260.082	.000[c]
	Residual	18.466	122	.151		
	Total	97.200	124			
3	Regression	79.386	3	26.462	179.743	.000[d]
	Residual	17.814	121	.147		
	Total	97.200	124			
4	Regression	80.013	4	20.003	139.666	.000[e]
	Residual	17.187	120	.143		
	Total	97.200	124			

a. Dependent Variable: Effective data-driven marketing providing customised solutions
a. Predictors: (Constant), Proactive Engagement
b. Predictors: (Constant), Proactive Engagement, and Customer satisfaction
c. Predictors: (Constant), Proactive Engagement, Customer satisfaction, and Targeted communication
d. Predictors: (Constant), Proactive Engagement, Customer satisfaction, Targeted communication, and Personalized products

Table 9. Coefficients

"Model"	"Unstandardized Coefficients"		"Standardized Coefficients"	"t"	"Sig."
	"β"	"Std. Error"	"Beta"		
(Constant)	4.120	.036		114.970	.000
Proactive Engagement	.790	.036	.893	21.966	.000
(Constant)	4.120	.035		118.397	.000
Proactive Engagement	.790	.035	.893	22.621	.000
Customer satisfaction	.102	.035	.115	2.906	.004
(Constant)	4.120	.034		120.051	.000
Proactive Engagement	.790	.034	.893	22.937	.000
Customer satisfaction	.102	.034	.115	2.946	.004
Targeted communication	.073	.034	.082	2.105	.037
(Constant)	4.120	.034		121.716	.000
Proactive Engagement	.790	.034	.893	23.255	.000
Customer satisfaction	.102	.034	.115	2.987	.003
Targeted communication	.073	.034	.082	2.134	.035
Personalized products	.071	.034	.080	2.093	.038

DV: Overall Effectiveness of Data-Driven Marketing for Providing Customised Solutions

Table 9 shows the significant effect of all the factors, namely Proactive Engagement, Customer satisfaction, Targeted communication, and Personalized products, in providing customized solutions to insurance customers.

DISCUSSION ON FINDINGS

This study proactive engagement, customer satisfaction, targeted communication and personalized products significantly affect the overall effectiveness of data-driven marketing for providing customized solutions (DV). Considering the 'β' value ("unstandardized beta") value from the table Proactive Engagement (β=0.790) is the most important variable affecting the DV followed by Customer Satisfaction (β=0.102), Targeted Communication (β=0.073) and Personalized Product (β=0.790). The first two IDVs are significant at 1% ($p<0.01$), however, the other two are significant at 5% ($p<0.05$). These findings indicate that proactive engagement is the most prominent variable. However, except for the four IDVs taken into consideration in this study there might be other variables also that have an impact on the overall effectiveness of data-driven marketing such as digital marketing, consumer behavior, value co-creation, artificial intelligence and other technological advancements (Borah et al., 2024; Mittal et al., 2024; Rosário and Dias, 2023).

CONCLUSION AND IMPLICATIONS

The study aims to role of data-driven marketing in providing customized solutions to insurance customers and the impact of effective data-driven marketing on insurance customers. It is found that Proactive Engagement, Customer satisfaction, Targeted communication, and Personalized products are different roles of data-driven marketing in providing customized solutions to insurance customers. The study concludes that there is a significant role of "data-driven marketing" in providing customized solutions for insurance customers. Future researchers can also focus on the flip aspect of technologies also, such as AI comes with both good and bad. Studies that may be conducted evaluate the role of AI in the ethical boundaries (Mittal et al., 2024). Further, there are many innovations. which can contribute to the data-driven marketing of insurance products. One such innovation is blockchain technology. The function of blockchain in fighting several frauds and its strength to enhance trust and transparency have been tested. The extant literature indicates that there is a need to explore role of value co-creation, personalization, data driven decision making, Customer relationship management, Customer journey mapping etc. (Rosário and Dias, 2023). The issues of scalability, standards, operational role, and privacy are well addressed, along with the techniques of a successful transition. Finally, the growing activities of tokenization, parametric insurance, and end-to-end insurance should be revisited. Future studies may also be conducted to investigate the role of perceived usage of blockchain on business performance in the insurance industry (Garg et al., 2020). Lastly, future studies may consider longitudinal methodology, demographic comparisons, and use of qualitative research methods. In the era of instant decision making, consumers do not want to analyze too much information to make a buying decision. Consumers expect that either the marketer or any other platforms the information and offer ready-made solutions to their insurance problems. The policymakers in insurance field must realize the value of data for providing most effective and close offerings to customers to compete in the data-drive world. In addition to this, for successful implementation of data-driven marketing, the marketers must ensure transparency, clear communication and secure technology adoption to build trust in insurance customers.

REFERENCES

Abdul-Rahman, S., Arifin, N. F. K., Hanafiah, M., & Mutalib, S. (2021). Customer Segmentation and Profiling for Life Insurance using K-Modes Clustering and Decision Tree Classifier. *International Journal of Advanced Computer Science and Applications*, *12*(9), 434–444. DOI: 10.14569/IJACSA.2021.0120950

Abu-Salim, T., Onyia, O. P., Harrison, T., & Lindsay, V. (2017). Effects of perceived cost, service quality, and customer satisfaction on health insurance service continuance. [IDEAS/RePEcmarketplace.copyright.com]. *Journal of Financial Services Marketing*, *22*(4), 173–186. DOI: 10.1057/s41264-017-0035-4

Ahmad, S., Saxena, C., Islam, S., & Karim, R. (2024). Impact of Insur-Tech on the premium performance of the insurance business. *SN Computer Science*, *5*(1), 138. Advance online publication. DOI: 10.1007/s42979-023-02462-0

Aloulou, M., Grati, R., Al-Qudah, A. A., & Al-Okaily, M. (2023). Does FinTech adoption increase the diffusion rate of digital financial inclusion? A study of the banking industry sector. *Journal of Financial Reporting & Accounting*, *22*(2), 289–307. DOI: 10.1108/JFRA-05-2023-0224

Arkorful, V. E., Lugu, B. K., Hammond, A., Basiru, I., Afriyie, F. A., & Mohajan, B. (2021). Examining quality, value, satisfaction, and trust dimensions: An empirical lens to understand health insurance systems' actual usage. *Public Organization Review*, *21*(3), 471–489. DOI: 10.1007/s11115-020-00498-x

Baranauskas, G. (2021a). Application of customisation and personalisation in digital solutions of the non-life insurance market: A case study of Lithuanian, Latvian and Estonian e-sales platforms. *Engineering Management in Production and Services*, *13*(2), 68–82. DOI: 10.2478/emj-2021-0013

Baranauskas (2021b). Expert-Based Evaluation of Digitalization and Mass Customization in the Baltic Non-Life Insurance Online Platforms 184-201. Journal of Eastern European and Central Asian Research, 8(2), 184-201.

Borah, P., Kv, R., Y, P., Prasanthi, M., & Duttagupta, A. (2024). A Study of the Factors that Influence the Success of Digital Marketing in a Dynamic Marketing Landscape. *Educational Administration: Theory and Practice*, 3956–3964. https://doi.org/DOI: 10.53555/kuey.v30i5.3554

Chakravaram, V., Ratnakaram, S., Vihari, N. S., & Tatikonda, N. (2021). The role of technologies on banking and insurance sectors in the digitalization and globalization era a select study. In Proceedings of the International Conference on Recent Trends in Machine Learning, IoT, Smart Cities and Applications (pp. 145–156). Springer. DOI: 10.1007/978-981-15-7234-0_12

Ebrahimi, A., Askarifar, K., & Nikbakht, A. (2023). Designing and evaluating insurance customer loyalty programs for different customer groups based on their lifetime value. *Journal of Financial Services Marketing*, *29*(3), 808–825. DOI: 10.1057/s41264-023-00242-8

Garg, P., Gupta, B., Chauhan, A. K., Sivarajah, U., Gupta, S., & Modgil, S. (2020). Measuring the perceived benefits of implementing blockchain technology in the banking sector. *Technological Forecasting and Social Change*, *163*, 120407. DOI: 10.1016/j.techfore.2020.120407

Grösch, M., & Steul-Fischer, M. (2017). Defaults and advice in self-customization procedures of insurance. *ZVersWiss*, *106*(3-4), 325–341. DOI: 10.1007/s12297-017-0390-1

Hassan, M. S., Islam, M. A., Abdullah, A. B. M., & Nasir, H. (2024). End-user perspectives on fintech services adoption in the Bangladesh insurance industry: The moderating role of trust. *Journal of Financial Services Marketing*, *29*(4), 1377–1395. DOI: 10.1057/s41264-024-00268-6

Kapse, M., Sharma, V., Vidhale, R., & Vellanki, V. (2025). Customization of health insurance premiums using machine learning and explainable AI. *International Journal of Information Management Data Insights*, *5*(1), 100328. DOI: 10.1016/j.jjimei.2025.100328

Krishnamurthy, S., Mony, S. V., Jhaveri, N., Bakhshi, S., Bhat, R., Dixit, M. R., & Maheshwari, S. (2005). Insurance industry in India: Structure, performance, and future challenges. *Colloquium*, *30*(3), 93.

Kudeshia, C., & Mittal, A. (2015). The journey of Chumbak: From mail to mall – leveraging social media networks for on-going dialogue with customers. *Emerald Emerging Markets Case Studies*, *5*(4), 1–20. DOI: 10.1108/EEMCS-09-2014-0209

Mesut, B., Başkor, A., & Aksu, N. B. (2023). Role of artificial intelligence in quality profiling and optimization of drug products. In Elsevier eBooks (pp. 35–54). DOI: 10.1016/B978-0-323-89925-3.00003-4

Mittal, A., Singh, S., & George, S. R. (2023). Role of artificial intelligence in knowledge management: An empirical study of industry experts using stepwise multiple regression. *International Journal of Electronic Finance*, *12*(1), 403–422. DOI: 10.1504/ijef.2023.10053587

Mittal, A., Chaturvedi, D. D., Chaturvedi, S., & Singh, P. K. (2024). "Impact of Negative Aspects of Artificial Intelligence on Customer Purchase Intention: An Empirical Study of Online Retail Customers Towards AI-Enabled E-Retail Platforms" In Dadwal, S., Goyal, S., Kumar, P., Verma, R. Demystifying the dark side of AI in business (1st ed., pp. 159-173). Hershey, Pennsylvania, 17033, USA): IGI Global.

Rahman, M. S., Abdel Fattah, F. A., & Mohamad, O. B. (2014). Service quality and customers' patronage decision of healthcare insurance products: In-depth interview approach. *International Journal of Academic Research in Business & Social Sciences*, *4*(7), 436–444. DOI: 10.6007/IJARBSS/v4-i7/1046

Rosário, A. T., & Dias, J. C. (2023). How has data-driven marketing evolved: Challenges and opportunities with emerging technologies. *International Journal of Information Management Data Insights*, *3*(2), 100203. DOI: 10.1016/j.jjimei.2023.100203

Shouri, S., & Ramezani, R. (2025). A blockchain-based health insurance model enhanced with quadratic voting. *Health Informatics Journal*, *31*(2), 14604582251339422. Advance online publication. DOI: 10.1177/14604582251339422 PMID: 40314149

Wong, Y., Chan, R. Y., Leung, T., & Pae, J. H. (2008). Commitment and vulnerability in B2B relationship selling in the Hong Kong institutional insurance service industry. *Journal of Services Marketing*, *22*(2), 136–148. DOI: 10.1108/08876040810862877

Yadav, M., Khurana, R., Vihari, N. S., Mittal, A., Balodi, A., & Srivastava, A. P. (2023, November). Virtual reality in human resource management: Past, present and future trends. In *2023 International Conference on Recent Advances in Science and Engineering Technology (ICRASET)* (pp. 1-5). IEEE.

Yadav, R., Yadav, M., & Nghiem, X. (2025). The influence of conversational AI on enhancing customer satisfaction in insurance claims handling. In IGI Global eBooks (pp. 489–504). DOI: 10.4018/979-8-3693-9944-6.ch023

Chapter 2
Data as an Asset:
From Raw Information to Revenue

Ajay Kumar
DAV University, India

Shamily Jaggi
https://orcid.org/0000-0002-6341-1582
Indus International University, India

Arvind Kumar
University of Strathclyde, UK

ABSTRACT

In the present digital economy, data has become one of the most powerful economic assets reshaping how businesses create value, consumers experience services and governments design policy. This chapter takes a deep dive into strategically transforming raw and unstructured data into monetizable economic value. It explores deeply how organizations use different types of data through structured processes of collection, preservation, integration, and analysis to drive efficiency, innovation, and competitive advantage. By highlighting different data monetization models ranging from direct commercialization to insight-driven service enhancement, this chapter presents a roadmap for leveraging data in ways that go beyond operational use. This chapter also explores methods of the institutional challenges related to data ownership, governance, regulatory compliance and implications of treating data as capital. This chapter explains that data is not just and digital outcome but also a valuable and useful resource that can be used as income source if it is properly managed.

DOI: 10.4018/979-8-3373-2772-3.ch002

INTRODUCTION

Data has become a key component of competitiveness, innovation, and value creation in the 21st-century information economy (Lim et al., 2018; Singh & Kumar, 2022). Globally, large volumes of data are produced with each click, sensor reading, transaction, and digital contact. Nowadays, most o people view what was formerly thought of as a technical by-product of operations as a vital organizational asset. Now institutions may use this data for product creation, strategic decision-making, consumer engagement and market growth in addition to operational efficiency thanks to the growing complexity of digital technology (Flyverbom et al., 2019). Data is influencing new business models and changing conventional value chains as economies become more linked and dependent on digital infrastructure. Adewusi et al. (2024) stated that organizations that successfully collect, handle, and evaluate data are now in a position to unlock substantial economic value, beat rivals, and more accurately predict changes in the market. Data is a catalyst for change at both the micro and macro levels, from projecting macroeconomic trends to streamlining supply chains and personalizing customer experiences, (Findikoglu, & Watson-Manheim, 2016).

As per Laitila (2017) the ability to monetize data does not stem merely from its availability or volume. Only when data is carefully chosen, put into context, and turned into useful insights does it become valuable (Fahey, 2019). Strong systems for data governance, integration, quality control, analysis, and, eventually, monetization are needed for this (Rothberg & Erickson, 2017). Furthermore, as data is non-depleting, intangible, and challenging to evaluate using conventional financial criteria, its recognition as an asset undermines accepted ideas of value in accounting and economic theory.

This chapter investigates how raw data can be strategically converted into economic value. It presents a structured view of the data lifecycle from collection and preparation to insight generation and revenue realization. It also highlights the valuation frameworks of data, various data monetization techniques, and critical concerns associated with ethics, data ownership, regulatory compliance and privacy. This chapter also provides an in-depth understanding of how organizations or businesses and institutions can transform data or information into long-term financial results by treating it as a purposefully managed and monetized asset.

UNDERSTANDING DATA AS AN ECONOMIC ASSET

Characteristics of Data Assets

Traditional intangible and tangible assets are not the same or equal as data as assets. It is non-rival, meaning that its use by one organizations or company does not make it less accessible to other organizations. It is easily replicated and scalable, and the more it is used especially with other data sources the more valuable it becomes (Chowdhury, 2020). Data does not deteriorate with use like tangible assets or equipment, although it can if it becomes irrelevant or obsolete over time. Compared to normal assets, managing data as an asset require distinct governance, monetization, and valuation strategies because of these unique qualities.

Additionally, data is highly contextual. Its usability, quality, and the insights derived from it determine its value (Canali, 2020). High-quality data that is accurate, timely, and well-organized is more likely to aid revenue-generating efforts and more useful (Diorio & Hummel, 2022).

Types of Data Assets

Not all data is created equal, and the quality, source, and usage rights (Mavrogiorgou et al., 2019) associated with data significantly affect how it can be treated as an asset. Generally, there are three categories of data assets that are first-party, second-party, and third-party (Corrado et al., 2022).

First-Party Data

When the information collected directly by an organization or company through its own sources it is known as First-party data (Long, 2022). This may include sales data, customer interactions, operational metrics and website behavior. It is highly relevant, exclusive and reliable, which makes it valuable (Long, 2022) for customer relationship management, personalized marketing and predictive analytics. It offers profound insights into the requirements, interests, and behavior of customers that may be utilized to develop focused marketing campaigns, enhance goods, build stronger bonds with customers, and personalize experiences (Latvala et al., 2022). In the current era of tighter privacy laws and limitations on third-party cookies, first-party data has emerged as a vital resource for companies looking to establish credibility, stay compliant, and gain a sustained competitive edge (Çınar & Ates, 2022).

Sources of First Party Data

1. **Mobile Applications: In current digital era mobile applications are the** powerful sources of first party data (Bins et al., 2018). With every click or visit activities on app can be observed. Firms or companies or businesses could keep an eye on every activity of customer doing on a specified app. By Keeping in mind that time spent and frequency are key indicators of good retention (Lin et al., 2020). For example a retail application monitors how users behave when searching for various products or deals or services.
2. **Websites:** For any company or firm one of the main sources of first-party data is a company's own website (Latvala et al., 2022). Automated data generated with the daily visiting of millions of people. This type of data provide important information and insight. It provides the behaviour data about customers purchasing decisions, their preferences etc.
3. **Customer Relationship Management, or CRM:** Lot of information of clients kept by systems customer relationship management or CRM (Ku, 2010). Contact details, past purchases, the course of a discussion and assistance requests, are among the details that are recorded (Gulati et al., 2023). In this way such data provide information that how customers have interacted. It informs organizations or companies about preferences and behavior of their customers. B2B businesses benefit greatly from CRMs.
4. **Surveys:** Direct customer feedback surveys and questionnaires serve as effective, sources of first-hand information (Dandekar, 2019). This type of information is more valuable than gold. It provides information about what clients think, how satisfied they are, and, of course, what they explicitly desire from companies or organizations. It also informs business people about how satisfied their client or customers are. Addition to this it may indicate whether their brand score achieves even greater success.
5. **Social Media Engagement (Owned Channels): In the era of digitalization** social media platforms are core for any business. It is a social media where engagement takes place for businesses (Hollebeek, 2019). Comments, Likes, and shares are all included. Except this, it also provides information about the demographics of followers. Click-through also occur. It also provides great insights into the interests of customers or client or people. A component of it all is brand perception. In this way data belongs to the company, unlike social listening tools. So, data ownership makes it first-party data.
6. **Email and SMS campaigns:** Campaigns using email and SMS generate useful data for companies of organizations (Păvăloaia, 2020). Such types of campaigns generate data of customers that help businesses to go deep insights about customers' preferences and their buying patterns. On the other hand, such types of

activities also help business to decide which segment of customer is beneficial for them.

7. **E-Commerce Transactions:** Transaction data is very important or crucial for online retailers (Akazue et al., 2024). Customers' purchase history provides information. Except this the frequency of customer purchases gives a clear picture of customers. On the other hand, mechanisms of payment are also important or crucial. Information provided by the average order value, is quite beneficial, particularly when monitoring product demand and customer loyalty, that helps in planning for inventory.
8. **Loyalty and Rewards Programs:** To encourage customers to provide information companies launches loyalty schemes. Customers are motivated by benefits (Nastasoiu & Vandenbosch, 2019). These benefits are included in the form of discounts and reward points. Companies or businesses may then monitor the frequency of purchases through such programs or campaigns (Liu, 2007). It is also possible to track product or services preferences. Organizations or company can also keep an eye on redemption patterns. In this way for companies data becomes precious or important. These items aid in the company's efforts to identify high-value clients. In this way customized retention tactics are being developed.
9. **Customer Support Interactions:** In the era of competition or digital age customer service is very essential (Lee & Lee, 2020). Customer helpline or support staffs communicate with clients through chatbots, phone conversations, and emails. These conversations or exchanges provide valuable first-party information. By considering the resolution time and the post-interaction feedback, data demonstrates the course of events. For any company or organization such information is quite useful or helpful in identifying trouble areas. Such information might be very beneficial to businesses or companies. Which help companies to improve the quality of their services.
10. **In-Store and Offline Interactions:** Organizations or companies also have physical locations or outlets. As a result, they have option of gathering offline data. Transactions take place at the POS (point of sale. The offline data is considered first-party data (Svikhnushina & PU, 2024). It helps to gain greater knowledge and benefit by combining it with online data; it provides a 360-degree view of all client activity.

Second-Party Data

When first party's data shared to another organization through partnerships or agreements, then it is known as second party data (Schneider et al., 2017). Information that a business obtains directly from its clients and subsequently sells or distributes to another reliable business is known as second-party data (Schneider et al., 2017). This data is basically "someone else's first-party data" that is collected or acquired through collaborations or partnerships, as opposed to first-party data, which is collected by a corporation itself. For example, a hotel chain or an airline may exchange booking information to develop customized vacation packages. Although there are number of limitations to its access and usage. It still retains a large portion of the context and reliability of first-party data. It is often used in joint ventures and strategic partnerships to enhance the mutual value creation.

Sources of Second Party Data

1. **Strategic Partnerships between Businesses:** One typical source of second-party data is direct commercial partnerships (Liu & Li,, 2024). For example, a hotel chain and a travel agency could work together; they might exchange booking or other information. It is beneficial for both companies. They start to comprehend customer groupings that overlap. In this way, they cross-sell services. For maintaining clarity and adhere to regulations, these strategic maneuvers and partnerships are codified through data-sharing agreements.
2. **Retailer and Brand Partnerships:** Retailers and product brands exchange data and their goal is to comprehend how clients consumers truly make purchases or do purchase decisions (Dyché & Levy, 2006). A chain of retail may provide or access consumer goods brands with access to consumer data, including buy frequency and demographics. Companies or store could get brand-specific insights or information on how clients or customers interact with the product brand. By doing this sales strategies will most likely grow better.
3. **Media and Publishing Companies:** Different media businesses and publishers maintained rich audience data (Cherubini & Nielsen, 2016). They are therefore reliable sources of second-party information. A company may collaborate with news websites or periodicals. Typically, the periodicals focus on lifestyle. Both have information of subscribers. Additionally, information on reading habits and content engagement are easily accessible. It enables the advertisers target consumers, interested in particular issues. Addition to this, it helps marketers who are interested in particular items; hopefully, these efforts lead to a marketing strategy that is optimized.
4. **Hospitality and Travel Industry Partnerships:** Partnerships make it simple and common for hotels, airlines, and travel companies to exchange client data (Taneja, 2024). For example, a hotels chain may decide to share the important information or insights from its loyalty program. In every instance, this data enables both firms (hotels and travel industry) to identify regular passengers. In this way packaged offerings are created as a result of these collaborations.

Such type of second-party data eventually provides valuable information or insights. Clients or customers spending patterns, tastes, and habits are all taken into account when they travel.

5. **Technology Companies and Telecommunication:** Operators of telecommunications gather user information. Information is gathered about mobile usage (Wang et al., 2017). Both app preferences and internet activity are gathered. This information is referred as first-party data. After collaboration between both business they get able to supply crucial second-party data. For example, to safeguard each particular consumer, a telecom provider can choose to provide anonymised location data to a retail establishment. On the other hand, the retail chain may use this shared data to better understand customer foot traffic patterns and perhaps enhance its displays.
6. **Event Sponsorships and Co-Branding Campaigns:** Different types of businesses can organize events together (Luckham, 2011). In this way attendee data is frequently disseminated with participant data. For example, in sports event different types of companies participate or collaborate in organizing event. They share information of attendees of data. In a similar vein, collaborative brand initiatives are known to share client or customer information in order to generate interest.
7. **E-Commerce Platforms and Marketplaces: Li & Zhang, (2021) stated that** big e-commerce sites are the main or big source of second party data. Such type of data provides deep insights about client or consumer's demographics and their purchasing patterns. This data also provides reviews about products or services. This information aids in the brands' comprehension. More expertise and information make More and better extensive customer involvement (Cui & Wu, 2016).
8. **Financial Institutions and Loyalty Programs:** Financial organizations, like banks have a lot of transactional data, which is referred to as first party data (Westermeier, 2020). When they share this important data with related businesses it becomes second party data. It builds strong collaboration between firms or companies.
9. **Educational Institutions and Training Providers:** Educational institutions or agencies collect information about students (De & Du, 2010). Hobbies, demographics and even professional aspirations are included in the data. Training platforms and online course providers follow suit. Student data becomes quite important or useful when coupled with recruiters or companies. Business shaped the plans for hiring. Addition to this, it makes it possible to develop beneficial training initiatives.

Third-Party Data

In the third-party data scenario data is collected, aggregated, and sold by external providers (Rahimzadeh et al., 2021), typically without a direct relationship with data subjects. Third-party data reaches a far wider audience than first- or second-party data, which enables businesses to connect with new client categories they don't normally deal with (Neumann et al., 2023). To operate advertising campaigns, for example, marketing companies could buy third-party interest or demographic based databases (Tucker et al. 2019). Because this data is not gathered directly from a company's own clients, its dependability may be weak even though it offers variety and size. While it provides breadth and scale to data, it often lacks context and depth, and its use is increasingly regulated. Neuman et al., (2019) stated that despite its limitations, third-party data remains useful for market research, benchmarking, and audience segmentation.

Sources of Third Party Data

1. **Data Brokers:** Data Brokers are the main sources of third-party data (Zhang et al., 2024). These organizations get or collect their information from number of sources. Before reselling it to interested companies, they carefully process it. Large dataset compilation is a specialty of industry titans like Oracle Data Cloud, Acxiom, and Experian. Information or data data sets may contain information about income, gender, or age. They research and classify people based on their values, lifestyle, conduct and hobbies. They buy data from sources such as surveys, publications, and online and offline platforms.
2. **Web Browsing Activities and Cookies:** Web browsing is a prominent source of data (Olejnik, 2014). It is followed using technologies like tracking pixels, tags and cookies. Cookies of third party track users of internet, across various apps and websites. They log data, such as pages visited products, time spent on pages and viewed links clicked.
3. **Mobile Applications:** A lot of data is collected by different types of applications for mobile devices (Wagner et al., 2014). Device use, location data, and in-app activity are a few examples of this type of data or information. Applications preferences are also noted or under consideration. Sometimes, extensive app permissions are provided, or user approval is gained, which makes it possible to share data. Collected information or data is subsequently sent to outside vendors, which may be concerning. Applications captured comprehensive behavior patterns, such as weather apps or even navigation software. Such type of information some time very beneficial for research agencies.

4. **Social Media Platforms:** Alaimo & Kallinikos (2017) stated that social media platforms are important sources of data or information. Businesses or companies obtain first-party data from different social media platforms. Huge amount of data is generated by social media like, comments, likes and demographics etc. This data provides deep insights to firms or companies about targeted markets.
5. **Public Records and Government Databases:** Various types of data or information may be found in government databases or records (Barber, 2006). They offer their data to third-party sources. Sometimes it provides as first party data. For example, in India if someone have to get information related to government or project then he can file RTI. Information about business permits, courts documents etc. are also available there. Such type of data may be accessed at very little cost, or sometimes free of cost. Brokers or aggregators collect it and arrange it in a methodical manner.
6. **Research Panels and Surveys:** Market research firms conduct in-depth polls and surveys (Mooi et al., 2018). Such type of data for market research firm is first party data. Additionally, consumer panels are conducted. People donate their personal information for these initiatives. Such type of data is gathered by research firms or organizations. They make the data anonymous, and then businesses sell the results. Some time they provide the data as third party data sources to different companies or firms. Number of interested parties then utilize the information or data.
7. **Location Data Providers:** Brennan et al., (2023) stated that location-based data has emerged as a crucial source of third-party datasets. Firms of location intelligence get information from navigation systems, beacons, and mobile apps. This anonymized data purchased by business to gain insight into regional activity trends, store visits and foot traffic patterns.
8. **Financial and Transactional Data:** The sale of anonymous expenditure data is common for credit card companies. Payment processors and providers of loyalty campaigns or programs also exchange information. Collected data is sent to aggregators or brokers. Buying behavior of customer and types of items purchased are frequently included in data. Not only this it also includes people average purchase amount. Aggregated transaction information, however, provide excellent perspectives and deep insights. It provides information to businesses on consumers' spending patterns and general preferences. So it's very important source of third party data.

RAW DATA TO INSIGHT: THE DATA VALUE CHAIN

To get economic benefits from raw data, organizations must transform raw data or information into structured and actionable insights. Which is possible through across a value chain consisting of several interconnected stages like:

Data Collection

The process of gathering information from number of sources to better understand a situation, solve problems or make decisions, is known and data collection (Taherdoost, 2021). It can be done through interviews, surveys, sensors, online forms, or by tracking user behavior on apps and websites. For accuracy of results the quality of the collected data is very necessary or important (Chang, 2019). For better data collection it is necessary that there should be careful planning, selection of right tools, and making sure the data is reliable and complete. After data collection it can be organized and analyzed to provide useful insights for researchers, businesses and decision-makers.

Data Processing and Cleaning

Data sorting, cleaning and processing, are important steps for converting raw data into final or productive data (Roy et al., 2018). Normally collected data contains missing values, errors, or duplicates that can affect final results. Data Cleaning means correcting these types of issues like filling in missing information, removing incorrect entries, and organizing it in a clear format. Processing of the data means converting the cleaned or error free data into a usable form, such as grouping, or calculating totals (Ganti & Shama, 2013). These steps ensure the data's consistency, accuracy, and readiness, which helps in providing meaningful insights when analyzed.

Data Integration and Storage

Integration of data and storage are main steps in managing information or data from different types of sources (Bergamaschi, 2017). Data integration is the process of combining data from different sources websites, databases or like apps into one unified view. For companies or firms to make better decision this facilitates or helps. After combining full data, the next step is to store in an organized and safely way. Storage of data can be done by the use of cloud services or physical servers, where the data is easy to access, secured, and ready for use. Integration and proper storage ensure that data is protected and useful (Gupta et al., 2022).

Data Analytics and Insight Generation

Vassakis (2017) stated that understanding of huge amounts of collected data requires the use of data analytics and insight development. In the other word the process of analyzing, organizing, and exploring data using methods and tools to find hidden correlations, patterns and trends is known as analytics. It can involve more complex strategies like machine learning, statistical analysis, and predictive modeling or straightforward techniques like charts and averages. As per Marr (2015) understanding what the data is telling us rather than merely focusing on numbers is the primary goal of data analytics.

After data analysis then insight generation takes place. It gives explanation that why something happens and what can be done about them (Sacha et al., 2014). For example, businesses or organizations can go deep about consumer or customer behavior, operational inefficiencies or market trends. In this way these insights help managers and leaders to make better decisions, create more efficient and effective strategies, improve services or products, and gain a competitive edge. It helps in predicting future outcomes and suggesting actions rather than only reporting what has already happened (Patel, 2016). The importance of data lies in how well it can help in support innovation and decision making. So, data analytics and insight generation is very important in turning raw data into powerful knowledge that drives growth and success.

MONETIZATION MODELS: CONVERTING INSIGHT TO REVENUE

Unlocking the economic value of data is the main goal of managing it as an asset; this process is known as data monetization (Gizelis et al., 2024). Use of data to make better decisions, provide services or develop new goods that increase revenue in order to produce quantifiable financial or strategic benefits is known as monetization. In this process, data work as valuable resource. When data is exploited properly, it can generate actual economic value, like tangible assets. Monetization has several forms.

Direct Monetization

The deliberate and transparent process of converting data into a product that generates income through license to outside parties or sale is known as "direct monetization" (Parvinen et al., 2020). According to Elvy (2018) data itself turns into a commodity or product that businesses can sell to other parties that are interested in it.

For example, credit bureaus collect, sort or arrange, and evaluate personal financial patterns before selling financial histories and credit scores to insurance companies, banks, and other financial organizations or companies for use in lending decisions or risk assessment. Same as, location data providers gather data of geographic in real time from mobile devices or sensors and then sell it to marketers, shops, or government organizations or companies and these companies or organizations use the data to target ads, design infrastructure, and understand traffic patterns. By developing value-added data products or commodities, organizations or businesses can also move beyond the sale of raw data (Monino, 2021). This could involve evaluating and selecting the data before making it available as real-time analytics services, market research studies, benchmarking tools, or dashboards that need a subscription. For example, a retail analytics company might collect point-of-sale data from numbers of retailers, examine buying patterns, and then can provide brands with access to these insights via a monthly subscription.

Direct monetization is particularly effective because the data is high-quality, unique, and difficult to replicate (Zhang et al., 2023), which makes it valuable to potential buyers. But it also necessitates paying close attention to security requirements, ethical issues, and data protection rules, particularly when handling personal or sensitive data. When done correctly, direct monetization helps companies to creates a new income and decision making process.

Indirect Monetization

When data is use strategically within an organization to improve or enhance internal processes is called indirect monetization of data (Maia et al., 2024). It also helps in improving decision-making, and delivering superior customer experiences that leads to increase profits or revenues, cost cutting, or competitive advantages. In direct monetization, data is used or treated as a commodity or product but in indirect monetization data is used as a tool for internal value creation.

As per Zhang et al., (2023) targeted marketing is a crucial component of indirect monetization. Organizations or businesses can segment their customers or audience and can create highly customized marketing campaigns by looking at past purchases, client demographics, social media activity and browsing patterns. It helps in lowering marketing expenses and waste, while improving client engagement, making promotions more effective and boosting conversion rates.

It is helpful and useful in product innovation and development (Johnson et al., 2017). Companies or organizations can collect and analyze data from market trends, customer feedback, and usage patterns to identify areas for improvement or unmet needs. This data-driven approach allows businesses to create better products, enhance existing features, and stay ahead of competitors by responding quickly to market demands (Glass & Callahan, 2014). On the other side, organizations or businesses can identify early warning indications of discontent or churn by keeping an eye on different types of metrics like complaint rates, engagement levels, and customer satisfaction scores. This makes organizations or companies possible to implement pro-active measures that assist them to retain valuable clients and lower the expenses associated with gaining new ones.

Data-as-a-Service (DaaS)

A cloud-based paradigm known as Data-as-a-Service (DaaS) allows data to be sent over the internet to systems, users, or applications whenever they require it (Ustundaug & Abe, 2018). In DaaS model, data is treated as a service or product that can be queried, accessed, and consumed without the need for users to manage the storage or infrastructure behind it. Same as Software-as-a-Service (SaaS), it provides real-time access to curated, clean, and organized data, often through dashboards, APIs, or web platforms (Ogeawuchi et al., 2024). DaaS allows organizations or companies to access ready-to-use and high-quality data without the overhead of cleaning, collecting, maintaining and integrating it themselves. DaaS's providers offer data from number of sources like weather trends, customer demographics, financial markets, geo-location or social media activity, which clients or customers can use for reporting, analytics, strategic planning and forecasting.

Scalability and flexibility is the key benefits of DaaS (Chinesta Llobregat, 2024). Organizations or businesses without investing in hiring specialized teams or expensive infrastructure can purchase specific data sets according to their need. This make DaaS especially attractive for startups, companies and small businesses.

CHALLENGES IN TREATING DATA AS AN ASSET

Data Ownership and Governance

It is very complex to determine who owns data in today's digital ecosystem, especially when numbers of stakeholders are involved (Kitsios & Kamariotou, 2023). In most of cases, data is generated or extracted through different parties' attraction such as users, service providers, platforms, and third-party applications. For example, data of patients may be collected by hospitals and it is processed by software vendors, cloud service providers stored it, and analyzed by researchers.

Now in such conditions, questions arise: Who is the owner of data? Who has the right to use this data? And under what conditions?

Such conditions or complexity makes it essential to have clear and comprehensive data governance policies. As per Marcucci et al., (2023) governance means framework of processes, rules, and responsibilities that define how data is accessed, managed, and protected. There is need to clearly establish data access rights, data usage permissions, data ownership, data-sharing protocols, and responsibilities across all concerned parties. Otherwise organizations or companies may face privacy violations, legal risks, potential misuse of data and ethical concerns. On the other hand, Hummel et al., (2021) stated that strict regulations like the California Consumer Privacy Act (CCPA) and General Data Protection Regulation (GDPR) and with rising public awareness defining ownership is not just a technical or business concern, but an ethical and legal imperative.

Privacy and Regulation

In the era of data-driven decision making and digital transformation Privacy and Regulation have become central issues (Sarioguz & Miser (2024). As organizations increasingly gathering or collecting data, analyzing, and sharing personal and sensitive information, such organizations must navigate a growing landscape of legal and ethical obligations, that are designed to protect individual rights.

For the protection of privacy and set precise rules for the collection or gathering, storage, sharing and processing of data a number of national and international laws and rules and regulations have been enacted. For example, General Data Protection Regulation (GDPR), has been enacted in the European Union. This law gives individuals strong rights over their personal data, including the right to access, delete, correct, or restrict its use (Hoofnagle et. al., 2019).

On the other hand, In the United States of America, the California Consumer Privacy Act (CCPA) grants similar rights to California residents. Such as the right to know what personal data is collected, to request its deletion and to opt out of its sale (Shatz & Chylik, 2019). Such types of laws have big impact on global data practices and encouraging companies to adopt privacy-by-design principles and to enhance their frameworks of data governance.

India has also taken an important step with the introduction of the Digital Personal Data Protection (DPDP) Act, 2023 (Bareh, 2024). In this act rules and norms has set down for how personal data should be processed. DPDP has introduced the concept of data principals and data fiduciaries, mandating informed consent, purpose limitation, and accountability. Given law also establishes a Data Protection Board to address grievances and oversee compliance.

CASE STUDIES

Netflix: Personalization Through Viewing Data

Raw data from user behavior, including search terms, watching history, watch time and device settings, is gathered by Netflix (Lall & Sivakumar, 2021). Machine learning algorithms that select personal content rows, personalize thumbnails, and suggest shows are used to enhance this enormous collection. Naglur & PS (2024) stated that by converting raw data into personalized experiences, Netflix lowers customer attrition, resulting in longer subscriptions and a better lifetime value per user. User data is at the heart of Netflix's subscription business model, which is thought to save the streaming service over $1 billion a year (Jenkins, 2022).

Spotify: Turning Listening Data into Viral Marketing

Spotify uses user information including songs listened to, songs skipped, playlists made, and genre preferences (Büyüksağnak, 2021). These insights not only improve user engagement but also produce viral social media content that draws in millions of new users and promotes upgrades to premium memberships. In this way, Spotify effectively converts listening habits into increased income and brand loyalty (Patria et al., 2023).

The Weather Company: Data Licensing and Forecasting

The Weather Company uses sensors, radars, satellites, and mobile devices to collect meteorological data (Binetti, 2022). It offers APIs and data solutions to sectors including retail, insurance, and aviation by transforming this raw data into high-resolution forecasts and insights (Jain & Jain, 2017). In addition to influencing company choices, this data supports digital advertising on consumer websites like weather.com. This exemplifies the dual usefulness of data as a product and as a service enabler by monetizing raw environmental observations through both B2B and B2C channels.

Mastercard Advisors: Financial Transactions to Market Insights

Purchase quantities, merchant classifications, and geographic trends are among the transaction data that Mastercard gathers (Lauer, 2020). This raw data is aggregated, anonymized, and then turned into benchmarking tools and market intelligence solutions that are sold through its consulting division. Given information is used by retailers and banks for targeted marketing, loyalty programs and strategic planning.

In this way beyond standard transaction fees, this idea is generating a sizable income stream by transforming payment data into business analytics.

John Deere: Using IoT Data for Precision Agriculture

Sensors installed on John Deere's farming machinery gather information on crop yields, soil conditions, and machine performance (Arsenoaia et al.,2023). The John Deere Operations Center processes this raw data to provide farmers better information about when and how to sow, fertilize, and harvest. Lee et al., (2024) stated that companies like John Deere increases farmer productivity and transforms agricultural machine data into a recurring software-driven income model by providing these insights through subscription-based platforms and collaborations with agronomists.

Airbus: Skywise as a Platform for Predictive Maintenance

Airbus collects operating records, maintenance logs, and raw flight data from its fleet of aircraft. This data is standardized and examined by the Skywise platform, which offers airlines efficiency and predictive maintenance options (Kabashkin & Susanin, 2024). In order to cut expenses and increase dependability, airlines use Skywise apps and pay membership fees (Henama et al., 2016). Thus, what starts out as aircraft sensor output is converted into a worldwide platform that brings in direct income for Airbus and operational value for airlines.

Zillow: Real Estate Data to Advertising Revenue

Zillow gathers raw data from price histories, user queries, government documents, and real estate listings (Gindelsky et al., 2019). It uses machine learning to create dynamic pages for almost every property in the United States including the well-known "Zestimate" home appraisal calculator (Flores, 2024). Massive consumer traffic is drawn by these data-driven features, and advertising, agent subscriptions, and premium services are how these features are made profitable. In this way Zillow serves as an example of how even publicly accessible data can be transformed into a lucrative commodity and a competitive advantage.

Flipkart: E-Commerce Behavior into Retail Media

One of the top e-commerce sites in India, Flipkart, gathers raw data on buyer searches, browsing patterns, purchases, and merchant activities (Karal, 2016). Flipkart's retail media business is fueled by the processing of this data into audience groups and shopping intent signals (Manikandan & Madhubala, 2024). Based on this information, advertisers buy tailored display advertisements, sponsored product listings, and promotional slots. So, behavioral data not only enhances the user experience, but also generates a rapidly expanding source of income from platform advertising (Theodorakopoulos & Theodoropoulou, 2024).

THE FUTURE OF DATA AS CAPITAL

In the future, data will play an important role in economic systems of every country. The way data is valued, managed, and shared will be totally redesigned by developments in blockchain, decentralized data ownership models and machine learning. National or International governments and organizations have started to investigate frameworks for acknowledging data as a type of capital that adds to wealth of nations. Proactive approach in investigating data strategy, governance and monetization will put organizations or businesses in better position to prosper in this changing environment. The idea of capital has evolved in the twenty-first century to include more than just conventional resources like land, labor, and money (Piketty, 2014). Now data is a new type of capital that propels economic development, competitiveness and innovation. There are number of factors that are contributing to the increasing acknowledgment of data as capital. It is becoming more important than ever because of the development of technology like machine learning, artificial intelligence, 5G connection and the Internet of Things. For proper functioning of technology large datasets are necessary (Chen et al., 2014). The more data they are fed, the more effective and precise they get. In current era of technology advancement data is essential for forecasting trends, comprehending customer behavior, and customizing services as a result of enterprises' growing transition from physical to digital models. Countries like the China and US viewing data as a strategic asset that affects economic supremacy, international commerce, and defense capabilities.

The official acknowledgement of data as an asset in accounting systems will be a significant advancement in the future (Chowdhury, 2020). Even most organizations now aren't able to fully represent the value of their data on their balance sheets. Emerging data markets allow structured datasets to purchase, trade, or exchange in a controlled setting.

CONCLUSION

In the new era of digital economy data is becoming a strategic asset with enormous economic potential. The examples that were highlighted from different companies like Flipkart's digital marketing and Netflix's customized recommendations demonstrate the power of information in new era. Companies or organizations, those are looking for the advantages have a strong foundation, thanks to this data that has been studied and turned into insight. Companies or organizations may acquire a competitive edge, increase productivity, and open up new sources of revenue by adopting organized procedures for data collection, processing, and analysis into place.

Issues with legislation, governance, valuation and ethics must be sorted out to reach this potential. In the current digital economy, long-term success will depend on handling data as a controllable, quantifiable, and marketable asset. And for the protection of data privacy there in need to set out strict rules and regulations. Which are very necessary. Adherence and privacy to regulations are very crucial. Organizations or enterprises should see them as unchangeable and unassailable. For the protection of data every country working on it and Global policies arise that shield information like Europe's General Data Protection Regulation (GDPR). In India digital personal information is protected by similar policies. Companies or firms that are doing misuse of information may face legal punishments. Organizations should create perfect or excellent practices to securely save, gather, and refine information.

REFERENCES

Abe, J. O., & Ustundaug, B. B. (2018). A data as a service (DaaS) model for GPU-based data analytics. *arXiv preprint arXiv:1802.01639.*

Adewusi, A. O., Okoli, U. I., Adaga, E., Olorunsogo, T., Asuzu, O. F., & Daraojimba, D. O. (2024). Business intelligence in the era of big data: A review of analytical tools and competitive advantage. *Computer Science & IT Research Journal, 5*(2), 415–431. DOI: 10.51594/csitrj.v5i2.791

Akazue, M. I., Okofu, S. N., Ojugo, A. A., Ejeh, P. O., Odiakaose, C. C., Emordi, F. U., Ako, R. E., & Geteloma, V. O. (2024). Handling Transactional Data Features via Associative Rule Mining for Mobile Online Shopping Platforms. *International Journal of Advanced Computer Science and Applications, 15*(3). Advance online publication. DOI: 10.14569/IJACSA.2024.0150354

Alaimo, C., & Kallinikos, J. (2017). Computing the everyday: Social media as data platforms. *The Information Society, 33*(4), 175–191. DOI: 10.1080/01972243.2017.1318327

Arsenoaia, V. N., Ra u, R. N., Vele cu, I. D., & enu, I. (2023). Field tests of a John Deere harvester for the purpose of production maps achievement.

Barber, G. (2006). Personal information in government records: Protecting the public interest in privacy. *Louis U. Pub. L. Rev., 25*, 63.

Bergamaschi, S., Beneventano, D., Mandreoli, F., Martoglia, R., Guerra, F., Orsini, M., & Magnotta, L. (2017). From data integration to big data integration. In *A Comprehensive Guide Through the Italian Database Research Over the Last 25 Years* (pp. 43–59). Springer International Publishing.

Binetti, M. S., Campanale, C., Massarelli, C., & Uricchio, V. F. (2022). The use of weather radar data: Possibilities, challenges and advanced applications. *Earth (Basel, Switzerland), 3*(1), 157–171. DOI: 10.3390/earth3010012

Brennan, S., Coulthart, S., & Nussbaum, B. (2023). The brave new world of third party location data. *Journal of Strategic Security, 16*(2), 81–95. DOI: 10.5038/1944-0472.16.2.2070

Büyüksağnak, M. (2021). The effect of Spotify playlists on the music consumption habits of music consumers.

Canali, S. (2020). Towards a contextual approach to data quality. *Data, 5*(4), 90. DOI: 10.3390/data5040090

Chen, M., Mao, S., Zhang, Y., & Leung, V. C. (2014). *Big data: related technologies, challenges and future prospects* (Vol. 100). Springer. DOI: 10.1007/978-3-319-06245-7

Cherubini, F., & Nielsen, R. K. (2016). Editorial analytics: How news media are developing and using audience data and metrics. *Available at SSRN* 2739328. DOI: 10.2139/ssrn.2739328

Chinesta Llobregat, S. (2024). Design of a Data Analysis Platform as a Multitenant Service in the Cloud: An Approach towards Scalability and Adaptability.

Chowdhury, R. H. (2020). Accounting for Data: A Framework for Valuing and Reporting Digital Intangible Assets. *Journal of Frontiers in Multidisciplinary Research, 1*(1), 16–23. DOI: 10.54660/.IJFMR.2020.1.1.16-23

Çınar, N., & Ateş, S. (2022). Data privacy in digital advertising: Towards a post-third-party cookie era. In *Privacy* (pp. 55–77). Routledge. DOI: 10.4324/9781003173335-3

Corrado, C., Haskel, J., Iommi, M., & Jona Lasinio, C. S. (2022). Measuring data as an asset: Framework, methods and preliminary estimates. *OECD Economics Department Working Papers, 1731.*

Cui, A. S., & Wu, F. (2016). Utilizing customer knowledge in innovation: Antecedents and impact of customer involvement on new product performance. *Journal of the Academy of Marketing Science*, *44*(4), 516–538. DOI: 10.1007/s11747-015-0433-x

Diorio, S. G., & Hummel, C. K. (2022). *Revenue Operations: A New Way to Align Sales & Marketing, Monetize Data, and Ignite Growth.* John Wiley & Sons.

Dyché, J., & Levy, E. (2006). *Customer data integration: Reaching a Single Version of the Truth.* John Wiley & Sons.

Elvy, S. A. (2018). Commodifying consumer data in the era of the internet of things. *BCL Rev.*, *59*, 423.

Fahey, L. (2019). Getting to insight: The value and use of small data. *Strategy and Leadership*, *47*(3), 27–33. DOI: 10.1108/SL-03-2019-0034

Findikoglu, M., & Watson-Manheim, M. B. (2016). Linking macro-level goals to micro-level routines: EHR-enabled transformation of primary care services. *Journal of Information Technology*, *31*(4), 382–400. DOI: 10.1057/s41265-016-0023-5

Flores, M. D. (2024). *Learning-Based Home Estimation: An Automated Data Pipeline Approach* (Master's thesis, San Diego State University).

Flyverbom, M., Deibert, R., & Matten, D. (2019). The governance of digital technology, big data, and the internet: New roles and responsibilities for business. *Business & Society*, *58*(1), 3–19. DOI: 10.1177/0007650317727540

Ganti, V., & Sarma, A. D. (2013). *Data cleaning: A practical perspective*. Morgan & Claypool Publishers. DOI: 10.1007/978-3-031-01897-8

Gindelsky, M., Moulton, J., & Wentland, S. A. (2019). Valuing housing services in the era of big data: A user cost approach leveraging Zillow microdata. In *Big Data for 21st Century Economic Statistics*. University of Chicago Press.

Gizelis, C. A., Panagiotidou, M., Petrova, S., Fuchs, D., Hofer, M., Plociennik, M., . . . Cauche, E. (2024, June). Data monetization opportunities and challenges: the European landscape by Datamite. In *IFIP International Conference on Artificial Intelligence Applications and Innovations* (pp. 62-79). Cham: Springer Nature Switzerland. DOI: 10.1007/978-3-031-63227-3_5

Glass, R., & Callahan, S. (2014). *The Big Data-driven business: How to use big data to win customers, beat competitors, and boost profits*. John Wiley & Sons.

Gulati, S., Singh, G., & Kumar, A. (2023). Interceding of Repurchase Intention between E-loyalty and Word of Mouth Advocacy: A Study of Behavioural Consequences and Antecedents of E-Loyalty. *International Journal of Electronic Business*, *18*(3), 299–319. DOI: 10.1504/IJEB.2023.132190

Gupta, I., Singh, A. K., Lee, C. N., & Buyya, R. (2022). Secure data storage and sharing techniques for data protection in cloud environments: A systematic review, analysis, and future directions. *IEEE Access : Practical Innovations, Open Solutions*, *10*, 71247–71277. DOI: 10.1109/ACCESS.2022.3188110

Henama, U. S., Acha-Anyi, P. N., & Sifolo, P. P. S. (2016). The low cost carrier bandwagon: Lessons for Skywise Airline. *African Journal of Hospitality, Tourism and Leisure*, *5*(2), 1–23.

Hollebeek, L. D. (2019). Developing business customer engagement through social media engagement-platforms: An integrative SD logic/RBV-informed model. *Industrial Marketing Management*, *81*, 89–98. DOI: 10.1016/j.indmarman.2017.11.016

Hoofnagle, C. J., Van Der Sloot, B., & Borgesius, F. Z. (2019). The European Union general data protection regulation: What it is and what it means. *Information & Communications Technology Law*, *28*(1), 65–98. DOI: 10.1080/13600834.2019.1573501

Hummel, P., Braun, M., & Dabrock, P. (2021). Own data? Ethical reflections on data ownership. *Philosophy & Technology*, *34*(3), 545–572. DOI: 10.1007/s13347-020-00404-9

Jain, H., & Jain, R. (2017, March). Big data in weather forecasting: Applications and challenges. In *2017 International conference on big data analytics and computational intelligence (ICBDAC)* (pp. 138-142). IEEE. DOI: 10.1109/ICBDACI.2017.8070824

Jenkins, J. J. (2022). Netflix. In *Encyclopedia of Big Data* (pp. 682–684). Springer International Publishing. DOI: 10.1007/978-3-319-32010-6_144

Johnson, J. S., Friend, S. B., & Lee, H. S. (2017). Big data facilitation, utilization, and monetization: Exploring the 3Vs in a new product development process. *Journal of Product Innovation Management*, *34*(5), 640–658. DOI: 10.1111/jpim.12397

Kabashkin, I., & Susanin, V. (2024). Unified ecosystem for data sharing and AI-driven predictive maintenance in aviation. *Computers*, *13*(12), 318. DOI: 10.3390/computers13120318

Karal, D. (2016). *E-Commerce in India: a case study of Amazon & Flipkart (India)* (Doctoral dissertation, Wien).

Kitsios, F., & Kamariotou, M. (2023). Digital innovation and entrepreneurship in open data ecosystems: stakeholder perspectives and challenges. *Handbook of Research on Artificial Intelligence, Innovation and Entrepreneurship*, 136-151.

Ku, E. C. (2010). The impact of customer relationship management through implementation of information systems. *Total Quality Management & Business Excellence*, *21*(11), 1085–1102. DOI: 10.1080/14783360903250514

Laitila, M. (2017). Data monetization: Utilizing data as an asset to generate new revenues for firms.

Lall, S., & Sivakumar, R. (2021, June). A Real-world Dataset of Netflix Videos and User Watch-Behavior: Analysis and Insights. In *ICC 2021-IEEE International Conference on Communications* (pp. 1-7). IEEE.

Latvala, L., Horn, J., & Bruno, B. (2022). Thriving in the age of privacy regulation: A first-party data strategy. *Applied Marketing Analytics*, *7*(3), 211–220. DOI: 10.69554/KMBL6487

Lauer, J. (2020). Plastic surveillance: Payment cards and the history of transactional data, 1888 to present. *Big Data & Society*, *7*(1), 2053951720907632. DOI: 10.1177/2053951720907632

Lee, B. G. (2024). Digital and AI Transformation of Industry. In *Understanding the Digital and AI Transformation* (pp. 163–184). Springer Nature Singapore.

Lee, S. M., & Lee, D. (2020). "Untact": A new customer service strategy in the digital age. *Service Business*, *14*(1), 1–22. DOI: 10.1007/s11628-019-00408-2

Li, L., & Zhang, J. (2021). Research and analysis of an enterprise E-commerce marketing system under the big data environment. [JOEUC]. *Journal of Organizational and End User Computing, 33*(6), 1–19. DOI: 10.4018/JOEUC.20211101.oa15

Lim, C., Kim, K. H., Kim, M. J., Heo, J. Y., Kim, K. J., & Maglio, P. P. (2018). From data to value: A nine-factor framework for data-based value creation in information-intensive services. *International Journal of Information Management, 39*, 121–135. DOI: 10.1016/j.ijinfomgt.2017.12.007

Lin, Y. H., Chen, S. Y., Lin, P. H., Tai, A. S., Pan, Y. C., Hsieh, C. E., & Lin, S. H. (2020). Assessing user retention of a mobile app: Survival analysis. *JMIR mHealth and uHealth, 8*(11), e16309. DOI: 10.2196/16309 PMID: 33242023

Liu, X., & Li, X. (2024). Acquiring Second-Party Transaction Data for Customer Analytics.

Liu, Y. (2007). The long-term impact of loyalty programs on consumer purchase behavior and loyalty. *Journal of Marketing, 71*(4), 19–35. DOI: 10.1509/jmkg.71.4.019

Long, L. (2022). Effective first-party data collection in a privacy-first world. *Applied Marketing Analytics, 7*(3), 202–210. DOI: 10.69554/NPRK2282

Luckham, D. C. (2011). *Event processing for business: organizing the real-time enterprise*. John Wiley & Sons.

Maia, C. R., Maçada, A. C. G., Lunardi, G. L., & Sengik, A. R. (2024). Data monetization capability: From the systematic literature review to the proposition of a multidimensional model. *Revista de Administração da UFSM, 17*(2), e6. DOI: 10.5902/1983465986416

Manikandan, M., & Madhubala, V. (2024). A study on the impact of seasonal sales on online shopping trends in India: A study of amazon and Flipkart.

Marcucci, S., Alarcón, N. G., Verhulst, S. G., & Wüllhorst, E. (2023). Informing the global data future: Benchmarking data governance frameworks. *Data & Policy, 5*, e30. DOI: 10.1017/dap.2023.24

Marr, B. (2015). *Big Data: Using SMART big data, analytics and metrics to make better decisions and improve performance*. John Wiley & Sons.

Mavrogiorgou, A., Kiourtis, A., Perakis, K., Miltiadou, D., Pitsios, S., & Kyriazis, D. (2019). Analyzing data and data sources towards a unified approach for ensuring end-to-end data and data sources quality in healthcare 4.0. *Computer Methods and Programs in Biomedicine, 181*, 104967. DOI: 10.1016/j.cmpb.2019.06.026 PMID: 31303342

Monino, J. L. (2021). Data value, big data analytics, and decision-making. *Journal of the Knowledge Economy, 12*(1), 256–267. DOI: 10.1007/s13132-016-0396-2

Nastasoiu, A., & Vandenbosch, M. (2019). Competing with loyalty: How to design successful customer loyalty reward programs. *Business Horizons, 62*(2), 207–214. DOI: 10.1016/j.bushor.2018.11.002

Neumann, N., Tucker, C. E., Subramanyam, K., & Marshall, J. (2023). Is first-or third-party audience data more effective for reaching the 'right' customers? The case of IT decision-makers. *Quantitative Marketing and Economics, 21*(4), 519–571. DOI: 10.1007/s11129-023-09268-7

Ogeawuchi, J. C., Uzoka, A. C., Abayomi, A. A., Agboola, O. A., Gbenle, T. P., & Owoade, S. (2024). Advancements in Scalable Data Modeling and Reporting for SaaS Applications and Cloud Business Intelligence'. *International Journal of Advanced Multidisciplinary Research and Studies, 4*(6), 2155–2162. DOI: 10.62225/2583049X.2024.4.6.4267

Olejnik, L., Castelluccia, C., & Janc, A. (2014). On the uniqueness of web browsing history patterns. *annals of telecommunications-annales des télécommunications, 69*(1), 63-74.

Parvinen, P., Pöyry, E., Gustafsson, R., Laitila, M., & Rossi, M. (2020). Advancing data monetization and the creation of data-based business models. *Communications of the Association for Information Systems, 47*(1), 25–49. DOI: 10.17705/1CAIS.04702

Patel, A. (2016). Gaining insight: Re-thinking at the edge. *Technological Forecasting and Social Change, 107*, 141–153. DOI: 10.1016/j.techfore.2015.12.002

Patria, D., Achmadi, H., Wuisan, D., & Purba, J. T. (2023). How brand engagement, brand experience on brand loyalty through brand trust and brand commitment: Spotify online music evidence. [Jurnal Ilmiah Manajemen Bisnis dan Inovasi Universitas Sam Ratulangi]. *JMBI UNSRAT, 10*(3), 1694–1710. DOI: 10.35794/jmbi.v10i3.50319

Păvăloaia, V. D., Anastasiei, I. D., & Fotache, D. (2020). Social media and e-mail marketing campaigns: Symmetry versus convergence. *Symmetry, 12*(12), 1940. DOI: 10.3390/sym12121940

Piketty, T. (2014). *Capital in the twenty-first century*. Harvard University Press. DOI: 10.4159/9780674369542

Rahimzadeh, V. (2021). A policy and practice review of consumer protections and their application to hospital-sourced data aggregation and analytics by third-party companies. *Frontiers in Big Data, 3*, 603044. DOI: 10.3389/fdata.2020.603044 PMID: 33693425

Rothberg, H. N., & Erickson, G. S. (2017). Big data systems: Knowledge transfer or intelligence insights? *Journal of Knowledge Management*, *21*(1), 92–112. DOI: 10.1108/JKM-07-2015-0300

Sacha, D., Stoffel, A., Stoffel, F., Kwon, B. C., Ellis, G., & Keim, D. A. (2014). Knowledge generation model for visual analytics. *IEEE Transactions on Visualization and Computer Graphics*, *20*(12), 1604–1613. DOI: 10.1109/TVCG.2014.2346481 PMID: 26356874

Sarioguz, O., & Miser, E. (2024). Data-Driven Decision-Making: Transforming Management in the Information Age. *International Research Journal of Modernization in Engineering Technology and Science*, *6*(02), 1642–1652.

Schneider, M. J., Jagpal, S., Gupta, S., Li, S., & Yu, Y. (2017). Protecting customer privacy when marketing with second-party data. *International Journal of Research in Marketing*, *34*(3), 593–603. DOI: 10.1016/j.ijresmar.2017.02.003

Singh, G., & Kumar, A. (2022). Impact of Firm Created, and User generated Social Media Communications on Consumer-Brand Metrics of Smartphones during COVID-19. *Journal of Content. Community & Communication*, *15*(1), 147–162. DOI: 10.31620/JCCC.06.22/11

Svikhnushina, E., & Pu, P. (2024). Online vs Offline: A Comparative Study of First-Party and Third-Party Evaluations of Social Chatbots. *arXiv preprint arXiv:2409.07823*.

Taherdoost, H. (2021). Data collection methods and tools for research; a step-by-step guide to choose data collection technique for academic and business research projects. [IJARM]. *International Journal of Academic Research in Management*, *10*(1), 10–38.

Taneja, N. K. (2024). *Air Travel Partnerships: How to Create Greater Value Through Collaboration*. Taylor & Francis. DOI: 10.4324/9781003483960

Theodorakopoulos, L., & Theodoropoulou, A. (2024). Leveraging big data analytics for understanding consumer behavior in digital marketing: A systematic review. *Human Behavior and Emerging Technologies*, *2024*(1), 3641502. DOI: 10.1155/2024/3641502

Tucker, C. E., Neumann, N., & Whitfield, T. (2019). Frontiers: How effective is third-party consumer profiling? Evidence from field studies. *Marketing Science*, *38*(6), 918–926.

Vassakis, K., Petrakis, E., & Kopanakis, I. (2017). Big data analytics: applications, prospects and challenges. *Mobile big data: A roadmap from models to technologies*, 3-20.

Wagner, D. T., Rice, A., & Beresford, A. R. (2014). Device Analyzer: Large-scale mobile data collection. *Performance Evaluation Review*, *41*(4), 53–56. DOI: 10.1145/2627534.2627553

Wang, Z., Wei, G., Zhan, Y., & Sun, Y. (2017). Big data in telecommunication operators: Data, platform and practices. *Journal of Communications and Information Networks*, *2*(3), 78–91. DOI: 10.1007/s41650-017-0010-1

Westermeier, C. (2020). Money is data–the platformization of financial transactions. *Information Communication and Society*, *23*(14), 2047–2063. DOI: 10.1080/1369118X.2020.1770833

Zhang, X., Yue, W. T., Yu, Y., & Zhang, X. (2023). How to monetize data: An economic analysis of data monetization strategies under competition. *Decision Support Systems*, *173*, 114012. DOI: 10.1016/j.dss.2023.114012

Chapter 3
Data-Driven Monetization Strategies for Economic Insights:
Models, Tools, and Impact on Decision-Making

Muhammad Usman Tariq
https://orcid.org/0000-0002-7605-3040
Abu Dhabi University, UAE & University College Cork, Ireland

ABSTRACT

This chapter examines data-controlled financialization strategies and their transformational impact on economic decision-making. With data in the digital economy becoming a central advantage, organizations use direct and indirect models to extract value from selling raw data and analytics services to improve internal processes and customer experiences and drive product innovation. Integrating advanced tools such as business intelligence, predictive analytics, and artificial intelligence allows businesses to generate implementable knowledge and gain competitive advantages. In addition to implementing technology, research highlights how important it is to foster a data-centric culture, bridge cross-functional expertise, and consider ethical considerations concerning privacy and transparency. Through industry-specific case studies and analysis, this work demonstrates how data control approaches increase profitability and support resilient, informed, and adaptive decisions.

DOI: 10.4018/979-8-3373-2772-3.ch003

INTRODUCTION

Data have evolved into one of the most valuable and transformative assets in the modern world economy. Data is no longer merely a product of digital activities but has become an engine of life exclusion, innovation, productivity, and competitiveness in the economic system. Digitalization permeates all aspects of business and society; therefore, the manner in which data are recorded, processed, and leveraged is important. This technical and deep economic transformation changes the fundamental structures of production, exchange, and value creation. Companies now recognize that data can rival strong resources using industrial-age oils but are likely to be versatile and scalable. Historically, strategic decisions have often been guided by management experience, gut emotions, or anecdotal evidence. Human intuition remains useful but is increasingly supplemented, and controlled knowledge temporarily replaces data. Advanced analytics, predictive modeling, and real-time feedback loops allow companies to make decisions based on empirical evidence rather than assumptions. This evolution has enabled customers to target offer chains, predict market demand and personalize services. Consequently, organizations that use data effectively gain competitive advantages and often surpass their competitors who maintain data maturity. This displacement of intuitive decisions about data-controlled decisions issues a fundamental redirection in function, strategy, and collaboration with stakeholders. Platform-based companies such as Amazon, Google, and Alibaba explain this paradigm, generating huge amounts of data through user interaction and providing this data to prepare improved algorithms, product recommendations, and user experience.

These companies use data to increase internal efficiency and monetize it through targeted advertisements, subscription models, and market analysis. These technologies not only improve decision-making but also create new ways of monetizing. For example, predictive analytics can reduce costs by predicting the likelihood of device failure. Simultaneously, customer segmentation models can increase sales through personalized marketing. Integrating mature AI and data analytics into business strategy is more necessary than luxury. The aim is to shed light on how data redefine value-added, redesign the industry, and influence the broader contours of business organizations. This text is structured to guide readers through the conceptual foundations, technical enablers, and strategic effects of data-controlled transformation. We begin by exploring the historical development of the economic role of data and how information has changed into dynamic assets that drive growth (Murray, 2024). The book focuses on data and artificial intelligence, examining how convergence enables new business models and interferes with existing challenges. It also examines the impact of data-oriented economies on the labor market, data protection rights, and regulatory frameworks. This raises important questions regarding inclusion, accountability, and power. The book envisions an interdisciplinary lens that includes insights from business, business strategy, computer science, and the public sector. This approach reflects a complex and interconnected data economy in which technical skills, economic incentives, and social norms overlap. Whether you are a company manager who delivers data strategies, a political decision-maker with regulatory challenges, or a scholar examining the developing digital economy, valuable perspectives are based on research and practice. By unlocking mechanisms and creating economic value through data, text contributes to a deeper assessment of one of the most consistent developmental outcomes of our time. The data journey to value is non-linear. However, with the right tools, framework conditions, and ethical considerations, there is a commitment to fostering integrated and sustainable growth in the next few years.

UNDERSTANDING DATA AS A FINANCIAL ASSET

In the development of the digital economy, data has not only proven valuable real estate, but its value is increasingly recognized economically and economically. However, quantifying the economic impact of data remains challenging. Traditional valuation frames cover material assets and inventories. They often cannot be recorded in a record of data's intangible but immeasurable value. The development of new methods for measuring, managing, and reporting data as economic assets is becoming increasingly urgent (Loers & Roye, 2025). Data assessment involves understanding the profits, relevance, and potential future income. In contrast to physical products, data are not a rival and do not worsen when used. This value is often increased when combined with other data sources, enriched by processing, and analyzed with patterns and predictions. This shift in the value structure requires innovative approaches to quantification, considering the role of data in improving decision-making, process automation, growth, and even opening up new markets. For example, companies that use customer analysis effectively have been shown to outperform their colleagues in terms of profitability and operational efficiency. The assessment approach considers sales surveys directly caused by data usage. Sales increase due to cost savings from personalized marketing campaigns or forecast expectations. Another model evaluates the contribution of data to enterprise value by measuring its impact on key performance metrics, such as customer loyalty, inventory sales, and innovation performance. Additionally, the developed framework includes the effect of data that exponentially increases the value of the data record when more users or systems are entered. Nevertheless, economic assessments of data remain a further developed area influenced by database and privacy-related analyses, consumer changes, and changes in the regulatory environment. Like physical machinery and intellectual property, this idea is to be treated as a form of capital investment, as it questions the traditional dichotomy between capital and work by creating a long-term economic value. From this perspective, operational activities are not the only companies that collect, curates, and analyzes data. They invest in assets that contribute to their competitive advantage. Some scientists and economists are working to ensure that data are included in annual financial statements, especially when used to develop proprietary algorithms, personalized services, or predictive models that improve sales and reduce risk. The impact of data perception as capital is severe and could change how companies are valued in financial markets, how taxes are collected, and how investments in data infrastructure are stimulated. It is not easy to objectively evaluate data, as its usefulness can vary dramatically across contexts and time frames. Furthermore, data quality, replication, dating, and security issues classify the classification as being stable and good. Supervisors are cautious, and accounting standards have not yet been fully developed to consider the economic realities of data. However, experimental models and pilot projects are underway in some jurisdictions, allowing us to examine how to consider corporate balance sheet data as intangible assets or through disclosures that can complement traditional financial metrics (Tripathi et al., 2024). These initiatives are part of a more comprehensive postponement to recognize the role of real estate in increasing the value of modern companies. This shift includes data, brand value, organizational culture, and technical expertise. Companies that translate raw data into implementable knowledge can respond faster to market changes, predict customer needs, and optimize their internal processes (Kargar, 2024). The data-rich to insightful transition is a key turning point in a company's digital maturity. It is not the data volume that provides the advantage but the ability to interpret it wisely, respond to it, and learn continuously from it. In this regard, data-controlled decision-making is a core capability. It affects all aspects of an organization's behavior, from product development and pricing to supply chain management and customer loyalty. Large companies embed fully embedded data in their strategic DNA, not just technology but also talent, governance frameworks, and cultural change. For example, a data-controlled supply chain uses real-time sensor data to optimize inventory and logistics routes, reduce costs, and simultaneously improve service levels. In marketing, advanced analytics enable micro-segmentation and targeted public relations activities, improving conversion rates and customer loyalty. In the case of product innovation, customer feedback and usage data are categorized to improve functionality and to forecast demand. This enables an agile development cycle. These skills are not easily replicated because they rely on sophisticated orientations of systems, processes, and human expertise. Therefore, data can be input and dynamic assets that affect competitive positioning and long-term profitability. Figure 1 provides an overview of how data become economic value.

Figure 1. The data-to-value flywheel: From assets to monetisation (direct & indirect)

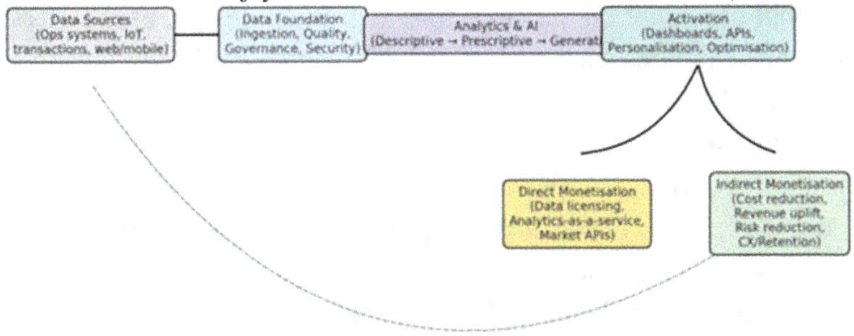

Many companies have demonstrated the transformational power of data systems. For example, Amazon built its empire based on data-controlled operations. Data drives virtually every aspect of a business, from recommendation engines and dynamic pricing algorithms to warehouse automation and logistical optimization. The company's vast repository of customer behavior data allows it to personalize experiences at scale, and its operational data supports rapid performance and customer satisfaction. Retail Beyond originally developed Amazon Web Services (AWS) infrastructure and analytics capabilities to support their businesses, creating businesses with billions of dollars that serve customers in all industries. By analyzing observational habits, search patterns, and user ratings, Netflix adapts its recommendations and makes decisions regarding content production. The success of original series such as House of Cards and Stranger Things could be partly due to findings derived from the user data. The company's ability to predict audience preferences allows it to strategically invest in content that is likely to resonate, maximize returns, and minimize risk. This model of data-controlled content creation sets new standards for the industry and emphasizes the value of data as a guide for creative investments. From the beginning, banks have embraced the philosophy of testing and learning. It has adapted loan offerings to use data to assess customer operational risks and optimize them. Analytics extends to fraud awareness, digital marketing, and customer service, creating a seamless and secure experience for users. Capital One's data capabilities allow us to remain competitive in rapidly developing situations and quickly adapt to regulatory changes, market volatility, and consumer expectations. Owing to its precision agricultural platform, the company collects data from sensors embedded in tractors combined with satellite imagery, weather data, and soil analysis. Farmers using John Deer technology can optimize planting plans, irrigation, fertilization, and harvesting, increasing yields and reducing input costs. John Deere provided these findings as part of an integrated digital platform, creating new revenue streams and deepening customer relationships. The company's evolution shows that even traditional industries can use data to create innovation and value-added products. The company emphasizes privacy and restricts third-party access to user data but uses internal data to improve product design, user experience, and service delivery. Features such as Siri, Face ID, and Health Monitoring are driven by sophisticated data analysis and machine learning algorithms.

Apple's ecosystem approach to hardware, software, and services also allows seamless data flows to support personalization, predictive capabilities, and customer loyalty. Company ratings reflect not only product quality but also the strategic use of data to strengthen the brand and build long-term customer loyalty. It also highlights the importance of investing in data infrastructure, talent, and governance to maximize the potential of data assets. If the digital economy matures, more companies will likely follow examples and data-controlled approaches for survival in increasingly competitive environments (Ahsan, 2024). Streets require ongoing innovation in data management, increased transparency in assessment practices, and thoughtful regulations to ensure fairness and accountability. By recognizing data as assets and strategic capabilities, organizations can position themselves at the forefront of economic transformation. The challenges of evaluation, accounting, and ethical use are substantial, but there are also significant opportunities for improvement. As data continue to permeate all aspects of economic activity, those who acquire the potential will impact the future of business and society.

EXTRACTING ACTIONABLE ECONOMIC INSIGHTS FROM DATA

As digital transformation is increasingly shaped, identifying and using key economic indicators is critical for businesses seeking to remain competitive and sustainable. Economic indicators are no longer limited to high-ranking indicators, such as sales growth, profit margins, and investments. They have expanded to include many data points that provide greater visibility into market dynamics, customer preferences, operational efficiency, and innovation possibilities. Companies that recognize which metrics are most important to their strategic goals and can monitor them in real time are better positioned to make sound decisions and adapt quickly. This ability is critical in volatile or fast-moving markets, where traditional decision models that rely on static reports and periodic checks often do not cover the nuances required for timely measures. Currently, metrics such as customer life, immigration probability, lead-fusion relationships, and cost of acquisition are pursued and dynamically modeled to predict performance and direct resource allocation (Tariq, 2025).

Market analysis is one of the most transformative applications of data. Companies do not rely solely on past sales data and regular consumer research to understand their market position. Through data-controlled market analysis, companies can assess actual trends, competitor movements, demographic changes, and emerging consumer needs. Companies can build multidimensional images of the market by mining unstructured data from point-of-sale transactions and CRM protocols into social media and online reviews. This approach allows for not only descriptive analysis (what happens) but also diagnostic (why), predictive (what happens), and even prescriptive (what should be done) analyses. Companies that can effectively predict customer behavior based on historical data, context-related factors, and behavioral signals will gain significant strategic benefits. For example, retailers can expect demand for the right product in seasonal patterns and on social media. Simultaneously, financial institutions can use behavioral and transaction data to predict credit cases or investment risks. AI-operated behavioral analysis allows businesses to map customer trips in detail to identify friction points, critical moments in decisions, loyalty, and attributes that drive resolution (Rodrigues Maia et al., 2024). These findings are invaluable for adapting experiences, optimizing communication strategies, and designing more relevant products or services. Customer behavior forecasting is not limited to e-commerce and digital services. It affects sectors such as healthcare (predicting patient compliance for treatment), education (before the risk of failure), and transportation (modeling of commuting behavior). Furthermore, this ability allows businesses to switch from reactive to aggressive commitment, increasing satisfaction while reducing immigration and operational inefficiencies. Business intelligence platforms, such as Tableau, Power BI, and Looker, provide intuitive dashboards and reporting tools that allow users to visualize their data and track KPIs in real time. These platforms democratize data access within an organization, allowing finance and HR departments to rely on general and reliable knowledge decisions through sales and marketing departments. Predictive analytics tools such as IBM SPSS, RapidMiner, and SAS are immersed in data, using statistical models and algorithms to uncover machine learning trends, predict results and propose the best course of action. These tools are useful for scenario management, risk assessment, and market forecasting. Artificial intelligence adds another depth, especially in natural language and computer vision processing, by analyzing unstructured data, automating content understanding, and improving personalization strategies. AI-powered recommendation engines, chatbots, and customer feedback analytics have become standard features for many customer-oriented companies, enabling improved user experience and operational understanding. These models can recognize patterns that are invisible to human analysts. B. Subtle changes in consumer mood or complex correlations between different operational factors. For example, machine learning models show that marketing teams will enhance localized campaigns as increased website data traffic from a given region correlates with increased sales of a given product. Simultaneously, business teams can use these findings to optimize their inventory and avoid stockouts. AI models also simulate business outcomes in various scenarios, allowing for more agile and reactive planning to be implemented. This type of strategic foresight, driven by sophisticated tools, lies where competitive advantages are fleeting and consumer expectations constantly evolve. An example is UPS, a global logistics giant called Orion, which is an advanced route optimization system (on-load integrated optimization and navigation). Orion uses telematics data, traffic patterns, and historical distribution data to determine the most efficient delivery routes. The system saves millions of gallons of water each year, reduces emissions, improves delivery times, and reduces operational costs. By integrating data into fleets and operations, UPS has transformed logistics optimization into strategic capital, increasing market management and achieving substantial environmental benefits. The company's data analysis system pursues real sales data across thousands of shops, enabling localized inventory and a rapid response to changes in demand. For example, in extreme weather events, Walmart can predict which products (such as bottled water or flashlights) in the affected area will have high demand levels if needed. The inventory will be adapted proactively (Ofulue & Benyoucef, 2024). These findings are because they increase sales, strengthen customer trust, and help buyers find what they need in critical situations. Walmart's ability to synthesize large data records into implementable knowledge demonstrates how data promote operational excellence and customer loyalty (Tariq, 2025).

Starbucks provides another compelling example of the process of controlling data. The company uses mobile app data, loyalty program analytics, and geolocation services to personalize customer interactions and optimize storage performance. Starbucks adapts advertising campaigns through customer preferences, history purchases, deep brewing AI platforms, proposing products, and analyzing information. This personalization increases commitment and costs per visit. However, operational findings help the managing director adjust resources to meet the expected demand. Starbucks also uses data to analyze factors such as street traffic, demographics, and proximity to competitors to manage site selection for new businesses and maximize potential sales (Khan & Fatima, 2025). By predicting maintenance requirements in front of information, GE helps customers avoid costly downtime and extend the life of their equipment. These prediction functions are made possible by huge data records and algorithms for machine learning to identify anomalies and model wear patterns. As a result, not only will it improve customer efficiency, but it will also be charged new revenue streams for GE through digital industrial services. This example shows how to embed data in a physical infrastructure to generate value beyond the initial product range. By analyzing patient data, including ANAMNESIS, diagnosis results, and treatment response, these agencies can identify high-risk patients, recommend preventive care, and adapt treatment plans to individual needs. Predictive analytics also help hospitals manage personnel, reduce acquisitions, and ensure the availability of critical resources (Ravat et al., 2024). For example, forecasting emergency room demand allows better shift planning and resource allocation, shorter waiting times, and improved supply regulations. In these settings, data is a tool for analysis and a catalyst for system-wide conversion.

Each Tesla vehicle continuously collects data from sensors, cameras, and user interactions. This data leads to Tesla A-AI systems that improve autonomous driving algorithms, predict maintenance requirements, and improve user experience through over-air software updates. The company's data control approach allows him to work more like a technology company than a traditional automaker who quickly iterates in response to actual feedback on features and services. Tesla's ability to monetize data on software, insurance, and autonomous driving services is a new limitation of its data-controlled business model. The shift in intuition-driven operations is more than just a matter of introducing technology. We need to rethink our organizational culture, government, and decision-making processes. Companies must invest in data capabilities, create infrastructure ensuring data quality, and support secure and scalable analytics. It is also essential to ensure the ethical use of data that ensures transparency, privacy, and fairness in the derivation and use of knowledge (Maaz & Ismail, 2024). Because organizations use data more strongly, the question is not whether or not data should drive it but how quickly it can do this. Successful people optimize their business and redefine what is possible in the industry.

FRAMEWORKS FOR DATA MONETIZATION

Data monetization has become one of the most powerful factors in economic value in the digital age. Companies collect vast amounts of information beyond their digital contacts but increasingly discover innovative options for converting this data into revenue. Overall, data supply strategies fall into two categories: direct and indirect. Direct monetization involves selling data or data-derived services to external companies. At the same time, indirect strategies focus on using data to improve internal processes, reduce costs, and improve customer loyalty (Bálint et al., 2025). Both approaches offer significant financial and strategic benefits, and many companies combine these methods to create robust, data-centric business models.

One of the simplest approaches to direct monetization is selling raw data. Organizations with unique or high proposal data records can pack this data into customers needed for their analysis, market research, or strategic planning (Alimi et al., 2024). For example, telecommunications companies often sell anonymous location data to retailers and urban planners, providing insights into traffic flows, consumer mobility patterns, and demographic behaviors. Similarly, financial data aggregators such as Bloomberg make billions of dollars yearly by selling financial information in real time to investors, dealers, and analysts. These data transactions are subject to strict licensing agreements to ensure compliance with data protection regulations and protect data asset ownership. Another growth trend is the provision of analysis as a service. Instead of selling raw data, some companies specialize in analyzing the data and providing customers who may not have internal analytics capabilities (Tariq, 2025). This model is particularly attractive for small and medium-sized businesses (small businesses) who want to benefit from data-controlled decisions but cannot afford a full-time data science team. Companies like Palantir and Snowflake provide a platform for customers to upload data, run complex queries, and extract intelligence that can be implemented without managing the infrastructure itself. This service model creates recurring revenue streams and deepens customer relationships because the findings generated by operations and strategic planning are essential (Cacho, 2024). In this model, companies often allow external companies to access data under certain conditions in exchange for subscription and license fees. For example, travel booking platforms such as Expedia and Airbnb can use search and booking data for tourism boards, airlines, or hotel chains to understand demand patterns and travelers. Social media platforms like LinkedIn monetized user data by providing human resource access to recruiters and advertisers, who relied on fine-grained audience segmentation. Not only does a license generate direct revenue, but it also allows the database to control how data is used by contracts that restrict resale or contracts that specify specific usage standards. In this case, companies use their data to create entirely new products or services that can be monetized independently of one another. A typical example is Spotify. It uses hearing data to develop curated playlists, personalized recommendations, and exclusive offers. These data-based capabilities are centrally crucial in user and subscription integration. Similarly, insurers such as Lemonade use their actions and information using data to design Taylormade insurance products, set dynamic prices, and optimize insurance procedures. These innovations create new revenue streams and improve customer satisfaction and competitive differentiation. Internally, one of the most common uses of data is to improve operational efficiency and reduce costs. Businesses can identify inefficiencies and make data-controlled adjustments by analyzing supply chain performance, employee productivity, and machine use. For example, manufacturers use sensor data and IoT devices to monitor devices in real time, identify performance abnormalities, and hear about maintenance needs before an error occurs (Sala et al., 2025). This forecasting expectation prevents costly drainage, increases machine lifespan, and optimizes resource allocation. Airlines, logistics companies, and service programs use this approach to optimize operations and increase margins. By segmenting customers based on preferences, behaviors, and commercial history, companies can send targeted messages that lead to conversions. Retailers such as Amazon and fashion brands such as ASOS use algorithms in machine learning to adapt product recommendations, advertising campaigns, and content to individual users. This personalization increases the average order value and promotes brand loyalty and repetitive business. In the media industry, platforms like Netflix rely on history and user exhibits to recommend content, attract users, and reduce immigration. The economic value here is improved customer acquisition and divisional rates, which are extremely important for long-term profitability.

Customer segmentation also allows for more efficient allocation of marketing editions. Instead of filling up a vast network, businesses can focus on high-quality segments most likely to respond positively. This accuracy leads to higher returns and better use of advertising budgets for marketing investments. For example, in the financial services sector, banks use transaction and demographic data to identify customers interested in new credit products, loans, or investment services (Syed et al., 2024). Adjusting campaigns created based on these findings often results in significantly higher commitment rates compared to general public relations. Prediction expectations already touched on in the cost-cutting context are essential in improving operational efficiency. It is not limited to industrial environments. Even in the serving industry, forecasting models can optimize HR management, stock filling, and resource planning. For example, restaurants and retailers use pedestrian traffic data and weather forecasts to predict customer volumes and adapt their HR departments accordingly. Hospitals and clinics use patient flow data to plan appointments, minimize wait times, and optimize employee allocation. These improvements will improve service delivery and customer satisfaction, increasing the most important drivers for repetitive business and positive brand recognition.

An example is a weather company currently part of IBM. It has merged from a traditional radio model into a data-centric company. Weather companies provide agriculture, aviation, and insurance industries with over-point forecasting and analytical services by collecting large amounts of weather and location data via apps and sensors. These customers use the data to make important decisions about planting plans, flight routes, and risk reviews, and they pay a significant fee for the value they offer. Zillow has built a vast repository of real estate data, including property values, transaction history, and user behavior. The company initially provided free access to attractions. Then, it developed premium services for brokers, real estate managers, and mortgage providers who pay for access to advertising and deeper analysis. Zillow Zillows' inbound model is an excellent example of data-controlled product innovation that has become centrally important for brand identity and user operations (George, 2025).

The company uses this data to meet supply and demand, set dynamic pricing, optimize routes, and even guide expansion into new markets. Uber has begun selling anonymized traffic data to urban planners and transport authorities, providing insight into mobility patterns and infrastructure requirements. It represents a direct and indirect financial model, as data affects internal decisions and generates external income simultaneously (Gizelis et al., 2024). Flatiron collects oncological data from treatment centers, cleanings, and structures. It sells anonymized data records to pharmaceutical companies that develop new cancer therapies. These findings accelerate drug development and improve clinical research design. It means that stakeholders provide enormous value and, at the same time, promote medical science. At the same time, providers using the Flatron platform will benefit from decision-making tools that improve the quality of care and operational efficiency. This information is sold to lenders, landlords, and employers to assess creditworthiness and reduce risk. In the meantime, fintech startups such as Plaid can easily exchange data between financial institutions and developers, allowing the creation of new apps and services and realizing license revenue. These examples highlight how data intermediaries can thrive by creating an ecosystem that benefits several parties (Tariq, 2025).

All these examples have created some essential principles. Privacy and governance are important, mainly when regulations such as the GDPR and CCPA impose stricter controls. Companies must implement robust framework conditions to ensure compliance and provide value simultaneously. Additionally, organizational culture must be developed to promote collaboration between technical and business teams, use data-driven thinking, and unlock value at all levels. Organizations that recognize the multifaceted nature of data from operational, strategic, and economic potential will likely be best positioned in the coming decades. As data grows, those with vision, tools, and ethics carefully monetize them and shape the outline of innovation, competitiveness, and social progress.

MANAGING DATA-DRIVEN TEAMS FOR BUSINESS SUCCESS

In today's digital economy, where data is often published as new oil, thriving organizations are not only incredible information but also in an effective way. At the heart of this transformation is leadership. The role of leadership in fostering a data-centric culture is not just about investing in technology and hiring data scientists. It involves designing mindsets, rigorously organizing the organization's values, and incorporating data-driven thinking into the company's strategic DNA. Effective managers are committed to a vision in which data is treated as core strategic capital rather than a by-product of operations. You need to clarify the value of your data at all levels of your organization and ensure that its importance is not limited to IT or analytics but is understood and understood by all functions, from marketing and HR to fundraising to customer service (Machado et al., 2024). You need to model what you want to see across your organization. For example, suppose key employees rely on data to ensure decisions during the board of directors or use efficient dashboards with regular updates. In that case, they demonstrate their obligations to evidence-based thinking. It is probably a precedent that follows others. Additionally, managers must create an environment where data-controlled experiments are facilitated, and failures are considered learning options rather than set-offs. This culture of psychological safety, where the investigation of assumptions and test hypotheses is welcome, is extremely important for innovation in data use. In companies with such leadership, data becomes a democratized instrument available to all sectors and is regularly used to refine strategy and operations. It also includes filling the communication gap between data analysts, economists, and decision-makers. It is one of the most continuous challenges in data-controlled organizations. Analysts often speak statistical and technical jargon, while managers focus on strategic outcomes and ROI. On the other hand, economists can emphasize mako trends or behavioral knowledge that require translation into implementable business initiatives. Managers need to act as translators and moderators in this ecosystem. You must ensure that the data perspective is presented to align with the business goals and that the decision-maker understands the assumptions, restrictions, and context behind the numbers. This ability to combine depth of analysis with narrative clarity is important to make data accessible and compelling. Instead of bombing managers with metric-filled dashboards, effective data narrators contextualize findings within a broader business narrative. Instead of reporting only a decline in customer loyalty, analysts can create stories that combine this data with recent changes in product features, customer feedback, and competitive moves. This narrative approach helps deciders see the perfect image and act accordingly. Leadership plays an important role in promoting the investment of communication skills in a team and recognizing that it is just as important as analytical accuracy. Data scientists bring algorithmic and modeling expertise (Kotonen, 2025). However, their work must be supplemented by domain experts who understand the company's nuances, designers who can effectively present discoveries, and strategists who can align their data initiatives with long-term goals. Managers who understand the value of such diversity are based on teams that can tackle complex issues from several perspectives.

For retailers who plan to optimize inventory, data scientists can model demand forecasts when optimizing inventory, Supply experts can provide logistics knowledge, marketing experts can ask about customer issues knowledge, and UX designers can ensure that insights are presented to the operations team. The fusion of these perspectives leads to a robust and implementable solution. Data-oriented innovation often requires cross-sectoral cooperation and can be restrained in hierarchical, functionally divided companies. Managers must promote and institutionalize cooperation through cross-functional project teams, general KPIs, or integrated data platforms allowing information exchange. Sometimes, the organization may assign a Chief Data Officer (CDO) or data steward to monitor integration of data efforts across all departments and ensure orientation and consistency. However, these roles require clear missions and support from the highest management level to be effective. Best results are achieved when these interdisciplinary teams are approved for autonomy, tools, and data access to promote experimentation and continuous improvement. Even the best-designed data strategies stall if the workforce cannot implement them. In data-centric organizations, training is not limited to data teams. It will expand into the company (Jiang & Yu, 2024). All employees should be employed to some extent, regardless of their role. It does not mean everyone must know how to create machine learning models. However, they must understand how to interpret data, questionable assumptions, and data tools related to their functionality. For example, marketers should be able to use dashboards to analyze campaign performance. Product Managers need to know how to interpret the results of A/B tests. Customer service managers should be familiar with the tools for mood analysis. Managers should prioritize these training courses, such as internal academies, partnerships with educational institutions, or online learning platforms.

Training is continuous and adaptive in major organizations, not a single event. Changes to analytical tools and a rapid pace of AI skills require a culture of continuous learning. Managers who work as central organizational values ensure their team is agile and in front of the curve. Some companies have developed data flow path structured programs that help employees develop from basic literacy to advanced analytical capabilities over time. These paths are often played, stimulated, and connected to career progress, making the ability of the data a recognized and rewarded skill. Managers should also invest in mentoring, peer learning, and knowledge exchange forums where employees can learn about the successes and mistakes of others. A notable example is Microsoft's conversion under Satya Nadella. When Nadella CEO came, he shifted the company's culture from "knowledge" to "learning," emphasizing data-oriented decision-making and empathy. This cultural pivot was supported by structural changes such as integrating data analytics across all product lines and promoting interdisciplinary collaboration. Using Microsoft data has underpinned innovation in Azure Cloud Services, personalized Office 365 capabilities, and customer loyalty strategies. The company also invested heavily in Upskymal workers through programs such as Microsoft Learn, and data capabilities have become core capabilities through roles. The company is "a culture of freedom and responsibility, and employees are familiar with the fact that it is based on data and is done for the outcome. Teams are encouraged to test hypotheses through experiments where knowledge across the organization is widely popular. Leadership ensures that data is not only a tool but also a goal for the company to improve offers and forecast market requirements constantly. With a combination of operational ladders from clinicians, data scientists, IT professionals, and unified teams, the emperor developed a predictive model that predicts patient needs, improves treatment outcomes, and optimizes resource allocation. For example, a risk definition model identifies patients at risk of regaining it and allows for active intervention. Data integrity, interdisciplinary collaboration, ethical government, and leadership supported these efforts, which ensured that data use was consistent with goals and patient care. Under his data-centric manager leadership, Walmart used data to translate everything from inventory management to pricing strategies. The company's data science team works closely with the department for business, logistics, and marketing to gain real-time knowledge. Walmart's retail linking platform allows suppliers to access performance data and enable a joint, transparent supply chain. This integration level is impossible without leadership understanding the value of data and investing in interdisciplinary and interdisciplinary collaborations of value chains. This transformation continues and requires continuous adjustment, learning, and orientation (Wang & Song, 2024). However, this reward is substantial for organizations that accept it.

DATA MONETIZATION IN DIFFERENT INDUSTRY SECTORS

At a time when data has become the backbone of economic strategy, the overall industry is exposed to profound changes through findings from the broader flow of information. Retail and e-commerce can be the most visible limits of this data revolution after being dramatically developed through customer knowledge of personalized technology and more (Bulani et al., 2025). These sectors have long depended on customer behavior. However, the advent of AI, machine learning, and real-time analytics allows us to adapt our experiences at the individual level. Data enables retailers to predict consumer needs with unprecedented accuracy, from personalized product recommendations and targeted ads to dynamic pricing and forecast inventory management. Amazon offers personalized product suggestions, for example, using highly developed algorithms that analyze browsing patterns and purchase history and provide life on specific pages (Schuurman, 2025). It improves your shopping experience and increases conversion rates and customer loyalty. Additionally, a dynamic pricing model operated by real-time data allows e-commerce platforms to adapt prices based on external factors such as requests, competition, inventory, and even weather and public holidays. This data agility allows businesses to maximize sales and maintain customer satisfaction simultaneously.

However, the benefits of personalization are related to the challenges. Data protection concerns are paramount as consumers increasingly know how data is collected and used. Companies must remove the delicate balance between personalization and intrusion and ensure transparency and compliance with regulations such as the General Data Protection Ordinance (GDPR) and the California Consumer

Privacy Act (CCPA). Another challenge is that many retailers work on several online and offline platforms on several platforms, and an overview of data from these contacts in a consistent customer profile remains a complex effort. Retailers who have overcome these hurdles offer compelling success stories. For example, Sephora is seamlessly integrated into your shop and online experience through data, offering personalized beauty recommendations, loyalty rewards, and tutorials based on previous purchases and preferences. Mobile apps use data for marketing, user development, and involvement. It increases brand affinity and repeat business. One of the most effective data applications in the industry is fraud detection. Financial transactions in global networks are insufficient to catch fraud in traditional rules-based systems due to real-time financial transactions (Olaleye et al., 2024). The AI control model analyzes vast amounts of transactional data and identifies subtle patterns and anomalies that can indicate fraud. These systems continue to learn from new fraud tactics. New fraud tactics constantly adapt to demanding threats in real time. For example, MasterCard and Visa use AI-based fraud marking engines that characterize unusual spending patterns and trigger immediate security controls or transaction blocks. These tools significantly reduced unauthorized losses while at the same time improving consumer confidence.

Credit valuations are another area in which data has made a distinct difference. Traditional credit ratings were firmly based on credit history and income reporting and often excluded segments of the population with limited financial history (Maia et al., 2024). We currently use alternative data such as payment usage, mobile phone usage, and even social media behavior numbers to achieve a more integrated and accurate credit score. Fintech companies such as Tala and ZestFinance have cast the pioneering work of this approach, allowing loans to population groups of emerging countries sizes by analyzing behavioral and smartphone usage data. It democratizes access to loans and opens up a new customer base for financial institutions. Investment banking and asset management use predictive analytics to model market trends, simulate portfolios, and identify new investment opportunities. Hedge funds such as Renaissance Technology and Two Sigma apply quantum-oriented strategies. It analyzes large data records to produce shops with speed and scale that people can't keep up with. However, the industry is challenging, particularly concerning data security, compliance with financial regulations, and the ethical use of data control models when making decisions with high inserts.

Traditionally cautious about technology adoption, healthcare systems are currently one of the most promising areas for AI and data analytics. Many institutions have already realized AI, diagnosis, treatment planning, and hospital operational possibilities. Machine learning algorithms trained on large data records using medical images can now identify abnormalities such as tumors, fractures, and organ abnormalities that compete with experienced radiologists. In some cases, AI tools act as second opinions that human clinicians can overlook. Although IBMS Watson Health was controversial on commercialized trips, it presented AI's early promises in integrating huge medical literature and patient files to support clinical decision-making. Additionally, predictive models are used to assess patient acquisition risk. Health service providers can implement precautions that improve outcomes and reduce costs. Hospitals and clinics are under immeasurable pressure to manage resources efficiently and, at the same time, maintain high care standards. Data analysis helps streamline planning, optimize employee allocation, and reduce wait times by predicting patient influx and service needs (Cahyono et al., 2025). Additionally, portable technology and remote monitoring devices create continuous currents of patient data that can be analyzed in real-time to recognize health degradation and attract attention to nursing staff. This approach is particularly advantageous for managing chronic diseases where timely interventions can prevent complications and hospitalization. However, the health sector came with strict regulatory frameworks such as data silos, inconsistent data formats, and HIPAA.

Integrating electronic medical records, insurance databases, and data from third-party providers requires robust infrastructure and governance. Nevertheless, institutions such as the Mayo Clinic and the Emperor decided on permanent benchmarks by granting integrated health systems and analytics platforms aggressive and personalized care. Traditional manufacturing models operate on static planning models, often leading to excess inventory or inventory. Real-time data from production management, supplier networks, and market trends introduce dynamic forecasting models that adapt procurement and production plans accordingly (Okeyo, 2024). For example, General Electric uses an industrial Internet platform to collect data from sensors embedded in a machine. It is then analyzed to predict device failures before they occur. This forecasting expectation approach reduces costly downtime and increases the lifespan of key assets. Supply chain analysis goes beyond inventory management. It also supports route optimization, supplier risk assessment, and demand recognition. During the COVID-19 pandemic, supply chain failures pose vulnerabilities in the global logistics system. Companies investing in data analytics quickly turned, redirected shipments, adapted production, and communicated effectively with customers. Walmart offers leading examples of using real-time analytics to monitor sales at the store level, predict replenishment needs, and maintain efficient delivery networks. Integrating blockchain technology and delivery fees will improve transparency, traceability, and fraud prevention, especially in industries such as food and drugs. Despite these advancements, harmonizing data among global partners and addressing large data volumes and cybersecurity assurances is challenging. However, the trend toward intelligent factories and Industry 4.0 continues to attract dynamics. This is due to the measurable benefits of efficiency and resilience. From internet service providers to social media platforms, these companies collect vast amounts of data about user behavior, preferences, locations, and communication patterns. This data is driven by advertising, content managers, and new revenue streams through data partnerships. For example, Google and Facebook have completed the art of action goals and use detailed user profiles to provide more profitable ads as they are more relevant. These companies have created an ecosystem that seamlessly flows data flow between services, strengthens user commitment, and generates constant feedback loops that improve the accuracy of their algorithms. For example, telecommunications providers use call data records to identify risks of deviation services, develop personalized service packages, and predict customer service needs. Some Telkos monetize aggregated anonymized data by selling survey results to urban planners, transportation authorities, and marketing companies. However, this sector exists intensively through data protection, primarily when user data is sold or shared with third parties. The balance between monetization and user trust remains sensitive, with some companies exposing public responses and regulatory punishments to over-control data protection restrictions.

Despite these challenges, there are many success stories. For example, Spotify uses auditory data to recommend songs and design content strategies, curate playlists, and guide artist collaborations. Their annual campaign transforms user data into personalized stories at the annual review level and their analytics into cultural events. Similarly, Telecom Giant Telefânica Luca has developed a unit that converts big data into commercial knowledge of customers in several industries, from retail to transportation. These cases illustrate the immeasurable possibilities of user data combined with ethical data practices, clear communication, and innovative applications. In retail, the omnichannel nature of customer interaction requires a unified data system, but the regulation requires strict data government. Healthcare must navigate ethical concerns and data-to-data maneuverability issues. At the same time, production fights against legacy systems and fragmented supplier networks. In technology, user privacy and data ethics dominate discourse. Despite these variations, successful organizations share common characteristics. It is a strategic vision of data, strong leadership, cross-functional collaboration, and willingness to invest in the infrastructure and skills needed to get data to work.

ETHICAL CONSIDERATIONS IN DATA MONETIZATION

In today's data-centric global economy, organizations are increasingly judged on their financial performance and how they collect, manage, and use responsibly. Data monetizing opened up key possibilities for profitability that promote personalized experience, increased efficiency, and predictive insights and raised considerable ethical questions. The voltage between maximizing the economic value of data and maintaining ethical responsibility was never noticeable. Consumers, supervisors, and stakeholders require businesses to deliver more than just results. You need to do this with integrity, fairness, and transparency. This ambitious paradigm encourages businesses to embed ethical data practices at the heart of their business, reverting guidelines and technology and fostering culture and management points. In landscapes where public trust is weak, and data injuries can lead to reputation and economic ruin, handling ethical data on data becomes a strategic obligation (Gizelis et al., 2024). Companies that prioritize ethical responsibility in the use of data often experience customer loyalty, brand value, and regulation - goodwill. Ethical data management protects consumer privacy, ensures data accuracy, prevents algorithm distortion, and makes data transparent. This responsibility is not merely a matter of compliance. It shows that data respects people who drive modern business models.

In particular, the GDPR has redefined the global data protection environment for global data protection by introducing principles such as data minimization, purpose limits, and the right to forgetting. According to the GDPR, organizations must obtain clear and positive consent from individuals before collecting data. They must clearly explain the purpose of data processing. Non-compliance can lead to fines, but more than anything, it can undermine public trust. The CCPA is built on similar principles and provides the sale of your data to the sale of your data for access to deletion and resignation. These regulations not only protect individuals but also determine standards of business behavior, and they also help companies tackle data governance. This allows businesses to align their data strategies with ethical best practices. For example, the assumption of privacy principles ensures that data protection is integrated into systems and processes rather than being treated as a subsequent thought. This proactive approach minimizes risk and increases the company's commitment to responsible data use.

Furthermore, the increase in data ethics management and data protection officers within the organization indicates a shift toward institutionalizing ethical supervision (Mirbagheri, 2025). These roles include monitoring data collection practices, assessing algorithm equity, and advising ethical dilemmas concerning data monetizing. The Cambridge Analytica scandal revealed how personal data from millions of Facebook users were harvested without consent and used for political profiles, serving as a global wake-up call. The way opaque data practices lead to manipulative results was highlighted, and public trust was disbanded (Sihotang et al., 2024). Consumer concerns require businesses to assume fundamental transparency beyond legal compliance. It includes what data is collected, how they are used, who they are shared, and which appropriate consumers have in managing the data. More transparency and trust are key currencies in the data industry.

Features like detailed data protection settings, dashboards in real-time, and user-friendly data access tools can dramatically improve the consumer experience. For example, Apple has established itself as a data protection company, allowing users to restrict tracking, check app permissions, and manage data through an intuitive interface. These features respond to regulations and reflect a broader commitment to autonomy and respect for users (Wei, 2025). Similarly, the Mozilla Firefox browser emphasizes privacy as a core value, blocks third-party trackers from third-party providers, and provides clear data protection controls. These approaches show that observing user privacy does not necessarily sacrifice functionality or profitability. It currently includes digital ethics and responsible data management. It is increasingly hoped that the wider social impact of data practices will be considered, particularly in terms of justice, inclusion, and equity. For example, algorithms for setting up, lending, or criminal justice should check for bias and unintended consequences. Using AI in these contexts has sparked critical debates about accountability, transparency, and human observation. Companies that do not consider these concerns will risk discrimination and undermine the legitimacy of their businesses.

Embedding CSRs into data strategies involves the introduction of ethical framework conditions. It guides analysis and application decisions through the collection and storage of the data lifecycle. This requires interdisciplinary collaboration between data scientists, ethicists, legal experts, and administrative supervision. It also requires ethical training and sensitization programs in which employees recognize and respond to data-related risks. For example, Google has founded the AI Ethics Board, revealing AI principles to lead responsible development and the use of artificial intelligence. Implementing these initiatives is not without controversy, but they represent steps to formalizing ethical considerations within corporate data practices. Microsoft was at the top of promoting responsible AI and data use. A great initiative, AI uses data and machine learning to support projects that address social challenges such as environmental compatibility, accessibility, and humanitarian responses. At the same time, Microsoft has implemented strong guidelines for data management, highlighting user control, approval, and security. His approach combines ethical engagement with innovation, demonstrating that profitability and purpose coexist.

Unilever offers another compelling example. As a consumer goods company, Unilever is extremely reluctant to know about consumer knowledge to promote marketing and product development. However, it is publicly disclosed for data transparency, and consumers are committed to consumers that data will not be sold to third parties and will only be used in ways that add value to the experience. This commitment is supported by a comprehensive framework of data ethics that leads the company's digital marketing efforts. By organizing data strategies across various CSR destinations, Unilever has developed stronger customer relationships and is differentiated in busy markets. The company has established an office for the ethical and humane use of technology. It ensures that Salesforce products are used in ways that promote trust, fairness, and respect. The office works closely with customers to develop responsible AI applications and provide ethical consulting services. Salesforce improves value supply by embedding ethical considerations into its service offers while envisaging growing concerns about data abuse.

Even in the rapidly growing world of digital advertising, some companies are setting new ethical standards. Behind the Brave Browser, Brave Software introduced innovative models that reward cryptocurrency users for displaying ads while maintaining privacy. This approach requires traditional advertising tech models based on invasive persecution and data harvesting (Homner et al., 2024). The brave model respects user privacy and creates new revenue streams based on consent and transparency. However, maintaining an ethical data strategy is not without its challenges. Businesses are often breached in terms of data use and privacy. More detailed data can lead to better personalization and insights, increasing the risk of new identification and data protection violations. The right balance requires robust anonymization techniques, an ethical review process, and an obligation to minimize data. Furthermore, the global nature of digital businesses means businesses must navigate a patchwork of data regulations across their jurisdiction. This complexity requires an adaptive compliance framework and continuous monitoring.

Another vital challenge is measuring the impact of ethical data practices. While profitability can be quantified, assessing the benefits of trust, brand reputation, and ethical leadership is more difficult. However, new trials show that consumers are more likely and likely to support brands that show ethical responsibility. Companies that become transparent through data practices and address consumer issues often enjoy higher customer satisfaction and lower immigration rates. Data ethical leadership reduces risk and contributes to long-term business sustainability. Future methods include collective efforts to establish and maintain ethical norms in the digital economy. Industry associations, academic institutions, and civil society organizations are responsible for designing standards, sharing best practices, and considering holding companies. Collaboration with multi-stakeholders can promote innovation in using ethical data while at the same time preventing commercial interests from overriding fundamental rights. For example, partnerships combine AI high-tech companies, researchers, and representative groups to promote responsible AI practices through dialogue, research, and joint obligations. Organizations that thrive in this new era recognize data as exploited assets and are responsible for managing them carefully. You will be the one who asks what data can do, as well as what to do. Build a culture of accountability, a system of transparency, and a strategy of inclusion. Redefine what it means to be a successful, reliable, ethical company in the data age.

SUSTAINABILITY AND THE FUTURE OF DATA-DRIVEN BUSINESS MODELS

Establishing a sustainable data strategy is essential to ensure long-term profitability when data is no longer just a production of operations but a fundamental asset. The early years of digital transformation were often rushed to collect, store, and analyze data without a consistent strategy or long-term vision. If organizations are ripe and data volume, speed, and diversity increase exponentially, data practice sustainability is no longer an option. A sustainable data strategy requires companies to think comprehensively about how data is collected, controlled, used, and ultimately eliminated. Not only should we consider immediate business benefits, but we also need to consider long-term impacts on privacy, costs, and social impact. This shift requires a balance of agility and structure. It includes clear database establishment, management, access control, and usage guidelines. When data governance is treated as a strategic asset, companies can ensure that data is reliable, compliant, and functional over time. It means investing in data quality initiatives, metadata management, and ongoing testing to avoid the risk of data drop and misuse. But governance is more than just a technical feature. It must be embedded in corporate culture and leadership. It encourages cooperation and avoids data silos and auction inefficiencies when managers treat data as a more general organizational resource than as a departmental asset. The spread of cloud-based infrastructure has made storing large amounts of data easy. However, the associated energy consumption and cost-effectiveness are often overlooked.

Sustainable data strategies include optimizing data lifecycle management for the data lifecycle and "when to archive, anonymize, or delete data that does not meet strategic objectives." Ethical considerations for the data collected are also required. Do I need data? Is it being used responsibly? Companies such as Patagonia and IKEA emphasize the sustainability of all aspects of operations. They are beginning to apply these principles to their digital strategies. Organize data practices with broader corporate value by limiting unnecessary data collection and prioritization. Open data and transparency, once considered radical concepts, are now envisaged as levers for innovation and economic growth. Governments, NGOs, and even private companies are increasingly aware of the value of data release in ways that benefit the wider ecosystem. The Open Data Initiative promotes cooperation, lane innovation, and supports evidence-based politicians. Open access to transportation, environmental, and health data has allowed cities to develop new solutions that improve their lives. For example, Transport for London (TFL) has made large amounts of transport data available to facilitate navigation app development, overload management tools, and research into guidelines. Companies create network effects by opening and accessing, increasing growth beyond their immediate limits. When businesses communicate data practices, what they have collected, how they use them, and what kind of consumers the right consumers have, they meet legal requirements and create stronger relationships with stakeholders. This transparency promotes accountability and allows third parties to check, criticize, and improve data models and algorithms. In the financial sector, data-controlled decision transparency can help to improve systematic bias regarding credit valuations and lending, for example. Opening a review model allows businesses to demonstrate fairness and gain public trust (Yusuf et al., 2024). Transparent data methods in journalism and research also communicate reliability and enable peer checking—blockchain, in particular, offers promising opportunities for improving data integrity, traceability, and user control. By providing immutable records and decentralized reviews, blockchain can reduce reliance on centralized data authorities and promote trust in data transactions. It is particularly relevant in industries such as supply chain management, with origin and reliability being very important. In healthcare systems, blockchain-enabled patient files allow people to control data access while maintaining safety and compliance with regulations such as HIPAA and GDPR.

In contrast to traditional models in which data is collected and controlled by central authorities, distributed ownership of data between users. Projects such as Solid, launched by the World Wide Web Inventor, aim to allow individuals more control over their data by separating it from their applications. This way, users can store their data in the pod and selectively grant access to third parties. Instead of treating users as mere data sources, these distributed models could redefine the digital business model by placing users at the heart of the data ecosystem. It also promotes ethical data consumption and increased competition by reducing monopoly control. Next-generation AI models can extract knowledge from unstructured data, predict trends with high accuracy, and even generate synthetic data to fill gaps in training rates. These skills allow for more detailed personalization, optimized operations, and new product innovation. But these advancements are a greater responsibility. Organizations should invest in AI ethics, model interpretability, and fairness testing to ensure that AI-controlled knowledge does not disproportionate inequality or violate user rights. The role of explainable AI (XAI) is significant so interest groups understand how decisions are made and identify potential distortions. The largest culture of data is one in which data is not only an analyst or IT sector but also a common organizational asset that influences decision-making at all levels. There is a need for a leadership cup, employee empowerment, and a shift in thinking from reactive to active use of data. In this culture, employees are encouraged to ask data-controlled questions, test hypotheses, and use evidence to support their strategies. This cultural change includes referring and increasing employee profiles, integrating data capabilities into training programs, and promoting unstable collaboration.

The structure of this type of culture is not simple. In many cases, habits need to be changed to overcome skepticism. Managers must model data-driven behavior, celebrate success, and learn from mistakes. You also need to invest in tools and infrastructure that will allow you to access your data. Self-service analytics platforms, data visualization tools, and co-dashboards can democratize data usage and enable better-established decisions. But beyond the tool, the actual conversion is in the value. Organizations that assess curiosity, evidence, transparency, and continuous learning are better positioned to thrive in the data industry. It includes increased agility, improved customer experience, more efficient processes, and the ability to anticipate and respond to market changes. During times of crisis, such as during the COVID-19 pandemic, organizations with strong data cultures could quickly realize resources, adapt their supply chains, and communicate effectively with stakeholders. The same principle applies to important competitive markets where speed, accuracy, and innovation highlight feature features. Rather than using technologies like blockchain and AI for innovation, it increases trust, strengthens, and improves resilience. Address regulators, communities, and partners to form a data economy that is useful to everyone. And they will continually adapt their strategies to reflect new challenges and opportunities.

CONCLUSION

Data-oriented monetarization strategies have transformed modern business by transforming information into powerful economic capital. Through both knowledge sales, licensing, and data-controlled innovation and direct models such as indirect approaches such as personalized marketing and operational efficiency, companies improve profitability and, at the same time, improve decision-making. Integrating business intelligence, predictive analytics, and AI tools allows businesses to extract implementable knowledge, optimize operations, and respond quickly to market requirements. However, success depends not only on technology but also on data-centric culture, ethical responsibility, and the promotion of interdisciplinary collaboration. Companies strategically investing in data governance, skill development, and sustainable practices are positioned for their long-term competitive advantage. Data monetization effectively requires economic benefits such as transparency, privacy, and social accountability. While the digital economy is developing, organizations that take thoughtful, ethical, and future data strategies have a path to innovation, resilience, and lasting impact in the industry.

REFERENCES

Ahsan, Z. (2024). *Data monetization and inequality: Evidence from case studies. The National High School Journal of Science*. https://nhsjs.com/2024/data-monetization-and-inequality-evidence-from-case-studies

Alimi, A., Grace, C., Oladele, S., & Mia, J. (2024). *Data-driven decision-making: Challenges and opportunities in business analytics* [Preprint]. ResearchGate.

Bálint, L. P., Várallyai, L., & Botos, S. (2025). Evaluation of data-driven sustainability potential at SMEs using an altered Ecocanvas model. *Economies*, *13*(2), 49. DOI: 10.3390/economies13020049

Bulani, P. R., & Jain, S. (2025). AI-driven predictive models for asset monetization. *International Journal of Research in All Subjects in Multi Languages*, *13*(1), 131–152.

Cacho, S. F. (2024). *The impact of data monetization in business models: A study on the Portuguese banking industry* (Master's thesis, Universidade Católica Portuguesa, Portugal). Repositório Institucional UCP.

Cahyono, D., Sijabat, A., Panjaitan, M. B., Julianingsih, D., & Lorenzo, A. (2025). Challenges and opportunities in implementing big data for small and medium enterprises (SMEs). *Journal of Computer Science and Technology Application*, *2*(1), 75–83.

George, A. S. (2025). Leveraging the new oil: An analysis of emergent data monetization models and their impact on corporate innovation. *PUIRP Journal of Business and Management*, *3*(2), 37–52.

Gizelis, C. A., Panagiotidou, M., Petrova, S., Fuchs, D., Hofer, M., Plociennik, M., . . . Cauche, E. (2024, June). Data monetization opportunities and challenges: The European landscape by DATAMITE. In *IFIP International Conference on Artificial Intelligence Applications and Innovations* (pp. 62–79). Springer Nature. DOI: 10.1007/978-3-031-63227-3_5

Homner, N., Bellin, P., Fielt, E., & Matzner, M. (2024). Data-driven business models. In *International encyclopedia of business management*. Elsevier.

Jiang, Y., & Yu, X. (2024). Theoretical and practical aspects of data asset monetization in maritime enterprises. *Fudan Journal of the Humanities and Social Sciences*, *17*(3), 479–506. DOI: 10.1007/s40647-024-00415-2

Kargar, B. (2024). *Data driven decision making for sustainable planning and operations of large scale networks* (Doctoral dissertation, New Jersey Institute of Technology). NJIT Digital Commons.

Khan, M. U., & Fatima, I. (2025). The role of big data analytics capability in the telecommunication sector of Pakistan: The chain mediating effect of data integration capability and data-driven decision making. *Quality & Quantity, 59*(1), 51–85. DOI: 10.1007/s11135-024-01923-9

Kotonen, A. (2025). *Data-driven product portfolio process development: Navigating growth and strategic decision-making* (Master's thesis, Aalto University, Finland). Aalto University Repository.

Loers, M., & Roye, D. (2025). DATAMITE: Effektive Datenmonetarisierungsstrategien zur Stärkung der europäischen Datenökonomie/DATAMITE: Effective data monetization strategies to strengthen the European data economy. *UdZ – The Data-driven Enterprise, 5*(1), 54–59.

Maaz, Z. N., & Ismail, M. Z. (2024). Data monetization strategies: The construction industry market analysis. *International Journal of Built Environment and Sustainability, 11*(3), 103–119. DOI: 10.11113/ijbes.v11.n3.1351

Machado, M. P., Klingenberg, C. O., Abreu, J. L., Barbastefano, R., & Lacerda, D. P. (2024). Business processes for data monetization: An exploratory analysis and proposition of design patterns. *Business Process Management Journal, 31*(4), 1528–1559. DOI: 10.1108/BPMJ-02-2024-0079

Maia, C. R., Maçada, A. C. G., Lunardi, G. L., & Sengik, A. R. (2024). Data monetization capability: From the systematic literature review to the proposition of a multidimensional model. *Revista de Administração da UFSM, 17*(2), e6. DOI: 10.5902/1983465986416

Mirbagheri, F. (2025). To sell or not to sell? Drivers and barriers to direct data monetization in incumbents. In *Proceedings of the 58th Hawaii International Conference on System Sciences (HICSS)*. ScholarSpace. DOI: 10.24251/HICSS.2025.485

Murray, J. (2024, September). Optimizing risk reduction: A data-driven approach for strategic preventive and mitigative action planning. In *International Pipeline Conference* (Vol. 88537, p. V001T01A003). American Society of Mechanical Engineers. DOI: 10.1115/IPC2024-132099

Ofulue, J., & Benyoucef, M. (2024). Data monetization: Insights from a technology-enabled literature review and research agenda. *Management Review Quarterly, 74*(2), 521–565. DOI: 10.1007/s11301-022-00309-1

Okeyo, M. (2024). *Customer-centric data strategies to drive revenue growth* (Master's thesis, Aga Khan University, Kenya). Aga Khan University Institutional Repository.

Olaleye, I., Mokogwu, V., Olufemi-Phillips, A. Q., & Adewale, T. T. (2024). Transforming supply chain resilience: Frameworks and advancements in predictive analytics and data-driven strategies. *Open Access Research Journal of Multidisciplinary Studies*, *8*(2), 85–93. DOI: 10.53022/oarjms.2024.8.2.0065

Ravat, L., Hemonnet-Goujot, A., & Hollet-Haudebert, S. (2024). Exploring how to develop data-driven innovation capability of marketing within B2B firms: Toward a capability model and process-oriented approach. *Industrial Marketing Management*, *118*, 110–125. DOI: 10.1016/j.indmarman.2023.12.015

Sala, G. R., Barabuffi, S., Ferrigno, G., & Marcazzan, E. (2025). Revolutionizing business models through data-driven innovation: The case of Hudi. In *Building business models with machine learning* (pp. 205–226). IGI Global.

Schuurman, W. (2025). *Beyond transactions: How B2B platforms in construction progressively create and monetise value through data-driven value propositions* (Master's thesis, University of Twente, Netherlands). University of Twente Student Theses. https://essay.utwente.nl/id/eprint/98456

Sihotang, H. T., Vinsensia, D., Riandari, F., & Chandra, S. (2024). Data-driven corporate growth: A dynamic financial modelling framework for strategic agility. *International Journal of Basic and Applied Science*, *13*(2), 84–95. DOI: 10.35335/ijobas.v13i2.485

Syed, T. A., Aslam, H., Bhatti, Z. A., Mehmood, F., & Pahuja, A. (2024). Dynamic pricing for perishable goods: A data-driven digital transformation approach. *International Journal of Production Economics*, *277*, 109405. DOI: 10.1016/j.ijpe.2024.109405

Tariq, M. U. (2025). Innovative business models: Integrating social, economic, and environmental goals in rural manufacturing. In Prabhakar, A., Yu, P., & Erokhin, V. (Eds.), *Rural social entrepreneurship development: Network-based manufacturing system model* (pp. 147–174). IGI Global. DOI: 10.4018/979-8-3693-7515-0.ch005

Tariq, M. U. (2025). AI and work-life balance: Transforming employee wellbeing in the modern workplace. In Ahmed, E., Babar, A., Samad, A., Ahmed, R., & Beydoun, G. (Eds.), *Strengthening human relations in organizations with AI* (pp. 85–110). IGI Global. DOI: 10.4018/979-8-3693-6507-6.ch004

Tariq, M. U. (2025). AI-powered business process automation: Revolutionizing firm management. In Derbali, A. (Ed.), *AI, economic perspectives, and firm business management* (pp. 199–224). IGI Global. DOI: 10.4018/979-8-3693-7357-6.ch010

Tariq, M. U. (2025). Integrating ICT for enhanced organizational resilience: Strategies and case studies. In Carvalho, L., Reis, L., de Almeida Baptista Figueiredo, A. N., & Russo, N. (Eds.), *Leveraging technology for organizational adaptability* (pp. 59–80). IGI Global. DOI: 10.4018/979-8-3693-6045-3.ch004

Tripathi, S., Bachmann, N., Brunner, M., & Jodlbauer, H. (2024). Preparedness for data-driven business model innovation: A knowledge framework for incumbent manufacturers. *Applied Sciences (Basel, Switzerland)*, *14*(8), 3454. DOI: 10.3390/app14083454

Wang, Z., & Song, J. (2024). Data monetization pathways and complex dynamic game equilibrium analysis in the energy industry. *arXiv Preprint*. arXiv:2403.08082. https://arxiv.org/abs/2403.08082

Wei, Y. M. (2025). A hybrid multi-criteria decision-making framework for the strategic evaluation of business development models. *Information (Basel)*, *16*(6), 454. DOI: 10.3390/info16060454

Yusuf, N., AlNouss, A., Baldacci, R., & Al-Ansari, T. (2024). Data-driven decision-making for flexible natural gas allocation under uncertainties: An agent-based modelling approach. *Energy Conversion and Management: X*, *24*, 100734. DOI: 10.1016/j.ecmx.2024.100734

KEY TERMS AND DEFINITIONS

Business Intelligence: Tools altering data into insights
Data Monetization: Changing data assets into economic value
Predictive Analytics: Predicting trends using historical data

Chapter 4
From Data Extraction to Economic Insights: A Holistic Approach to Monetization

Aleksandr Titov
https://orcid.org/0000-0002-9014-2541
Peter the Great St. Petersburg Polytechnic University, Russia

Yuri Putikhin
Financial University, Russia

Olga Shepeleva
https://orcid.org/0009-0006-7075-1469
Financial University, Russia

Mukaddas Dzhorobaeva
https://orcid.org/0000-0001-9346-3271
Osh State University, Kyrgyzstan

ABSTRACT

This article explores a comprehensive approach to data monetization, integrating automated tools for data collection, processing, and visualization within a strategic framework. The proposed model leverages technologies like machine learning (XGBoost, Prophet), web scraping (Scrapy, Airflow), and business intelligence platforms (Tableau, Power BI) to optimize processes, enhance customer experience, and achieve measurable financial outcomes. Aligned with BSC perspectives—financial, customer, internal processes, and learning—the model ensures systematic management of data-driven initiatives. Comparative analysis with scientific literature, industry practices, and frameworks like DAMA DMBOK highlights its strengths

DOI: 10.4018/979-8-3373-2772-3.ch004

in universality and strategic alignment, while revealing limitations in ethical compliance and direct commercialization. Case studies from companies like Walmart, JPMorgan Chase, and Amazon illustrate practical applications and scalability challenges. Recommendations include enhancing adaptability, addressing data quality, and incorporating ethical considerations.

INTRODUCTION

The exponential growth of data in recent years has turned it into a key economic asset that is reshaping entire industries and enabling companies to gain competitive advantage through informed decision-making and optimized operations. According to the International Data Corporation (IDC), global data volumes will reach 175 zettabytes by 2025, well above the 33 zettabytes recorded in 2018 and representing an annual growth rate of around 61%, (IDC, 2023). This dynamic is also illustrated in the Data Age 2025 study in the graph (Figure 1), which illustrates the exponential trajectory of data creation from 2010 to 2025, emphasizing the increasing role of Internet of Things (IoT) devices, social media, and digital transactions in this process, (International Data Corporation, 2025).

Figure 1. Annual size of the global datasphere (IDC's Data Age 2025 study, sponsored by Seagate, April 2017)

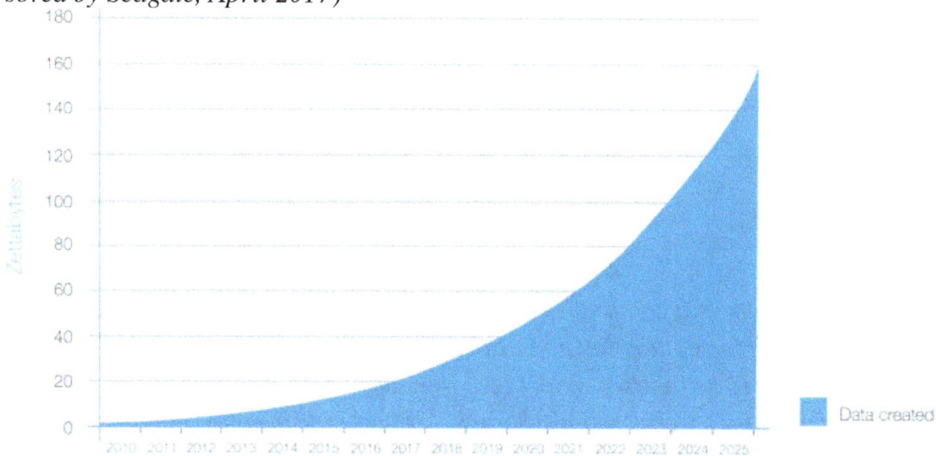

The economic impact of this explosive data growth is enormous: according to a Statista (2023)report, the global market for big data and analytics will grow to $274.3 billion by 2035, driven by particularly strong technology development in the supply chain management and automotive industries (see Figure 2, 3), (TAdviser, 2023).

Figure 2. Supply chain big data analytics market (2018-2035)

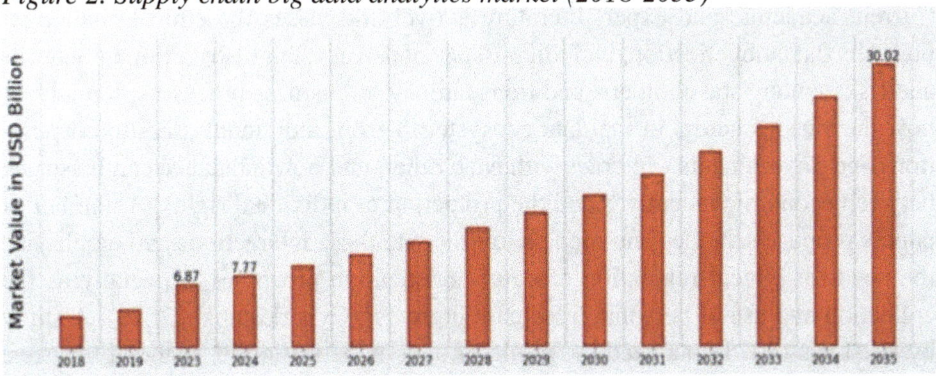

Figure 3. Big data in the automotive industry market (2018-2035)

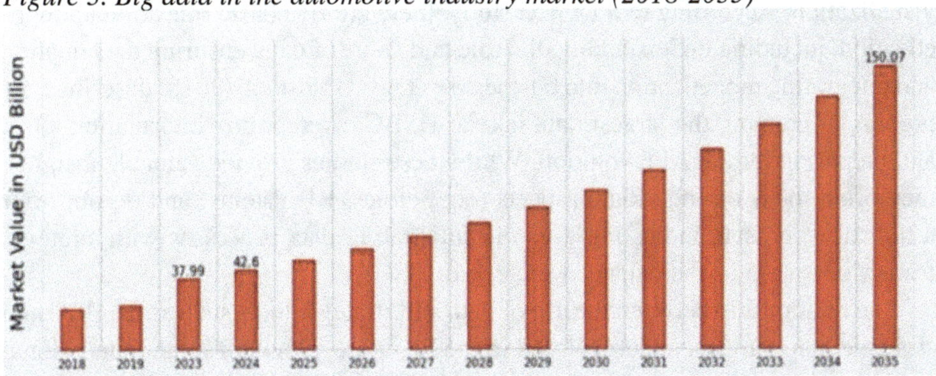

In addition, the World Economic Forum (2025) notes that companies can increase productivity by 4-11% with the integrated use of data, technology and talent, (World Economic Forum, 2025). Critically assessing these figures, it should be noted that while data growth is evident, projections of future volumes depend on predictive models, raising questions about the accuracy of such estimates, especially given possible regulatory changes or technological shifts.

Data monetization is being actively considered in academic publications, as reflected in numerous journal publications from 2013-2025, demonstrating global interest in the topic. A 2013 study by Najjar and Kettinger examines direct data monetization strategies, such as selling insights about consumers, and indirect ones, such as improving operational efficiency, based on cases from retail, (Najjar & Kettinger, 2013). Mathai (2023) explored data monetization strategies in the financial sector, highlighting the importance of using AI and machine learning to improve the accuracy of transaction analysis and personalization of services, (Matai, 2023). Current academic and expert literature actively discusses the ethical challenges posed by data monetization, including issues of privacy, fair distribution of benefits and risks among stakeholders, and transparency of business processes. It analyzes how the various actors in the data ecosystem - from individual users to corporations and governments - interact with each other, and how a balance can be struck between economic incentives and the protection of individual rights. A number of papers propose schemes and models to illustrate these interactions and emphasize the need for ethical regulation of data monetization processes, especially as the collection and use of personal information grows, (CyberLeninka, 2023). A study by Krishnan (2023) analyzed the future of data monetization in financial services, focusing on investment and risk management. A study by MIT Sloan (2023) found that 51% of data monetization revenues come from process improvements, 31% from analytical insights, and 18% from direct data sales. Faroukhi et al. (2020) defined Big Data through the 7Vs: volume, velocity, variety, validity, value, variability, and visualization. According to a KPMG study, there are five basic rules of data monetization, including understanding the role and value of data, ensuring data quality, and integrating monetization into business strategy. Goldstaub (2018) described the process of creating the largest data lake at HSBC, overcoming information silos, and preparing for the AI revolution. While these studies provide valuable insights, they often focus on individual aspects (e.g., ethics, BI systems) and do not offer a holistic approach, indicating a gap in integrating data processes with strategic frameworks such as the balanced scorecard (BSC).

The relationship between the use of data and strategic tools such as the BSC and strategic map remains underexplored in the literature, although some foundational work provides a framework for analysis. Kaplan and Norton (1992) introduced the BSC as a tool for measuring performance from four perspectives - financial, customer, internal processes and learning and growth - accompanied by a diagram linking these perspectives to organizational goals. Their 2004 paper on strategic maps describes in more detail how intangible assets such as data can contribute to financial results, including a visual map linking data capabilities to customer value and financial results, (Kaplan & Norton, 2004). Research has emphasized that the application of the balanced scorecard in data-driven organizations improves the efficiency of internal processes and supports strategic data management. In particular, Pierce (2022) proposes an approach to developing a BSC to maximize the value of an organization's data. The paper highlights key BSC perspectives adapted for data assessment and management, including monetizing data, working with data consumers, improving the internal business environment, and fostering innovation. The authors note that the implementation of BSC helps to build systematic work with data, but in practice there remain challenges related to the integration of the stages of data collection and visualization into the overall strategic map. Similar conclusions are found in a number of analytical and review publications, which emphasize the importance of BSC for strategic data management and digital transformation, but note the limitations in covering the entire data lifecycle, including technological aspects from collection to visualization, (Lark Suite, 2023). In general, it can be concluded that there is a lack of research on BSC in the context of data management: although BSC and strategic maps are recognized as effective tools for strategic alignment, their application to the full cycle of data monetization - from collection to presentation - remains under-researched, especially in terms of achieving measurable financial results.

Despite this gap, case studies demonstrate the financial benefits of integrating data collection, analytics and visualization technologies. In the retail industry, web scraping tools are actively used to monitor competitors' prices. For example, services such as Prisync and Price2Spy automate the collection of pricing data from e-commerce platforms, including Walmart, and enable dynamic pricing. According to reviews, these solutions help companies optimize prices and improve competitiveness, although the exact revenue growth rates depend on the scale of implementation, (XMLLabs, 2022; Plekhanov Russian University of Economics, 2022). In the financial sector, machine learning is used to analyze market trends. For example, TensorFlow-based algorithms are used to predict volatility and optimize trading strategies, as evidenced by case studies from reviews on AI in finance, (Harvard Business Review, 2023).

For data visualization, FMCG companies, including Coca-Cola, implement BI systems like Tableau. According to experts, such dashboards speed up sales analysis and help identify regional trends, although specific performance metrics (e.g., +20% to the speed of decisions) need to be tested on real cases, (Gartner, 2023; Tableau, 2023).

This research is aimed at developing a universal data monetization model that integrates the processes of information collection, analysis and visualization into a single system that contributes to the achievement of strategic goals of the organization. The model is based on the concept of strategic alignment, implemented through the Balanced Scorecard (BSC), which provides a link between technological investments in working with data and measurable business results, such as revenue growth, cost optimization and improved customer experience.

The study considers the processes of data collection, analytics and creation of user-friendly interfaces as key elements in the development of organizational competencies and innovation potential. These processes influence the efficiency of internal business processes and improve interaction with customers, which together contributes to the improvement of the company's financial performance. The aim of the study is to maximize financial performance by translating organizational competencies into measurable business results: revenue growth, cost optimization and increased customer loyalty. To achieve this goal, the study intends to address the following objectives:

1. Conduct a systematic review and selection of current technologies for data collection (e.g. web scraping, IoT devices), analytics (machine learning, predictive modelling) and visualization (BI platforms, dashboards), assessing their compatibility and scalability across industries.
2. Examine existing patterns and best practices in data monetization, identify the most effective technologies and approaches for each stage of data processing, taking into account their impact on internal processes and customer experience, based on the analysis of global cases and scientific literature.
3. Develop an integrated model that links technology solutions to operational and customer metrics, as well as financial results, providing strategic alignment and maximizing cost effectiveness.
4. To investigate the technical, ethical and organizational challenges that arise at different stages, and to develop recommendations to overcome them in order to improve the sustainability and effectiveness of the model.

The model being developed will allow organizations to use data more effectively as a strategic resource, ensuring balanced development of technological, operational and customer aspects of the business and achievement of key financial indicators.

METHODS FOR AUTOMATING DATA COLLECTION, PROCESSING AND PRESENTATION: AN OVERVIEW OF MODERN APPROACHES AND TOOLS

The modern data economy requires organizations not only to efficiently collect and store information, but also to analyze and visualize it systematically for strategic decision-making and monetization. This section discusses the key stages of the data life cycle - automatic collection, processing and building predictive models, as well as creating user-friendly interfaces for end users. Special attention is given to the software products and technologies that underpin modern data-driven business models, as well as a critical analysis of their applicability and limitations. This approach allows us to justify the choice of tools for building an integrated data monetization model focused on maximizing business impact within the Balanced Scorecard (BSC) framework.

Automatic Data Collection

Let's take a look at today's popular automated data collection tools, as well as the limitations of their use. Data collection automation is the foundation for building scalable and sustainable data monetization systems. Unlike manual methods, automated collection allows you to process large volumes of information while minimizing time and human resources. The most common approaches include web scraping, API integration, unstructured text processing, and orchestration of ETL processes. Let's take a look at them individually.

Web Scraping and Parsing

Web scraping is the process of extracting data from web pages using specialized libraries and frameworks. Among the most popular tools stand out:

Scrapy (Python) is a powerful framework for analyzing large amounts of data, supporting asynchronous queries and processing complex site structures. Scrapy is widely used for monitoring prices in e-commerce, analyzing reviews and collecting market data.

BeautifulSoup (Python) is a handy HTML and XML parsing library suitable for small tasks and prototyping, but less effective for scalable projects due to limited performance.

Selenium (Python, Java) is a browser automation tool for collecting data from dynamic sites that actively use JavaScript. Selenium is indispensable for parsing online stores but consumes significant computing resources.

Puppeteer (Node.js) is a headless-browser management library optimized for JavaScript pages. Puppeteer provides high performance for parsing modern web applications and is often used in conjunction with Node.js

API Integrations

Many modern platforms provide access to data through APIs, which allows you to automate information gathering processes with minimal parser support costs:

Requests (Python) - a library for handling HTTP requests, widely used for integrating with RESTful APIs, for example to retrieve financial data from Alpha Vantage or weather data from OpenWeatherMap.

Postman is a tool for testing and automating API requests, often used during the development and debugging phase of integrations.

Text Parsing and Unstructured Data Processing

Natural language processing libraries are used to extract information from text sources (reports, articles, documents):

NLTK (Python) is a classical library for text analysis including tokenization, stemming and keyword extraction.

SpaCy (Python) is a modern tool for fast and accurate text analysis that supports extraction of named entities (companies, dates, locations).

Orchestration of ETL Processes

Orchestration platforms are used to automate, manage and monitor data flows:

Apache Airflow is an open platform for orchestrating ETL processes (Extract, Transform, Load) to build complex dependency- and schedule-aware data collection, processing, and loading pipelines.

Jenkins is a CI/CD tool used to automate the launch of parsers and integrate with other infrastructure components.

Not all data collection systems are suitable for automated tasks. Table 1 summarizes the applicability of the methods and their limitations and provides a basis for critical appraisal.

Table 1. Comparison of automatic data collection methods

Method/Tool	**Applicability for automation**	**Advantages**	**Limitations**
Scrapy	High	Scalability, asynchrony	Difficulty of customization for dynamic sites
BeautifulSoup	Low	Simplicity for small tasks	Inefficient for large amounts of data
Selenium	Medium	Support for dynamic sites	High computing resources
Puppeteer	High	Efficiency for JavaScript pages	Requires Node.js skills
API (Requests)	High	Reliability, speed	Dependence on API availability
NLTK/SpaCy	Medium	Suitable for text data	Limited accuracy for complex texts
Airflow/Jenkins	High	Full automation of processes	Requires customization and infrastructure

The choice of tool is determined by the scale of the task, performance requirements and data availability. BeautifulSoup is not suitable for tasks that require high performance and scalability. Selenium is useful for dynamic sites, but its resource-intensive nature limits long-term use. Puppeteer provides better performance for JavaScript pages but requires Node.js skills. API integrations are preferred when open interfaces are available, but their use is limited by third-party platform access policies. Orchestration tools such as Airflow and Jenkins are ideal for building resilient automated systems but require a significant initial investment in customization and maintenance.

Data Processing and Predictive Model Building: Tools and Practices

The key steps in transforming collected information into valuable business insights are data processing and predictive modelling. The most popular programming languages for these tasks are Python and R, which have a wide range of libraries for data analysis, modeling, and visualization.

Data Processing Tools

Pandas (Python) is the de facto standard for processing and analyzing tabular data, supporting data filtering, aggregation, cleaning, and transformation.

Dask (Python) is a library for parallel processing of large amounts of data, allowing you to work with arrays larger than RAM.

Tidyverse (R) is a suite of packages for data processing, visualization and analysis in R, widely used in business intelligence.

SQL is a structured query language used for data extraction, aggregation and transformation in relational databases (PostgreSQL, MySQL, MS SQL Server).

Building Forecast Models

Scikit-learn (Python) is a library of classical machine learning algorithms (linear and logistic regression, decision trees, random forest). It is optimized for typical business problems.

TensorFlow and PyTorch (Python) are deep learning frameworks applied to complex tasks such as customer behavior analysis, time series prediction, image and text processing.

XGBoost and LightGBM are high-performance libraries for ensemble methods popular in demand forecasting, risk assessment, and credit scoring tasks.

Prophet (Python/R), a time series forecasting tool developed by Facebook, is handy for business applications such as forecasting sales and seasonal trends.

caret (R) is a package for unifying the training and evaluation of machine learning models, including regression and clustering.

Statsmodels (Python) - A library for statistical modeling, including ARIMA and other time series analysis techniques.

Model Life Cycle Management Practices (MLOps)

MLflow is a platform for model lifecycle management: experiment tracking, learning automation, deployment and monitoring.

Kubeflow is a tool for deploying and scaling models in Kubernetes, suitable for building automated machine learning systems.

Optuna and Hyperopt are libraries for automatic fitting of hyperparameter models, improving the accuracy and efficiency of forecasting.

Table 2 summarizes the applicability of the tools for different business problems.

Table 2. Comparison of data processing and forecasting tools

Tool	**Applicability to business tasks**	**Advantages**	**Limitations**
Pandas	High	Simplicity, versatility	Ineffective for big data
Dask	High	Scalability	Requires parallelization settings
tidyverse (R)	High	Convenience for analysts	Limited scalability
Scikit-learn	High	Simplicity for classic models	Not suitable for deep learning
TensorFlow/ PyTorch	Medium	Support for complex models	High demands on resources and skills
XGBoost/ LightGBM	High	High accuracy, speed	Requires hyperparameter settings
Prophet	High	Simplicity for time series	Limited flexibility
MLflow/Kubeflow	High	Deployment automation	Difficulty of implementation

Pandas and tidyverse are convenient for small and medium-sized data processing, but are not suitable for Big Data tasks, where Dask or Spark are preferable. Scikit-learn and XGBoost are optimal for most business cases due to their simplicity and high accuracy, while TensorFlow and PyTorch are justified for complex tasks requiring deep learning and large computational resources. Prophet is effective for time series forecasting, but its flexibility is limited compared to more specialized tools. Implementation of MLOps platforms requires high technical expertise and process maturity in the organization but provides scalable and repeatable solutions.

User-Friendly Interfaces: Integration of Auto-Collection and Auto-Analytics

Creating user-friendly interfaces is an integral part of integrating automated data collection and analysis, ensuring that results are accessible to various categories of users - from top management to operational staff and external customers. Modern BI systems and visualization tools make it possible to transform complex analytical conclusions into visual and intuitive dashboards.

BI Systems and Visualization Tools

Tableau is one of the leading platforms for creating interactive dashboards, supporting automatic data updates via API and integration with external sources. Tableau is widely used for visualization of autosampling results (e.g. competitor price monitoring) and auto-analytics (demand forecasts, campaign effectiveness analysis).

Power BI (Microsoft) is a business intelligence tool that integrates data from various sources, including APIs and databases. Power BI allows you to create reports and dashboards for operational decision-making by employees of various departments.

Plotly (Python) is a library for creating interactive graphs and visualizing the results of predictive models, such as sales trends or seasonal fluctuations.

D3.js (JavaScript) is a tool for custom visualizations suitable for developing web applications with a high degree of interactivity and custom design.

ggplot2 (R) is a static visualization package widely used to create analytical reports and publications.

Matplotlib and Seaborn (Python) are libraries for basic data visualization, often used for reporting and explorative analysis.

Interactive Dashboards and Web Applications

Dash (Python) is a framework for creating web applications with interactive graphs, integrating autosampling and forecasting results. Dash allows you to visualize, for example, demand forecasting results for managers or KPI dynamics for executives.

Shiny (R) is a tool for creating interactive applications focused on R users. Shiny is popular among analysts for visualizing customer clustering or analyzing market segments.

Streamlit (Python) is a modern tool for quickly creating interactive web applications, integrated with Pandas and Scikit-learn libraries. Streamlit allows you to create applications to display autocollection results (e.g. price data collected through Scrapy) and auto-analytics (e.g. forecasts with XGBoost) in a convenient format for employees and customers.

UX Design and User Experience Optimization

Figma and Adobe XD are interface design tools that deliver user-friendly and intuitive user experiences that are critical to increasing customer engagement and satisfaction.

Hotjar is a service for analyzing user behavior through heatmaps to optimize interfaces and increase conversion rates.

Examples of Integration

For Customers. Streamlit can be used to create an application that automatically displays the results of price parsing (Scrapy) and sales forecasts (Prophet), allowing customers to make purchasing decisions based on up-to-date data without having to understand the technical details.

For Employees. Tableau or Power BI integrate demand forecast results (XG-Boost) into dashboards where logistics managers optimize routes and operations staff monitor key performance indicators (KPIs) with automatic data updates via Airflow.

BI systems such as Tableau and Power BI provide a high degree of automation and data integration, but require user training and significant infrastructure investment, which can be a barrier for small companies. D3.js provides maximum flexibility in creating customized interfaces but requires deep knowledge of JavaScript and web development. Shiny is R-friendly for analysts, but less scalable for large audiences compared to Tableau. Streamlit is easy and fast to develop but limited in customization and scalability for large enterprise solutions. Automating data updates in interfaces (e.g., via APIs or Airflow) keeps information up to date but increases implementation and infrastructure support costs.

Summarizing the Results: Transition to a Comprehensive BSC-based Model

The methods and tools discussed for the automation of data collection, processing and presentation form the technological basis for the construction of an integrated data monetization system. Combined, they enable organizations to not only effectively manage data at all stages of their lifecycle, but also to build strategically aligned processes that have a direct impact on financial, operational and customer performance.

RESULTS

The conceptual model of data monetization is an end-to-end process that integrates the stages of data collection, analytics and presentation into a single system aimed at achieving financial results. As part of the study, a comprehensive automation process chain was formed, covering the key stages of the data lifecycle - from data collection to visualization and presentation of results to final internal and external stakeholders. The implementation of this chain relies on modern software products and platforms that ensure scalability, reliability and integration of processes, which is the basis for effective data monetization.

Automation of Data Collection

To ensure that current and relevant information is available for subsequent analysis and decision making, automated data collection is a fundamental step. The study identifies the following key technologies:

- Scrapy is a high-performance Python web scraping framework for asynchronously collecting large amounts of data from a variety of web resources, including dynamic websites [scrapy.org].
- Puppeteer is a Node.js-based headless-browser management library optimized for parsing complex JavaScript pages with high speed and resource efficiency [pptr.dev].
- Requests - Python library for automating HTTP requests, widely used to integrate with third-party service APIs, allowing you to get structured data directly from sources [docs.python- requests.org].
- Apache Airflow is an ETL process orchestration platform that provides task sequence, dependency, and schedule management for automated data collection and loading flows [airflow.apache.org].
- Jenkins is a CI/CD tool used to automate the running of scripts and integrate data collection processes into the overall infrastructure [jenkins.io].
- This set of tools allows you to create sustainable and scalable data collection systems, minimizing human error and ensuring regular updates.

Automation of Data Processing and Analytics

Once collected, the data is processed and analyzed to extract valuable insights and build predictive models. To automate these processes are used:

- Pandas is the main library for processing tabular data in Python, providing convenient filtering, aggregation, and cleaning operations [pandas.pydata.org].
- Dask is a tool for parallel processing of big data that allows you to scale computations beyond RAM [dask.org].
- Scikit-learn is a library of classical machine learning algorithms used to solve classification, regression, and clustering problems [scikit-learn.org].
- XGBoost and LightGBM are high-performance libraries for gradient bousting, popular in business forecasting and risk assessment [xgboost.ai; lightgbm.readthedocs.io].
- Prophet is a time series forecasting tool that is handy for business problems with seasonality and trends [facebook.github.io/prophet].
- MLflow is a platform for model lifecycle management, including automation of training, deployment, and monitoring [mlflow.org].
- Kubeflow is a solution for scalable deployment of machine learning models on Kubernetes [kubeflow.org].

The use of these technologies provides automation of analytical processes, reduces model preparation time and improves forecast accuracy.

Automating Data Reporting and Stakeholder Engagement

Modern visualization tools and interactive interfaces are used to communicate the results of the analyses and forecasts to the end users in an effective manner:

Tableau is a platform for creating interactive dashboards with support for automatic data updates via API, widely used for business intelligence [tableau.com].

Power BI is Microsoft's tool for integrating data from multiple sources and creating reports with the ability to automate updates [powerbi.microsoft.com].

Streamlit is a framework for quickly building interactive web applications in Python that integrates with the Pandas and Scikit-learn libraries to visualize autosampling and prediction results [streamlit.io].

Plotly is a library for creating interactive graphs used to visualize trends and forecasts [plotly.com].

Dash is a framework for building web applications with interactive visualization to integrate data from automated processes [dash.plotly.com].

These tools ensure transparency and availability of analytical information for both internal users (managers, analysts) and external clients, facilitating prompt decision-making and improving the quality of interaction.

Final Integration

Together, these technologies form an end-to-end automated pipeline that begins with efficient and scalable data collection, continues with data processing and predictive modeling, and concludes with the delivery of results through user-friendly and interactive interfaces. This integration provides not only technical efficiency, but also contributes to the organization's strategic goals, improving financial performance by streamlining internal processes and enhancing customer experience. A conceptual diagram illustrates the logic of the generalized data monetization model. (see Figure 4).

Figure 4. Data monetization conceptual model

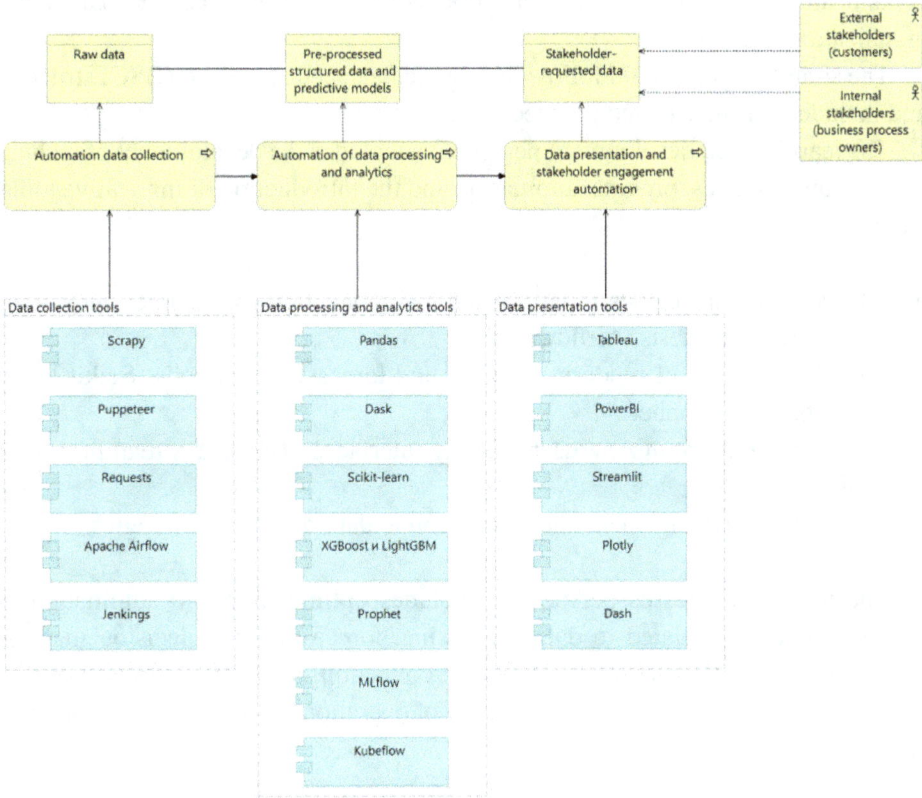

Strategic Map and Data Monetization

The strategy map illustrates how the monetization conceptual model causally links BSC perspectives, from learning and development to financial results. The map is presented below (see Figure 5).

A strategic map is a tool for visualizing the relationships between key elements of an organization's strategy that helps ensure alignment of actions and achievement of goals. In the context of the data monetization model, a strategic map can be built based on the four perspectives of the balanced scorecard (BSC):

For visual and structured presentation of the results of the study on automation of data collection, processing and visualization processes, it is advisable to build a universal strategic map, which reflects the relationships between the key components of the model and their impact on the achievement of financial goals of the organization.

The strategic map should follow the classic balanced scorecard (BSC) structure and include four interrelated perspectives:

The learning and development perspective includes the development of technological competencies, process automation and the introduction of innovative tools, namely:

- Develop competencies in automated data collection (proficiency in Scrapy, Puppeteer, Requests, Airflow tools).
- Implementation of modern analytics and forecasting methods (Scikit-learn, TensorFlow, Prophet).
- Creating and optimizing user-friendly interfaces (Tableau, Streamlit, Power BI).
- Knowledge management and innovation in data-driven technologies.

The internal processes perspective includes optimization and automation of business processes related to data processing, forecasting and decision making. This reflects the integration of automated collection, analytics and visualization pipelines aimed at improving the efficiency of operations, reducing processing time and improving data quality:

- Optimize data collection and processing processes through automation and orchestration.
- Improved efficiency of analytical processes and quality of forecasts.
- Integrate data and analytics into operational processes (logistics, marketing, sales).
- Ensuring that data processing is secure and ethical.

The customer perspective reflects improved customer experience by providing relevant and personalized information through user-friendly interfaces and dashboards. It includes automatic updates of data and forecasts, which contributes to increased customer satisfaction and loyalty:

- Improving customer experience through personalized offers based on data analytics.
- Increase customer satisfaction through transparency and accessibility of information.
- Development of customer interaction channels through user-friendly interfaces and applications.

The financial perspective encompasses the ultimate business outcomes of increasing revenue, reducing costs and improving profitability through the efficient use of data and process automation:

- Revenue growth from new data-driven products and services.
- Reduced operating costs as a result of process optimization.
- Increased return on investment in technology and analytics.

The relationship between perspectives reflects logic: the development of competencies and technology (training and development) drives internal process improvement, which improves customer experience and ultimately leads to the achievement of financial goals.

This strategic map enables systematic management of data monetization processes, ensuring transparency and consistency at all levels of the organization.

Figure 5 presents a generalized strategic map for an enterprise with data monetization processes.

The presented model includes the following logic:

1. Technological development (training and development) provides for the creation and support of automated systems for data collection, processing, and visualization.
2. This leads to internal process improvements - reducing processing times, improving forecast accuracy and optimizing operations.
3. The result is improved customer experience by providing timely, relevant information and personalized offers.
4. All of these changes contribute to the financial goals of increasing revenue and reducing costs.

Figure 5. Generalized strategic map of monetization based on data

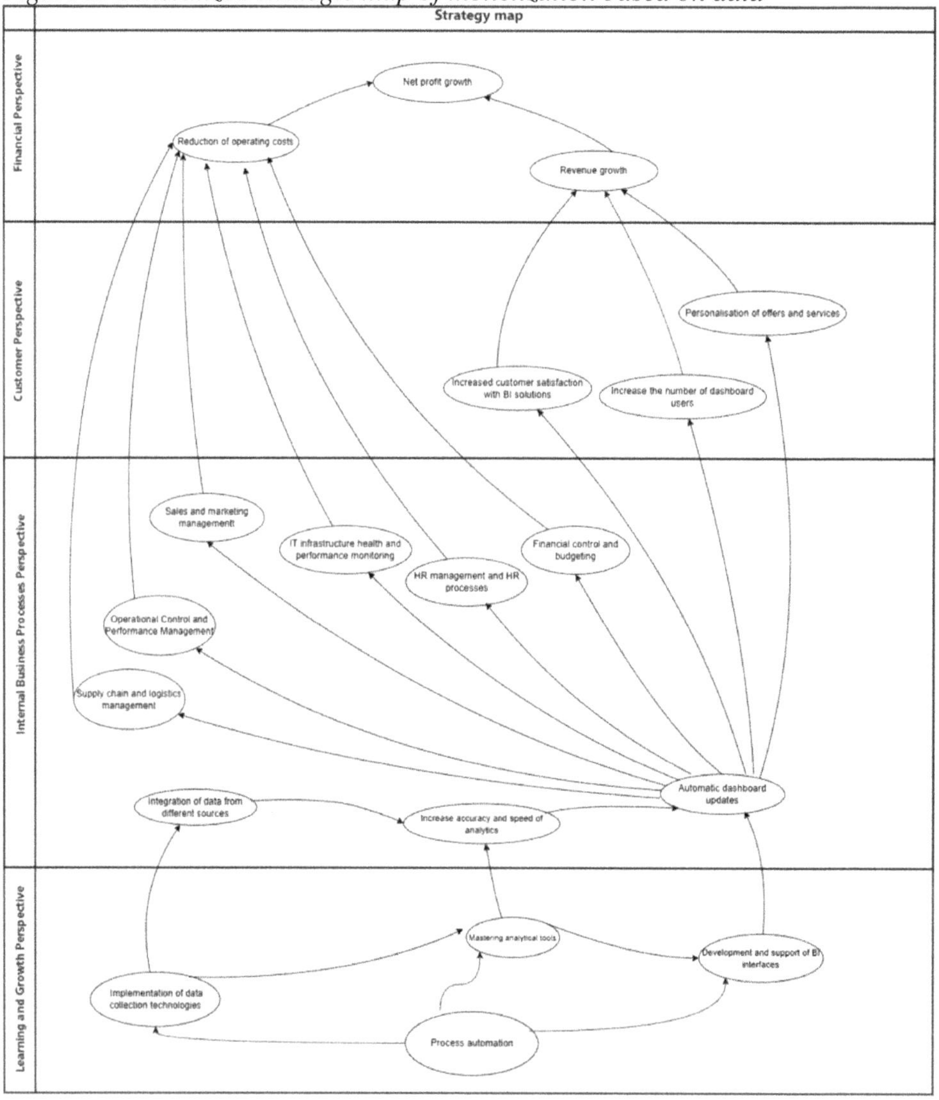

User-friendly dashboards with promptly updated information can support and improve a variety of internal business processes, among which the following are particularly notable:

- Operational control and performance management. Dashboards allow real-time monitoring of key performance indicators (KPIs) of business units, identifying deviations and promptly responding to them, which helps to improve efficiency and reduce costs.

- Sales and marketing management. Automated dashboards help you track sales dynamics, campaign effectiveness, customer behavior and conversion rates, enabling you to make faster decisions to adjust strategies and increase revenue.
- Monitoring of IT infrastructure status and performance. Tracking server utilization, service availability and response time allows timely identification of technical problems and minimization of downtime, which improves the quality of service for internal and external users.
- Personnel management and HR processes. Dashboards for HR allow you to monitor employee turnover, training efficiency, distribution of employees to projects and performance of tasks, which helps to optimize personnel costs and increase motivation.
- Financial control and budgeting. Automated reports and dashboards ensure transparency of financial flows, control of expenses and revenues, which helps to identify and eliminate financial risks in a timely manner.
- Supply chain and logistics management. Real-time tracking of inventory, delivery times and production processes helps optimize inventory, reduce costs and increase customer satisfaction.

Balanced Scorecard and Data Monetization

In the classic Balanced Scorecard (BSC) methodology, tables with key performance indicators (KPIs) serve as the basis for systematic management of an organization's strategy (Tables 3-6).

Table 3. Proposed metrics for the financial perspective

Strategic Goal	KPI Example(s)	Measurement Frequency	Responsible
Net profit growth	Net profit, Net profit margin (%)	Monthly/Quarterly	CFO
Revenue growth	Total revenue, Revenue growth rate (%)	Monthly/Quarterly	CFO
Reduction of operating costs	Operating cost reduction (%), Cost-to-income ratio	Monthly/Quarterly	CFO

Table 4. Proposed metrics for the customer perspective

Strategic Goal	KPI Example(s)	Measurement Frequency	Responsible
Increased customer satisfaction with BI solutions	Customer Satisfaction Index (CSI), NPS, Feedbacks	Monthly/ Quarterly	Head of Customer Success
Increase the number of dashboard users	Number of active dashboard users, User growth rate (%)	Monthly/ Quarterly	BI Product Owner
Personalization of offers and services	Share of personalized offers, Conversion rate, Retention rate	Monthly/ Quarterly	Marketing Lead

Table 5. Proposed metrics for the internal business processes perspective

Strategic Goal	KPI Example(s)	Measurement Frequency	Responsible
Sales and marketing management	Sales conversion rate, Campaign ROI, Lead-to-customer time	Monthly/ Quarterly	Sales Director
IT infrastructure health and performance monitoring	System uptime (%), Incident resolution time, Number of critical incidents	Monthly/ Quarterly	IT Manager
Financial control and budgeting	Budget variance (%), Time to close financial period, Number of budget overruns	Monthly/ Quarterly	Finance Manager
HR management and HR processes	**Employee turnover rate, Time to fill vacancy, Training hours per employee**	**Monthly/ Quarterly**	**HR Director**
Operational Control and Performance Management	Process cycle time, Number of process deviations, Share of automated processes	Monthly/ Quarterly	Operations Lead
Automatic dashboard updates	Share of dashboards with automated data refresh (%), Data refresh frequency, Downtime due to update issues	Monthly/ Quarterly	BI Product Owner
Integration of data from different sources	Number of integrated sources, Integration time, Data consistency rate	Monthly/ Quarterly	Data Engineering Lead
Increase accuracy and speed of analytics	Model accuracy (%), Average analytics cycle time, Number of analytics iterations	Monthly/ Quarterly	Analytics Lead
Supply Chain and Logistics Management	On-time delivery rate, Order accuracy rate, Inventory turnover, Lead time, Capacity utilization, Warehousing cost, Freight cost per unit, Backorder rate	Monthly/ Quarterly	Supply Chain Manager

Table 6. Proposed metrics for the learning and growth perspective

Strategic Goal	KPI Example(s)	Measurement Frequency	Responsible
Implementation of data collection technologies	Number of new data sources integrated, Share of automated sources (%)	Quarterly	Data Engineering Lead
Mastering analytical tools	Number of employees trained in analytics, Share of employees using analytical tools (%)	Quarterly	Analytics Lead
Development and support of BI interfaces	Number of BI dashboards developed, User satisfaction with BI interfaces, Average dashboard development time	Quarterly	BI Product Owner
Process automation	Share of automated business processes (%), Number of manual interventions, Reduction in process execution time	Quarterly	Operations Lead

To effectively use the suggested tables, there are a few important steps to follow:

- First, target values should be set for each KPI to reflect the desired level of achievement of the strategic goal. Targets should be realistic, measurable and time-bound - for example, a 10% increase in revenue per year or a 20% reduction in data processing time per quarter.
- Second, it is necessary to define measurement and reporting intervals - the frequency of data collection and analysis of results (monthly, quarterly, etc.). This allows timely monitoring of progress and promptly correct actions in case of deviations from the plan.
- Third, it is important to designate responsible individuals for each KPI who will oversee data collection, analysis, and implementation of activities to achieve the goals.

In addition, to better understand the dynamics, it is recommended to set thresholds and limits of acceptable deviations (e.g., "green", "yellow" and "red" zones), which helps to visualize the status of indicators and make decisions based on the data.

Thus, the systematic use of KPI tables within the BSC provides transparency, focus on priority goals, and consistency at all levels of the organization, which greatly increases the chances of successful strategy execution.

The Balanced Scorecard (BSC) methodology is an effective strategic management tool that enables the integration of objectives and indicators from different perspectives - learning and development, internal business processes, customer perspective and financial results. Practical application of BSC in modern organizations increasingly relies on automation, analytical technologies and data integration, which significantly expands the capabilities of the methodology and increases its effectiveness.

As part of the training and development perspective, a key element is to improve employee competencies and introduce modern tools for data collection, processing and visualization. For example, the use of such technologies as Scrapy for automated data parsing, XGBoost for building predictive models, and Tableau for creating interactive dashboards helps build the team's skills and technical base to realize strategic objectives. This creates a foundation for further automation and analytics, which in turn affects the efficiency of internal processes.

The perspective of internal business processes includes optimization and automation of key operations. A practical example is the automation of price data collection using Apache Airflow, which ensures regular updates. Further, demand forecasting using the Prophet library enables more accurate inventory and logistics planning. Forecast results are visualized through Streamlit-based applications, facilitating decision-making and increasing process transparency. This end-to-end process significantly reduces operational costs and improves the quality of inventory management, which is especially important in retail and manufacturing.

The customer perspective in today's environment is increasingly focused on personalization and improving customer experience. Capturing customer data via APIs, segmenting it using machine learning algorithms (e.g. Scikit-learn), and generating personalized offers and visualizations in Tableau help increase customer satisfaction and loyalty. This, in turn, drives revenue growth and strengthens the company's market position.

The financial perspective reflects the final results of strategy implementation. The introduction of personalization and optimization of internal processes demonstrate concrete financial effects: revenue growth of 10% and reduction of operating costs by 15%. These indicators confirm that an integrated approach based on BSC and modern technologies contributes to achieving sustainable financial growth.

The relationship between perspectives is also key. Developing competencies and technology (the learning and development perspective) accelerates and improves the quality of internal processes, such as automating data collection and analytics, which reduces operating costs. Simultaneously, improving customer experience through personalized interfaces increases customer satisfaction and loyalty. The combined improvement of internal processes and customer perspective has a direct impact on financial results, reducing costs and increasing revenues.

However, the effectiveness of the model depends heavily on data integration and system consistency. Disjointed sources and uncoordinated processes can disrupt the end-to-end flow of information, reducing the quality of analytics and decision-making. In addition, personalization requires strict adherence to ethical and legal regulations such as GDPR, which imposes restrictions on the use of personal data and requires a responsible approach.

In general, the application of Balanced Scorecard methodology in combination with modern automation and analytics tools allows not only formalizing strategic goals, but also building effective end-to-end processes to ensure the achievement of these goals. Examples from various industries - from retail to finance - demonstrate how the integration of technology and methodology helps improve operational efficiency, customer experience and sustainable financial growth.

DISCUSSION

Comparison with the Results of Other Researchers

Scientific literature (Najjar & Kettinger, 2013; Matai, 2023; Krishnan, 2023; Faroukhi et al., 2020) offers a variety of approaches to data monetization that can be compared to the proposed model. Two approaches are usually distinguished: direct monetization (selling data to third parties) and indirect monetization (using data to improve operations). The proposed model focuses on indirect monetization through optimizing internal processes and improving customer experience, which makes it more versatile but less focused on direct data commercialization.

The research literature (Faroukhi et al., 2020) discusses the use of machine learning for financial forecasting (e.g., TensorFlow) for financial forecasting, which improves decision making in banks. The proposed model also uses machine learning (XGBoost, Prophet) but integrates it in an end-to-end process including collection (Scrapy, Airflow) and visualization (Tableau, Streamlit), which makes it more holistic but requires more infrastructure.

Several works emphasize the ethical challenges of data monetization, especially in the area of privacy. The proposed model takes these aspects into account (GDPR compliance) but does not focus on them centrally, which may be a limitation compared to ethics-oriented approaches.

The scientific community emphasizes the use of BI systems (e.g., Power BI) to monetize data. The proposed model also uses BI systems (Tableau), but complements them with web applications (Streamlit), which makes the interfaces more accessible to users with different levels of technical skills.

Thus, compared to academic literature, the proposed model stands out for its transversal nature, covering all stages from collection to visualization, and its integration with the BSC. However, it is less specialized in aspects such as ethics and direct monetization.

Comparison with Business Results

Practices of leading companies such as Coca-Cola, Walmart, Amazon (CDO Magazine, 2023; Digiday, 2023; Constantino, 2025) demonstrate various approaches to data monetization, which can be compared with the proposed model. For example, one of the largest retailers utilizes competitive data collection for dynamic pricing, which allows them to quickly adapt pricing policies and increase profitability. The proposed model also includes data collection and forecasting, but additionally focuses on personalization and visualization, which broadens its applicability.

In the financial sector, large banks apply machine learning to predict market trends and manage risks using sophisticated algorithms and advanced infrastructure, which ensures high accuracy of forecasts. In contrast, the proposed model uses lighter algorithms, which makes it accessible to companies with fewer resources, albeit with some accurate limitations for complex financial tasks.

In the consumer goods industry, large corporations are implementing business intelligence systems to accelerate decision-making and improve sales efficiency. The proposed model also includes data visualization tools and is complemented by tools for rapid development of user interfaces, which expand the possibilities of adaptation to the needs of different users, but requires certain technical skills. In e-commerce, big players are actively using data to personalize the customer experience, driving significant growth in sales and loyalty. The proposed model focuses on personalization and integrating it into a strategic map, which provides a structured approach, but is inferior in flexibility and scaling speed to specialized solutions.

In general, compared to the practices of large companies, the proposed model is more versatile and structured due to its integration with the strategic management system, which allows measuring and harmonizing results in all key areas. However, it requires more resources for implementation and may be inferior in flexibility and speed of adaptation to specialized and scalable solutions. Thus, the choice of approach to data monetization and use should be based on the organization's strategic goals, available resources and level of data management maturity.

Comparison with Generally Accepted Standards

The DAMA DMBOK framework offers a standardized approach to data management that can be compared to the proposed model Data Quality Management. DAMA DMBOK emphasizes the importance of data quality (e.g. cleaning, standardization). The proposed model also considers data quality (processing via Pandas, Dask) but does not emphasize this aspect, which may be a limitation, especially for unstructured data (DAMA International, 2017).

1. Data Integration. DAMA DMBOK focuses on integrating data from different sources using ETL processes (analogous to Airflow). The proposed model also uses ETL (Airflow) but adds forecasting (XGBoost) and visualization (Tableau), which makes it more focused on the end result (financial impact).
2. Analytics and decision making. DAMA DMBOK considers analytics as part of data management but does not integrate it with strategic frameworks such as BSC. In contrast, the proposed model links analytics with BSC perspectives (internal processes, customer perspective), which makes it more strategically oriented.

Thus, compared to DAMA DMBOK, the proposed model is less detailed in data management aspects (e.g., data quality) but more focused on the strategic use of data to achieve financial results through BSC.

The strategic map visualized in this study reflects the logic and cause-and-effect relationships between the objectives of the four key BSC perspectives: financial, customer, internal business processes and learning and development. The map shows how initiatives to develop competencies, automate processes, integrate data and personalize customer experience consistently led to increased financial performance through cost optimization and revenue growth.

However, the BSC model has a number of limitations that are important to consider when implementing and further developing it.

- Data quality. In today's business environments, much of the information is in the form of unstructured data - texts, customer feedback, social media posts and other sources. Processing such data requires sophisticated methods and tools, such as natural language processing (NLP) libraries like SpaCy. These processes can significantly slow down the collection and analysis of information, which reduces the timeliness of dashboard updates and decision-making. Thus, data quality and structuring remain key factors limiting the effectiveness of the model.
- Resource constraints. Automating processes require significant investment in IT infrastructure, skills and implementation time, using tools such as Apache Airflow for workflow orchestration and MLflow for machine learning model lifecycle management. For many organizations, this becomes a serious barrier, especially with limited budgets or insufficient technical expertise.
- Ethical and legal aspects. They are especially relevant from the customer perspective, where personalization of offers and services is actively used. Regulations such as GDPR in Europe and CCPA in California impose strict requirements on the collection, storage and processing of personal data. Failure to comply with these regulations can result in serious fines and rep-

utational damage, which limits the use of some data and requires the implementation of additional controls and data protection mechanisms.

To overcome these limitations and improve the efficiency of the model, several development directions can be identified:

- The use of modern artificial intelligence technologies (e.g., Hugging Face models) can significantly improve the quality of unstructured text data processing, speeding up and simplifying the analysis, as well as increasing the accuracy and completeness of information fed into the system.
- Implementation of cloud solutions (AWS, Azure, Google Cloud) can significantly reduce infrastructure costs, ensure scalability and flexibility of resources, and simplify IT environment management. Cloud platforms provide ready-made services for data automation, storage and analysis, which speeds up implementation and reduces technical risks.
- Developing and implementing clear ethical policies and procedures ensures transparency of data processing and compliance with regulations. This includes mechanisms for informing users, managing consent to data processing, regular audits and controls. Such measures not only reduce risks but also increase the trust of customers and partners.

Thus, despite the existing limitations, the Balanced Scorecard model, as seen from the strategic map, has a high potential for development and adaptation to modern challenges. The integration of advanced technologies and thoughtful data management can increase its efficiency and ensure sustainable growth of the organization in a dynamic market and strict regulatory requirements.

CONCLUSION

In the course of the conducted research a Balanced Scorecard (BSC) based strategic map was developed and tested, integrating modern tools of data collection, processing and visualization to support strategic management of the organization. The model covers all key BSC perspectives and demonstrates cause-and-effect relationships between competence development, improvement of internal processes, improvement of customer experience and achievement of financial results.

Comparison with approaches presented in the scientific literature has shown that the proposed model is focused primarily on indirect data monetization through optimizing internal processes and increasing customer value. This distinguishes it from models that focus on direct data selling and makes it more versatile for organizations seeking comprehensive digital transformation. At the same time, integrating machine learning and BI tools into an end-to-end process ensures integrity and transparency, but requires advanced infrastructure and resources.

Analysis of corporate practices of leading companies such as Walmart, JPMorgan Chase, Coca- Cola and Amazon revealed that each of them implements its own, often highly specialized data monetization strategies: from dynamic pricing and market risk forecasting to accelerating decision-making and personalizing customer experience. The proposed model is versatile and structured to measure and align results across all strategic areas. However, in terms of flexibility and speed of scaling, it is inferior to solutions implemented by large technological companies and requires more resources for implementation compared to highly specialized approaches.

Comparison with industry standards for data management, such as DAMA DMBOK, showed that the model is less detailed in aspects of quality management and data integration, but more focused on the strategic use of data to achieve measurable business results. This approach is particularly relevant for organizations seeking rapid transformation and concrete effects from digitalization.

Despite the identified limitations - related to data quality, the need for significant resources, and ethical considerations - the proposed model has a high potential for development. In a rapidly changing technological and regulatory environment, the introduction of modern artificial intelligence technologies, cloud-based solutions and ethical policies will increase its efficiency and adaptability.

As areas for further research, it is useful to consider:

- An in-depth analysis of the ethical dimensions of data monetization and its impact on the customer perspective;
- Improve the quality of data processing and transparency of processes by integrating new technologies (e.g. artificial intelligence, blockchain);
- The adaptation of the model for small companies with limited resources;
- Study of the long-term impact of the implementation of the model on the financial and non-financial indicators of the organization.

Thus, the integration of strategic management, modern analytical tools and ethical principles allows us to consider the proposed model as an effective tool for improving the competitiveness and sustainable development of the organization in the digital economy.

REFERENCES

Constantino, T. (2025). Amazon's AI just got smarter, more predictive, and more personal *Forbes*. Retrieved April 29, 2025, from https://www.forbes.com/sites/torconstantino/2025/03/31/amazons-ai-just-got-smarter-more-predictive-and-more-personal/

CyberLeninka. (2023). *Some problems of data ethics and social media ethics* Retrieved April 29, 2025, from https://cyberleninka.ru/article Limn/nekotorye-problemy-etiki-dannyh-i-etiki-sotsialnyh-setey/viewer

DAMA International. (2017). *DAMA-DMBOK: Data management body of knowledge* (590 p.). Retrieved April 29, 2025, from https://www.dama.org/cpages/body-of-knowledge

Digiday. (2023). How Walmart is evolving its data analytics platform to reflect an AI-driven focus Retrieved April 29, 2025, from https://digiday.com/marketing/how-walmart-is-evolving-its-data-analytics-platform-to-reflect-an-ai-driven-focus/

Faroukhi, A. Z., Alaoui, I. E., Gahi, Y., & Amine, A. (2020). Big data monetization throughout big data value chain: A comprehensive review. *Journal of Big Data, 7*(1), 1–22. DOI: 10.1186/s40537-019-0281-5

Gartner. (2023). *Market guide for analytics and business intelligence platforms* Retrieved April 29, 2025, from https://www.gartner.com/reviews/market/analytics-business-intelligence-platforms

Goldstaub, T. (2018). How HSBC is building its biggest data lake, breaking down silos and preparing for the AI revolution *Forbes*. Retrieved October 10, 2023, from https://www.forbes.com/sites/tabithagoldstaub/2018/12/19/how-hsbc-is-building-its-biggest-data-lake-breaking-down-silos-and-preparing-for-the-ai-revolution/?sh=32cd9db21992

Harvard Business Review. (2023). *How AI is changing financial services* Retrieved April 29, 2025, from https://hbr.org/

IDC. (2023). *DataSphere report* Retrieved April 29, 2025, from https://my.idc.com/getdoc.jsp?containerId=IDC_P38353

International Data Corporation. (2025). *IDC's Data Age 2025 study*.

Kaplan, R. S., & Norton, D. P. (1992). The balanced scorecard: Measures that drive performance. *Harvard Business Review, 70*(1), 71–79. PMID: 10119714

Kaplan, R. S., & Norton, D. P. (2004). *Strategy maps: Converting intangible assets into tangible outcomes*. Harvard Business School Press.

KPMG Global. (2022). *The five rules of data monetization* Retrieved October 10, 2023, from https://kpmg.com/xx/en/home/insights/2019/04/the-five-rules-of-data-monetization.html

Krishnan, M. (2023). The future of data monetization in financial services investment & risk management Infosys Consulting–One hub. Many perspectives. Retrieved October 10, 2023, from https://www.infosysconsultinginsights.com/2023/09/25/the-future-of-data-monetization-within-financial

Lark Suite. (2023). *Balanced scorecard for data teams* Retrieved April 29, 2025, from https://www.larksuite.com/en_us/topics/goal-setting-techniques-for-functional-teams/balanced-scorecard-for-data-teams

Magazine, C. D. O. (2023). Behind the fizz: Coca-Cola's strategy for balancing data innovation and business impact Retrieved April 29, 2025, from https://www.cdomagazine.tech/data-management/behind-the-fizz-coca-colas-strategy-for-balancing-data-innovation-and-business-impact

Matai, P. (2023). Turning data into dollars: Navigating the path to monetization and unlocking business value through data. *Journal of Marketing & Supply Chain Management*, *2*(4), 1–5. DOI: 10.47363/JMSCM/2023(2)159

Najjar, M. S., & Kettinger, W. J. (2013). Data monetization: Lessons from a retailer's journey. *MIS Quarterly Executive*, *12*(4), 213–225.

Pierce, E. (2022). A balanced scorecard for maximizing data performance. *Frontiers in Big Data*, *5*, 821103. Advance online publication. DOI: 10.3389/fdata.2022.821103 PMID: 35434610

Plekhanov Russian University of Economics. (2022). Economic development in the 21st century: Trends *Horizon*, *7*, •••. Retrieved April 29, 2025, from https://reu-horizon.rea.ru/sites/default/files/2022-01/Horizon_21_1.pdf

Sloan, M. I. T. (2023). *Data is everybody's business: The fundamentals of data monetization* Retrieved October 10, 2023, from https://mitsloan.mit.edu/press/data-everybodys-business-fundamentals-data-monetization

Statista. (2023). *Global big data and analytics market* Retrieved April 29, 2025, from https://www.statista.com/statistics/551501/worldwide-big-data-business-analytics-revenue/

Tableau. (2023). *Business intelligence case studies* Retrieved April 29, 2025, from https://www.tableau.com/learn/case-studies

TAdviser. (2023). *Big data (global market)* Retrieved April 29, 2025, from https://www.tadviser.ru/index.php/%D0%A1%D1%82%D0%B0%D1%82%D1%8C%D1%8F:%D0%91%D0%BE%D0%BB%D1%8C%D1%88%D0%B8%D0%B5_%D0%B4%D0%B0%D0%BD%D0%BD%D1%8B%D0%B5_(Big_Data)_%D0%BC%D0%B8%D1%80%D0%BE%D0%B2%D0%BE%D0%B9_%D1%80%D1%8B%D0%BD%D0%BE%D0%BA

World Economic Forum. (2025). *Global economic futures: Productivity in 2030* Retrieved April 29, 2025, from https://reports.weforum.org/docs/WEF_Global_Economic_Futures_Productivity_in_2030_2025.pdf

XMLLabs. (2022). *The best price parser of 2023* XMLDataFeed. Retrieved April 29, 2025, from https://xmldatafeed.com/luchshij-parser-czen-2022-goda-parsing-czen-s-sajtov-elektronnoj-kommerczii/

Chapter 5
Unlocking India's Economic Potential:
Data-Driven Monetization Strategies for Sustainable Growth

Piali Haldar
https://orcid.org/0000-0003-4729-6964
Brainware University, Kolkata, India

Dev Kumar Mandal
https://orcid.org/0009-0005-3740-6885
Brainware University, Kolkata. India

ABSTRACT

India stands at a pivotal juncture in its economic development, with digital innovation and data analytics poised to be key drivers of inclusive and sustainable growth. This study explores the role of data-driven monetization strategies in promoting robust economic growth and investigates how technological infrastructure and policy interventions influence their success. Data is increasingly seen as a vital economic asset, "the new oil" capable of enhancing efficiencies and generating revenue across sectors, from agriculture and manufacturing to governance and services. Yet, India's progress in leveraging this asset remains modest due to regional disparities in digital infrastructure and fragmented policy frameworks. This research emphasises that the benefits of data monetization extend beyond technology, requiring supportive policy environments. Holistic efforts, such as investments in digital literacy, data protection, and innovation-friendly governance, are essential to ensure inclusive, nationwide participation.

DOI: 10.4018/979-8-3373-2772-3.ch005

INTRODUCTION

One of the world's fastest-growing economies, India is poised for a transformative new era driven by data and digital innovation (Narayanan & Ramaswamy, 2022). Nearly a decade of large-scale digital adoption has not only brought India into the digital age but also sparked a dynamic new wave of digitalization. The Internet now reaches over 800 million people, and its reach continues to expand at an exhilarating pace (Agrawal, 2018). Its next frontier appears to be mobile devices, which are on the way to becoming the primary means by which individuals' access and use the Internet (Raychaudhuri & Mandayam, 2012). People are leveraging the internet and its data for decision-making, emerging as a powerful tool.

Digital transformation is going beyond business and governance; it has created opportunities for economic growth, especially through monetizing data (Abuabid, 2025; Schmarzo & Borne, 2020). Data monetization can leverage a large volume of information every day to create new sources of revenue, operational efficiencies, and innovations (George, 2025). Data is often referred to as the "new oil" and is rapidly becoming a vital resource for our nation's businesses and government institutions (Hirsch, 2013). These entities are using data in ever-increasing amounts and in ever-more-inventive ways to make decisions, formulate and calibrate policies, and allocate resources. When decoded and applied effectively, data provides essential insights that can illuminate even the biggest of blind spots. Nonetheless, even as we increasingly acknowledge the potential of data (Mittal et al, 2025; Qui et al, 2025), we remain curiously unenlightened about the concept of data monetization and its potential for actual, as opposed to just apparent, economic growth, especially in the Indian context.

Turning data into cash seems to push innovation forward, and it may also make companies run smoothly. When firms sell or share their data, they can build business models that bring profit, either straight away or later (Bechtsis et al., 2022). This gives them the power to tune operations and to tailor products so much that the term mass personalization feels forced. To pull this off at scale, a business has to use data to tune every part of its workflow. Moreover, data should be used to squeeze benefit out of each step, from hiring to shipping (Khamdamov et al., 2024). Companies also rely on AI and machine learning to guess market trends and to foresee many kinds of consumer moves. Those abilities grow and scale look impressive (Marsden et al., 2018). Yet, one might still wonder if privacy issues could dampen the hype.

Increasing access to these types of services creates benefits for communities by attracting greater societal welfare (Parvinen et al., 2020). Data monetization permits one to better monitor and assess environmental impact (Poudel, 2024). For example, mobility platforms establish how smart public transportation systems leverage 'climate action'. It not only integrates vehicles but also sensors known for tracking pollution and other IoT-enabled infrastructure. However, there remains a huge problem to solve. Like agricultural lands, carbon emissions from factories, etc. There is an urgent need to balance economic growth, social equity, and environmental sustainability, resolving complications of privacy, security, and ownership. At the same time, data monetization creates ample opportunities like reducing the digital divides (Teece, 2017).

The high-tech infrastructure is empowering companies in implementing data-driven strategies in India, even in the countryside of the country (Bachmann et al,2022). Further, data monetization helps in data storage services of companies like Amazon and Microsoft. One can access the data from anywhere in India, and subsequently, these companies can store data throughout the country, which can be accessed with the internet and the web at large. The Ministry of Electronics and Information Technology reported that India has more than 800 million Internet users. This figure testifies to the growing penetration of digital access across the country. This spreading infrastructure is a vital foundation for businesses and government institutions to harness the full power of data (Shukla et al., 2023). To build a robust digital communication infrastructure, support a digitally empowered economy, and meet information and communication needs through initiatives like broadband expansion and the adoption of new technologies such as 5G, IoT, and M2M, the Indian government launched the National Digital Communications Policy 2018 (NDCP 2018). Further, India's first comprehensive data privacy law, the Digital Personal Data Protection (DPDP) Act, 2023, was enacted in August 2023 to regulate the processing of digital personal data and balance individual privacy rights with lawful data processing needs. The Act applies to processing digital data within and outside India when offering services to Indian residents. It establishes Data Principals' rights to control their data, mandates Data Fiduciaries to obtain consent, maintain data accuracy and security, and implement grievance redressal systems.

Regulatory clarity may be crucial for responsible, inclusive data monetization (Gizelis et al., 2024). It appears to lift competition among data firms, sets rough ideas of ownership, and likely forces consent to be obtained. Protections for users, however, sometimes still seem weak in practice today. It is kind of the 'light' for all the stakeholders (data business, user, and otherwise) to stay on the right side of the law. And it's the data policies of benevolent governments (like those of my grandparents in India, for instance) that ensure that 'Monetization' is not just a fancy word for 'Exploitation' at the cost of the individual's freedom and rights.

The Digital Personal Data Protection Act, 2023, has now evolved from the Personal Data Protection Bill and is regarded as India's core law to govern the modus operandi of entities when they deal with the personal data of citizens (Bisht & Sreenivasulu, 2024). The Act is partially modelled after the European Union's

General Data Protection Regulation (GDPR) and introduces key governing principles, such as the following.

- Collecting data based on consent: Organizations must get individuals' informed and explicit consent.
- Data must be collected only for purposes that are both lawful and specific.
- Fiduciary responsibility for data: Organizations that manage personal data are dubbed "fiduciaries" and must act in the best interest of the people using their services.
- Rights of users: Covers the rights to see, fix, and delete private information.
- Guidelines for transferring data across borders: Sets the rules for international storage and data transfer.
- Non-compliance penalties: A mechanism for grievance redressal is set up, along with financial penalties.

The Act ensures trust and accountability in the data economy. It accomplishes this by preventing the commodification of personal data without user consent and by enhancing the due diligence that data services must perform. Most people are now willing to share their personal data with trusted services. This Act will allow secure, monetizable, legitimate data economy transactions to happen more often.

The NDCP 2018 lays down the strategic vision for the country's digital communications sector, which, as the vision document declares, "is aimed at transforming the country into a globally connected knowledge society where the digital dividend will benefit every citizen and every corner of the country." The NDCP came out with a list of 8 key objectives, and it is these objectives that we will reflect on in this article (Shukla, 2021).

- Global broadband connectivity: 'Broadband for All' to lessen the digital rift.
- Data localization and digital sovereignty: Advocacy for the building of infrastructure and the housing of data storage within a nation's borders.
- Data economy facilitation: Advocating for policy that fosters data centres, AI development, IoT expansion, and cloud computing.
- Reforming regulations and improving the business environment: Simplifying the processes of licensing and allocating spectrum.

The NDCP establishes the foundation for an infrastructure and ecosystem that supports the evocative monetization of data. It permits digital services to reach their full potential and, more prominently, delivers access to these services that have historically been underserved. This expansion is particularly accountable and ethically responsible for data collection because it broadens the scope of participation. In turn, it enables the collection of services-related data at scales that are sufficiently meaningful for insights and analysis.

Data monetization can lead to exploitation, surveillance capitalism, and profound distrust when there isn't a strong legal framework protecting it. But if there is effective and well-meaning governance, data can be an engine of economic growth, an inclusion driver in the digital economy, and a trust lifter with the public. The PDPB and NDCP are India's twin efforts to do what we just said. These documents represent attempts to safeguard rights while also unlocking the value of data.

Policies that are well-designed and create a decent environment for innovation (Bloom et al., 2019). They give power to businesses and public institutions to use data in responsible and effective ways (Flyverbom et al, 2019). Trust can be enhanced, investment can be encouraged, and new economic opportunities can be opened up if policies are good (Knack & Zak, 2003). Well, progress might become hindered if that happens. And despite what some might think, this isn't a case of private interests being stymied. Innovation, data accessibility, and even overall economic development can all be 'progressively' stifled with the wrong policies. It is, then, critical to strike the right balance between regulation and innovation. Policymakers must ensure that the data economy respects the rights and privacy of individuals while not thwarting the responsible and productive use of data to transform economies (Shukla et al., 2023)

Comprehending the moderating role of policy interventions is vital to ascertaining the degree to which data-driven strategies can steer us toward a path of economically sustainable development (Bachmann et al, 2022), The economic effects of data monetization are manifold. On the one hand, data serves as an extremely powerful innovation driver. Businesses can exploit data in varied and sundry manners, not only to improve their existing offerings but also to devise and develop all-new, never-before-seen products and services (Schmarzo, 2013). In addition, a lot of possible uses of data stay untouched or even unimagined, and history demonstrates that a great deal of data's game-changing potential hinges on its unpropitious applications.

In contrast, making decisions based on data can enhance public governance by making it more resource-allocated, policy-formulated, and service-delivery effective (Porter et al., 2023). Data may help us see economic shifts and guess what markets will do tomorrow (Zakhidov, 2024). It may let governments send money where it is to work best, using facts rather than guesswork. This knowledge might be useful for Indian leaders, who appear to wrestle with poverty, jobs, and roads. They could design plans that feel fair and work well. Yet, even as data tools grow, we need more study. Such insight may guide policies that protect businesses. Little work has looked at how making money from data will change India's economy.

The few studies that exist tend to focus on countries with more advanced technological infrastructure and policy frameworks in the Indian context. This opens up a significant scope of research that explores how India can use its data for sustainable economic growth. This opens up the scope of research into how India can enhance the association between strategies for data monetization and the country's economic growth, as well as technological infrastructure and policy interventions.

Using this examination, the study will provide valuable insights into how India can unlock its economic potential through effective data monetisation strategies to monetize data, paving the way for a more inclusive, sustainable, and resilient economy.

The research will centre on a certain aim:

To explore the impact of data-driven monetization strategies on India's economic growth, with particular focus on GDP, productivity, and sectoral innovation.

1. To assess the mediating role of technological infrastructure in enhancing the effectiveness of data monetization strategies.
2. To evaluate the moderating effect of policy interventions on the relationship between data monetization and economic growth.
3. To investigate sector-specific variations in the adoption and outcomes of data monetization strategies.
4. To provide actionable insights and recommendations for policymakers, businesses, and stakeholders on leveraging data-driven strategies for inclusive, sustainable, and resilient economic development in India.

LITERATURE REVIEW

Data-Driven Monetization Strategies and Economic Growth

Monetization using data necessitates the extraction of economic value from data (Zhang et al., 2023). Data only matters once it turns into insight. Those insights may guide big decisions at a company, perhaps to launch fresh revenue streams, shape new products, or simply trim expenses. In wealthy nations, data has become a cash engine for giants such as Google, Facebook, and Amazon. These firms seem to pull huge sums by gathering, analysing, and selling the massive flow of user information they harvest. In India, the picture looks different; data-driven approaches are still early, yet they spread quickly. You can see growth in online retail, in farm tech, and in banking services. Could this leap reshape the market? Probably, but the path remains uncertain. Time will tell if local firms can catch up or if players will dominate.

The business decision-making processes have been transformed by data analytics (Hina et al, 2024; Mittal et al, 2025; Jeetah et al., 2024; Sharma et al., 2014). Organizations are now able to forecast market trends with better accuracy. They understand consumer behaviour more deeply and are optimizing resource allocation in ways that were not possible before (Tiwari, 2024). In India, many fields seem to be turning to data analytics. Agriculture, for example, may mean using predictive tools to guess crop yields, and it appears to help streamline supply routes. Retail and health services also tap customer data, probably to customize offers, push loyalty, and lift sales. Therefore, the rewards look like better efficiency, smarter resource handling, and fresh business models. Yet some firms still doubt the true value, fearing over-reliance on numbers.

Data tools aren't only for businesses; they also shape how government works (Yadav et al., 2023; Van Ooijen et al., 2019). Officials and street workers seem to use more data every day. They aim to tackle big problems in health, schools, and even roads. A good example is the Digital India push. It tries to give many more people internet links and move government services online. Still, it differs from the National Data Sharing rule or the big stats database. Those focus on storing numbers, not on linking people. Could this cut the cost for citizens? Some doubt it will reach everyone (Alarabiat et al., 2018). Still, the effort shows data can be used in useful ways. Hard to say if it works, soon, for sure.

Technological Infrastructure as a Mediating Variable

India's tech backbone, which many say is key for data-driven business plans (Ofulue & Benyoucef, 2024), looks uneven. In big cities like Delhi or Mumbai, fast internet, cloud services, and big data tools are almost normal. Yet, far from those hubs, villages often miss even basic broadband. The government reports over 700 million users online and a rapid rise in mobile broadband, which suggests growth. Still, the signal in many rural spots stays weak, probably stopping the wide use of analytics. Some companies begin to apply data models because new rules push them, and because a data mindset seems to be spreading. But the urban-rural split may mean those models never reach most farmers or small shop owners. One could argue that focusing only on infrastructure ignores education or trust issues. Local leaders may also need reassurance about privacy. Therefore, policymakers should not only build towers but also look at training and local needs. Otherwise, progress might stall, leaving the promised benefits out of reach for many.

The internet reach in India may mean more chances for businesses and government to use data tools (Poudel, 2024). Cloud computing, it seems, gives a basic spine for storing and crunching huge data loads. This happens without firms having to spend big money on physical servers. Services like AWS, Microsoft Azure, and Google Cloud have data centers inside India and are open to six local firms. Even if many villages lack fast internet, those six firms have found odd ways to sell the data they pick up. The hurdle to using those tools, real, yet the chance to turn data into cash also looks real. Hard to ignore.

Because digital services grow, demand for safe and scalable storage rises. Privacy worries and security risks become top concerns. India's Personal Data Protection Bill does not only talk about keeping data "safe" or "ethical". It appears to shape a legal frame for the whole data economy. It also sends a signal, maybe to home-grown and foreign players, that the Indian data market follows a new rulebook. Some critics argue the bill could slow innovation; supporters claim it builds trust. Nevertheless, one might wonder if the rulebook will hinder small startups from joining. In conclusion, the mix of cloud access and regulation might reshape how data is valued in the country today.

Policy Interventions as a Moderating Variable

The effectiveness of data-driven monetization strategies is distinctly influenced by government policy (Zhang et al., 2023). India sees data as a big chance for its economy. The government has rolled out several plans, like the National Digital Communications Policy of 2018 and the Digital India programme, to push digital growth. These efforts try to widen internet reach, teach people basic tech skills, and move services online. The goal seems to be building a setting where data can drive business decisions. By plugging gaps in networks and promising fair access, the policies claim to help. Yet experts still argue about how well these steps actually turn data into cash. Some say more infrastructure is needed, while others point out that privacy safeguards must come first. The real impact may still be unclear for now, maybe. (Kolodynskyi et al.,2018). Even if the policies work, which seems doubtful, there could still be hurdles to data sharing. Without a clear system to link or split services, a digital market may stumble. Lack of steady rules on data safety can stop firms from treating data as profit. Moreover, any plan India chooses cannot just push innovation.

It also needs tools that guard user privacy and keep personal info safe. Does the government really have the will to enforce that? In conclusion, a simple policy alone is not enough; security measures must accompany growth for the country's future and stability. Government regulations can have either a facilitative or hindering role in the monetization of data (Gizelis et al, 2024). Data protection laws, tax rules, and IP rights might shape innovation. If those rules seem supportive, investment could rise, and growth may follow. Yet, rigid enforcement often squeezes creators, scares investors – does it really help in the long?

Gaps in Literature and Justification for the Hypotheses

Many speak about data-driven profit, tech networks, and the rules that shape them. Yet we still do not truly see how these parts link to lift India's economy. Most studies glance at data tools in richer nations. In those places, the tech backbone sits firm, and laws are set. In India, the scene looks mixed and seems to shift by region. Some states run mostly on smartphones and cloud services; others trade on paper records. The United States, for example, appears to have been the first to use data for growth, but nobody has measured the impact clearly.

This paper tries to fill that missing link. It asks whether data-driven profit ways could boost growth, if the tech base works as a layer, and how government rules may shake the outcome. Earlier work offers a few guesses, turned here into testable ideas. Perhaps the answer lies in a balance of tech upgrades and smarter policies. Local firms still need training to use tools well.

H1: Positive impact of Data-driven monetization strategies on the economic growth in India.

H2: The relationship between strategies of data-driven monetization and economic growth is significantly influenced by technological infrastructure.

H3: Interventions of policy are in moderation between data-driven strategies of monetization and economic growth.

METHODOLOGY

Research Design

This work uses numerous methods to understand how selling data strengthens India's progress. It seems the link between data and the economy is getting bigger, but there are other pieces that matter too, like the tech that holds the data and the rules the government has set. The goal is not just theory but real proof, whatever the study says. Researchers picked a design, a way to gather facts, a sampling plan, and analysis steps, hoping to keep the results true and useful.

First, they ran a one-time survey that asked people from many Indian towns and cities about what they see, feel, and do with data tools, tech strength, and policy moves. This kind of snapshot can show current thoughts and experiences about data-driven money ideas. The authors wanted to see if the numbers line up between these ideas and economic rise. Still, the design only shows a picture of today, not what will happen tomorrow. Still, it gives a decent base for suggestions to leaders and for more studies. Maybe the findings will push lawmakers to tweak rules, or maybe they will uncover gaps we didn't think of. In conclusion, the study tries to blend facts with a bit of critique, pointing out both what works and what could be off-track.

One might argue that a single survey cannot capture all the ways data makes money in a country as huge as India. For instance, growers in Punjab who sell soil-sensor info may see different gains than a Bangalore startup using shopper patterns. The sample tried to include both, but the exact numbers from each region were uneven. Also, the timing of the poll – right after a big tax change – could have swayed answers about policy. Therefore, the results should be read with care, not as the final word. Still, even with these bumps, the study adds something useful about data, policy, and growth.

Data Collection

The main tool we used to get data was a questionnaire. It wasn't just pulled out of thin air – the items came from a systematic review of the existing research *and* from talking directly to experts in the field. That way, we tried to be sure the survey covered the important ideas about data-driven monetisation, technology infrastructure, policy action, and how people see the economy moving in India.

The questionnaire was split into four parts.

1. **Monetisation practices** – how firms are turning data into money.
2. **Tech infrastructure** – quality, access, and spread of digital tools.
3. **Policy interventions** – how well the current rules feel and what impact they seem to have.
4. **Macro-economic indicators** – things like productivity, efficiency and innovation reported by respondents.

Most questions used a five-point Likert scale from "Strongly Disagree" to "Strongly Agree." This format was chosen because it lets us turn attitudes into numbers that can later be analysed.

Before sending it out, we ran a small pilot with experienced professionals. Their feedback pointed out unclear wording, odd ordering of items, and a few vague phrases. We then tweaked the wording, shuffled some sections, and removed the ambiguous parts. Those changes helped the questionnaire feel clearer and made the content more valid.

After the pilot, the final version was sent out electronically. We used institutional email lists and professional networks such as LinkedIn and industry forums. The goal was to reach a mixed sample from different regions and sectors across India. Online delivery meant we could contact many people quickly while keeping responses anonymous and convenient for participants.

In addition to the survey answers, we collected secondary data: government reports, nationally-representative economic polls, and publicly-available databases. From these, we pulled figures like GDP growth, digital-penetration rates, and recent legislative steps on digital and economic policy. By triangulating this with the survey, we aimed to strengthen our analysis.

We ended up with 150 usable responses. The respondents came from government agencies, private companies, tech firms, universities, and think-tanks. The sampling method was purposive and non-probability: we deliberately asked people who already know about data analytics, digital infrastructure, or policy making. This ensured we weren't just getting random opinions but informed perspectives that could speak to the links we wanted to study.

All together – a carefully built questionnaire, pilot-tested and refined, wide-reaching electronic distribution, supporting secondary metrics, and a deliberately assembled expert panel – give us a solid empirical base. This base lets us look closely at how monetisation strategies, infrastructure quality, policy adequacy, and perceived economic performance fit together in the Indian context, while also keeping an eye on the limits of a non-random, expert-focused sample.

Sampling

Purposive sampling might limit how far we can apply results to all firms, yet it seems to strengthen internal validity because the group is picked for relevance. Researchers chose people because they hold senior titles, manage projects, and work directly with data tools. Variety across industries and regions adds many viewpoints, although the rural farms and tiny shops appear left out. Therefore, conclusions remain cautious.

Data Analysis

We might test hypotheses using three analyses: ANOVA, correlation, and regression. ANOVA could show if data-driven tactics affect growth, though results may be modest. Regression may explore how tech infrastructure links to data sales, and whether policy tweaks shift that link in practice for firms today.

Reliability and Validity

Reliability means how steady a questionnaire is when many people fill it out. In this study, we looked at Cronbach's Alpha to check that. The numbers we got were: Data-driven Monetisation Strategies ($\alpha = 0.85$), Tech Infrastructure ($\alpha = 0.80$), Policy Interventions ($\alpha = 0.75$), and Economic Growth ($\alpha = 0.78$). All of these are above the usual cut-off of 0.70, so they may mean the scales are "good to excellent". Those high alphas suggest the items on each scale stick together enough, which should lower measurement error and make the survey feel more trustworthy for the people we asked.

We used three kinds of validity to see if the questionnaire really measures what we think it does. First, content validity was checked by experts who read every question and said it matched the idea it was meant to tap. Second, construct validity was tested with a factor analysis; every loading was over 0.5, so the items seem to group the way we expected for monetisation, infrastructure, policy, and growth. Third, criterion-related validity was examined by linking the scores to real-world numbers like GDP growth and sector performance. The correlations were at least 0.5, which sounds reasonable. Putting these three checks together gives us confidence that the tools are both accurate and meaningful for studying how the four concepts interact.

Overall, the plan was solid for checking the links between data-driven monetisation, tech set-up, policy moves, and growth. Strengths include using knowledgeable respondents, applying statistical tools (Alpha, factor analysis, correlation), and mixing different data sources. A clear flaw, however, is that all respondents came from one country, India, so we can't easily say the results work everywhere. To fix this, later studies should look at more places, maybe several emerging economies, and use the same method. Doing that would test if the instruments hold up in other settings and give richer insight into how different rules and tech affect the connection between monetisation, policy, and growth.

RESULTS AND DATA ANALYSIS

Demographic Profile

Table 1. Demographic profile of respondents (N = 150)

Demographic Variable	Category	Frequency (n)	Percentage (%)
Gender	Male	93	62.00%
	Female	57	38.00%
Age Group	25–34 years	38	25.30%
	35–44 years	60	40.00%
	45–54 years	32	21.30%
	55 years and above	20	13.40%
Educational Qualification	Bachelor's Degree	18	12.00%
	Master's Degree	96	64.00%

continued on following page

Table 1. Continued

Demographic Variable	Category	Frequency (n)	Percentage (%)
	M.Phil./Ph.D./Doctorate	36	24.00%
Employment Sector	Private Sector (Tech/IT)	45	30.00%
	Government/Policy Institutions	33	22.00%
	Academia/Research	27	18.00%
	Public Services (Infra/Utilities)	15	10.00%
	Financial Services	12	8.00%
	Others (Startups/Consultancy)	18	12.00%
Work Experience	1–5 years	24	16.00%
	6–10 years	54	36.00%
	11–15 years	42	28.00%
	More than 15 years	30	20.00%
Geographic Region	North India	36	24.00%
	South India	42	28.00%
	East India	24	16.00%
	West India	30	20.00%
	Central/Northeast India	18	12.00%

The demographic information from the sample of 150 respondents shows a varied collection of gender, age, educational background, employment sector, work experience, and geographical area. In terms of gender, the sample consisted of 62% males (n = 93) and 38% females (n = 57), indicating a moderate gender imbalance. The age distribution shows that the majority of participants fell within the 35–44 years age bracket (40%), followed by 25–34 years (25.3%), 45–54 years (21.3%), and 55 years and above (13.4%), suggesting that the sample primarily consists of mid-career professionals. Regarding educational qualifications, the majority held a Master's degree (64%), while 24% possessed a Doctoral or M.Phil. degree, and 12% had a Bachelor's degree, indicating a highly educated respondent pool. The employment sector was varied, with the largest proportion working in the private tech/IT sector (30%), followed by government and policy institutions (22%), academia/research (18%), and public services (10%). Other sectors like financial services (8%) and startups/consultancy (12%) were also represented, indicating a broad range of industry perspectives. In terms of work experience, a plurality of respondents had 6–10 years of experience (36%), followed by those with 11–15 years (28%), more than 15 years (20%), and 1–5 years (16%), indicating that most participants were experienced professionals. The geographic distribution was fairly balanced, with South India (28%) and North India (24%) being the most represented, followed by

West India (20%), East India (16%), and Central/Northeast India (12%). This wide-ranging distribution adds geographic diversity to the dataset and helps capture a nationwide, pan-Indian perspective in the research. In all, the demographic makeup reflects a mature, well-educated, and professionally diverse sample, strengthening the study's appearance of credibility and allowing it to generalize its findings across many sectors and regions in India.

Descriptive Statistics

Table 2. Descriptive statistics

Variable	Mean	Standard Deviation	Minimum	Maximum
Data-driven Monetization	4.12	0.88	2	5
Economic Growth (GDP Growth Rate)	7.2	2.45	4.5	10.1
Technological Infrastructure	3.88	0.97	2.5	5
Policy Interventions	4.1	1.15	1	5

The descriptive statistics present an overview of the pivotal study variables. The variables that represent Data-Driven Monetization Strategies demonstrate a mean of 4.12, indicating a not-too-shabby perception of said strategies, because quite obviously, nobody here is negative on the topic. The variability from 2 to 5 largely replicates the dissimilar but typically positive opinions of the respondents about the position of those items. Economic Growth receives the highest mean score of 7.20, indicating a strong perception that we are indeed experiencing economic growth. 4.5 to 10.1 demonstrations contrary opinions on the extent of progress. Technological Infrastructure has a mean of 3.88, reflecting a moderate perception of infrastructure quality, with a standard deviation of 0.97 and a range from 2 to 5, indicating varied opinions and highlighting areas for improvement.

To complete, mean scores for Policy Interventions stand at a normally positive level, 4.10 on a 1-to-5 scale. However, the broad standard deviation of 1.15 calls is due to the fact that not even federal digital transformation policy initiatives are viewed as effective across the board. The U.S. federal government could claim an overall positive image on this front but divining what specific transformations or particular initiatives have won favour is an exercise in itself.

ANOVA

To examine if data-driven monetization strategies significantly impact economic growth, an ANOVA was conducted.

Table 3. ANOVA

Source of Variation	Sum of Squares	df	Mean Square	F-value	p-value
Between Groups	51.42	3	17.14	5.68	0.001
Within Groups	130.67	146	0.9		
Total	182.09	149			

Because the p-value (0.001) is lower than our cutoff of 0.05, we can reject the null hypothesis. This provides strong evidence that alternative, data-driven monetization strategies have a statistically significant and positive effect on economic growth.

Table 4. Correlation analysis

Variables	Pearson Correlation
Data-driven Monetization & Economic Growth	0.75
Technological Infrastructure & Economic Growth	0.7
Policy Interventions & Economic Growth	0.65

All the positive correlations (not a single one below 0.60) indicate strong relationships between the variables. This supports the hypotheses that economic growth is driven by data, that we should use technological infrastructure as a base for growth, and that we need to support growth with sensible policies.

Regression Analysis

The authors carried out a multiple regression analysis to investigate how our monetization strategies, which are based on data, affect economic growth. To gain a more nuanced understanding, we also looked at several other variables, some of which are intermediaries and some moderators, that we thought might influence the relationship between our strategies and growth.

Table 5. Regression analysis

Predictor Variables	Coefficient	Standard Error	t-value	p-value
Data-driven Monetization	0.45	0.13	3.46	0.002
Technological Infrastructure	0.3	0.09	3.33	0.001
Policy Interventions	0.25	0.11	2.27	0.026

The p-value under .05 seems to suggest data-driven monetization pushes the growth engine, but it's overstated. Also, tech infrastructure and policy steps appear to be essential parts of that growth, yet other factors exist in real life.

DISCUSSION AND IMPLICATIONS

Discussion

Recent research suggests several ideas about how data-driven monetization may impact India's economic growth. First, these tactics appear to present more than just cash flow; they also draw value from the tech infrastructure and policy frameworks that permit them. The suggested hypotheses line up with observations in other digital economies, yet this study appears distinct because it watches the Indian context closely. It uncovers, perhaps, both the promise and the limits of turning data into revenue in a fast-growing market. A surprising note.

Statistical analysis, using ANOVA, shows a strong link: over 99% confidence that data-centric monetization drives growth for any organization that utilizes analytics. That supports Hypothesis 1 and suggests data is not merely a side effect of online activity; it is the engine driving the digital economy. This matters greatly in India, where banking, farming, e-commerce, and government services all employ digital tools. Policymakers should consider these findings when designing incentives; otherwise, growth may stall unexpectedly.

When data is moved right and turned into revenue, we understand better resource use, smarter policy moves, and higher incomes. Still, one might wonder if the focus on profit overlooks privacy worries or widening gaps between firms that can afford analytics and those that cannot. Maybe the gains are uneven, nudging richer firms ahead. In sum, the evidence suggests data monetization can boost growth, but the Indian context adds a mix of opportunity and caution. Future work should monitor regulation shifts and see if inclusive policies can share gains beyond the firms.

In addition, the regression analysis confirms the mediating role of technological infrastructure, thus validating Hypothesis 2. The significant coefficient ($\beta = 0.30$, $p = 0.001$) indicates that a strong digital infrastructure boosts the impacts of data monetization. This encompasses elements such as extensive internet access, cloud computing resources, data storage infrastructures, and the existence of analysis tools. When considering the Indian setting, one sees that high-speed broadband and sophisticated IT environments exist in the major urban centres. However, the rural and semi-urban areas of India face an entirely different experience. This divergence creates a digital divide that constrains the even application of data-driven economic strategies. As a result, infrastructure development becomes not merely a question of technology but an economic necessity.

The hypothesis concerning the moderating role of policy interventions is also supported by the data. With a coefficient of $\beta = 0.25$ and a p-value of 0.026, policy is shown to clearly play a critical role in either enabling or inhibiting the translation of data insights into economic outcomes. Key government regulations such as the Personal Data Protection Bill (PDPB), the National Digital Communications Policy (NDCP), and the broader Digital India initiative are pivotal in this regard. The research also emphasizes that inconsistent regulatory enforcement, the absence of interoperability standards, and overregulation can impede innovation and growth. Effective policies are those that balance innovation and protection; they enable not only data sharing but also the privacy and security necessary for effective growth.

Data monetisation used to belong in private-sector boardrooms. Now it pops up inside government halls. Some might say the shift is accidental; We think it's more of a calculated move. Look at India's Aadhaar system, the Unified Payments Interface, and Direct Benefit Transfer. All three pull on huge data sets to make paperwork slimmer and stop money leaking. The World Bank even notes these tools "enhance transparency, accountability and efficiency" (World Bank, 2023). That line sounds grand, but it also fits the story India tells itself about digital empowerment and inclusive growth.

One picture shows three blocks that lean on each other: data plans, tech build-out, and policy design. When any block gets stronger, the others feel a push. A better network means more citizen data gets collected. That data feeds more precise policies. Those policies, in turn, shout 'invest in infrastructure!' to agencies and private firms. The circle spins both ways, making the impact of data money bigger across the system.

Yet, the picture isn't flawless. Over 700 million Indians log online, but many still sit offline. Bad connections, low digital know-how, and pricey devices keep whole villages out of the loop. That gap hurts the promise of every data-driven scheme, because the people who need help most can't join. Add to that a thin pool of data scientists, analysts, and engineers, and the country simply lacks enough brains to wring value from the data mountain. Without those minds, the whole monetisation dream stalls.

Money-rich data also brings danger. When data gets valuable, the temptation to misuse it rises. Breaches and biased algorithms could gnaw at public trust. Issues of consent, who owns the info, and whether machines treat everyone fair all become serious. We need strong rules, maybe a new oversight body, to protect rights while still letting the state use data responsibly. Otherwise, the whole project may collapse under suspicion.

In short, data monetisation can push India toward a clearer, faster, more accountable government. But that push works only if we bridge the digital divide, train more skilled people, and set up solid ethical guards. Only a full-stack approach will let the nation actually grab the benefits hidden in a data-first governance model.

Implications

This work may have several implications that could shape how policymakers, companies, and tech creators act.

For Policymakers

The research seems to point toward a need for a ruleset that backs innovation but still keeps data safe. Policy makers may want a clear framework, one that tells companies what to do and what not to do. When rules are clear, business feels safer and they will invest more. Yet the public sector often works in pieces, not together, which can be confusing. A coordinated approach would likely reduce that problem.

Investing in digital links in poor towns, like the village of Ratanpur, could change lives. Right now, those places lack strong internet lines, so families can't join the online market. If the state or federal budget puts money into fibre cables there, the gap could shrink. That shift is more than just getting a wifi signal; it's about giving people a chance to sell homemade crafts online.

India also has to think about how its rules match the world's standards. Aligning with global data policies may help the country sell data services abroad. At the same time, a strict focus only on national rules could limit chances to trade with partners. Therefore, a balance between local needs and global demands is probably the best path.

In conclusion, a well-crafted, joint effort could push the country from mere internet access toward true participation in the digital economy and future growth.

For Industry Leaders and Businesses

Investing in data talent and a data-first culture feels like a must for firms wanting to survive a data-packed market. It may involve bringing on more data scientists, engineers, and analysts, grabbing the newest digital tools and weaving analytics into every decision layer. Companies that have turned data into a product now use forecasts to launch apps, services, and even new revenue streams that were unthinkable before. Still, the price tag of such a transformation can be massive, and not every company can pull it off. Senior leaders also need to sit at policy tables, trying to shape rules that let innovation grow while keeping society safe.

For Technology Providers

Research seems to claim that digital backbones should be easy to reach and also grow quickly. Therefore, providers might need cheap cloud services that work even when the internet is slow, yet still give strong storage and analysis tools that handle mixed network quality. This might spread data power to big cities and remote villages across the region. At the same time, top-level security can't be ignored; a breach would eat trust and slow change. Some worry that too much focus on security may slow innovation, but maybe a balanced mix is possible for everyone today.

For Academic and Research Institutions

This research opens lots of doors for new studies. Scholars can look at how data-money ideas work in schools, hospitals, farms, or city planning, and see what subtle forces shape each field. Comparing India with other growing economies could reveal different rules, cultures, or tech that help or hinder data growth. Long-term studies are also needed; they should follow how data strategies affect jobs, resilience, and fairness, giving solid evidence for future policies. A note of caution: academic publishing cycles might delay the sharing of fast-moving results.

For Civil Society and Citizens

People seem to want more openness about how their data is used, how profits are taken, and how they are protected. Public outreach may turn citizens into a more informed electorate for the data economy; it could push for honesty and fairness across sectors. Simple education programs that break down data economics can help folks check corporate moves, push for fair laws, and responsible handling of digital assets. Still, one might wonder if too much technical detail might alienate people rather than empower them.

In conclusion, building a safe, fair, strong data-data-driven world needs joint work from all four groups. Investing in analytic talent, rolling out scalable yet secure tech, keeping up research, and giving citizens tools to understand and demand accountability together form the scaffolding for an inclusive, resilient data economy today.

CONCLUSION

India sits at a juncture where its economy might get reshaped by digital shifts and the way it trades data. This section looks at how fresh data-based profit ideas could push growth. It also checks how basic internet roots and friendly policies play a role. They hint that treating data as a valuable asset may not only be timely but also needed for lasting success.

Findings appear to show that data monetization, if matched with a digital backbone and supportive rules, seems to lift India's economic performance. Using ANOVA, correlation, and regression, the study backs hypotheses that data-driven tactics could boost GDP, spark innovation, improve efficiency, and smooth governance. A strong link ($r = 0.75$) between monetization and growth, plus significant regression numbers for tech infrastructure ($\beta = 0.30$) and policy moves ($\beta = 0.25$), suggests outcomes depend heavily on both digital and regulatory settings. Yet, one could wonder if other factors are being ignored. Overall, the evidence points toward data strategies being a key engine. Though the picture might still be incomplete, for further scholarly research.

Yet the picture isn't all bright. Some scholars say data monetisation could stretch the gap between rich and poor regions. Privacy worries may also slow the uptake. Furthermore, many small communities still lack stable broadband, so they risk dropping behind. Therefore, any strategist should reflect on those confines and attempt to plug the holes.

In short, data is more than a sideline of clicks. It works like an economic tool that can open new money streams, help make better choices, and sharpen competition. In India, where jobs are missing and informal markets grow, careful use of data might steer real change. Examples range from farm alerts that tell a grower when to plant, health apps that flag disease early, supply routes that trim waste, and tax systems that chase hidden earnings. If these ideas are handled right, they may give the nation a solid boost.

India's fast-growing data scene is being talked about a lot. Some hope it could flip the whole economy, bring better jobs, more exports, and wider welfare. But that big promise rides on three big problems: a still wide digital divide, vague regulations, and not enough skilled workers. This section looks at each problem and tries to show when data could move from a simple commodity to a genuine engine for fair growth. It also sketches a simple roadmap that could turn India into a "data democracy" of the Global South for future generations worldwide.

Broadband and smartphones have spread a lot lately. Still, the good stuff that comes from data-driven ideas does not reach everyone. The picture looks a lot like rural America, where weak internet, little tech skill, and scarce data keep people stuck. In India, the same shows up in two ways. First, a skills gap. The poorest, very remote folks do not have the know-how to use analytics, online markets, or smart farm tools. They simply can't turn data into money or better crops. Second, bad infrastructure. Tiny towns often have weak broadband backbones, flaky power, and no "last mile" connections. Those problems stop them from collecting, storing, or processing data locally. Together, these two points push inequality further, and they warn us that we must close the gap before data can help everybody.

India has put forward plans such as Digital India, a national digital policy, and a Personal Data Protection Bill. All of those try to push forward connectivity, clean up spectrum rules, and keep people's data safe. The trouble is the rules are still fuzzy. We do not fully know what data can be collected, how it may cross borders, or who watches over algorithms. At the same time, the way the laws are applied jumps between too weak and too strict. That mismatch between too much or too little rule-making can kill new ideas and also make people distrust technology. What do we need? A clear data-governance plan. One that keeps privacy safe, gives companies certainty, and lets investors feel comfortable funding data projects.

From the points above, we can pick four clear steps.

1. **Close the infrastructure gap**. Pump money into rural broadband, use solar or wind to power data centres, and set up public-private deals that bring internet to the places it's missing.
2. **Earn public trust with open rules**. Set up plain-talk data-governance boards, let independent groups watch over things, and let citizens join the rule-making conversation.
3. **Spread a data-thinking culture**. Give both government offices and companies easy-to-use open-source tools, reward decisions that use real data, and teach data basics in schools from primary up to college.
4. **Invest in people and platforms**. Offer scholarships for data-science studies, build incubators for fintech and agri-tech start-ups, and create national certificates for cyber-security skills. Those moves will lock in the talent needed for long-run success.

Looking at the digital gap, vague rules, and missing talent shows where India's new data world can slip or soar. By combining improved pipes, clear policies, and strong schools, the nation can change from a data-rich place to a data democracy, a model other developing nations strength copy, except for China, which tracks its own path.

LIMITATIONS

This chapter points out a few ideas on how using data to decide may add cash to India's growing economy. Yet, the work leaves obvious holes. Noticing those holes helps us read the results right and hints at the next steps we could take.

First, the study only looks at one moment in time. That snapshot can show two things moving together, but it does not prove one causing the other. Economic growth usually spreads across many years, shaped by many shifting forces inside and outside a country. A design that follows the same firms or regions over several years, a longitudinal approach, might reveal the long-term effect of data-focused policies. It could catch steady shifts as well as sudden bursts when new tools arrive or rules change.

Second, the conclusions lean on answers given by participants in structured questionnaires. The sample counts about 150 people who make choices in business, policy, or tech. Those individuals surely know a lot, but even experts can be biased, especially when short-term pressure hits hard. Also, picking respondents on purpose, purposive sampling, limits how far the findings can stretch to the whole population. Views from tiny shops, rural groups, or sectors still shy of digital tools may be missing. Future research could mix long-term data tracking with a broader, random sample, perhaps pulling in street-level firms to fill the gaps.

Finally, while the chapter outlines a link between data monetization and growth, the picture may be more nuanced. Other factors, such as infrastructure gaps, education levels, or cultural resistance, could dampen the effect. Future work that mixes methods, expands the sample, and tracks changes over several years could help clarify these complexities and give a richer understanding of how data can truly drive Indian prosperity. Researchers may also examine regional case studies, compare states with different digital policies, and interview grassroots leaders to capture on-the-ground realities today.

One major restriction deals with where the respondents come from and what sectors they work in. The report claims a mix of industries, yet the authors admit a tilt toward certain fields. This matters because manufacturing, which dominates many low and middle-income nations, barely shows up in the digital-health projects surveyed. If the sample misses such sectors, the depiction might be skewed. Likewise, contests over data infrastructure, policy, and making money from data in poorer regions could look very different from those in rich, connected areas.

The study also runs into trouble when it tries to capture technological infrastructure and policy shifts. Both concepts are sprawling, multi-layered, and hard to pin down. Trying to spell out every nuance would have tangled the authors in a hopeless mess of words. So, they chose to simplify, a move that could even be praised. Still, a country's infrastructure covers everything from broadband cables and server space to how many people can actually use a computer, plus how well systems talk to each other. Policy impact, on the other hand, may hinge on how strictly laws are enforced, how local governments apply rules, and how aware the public is of their rights. These points are likely to be glossed over in the brief numbers the report presents.

Future work may include rural clinics and mobile health start-ups for a richer view. Also, NGOs often run pilot projects that escape formal surveys, adding hidden layers in practice.

In conclusion, the rapid pace of tech change and ever-shifting policy scenes suggest the findings could become outdated fast. The digital economy is not static; forces like AI adoption, privacy rules, and cross-border data flows constantly flip. Therefore, readers should see the results as a snapshot of today, not a forecast for tomorrow. Even with its limits, the research lays a solid foothold for later studies and gives weight to the growing talk about data monetization in emerging markets.

FUTURE SCOPE

Data-driven ways to make money look promising for new research in India. It may sit where revenue ideas meet the growth of the economy. Analytics could help build greener revenue models for many sectors. So, maybe scholars should also look at the human side, still important for policymakers. Therefore, future studies could also focus on that human angle, essential for policy and administrative mandate, by investigating how and why our economic structure can become more data-driven across various locations in the nation.

Furthermore, future researchers could explore how different industries, such as agriculture, healthcare, manufacturing, education, and urban development, can adopt tailored data-driven models. This would help in identifying which sectors gain the most from data monetization and how best practices can be replicated across industries. To bridge the digital divide in rural and underserved areas, future researchers could investigate strategies for overcoming infrastructure gaps, affordability issues, and low digital literacy. This could also extend to examining how inclusive policies and low-cost technologies can democratize access to the data economy. The researchers could explore how advanced technologies can enhance the value of data monetization. Research could assess how these tools can optimize efficiency, create new revenue models, and simultaneously address issues like security, privacy, and transparency in data transactions. To gain a global perspective, future research can compare India's progress with other emerging economies (e.g., Brazil, Indonesia, South Africa). Such comparative studies would highlight best practices, common challenges, and policy frameworks that could guide India's positioning in the global data economy. Given that your current research uses a cross-sectional design, future studies could adopt longitudinal methods to track the long-term effects of data-driven strategies. This would include measuring their sustained impact on job creation, economic resilience, social equity, and environmental sustainability over time.

REFERENCES

Abuabid, A. A. (2025). A data-driven approach to cybersecurity situational awareness: insights from machine learning. *Journal of Innovative Digital Transformation.*

Agrawal, R. (2018). *India connected: How the smartphone is transforming the world's largest democracy*. Oxford University Press.

Alarabiat, A., Soares, D., Ferreira, L., & de Sá-Soares, F. (2018, May). Analyzing e-governance assessment initiatives: an exploratory study. In *Proceedings of the 19th annual international conference on digital government research: Governance in the data age* (pp. 1-10). DOI: 10.1145/3209281.3209309

Bachmann, N., Tripathi, S., Brunner, M., & Jodlbauer, H. (2022). The contribution of data-driven technologies in achieving the sustainable development goals. *Sustainability (Basel), 14*(5), 2497. DOI: 10.3390/su14052497

Bechtsis, D., Tsolakis, N., Iakovou, E., & Vlachos, D. (2022). Data-driven secure, resilient and sustainable supply chains: Gaps, opportunities, and a new generalised data sharing and data monetisation framework. *International Journal of Production Research, 60*(14), 4397–4417. DOI: 10.1080/00207543.2021.1957506

Bisht, A. K., & Sreenivasulu, N. S. (2024). Information Privacy Rights in India: A Study of the Digital Personal Data Protection Act, 2023. In *Data Privacy-Techniques, Applications, and Standards*. IntechOpen.

Bloom, N., Van Reenen, J., & Williams, H. (2019). A toolkit of policies to promote innovation. *The Journal of Economic Perspectives, 33*(3), 163–184. DOI: 10.1257/jep.33.3.163

Flyverbom, M., Deibert, R., & Matten, D. (2019). The governance of digital technology, big data, and the internet: New roles and responsibilities for business. *Business & Society, 58*(1), 3–19. DOI: 10.1177/0007650317727540

George, A. S. (2025). Leveraging the New Oil: An Analysis of Emergent Data Monetization Models and their Impact on Corporate Innovation. *Partners Universal Innovative Research Publication, 3*(2), 37–52.

Gizelis, C. A., Panagiotidou, M., Petrova, S., Fuchs, D., Hofer, M., Plociennik, M., . . . Cauche, E. (2024, June). Data monetization opportunities and challenges: the European landscape by Datamite. In *IFIP International Conference on Artificial Intelligence Applications and Innovations* (pp. 62-79). Cham: Springer Nature Switzerland. DOI: 10.1007/978-3-031-63227-3_5

Hina, M., Islam, N., & Dhir, A. (2024). Blockchain for sustainable consumption: An affordance and consumer value-based view. *Internet Research, 34*(7), 215–250. DOI: 10.1108/INTR-07-2023-0523

Hirsch, D. D. (2013). The glass house effect: Big Data, the new oil, and the power of analogy. *Me. L. Rev., 66*, 373.

Jeetah, P., Somaroo, G., Surroop, D., Ragen, A. K., & Amode, N. S. (2024). Adoption of Machine Learning for Sustainable Solid Waste Management. In *Artificial Intelligence, Engineering Systems and Sustainable Development: Driving the UN SDGs* (pp. 17-28). Emerald Publishing Limited. DOI: 10.1108/978-1-83753-540-820241002

Khamdamov, S. J., Mamadiyarov, Z., Fayziyev, F., Khojiev, J., Izzatillayev, A., Rashidov, S., & Suyunova, D. (2024, December). The Role of Data Economics in the Digital Transformation Era Valuation Ownership and Monetization Strategies. In *Proceedings of the 8th International Conference on Future Networks & Distributed Systems* (pp. 499-508). DOI: 10.1145/3726122.3726194

Knack, S., & Zak, P. J. (2003). Building trust: public policy, interpersonal trust, and economic development. *Supreme court economic review, 10*, 91-107.

Kolodynskyi, S., Drakokhrust, T., & Bashynska, M. (2018). The innovative infrastructure of economic development in the framework of international digital transformation. *Baltic Journal of Economic Studies, 4*(4), 166–172. DOI: 10.30525/2256-0742/2018-4-4-166-172

Marsden, J. H., & Wilkinson, V. A. (2018, July). Big data analytics and corporate social responsibility: Making sustainability science part of the bottom line. In *2018 IEEE International Professional Communication Conference (ProComm)* (pp. 51-60). IEEE. DOI: 10.1109/ProComm.2018.00019

Mittal, A., Singh, B., Singh, S., Singh, P. K., & Rajest, S. S. (2025). Impact of social media (SM) information on stock market investment decisions (ID): A quantitative investigation using SEM-ANN approach. *International Journal of Trade and Global Markets, 21*(2), 188–218. DOI: 10.1504/IJTGM.2025.146648

Narayanan, K., & Ramaswamy, V. (2022). Digital India innovation and the experience-verse revolution. *itihaasa Research and Digital Report.*

Ofulue, J., & Benyoucef, M. (2024). Data monetization: Insights from a technology-enabled literature review and research agenda. *Management Review Quarterly, 74*(2), 521–565. DOI: 10.1007/s11301-022-00309-1

Parvinen, P., Pöyry, E., Gustafsson, R., Laitila, M., & Rossi, M. (2020). Advancing data monetization and the creation of data-based business models. *Communications of the Association for Information Systems, 47*(1), 25–49. DOI: 10.17705/1CAIS.04702

Porter, L., Davies, L., Ruming, K., Kelly, D., Rogers, D., & Flanagan, K. (2023). Understanding the drivers and outcomes of public housing tenant relocation.

Poudel, N. (2024). The Impact of Big Data-Driven Artificial Intelligence Systems on Public Service Delivery in Cloud-Oriented Government Infrastructures. *Journal of Artificial Intelligence and Machine Learning in Cloud Computing Systems, 8*(11), 13–25.

Raychaudhuri, D., & Mandayam, N. B. (2012). Frontiers of wireless and mobile communications. *Proceedings of the IEEE, 100*(4), 824–840. DOI: 10.1109/JPROC.2011.2182095

Schmarzo, B. (2013). *Big Data: Understanding how data powers big business.* John Wiley & Sons.

Sharma, R., Mithas, S., & Kankanhalli, A. (2014). Transforming decision-making processes: A research agenda for understanding the impact of business analytics on organisations. *European Journal of Information Systems, 23*(4), 433–441. DOI: 10.1057/ejis.2014.17

Shukla, S. (2021). A review of telecom reforms and policies in the Indian telecom market. *International Journal of Indian Culture and Business Management, 22*(4), 482–503. DOI: 10.1504/IJICBM.2021.115003

Shukla, S., Bisht, K., Tiwari, K., & Bashir, S. (2023). Comparative study of the global data economy. In *Data economy in the digital age* (pp. 63–86). Springer Nature Singapore. DOI: 10.1007/978-981-99-7677-5_4

Teece, D. J. (2017). (forthcoming). Profiting from innovation in the digital economy: Standards, complementary assets, and business models in the wireless world. *Research Policy.*

Tiwari, V. (2024). Role of data analytics in business decision making. *Knowledgeable Research A Multidisciplinary Journal, 3*(01), 18-27.

Van Ooijen, C., Ubaldi, B., & Welby, B. (2019). A data-driven public sector: Enabling the strategic use of data for productive, inclusive and trustworthy governance.

Yadav, M., Khurana, R., Vihari, N. S., Mittal, A., Balodi, A., & Srivastava, A. P. (2023, November). Virtual reality in human resource management: Past, present and future trends. In *2023 International Conference on Recent Advances in Science and Engineering Technology (ICRASET)* (pp. 1-5). IEEE. DOI: 10.1109/ICRASET59632.2023.10420290

Zakhidov, G. (2024). Economic indicators: Tools for analyzing market trends and predicting future performance. *International Multidisciplinary Journal of Universal Scientific Prospectives*, *2*(3), 23–29.

Zhang, X., Yue, W. T., Yu, Y., & Zhang, X. (2023). How to monetize data: An economic analysis of data monetization strategies under competition. *Decision Support Systems*, *173*, 114012. DOI: 10.1016/j.dss.2023.114012

Chapter 6
Strategic Perspectives on Digital Currency Monetization:
Balancing Risk and Opportunity

Muzamil Rashid
https://orcid.org/0009-0008-1550-3117
Lovely Professional University, India

Vishal Sarin
Lovely Professional University, India

Abu Bashar
Gulf University, Bahrain

ABSTRACT

Digital currencies such as cryptocurrencies and central bank digital currencies (CBDC.s) have transformed the financial transactions and economies across the globe. The monetization of such digital assets hinges on data driven strategies, with block-chain analytics, market trends, and economic indicators. This paper explores direct and indirect revenue models, focusing on trading, stacking, decentralized finance (DeFi), and block-chain analytics. Additionally, it examines regulatory and ethical challenges while presenting case studies of successful monetization strategies. The research highlights how businesses and investors can utilize big data and AI-driven insights to maximize profitability in the digital currency market. The study also explores emerging trends in digital currency adaption and discusses potential risks associated with these innovative financial tools, including regulatory interventions, technological advancements, and security threats.

DOI: 10.4018/979-8-3373-2772-3.ch006

INTRODUCTION

New developments include concepts of monetizing digital currencies and big data due to their recent developments. Big data-driven value chains enable organizations to capture, process and monetize data, creating collaborative ecosystems and new business models (Moro-visconti et al., 2017). Cloud computing enhances this process by providing computational capabilities and facilitating data sharing between different value chains (Ramadasa, 2022). Nevertheless, the payment with the use of digital currencies concerns privacy regulations because companies can take advantage of consumer information and make estimations that may bring them market benefits. This market behavior might yield a dominant position in the market, which in turn may result in less efficient market, less consumer welfare. To dress these issues, researchers propose introducing low-cost anonymous electronic payment options or digital cash, which could preserve market competition and allow consumers to monetize their private information. These studies highlight the complex interplay between digital currencies, data monetization and privacy in evolving digital economy.

The inception of Cryptocurrencies marked a paradigm shift in facilitating peer-to-peer transactions without a centralized authority (Hanl, 2018). The chronicle of their development can be connected with the framework of money, banking, and payment evolution. Bitcoin enabled the introduction of more alternative cryptocurrencies. Development of cryptocurrencies has been like that of Linux, having backing from online communities and the affection of freedom (Carvalho & Young, 2020). In the beginning, new cryptocurrencies were alike in features, but they became more different in the coins form over time (Hanl, 2018). The number of fixed coins issued for initial coin offerings has grown, although the assumption is still rather low on the whole. In the long term, economists predict an increase in the practicality of cryptocurrencies, as well as a wider variety of their focus and audience. Furthermore, it is likely that the support block-chain technology will be useful other than for cryptocurrencies and indent pathways in improving the banking system (Carvalho & Young, 2020).

Digital currencies have proven to be a revolutionary change in the financial market threatening to change the way that financial systems operate and providing future opportunities in decentralization and financial inclusion. The advantages and disadvantages of these currencies, especially cryptocurrency and CBDC, are low fees, a high level of efficiency in international payments, regulatory and cybersecurity problems (Juminawati et al., 2024). Bitcoin, the foremost digital currency, has raised important questions regarding the concept of money, modes of exchange, the functioning of monetary policy, and the economic system of the world (Yu, 2024). The emergence of digital currencies in general effects the operations of traditional banks and their competition in the finance world currencies in general affects the operations of traditional banks and their competition in the finance world by providing new channels for creativity while simultaneously endangering the condition of financial stability (Ahmad, 2023). The continued evolution of digital currencies will further deepen the impacts of innovation of traditional digital financial institutions, which need to implement countermeasures to such effects through coordinated regulatory measures and framework as technology evolves (Juminawati et al., 2024).

The cryptocurrency market has rapidly expanded from the first decentralized currency of Bitcoin in 2009 to a treasury of digital assets and decentralized applications (Grasic & Vidnjevic, 2024). Bitcoin set the standard for crypto trade in a peer-to-peer network, which was followed by Ethereum with its expansion of computer functionalities through smart contracts, the number of cryptocurrencies available to trade exceeded 1400 from 2013 to 2017, contributing to the total market capitalization of over $100 billion by June 2017 (Elbahrawy et al., 2017).

Nevertheless, there have been no significant changes in market share properties such as the number of active cryptocurrencies and their market share distribution despite the occasional emergence and disappearance of cryptocurrencies. The blockchain technology cryptocurrencies are based on allows decentralization, security, and transparency, and thus it has the potential to change several industries (Dandanayakula & Chandana, 2024). Some issues include scalability, power consumption and regulatory issues. Continued innovation and cooperation push the discipline further, and it promises to transform the old ways of financial systems and help new people participate in the economy (Grasic & Vidnjevic, 2024).

The advent of digital currencies is profoundly affecting the economies of today and offers perks like increased financial inclusion, efficiency in transactions, and even affects monetary policy. Although these currencies only exist in the digital domain and their purpose is limited to certain virtual circles, they can be utilized for procuring goods and services. The introduction of digital currencies, especially central bank digital currencies such as e-rupee of India, offers new prospects but also threats to the financial systems and the balance of economic relations internationally (Yasir, 2024). Like any cutting-edge technology, the development of digital currencies comes with promises for economic growth and development, as well as grave threats in the form of cyber-attacks, financial chaos, and infringement of rights and liberties (Arumugam & Manida, 2023). For a digital currency system to be successfully integrated, there must be a corresponding legal framework and strong governance of risk.

Even with the variety of opportunities that may appear on the scene of digital currencies, the process of their monetization is connected with a series of regulatory and ethical issues. Both governments and financial institutions are constantly creating policies to ensure they curtail issues associated with security, fraud, money laundering, and the protection of consumers Other than that, the rate of innovation and new threats to cybersecurity also pose a risk that the investors and businesses exposed to the digital currency trading are forced to tackle. The information about these risks and the creation of comprehensive strategies considering such risks is of the first priority of achieving sustainable digital financial ecosystems.

The purpose of this paper is to discuss the different monetization efforts in the digital currency sector, as well as presenting successful case examples and possible risks. It offers an in-depth report on indirect and direct sources of revenue and the implications of using block-chain analytics, AI-based insights, and regulations in the future of digital money monetization. By applying quantitative design of research, the present research is important to businesses, investors and government in enhancing profitability and financial stability of business in this ever-changing digital economy.

METHODOLOGY

This paper uses data-driven and qualitative methods. Academic literature, reports issued by industry and regulatory frameworks are examined to determine revenue models and risk factors. Case studies of the most successful digital currency platforms (e.g., Binance, Coinbase, Ethereum-based DeFi protocols) are considered in order to demonstrate effective monetization strategies. Comparative analysis is applied in the comparison of direct and indirect revenue streams, whereas the events of a regulatory nature on major economies (U.S., EU, China and India) are considered in their role of affecting the opportunities related to the field of monetization.

Monetization Strategies

Direct Monetization explicit, immediate sources of income tied to the functioning of digital currency ecosystems. Examples include exchange fees, token issuance, and mining or staking rewards. Indirect Monetization revenue potential arises as a result of involvement in a wider digital ecosystem. This is in addition to value creation in financial instruments, information services, collectibles and tokenization of real-world assets.

A data-based framework is at the core of treating these dynamics, as it allows the businesses, investors, and regulators to measure transaction volumes, liquidity proportions, volatility rates, and adoption metrics, across myriad approaches to monetization (Catalini & Gans, 2020)

Table 1 summarizes the two main monetization channels in the digital currency world, direct and indirect revenue. The core blockchain activity used to drive direct revenues is usually transaction fees, mining or staking rewards, and issuing token as part of ICO, IEO, or STOs. As an example, there is gas fees on Ethereum and mining rewards on Bitcoin, which can be seen as prominent instances of direct monetization. Indirect revenues, in turn, will occur because of added value services and applications based on blockchain, such as analytics tools, AI-based trading suggestions, advertisement mechanisms and decentralized finance (DeFi) yield farming. Examples of this category of companies include Chainalysis, a blockchain analytics company, Uniswap and Aave, which allows generating income through DeFi. All these streams show that digital currencies can be a source of revenue not only because of the use of the network itself but also due to the surrounding ecosystem of products and services.

Table 1. Direct vs indirect revenue streams in digital currencies

Revenue Stream	Type	Example
Transaction Fees	Direct	Coin base, Binance
Mining/Staking Rewards	Direct	Ethereum 2.0, Bitcoin
Token Issuance (ICO/IEO/STO)	Direct	EOS ICO, File coin STO
DeFi Lending & Borrowing	Indirect	Aave, Compound, Maker DAO
NFT Marketplaces	Indirect	OpenSea, Rarible
Blockchain Analytics	Indirect	Chainalysis, Elliptic
AI-driven Trading Insights	Indirect	Crypto Hedge funds
Tokenization of Assets	Indirect	Real Estate, Commodities

Source: Authors Compilation.

It shows that monetization within the digital currency ecosystem is multi-dimensional, with additional functionalities beyond the basic roles of transaction processing and mining. Direct revenue streams will make blockchain networks sustainable in the sense that they reward participants with securing and validating transactions, whereas the second category reveals the broadening business potential that blockchain innovation opens up. Such dual structure shows that profitability within digital currencies is not solely a matter of token economies but also due to underpinning services, analytics and decentralized applications. Notably, it indicates that ecosystems presented around blockchain are maturing to self-sustaining business models, that present not only stability in the operations of the networks, but also the opportunity to perpetually innovate.

GLOBAL TRENDS IN MONETIZATION

Currently, the digital currency market is undergoing fast development and evolution due to the technological progress and spreading trend (Sintsova & Vitsko, 2021). Cryptocurrencies, especially Bitcoin, have caused investor interest to take a significant market value because they currently have more than 4,000 cryptocurrencies in the market (Masiha, 2022). The bank reserves all over the world are studying the possibility of launching Central Bank Digital Currencies (CBDCs) in order to increase financial stability and the effectiveness of monetary policy (Sintsova & Vitsko, 2021; Koshelev K.A, 2022) . The feasibility of the CBDC initiatives relies on various dimensions, i.e., money, technical expertise, and entrepreneurial skills (Koshelev K.A, 2022).The market with digital currencies offers opportunities and challenges, which requires a complete overview of the systemic, technical, legal, and industrial characteristics (Tasca, n.d.). Of particular importance is the development of digital financial assets market and the growth of distributed ledger technologies as the global economy is experiencing digital changes (Koshelev, 2022).

The monetization landscape of digital currencies has evolved dramatically over the past decade. At the initial phases, mining rewards and transaction fees were the main sources of the revenue, and Initial Coin Offerings (ICOs) and subsequent Initial Exchange Offerings (IEOs) became the most notable fundraisers of block chain projects (Adhami et al., 2018). Nonetheless, the increasing regulatory attention and allegations of fraud and speculative bubbles saw a corresponding steep drop in funding of ICOs after 2018 (Howell et al., 2020). Meanwhile, the ecosystem also saw the emergence of Decentralized Finance (DeFi), with the provision of lending and borrowing capabilities along with generation of yield, which turned into a massive value creation engine (Chen, 2020). Moreover, the new directions of monetization presented by the Non-Fungible Token (NFT) market included the possibility to own digitally art, collectibles and any virtual asset and represented the cultural and financial mainstreaming of the blockchain technology (Dowling, 2022). This represents a transition in the paradigm of fundraising and toward more practically driven and innovation-oriented revenue streams, with DeFi and NFTs as the emerging cornerstones of digital currency monetization.

As Table 2 shows, there is a clear pattern of the way monetization in the digital currency ecosystem has changed since 2017 till 2024. During these early years (20172018), Initial Coin Offerings (ICOs) became the predominant monetization model and was able to receive USD 6.2 billion in 2017 and USD 7.8 billion in 2018. This was in response to a popular euphoria on fundraising through blockchain. Nevertheless, the amount of money raised in ICO has been decreasing dramatically and steadily due to the emergence of fraud, regulators violations, and infeasible projects.

ICO funding declined to fewer than USD 0.2 billion by 2024, as it can barely be considered a stable source of income any longer.

On the other hand, Decentralized Finance (DeFi) experienced exponential growth beginning in 2019, when its Total Value Locked (TVL) was only USD 0.6 billion. Within just two years, it surged to USD 98 billion in 2021, underscoring the rapid adoption of decentralized lending, borrowing, and yield farming. Although DeFi TVL contracted to USD 50 billion in 2022 due to market corrections, it recovered slightly and stabilized at USD 60 billion by 2024, indicating resilience and continued relevance in the crypto economy.

Non-Fungible Tokens (NFTs) followed a similar trajectory of rapid growth. Starting from modest sales of USD 0.03 billion in 2017, NFT revenues expanded steadily, peaking at USD 24.7 billion in 2021 as digital art, collectibles, and blockchain-based gaming gained global traction. While NFT sales declined after the 2021 boom, they have maintained a strong position, reaching USD 13 billion in 2024, which highlights their continued role in monetizing creativity and digital ownership.

Overall, the data illustrates a structural shift from speculative ICO-based funding to more sustainable and innovative models such as DeFi and NFTs. While ICOs have nearly vanished, DeFi and NFTs have established themselves as enduring pillars of the digital economy, supported by user participation, tokenized assets, and decentralized governance.

Table 2. Global crypto monetization trends (2017–2024)

Year	ICO Funding (Billion $)	DeFi TVL (Billion $)	NFT Sales (Billion)
2017	6.2	0.02	0.03
2018	7.8	0.1	0.04
2019	4.1	0.6	0.08
2020	3.0	12.0	0.25
2021	2.5	98.0	24.7
2022	1.5	50.0	11.1
2023	0.9	52.0	12.5
2024	0.2	60	13.0

Source: Authors Compilation.

Table 2 not only captures the rise and fall of ICOs but also tracks the parallel growth of DeFi and NFTs, presenting a holistic picture of the industry's evolution. Unlike studies that focus on one revenue stream, this comparative framework demonstrates how financial and cultural dimensions of digital currencies have co-existed and reshaped global economic trends. By combining different monetization channels across a seven-year horizon, the table provides a distinctive narrative of transition from speculative fundraising to value-driven ecosystems, making it a valuable reference for understanding the structural maturity of the crypto economy.

Figure 1. Global crypto monetization trends (2017–2024) (Authors Compilation)

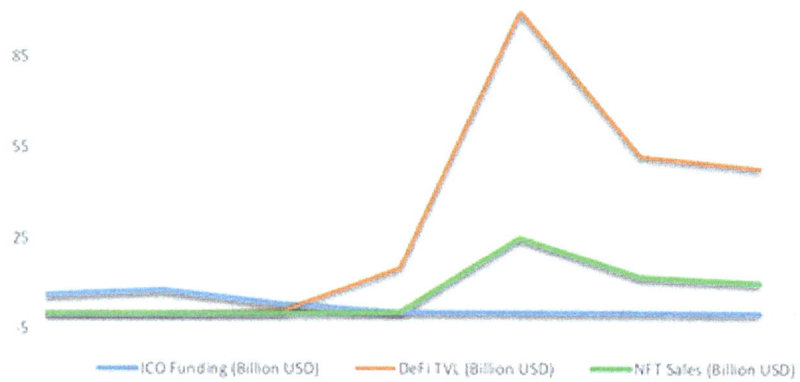

Figure 1 captures the rapid transformation of monetization models in the digital currency space, but the trends unfold differently across advanced and emerging economies. In advanced economies such as the United States, Japan, and parts of Europe, the decline of ICOs after 2018 coincided with tighter regulatory oversight and greater demand for investor protection, which pushed innovation toward more compliance-oriented models like regulated DeFi platforms and tokenized securities. By contrast, emerging economies including India, Southeast Asia, and parts of Africa saw DeFi and NFTs gain traction not only as speculative investments but also as alternative financial infrastructures to address gaps in banking access and cross-border remittances. The NFT surge of 2021 also revealed cultural asymmetries: while advanced markets emphasized digital art, entertainment, and gaming ecosystems, emerging markets embraced NFTs as a means of identity verification, micro-entrepreneurship, and community-driven finance. Thus, Figure 1 highlights not just a linear shift from ICOs to DeFi and NFTs, but also a geographically uneven evolution where blockchain monetization reflects distinct socio-economic realities across regions

RISK–OPPORTUNITY DYNAMICS AND ROLE OF BLOCKCHAIN ANALYTICS AND AI

In the current financial structures, there is a need to ensure that the risks involved in banking are managed and also that credit card frauds are detected to maintain stability. Fraudsters are more advanced as it has been shown that they keep up with the pace of conventional risk management practices as transactions become more digital (Adepoju & Chianumba, 2025). The traditional techniques, e.g., rule-based systems, worked well a while back, but not with the increased complexity and explosion of the volume transactional data today in a high-frequency setting (Aslam & Hussain, 2024). Machine learning has therefore become a dominant force in the banking sector, where it has been used in the prevention of fraud by real-time monitoring, detection of analytics patterns, and flexibility (Sarkar & Paul, 2024).

To better illustrate the trade-offs between risks and opportunities in digital currency monetization, a Risk Opportunity Matrix is developed in Table 3. This matrix positions different monetization models such as token issuance, DeFi lending, transaction fees, NFT marketplaces, mining, and blockchain analytics along two axes: the level of risk involved, and the scale of opportunity offered. By mapping these strategies visually, the matrix highlights the inherent tension between innovation driven models that offer high returns but also carry regulatory and technological vulnerabilities, and infrastructure-based models that ensure stability with comparatively lower risk. Figure 2 provides a clear framework to understand where each monetization approach stands in the broader landscape of digital currency adoption.

Table 3. Risk–opportunity matrix

Category	Risk	Opportunity
Transaction Fees	3 (Medium)	4 (High)
DeFi Yield Farming	4 (High)	5 (Very High)
NFT Royalties	3 (Medium)	3 (Medium)
CBDCs	2 (Low)	4 (High)
Tokenization of Assets	3 (Medium)	5 (Very High)
Token Issuance (ICO/IEO/STO)	5 (Very High)	5 (Very High)
AI-driven Trading	5 (Very High)	5 (Very High)
Mining/Staking	3 (Medium)	3 (Medium)

Source: Authors Compilation.

The Risk Opportunity Matrix for Digital Currency Monetization (Figure 2) evaluates different revenue strategies by plotting them against risk and opportunity, each measured on a scale from one to five. Token issuance methods such as ICOs, IEOs, and STOs fall into the high-risk, high-opportunity category, reflecting their potential for substantial returns but also significant uncertainty. Similarly, DeFi lending and AI-driven trading are positioned in the high-opportunity zone, though they also carry considerable volatility. In contrast, NFT marketplaces and mining or staking strategies are considered moderately risky, with NFTs offering higher opportunity while mining and staking present steadier but lower returns. Models like blockchain analytics and transaction fees occupy the low-risk, medium-opportunity space, making them more reliable and sustainable for long-term monetization. Likewise, asset tokenization is viewed as a relatively safe approach with strong potential, appealing to those seeking stability alongside growth. Overall, the matrix illustrates that innovative approaches such as DeFi, AI-based trading, and token issuance provide the greatest opportunities but also the highest risks, whereas transaction-focused models and analytics deliver more stable, long-term revenue streams.

Figure 2. Risk–opportunity matrix for monetization strategies (Authors Compilation)

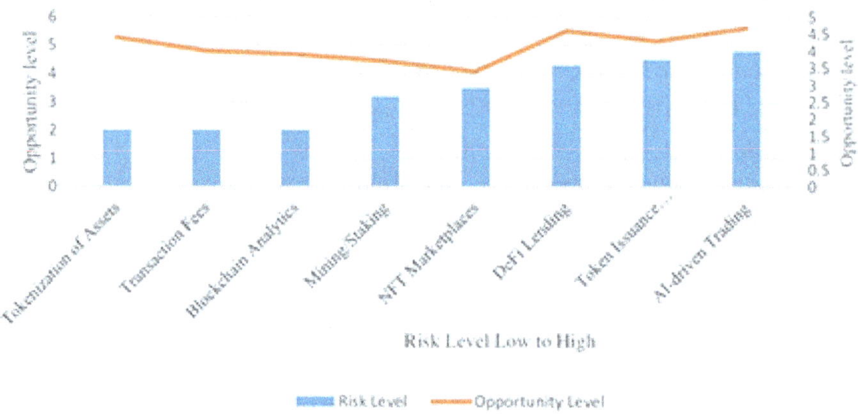

Machine learning techniques, by examining large volumes of historical transaction records, can effectively detect suspicious activities with strong accuracy. These methods are particularly skilled at uncovering valuable patterns in extensive datasets and allowing rapid responses to unusual transactions (Liu, 2024). Still, several ongoing issues limit their effectiveness. A key challenge is data silos, where critical information remains confined within separate institutions or departments, reducing the efficiency of fraud detection (Xu et al., 2024). Additionally, financial institutions face serious data privacy concerns, as protecting sensitive customer details is essential. Another major limitation is the lack of generalization and adaptability of machine learning models, which often perform poorly when transferred to different environments or real-world conditions (Wang, 2024).

In contrast, blockchain technology has recently emerged as a promising tool. With its decentralized, tamper-proof, and transparent structure, blockchain can help address many of the weaknesses of current machine learning models (Zhu et al., 2024). It enables security for data sharing across multiple parties and strengthens privacy safeguards, thereby reducing the impact of data silos. Moreover, combining blockchain with machine learning could establish a more resilient system for fraud detection and risk control. For example, smart contracts embedded in blockchain networks can automatically execute risk management protocols, ensuring the safety of real-time financial transactions. However, despite these advantages, blockchain–machine learning integration is still at an early stage, with limited real-world applications and significant technical challenges in deployment (Xu et al., 2024).

REGULATORY AND ETHICAL CHALLENGES

There are new trends in the world regarding digital currency monetization and different strategies are being developed in the various sectors. Every organization is using subscription models and consumptive pricing and data-driven strategies to monetize digital assets (Brji, 2025). In Africa, some factors which affect adoption include the financial inclusion, regulatory, and the technological infrastructure (Adeleye et al., 2024). The spread of digital currencies is changing the existing financial power structure among the world players with the significant players adopting various approaches in regard to technology, regulation and policy. The transformation has an effect on world commerce and investment, decreasing the expense of transactions and increasing rates of speed and availability (Gao, 2024). The CBDCs are a growing mechanism in the digital finance future (Gao, 2024). With the changes that take place in the digital currency industry, effective monetization strategies should be approached in line with other digital transformations that are aimed at creating a long-term competitive advantage (Brji, 2025).

The issue of monetizing digital currencies is highly regulated and subject to ethical opinions, which changes significantly depending on the territory and determines the approach of businesses and investors. Regulatory regimes are very much in a fragmented and dissimilar state, and this presents an opportunity as well as a source of uncertainty. The table 4 illustrates that United States cryptocurrencies are subject to various legal frameworks by the different agencies: The Securities and Exchange Commission (SEC), the Commodity Futures Trading Commission (CFTC) and the Financial Crimes Enforcement Network (FinCEN) treat certain tokens as securities, commodities, and money equivalents respectively. This duplication of jurisdiction makes compliance hard yet gives direction to the firms who are ready to conform their operations to the legal provisions. Comparatively, the EU has proposed the Markets in Crypto-Assets (MiCA) regulation, an attempt to create standardized laws across countries and a harmonized regulatory framework on stablecoins and digital asset service providers. In Asia, there are more varied strategies, with China prohibiting cryptocurrency trading and mining as well as developing its central bank digital currency (CBDC) the Digital Yuan, whereas Singapore has implemented the Payment Services Act and is looking to be a global center of digital finance. India, on the other hand, has shown a reserved approach imposing heavy taxes on cryptocurrency profit and development of a elaborate regulatory framework in line with G20 principles. Such differences in regulation have a direct effect on the way companies monetize digital assets, and exchanges, DeFi platforms, and blockchain analytics firms all need to adjust their models to fit certain regulatory frameworks in various jurisdictions.

Table 4. Regulatory and ethical challenges in monetizing digital currencies

Dimension	**Region /Context**	**Key Features**	**Impact on Monetization**
	United States	Overlapping jurisdictions: SEC (securities), CFTC (commodities), FinCEN (money equivalents)	Creates compliance complexity but offers clarity for firms aligning with laws
	European Union	Markets in Crypto-Assets (MiCA) framework for harmonized regulation	Provides uniformity, enabling cross-border monetization strategies
Regulatory Frameworks	China	Ban on crypto trading and mining; promotion of Digital Yuan (CBDC)	Limits private monetization but expands state-driven digital finance
	Singapore	Payment Services Act supports digital finance ecosystem	Fosters innovation, attracting global crypto firms
	India	High taxes on crypto gains; cautious regulatory stance under G20 guidelines	Discourages retail speculation, but ensures gradual ecosystem development
Ethical Challenges	Accountability	Privacy vs. misuse (money laundering, tax evasion, illicit trade)	Forces firms to adopt stronger KYC/AML measures
	Market Volatility & speculation	Extreme price swings impacting retail investors	Raises concerns on fairness, consumer protection, and sustainability of profits
	Environmental sustainability	High energy use in proof-of-work mining (e.g., Bitcoin)	Pushes adoption of greener proof-of-stake mechanisms
	AI & Algorithmic Bias	Use of AI in trading, DeFi lending, and credit scoring	Risk of reinforcing systemic inequalities and reducing transparency

Source: Authors Compilation.

In addition to regulatory obstacles, there are ethical issues that make it all the more difficult to drive the monetization strategy. Among the most burning topics is the anonymity vs accountability balance. Even though cryptocurrencies can be viewed as a way of empowerment due to their privacy and decentralization, they are often related to illegal purposes involved with money laundering, tax avoidance and the financing of illegal trade. The speculative aspects of the crypto markets form yet another ethical dilemma. Despite the potential of digital currencies to bring financial inclusion, the inexperienced retail investors are being exposed to huge losses through the extreme volatility in this asset, which renders itself unfair and lacking consumer protection. Environmental sustainability is one other major issue, especially with regards to the energy-intensive proof-of-work mining systems such as Bitcoin. With the growing controversy over climate change, the carbon emissions associated with such networks pose a dilemma to the industry to consider the use of green alternative networks, like proof-of-stake mechanisms. Besides, because artificial intelligence is increasingly being used in crypto trading, lending, and credit scoring platforms in DeFi ecosystems, new risks appear on the algorithmic bias and transparency aspect. Bias data models have the potential to replicate systemic disparities, a situation that goes against fairness and accessibility values that digital finance intends to introduce.

The regulatory and ethical problems are neither challenges nor games of chance in this context because they have proactive roles in driving monetization strategies. A company that disregards them suffers reputational and legal sanctions, as well as a loss of confidence in the market, whereas those companies that respond to the changes in regulations, take sustainability into account, and implement ethical values in the model have an opportunity to transform the challenge into a benefit.

CASE STUDIES OF SUCCESSFUL MONETIZATION STRATEGIES

The recent studies examine various monetization options in different business spheres in telecom, 5G is opening new revenue opportunities with the introduction of network slicing, edge cloud, and IoT based applications, and those would be successful through managed services, partner ecosystems, and vertical-based solutions. Creative industries make use of different strategies, such as custom work, subscription, advertising, and some innovation, such as crowdfunding and consulting (Golmgrein, 2023). Monetization of data is in the form of sale of assets, or strategic sharing of data and it can give businesses an insight on how to cut profit on data assets (Baecker et al., 2020). Among the most important strategies that can be recommended to content creators are sponsorships, merchandizing, and subscription, as these strategies are the most adaptive and diversified in relation to the possibility of a continuing source of income (Adewunmi, 2024). In all these studies, however, the role of innovation, ecological collaboration, and leading market shifts will be significant in the success of monetization within different sectors.

The implications of regulatory and ethical issues can be best explained by the real-life examples of firms who managed to monetize digital currencies successfully, despite the complexities mentioned in table 5. One of the most evident instances of monetization that complies with the law is Coinbase. In the United States, by being a first or early mover in the adoption of regulation, Coinbase seeded its revenue stream with transaction fees and institutional services. Not only did this not restrain growth, but it also became a competitive strength, as the company received the confidence of investors and became the subject of a historic IPO in 2021, raising $100 billion. This is how compliance with the regulatory requirements can result in legitimacy as well as profitability.

Another example of how ethical and technological concerns can be utilized to make money is the changes to Ethereum that saw it move to a Proof-of-Stake system. The move, which was finished in 2022, dramatically decreased the overall energy use of the network, soaring criticisms over the environmental effect of cryptocurrencies. At the same time, it introduced new revenue streams by providing staking opportunities such that token holders can generate passive revenues as well as enhance network security. This indicates clearly that profitability and sustainability can complement one another.

The blistering ascent of OpenSea signifies the potential and the threat of emerging electronic markets including non-fungible tokens (NFTs). Charging transaction fees and selling premium listings, as well as accepting exclusive NFT drops, OpenSea quickly became the biggest NFT marketplace in the world, generating a peak of $4.8 billion in sales in January 2022. The platform was however subjected to ethical and regulatory interference with wash trading and market manipulation practices that propelled it to install more stringent fraud prevention tools. This case relates to how unregulated development among emerging markets may result to credibility crisis given that transparency was not prioritized.

Lastly, Chainalysis also shows another way of going about its own monetization with indirect services. Instead of trading and issuing tokens, the company works in the blockchain analytics segment and offers governments, financial services and trading exchanges with compliance, fraud detection, and the ability to investigate operations. The subscription-based model has been succeeding especially as regulatory intervention is heightening globally. In such a manner, Chainalysis has managed to make regulation a way of monetization itself by demonstrating how oversight can actually act as the driving force behind new industries within the digital currency space.

Table 5. Case studies of successful monetization strategies in digital currencies

Company / Platform	Monetization Model	Regulatory / Ethical Challenge	Key Lesson Learned
Coinbase (USA)	Transaction fees, institutional trading services	Navigating overlapping U.S. regulations (SEC, CFTC, FinCEN)	Compliance-first strategies can enhance legitimacy and attract institutional investors, turning regulation into a competitive advantage.
Ethereum (ETH 2.0)	Staking rewards under Proof-of-Stake consensus	Criticism of energy-intensive Proof-of-Work mining	Technological upgrades that address ethical/environmental concerns can simultaneously open new monetization opportunities.
OpenSea (NFT Marketplace)	Transaction fees, premium listings, exclusive NFT drops	Accusations of wash trading, market manipulation, lack of transparency	Rapid growth must be balanced with transparency and oversight to sustain credibility in emerging digital markets.
Chainalysis (Blockchain Analytics)	Subscription-based compliance and fraud detection services	Growing demand for regulatory oversight and anti-money laundering (AML) compliance	Regulation itself can create monetization opportunities by driving demand for compliance-focused data solutions.

Source: Authors Compilation.

As illustrated in the table case studies have shown that effective monetization of digital currencies requires not only innovative business models, but the extra ability to adapt to the regulatory environment and ethical reality. Compliance-driven approaches can earn investor confidence; technological innovations coupled with principles of sustainability can create new sources of revenue; fast growth into new markets can be both a boon and a bane, and sitting at the edge of regulatory certainty, compliance business can be a significant source of new business opportunities. Coming together, these examples support the idea that having a data-driven approach, the companies will use blockchain analytics, market intelligence, and AI insights so as to anticipate the risks, react to the changes in regulatory environment and develop resilient monetization strategies in the new digital economy.

EMERGING TRENDS AND FUTURE OUTLOOK

The monetization of digital currencies is reaching its next phasc of a faster technological development and a change of the global regulations. Emerging trends suggest a more solid institutional presence, where the crypto-focused products are gaining traction with major banks and asset managers circling in, therefore legitimizing the digital finance sector on the mainstream markets. The introduction of Central Bank Digital Currencies (CBDCs) may also shake-up the market, with nations as China, India, and those that are members of the European Union working on their own forms of sovereign-backed coins that may be efficient and stable in comparison to privately run cryptocurrencies. The other important tendency is the growing speed of decentralized finance (DeFi) and tokenization of the real-world assets like property, carbon credits and intellectual property, which expand the range of monetization opportunities beyond speculative trading.

Ethical and environmental issues are simultaneously pushing innovation towards sustainability. The transition to proof-of-stake-based consensus systems such as that proposed by Ethereum is an indication of how the industry is adapting to international climate pledges. Further, regulatory transparency will play a critical role in determining future opportunities as shown in Table 2.1. Whole-sale jurisdictions that are collaborative between the investor protection and innovation such as Singapore and European Union will attract global digital asset monetization to be naturally establish there. The last area is the combination of artificial intelligence and blockchain analytics, which can allow more intelligent trading tools, improved fraud identification, and increased levels of transparency, but also bring new concerns about bias and responsibility. Taken together, all these trends indicate that digital currency monetization in the future will be more institutionalized, regulated, sustainable and technologically advanced.

POLICY IMPLICATIONS

The implications of the findings of this chapter are significant to policymakers and those practicing in the digital economy. To regulators, close to the top of the list is bridging the digital divide through substantial investment in large-scale infrastructure like broadband connectivity and cloud services, thus facilitating enhanced involvement in international trade. Looking at the gaps between digitally advanced and less-developed economies, the following measures can be taken to mitigate the situation: public-private partnerships and targeted subsidies. It is also crucial that effective governance systems to safeguard and preserve data, privacy, and cross-border sharing of data be established since harmonized international laws are needed to reduce uncertainty among companies involved in online transactions. There is also the emergence of digital currencies, such as cryptocurrencies and central bank digital currencies, which need to be regulated to achieve interoperability, transparent taxation, and anti-money laundering measures, and to balance innovation with financial stability. Besides this, regulators must implement innovation-friendly policies including regulatory sandboxes and fintech, block chain, and artificial intelligence pilot projects, which can encourage experimentation and reduce risks.

As a practitioner, I believe that the main solution to improving efficiency and resilience in trade and supply chains is to integrate sophisticated digital tools. To remain competitive in the digital market, businesses need to consider the use of artificial intelligence, block chain, and big data analytics more. Simultaneously, companies need to focus on cybersecurity and open data management because consumer confidence is closely tied to responsible data management and a stable system. Capacity building is also vital, and there must be constant investment in digital capabilities and staff training to leverage the opportunities offered by automation and digital platforms to the fullest. Lastly, companies need to adopt sustainable digital approaches, such as energy-efficient data centers, environmentally-friendly block chain models, and other green technologies that comply with global sustainability goals.

CONCLUSION

Digital currency by its monetization has developed at an unprecedented pace shifting from wild speculation to a much more diverse revenue stream comprising of direct and indirect monetization dimensions such as DeFi, NFTs, block chain analytics and CBDCs. The case studies of Coinbase, Ethereum, and OpenSea demonstrate that today profitability is much more about regulatory compliance, transparency, and ethical responsibility than it is about scientific innovations. Existence of regulatory disparities between regions, ethical issues (privacy, volatility, and environmental sustainability), and the necessity of finding the middle ground between innovation and accountability need to be mentioned.

In the future, it is expected that digital currency monetization will take place in the context of institutional embracement, the growth of CBDC, asset tokens, and the integration of AI. The key to success will be to make sustainability and regulatory clarity competitive advantages by the firms and policymakers. Digital currencies ceased to be a peripheral novelty: they are taking a central position in the global economy, the future of which will depend on how well stakeholders can balance profitability and responsible governance.

IMPLICATIONS (COMPARATIVE PERSPECTIVE)

These global trends in monetization carry significant international implications. In advanced economies, the transition toward DeFi and NFTs signals a gradual embedding of blockchain into mainstream financial markets, with institutions exploring asset tokenization, decentralized finance products, and blockchain-based settlement systems under regulated environments. For emerging economies, however, the implications are more transformative: DeFi protocols and blockchain-based assets offer low-cost alternatives to traditional banking, expand access to credit and investment opportunities, and create new income streams through digital entrepreneurship. This divergence suggests that while advanced economies are focused on integrating blockchain within existing financial frameworks, emerging economies are leveraging it to leapfrog institutional gaps and foster financial inclusion. For global policymakers and investors, this dual trajectory underscores the need for context-specific strategies, balancing innovation with regulatory clarity, while recognizing that the global digital economy will increasingly be shaped by a mosaic of regional adoption patterns rather than a single universal model.

REFERENCES

Adeleye, R. A., Asuzu, O. F., Bello, B. G., & Oyeyemi, O. P. (2024). *Digital currency adoption in Africa : A critical review and global comparison*. World Journal of Advanced Research and Reviews.

Adepoju, A., & Chianumba, E. C. (2025). AI-driven fraud detection in banking : A systematic review of data science approaches to enhancing cybersecurity. *GSC Advanced Research and Reviews*, (January). Advance online publication. DOI: 10.30574/gscarr.2024.21.2.0418

Adewunmi, O. (2024). Monetization Strategies For Content Creators. *Iosr Journal Of Economics And Finance (Iosr-Jef), 15*(6), 57–66. DOI: 10.9790/5933-1506055766

Adhami, S., Giudici, G., & Martinazzi, S. (2018). Why do businesses go crypto? An empirical analysis of Initial Coin Offerings. *Journal of Economics and Business, 100*, 1–36. DOI: 10.1016/j.jeconbus.2018.04.001

Ahmad, S. (2023). The impact of digital currencies on traditional banking systems : An analysis. *Journal of Economics and Business Letters, 3*(2), 22–23. DOI: 10.55942/jebl.v3i2.277

Arumugam, U., & Manida, M. (2023). *Prospects and Problems of Digital Currency*.

Aslam, A., & Hussain, A. (2024). A Performance Analysis of Machine Learning Techniques for Credit Card Fraud Detection. *Journal on Artificial Intelligence, 6*(January), 1–21. Advance online publication. DOI: 10.32604/jai.2024.047226

Baecker, J., Engert, M., Pfaff, M., & Krcmar, H. (2020). *Business Strategies for Data Monetization : Deriving Insights from Practice*. Meist Angesehene Beiträge.

Brji, V. K. T. (2025). The Monetization Playbook: Digital Transformation Success in the Digital Economy. *Journal of Computer Science and Technology Studies*, 116–124. https://doi.org/DOI: 10.32996/jcsts

Carvalho, A., & Young, P. (2020). What the History of Linux Says About the Future of Cryptocurrencies. *Communications of the Association for Information Systems, 46*(January), 18–29. DOI: 10.17705/1CAIS.04602

Catalini, C., & Gans, J. S. (2020). *Some Simple Economics of the Blockchain*. ACM Digital Library., DOI: 10.1145/3359552

Chen, Y. (2020). Decentralized Finance: Blockchain Technology and the Quest for an Open Financial System. *Stevens Institute of Technology School of Business Research Paper*, 1–27.

Dandanayakula, S., & Chandana, P. (2024). Blockchain Technology and Cryptocurrencies : A Review Paper. *International Journal of Scientific Research in Engineering and Management, 8–12*(12), 1–7. Advance online publication. DOI: 10.55041/IJSREM40122

Dowling, M. (2022). Is non-fungible token pricing driven by cryptocurrencies ? *Finance Research Letters, 44*(April 2021), 102097. DOI: 10.1016/j.frl.2021.102097

Elbahrawy, A., Alessandretti, L., Kandler, A., Pastor-satorras, R., & Baronchelli, A. (2017). *Evolutionary dynamics of the cryptocurrency market.* 1–16.

Gao, J. (2024). The Impact of Digital Currency Policies on International Trade and Investment. *The 3rd International Conference on Financial Technology and Business Analysis, 0*, 29–35. DOI: 10.54254/2754-1169/89/20241905

Golmgrein, I. (2023). A Comprehensive Overview of Monetization Strategies in Creative Industries A Comprehensive Overview of Monetization Strategies in Creative Industries. [IJLEMR]. *International Journal of Latest Engineering and Management Research, 8*(December). Advance online publication. DOI: 10.56581/IJLEMR.8.4.90-100

Grasic, A., & Vidnjevic, M. (2024). Evolution of cryptocurrencies and their utilization in the digital economy. *MEST Journal, 12*(July), 36–42. Advance online publication. DOI: 10.12709/mest.12.12.02.05

Hanl, A. (2018). *Some Insights into the Development of Cryptocurrencies* (Issue February). DOI: 10.13140/RG.2.2.33318.01601

Howell, S. T., Niessner, M., & Yermack, D. (2020). Initial Coin Offerings: Financing growth with cryptocurrency token sales. *Review of Financial Studies, 33*(9), 3925–3974. DOI: 10.1093/rfs/hhz131

Juminawati, S., Macpal, S. J., & Tuwi, I. W. (2024). *Exploring the Economic Impact of Digital Currencies on Traditional Financial Systems : Challenges and Opportunities.*

Koshelev, K. A. (2022). Trends in the Evolution of the Digital Financial Assets Market in the Context of the Digital Transformation of the Global Econfile. In *Finance* (Vol. 26). Theory and Practice., DOI: 10.26794/2587-5671

Liu, Z. (2024). *A Comparative Study of Machine Learning Methods in Financial Fraud Detection* (Issue Ftbm). Atlantis Press International BV. DOI: 10.2991/978-94-6463-546-1

Masiha, R. Y. (2022). Effects of Cryptocurrencies on Global Economics : A Review Study. *Qubaham Academic Journal, 2*(2), 9–15. DOI: 10.48161/qaj.v2n2a138

Moro-visconti, R., Larocca, A., & Marconi, M. (2017). *Big data-Driven Healthcare Project Financing. March 2018.* DOI: 10.2139/ssrn.2903799

Ramadasa, I. (2022). *How Telco ' s use Big Data for Monetization & Revenue Maximization. September.*

Sarkar, A., & Paul, R. (2024). Artificial Intelligence in Fraud Detection and Financial Risk Mitigation : Future Directions and Business Applications. *International Journal For Multidisciplinary Research, 6*(October), 28496. Advance online publication. DOI: 10.36948/ijfmr.2024.v06i05.28496

Sintsova, E. A., & Vitsko, E. A. (2021). Current Development Trends in the Digital Currency Market. *Economics and Management, 27*(7), 504–511. DOI: 10.35854/1998-1627-2021-7-504-511

Tasca, P. (n.d.). Digital Currencies : Principles, Trends, Opportunities, and Risks Summary : *Deutsche Bundesbank and ECUREX Research*, 1–110.

Wang, C. (2024). Evaluating Supervised Learning Models for Fraud Detection : A Comparative Study of Classical and Deep Architectures on Imbalanced Transaction Data. *ArXiv Preprint ArXiv, Ml.*

Xu, J., Yang, T., Zhuang, S., Li, H., & Lu, W. (2024). AI-Based Financial Transaction Monitoring and Fraud Prevention with Behaviour Prediction. *Preprints.Org*. DOI: 10.20944/preprints202407.1107.v1

Yasir, M. (2024). E-Rupee : Unlocking India ' s Digital Economy, Challenges, and. *South Asian Journal of Social Studies and Economics, 21*(July), 1–13. Advance online publication. DOI: 10.9734/sajsse/2024/v21i8860

Yu, B. (2024). Research on the Features and Functions of Bitcoin and Digital Currencies. *Proceedings of the 2nd International Conference on Management Research and Economic Development, 0*, 55–60. DOI: 10.54254/2754-1169/86/20240942

Zhu, M., Zhang, Y., Gong, Y., Xu, C., & Xiang, Y. (2024). *Enhancing Credit Card Fraud Detection : A Neural Network and SMOTE Integrated Approach.* ArXiv Preprint ArXiv.

Chapter 7
Digital Transformation in Banking:
Enhancing Customer Experience Through Technological Innovation

Animesh Kumar Sharma
https://orcid.org/0000-0002-6673-319X
Lovely Professional University, India

Rohit Duggal
CIC Higher Education, Australia

Rahul Sharma
https://orcid.org/0000-0001-8880-7527
Lovely Professional University, India

ABSTRACT

The integration of digital technology in banking is examined in this study with an emphasis on improving client experiences and associated services. Adoption of cutting-edge technology like chatbots powered by AI, blockchain for safe transactions, and mobile banking apps is a prerequisite for the digital revolution in banking. Customers can access a variety of banking services anytime, anyplace with digital platforms, negating the necessity for in-person branch visits. Digitalization has also completely changed the way that banks provide customer support. Stronger client relationships and loyalty are fostered by personalized recommendations that are based on customer data and improve the entire banking experience. In addition, the digital revolution has sparked the creation of new financial services and products

DOI: 10.4018/979-8-3373-2772-3.ch007

that are suited to changing consumer demands. This study not only contributes to understanding the theoretical knowledge but also provides the practical implications of digital technology in the banking sector.

INTRODUCTION

The emergence of digital technologies has resulted in a paradigm change in client services within the constantly changing banking industry (Pazouki et al., 2025). Customers' interactions with financial institutions have changed because of the growing replacement of the conventional brick-and-mortar banking paradigm with more dynamic and accessible digital frameworks. The banking industry has entered a new phase of innovation and customer-centricity because of the COVID-19 epidemic, which has accelerated the adoption of digital technologies (Pal, 2022). The importance of seamless integration, individualized experiences, and improved security measures has been emphasized by the most recent developments in the field of digital banking. Banks are revolutionizing their service offerings by utilizing cutting-edge technology like blockchain, artificial intelligence (AI), and machine learning to meet clients' growing demands for efficiency and convenience. Financial institutions are using a wide range of tools to meet the changing demands and tastes of their customers, from user-friendly mobile banking apps to chatbots driven by artificial intelligence (Khandelwal & Kapoor, 2024).

From basic internet banking platforms to complex mobile applications and cutting-edge financial technologies (fintech), digital banking has come a long way (Murinde et al., 2022). The transfer of banking services from traditional brick-and-mortar branches to digital platforms emphasis on the accessibility and convenience provided to customers (Mishra & Prashar, 2021). Digital technological advances have had a significant impact on banking customers' experiences. Digital banking improves consumer happiness by increasing convenience, efficiency, and customization (Dağaşaner & Karaatmaca, 2025). Banks have adapted their client services through a variety of tactics to prosper in the digital age. Tran Xuan et al., (2023) highlighted the importance of omnichannel banking, which improves client engagement through smooth integration across various digital and physical touch points. Banks are now able to enhance decision-making processes and customize services thanks to the implementation of artificial intelligence and data analytics (Mahalakshmi et al., 2022). Moreover, collaborations with fintech companies have become a critical strategic requirement for conventional banks looking to capitalize on disruptive technology and broaden their range of services (Anagnostopoulos et al., 2025). The banking sector is cultivating a culture of cooperation and experimentation thanks to legislative developments and partnerships with fintech startups (Riikkinen

& Pihlajamaa, 2022). For example, open banking projects are facilitating increased interoperability between financial institutions and outside service providers, which benefits customers by increasing choice and innovation. In addition, traditional incumbents are facing new challenges from the emergence of digital-only banks and neobanks, which will require them to innovate and adapt to remain competitive in the digital age. Chan et al. (2022) has done a case study about the understanding of consumers' FinTech adoption: the case of Open Banking where they found that financial knowledge reduces customer mistrust and initial faith in Open Banking.

Digital technologies have brought about a new age of customer expectations: seamless, personalized, immediate services (Lee & Lee, 2020). Banking services are now available anytime, anywhere, and are no longer limited to physical branches due to the widespread use of smartphones and internet connectivity (Chaimaa et al., 2021). Customers now consider online and mobile banking platforms and applications to be essential tools since they provide them with access to a wide range of services, including loan applications and account management. The banks offer their clients customized solutions and predicted insights thanks to the integration of machine learning algorithms and artificial intelligence (AI) (Bhattacharya & Sinha, 2022). Financial organizations may improve the whole banking experience by using data analytics to predict consumer demands, identify fraudulent activity, and provide personalized suggestions.

The rivalry in the banking industry has increased due to the emergence of fintech firms and challenger banks that prioritize digitalization (Murinde et al., 2022, Lauterbach et al., 2020). Traditional banks are being challenged to adapt and innovate by these nimble and creative players who use technology to offer cutting-edge goods and services. As a result, in order to remain relevant and competitive in the modern digital economy, established banks are investing more money in digital transformation projects (Pan et al., 2022). But amid the digital boom, worries about cybersecurity, data privacy, and digital literacy remain prevalent. Large-scale consumer data collection by banks necessitates protecting this data from cyberattacks and making sure strict standards are followed (Ionescu et al., 2025). To guarantee that every member of society has fair access to banking services, it is still imperative to close the digital divide and promote digital literacy among consumers. The digital transformation of banking services has changed the customer experience while streamlining old operations using chatbots powered by artificial intelligence and mobile banking apps (Alam et al., 2025; Keil & Ongena, 2024).

Personalized experiences and real-time interactions have become increasingly important in recent advancements in digital banking (Sheth et al., 2022). With the development of big data analytics and machine learning algorithms, banks are now able to examine enormous volumes of consumer data to customize their offerings based on unique interests and behaviors. In addition to strengthening customer relations, hyper-personalization enables banks to anticipate demand and provide proactive solutions. Virtual platforms, smartphone applications, and chatbots are driven by artificial intelligence are progressively complementing, and in some cases replacing, traditional brick-and-mortar branches. The acceleration of digital adoption brought about by pandemics has highlighted the need for strong digital infrastructures to guarantee the provision of financial services even in times of global crisis (Theiri & Alareeni, 2023). The emergence of digital-only banks and fintech companies has increased competition in the banking industry, pushing established players to change and innovate. Peer-to-peer payments, robo-advisors, and digital wallets are just a few of the cutting-edge services that have proliferated as a result, all geared toward giving users easier access to and convenience with their money. Notwithstanding the enthusiasm surrounding digital banking, worries about privacy and data security remain significant. Cyberattacks and high-profile data breaches have highlighted the necessity of strong cybersecurity defenses to protect private financial data (Ahmad et al., 2023). To reduce risks and reassure clients about the security of their digital transactions, banks are consequently making significant investments in cybersecurity infrastructure and implementing cutting-edge encryption techniques (Alsaghir, 2023).

The fast progress of digital technology has substantially transformed the way bank's function, transforming conventional brick-and-mortar services into a more dynamic, accessible digital environment. The worldwide COVID-19 epidemic has hastened this shift, causing banks to explore digital technologies to address the increased need for accessible, safe, and efficient financial services (Pazouki et al., 2025). Banks are not just adopting new technology but also reinventing their whole service delivery strategies to be competitive in a quickly changing digital economy. In the banking industry, digital transformation refers to the incorporation of advanced technologies such as artificial intelligence (AI), machine learning (ML), blockchain, and data analytics into bank operations to improve efficiency, improve customer experiences, and create new economic opportunities (Srivastava et al., 2021). This transformation goes beyond just digitising services; it also includes a culture shift towards customer-centricity and innovation (Mahalakshmi et al., 2022). In an increasingly linked world, banks are focussing on offering consumers with smooth, personalised experiences while maintaining security and regulatory compliance (Sheth et al., 2022).

Digital Transformation

Digital transformation is the use of digital technology to simplify processes, improve customer relations, and open up new opportunities for economic development (Bresciani et al., 2021; Mann et al., 2022). In banking, it ranges from mobile banking applications to AI-powered decision-making and blockchain-based transaction platforms.

Customer Experience (CX)

In the digital era, customer experience has become an important distinction for banks. The capacity to provide seamless, personalised, and real-time services is critical to consumer happiness. Financial institutions use digital technology to better predict and meet client wants (Dağaşaner & Karaatmaca, 2025).

Data Monetization

With the growth of digital technology, banks now hold massive volumes of client data. Data monetisation is the process of using this data to produce value, whether by enhancing services or developing new income sources. Banks may use analytics to provide personalised services, prevent fraud, and make data-driven business choices, increasing their economic value (Bhattacharya and Sinha, 2022).

RESEARCH PROBLEM

The central question guiding this study is: *How do digital innovations in banking contribute to customer experience enhancement and economic value creation?* As the banking sector embraces digital transformation, it is critical to understand how technology improvements affect both consumer experience and financial institution profitability. The purpose of this study is to investigate the relationship between digital innovations and increased customer happiness, as well as how these breakthroughs translate into concrete economic advantages for both consumers and banks.

CONCEPTUAL BACKGROUND

The Strategic Importance of Digital Transformation in Banking

The digital transformation of the banking sector has emerged as a strategic need for financial institutions striving to remain relevant and competitive in an increasingly technologically driven world. Historically, banks relied on legacy systems that prioritised physical branches, manual processes, and in-person encounters. However, as consumer behaviour and expectations shift due to the growth of digital technology, banks have been forced to embrace new models that give better efficiency, flexibility, and convenience. Digital transformation in banking entails more than just upgrading technology; it necessitates a fundamental change in how banks function, interact with clients, and make decisions. It enables financial organisations to improve customer happiness, optimise processes, and generate new income streams by implementing cutting-edge technologies like artificial intelligence (AI), blockchain, big data analytics, and the Internet of Things (IoT) (Kreuzer et al., 2020). This change is crucial not just for enhancing the customer experience, but also for optimising internal operations, lowering costs, and promoting innovation. Banks that do not embrace digital transformation risk losing their competitive advantage as customers want quicker, more personalised, and secure services (Pal, 2022).

Key Drivers of Digital Innovation in Financial Services

Several factors have led to the rapid acceleration of digital innovation in the banking sector. These drivers can be classified as technical, customer-centric, and competitive reasons.

Technological Advancements

Artificial intelligence, machine learning, blockchain, and data analytics are transforming the financial services industry (Nguyen et al., 2023). AI-powered chatbots, for example, provide real-time consumer contacts, and blockchain technology assures safe and transparent transactions. Furthermore, the utilisation of big data enables banks to deliver personalised services by analysing consumer behaviour and forecasting future financial requirements.

Changing Consumer Expectations

Consumer expectations have shifted significantly, accelerating digital innovation. Customers increasingly expect seamless, rapid access to financial services, with an emphasis on simplicity of use and personalised solutions. The proliferation of smartphones and the growing acceptance of mobile applications have created the expectation of 24-hour access to financial services from anywhere in the globe (Hazar & Babuşcu, 2023). As a result, banks must constantly innovate to fulfil increased demands and stay ahead of the competition.

Increased Competition from Fintechs

The growth of fintech startups has posed significant challenges to traditional banks (Boustani, 2020). These digital-first, agile firms employ technology to offer speciality, customer-focused services such as peer-to-peer lending, robo-advisory, and rapid payments, sometimes at cheaper costs. As fintechs continue to disrupt the financial services industry, established banks must speed their digital transformation to preserve a competitive advantage.

Regulatory Pressure

Regulatory authorities have also contributed to digital innovation in banking (Tsindeliani et al., 2022). Open banking regulations have encouraged banks to implement interoperable systems and partner with third-party fintechs to provide clients with a greater choice of services. These regulation measures are intended to promote competition and guarantee that customers benefit from improved services, reduced costs, and more transparency in financial transactions (Diener & Špaček, 2021).

Industry Trends: Post-COVID Acceleration, Regulatory Changes, Fintech Disruption

The COVID-19 pandemic has had a significant influence on the banking industry, serving as a driving force for digital transformation (Yıldırım & Erdil, 2024; Demirgüç-Kunt et al., 2021). As lockdowns and social distancing tactics drove physical bank offices to collapse, banks were compelled to swiftly adapt to digital platforms. The epidemic has hastened the use of mobile banking, internet payments, and remote customer service systems. With continuous instability and a move towards remote work, the need for digital banking services has only grown, prompting banks to spend more extensively in digital infrastructure and customer-centric technologies.

Post-COVID Acceleration

The epidemic underlined the importance for banks to be technologically nimble and capable of serving customers remotely (olak & Öztekin, 2021). During this time, digital channels including mobile banking apps, online loan applications, and virtual financial advice services saw exponential development. Many banks saw the crisis as a chance to accelerate their digital activities, from releasing new applications and tools to improving cybersecurity and fraud prevention (Ionascu & Barbu, 2023; Silva et al., 2023). As customers abandoned cash in favour of safer, more convenient payment alternatives, demand for contactless payments, digital wallets, and peer-to-peer (P2P) payment systems skyrocketed (Pal, 2022).

Regulatory Changes

Regulatory frameworks have developed in response to the changing landscape to accommodate the advent of digital banking (Omarini, 2022). Open banking, for example, promotes banks to share data with third-party suppliers in order to foster a more competitive, innovative economy. This legislative drive for openness and data sharing has compelled conventional financial institutions to adopt new digital technologies that allow them to collaborate smoothly with fintechs and offer consumers a broader range of services. More, authorities are increasingly concerned with ensuring that banks prioritise data privacy, cybersecurity, and consumer safety when they embrace digital advances.

Fintech Disruption

Fintech companies continue to challenge the traditional banking paradigm by providing new financial products and services (Cornelli et al., 2023). Fintech businesses, ranging from digital-only banks (neobanks) to peer-to-peer lending platforms, are challenging existing financial institutions by offering faster, cheaper, and more user-friendly alternatives to traditional banking services (Grabovets & Temelkov, 2024). The success of these fintech companies has led banks to reconsider their service offerings and digital strategy. Many conventional banks are increasingly collaborating with or even purchasing fintechs to incorporate cutting-edge technology into their business models and remain competitive in the digital age (Mogaji, 2023).

The digital transformation of banking is being driven by a combination of technological innovations, evolving consumer expectations, and increased competition from fintechs. The COVID-19 pandemic has only accelerated this shift, pushing banks to enhance their digital capabilities to meet the demands of an increasingly digital-savvy customer base. At the same time, regulatory changes are helping shape the direction of digital banking by encouraging interoperability, data sharing, and enhanced security standards. As banks continue to navigate this digital revolution, they must stay ahead of industry trends to ensure they remain relevant and competitive in the rapidly evolving financial services landscape.

REVIEW OF LITERATURE

Due to the incorporation of digital technologies into numerous facets of its operations, the banking sector has experienced tremendous changes in recent years.

Digital Banking Channels

Emergence of digital banking channels including internet, mobile, and digital wallets is a result of the revolution in banking brought about by the introduction of digital technology (Kaur et al., 2021). Customers' interactions with banks have changed because of these channels, which make banking services accessible anytime, anywhere. Customers' need for contactless and remote banking solutions further accelerated the adoption of digital banking because of the COVID-19 epidemic (Ahmed & Sur, 2021). For banks to remain competitive in today's market, digital transformation has become essential. The COVID-19 epidemic, according to McKinsey & Company, significantly increased online transactions and mobile banking usage, marking an acceleration in the adoption of digital banking (Ramaswamy et al., 2021). To meet customer expectations and minimize expenses, banks have been forced to adopt digitization. The way banks engage with their consumers has been completely transformed by digital technologies, such as blockchain, artificial intelligence, internet banking, and mobile banking. The consumer experience is improved overall by these technologies' ease of use, accessibility, and customized offerings (Gonçalves et al., 2020).

Digital Transformation

Digital transformation is a multifaceted process that includes, among other things, data analytics, blockchain technology, artificial intelligence (AI), mobile banking, and online transactions (Dutta et al., 2022). Banks are spending more on digital infrastructure to improve efficiency, streamline procedures, and provide clients with individualized services (Bueno et al., 2024). Technological developments, shifting consumer expectations, and competitive pressures have all contributed to the digital revolution of banking (Broby, 2021). To improve client interactions and service delivery, banks have been using digital channels including chatbots, online platforms, and mobile banking apps increasingly (Manser Payne et al., 2021). The manner that financial services are provided and used has been completely transformed by digital technologies like big data analytics, blockchain and artificial intelligence (AI). Blockchain, big data analytics, machine learning, artificial intelligence, and other technological breakthroughs have all contributed to the banking industry's digital revolution. With the use of these technologies, banks are now able to improve productivity, customize client care, and streamline operations (Boute et al., 2022). Banks must undergo digital transformation to be competitive in an increasingly digitalized market world (Tsindeliani et al., 2022). Customers may conduct transactions, check balances, and pay bills whenever and wherever they choose thanks to digital banking services that give them constant access to their accounts (Qatawneh & Makhlouf.,

2025). Customer loyalty and satisfaction are raised by this improved accessibility. Banks can tailor their services to each individual customer's interests and behavior by integrating AI and data analytics (Tulcanaza-Prieto et al., 2023). Luu et al. (2025) tailored recommendations and focused marketing techniques improve client engagement and retention. Banks can save money by using digital banking, which eliminates the need for manual procedures and physical infrastructure. Chatbots and robo-advisors are examples of automated services that increase productivity and streamline processes for the benefit of both banks and clients (Kediya et al., 2023). The integration of digital technologies with banking services, which enables clients to execute transactions and access financial services remotely, is referred to as digital banking (Indriasari et al., 2022). Banks are now able to provide improved consumer services through a variety of digital channels, including automated teller machines (ATMs), internet banking, and mobile banking, thanks to the digital banking revolution that has completely changed traditional banking processes. Banks now operate more efficiently because of the incorporation of digital technologies (Li et al., 2025). The automation of standard procedures like loan approvals and account opening cuts down on processing times and human error. Banks can detect fraudulent activity, optimize resource allocation, and tailor services based on consumer behavior by utilizing machine learning algorithms and AI (Akyüz & Mavnacıoğlu., 2021). For banking institutions, the digital revolution has also significantly increased operational effectiveness and decreased costs (Mavlutova et al., 2022) Routine functions, like processing transactions and account queries, have been automated to expedite internal processes and save money. Moreover, banks can leverage data analytics to obtain insightful knowledge about consumer behavior, which facilitates focused marketing campaigns and customized products (Maja & Letaba, 2022).

Customer Experience

Dhamija et al. (2025) conducted studies that highlight the significance of customer experience in digital banking. They contend that the provision of round-the-clock accessibility, tailored services, and flawless user interfaces are essential for improving consumer satisfaction in digital banking platforms. The importance of client-centric digital strategies in promoting customer engagement and loyalty in the banking industry is in the study. A key effect of digital technologies on banking is improved customer experience. Digital banking channels offer clients round-the-clock service accessibility, tailored suggestions, and expedited procedures. Banks can anticipate client wants and provide customized solutions in real-time by utilizing machine learning algorithms and data analytics. Research indicates that the adoption of personalized banking experiences leads to higher levels of client satisfaction and loyalty (Taghizadeh et al., 2021). Enhancing the client experience is one of the main motivations for digital technology adoption in banking (Chauhan et al., 2022). Customers can conduct transactions via digital channels at any time and from any location thanks to their ease, flexibility, and accessibility (Shankar & Rishi, 2020). With capabilities like account management, bill payment, and remote deposit capture, mobile banking apps have become essential to the client journey (Kandpal et al., 2025). Moreover, chatbots and virtual assistants driven by AI have become indispensable instruments for offering clients immediate assistance and tailored suggestions (Nirala et al., 2022). The convenience, accessibility, and customization that digital technologies provide have completely changed consumer experience. Mobile banking apps increase customer happiness and loyalty by enabling users to conduct transactions, check balances, and access support services whenever and wherever they are (Zhou et al., 2021). Additionally, engagement is increased, and customer relationships are strengthened through tailored recommendations and focused marketing strategies made possible by data analytics. Customer services in the banking industry have been significantly changed by digital technology. The consumer experience is a crucial sector undergoing change. Studies show that tailored services, quick transaction processing, and 24/7 support are some of the ways that digital banking improves the client experience (Hoyer et al., 2020). Additionally, digital channels' self-service features enable clients to complete transactions on their own, eliminating the need for in-person bank visits and raising client satisfaction.

Digital Technologies

Digital technologies have also made it easier to automate standard banking procedures, which has improved bank operational efficiency and reduced costs. Consequently, this makes it possible for banks to make investments in cutting-edge digital solutions that enhance customer services. Villar and Khan (2021) conducted a case study on Deutsche Bank's implementation of Robotic Process Automation (RPA) in the banking sector. Their study highlights how the bank automated Adverse Media Screening (AMS) processes to strengthen compliance, expand the scope of adverse media searches, and significantly reduce the occurrence of false positives. To improve the overall customer service experience, banks can provide proactive customer support, tailored recommendations, and predictive analytics by integrating AI and machine learning (ML) algorithms (Maseke, 2024). Because digital technologies offer efficient and easy-to-use services, they have completely changed clients' banking experience. Customers now have 24/7 access to banking services thanks to chatbots, online account management tools, and mobile banking applications (Mogaji et al., 2021). According to studies, consumers view digital banking as more practical and effective than traditional banking methods (Melnyk, 2024). Enhanced customer involvement and happiness have been facilitated by AI algorithms' ability to provide tailored recommendations and targeted marketing strategies (Huang & Rust, 2021).

Innovations in digital banking have sparked worries about consumer trust and security. Building trust and confidence among consumers of digital banking requires implementing strong cybersecurity safeguards and clear data protection regulations. Geebren & Jabbar (2021) conducted research that highlights the significance of trust in influencing customers' perceptions of digital banking platforms. The study emphasizes the need for banks to give priority to security and privacy concerns. Even though there are many advantages to digital technologies, security and trust issues are still quite important. The escalation of cyberattacks and data leaks presents major obstacles for banks to protect client data and uphold confidence. Therefore, to reduce risks and guarantee that customers have faith in digital banking services, financial institutions must invest in strong cybersecurity safeguards and compliance frameworks. The introduction of omni-channel banking has changed how clients communicate with banks at many points of contact. The notion of an omni-channel customer experience is examined in a study which emphasizes the significance of smooth integration and uniformity between digital and physical channels (Nguyen & Tran, 2023). Moreover, banks that implement omni-channel strategies have better customer satisfaction and retention rates than those that only use traditional channels (Xuan et al., 2023).

Banks can now use client data to provide individualized services thanks to developments in big data analytics. The use of predictive analytics to provide customized banking solutions and increase client engagement and loyalty (Patel & Trivedi, 2020). Lóska & Uotila (2023) underscore the possibility of utilizing data-driven insights to comprehend consumer behaviors and inclinations, hence empowering banks to provide customized advice and focused marketing efforts. Digital technologies facilitate banks' ability to utilize extensive consumer data to customize services and offerings based on individual preferences. Banks may anticipate client demands, provide pertinent products, and launch focused marketing efforts by utilizing advanced analytics and machine learning algorithms.

Technological Innovations and Service Transformation

Technological advancements have transformed the banking business dramatically. Artificial intelligence, chatbots, mobile banking, and big data analytics have transformed how financial services are delivered. AI-powered chatbots, for example, offer real-time customer service, improving user experience and operational efficiency (Campino et al., 2021). Mobile banking has become crucial, allowing users to access financial services while on the go, free from the limits of traditional banking hours and locations (Kaur et al., 2021). Big data analytics has enabled banks to forecast client behaviour, resulting in personalised services and targeted marketing (Gonçalves et al., 2020). These technologies not only increase operational efficiency, but also the whole client experience, making financial services more accessible and personalised to individual requirements (Ramaswamy et al., 2021).

Business Model Innovation in Digital Banking

The digital revolution of banking has had a tremendous impact on business model innovation. Traditional banking models have been challenged, and banks are rapidly implementing new value propositions based on digital technology. Digital banking has emerged as a significant engine of innovation, enabling banks to decrease operating costs, provide personalised services, and reach new consumer groups (Dutta et al., 2022). For example, digital platforms have enabled banks to offer remote account opening, real-time loan approvals, and personalised financial advising. These innovations not only improve client happiness, but also enable banks to diversify their income sources, such as fee-based services and data monetisation (Broby, 2021). As competition heats up, banks are looking for novel methods to incorporate AI, machine learning, and data analytics to generate new revenue streams while keeping costs down (Tsindeliani et al., 2022).

Data Monetization and Economic Value Creation

The digital banking revolution has also offered data monetisation as a new source of economic value generation. Banks have huge volumes of client data that may be used for predictive analytics, cross-selling, and increasing customer lifetime value (CLV). Predictive analytics forecasts future behaviour from client data, allowing banks to provide personalised goods and services (Tulcanaza-Prieto et al., 2023). AI and machine learning integration enables banks to boost their marketing operations by targeting the appropriate clients with the right offers at the right time (Mogaji et al., 2021). Data monetisation frameworks, such as using customer data for personalised suggestions and targeted advertising, have emerged as important revenue growth drivers in the banking industry.

Data Storytelling and Business Process Visualization

Data storytelling improves consumer engagement by translating complex facts into simple, narrative-driven visuals that enlighten and assist decision-making. Schröder (2021) highlights that data-driven storytelling not only enhances comprehension but also fosters trust, which is an important aspect in consumer loyalty on digital banking platforms. Integrating data storytelling into dashboards and personal finance tools allows clients to better understand their financial situation, manage savings goals, and interact with banking services. Santoro et al. (2020) argue that business process visualisations promote user interaction and comprehension, particularly in service delivery processes. Banks can minimize cognitive load and increase consumer satisfaction by visualizing transaction flows, investment paths, or loan application stages. This is especially important in omnichannel platforms, where consumers expect transparency and real-time status updates. Makudza (2021) investigated and evaluated the effect of customer experience management (virtual, physical, and service interactions) on customer loyalty in the banking business. They discovered in their study that there is a positive correlation between customer experience management and client loyalty.

Gaps in Existing Literature

Despite substantial advances in digital banking, there are some gaps in the literature that need to be filled. One of the most significant gaps is the absence of integration of customer experience, strategic value, and data monetisation views. While many studies focus on technical improvements, few examine how these breakthroughs affect financial organisations' long-term strategic value and capacity to monetise consumer data (Melnyk, 2024). There has been little study into the significance of omnichannel banking strategies in improving customer experience and retention (Xuan et al., 2023). Addressing these gaps can assist create a more complete picture of the changing digital banking ecosystem and the issues that banks confront as they navigate this shift. The studied literature emphasises the critical significance of digital technology in altering financial services. Digital transformation is transforming how financial institutions operate and interact with their customers, from improving consumer experiences to increasing operational efficiency. However, there is a definite need for more integrated research into strategic value generation via data monetisation and customer experience, as well as addressing trust and security problems in the digital banking sector.

RESEARCH METHODOLOGY

This study utilizes a qualitative, conceptual, literature-based approach to investigating the influence of digital technology on customer service in the banking sector (Sebastian et al., 2017). The study attempts to synthesize current trends and insights on the acceptance and transformation of digital banking services by drawing on existing research and secondary sources. This study mainly uses secondary data analysis, gaining knowledge from reports, conference proceedings, book chapters, reviews, articles that have already been published, and online resources. By utilizing the vast amount of knowledge that has been amassed in the field throughout time, the methodology that has been selected enables a thorough investigation of the issue. Secondary sources, such as academic journals, conference proceedings, book chapters, review papers, reports, and online study materials, serve as the study's main source of data. These resources offer a wealth of knowledge about the acceptance, application, and outcomes of digital technology in banking customer care. Key themes, patterns, and insights pertinent to the study objectives are identified through the process of synthesizing data collected from secondary sources.

To thoroughly investigate the topic, a systematic review technique was used. This included scanning numerous academic and professional databases, including Scopus. The criteria used to identify studies included: Relevance to study topics on digital technology in the banking industry. The study's sources included peer-reviewed publications, conference papers, reports, and book chapters. Studies on the impact of technology such as artificial intelligence, mobile banking, chatbots, and big data analytics on customer service in banks. Studies were omitted if they did not explicitly address the influence of digital technology on customer service, were inaccessible, or lacked adequate data for analysis. The evaluation contains articles published during the previous four years (2020-2024) to provide a focus on the most recent research in the field. This period allows for the assimilation of tendencies accelerated by the worldwide COVID-19 epidemic, which had a significant impact on digital banking transformation. The combination of keywords used in the search was *"digital banking," "customer service," "artificial intelligence in banking," "mobile banking adoption," "chatbots in customer care,"* and *"big data analytics in banking."*

The use of secondary data is critical in this study because it enables for a thorough analysis of a large body of literature, providing a full and comprehensive picture of the present status of digital banking technology. Secondary data offers insights from numerous sources without the need for original data collection, making it both efficient and cost-effective. Thematic synthesis allows for the identification of repeating patterns, concepts, and linkages across research, resulting in a more in-depth knowledge of how digital technologies have altered customer service in the banking industry. This technique is especially appropriate for conceptual research that seeks to consolidate information from current literature to provide new interpretations and frameworks. This study intends to contribute to the current body of knowledge on digital banking transition by synthesising data from several scholarly and industry sources, emphasising major trends, gaps, and opportunities for further research.

DISCUSSIONS

The integration of digital technology in the banking sector has had a revolutionary impact, increasing operational efficiency, improving customer experiences, and opening new opportunities for value creation. In this section, the strategic and economic influence of important digital technologies in banking, with a particular emphasis on their commercial implications are discussed.

Artificial Intelligence and Automation

AI and automation are transforming customer service in the banking industry (Maseke, 2024). AI solutions, such as chatbots, virtual assistants, and automated advisory services, help banks manage regular client enquiries and transactions more effectively. This not only results in huge cost savings, but it also increases consumer engagement by providing personalised and timely replies. AI-powered systems continually learn from consumer encounters, allowing them to tailor services and offers to specific requirements and preferences (Sekarini & Selvabaskar, 2024). Beyond operational automation, AI empowers hyper-personalized service, which enhances emotional resonance and user satisfaction. Features like intelligent recommendations and conversational interfaces contribute to a seamless customer journey. HDFC Bank's "Eva" chatbot is an excellent example of AI-driven client interaction. Eva is a virtual assistant that offers consumers real-time help for several financial services. Eva's natural language processing skills enable personalised replies, making banking easier for clients. Similarly, JPMorgan's COiN (Contract Intelligence) technology employs AI to analyse legal texts, considerably increasing contract review efficiency. Both scenarios demonstrate how AI may not only automate regular processes but also provide more personalised client experiences, lowering operational expenses.

Big Data and Predictive Analytics

Big data and predictive analytics are key to the transformation of banking client services (He et al., 2023). The fundamental strength of big data is its capacity to anticipate demands and give context-aware content, changing passive interfaces into proactive, intuitive experiences. Banks may get important insights into client behaviour, preferences, and requirements by collecting and analysing massive amounts of transactional data. These insights are critical for improving client connections and developing new service offers. Banks may use big data to forecast customer lifetime value (CLV), detect possible churn concerns, and offer personalised product recommendations (Pathak et al., 2024). Banks may use sophisticated analytics to proactively address consumer problems and personalise their services, improving customer retention and satisfaction (Famoti et al., 2024). Predictive analytics also allows banks to predict future trends, which helps them stay competitive in a continuously changing market (Broby, 2022).

Blockchain and Secure Digital Transactions

Blockchain technology is rapidly being used in the banking industry due to its capacity to improve transaction security, expedite procedures, and assure compliance (Laroiya et al., 2020). While blockchain functions in the background, its security benefits translate into increased client trust, an important aspect of user experience, particularly in digital finance (Chong, 2021). The decentralised structure of blockchain means that all transactions are visible and tamper-proof, hence increasing customer confidence. It may also automate complicated operations like as cross-border payments and trade settlements, which saves time and money over traditional approaches. Blockchain also improves regulatory compliance by creating an immutable record of transactions, which may be useful for auditing and reporting (Bakhshi & Ghita, 2021). This improves efficiency and minimises the chance of fraud and mistakes, resulting in more reliable financial transactions.

Omnichannel and Mobile Banking Platforms

Omnichannel and mobile banking systems are critical drivers of accessibility, client retention, and competitive advantage (Mainardes et al., 2020). These platforms let users to access their financial services through a variety of channels, including mobile applications, web portals, and even voice-activated assistants. Banks can accommodate to clients' growing tastes by delivering seamless, integrated experiences across many touchpoints, allowing for ease and flexibility. Omnichannel platforms boost client happiness and retention by providing personalised services (Xuan et al., 2023). Mobile banking applications also provide banks a competitive advantage, as clients increasingly choose easy, on-the-go access to their financial services (Singh & Srivastava, 2020). Integrated mobile ecosystems allow users to engage with financial tools in a personalized, accessible, and real-time manner, supporting financial literacy and user empowerment.

Monetization Strategies in Digital Banking

Digital banking has created new prospects for income generating. Banks may generate income from both direct and indirect channels by using consumer data, forming strategic alliances, and collaborating across industries (Grassi et al. 2022).

Direct income streams include transaction fees, loan origination fees, and subscription-based premium services. Indirect revenue channels entail using customer data to target marketing, upsell, and cross-sell. Understanding consumer behaviour through data analytics allows banks to provide personalised services that respond to individual requirements, improving sales and income. Banks are increasingly exploiting client data to modify their offers, such as loan products, insurance services, and investment options. Data-driven personalisation boosts the possibility of upselling by presenting clients with items that are relevant to their needs and interests. DBS has been able to extend its digital products through these agreements, giving consumers with enhanced services like as robo-advisory and digital lending platforms, which have contributed to revenue growth.

Strategic Partnerships with Fintechs

Collaboration with fintech firms may also help banks broaden their service offerings and revenue streams (Elsaid, 2023). Banks may reach new customer segments and increase profits by embracing fintech technology such as peer-to-peer lending, digital wallets, and robo-advisory services. Banks can use monetisation tactics similar to those employed in the telecom and e-commerce industries. Telecom companies, for example, use data analytics to upsell mobile subscriptions, whilst e-commerce platforms tailor product recommendations. Banks may employ similar strategies to boost income, such as targeted marketing and product recommendations based on customer data. DBS Bank's engagement with fintech startups is an example of digital banking monetisation.

Challenges, Ethics, and Data Governance

Despite the benefits of digital technologies, banks face substantial problems and ethical considerations. With the increased usage of consumer data, data privacy has become a big issue (Bleier et al., 2020). Banks must comply with data protection legislation such as GDPR and RBI standards, which regulate how consumer data should be acquired, kept, and processed. Noncompliance can result in hefty fines and harm to the bank's image. The use of artificial intelligence and predictive analytics in customer personalisation poses ethical problems (Saxena & Muneeb, 2024). Decisions made by algorithms, such as loan approvals or credit rating, may unintentionally perpetuate bias or discrimination. Banks must guarantee that their algorithms are transparent and equitable, and that they do not unintentionally hurt certain client groups. Digital transformation incurs significant costs and risks, such as the initial investment in new technology, cybersecurity concerns, and operational issues (Stewart, 2023, Brunetti et al., 2020). Banks must weigh the advantages of digitalisation against the dangers associated with implementation and integration. The regulatory landscape changes in tandem with the evolution of digital banking. Banks must remain on top of emerging legislation governing digital transactions, data security, and customer safety. Failure to comply with rising legal standards might result in severe fines. The future of digital banking is bright, as innovative technologies continue to alter the sector. The Internet of Things (IoT), Extended Reality (XR), and Virtual Reality (VR) are about to transform client interactions in banking. IoT can give banks with real-time client data, whilst XR and VR deliver immersive experiences that help improve financial education and remote banking services (Bhat et al., 2023). Platform-based banking models and open banking efforts are gaining popularity, allowing third-party providers to access banking data (with client authorisation) to provide new financial products and services. This move encourages innovation and collaboration in the financial sector. Banks may gain useful lessons from industries that have effectively implemented digital transformation initiatives, such as retail and healthcare. For example, the retail sector's use of data analytics for personalised marketing and the healthcare industry's incorporation of telemedicine might give banks with information about how to improve their client experiences and services. Figure 1 shows the detailed flow of digital transformation in banking.

Figure 1. Digital transformation in banking (Authors' Own Compilation)

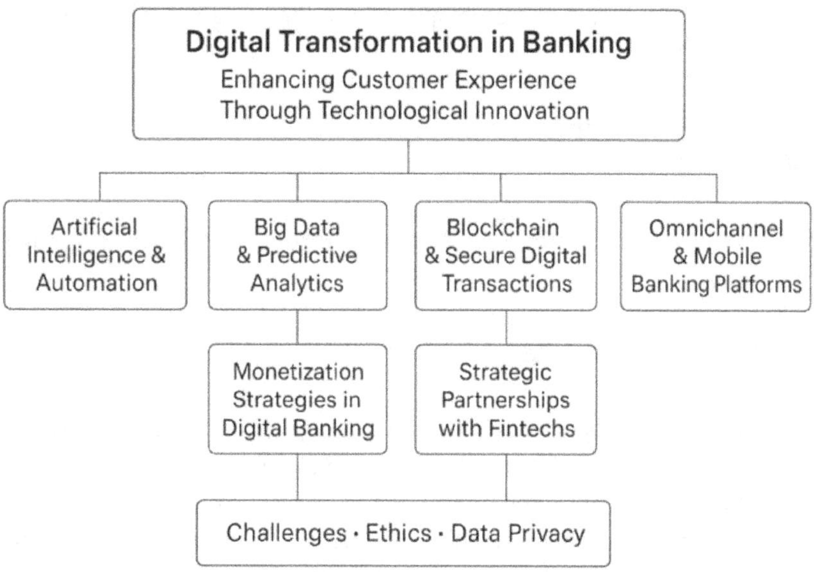

CONCLUSION

This study examined the strategic features of digital transformation in the banking industry, with a particular emphasis on how new technologies contribute to both customer experience and economic value generation. While AI, big data analytics, blockchain, and mobile platforms improve operational efficiency and consumer engagement, their ultimate effect is determined by how banks use them to monetise data, optimise business models, and promote long-term development. This study reveals that most banks are still in the early stages of fully leveraging data as a monetizable asset. Strategic alignment, regulatory compliance, and consumer trust are still essential facilitators of effective digital transformation. Findings of the study underscore the importance of AI and big data analytics in improving personalisation and operational efficiency, as well as allowing predictive monetisation and increasing revenue generation. Blockchain technologies do not provide immediate profits however they do lead to long-term cost reductions and improved operational transparency. Mobile platforms have evolved into dynamic ecosystems that not only enable cross-selling and user acquisition but also play an important role in increasing long-term client retention. Banks must consider the digital transformation as a vital component of their business strategy rather than a technical exercise. Future study should focus on observable economic effects, comparative studies of monetisation models, and the ethical implications of data use in banking. In an increasingly digital market, financial institutions may gain a competitive edge, develop client loyalty, and uncover new income prospects by combining digital innovation with value-driven goals.

IMPLICATIONS

The implications of the current study are in the theoretical and managerial sections below.

Theoretical Implications

This study provides important contributions to digital strategy, service innovation, and consumer value theory. It provides a complete framework for understanding how digital technologies influence customer service dynamics by combining various theoretical viewpoints and actual data. It specifically improves our understanding of innovation dissemination and organisational preparedness, providing fresh insights into the use of digital technologies in customer service operations. This study also highlights the obstacles and possibilities that organisations face when integrating digital technologies, such as the influence of organisational culture, leadership, and resource allocation. Additionally, it sheds light on how digital technologies alter the customer experience and impact consumer behaviour, expanding current ideas of customer engagement and value generation in service contexts.

Managerial Implications

This study outlines many crucial strategic factors for banking managers to consider while embracing digital innovation. To generate development and customer satisfaction, bank management should prioritise digital initiatives that are aligned with business objectives. Managers may strengthen customer connections and increase engagement by investing in technology that improve communication channels, including as chatbots, mobile applications, and social media platforms. Personalised customer experiences powered by data analytics and AI have the potential to greatly increase loyalty and happiness, both of which are crucial for long-term success. Managers could also explore strategic investments in automation to simplify processes and cut costs while preserving service quality. AI-powered chatbots and predictive analytics, for example, can increase service delivery efficiency and value by lowering human error and response times. However, such expenditures need a strong organisational infrastructure to successfully support digital technologies. Industry leaders should prioritise developing digital skills and creating an atmosphere receptive to innovation. In terms of data security, managers must acknowledge the increased dangers connected with digital transactions and interactions. With rising data breaches and privacy concerns, prioritising cybersecurity investments and ensuring compliance with regulatory requirements such as GDPR and local data protection legislation will be critical for maintaining consumer confidence. As digital technologies advance at a rapid pace, bank management must stay flexible and sensitive to market developments. Establishing a culture of continual learning and innovation can assist organisations in remaining competitive, adapting to changing customer expectations, and capitalising on new technology opportunities. Managers should also invest in staff training and skill development to ensure that the workforce is capable of efficiently managing and utilising new technology, hence driving overall organisational performance.

LIMITATIONS AND SCOPE OF FUTURE RESEARCH

Despite the advantages of secondary data analysis, certain limitations are inherent in this methodology. These could include the quality and accessibility of the data, possible biases in the body of current literature, and the inability to perform primary data collection or directly control factors. Accurate interpretation of the study's conclusions depends on being aware of these limitations. The investigation of secondary sources and current literature within the narrowly defined parameters of digital technologies and customer services in the banking industry is the only way in which the study's conclusions may be applied. The type and volume of available secondary data may limit the generalizability of findings, despite efforts to offer insights applicable to wider contexts. Subsequent investigations may explore the ways in which various digital technologies, such chatbots, virtual reality, augmented reality, and artificial intelligence, can be utilized to improve consumer experiences. Investigating how to increase satisfaction and loyalty through tailored recommendations, interactive interfaces, and immersive settings is part of this. Examining consumer preferences, worries, and obstacles regarding utilizing digital platforms for customer service interactions could be the subject of future research. Concerning algorithmic bias, consent, transparency, and data security could all be investigated in the context of online customer support transactions. Building trust and reducing possible dangers can be achieved through the development of ethical frameworks and best practices for the responsible use of customer data. Future studies might examine how different cultures communicate, whether they prefer human to automated contacts, and how different regions and demographics feel about data privacy.

REFERENCES

olak, G., & Öztekin, Ö. (2021). The impact of COVID-19 pandemic on bank lending around the world. *Journal of Banking & Finance, 133*, 106207. DOI: 10.1016/j.jbankfin.2021.106207

Ahmad, A. Y. A. B., & Kumari, S. S., MahabubBasha, S., Guha, S. K., Gehlot, A., & Pant, B. (2023, January). Blockchain Implementation in Financial Sector and Cyber Security System. In *2023 International Conference on Artificial Intelligence and Smart Communication (AISC)* (pp. 586-590). IEEE. DOI: 10.1109/AISC56616.2023.10085045

Ahmed, S., & Sur, S. (2021). Change in the uses pattern of digital banking services by Indian rural MSMEs during demonetization and Covid-19 pandemic-related restrictions. *Vilakshan-XIMB Journal of Management, 20*(1), 166–192. DOI: 10.1108/XJM-09-2020-0138

Akyüz, A., & Mavnacıoğlu, K. (2021). Marketing and financial services in the age of artificial intelligence. *Financial Strategies in Competitive Markets: Multidimensional Approaches to Financial Policies for Local Companies*, 327-340. DOI: 10.1007/978-3-030-68612-3_23

Alam, Y., Azizah, S. N., & Caroline, C. (2025). Digital Transformation in Banking Management: Optimizing Operational Efficiency and Enhancing Customer Experience. *International Journal of Management Science and Information Technology, 5*(1), 46–55. DOI: 10.35870/ijmsit.v5i1.3646

Alsaghir, M. (2023). Digital risks and Islamic FinTech: A road map to social justice and financial inclusion. *Journal of Islamic Accounting and Business Research*. Advance online publication. DOI: 10.1108/JIABR-10-2022-0262

Anagnostopoulos, I. Y., Sails, T., & Alexandrou, G. (2025). FinTechs, BigTechs and diminishing bank franchise values: Stakeholder perspectives on a disruptive emerging financial ecosystem. *Technological Forecasting and Social Change, 212*, 123924. DOI: 10.1016/j.techfore.2024.123924

Bakhshi, T., & Ghita, B. (2021). Perspectives on Auditing and Regulatory Compliance in Blockchain Transactions. In *Trust Models for Next-Generation Blockchain Ecosystems* (pp. 37–65). Springer International Publishing., DOI: 10.1007/978-3-030-75107-4_2

Bhat, J. R., AlQahtani, S. A., & Nekovee, M. (2023). FinTech enablers, use cases, and role of future internet of things. *Journal of King Saud University. Computer and Information Sciences, 35*(1), 87–101. DOI: 10.1016/j.jksuci.2022.08.033

Bhattacharya, C., & Sinha, M. (2022). The role of artificial intelligence in banking for leveraging customer experience. *Australasian Accounting. Business and Finance Journal, 16*(5), 89–105. DOI: 10.14453/aabfj.v16i5.07

Bleier, A., Goldfarb, A., & Tucker, C. (2020). Consumer privacy and the future of data-based innovation and marketing. *International Journal of Research in Marketing, 37*(3), 466–480. DOI: 10.1016/j.ijresmar.2020.03.006

Boustani, N. M. (2020). Traditional banks and fintech: survival, future and threats. *ICT for an Inclusive World: Industry 4.0–Towards the Smart Enterprise*, 345-359. DOI: 10.1007/978-3-030-34269-2_24

Boute, R. N., Gijsbrechts, J., & Van Mieghem, J. A. (2022). Digital lean operations: Smart automation and artificial intelligence in financial services. *Innovative Technology at the Interface of Finance and Operations, I*, 175–188. DOI: 10.1007/978-3-030-75729-8_6

Bresciani, S., Huarng, K. H., Malhotra, A., & Ferraris, A. (2021). Digital transformation as a springboard for product, process and business model innovation. *Journal of Business Research, 128*, 204–210. DOI: 10.1016/j.jbusres.2021.02.003

Broby, D. (2021). Financial technology and the future of banking. *Financial Innovation, 7*(1), 47. DOI: 10.1186/s40854-021-00264-y

Broby, D. (2022). The use of predictive analytics in finance. *The Journal of Financial Data Science, 8*, 145–161. DOI: 10.1016/j.jfds.2022.05.003

Brunetti, F., Matt, D. T., Bonfanti, A., De Longhi, A., Pedrini, G., & Orzes, G. (2020). Digital transformation challenges: Strategies emerging from a multi-stakeholder approach. *The TQM Journal, 32*(4), 697–724. DOI: 10.1108/TQM-12-2019-0309

Bueno, L. A., Sigahi, T. F., Rampasso, I. S., Leal Filho, W., & Anholon, R. (2024). Impacts of digitization on operational efficiency in the banking sector: Thematic analysis and research agenda proposal. *International Journal of Information Management Data Insights, 4*(1), 100230. DOI: 10.1016/j.jjimei.2024.100230

Campino, J., Brochado, A., & Rosa, Á. (2021). Digital business transformation in the banking sector. In *Research Anthology on Concepts, Applications, and Challenges of FinTech* (pp. 186-215). IGI Global. DOI: 10.4018/978-1-7998-8546-7.ch012

Chaimaa, B., Najib, E., & Rachid, H. (2021). E-banking overview: Concepts, challenges and solutions. *Wireless Personal Communications, 117*(2), 1059–1078. DOI: 10.1007/s11277-020-07911-0

Chan, R., Troshani, I., Rao Hill, S., & Hoffmann, A. (2022). Towards an understanding of consumers' FinTech adoption: The case of Open Banking. *International Journal of Bank Marketing*, *40*(4), 886–917. DOI: 10.1108/IJBM-08-2021-0397

Chauhan, S., Akhtar, A., & Gupta, A. (2022). Customer experience in digital banking: A review and future research directions. *International Journal of Quality and Service Sciences*, *14*(2), 311–348. DOI: 10.1108/IJQSS-02-2021-0027

Chong, F. H. L. (2021). Enhancing trust through digital Islamic finance and blockchain technology. *Qualitative Research in Financial Markets*, *13*(3), 328–341. DOI: 10.1108/QRFM-05-2020-0076

Cornelli, G., Frost, J., Gambacorta, L., Rau, P. R., Wardrop, R., & Ziegler, T. (2023). Fintech and big tech credit: Drivers of the growth of digital lending. *Journal of Banking & Finance*, *148*, 106742. DOI: 10.1016/j.jbankfin.2022.106742

Dağaşaner, S., & Karaatmaca, A. G. (2025). The Role of Online Banking Service Clues in Enhancing Individual and Corporate Customers' Satisfaction: The Mediating Role of Customer Experience as a Corporate Social Responsibility. *Sustainability (Basel)*, *17*(8), 3457. DOI: 10.3390/su17083457

Demirgüç-Kunt, A., Pedraza, A., & Ruiz-Ortega, C. (2021). Banking sector performance during the COVID-19 crisis. *Journal of Banking & Finance*, *133*, 106305. DOI: 10.1016/j.jbankfin.2021.106305 PMID: 34548747

Dhamija, A., Manrai, R., & Dhamija, D. (2025). Impact of Financial Service Quality on Customer Loyalty and Satisfaction Among Indian Consumers Utilizing Digital Payments. In *Insights Into Digital Business, Human Resource Management, and Competitiveness* (pp. 251-276). IGI Global Scientific Publishing. DOI: 10.4018/979-8-3693-9440-3.ch011

Diener, F., & Špaček, M. (2021). Digital transformation in banking: A managerial perspective on barriers to change. *Sustainability (Basel)*, *13*(4), 2032. DOI: 10.3390/su13042032

Dutta, S., Pramanik, H. S., Datta, S., & Kirtania, M. (2022). Imperatives, Trends and Dynamics of Digital Transformation as Banks Adopt Technology and Intelligent Systems. In *Intelligent Systems in Digital Transformation: Theory and Applications* (pp. 323–348). Springer International Publishing., DOI: 10.1007/978-3-031-16598-6_14

Elsaid, H. M. (2023). A review of literature directions regarding the impact of fintech firms on the banking industry. *Qualitative Research in Financial Markets*, *15*(5), 693–711. DOI: 10.1108/QRFM-10-2020-0197

Famoti, O., Omowole, B. M., Okiomah, E., Muyiwa-Ajayi, T. P., Ezechi, O. N., Ewim, C. P. M., & Omokhoa, H. E. (2024). Enhancing Customer Satisfaction in Financial Services Through Advanced BI Techniques. *International Journal of Multidisciplinary Research and Growth Evaluation*, *5*(06), 1558–1566. DOI: 10.54660/.IJMRGE.2024.5.6.1258-1266

Geebren, A., & Jabbar, A. (2021). Factors that influence customer trust and satisfaction in mobile banking: A problematization approach. [IJEBR]. *International Journal of E-Business Research*, *17*(3), 66–82. DOI: 10.4018/IJEBR.2021070105

Gonçalves, L., Patrício, L., Grenha Teixeira, J., & Wuenderlich, N. V. (2020). Understanding the customer experience with smart services. *Journal of Service Management*, *31*(4), 723–744. DOI: 10.1108/JOSM-11-2019-0349

Grabovets, K., & Temelkov, Z. (2024). Interplay between digital-only strategy and financial performance: A case of neobanks. In *New Strategy Models in Digital Entrepreneurship* (pp. 214–235). IGI Global., DOI: 10.4018/979-8-3693-3743-1.ch011

Grassi, L., Figini, N., & Fedeli, L. (2022). How does a data strategy enable customer value? The case of FinTechs and traditional banks under the open finance framework. *Financial Innovation*, *8*(1), 75. DOI: 10.1186/s40854-022-00378-x PMID: 36158456

Hazar, A., & Babuşcu, Ş. (2023). Financial Technologies: Digital Payment Systems and Digital Banking. Today's Dynamics. *Journal of Research. Innovation and Technologies*, *2*(4), 162–178.

He, W., Hung, J. L., & Liu, L. (2023). Impact of big data analytics on banking: A case study. *Journal of Enterprise Information Management*, *36*(2), 459–479. DOI: 10.1108/JEIM-05-2020-0176

Hoyer, W. D., Kroschke, M., Schmitt, B., Kraume, K., & Shankar, V. (2020). Transforming the customer experience through new technologies. *Journal of Interactive Marketing*, *51*(1), 57–71. DOI: 10.1016/j.intmar.2020.04.001

Huang, M. H., & Rust, R. T. (2021). A strategic framework for artificial intelligence in marketing. *Journal of the Academy of Marketing Science*, *49*(1), 30–50. DOI: 10.1007/s11747-020-00749-9

Indriasari, E., Prabowo, H., Gaol, F. L., & Purwandari, B. (2022). Intelligent Digital Banking Technology and Architecture: A Systematic Literature Review. *Int. J. Interact. Mob. Technol.*, *16*(19), 98–117. DOI: 10.3991/ijim.v16i19.30993

Ionascu, A. E., & Barbu, C. A. (2023). Digital transformation in the banking sector: A pre-and post-Covid-19 analysis. *Management Research and Practice*, *15*(3), 55–69.

Ionescu, S. A., Diaconita, V., & Radu, A. O. (2025). Engineering Sustainable Data Architectures for Modern Financial Institutions. *Electronics (Basel), 14*(8), 1650. DOI: 10.3390/electronics14081650

Kandpal, V., Ozili, P. K., Jeyanthi, P. M., Ranjan, D., & Chandra, D. (2025). Factors Reshaping the Digital Banking Sectors. In *Digital Finance and Metaverse in Banking: Decoding a Virtual Reality towards Financial Inclusion and Sustainable Development* (pp. 33–67). Emerald Publishing Limited., DOI: 10.1108/978-1-83662-088-420251002

Kaur, S. J., Ali, L., Hassan, M. K., & Al-Emran, M. (2021). Adoption of digital banking channels in an emerging economy: Exploring the role of in-branch efforts. *Journal of Financial Services Marketing, 26*(2), 107–121. DOI: 10.1057/s41264-020-00082-w

Kediya, S. O., Dhote, S., Singh, D. K., Bidve, V. S., Pathan, S., Mohare, R. V., & Suchak, A. (2023). Are AI and Chat Bots Services Effects the Psychology of Users in Banking Services and Financial Sector. *Journal for ReAttach Therapy and Developmental Diversities, 6*(9s (2)), 191–197. https://jrtdd.com/index.php/journal/article/view/1223

Keil, J., & Ongena, S. (2024). The demise of branch banking–Technology, consolidation, bank fragility. *Journal of Banking & Finance, 158*, 107038. DOI: 10.1016/j.jbankfin.2023.107038

Khandelwal, R., & Kapoor, D. (2024). The Use of Digital Tools for Customer Engagement in the Financial Services Sector. In *Revolutionizing Customer-Centric Banking Through ICT* (pp. 29–55). IGI Global., DOI: 10.4018/979-8-3693-2061-7.ch002

Kreuzer, T., Röglinger, M., & Rupprecht, L. (2020). Customer-centric prioritization of process improvement projects. *Decision Support Systems, 133*, 113286. DOI: 10.1016/j.dss.2020.113286

Laroiya, C., Saxena, D., & Komalavalli, C. (2020). Applications of blockchain technology. In *Handbook of research on blockchain technology* (pp. 213–243). Academic press., DOI: 10.1016/B978-0-12-819816-2.00009-5

Lauterbach, J., Mueller, B., Kahrau, F., & Maedche, A. (2020). Achieving Effective Use When Digitalizing Work: The Role of Representational Complexity. *Management Information Systems Quarterly, 44*(3), 1023–1048. Advance online publication. DOI: 10.25300/MISQ/2020/14583

Lee, S. M., & Lee, D. (2020). "Untact": A new customer service strategy in the digital age. *Service Business, 14*(1), 1–22. DOI: 10.1007/s11628-019-00408-2

Li, C., Li, Y., Xu, Y., & Sun, G. (2025). Research on the Impact of Financial Technology on Risk-taking of Commercial Banks. *Research in International Business and Finance, 102804*, 102804. Advance online publication. DOI: 10.1016/j.ribaf.2025.102804

Lóska, G., & Uotila, J. (2023). Digital Transformation in Corporate Banking: Toward a Blended Service Model. *California Management Review, 00081256231207429*. Advance online publication. DOI: 10.1177/00081256231207429

Luu, T. M. N., Mittal, S., & Gupta, S. (2025). Leveraging AI to Tailor Customer Engagement With Personalized Marketing Strategies. In *AI, Corporate Social Responsibility, and Marketing in Modern Organizations* (pp. 195-220). IGI Global Scientific Publishing. DOI: 10.4018/979-8-3373-0219-5.ch010

Mahalakshmi, V., Kulkarni, N., Kumar, K. P., Kumar, K. S., Sree, D. N., & Durga, S. (2022). The role of implementing artificial intelligence and machine learning technologies in the financial services industry for creating competitive intelligence. *Materials Today: Proceedings, 56*, 2252–2255. DOI: 10.1016/j.matpr.2021.11.577

Mainardes, E. W., Rosa, C. A. D. M., & Nossa, S. N. (2020). Omnichannel strategy and customer loyalty in banking. *International Journal of Bank Marketing, 38*(4), 799–822. DOI: 10.1108/IJBM-07-2019-0272

Maja, M. M., & Letaba, P. (2022). Towards a data-driven technology roadmap for the bank of the future: Exploring big data analytics to support technology roadmapping. *Social Sciences & Humanities Open, 6*(1), 100270. DOI: 10.1016/j.ssaho.2022.100270

Makudza, F. (2021). Augmenting customer loyalty through customer experience management in the banking industry. *Journal of Asian Business and Economic Studies, 28*(3), 191–203. DOI: 10.1108/JABES-01-2020-0007

Mann, G., Karanasios, S., & Breidbach, C. F. (2022). Orchestrating the digital transformation of a business ecosystem. *The Journal of Strategic Information Systems, 31*(3), 101733. DOI: 10.1016/j.jsis.2022.101733

Manser Payne, E. H., Peltier, J., & Barger, V. A. (2021). Enhancing the value co-creation process: Artificial intelligence and mobile banking service platforms. *Journal of Research in Interactive Marketing, 15*(1), 68–85. DOI: 10.1108/JRIM-10-2020-0214

Maseke, B. F. (2024). The Transformative Power of Artificial Intelligence in Banking Client Service. *South Asian Journal of Social Studies and Economics, 21*(3), 93–105. DOI: 10.9734/sajsse/2024/v21i3787

Mavlutova, I., Spilbergs, A., Verdenhofs, A., Natrins, A., Arefjevs, I., & Volkova, T. (2022). Digital transformation as a driver of the financial sector sustainable development: An impact on financial inclusion and operational efficiency. *Sustainability (Basel), 15*(1), 207. DOI: 10.3390/su15010207

Melnyk, V. (2024). Transforming the nature of trust between banks and young clients: From traditional to digital banking. *Qualitative Research in Financial Markets, 16*(4), 618–635. DOI: 10.1108/QRFM-08-2022-0129

Mishra, B., & Prashar, A. (2021). Customers' readiness for a paradigm shift towards cyberspace: An exploratory investigation in Indian retail banking. *International Journal of Financial Innovation in Banking, 3*(1), 1–25. DOI: 10.1504/IJFIB.2021.114924

Mogaji, E. (2023). Redefining banks in the digital era: A typology of banks and their research, managerial and policy implications. *International Journal of Bank Marketing, 41*(7), 1899–1918. DOI: 10.1108/IJBM-06-2023-0333

Mogaji, E., Balakrishnan, J., Nwoba, A. C., & Nguyen, N. P. (2021). Emerging-market consumers' interactions with banking chatbots. *Telematics and Informatics, 65*, 101711. DOI: 10.1016/j.tele.2021.101711

Murinde, V., Rizopoulos, E., & Zachariadis, M. (2022). The impact of the FinTech revolution on the future of banking: Opportunities and risks. *International Review of Financial Analysis, 81*, 102103. DOI: 10.1016/j.irfa.2022.102103

Nguyen, D. K., Sermpinis, G., & Stasinakis, C. (2023). Big data, artificial intelligence and machine learning: A transformative symbiosis in favour of financial technology. *European Financial Management, 29*(2), 517–548. DOI: 10.1111/eufm.12365

Nguyen, H. N., & Tran, M. D. (2023). Antecedents and outcomes of omnichannel retail customer experience. *International Journal of Electronic Marketing and Retailing, 14*(2), 171–189. DOI: 10.1504/IJEMR.2023.129883

Nirala, K. K., Singh, N. K., & Purani, V. S. (2022). A survey on providing customer and public administration based services using AI: Chatbot. *Multimedia Tools and Applications, 81*(16), 22215–22246. DOI: 10.1007/s11042-021-11458-y PMID: 35002470

Omarini, A. (2022). The changing landscape of retail banking and the future of digital banking. In *The Future of Financial Systems in the Digital Age: Perspectives from Europe and Japan* (pp. 133-158). Singapore: Springer Singapore. DOI: 10.1007/978-981-16-7830-1_8

Pal, P. (2022). The adoption of waves of digital technology as antecedents of digital transformation by financial services institutions. *Journal of Digital Banking*, *7*(1), 70–91. DOI: 10.69554/QHFT9370

Pan, W., Xie, T., Wang, Z., & Ma, L. (2022). Digital economy: An innovation driver for total factor productivity. *Journal of Business Research*, *139*, 303–311. DOI: 10.1016/j.jbusres.2021.09.061

Patel, N., & Trivedi, S. (2020). Leveraging predictive modeling, machine learning personalization, NLP customer support, and AI chatbots to increase customer loyalty. *Empirical Quests for Management Essences, 3*(3), 1-24. Retrieved from https://researchberg.com/index.php/eqme/article/view/46

Pathak, P., Chandgadkar, V., Solanki, A., Shrivastava, A., Pulgam, N., & Maktum, T. (2024, March). Customer churn prediction and personalised recommendations in banking. In *International Conference on Artificial Intelligence and Smart Energy* (pp. 409-421). Cham: Springer Nature Switzerland. DOI: 10.1007/978-3-031-61475-0_32

Pazouki, S., Jamshidi, M. B., Jalali, M., & Tafreshi, A. (2025). Transformative impact of AI and digital technologies on the FinTech industry: A comprehensive review. *International Journal of Advanced Research in Humanities and Law*, *2*(2), 1–27. DOI: 10.63053/ijrel.37

Qatawneh, A. M., & Makhlouf, M. H. (2025). Influence of smart mobile banking services on senior banks' clients intention to use: Moderating role of digital accounting. *Global Knowledge, Memory and Communication*, *74*(3/4), 1028–1044. DOI: 10.1108/GKMC-01-2023-0018

Ramaswamy, S., Khande, R., Patil, Y. S., & Kalkar, P. (2021). Adapting digital banking services during covid-19 pandemic: A study on customer experiences in selected district of maharashtra state, India. [IJEET]. *Journal of Electrical Engineering & Technology*, *12*(5), 8–17. DOI: 10.34218/IJEET.12.5.2021.002

Riikkinen, M., & Pihlajamaa, M. (2022). Achieving a strategic fit in fintech collaboration–A case study of Nordea Bank. *Journal of Business Research*, *152*, 461–472. DOI: 10.1016/j.jbusres.2022.05.049

Santoro, G., Bresciani, S., & Papa, A. (2020). Collaborative modes with cultural and creative industries and innovation performance: The moderating role of heterogeneous sources of knowledge and absorptive capacity. *Technovation*, *92*, 102040. DOI: 10.1016/j.technovation.2018.06.003

Saxena, A., & Muneeb, S. M. (2024). Transforming Financial Services Through Hyper-Personalization: The Role of Artificial Intelligence and Data Analytics in Enhancing Customer Experience. In *AI-Driven Decentralized Finance and the Future of Finance* (pp. 19-47). IGI Global. DOI: 10.4018/979-8-3693-6321-8.ch002

Schröder, A. M. (2021). Unboxing The Algorithm: Understandability And Algorithmic Experience In Intelligent Music Recommendation Systems.

Sebastian, Y., Siew, E. G., & Orimaye, S. O. (2017). Emerging approaches in literature-based discovery: Techniques and performance review. *The Knowledge Engineering Review*, *32*, e12. DOI: 10.1017/S0269888917000042

Sekarini, S., & Selvabaskar, S. (2024). AI-powered branding: enhancing consumer experience in emerging markets. In *Integrating AI-Driven Technologies Into Service Marketing* (pp. 19–48). IGI Global., DOI: 10.4018/979-8-3693-7122-0.ch002

Shankar, A., & Rishi, B. (2020). Convenience matter in mobile banking adoption intention? *Australasian Marketing Journal*, *28*(4), 273–285. DOI: 10.1016/j.ausmj.2020.06.008

Sheth, J. N., Jain, V., Roy, G., & Chakraborty, A. (2022). AI-driven banking services: The next frontier for a personalised experience in the emerging market. *International Journal of Bank Marketing*, *40*(6), 1248–1271. DOI: 10.1108/IJBM-09-2021-0449

Silva, T. C., de Souza, S. R. S., Guerra, S. M., & Tabak, B. M. (2023). COVID-19 and bank branch lending: The moderating effect of digitalization. *Journal of Banking & Finance*, *152*, 106869. DOI: 10.1016/j.jbankfin.2023.106869

Singh, S., & Srivastava, R. K. (2020). Understanding the intention to use mobile banking by existing online banking customers: An empirical study. *Journal of Financial Services Marketing*, *25*(3), 86–96. DOI: 10.1057/s41264-020-00074-w

Srivastava, V., Kishore, S., & Dhingra, D. (2021). Technology and the future of customer experience. In *Crafting customer experience strategy* (pp. 91–116). Emerald Publishing Limited., DOI: 10.1108/978-1-83909-710-220211006

Stewart, H. (2023). Digital transformation security challenges. *Journal of Computer Information Systems*, *63*(4), 919–936. DOI: 10.1080/08874417.2022.2115953

Taghizadeh, H., Panahi, K., & Iranzadeh, S. (2021). The Impact of Personalization on Customers' Loyalty and the Intention to Use E-banking Services. *International Economics Studies*, *51*(2), 37–52. DOI: 10.22108/ies.2022.132161.1125

Theiri, S., & Alareeni, B. (2023). Perception of the digital transformation as a strategic advantage through the Covid 19 crisis? case of Tunisian banks. *Journal of Sustainable Finance & Investment*, *13*(1), 477–498. DOI: 10.1080/20430795.2021.1964809

Tran Xuan, Q., Truong, H. T., & Vo Quang, T. (2023). Omnichannel retailing with brand engagement, trust and loyalty in banking: The moderating role of personal innovativeness. *International Journal of Bank Marketing*, *41*(3), 663–694. DOI: 10.1108/IJBM-07-2022-0292

Tsindeliani, I. A., Proshunin, M. M., Sadovskaya, T. D., Popkova, Z. G., Davydova, M. A., & Babayan, O. A. (2022). Digital transformation of the banking system in the context of sustainable development. *Journal of Money Laundering Control*, *25*(1), 165–180. DOI: 10.1108/JMLC-02-2021-0011

Tulcanaza-Prieto, A. B., Cortez-Ordoñez, A., & Lee, C. W. (2023). Influence of customer perception factors on AI-enabled customer experience in the Ecuadorian banking environment. *Sustainability (Basel)*, *15*(16), 12441. DOI: 10.3390/su151612441

Villar, A. S., & Khan, N. (2021). Robotic process automation in banking industry: A case study on Deutsche Bank. *Journal of Banking and Financial Technology*, *5*(1), 71–86. DOI: 10.1007/s42786-021-00030-9

Xuan, Q. T., Truong, H. T., & Quang, T. V. (2023). The impacts of omnichannel retailing properties on customer experience and brand loyalty: A study in the banking sector. *Cogent Business & Management*, *10*(2), 2244765. DOI: 10.1080/23311975.2023.2244765

Yıldırım, A. C., & Erdil, E. (2024). The effect of Covid-19 on digital banking explored under business model approach. *Qualitative Research in Financial Markets*, *16*(1), 87–107. DOI: 10.1108/QRFM-08-2021-0142

Zhou, Q., Lim, F. J., Yu, H., Xu, G., Ren, X., Liu, D., Wang, X., Mai, X., & Xu, H. (2021). A study on factors affecting service quality and loyalty intention in mobile banking. *Journal of Retailing and Consumer Services*, *60*, 102424. DOI: 10.1016/j.jretconser.2020.102424

Chapter 8
Leveraging Artificial Intelligence for Tax Monetization

Pitresh Kaushik
https://orcid.org/0000-0002-9168-2494
DBS Global University, India

Pooja Kansra
https://orcid.org/0000-0003-2229-0662
Lovely Professional University, India

Neha Kukrety
https://orcid.org/0009-0004-7374-688X
Shoolini University, India

ABSTRACT

The study seeks to investigate the intensification of quality and effectiveness in the tax collection system of India. The focus is to study the compliance and efficiency in the revenue forecasting with the use of digitisation and artificial intelligence (AI) in Indian Tax System. The upgradation of the system integrating the AI technologies, shows the environment a rise in the Indian Tax administration with the well-maintained records and principle responsibilities. The entire study resolves around the advance application of AI-driven methods and its relevant implications for the future research which will be a support for the policymakers. The aim of this study is to make sure that artificial intelligence helps to leverage the righteous system to generate tax-related income for the future.

DOI: 10.4018/979-8-3373-2772-3.ch008

INTRODUCTION TO AI AND TAX MONETISATION

Various studies show the efficiency and transparency in the Indian tax administration and these studies focus on the level of accomplishment which the tax system is benefited with because of the artificial intelligence (AI). The previous results confirmed that all those AI-based strategies effortlessly enhance calculations for tax accuracy. The issues in compliance related to the taxpayers shows a pivot with and improved administrative efficiency (Aladebumoye, 2025; Kaushik et al., 2025).The involvement of artificial intelligence into the Indian tax system with the prototype towards the best of the operational efficiency and the transparency in the set revenue system of administration leads to set a model for accuracy in the tax system. With the support of which the tax assessments become more accurate as these are backed using AI-based system. The escalation of the compliance can be notified by the innominate assessment mechanism, which supports to reduce personal interaction processes. The advancement and automation of the process with the effective application of Automated Information Systems, (Kaushik et al., 2024).

Artificial intelligence (AI) is a disruptive technology that, if effectively harnessed, can improve revenue mobilisation, compliance, and enforcement efforts for tax administrations all over the world. In India, AI's relevance is particularly pronounced given the nation's expanding digital tax landscape and persistent challenges in broadening the tax base and addressing non-compliance (NIPFP, 2023) Tax monetisation refers to the strategic maximisation of government tax revenue via policy, technology, and administrative innovation. According to Use of artificial intelligence in scrutiny selection of income tax returns in tax administration (2024), the adoption of AI in tax administration enhances scrutiny efficiency.

KEY TERMS

The Artificial Intelligence is a subfield of computer science dealing with the theoretical and practical development of algorithmically based systems that imitate the process of human thought. India's National Strategy for Artificial Intelligence by NITI Aayog defines AI as machines that demonstrate the high-level processes we associate with human intelligence including thinking, perceiving, learning, problem-solving and decision-making capabilities. According to the Ministry of Electronics and Information Technology (MeitY), AI is the ability of a system to perform tasks that typically require human intelligence and that can operate independently in complex environments. Studies show that approaches such as machine learning paradigms, natural language processing frameworks, and neural network architectures have the capacity to sense inputs from the world, infer meaning from environmental data, and adapt actions to maximize impact.

The India AI Mission, as it elaborates on its efforts towards using artificial intelligence mentions how the characteristic of artificial intelligence to change its behaviour and adapt through repeated learning cycles to refine behavioural strategies allows computational systems to autonomously enhance performance on some tasks in the decision or control domain without having to be specifically reprogrammed. Recent views suggest that AI systems act intelligently here by generalizing from experiences gained through training to novel situations, and adapting templates learned through training to the current dynamic context thus acting as exhibiting computational intelligence in analysis of dynamic circumstances. All measures and actions taken to maximise tax in the economy and for the benefit of tax compliance.

In other words, data analytics is a process that uses a variety of mathematical techniques and computational procedures to extract valuable information from large data sets (Davenport & Harris, 2007), that would assist a tax administration in taking decisions. Predictive analytics employs complicated statistical functions and AI-based algorithms that forecast upcoming trends in the amount of tax revenue by using both historical accounting and present economic data (Shmueli & Koppius, 2011).Tax compliance is the extent to which a taxpayer follows a tax system and pays his or her correct tax liability on time (Allingham & Sandmo, 1972). Blockchain is a scalable, decentralized ledger framework that can enhance the reliability, traceability and confidentiality of the tax journal entries (Nakamoto, 2008).

Machine Learning is a subfield of artificial intelligence that consists of algorithms that change their behaviour in response to input data in a way that improves their performance over time without the need for further explicit reprogramming (Mitchell, 1997). Tax policy refers to the laws and rules that governments design to determine tax bases, rates, and administrative procedures (Bird & Zolt, 2008). Tax evasion is the illegal use of methods to not pay taxes owed to the government (Slemrod, 2019).

In the cycle of tax filling, the automation of the tax administration enforced the digital applications, with the implementation of the right and real time implementation of the administrative system. This helps the system to improve the efficiency and be transparent enough for the users which helps the system to experience the flawless administration (OECD,2024)

OVERVIEW OF TAX COLLECTION AND ADMINISTRATION

When AI is being used in the tax system it leads to generative evaluation. There is a decisive base focusing on the system for building the part which can be fairer and efficient for the revenue collection. There are various long-standing challenges for the compliance and its implementation which is seen to be supported by the AI-powered tools. The system Indian Annual Information Statement (AIS) made it such an easier way out for taxpayers by keeping the digital transaction records. Because of such an efficient system the tax collection efficiency is enhanced along with the extreme reduction in evasion. Also, cannot miss to adhere with the fact that linking Aadhar and PAN makes all transactions across bank accounts will be easily tracked.

Ensuring Effective and Ethical AI Deployment

The instant delivery and availability of these innovations made in technologies achieved success in operational instances and implementation by the tax authorities along with the ethical level available at one's fingertips (de la Feria & Grau Ruiz, 2021). The qualities which is available with AI as a tool, progress with all assurances of taxpayers and all stakeholders. The entire system is transparent and clearly accountable (Antón,2021). The tax system is now showing us all complex presence and shows the entire management backed by available technologies.

Importance of Tax Monetisation in India

When the technology was introduced and adopted in the tax system identifying the non-compliant taxpayers showed an amicable operations and great contribution in efficiency. This has led to better transparency in the system and to steal a march on tax evasion (Deloitte India 2024). In a like manner, dispensing of personal interaction, reducing discretionary powers and making assessments fair has been the goal of the faceless assessment project, introduced by Central Board of Direct Taxes (CBDT) in FY 2019-20.

Although, we can see that tax authorities around the world are applying techniques in machine learning and data mining for example, in artificial intelligence (AI). They allow risk-based audit selection, anomaly detection in filings and better responses to compliance (OECD 2017) almost half (49 percent) of the taxpayers surveyed in 2024 by Deloitte said the notices generated by AI initially seemed accurate, and another 37 percent said they seemed somewhat accurate.

In fact, sufficient and just taxation is still at the heart of the larger structural goals of inclusive growth and equity. Tax systems have generally battled under-reporting, a small tax base and dynamic avoidance rates throughout history. Leakages can be minimized with the benefit that AI can bring to the system will be by minimizing leakages and ensuring better compliance with incentives Management.

How to mitigate corruption with use of AI-based protocols like., minimizing the part of the personality in the processes of assessment and decision-making needs to be performed in mediums of operation with no physical contact with human. While at the same time, recent research indicates that the velocity and efficacy of income tax management procedures may result in accelerating due to systems like the Annual Information Statement (AIS).

OVERVIEW OF AI TECHNOLOGIES

Recent advancements in ML methods allow us to examine large datasets for subtle behaviours to identify suspicious transactions, as well as to create detailed taxpayer risk profiles (Mitchell, 1997). In the same vein, the natural language processing systems help in automating the examination of the unstructured textual input that enable reviews for compliance in a shorter time as well as allow for efficient automated responses to taxpayer's queries .Moreover, they combine historical and recent financial information, thereby deriving revenue forecast that improves the ability of the policy makers to plan for changes in the budget and allocation of resources (Shmueli & Koppius, 2011; Indian Journal of Integrated Research in Law, 2024).

In parallel, the blockchain technology creates a tamper-proof record of tax transactions and thus enhances transparency and provides a non-repudiable audit trail for tax auditors (Nakamoto, 2008). Automatic conversational agents and virtual assistants also promote greater taxpayer engagement by providing real-time guidance on how to file and regulatory requirements, thus alleviating tax office administrative load (Woods, 2019). Like never before, the incorporation of these artificial intelligence–driven capabilities have the potential to take revenue administrations from providing a traditional digital service-based architecture to a more agile, accurate, and secure infrastructure underpinned by technology as the bedrock of a modernised and trusted tax ecosystem (Indian Journal of Integrated Research in Law, 2024).

Historical Context of Taxation in India

Taxation system in India is evolving through layers which can be roughly traced back to colonial regime, pre-liberalised and post-liberalised phase where recent introduction of Goods and services Tax (GST) is the recent significant development towards broadening of tax base and modernisation of compliance systems (NIPFP, 2023). AI-based applications could be visualised as the last mile in this continuum where tax liability has already been directly computed and AITP compliance body (including non-compliance behaviour) has already been enabled AI (Ademofe et al.,2016 & Aladebumoye, 2025) also recognises these abilities as necessary to building an effective resilient tax system.

AI is touted to revolutionise the workplace, but wider adoption increases the risk and reward when it comes to protecting data privacy and the security of systems. Therefore, this requires that in order to maintain the rights of taxpayers in relation to the lack of standards with respect to non-designated access to data and cyber-threats, there is a need for a suitable balance to be achieved between the rate of technological advancement and regulatory measures (Wang, 2024).

Although, the interviews with technologists, policymakers, and tax authorities revealed that the effective use of AI for tax enforcement will ask for the high levels of collaboration across all three types of entities. Interdisciplinary merging of this kind can lock in ethical safeguards and procedural transparency, but they can only do so at the expense of protecting ai systems from breaches of legal and ethical barriers. These synergies not only help digest accountability needed to form stronger tax systems, but also develop auditory, equitable and stakeholder-aligned AI technologies. Indian tax system attached with pre-colonial, post-colonial and post-liberalised period. Core reforms are mostly like, Goods & Services Tax (indicating the expanding face of the tax net as well as further modernisation of compliance framework (NIPFP, 2023).

EVOLUTION OF TAX POLICIES

We should see tax policy through this prism of evolution from the colonial centre of extraction to post-colonial but misfortune too-big-to-fail blocks, now stumbling on to viable-market principles, personified in tax policy with aspirational developmental economic and political change. Taxation was primarily used as a device to raise resources to meet expenditures which the British levied on colonial India to pay for the costs incurred in administering the colony and costs associated with military forces stationed in India, exemplified when the Income Tax Act of 1860 was introduced post-1857 when the British exchequer was significantly strained (NIPFP, 2023; Agrawal et al. 2025). Post Independence era has witness a paradigm shift in the view point of tax as an instrument of economic development and social justice, which is reflected in the Income Tax Act, 1961, which is brought into force universally in India and which classifies the crossheads of income into five categories and redefine the real direct taxation (Singh, 2019 & CBDT, 2022). This was followed by an appropriate sequencing of reforms in the 1990s towards broadening the tax base, rationalization of rates, and simplification of administration as recommended by the Chelliah Committee earlier such that by 2017, GST, a comprehensive indirect tax regime was realized (NIPFP, 2023; Rao & Kumar, 2016).

Previous Approaches to Tax Monetization

The strategy until now has been to carry out manual audits, voluntary disclosures, information exchange mechanisms, and under-utilization of IT. These approaches realised at best incremental benefits but were plagued by challenges of scalability and speed of precision-attuned enforcement (NIPFP, 2023). Tax monetization is currently not up to mark in three areas- retrospective and offline capitalized compliance verification using physical documentation, periodic amnesty schemes like the Voluntary Disclosure of Income Scheme (1997) and National Income Declaration Scheme (2016) and bilateral information sharing mechanisms with foreign tax authorities (Deloitte India, 2024; Singh, 2019). Such traditional approaches had inherent limitations in addressing the growing complexity of financial transactions and cross-border economic interactivity and required a tech reboot. Indian tax policy has adopted technology from e-filing to real time tax analytics overtime The pandemic period and consequent crisis has brought digitalisation to the fore for most of the governments, hence paving the way for creeping in the integration of AI in the governance as had already been proven earlier in case the Income Tax Department took initiatives for collecting analytics based information with respect to adherence where such a risk based assessment mechanisms based again on the basis of experience with modern data mining techniques were put to avail for a non-discretionary faceless assessment (CBDT, 2025; Agrawal, 2025).

THE ROLE OF AI IN TAXATION

By introducing artificial intelligence (AI), tax authorities will be able to scan big datasets, searching for signs of noncompliance as well as revenue shortfalls, which will be a new approach for risk assessment (Indian Journal of Integrated Research in Law, 2024).AI helps the system to scan and record the documents of taxpayers and details of the transaction which are automated and reducing the man-made hours. The operational efficiency leads to automation and its finally supplements the enforcement for maintaining the compliance.

The tax administration works basis AI protecting risk and then finding out which taxpayer group holds probable higher risk. The system strengthens the tax administration which is more adaptive leading to balance and optimisation in the data-driven high-scale implications of compliance (Indian Journal of Integrated Research in Law, 2024).

Predictive Analytics for Tax Revenue Forecasting

Predictive analytics helps to access the regression testing for the tax administration helping the authority to fix and identify these non-compliance risk. The models which are data-driven and supports the enforcement of detailed efforts of the tax agencies. There are sub-population of the taxpayers who faces complex issues for non-compliance and tax-evasion. Continuous investment in personnel development is just as important; equipping tax officials with the knowledge to interpret analytical outputs and manage AI-enabled processes is vital for maintaining a robust, equitable and transparent tax environment (Pamisetty et al., 2022).

Successful Implementations of AI in Tax Collection

Additionally, examination of AI use in tax collection provides valuable insights on how to prepare for compliance and efficiency. As AI, machine learning and generative AI technologies grow in confidence regarding compliance, reconciliation and fraud detection solutions, more organizations are prepared to deploy solutions in a tax function today (16%) or at least in limited use (35%), according to a 2024 Deloitte survey. AI-driven e-invoicing systems have achieved real-time monitoring of VAT/GST, doubled VAT gap-reduction effect, and accelerated VAT refund process in countries like Brazil and Mexico as an illustration. Just as the UK HM Revenue Customs uses its Connect system to ensure this massive array of data can find the unreported income and reclaim £millions in lost revenues every year. A strong message from taxpayers about their confidence in these technologies can be seen where nearly half of taxpayers surveyed regarding their interaction with an AI-generated notice believed the notice was probably correct.

Given the rapid pace of innovation, creating new risks but also unique challenges for tax authorities, they will need to be flexible in their working approach to potentially integrate AI into tax administration, when necessary. Which shows that there is an openness in iterating compliance and enforcement to make it fit into an actual and transparent tax system. Consequently, these international implementations also act as a necessary guide to encourage both tax compliance and tax administration in an imminent, fast-moving digital world.

Figure 1. Rating technology automation in tax function (Deloitte, Survey on Income Tax Digitalisation in India 2.0)

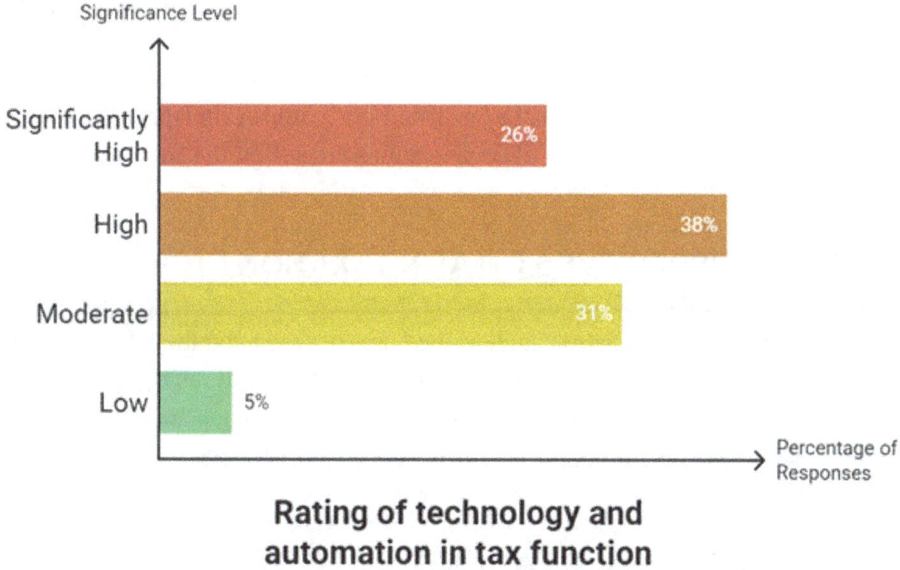

Figure 2. Comfort level with AI/ML and gen AI for tax function (Deloitte, Survey on Income Tax Digitalisation in India 2.0)

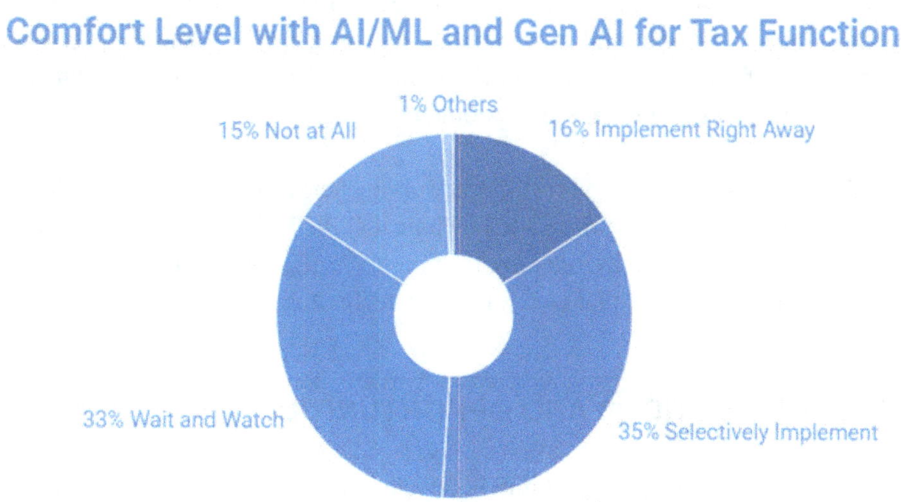

Like the data shown in a prior chart, recent 2024 results from Deloitte indicate that respondents feel more comfortable with next-gen tech applied in tax. More than half of the survey respondents say they are ready for AI, ML, and GenAI in their tax functions, with 16% saying they can deploy immediately and another 35% saying they are prepared to do so in some select use cases. At the same time though, only a third of organisations (33%) are in the "wait and see" camp (a sign that caution is still a virtue, too), and as few as 15% of organisations are still in the "not for us" camp.

GLOBAL PERSPECTIVES ON AI IN TAXATION

Tax authorities across nation such as the UK, Australia and the US have widely adopted AI-based systems for taxpayer communication, audit analytics, and compliance screening. As their experience reveals, inter-related legal, technological, and institutional reforms work together to achieve the best outcomes.

CHALLENGES AND LIMITATIONS

The growing use of technology and algorithm-based systems in tax administration has also created concerns about the safety of taxpayer data. People need to feel confident that their personal information is well-protected, which is why strong rules and safeguards should be in place to prevent data breaches.

Another challenge is the lack of reliable technology in some areas, especially in rural regions. Weak digital infrastructure makes it hard to scale these projects effectively. To fix this, governments need to invest in better infrastructure and also provide training programs that give people the skills and knowledge to use these systems.

A final issue is the hesitation within some tax agencies to adopt new technologies. This often happens because of limited technical skills and a resistance to change. Overcoming this will require ongoing training for staff, change management programs, and a work culture that welcomes new technology.

FUTURE DIRECTIONS AND OPPORTUNITIES

There exists enamours opportunities for the purpose of leverages for improvements of tax compliance which can be processed by automated resolution. The entire system can be personalised based on AI interfaces using the ML algorithms. Emerging evidence indicates that these innovations can minimise compliance overloads and increase revenue leakages. For experiencing the benefits of the tax policy these frameworks, the entire tax administration will evolve and enhance the operation in technology.

RECOMMENDATIONS FOR POLICYMAKERS

Since the transaction cost economics etc, started at organizational economics, it also explains why India needs to invest in robust support systems like reliable digital infrastructure as well as safe data frameworks. This is vital groundwork for using advanced computational technologies at scale in tax administration. For AI tools to be used throughout the tax system, they must develop skills in data analytics and other technology fields. The public and private sectors can also work together in this effort piloting new AI applications and scaling those that succeed across multiple tax functions.

Finally, we need strong legal protections against the misuse of the technology. These protections should ensure taxpayer rights are preserved while protecting equity and transparency in the system. These measures, collectively, are vital in making for a tax administration that uses AI in an efficient, responsible manner.

CONCLUSION

The tools can enhance and pivot the improvement in the tax administration with great potential for automation. There will seen enhancements and reductions in the risk existence of the automation. These benefits, however, will only arise if important obstacles can be overcome. Data privacy, the robustness of the technology ecosystem and workforce readiness need to be carefully managed. At once, however, robust ethical governance principles are equally critical. And clear rules are necessary to clarify technology's place in democracy, defend citizens' rights, and uphold public faith.

In tax administration, the responsible, fair, and equitable use of technology reforms has the potential to deliver high dividends for India. Succeeding will require a combination of good policy design, thoughtful technology development, and meaningful stakeholder involvement. This balance is crucial as tax systems must radically change, not only by the rapid advancement of technology but also by the pressing need for innovation in tax policy and accountability. In addition, those areas that are best suitable for conducting empirical research, large-scale pilot plans and evidence-based research on the socio-economic impact of AI-assisted tax administration require further study.

REFERENCES

Agrawal, R. (2025). CBDT using AI tools to boost income-tax compliance. *The Indian Express*, July 24, 2025.

Aladebumoye, T. (2025). The role of AI in enhancing tax transparency and reducing evasion. *World Journal of Advanced Research and Reviews*, *25*(1), 206–217. DOI: 10.30574/wjarr.2025.25.1.0023

Allingham, M. G., & Sandmo, A. (1972). Income tax evasion: A theoretical analysis. *Journal of public economics, 1*(3-4), 323-338.Antón, F. S. (2021). Artificial intelligence and tax administration: strategy, applications and implications, with special reference to the tax inspection procedure. *World Tax J.*, 575.

Bird, R. M., & Zolt, E. M. (2008). Technology and taxation in developing countries: From hand to mouse. *National Tax Journal, 61*(4), 791–821. DOI: 10.17310/ntj.2008.4S.02

Central Board of Direct Taxes (CBDT). (2022). *Annual report 2021-22*. Ministry of Finance, Government of India.

Davenport, T. H., & Harris, J. G. (2007). Competing on analytics: The new science of Winning. *Harvard business review press. Language*, *15*(217), 24.

de la Feria, R., & Grau Ruiz, M. A. (2021, May). The robotisation of tax administration. In *International Conference on Inclusive Robotics for a better Society* (pp. 115-123). Cham: Springer International Publishing.

Deloitte India. (2024). *Income tax digitalisation survey 2.0: Taxpayer perspectives on digital transformation*. Deloitte Touche Tohmatsu India LLP.

Indian Journal of Integrated Research in Law. (2024). Overview of AI technologies in tax administration. *Indian Journal of Integrated Research in Law*, *2*(1), 45–58.

Kaushik, P., Brahmi, M., Kakran, S., & Kansra, P. (2024). The Predictive Grey Forecasting Approach for Measuring Tax Collection. *Journal of Risk and Financial Management, 17*(12), 558. DOI: 10.3390/jrfm17120558

Mitchell, T. M. (1997). Does machine learning really work? *AI Magazine*, *18*(3), 11–11.

Nakamoto, S. (2008). Bitcoin: A peer-to-peer electronic cash system. *Available at SSRN* 3440802.

NIPFP. (2023). *Tax administration reforms in India*. National Institute of Public Finance and Policy. [REMOVED HYPERLINK FIELD]

OECD. (2017). *Technology tools to tackle tax evasion and tax fraud*. OECD Publishing., DOI: 10.1787/9789264271401-

OECD. (2024). *Digital solutions in tax administration*. OECD Publishing.

Pamisetty, V., Pandiri, L., Annapareddy, V. N., & Sriram, H. K. (2022). Leveraging AI, Machine Learning, And Big Data for Enhancing Tax Compliance, Fraud Detection, And Predictive Analytics in Government Financial Management. Machine Learning, And Big Data for Enhancing Tax Compliance, Fraud Detection, And Predictive Analytics in Government Financial Management (June 15, 2022).

Rao, M. G., & Kumar, S. (2016). Envisioning tax policy for accelerated development in India. *NIPFP Working Paper No. 190*. National Institute of Public Finance and Policy.

Shmueli, G., & Koppius, O. R. (2011). Predictive analytics in information systems research. *Management Information Systems Quarterly*, *35*(3), 553–572. DOI: 10.2307/23042796

Singh, P. (2019). Tax revenue in India: Trends and issues. *Working Paper 448*. Institute for Social and Economic Change.

Slemrod, J. (2019). Tax compliance and enforcement. *Journal of Economic Literature*, *57*(4), 904–954. DOI: 10.1257/jel.20181437

Wang, M. (2024). AI Technologies in Modern Taxation: Applications, Challenges, and Strategic Directions. *International Journal of Finance and Investment*, *1*(1), 42–46. DOI: 10.54097/v2kgty49

Chapter 9
Navigating the Social Media Landscape:
Strategies for Effective Marketing

Azamat Ali
https://orcid.org/0000-0003-2931-2166
Lovely Professional University, India

ABSTRACT

Social media platforms are among the most effective tools for modern marketing. They help increase brand awareness and allow direct communication with consumers. This chapter discusses the steps needed to effectively manage social media marketing. It provides guidance for marketers aiming to achieve better results. The chapter highlights the importance of using data to create effective social media plans. It emphasizes selecting the right channels for target audiences and developing engaging content. Key topics include audience segmentation and defining audience personas. Understanding user behaviour and preferences is crucial for success. Real-life examples and case studies are included to show how to improve campaigns. The chapter also explores new trends and developments in social media marketing. It discusses how businesses can adapt to innovations in the digital environment. Whether you are new to marketing or experienced, this chapter helps you confidently navigate and succeed in social media marketing.

INTRODUCTION

Marketing communication through social media has become a prominent tool especially to business organizations. It has come out as a key approach of placing products in the market for sale through advertising. These sites include; Facebook,

DOI: 10.4018/979-8-3373-2772-3.ch009

Instagram, Twitter, linkedin, and Tiktok are relevant in driving brand presence. They allow businesses to build communities hence promoting the development of business entities. It has improved on the prior mode of communication, which only involved one party, the consumer, and the brand, to include real time communication (Wang, 2021). According to the latest statistics for 2023, social networking will include person's number around 5. 7 billion people, or about 62 percent of the world's population (Statista, 2023). This huge population of users provides marketers the unique opportunity for coverage and reach out to the target consumers. Moreover, the time spent in the social networks has also risen to the greater extent. DataReportal (2024) informs that users spend 2 hours and 23 minutes of their time using social networks every day. Such involvement underlines the opportunity for brands for the consistent and highly relevant communication with the consumers.

Brand awareness is a major reason why social media marketing (SMM) proves to be effective to companies. The use of the social media is therefore effective for enhancing visibility since brands can post content often, target individual customers and present good information to consumers. Unlike the conventional direct marketing technique that may at times, have restricted coverage, social marketing tools such as Instagram and Facebook come with enhanced filtering that can allow the business-person to get through certain demography, activities and interests (Singha, 2024). Another major benefit of the SMM is that the customers can be engaged well. On social media, the communication between the brands and the consumers is a two-way communication through the posting, comments, tweeting, messages and status updates (Zhou et al., 2025). It can be seen that by this means, the engagement deepens the bonding between the brand and consumer making customers feel linked to the brand. Also, today's customers, especially on social media, expect quick responses, and a majority of them (69%) expect replies within 24 hours (Sprout Social, 2023). Quick and timely responses are very vital in formation and maintaining healthy relations with the customers.

Social media marketing is cheap and provides high value thus making it ideal for small businesses and 'new kids on the block'. While paid advertising strategies require some level of expenditure, the enhanced advertising can be adopted by posting certain content that will be useful to the customers and this will not only bring down the amount of money required for marketing but it will also be cost effective as it helps to improve the return on investment (Saxena, 2021). It brings benefits that permit small business enterprises to confront mammoth and well-established organizations. Social networks also have analytics and give information concerning users and performance of the content posted. These tools assist the marketers in decision making when targeting the right audience with the right strategy (Palle, 2021). For instance, Facebook Ads and Instagram have metrics for reach and awareness as well as followers which can guide brand's strategies. Still, it remains for some issues as, for instance, algorithm changes, or learning how to deal with negativity appropriately can be quite tricky. This is because the algorithms on social media platforms change very frequently, which puts the marketers in an unfamiliar ground and negative comments must be dealt with adequately enough to not tarnish the image of the brand. Campaign improvement is also made possible by analysing consumer reactions and competitor actions where detailed metrics like engagement or click-though and conversion rates can be utilized (Rosário & Dias, 2023).

PROBLEM STATEMENT

Social media has emerged as a key player in marketing yet there are also challenges facing most businesses when it comes to its effective use. The central issue is that digital platforms are changing rapidly, due to shifting algorithms, user behaviour and competition. Social media has potential advantages in terms of access and engagement, although, small and medium businesses find it difficult to make appropriate platform decisions and to make effective relevant content. The second problem is data utilization. Even although platforms give in-depth analytics, most marketers fail to utilize such analytics to inform their campaigns. This means incoherent and less effective campaigns. Besides, it is hard to control brand reputation on the Internet as negative posts and fake information may spoil the trust within a short period of time. As new platforms and technologies continue to emerge including artificial intelligence and augmented reality, it is critical to have clear strategies to enable business adjust to the changes and thrive.

METHODOLOGY

The approach used in this chapter is qualitative and exploratory research approach which backs up secondary data analysis. The methodology has been organized such that:

Literature Review

- The literature has been thoroughly reviewed on specific academic journals, reports in the industry, and statistical databases (e.g., Statista, Data Reportal, Sprout Social), in order to define the status quo of social media marketing.
- The review points at concept frameworks of audience segmentation, content strategy and data driven marketing and points out their lack of practical application.

Case Study Analysis

- Real life examples of companies and various businesses have been discussed including that of multinational companies, small enterprises to illustrate different approaches to social media marketing.
- These examples give insight into the best practice, challenges encountered and innovative ways that has led to a better engagement, brand awareness and customer retention.

Comparative Platforms Analysis

- Access to the social media, including Facebook, Instagram, LinkedIn, Twitter (X), and TikTok is contrasted on the basis of the demographics of the users, the tools of engagement, and advertising opportunities.
- Such comparative lenses offer ideas about how to approach various segments of the audience differently according to the platform.

Thematic Analysis of Emerging Trends

- Trends like AI driven analytical insights, working with influencers, customised marketing and leveraging immersive technologies (e.g., AR/VR) are covered.
- The thematic structure is employed to forecast the future paths of the social media marketing.

Synthesis for Strategy Development

- Data is summarized and converted into powerful strategies that a marketer can use to improve the efficacy of his or her campaigns.
- The synthesis draws focus upon the reconciliation between data-driven decision-making and creativity, flexibility, and ethics.

The above methodology also blends academic findings with the industry best practices to help in delivering a chapter applicable in not only the knowledge but also to offer guidelines to businesses and marketers to operate in the digital ecosystem.

UNDERSTANDING YOUR AUDIENCE

As much as we know in marketing research, the "know thy audience" adage has never been truer. The development of the diverse online platforms has increased the canvassing of marketing promotions. But it has also created more convolutions in regard with understanding of different audiences. Solving this issue is possible through the audience segmentation and persona approach. This section gives insight into the rationale as to why these practices are important. It also discusses ways to segment the audience, their characteristics, as well as behaviour besides the acceptable advertisement tactics.

Importance of Audience Segmentation and Persona Development

Audience Segmentation

Audience segmentation is the process of classifications of large market into submarkets based on certain similarities. This process can help marketers improve the persuasiveness of its promotions by directly targeting the customers' specific wants and needs in a particular category. Mentioned necessary segment requirements allow personalizing the communication with the organization's customers, which will result in enhanced satisfaction (Mustak et al., 2024). Another benefit of segmentation is that it helps to use the marketing communication resources efficiently since the concentrating is done on the most profitable segments. These segments are usually recognised based on aspects like age, gender, income, lifestyle, values, geographic location, and purchasing behaviour (Vamsee et al., 2023).

Persona Development

Persona development refines audience segmentation by establishing concrete and elaborate descriptions, called buyer personas, of the targeted consumers in each segment. These personas embody certain features, patterns of conduct, and requirements, thereby enabling marketers to come up with messages that will appeal to their targeted consumers. In doing so, personas help marketers to focus more on the audience, resulting in the creation of more persuasive content. The significance of the customers' personas cannot be overestimated as they help to shape further product development, communicate with clients, and promote a brand image to potential buyers (Salminen et al., 2023).

Techniques for Analysing Audience Demographics, Interests, and Behaviours

Audience profiling does not only entail knowing who the audience is or where they are from in terms of demographics. Instead it demands going further than the hobbies, activities, concerns, and actions of participants. Below are some of the ways through which marketers try to analyse these factors.

Demographic Analysis

Demographic analysis is often considered as the starting point while analysing and trying to understand an audience. It entails collection of information involving demographics including age, sex, income, and education. Other quantitative variables that relate to the clients are also factored in like the occupation status and the marital state. This information gives elementary information about the audience. This makes it possible to determine trends or patterns which exist in the demographic strata. For instance, a brand selling its products to millennials has to ensure its products are promoted on the social media apps Instagram or TikTok. At the same time, a brand that sells products for elderly will be better off focusing on Facebook or email marketing. Demographic analysis is useful in the first step of segmentation. It enables the marketers to segment broad categories within the population of viewer/listener/reader (Ashton & Gowland-Pryde, 2023).

Psychographic Profiling

In fact, though psychographic profiling is more extensive than demographic profiling it. It involves the mental processes of the individual in terms of values, attitudes, interest and life style. This analysis plays a very critical factor when studying or attempting to find out why individuals act the way they do. It also gives insight into the things that compel the people to make a purchase as stated (Wardana et al., 2023). Some of the strategies marketers apply for psychographic profiling include surveys, interviews and social media listening. It helps them also explain the psychological aspect of the consumer in as much as they do their shopping. From this, it enables brands to come up with more focused and emotionally charged campaigns. For instance, a brand that shares its targeted audience's environmental concern has better chances of getting closer emotionally. This proportion promotes brand loyalty that they tend to stick with the brand which has been found to have an influence in the market.

Behavioural Analysis

Behavioural analysis centres of how consumers relate with a brand. This includes; purchasing behaviour, website interactions, and interaction with marketing stimuli. It also takes a look into the concept of brand loyalty. Behavioural analysis is of most benefit when trying to locate the top clients. It also assists in the determination of customer experience map as a marketing concept (Chaffey & Ellis-Chadwick, 2019). Such tools as Goggle Analytics and CRM help in analysing the audience's behaviour. Social media analytics dashboard also comes in to the picture. Based on the number of page views, click through rates, conversions, one is in a position to estimate what type of content is well received. They can then change their strategies in relation to this discovery (Theodorakopoulos & Theodoropoulou, 2024).

Social Media Analytics

The social media channels are a treasure trove of qualitative information about the target audience. Specific social media monitoring identifies engagement indicators. These are likes, shares, comment, and mentions. It also affords marketers a live idea of what content is popular among the people (Tuten, 2023). Social listening tools enable marketers to track, listen to conversations that relate to their brand. It can also monitor the talk about competitors as well as develop trends in the industry. These are new areas of interest or concern and novel contact points for engaging with the audience. For instance, the number of posts with focus on certain product feature might increase, thus revealing a growing desire for it. This is usually followed by brands amplifying that feature in future marketing communications (Zhou et al., 2025).

Customer Surveys and Feedback

Of all the audience information types, feedback from customers is amongst the most useful and preferred by marketers. What customers like or dislike makes use of surveys, polls, and customer reviews that offer a primary source of information. Involving and responding to feedbacks frequently is a way that proves that the brand cares for its customers. Thus it can improve customer patronage. Feedback also identifies some issues that might be out of reach of other types of analysis, thus creating an opportunity to enhance certain products or services or redesign a marketing campaign (Priyono & Hidayat, 2024).

PLATFORM SELECTION AND STRATEGY DEVELOPMENT

In today's world, e-commerce is succeeding and depends on social media channels in order to find clients and increase the brand's recognition. However, care must be taken to select the correct marketing social site and a proper design the scheme of action to be taken. This section gives information on social networking sites and who uses them; a brief description of the most used sites is given below.

Overview of Popular Social Media Platforms and Their Demographics

Facebook

At the current time, Facebook has more than three billion monthly active account holders, which put it as the social media with the most active users all over the world. It has become one of the most popular sites to-date with regard to the ages, gender, as well as marital status of the users. Being the main social platform among the selected age group – those aged 25-34 years Facebook is flexible it can contain text, images, videos, and even live stream. For this reason, it can be adopted by companies in almost any industry. First, it is significant to notice that Facebook is rather non selective in the choice of its audience and foresees the increased range of active users among those people who are 50+ years old, simultaneously, it does not lose its popularity among young individuals (Pew Research Center 2023, Statista 2024).

Instagram

Instagram is popular among the active users with under 35 years of age, especially among 18-29 years age group. Instagram's major feature is a reliance on images, short videos, and stories to pass on information. That makes it suitable to be used in reaching urban consumers slightly more than half of them are women. B2C companies especially from benchmarks such as fashion, beauty, lifestyle, and travel get the most out of Instagram, as revealed by Statista (2023). New products such as shopping posts, influencer marketing, and Instagram stories represent specific ways through which companies can interact with the consumers. Indeed, the algorithm used by IG prefers post that indeed receives massive engagement, which means that business needs to come up with good looking content and more engaging posts (Pew Research Center, 2023).

Twitter

This is a social media whose trends are often associated with real time information-sharing mechanisms. This includes news, customer service, and public relations are some of the areas where it is commonly used. Twitter currently boasts 330 million monthly active users, and mostly actively used by audiences that are between 18 and 49 years old. It has fairly broad audience, however, it targets mainly a business, readers mostly are professionals, lecturers, journalists, and politicians (Statista, 2023). The platform works with the limit of 280 characters, so the messages are concise. This makes it favourable when used by companies that would wish to post brief status, give and receive comments or contribute to trends. From the analysis it can be seen that Twitter helps in increasing the reach of a brand especially during event or product launch through hashtags and trending topics (Pew Research Center, 2023).

LinkedIn

LinkedIn is the social media for business use that connects millions of professionals across the globe; now, it has counted up to 900 million individuals. LinkedIn is mostly popular among the businesspeople, managers and the B2B marketers, majority of the users are of the aged between twenty five and fifty four years. This makes it ideal for companies planning or targeting to provide a certain kind of message to the professionals, leaders, and decision-makers (Statista, 2023). As an important B2B, recruitment and professional services' platform, LinkedIn focuses on providing thought leadership, industry news and career advancement updates with its business features where organizations can post updates, recognize talents and build professional profiles (Pew Research Center, 2023).

TikTok

TikTok is a rapidly-altering socializing website that has rapidly been adopted in talking circles, more so among Generation Z users; it has monthly active users standing at over 1 billion, and through which the young users below 30 years are mostly served. The content of TikTok is short, bright videos that include such genres as comedy, music, trends, and challenges or allow creating a video in any genre. The platform has a set of recommendation features that adapts the content that is available according to the user's content interests and engagement activity. This makes it easier for the brands to get in front of a large audience. It is most suitable for business in the entertainment, fashion, and beauty industries (Pew Research Center, 2023; Statista, 2023).

YouTube

YouTube is the biggest social media for sharing videos on the Internet. It has over 2.5 billion monthly active users. The platform established in the year 2004 and has redesigned the logo and their interface many a times to attract the younger generation. It is also used in all age brackets but highly prevalent in persons within the ages of 18-49 years. YouTube is crucial for companies, creating videos, like tutorials, product reviews, and entertaining videos (Statista, 2023). Its long form content successful gives the platform an ability to tell many stories in depth. This makes it suitable for brands who would wish to pass detailed information to their audience. Another capability of YouTube is in search to promote SEOs for the growth of businesses (Pew Research Center, 2023).

Criteria for Selecting the Right Platforms for Target Audiences and Marketing Goals

The following factors are important when choosing the appropriate social media tools in marketing a strategy. These factors guide businesses in making informed decisions:

Audience Demographics

An important aspect to consider is mainly the areas where the target customers are found to spend most of their time on the internet. All these social platforms are comprised of a different population with different demographic characteristics. For instance, a brand interested in younger audiences might focus on Instagram, Tik Tok, to name but a few examples. However, a B2B company may find Twitter useful while a B2C business may concentrate on linkedIn. Selecting the appropriate platform correlates the platform to the targeted audience thereby increasing chances of the intended marketing strategy reaching out to the intended individuals (Kotler & Keller, 2016).

Content Type

Some sites may concentrate on articles whereas other sites may focus on specific stories or particular topics. Hence, Instagram and Pinterest are image-centered which makes them perfect for brands that relay on good pictures. LinkedIn fits well for professional materials as well as the content related to a particular field. Awareness of the unique qualities that each platform holds aids in selecting the platforms best suited to deliver the business' content and effective in reaching the clientele (Chaffey and Ellis-Chadwick, 2019).

Marketing Goals

This reason for platform selection must be based with the general marketing objectives of the business. For instance, if the dominant objective of the intended social media outreach is increasing brand recognition, then high Friending sites such as Face book or YouTube may be suitable. If the aim is to get the leads, then LinkedIn and twitter would be more appropriate as they are more professional oriented. To this, there is a need to match the capabilities of the chosen platforms with the required marketing goals and objectives (Kotler & Armstrong, 2018).

Budget and Resources

Some platforms incite fewer requirements from the consumers concerning time, money and resources as compared to others. Applications such as Tik Tok or Instagram can be largely creative compared to others. Similarly, it might call for a strategy centered on specific topics such as thought leadership, and professional content. Tuten (2023) has noted that budget and resources should be taken into consideration when selecting platforms to avoid an inconsistent and low quality of the business's presence.

Competitor Presence

Checking where competition is present can be helpful in identifying where they may authoritatively be useful. But it is equally crucial to know the areas that one might lack might be an area of weakness to the competitors. This in turn enables the business set a new identity and reaches other audiences it had not gained before (Chaffey & Ellis-Chadwick, 2019).

Developing a Cohesive Social Media Strategy Aligned with Business Objectives

Once the right platforms are identified, the next action is to create a consistent approach to building the social media strategy that will support business goals. This process includes several key components: This process includes several key components:

Defining Clear Objectives

Many have proposed a concept of social media objectives that can be understood as a basis for creating a plan for activity on this platform: These may be awareness, leads for the company and its products, visitors to the company or organization's website, or enhanced user engagement. Outlines goals give a clear focal point and help evaluate results as to whether or not they were achieved based on stated objectives (Smith & Zook, 2024).

Content Planning and Creation

Social Media is all about content hence content is the key in any social media planning. Organization has to develop information that would be useful to the target market and be in accordance to the goals set forth. This can include schoolwork such as writing blog posts to informative, fun videos to watch or interesting posts shared on social media platforms. A content calendar is useful in the planning and also in mapping when the content is to be posted and also is effective in the cross-checking of the content which is posted on the various platforms (Chaffey & Ellis-Chadwick, 2019).

Audience Engagement

It is important in creating the relationship with the audience. While it is more than just posting content, it requires much more than that. Engaging with the followers, replying to the comments, and messages and much more are significant. That way engagement can assist in increasing the confidence level with the audience, and there are superior chances that the audience will give support to the brand (Tuten, 2023).

Monitoring and Analytics

To look at the performance of the social media strategy, there is a need to constantly monitor and analyse the results. Information found from tools such as Google Analytics, platforms such as Instagram built-in analytics, and other third-party tools are insightful. Gross measures include reach, levels of engagement and the resulting conversion rates, which aid in decision making as well as improving the advertising strategy in the long run (Theodorakopoulos & Theodoropoulou, 2024).

Flexibility and Adaptation

Social media platforms are dynamic in nature, and it definitely is a raging issue of the contemporary world. New sites come up or the existing ones modify their workings and the services they offer. In order to have a good end result in a social media campaign, one must be willing to be somewhat fluid in his/her approach. This also makes it possible for the business to be agile in the event of changes in the environment linked with digital technology. This indicates that the strategy should be reviewed and updated frequently, in order to be relevant to the business goals (Smith & Zook, 2024).

CRAFTING COMPELLING CONTENT

The use of social media marketing is only as good as the content given to the consumers. Interactive contents attract attention, encourage people to get involved and make the viewer's turn into clients. This section groups recommendations for graphics, videos and writings, as well as some ideas on where to get content and how to aggregate some of it.

Principles of Effective Content Creation for Social Media

Understanding the Audience

Brand awareness is another important principle of content creation as every content creator should know his/her audience. This is a matter of determining what they want, what challenges they face or what they would like to see the most when it comes to content. It is necessary to use detailed descriptions of target customers including demographic and psychographic data called audience personas in this process. Marketers can therefore appeal to their target audience's emotions and visually perceive their personalities to foster better contact and consequently improve the impact of marketed material (Chaffey & Ellis-Chadwick, 2019).

Consistency and Cohesion

Consistency will be the key to social media branding in terms of language, graphics and amount of content frequency in the blogging activity as well as the social media posts. This helps in sustaining the intended message without any interference by other people or even the media. Consistency creates a consistent image of the brand and also increases the belief of the audience because audiences always expect similar reporting in different media outlets. This consistency contributes to ensuring the constant impact on consumers' memory and improvement of the brand's image, as Kotler and Armstrong (2018) pointed out in their work, while discussing the brand-building process.

Value-Driven Content

Experience always plays a significant part in persuading other followers as to the value of content. Such content can be enlightening, entertaining, and fun, inspiring, motivating or just make people feel great. Value-driven content as advocated here should seek to satisfy the audience needs in a way that makes them feel that the content is a stronger link with them in that they solve their problems, answer their questions or meet their basic needs. It not only helps in grabbing the attention but also helps one to go back again and again to the same place. Real creators, however, recognize the fact that concentrating on creating real value improves engagement and attracts more traffic, which translates to long-term investment (Smith & Zook, 2024).

Authenticity and Transparency

Loyalty cannot be bought but sustained attention can only be managed and so audiences look for and require authenticity. Organic content is real and specific which makes customer have trust in a particular brand. Authenticity is relatable because it means what people see and hear or interact with is the real thing and not a figment of the brand's imagination. When it is a question of the brands' values, relevant business strategies, successes, and even failures, such an approach increases trust and strengthens the ties with the audience. It also serves to enhance trust in the brand while showing that the latter is not afraid of being honest and transparent. By going the more accurate and sincere approach in engaging the public, brand are able to develop better and healthier relations with the audience (Tuten, 2023).

Call to Action (CTA)

There is always a persuasive and persuasive Call to Action (CTA) that elicits certain behaviour form the audience. This could be the purchase of product, subscription to a magazine or even sharing of the content. It should be also noted that effective calls-to-action are short and encouraging. Many of them are in harmony with the general content approach. CTAs also contain guiding instructions as to what the audience is supposed to do next. This does not only make the content relevant and interesting but also informative and capable of being implemented. Through leading users on the next course of action to be taken, CTAs assist in transforming visitors' attention into tangible actions. They make certain that the content has the purpose it was meant to (Kotler & Keller, 2016).

Strategies for Creating Engaging Visuals, Videos, and Written Content

Visual Content

Indeed, visuals serve as an effective way of grabbing a viewer's attention and in general passing over information. Below are strategies for creating engaging visual content:

- *High-Quality Imagery:* The next level of quality of the images is obtained where there is a clear and sharp focus and adequate levels of lighting. Below par performances are expected in highly manipulated images which are often used in place of lowly manipulated or even raw images or as general pictures (Chaffey & Ellis-Chadwick, 2019).
- *Infographics:* This way of information representation has several advantages: it is more convenient to decode than the enlarged written text, while the essence of the information is intensified, which makes it possible to simultaneously consider many aspects. They are images that contain both graphics and texts thus being very suitable for portraying information more so educational information. Canva and Piktochart are among the tools for designing pictures with nice looking even if the creator is not a designer (Tuten, 2023).
- *Branded Visuals:* Using the same logos, colours, and fonts also makes it possible to build brand identity in as far as visuals are concerned. This means that consistency of content makes it easy for the target audience to relate with content and carry it in their memories. Adobe Spark and Crello are examples of design tools which provide templates to ensure that the brand image is coherent with previous materials (P. F. Kotler and G. Armstrong, 2018).

Video Content

Sharing video content on social media platforms has been on the rise due to its effectiveness to capture audience's attention and spike their interest, rather than posting photos or texts. Below are strategies for creating compelling video content:

- *Short-Form Videos:* Reels on Instagram or TikTok accounts contain images and short videos that are very much in trend these days. It is applicable better when used in videos which are effective in grabbing the attention of the audience. That they should be short, memorable, and well-designed more often than not, they contain one clear message or prompt for action (Chaffey and Ellis-Chadwick, 2019).

- *Live Streaming:* Live videos give meaningful chance to interact with the audience as the video is being broadcasted. They can be applied to events such as new product releases, question and answer sessions or even the vantage point into the brand's operations. Thus, due to the live stream appeal, the audience interaction contribution, viewers' trust building, and enhanced emotional connection, live streaming results in improved audience loyalty (Tuten, 2023).
- *Storytelling:* Videos are best used for storytelling. They appeal to emotions of the audience. Video storytelling helps to make content more personal and memorable, when telling the customers' stories, brand story, or demonstration of products (Smith & Zook, 2024).

Written Content

It is, however, worth to note that text-based posts still form a large part of social media marketing. Its strengths are in its simplicity, its applicability to the real world and its fun factor. Below are strategies for crafting compelling written content:

- *Crafting Headlines:* Since they are the first thing that the audience gets to see they have to catch their attention from the onset. There are three things that can be said about good headlines: They should be short, understandable, and should contain an appeal to the audience's rational self-interest. They should also be developed with specific emphases on Search Engine Optimization with some key words (Kotler and Keller, 2016).
- *Engaging Copy:* The body of the section needs to be interesting, to teach, and to be in tune with what the audience wants to hear. The use of subheadings, bullet points, and short paragraphs are effective to create break-points and make passage easy to read. In regards to the content, it should be done in the brand's voice and be appealing to the target consumers (Chaffey & Ellis-Chadwick, 2019).
- *Interactive Content:* Games and polls, quizzes, and Q&A sessions - are the best way to engage the audience. This enhances audience participation and also helps deliver insights regarding customers' interests and behaviour (Tuten, 2023).

Tools and Resources for Content Creation and Curation

Building high-quality content every time can at times be a project. But still it is not a problem and different tools and resources can help in this process. Below are some popular tools for content creation and curation:

- *Canva:* Canva is a multi-functional graphic design platform, which helps to create great and aesthetic pieces of content. It is suitable for use in tweets, shareable images and posters, slide sharing among others. Canva helps in availing several templates, fonts, and images that are readily suitable for incorporation into the branding of a brand. It is also easy to use meaning users even those without any background in design can use this tool effectively (Chaffey and Ellis-Chadwick, 2019).
- *Adobe Creative Cloud:* Adobe Creative Cloud gives a central platform, where all the application for creating contents is installed. These are in the form of image editing such as Photoshop, video editing like Premiere Pro and vector graphics like Illustrator. These tools are more enhanced than the previous ones but they allow freedom and customization for creating high-quality content (Kotler & Armstrong, 2018).
- *Hootsuite:* Hootsuite is a tool that assists with posting in the social networks, as well as monitoring of the visibility and engagement. It offers administration to post and interact with the audience on several social media pages at the same time which makes it convenient to be on schedule when posting (Tuten, 2023).
- *BuzzSumo:* BuzzSumo is a tool that is used for content research by helping the user to find topics that are currently popular and to also search for content that are currently popular and to also check on the competitors. Data collected from here facilitates the collection of materials that would interest the audience and feed into the generation of new material that would most likely appeal to the audience as created by Smith & Zook (2023).
- *Lumen5:* Lumen5 is a video maker used and effective in how it transform blogs and articles into videos. It employs the use of Artificial Intelligence in the selection of text to match with appropriate visuals and music hence helping creators of content to create videos that are professional without the need for special video editing skills. This tool is especially helpful in converting written content for, for example, YouTube and other social media accounts (Chaffey & Ellis-Chadwick, 2019).

LEVERAGING DATA FOR OPTIMIZATION

Analytics plays a significant role when it comes to the effectiveness and efficiency of social media marketing especially when the world is experiencing the evolution of social media. Collected data allows businesses to evaluate their social media activities, the effectiveness of campaigns, determine key performance indicators or the KPI's and use the findings to modify and enhance the strategies.

Role of Data Analytics in Observing Social Media Metrics

Analysing customers' data is vital in social media marketing. It assists brands in measuring the effectiveness of their content they also help the brands to understand how best their content could perform. Measures such as engagement, clicks, and conversions can all be viewed so that businesses understand what brings forth the best results as well as what does not work at all. It thus proves beneficial to marketers as it provides them with right nuggets of information to help enhance their endeavours. Another benefit that one can derive from data analytics is quick feedback, feedback which is as immediate as the data being fed to the system. Due to this, marketers can easily identify which posts go well with their audience and the reasons as to why they are well received. For example, if a particular post has many likes or shares, then they can know what made it to be successful in terms of time it was posted or the type of content that is posted.

Apart from enhancing the content, data analytics also help in knowing the target public more. Subsequently, depending upon the followership of organizations, business houses can understand how best to attend to the needs and wants of the respective group. This increases brand awareness and makes clients be loyal to the brand, making this personalization effective for marketers. This over time builds a better relationship with the audience hence becoming the ultimate secret to long-term success in social media marketing (Chaffey & Ellis-Chadwick, 2019).

Key Indicators & Social Media Success Factors

Twitter marketing therefore to be effective requires a good understanding on how to measure social media success; that is simply by identifying the key metrics and KPI's. These metrics offer objective methodology to assessing performance of social media campaign and establish if goals and objectives have been achieved. Important metrics and KPIs include:

- *Engagement Rate:* This is usually the level of engagement of a post or a video in terms of likes, comments, shares, etc. to the number of followers or number of views. The high engagement rate suggests that the content finds a good reception with the target users (Tuten, 2023).

- *Reach and Impressions:* Impressions equals to the number of users that came across something at least once. Impression relates to the overall view and highlights the overall incidence of content display. These 'track' content's reach and its ability to entice new followers (Kotler and Keller, 2016).
- *Click-Through Rate (CTR):* CTR defines the ratio between the number of click through rate and the number of people who view the post. As the name suggests, a higher CTR means that the content used convinces users to take an action, (Smith and Zook, 2024).
- *Conversion Rate:* This KPI calculates the number of people, who perform a specific action, be it purchasing a product, subscribing or following a page, after exposure to social media content. It provides insight into the content performance in realising targeted organisational objectives (Chaffey & Smith, 2022).
- *Follower Growth:* Growth rate of the followers gives a clear indication of the effectiveness of the brand in expanding its coverage on the social media platforms. The gradual growth in the visitor count means that people are interested in the content created by the brand (Kotler & Armstrong, 2018).
- *Sentiment Analysis:* This entails determining the stance that the users take in regard to products, services, or brands by analysing sentiments or sentiments analysis. By capturing the sentiment of the public regarding the brand and content, it makes it easier to improve on strategies that are used (Thaichon & Quach, 2023).

Techniques for Using Insights to Refine Strategies and Optimize Campaigns

Afterward, the trends and the KPIs collected are used to review the data collected and used to improve the social media strategy. Effective techniques for leveraging data to optimize campaigns include:

- *A/B Testing:* A/B testing therefore means dividing a piece of content to two versions and testing the two in order to find out which one is more effective. This technique proves useful in understanding which component of the marketing message is performing well, whether it is the headings or the images or the call to actions, and so on; it can help marketers fine tune the content based on proof of performance as it were (Singh & Shukla, 2024).
- *Trend Analysis:* The time series analyse is used in business for identification of tendencies and modifications in behaviour of the audience. Some of the

uses include the ability to modify content strategies in relation to trends and preferences towards keeping the brand topical and enjoyable for the end users (Revella, 2015).

- *Audience Segmentation:* Audience targeting: users can effectively categorize its audience according to the demographics, affinity, and behaviour. Knowing the specific wants and needs of each audiences segment also helps marketers to being able to develop content that would be most relevant and appealing to each category (Chaffey & Smith, 2022).
- *Competitor Analysis:* Competitors' analyses on social media are useful to identify the tendencies of the industry and the excellence exemplars. That way, it becomes possible for businesses to weigh their performance against others and implement tactics that improve results seen in the competitors' performances (Tuten, 2023).
- *Content Optimization:* Based on data, content strategies are fine-tuned as one is able to determine which content attracts more engagement and sales. For instance, if videos outdo images, it suggests that business organizations should invest more on this so as to impact overall performance (Kotler & Armstrong, 2018).
- *Feedback Integration:* It is crucial to use social media feedbacks in an organization's planning process when developing content. Whenever user queries or doubts regarding a particular topic are many, this topic can be included in future posts to satisfy the target group and enhance its interaction with the blog (Smith & Zook, 2024).

EMERGING TRENDS AND TECHNOLOGIES IN SOCIAL MEDIA MARKETING

There is a continuous change in the social media marketing strategies mainly because of the shift in trends and innovations. It means that such changes need to be tracked properly to be aware of any shifts that can take place in such markets to remain competitive. This section examines important trends today, how these new technologies as Artificial Intelligence (AI),Augmented Reality (AR), and Virtual Reality (VR) will influence the hiring process and what tips can help you to be a step ahead.

Current Trends Shaping the Social Media Landscape

Current social media marketing trends include the rise of fast media content, exemplified by short-form videos on platforms like TikTok, Instagram Reels, and

YouTube Shorts (Babu et al., 2024). These platforms captivate users with concise, engaging videos that quickly grab attention. This shift towards visually formatted, instant media reflects audiences' preference for simple, easily digestible content. Consequently, brands need to adapt by creating visually appealing, relevant content to meet contemporary market demands. Another key trend is the growth of social commerce, where purchases are made directly within social networks like Instagram, Facebook, and Pinterest (Attar et al., 2022). This seamless integration from product discovery to purchase transforms social media from a marketing tool to a crucial part of the sales process. Additionally, influencer marketing is evolving towards more authentic, niche influencers with smaller but dedicated followings, enhancing credibility and engagement.

Emerging Technologies: AI, AR and VR in Social Media Marketing

The advanced technologies which are trending in the market like Artificial Learning, Augmented Reality, and Virtual Reality are changing the social media marketing. AI is best used for individualization or targeting and for providing its clients with helpful assistance. Social media customer support is availed by the instant use of chatbots which are in the majority powered by Artificial Intelligence. It increases the interaction and the satisfaction of the user. AI also promotes enhanced data analysis, to provide better knowledge and understanding, on the costumer's trends and demands (Haleem et al., 2022). Instagram is an example of a social media platform which is increasingly adopting AR into its marketing strategies. It superimposes the digital on top of reality through gadgets such as smartphone. AR is applied in advertising campaigns such as those involving the application of funny lenses like Snapchat filters and AR effects from Instagram. These technologies produce user engagement and interaction technologies for the users. Thus, VR, which is still in its infancy, provides even more immersive experiences. It created immersive spaces in which people can go and engage with brands in novel ways. With the availability of VR increasing in the future it can cause virtual events, demonstrations and even virtual shopping (Jafar et al., 2025).

Strategies for Staying Ahead of the Curve

In order to remain effective in social media marketing, the manufacturers must step up with the latest trends and technologies by learning. This means as a company, you should keep abreast with such trends, attend conferences where such trends are discussed and try out such technologies. Promoting the culture of experimentations will enable the brands to look forward to new concepts as solutions rather than problems and work effectively in a dynamic market (Vetrivel et al., 2024). No less important is the focus on analysis of data. Such of these are the evaluation of the tactic and effectiveness of the social media platforms as well as the modification of on-going campaigns. In the current world, it is much easier for the brands to utilize the data in order to manage better and more effective campaigns, as it also enables them detect key trends. In the same way, if data show that short-form videos play a crucial role that brands can focus on this content type. Influencers and content producers involved in IT, which is aware of the latest trends, can also complement a brand's approach. This allows the brand to be well-positioned this way, to manage its social media campaigns agility to respond to changes effectively (Foltean & van Bruggen, 2022).

CASE STUDIES AND BEST PRACTICES IN SOCIAL MEDIA MARKETING

This section looks at case studies of social marketing using the social media platform. From these case studies, we derive obvious and useful insights and lessons for obtaining successful social media initiatives.

Case 1: Amul's Topical Advertising Campaigns

Amul is India's largest selling dairy product which is known for its 'tongue-in-cheek' ad campaigns. Sometimes these ads are even in the form of animations of a character named Indica the Amul girl making fun of current issues, trend or events. It makes the brand very much top of mind and interesting for its target public at the same time.

Strategy and Tactics

Amul's strategic plan lays down procedures that include making advertisements familiar as soon as anyone comes across them. The ads are of similar style and offer a comic perspective to the particular topics. These ads are posted by Amul on their Social Media sites such as Twitter & Facebook. This is important in making the connection with the larger public as it creates a way through which people can take information lightly and in a fun way that does not take much of their time. This makes the ads very interactive and easily share-able, thus creating a large impact.

Results

Amul's topical ads are meanwhile having become somewhat of a cultural touch point in India. They create a lot of awareness in the media outlets and the social platforms. The campaign has managed to ensure that the brand is present in the market for the last three decades. It has also had established a very emotional appeal to the consumer. In a nutshell, it can be said that knowing ability to remain relevant through these ads has helped Amul in boosting up the brand loyalty tremendously.

Lessons Learned

Consistent branding is very important, and this can be evidenced by the growth of Amul. This demonstrates that to be close to the audience relevance through writing on trending issues is essential or simply valuable. The case also shows the usefulness of humour in marketing while developing content that can be easily consumed by the audience.

Case 2: Swiggy's #WhatsInAName Campaign

The food delivery platform in India named Swiggy came up with a campaign known as #WhatsInAName. The campaign was to make consumers aware of the fact that it is convenient to order food online without necessarily remembering the restaurant names. It involved the users by asking them to share their food stories and experience but avoided the use of brand names of the restaurants emphasizing on the quality of food and service that is available (Mudgal & Rana, 2023).

Strategy and Tactics

The popularity of the campaign was established through the utilization of User Generated Content, Influencer Marketing and Social Media Engagement by Swiggy. The brand encouraged the users to tell about what type of food they like and their experiences related to it. The above mentioned stories were posted on the Swiggy social media handles. Together with famous food bloggers, Swiggy also helped to expand the impact of the campaign and make it wide known.

Results

Through #WhatsInAName campaign, Swiggy was able to reach out its customers. This led to massive generation of content from the users and a higher interaction on the social media platforms. The campaign translated because it targeted the heart, the actual food, not the logos of the restaurant companies. It was useful in further consolidating Swiggy's stance as a service provider that is loyal to the customers.

Lessons Learned

The truth behind Swiggy's approach is that it is a way of emphasizing consumer experience. Swiggy was highly effective in making people care for food emotionally, and that is how it formed a successful campaign. The case also shows how word of mouth advertising plays an important role in developing community and brand identity.

Case 3: MakeMyTrip's Holi Campaign

A leading online travel company in India MakeMyTrip came up with a Holi promotions campaign. During the Holi festival, it supported travelling within the country. It was launched with Bollywood actress Alia Bhatt and actor Ranveer Singh and the campaign encouraged the local population to travel around India during the festive season.

Strategy and Tactics

As we can see MakeMyTrip capitalized on Holi and its celebrity brand endorsers. The campaign in question produced creative and touch Amazing graphical and emotional appeal. It was done through the use of television commercials, social media shares and creations from the general public. On the occasion of Holi festival, MakeMyTrip launched some attractive offers and hot selling tour deals too many Holi based flora fares.

Results

The Holi campaign was good and effective in making more and more people acknowledged the brand and getting more bookings. Bright colours and images, partnering with the popular celebrities ensured that MakeMyTrip succeeded at gaining the interest of many users. This made it easier for the clients to be attracted to book through the platform due to the exclusive offers it came with. It also got massive engagement on the social sites with regards to people sharing their travel experiences during the Holi.

Lessons Learned

The case of MakeMyTrip's Holi proves how wise it is to synchronize the marketing campaign with the cultural calendar. Chasing the spirits of Holi, MakeMyTrip embarked on a campaign that was touching the hearts of its audience while growing the sales. About timing and cultural sensitivity about the product being marketed, use of popular personalities to popularize the campaign message is well illustrated by this case.

Case 4: Zomato's "Meme Marketing" Strategy

Zomato, an Indian food delivery aggregator, is one of the best examples of Social Media Marketing through memes. Through amusing content and making references to current affairs and everyday life occurrences, Zomato has definitely reached out to its target group especially the youth through memed that the company often posts and shares (Mudgal & Rana, 2023).

Strategy and Tactics

The social media team at Zomato come up with jokes that lampoon the Indian market, food allergies, and current events hence the jokes are usually funny and hence can be spread from one person to another. It also actively fosters user interactiveness by engaging such notices with the brand while responding to user commentaries, and participates in trending popular items online. Not only does this increase interaction but it is a way to develop your brand personality to be more friendly and light-hearted.

Results

I began my analysis of Zomato's performance by looking at its overall number of followers and engagement in social media, and I can say that the meme marketing strategy has boosted the company's numbers. The pages' posts are often shared by other users, and thousands of likes, shares or comments can be seen on the branded ones. This has led to more brand recognition and brand advocacy with clients especially the growing population of the millennial and Gen Z. The regular weekly update and the humour that they use to bring people together make the brand very popular among social users in India.

Lessons Learned

The meme marketing of Zomato is also the best example of using humour and things which people can easily relate to for improving its social media presence. The case shows that brands can indeed employ memes as a strategy of maintaining the connection with the audience as natural as possible. It also portrays the effectiveness of updating himself or herself with knowledge regarding the trends as well as the capability to counter act with what is current in the society.

Case 5: BYJU'S Digital Learning During COVID-19 Campaign

Kite, which was launched in 2012 became the largest learning application in India and during the Covid-19 Lockdown, BYJU'S has come up with several campaigns. The campaigns related to the necessity of the studying process continuation during the pandemic and familiarized audiences with BYJU'S as an effective learning tool.

Strategy and Tactics

Bill gates a parent which means BYJU'S used different platforms like social media platforms, television ads and online ads to target parents and students across the country. Other highlights of the video campaigns that have worked were stories of change from students and parents, success stories, and the showcasing of BYJU's products as highly interactive educational tools. It also provided a free trial of its learning app during the initial days of the lockdown to ensure the public get to taste what the brand has to offer to them.

Results

The given campaign was very effective owing to the fact that it resulted in millions of installations of the app and active usage among the users. BYJU'S got a strong demand and millions of new students joined the platform to learn from it. Apart from the above, the particular campaign was beneficial in helping BYJU'S to carve a niche for the brand in the edtech industry during one of the most challenging and difficult times of the market.

Lessons Learned

This case of BYJU'S during a COVID-19 shows that one of the key aspects of marketing that can significantly affect the effectiveness of the formulated and implemented strategies is responsiveness. Due to the lockdown, students and parents were in dire search of digital learning solutions and thus, BYJU'S successfully captured the market by being a reliable and necessity service provider. The case also highlights the importance of free trial or getting a chance to sample some of the service provided to customer first before they subscribe to the paid services.

CONCLUSION

This chapter emphasizes the fact that social media marketing relies on targeting a specific audience, the choice of a media platform, the innovative content, and the constant usage of information analysis. The analysis of the effective campaigns reveals that they should be authentic, emotional and based on the content created by customers. It is important to understand that marketers have to be dynamic and adaptive because the world of social media is evolving at a fast rate with new technologies, and new user behaviour trends. In the future, artificial intelligence, augmented reality, and virtual reality are likely to change the face of social media marketing and provide more personal and immersive content to the consumers. Concurrently, the trend of influencer marketing and mobile-based social commerce will remain at the core of such changes amid changing consumer habits. Social media marketing is work in progress and continuous learning. Essentially, business that keep up with trends, utilise new technologies and that can continue to engage authentically will be better placed to achieve a sustainable growth in the digital market.

REFERENCES

Ashton, D., & Gowland-Pryde, R. (2023). Arts audience segmentation: data, profiles, segments and biographies. In *Audience Data and Research* (pp. 66–81). Routledge. DOI: 10.4324/9781032632452-6

Attar, R. W., Almusharraf, A., Alfawaz, A., & Hajli, N. (2022). New trends in e-commerce research: Linking social commerce and sharing commerce: A systematic literature review. *Sustainability (Basel)*, *14*(23), 16024. DOI: 10.3390/su142316024

Babu, S., Iqbal, A., Saha, S., Koneti, C., Eni, L. N., Premkumar, I., & Suman, S. (2024). Content marketing in the era of short-form video: TikTok and Beyond. *Journal of Informatics Education and Research*, *4*(2). Advance online publication. DOI: 10.52783/jier.v4i2.1179

Chaffey, D., & Ellis-Chadwick, F. (2019). *Digital marketing: strategy and implementation*. Pearson Education.

Chaffey, D., & Smith, P. R. (2022). *Digital marketing excellence: Planning, optimizing and integrating online marketing*. Routledge. DOI: 10.4324/9781003009498

DataReportal. (2024). The time we spend on social media. https://datareportal.com/reports/digital-2024-deep-dive-the-time-we-spend-on-social-media

Foltean, F. S., & van Bruggen, G. H. (2022). Digital Technologies, marketing agility, and Marketing Management Support Systems: How to remain competitive in changing markets. In *Organizational Innovation in the Digital Age* (pp. 1–38). Springer International Publishing. DOI: 10.1007/978-3-030-98183-9_1

Haleem, A., Javaid, M., Qadri, M. A., Singh, R. P., & Suman, R. (2022). Artificial intelligence (AI) applications for marketing: A literature-based study. *International Journal of Intelligent Networks*, *3*, 119–132. DOI: 10.1016/j.ijin.2022.08.005

Jafar, R. M. S., Jabeen, M., Hussain, S., Niu, B., Sham, R., & Al-Adwan, A. S. (2025). Cyber Shopping Beyond Boundaries: The Metaverse Revolution in e-Commerce and Consumer Behavior. *Human Behavior and Emerging Technologies*, *2025*(1), 5559234. DOI: 10.1155/hbe2/5559234

Kotler, P., & Armstrong, G. (2018). *Principles of marketing* (17th ed.). Pearson.

Kotler, P., & Keller, K. L. (2016). *Marketing management* (15th ed.). Pearson Education.

Mudgal, R., & Rana, P. (2023). Comparison of two most popular food delivery apps in India: A case study of Swiggy and Zomato. *International Journal of Research in Social Sciences*, *13*(02).

Mustak, M., Hallikainen, H., Laukkanen, T., Plé, L., Hollebeek, L. D., & Aleem, M. (2024). Using machine learning to develop customer insights from user-generated content. *Journal of Retailing and Consumer Services*, *81*, 104034. DOI: 10.1016/j.jretconser.2024.104034

Palle, R. R. (2021). Discuss the role of data analytics in extracting meaningful insights from social media data, influencing marketing strategies and user engagement. *Journal of Artificial Intelligence and Machine Learning in Management*, *5*(1), 64–69. https://journals.sagescience.org/index.php/jamm/article/view/131

Pew Research Center. (2023). Social media and news fact sheet. https://www.pewresearch.org/journalism/fact-sheet/social-media-and-news-fact-sheet/

Priyono, A., & Hidayat, A. (2024). Fostering innovation through learning from digital business ecosystem: A dynamic capability perspective. *Journal of Open Innovation*, *10*(1), 100196. DOI: 10.1016/j.joitmc.2023.100196

Revella, A. (2015). *Buyer personas: how to gain insight into your customer's expectations, align your marketing strategies, and win more business*. John Wiley & Sons.

Rosário, A. T., & Dias, J. C. (2023). How has data-driven marketing evolved: Challenges and opportunities with emerging technologies. *International Journal of Information Management Data Insights*, *3*(2), 100203. DOI: 10.1016/j.jjimei.2023.100203

Salminen, J., Şengün, S., Santos, J. M., Jung, S. G., Nielsen, L., & Jansen, B. (2023). The choice of a persona: an analysis of why stakeholders choose a given persona for a design task. In *International Conference on Human-Computer Interaction* (pp. 288-310). Cham: Springer Nature Switzerland. DOI: 10.1007/978-3-031-48038-6_18

Saxena, C. (2021). Effectiveness of advertisement: Traditional vs. new media. *Journal of Contemporary Issues in Business and Government*, *27*(1), 2447–2455. https://cibgp.com/au/index.php/1323-6903/article/view/719

Singh, J., & Shukla, P. (2024). *Brand management: Principles and applications for effective branding*. Kogan Page Publishers.

Singha, S. (2024). Navigating the Social Media Maze: Strategies for Effective Digital Marketing in a Fragmented Landscape. In *Changing Global Media Landscapes: Convergence, Fragmentation, and Polarization* (pp. 84-106). IGI Global.

Smith, P. R., & Zook, Z. (2024). *Marketing communications: Integrating online and offline, customer engagement and digital technologies*. Kogan Page Publishers.

Sprout Social. (2023). Why you need to speed up your social media response time (and how). https://sproutsocial.com/insights/social-media-response-time/

Statista (2023). Number of social network users of select social media platforms worldwide in 2019 and 2023. https://www.statista.com/statistics/1109866/number-social-media-users-worldwide-select-platforms/

Statista (2024). Most used social networks 2024, by number of users. https://www.statista.com/statistics/272014/global-social-networks-ranked-by-number-of-users/

Thaichon, P., & Quach, S. (Eds.). (2023). *Artificial intelligence for marketing management*. Routledge.

Theodorakopoulos, L., & Theodoropoulou, A. (2024). Leveraging big data analytics for understanding consumer behavior in digital marketing: A systematic review. *Human Behavior and Emerging Technologies*, *2024*(1), 3641502. DOI: 10.1155/2024/3641502

Tuten, T. L. (2023). *Social media marketing*. Sage publications limited.

Vamsee, C. S., Rakesh, D., Prathyusha, I., Dinesh, B., & Bharathi, C. (2023, May). Demographic and psychographic customer segmentation for ecommerce applications. In *2023 2nd International Conference on Applied Artificial Intelligence and Computing (ICAAIC)* (pp. 615-622). IEEE. DOI: 10.1109/ICAAIC56838.2023.10140861

Vetrivel, S. C., Gomathi, T., Sowmiya, K. C., & Sabareeshwari, V. (2024). Customer-centric excellence in the marketing 6.0 era: Industry 6.0. In *Advanced Businesses in Industry 6.0* (pp. 192-219). IGI Global. DOI: DOI: 10.4018/979-8-3693-3108-8.ch013

Wang, C. L. (2021). New frontiers and future directions in interactive marketing: Inaugural Editorial. *Journal of Research in Interactive Marketing*, *15*(1), 1–9. DOI: 10.1108/JRIM-03-2021-270

Wardana, M. A., Masliardi, A., Afifah, N., Sajili, M., & Kusnara, H. P. (2023). Unlocking purchase preferences: Harnessing psychographic segmentation, promotion and location strategies. *Jurnal Informatika Ekonomi Bisnis*, 713-719. DOI: 10.37034/infeb.v5i3.624

Zhou, X., Lou, C., & Huang, X. (2025). When social media gets political: How message–platform match affects consumer responses to brand activism advertising. *Journal of Advertising*, *54*(3), 342–358. DOI: 10.1080/00913367.2024.2347271

Chapter 10
Gender Pay Gap in India: Causes, Consequences, and Cures

Aayisha Ahamed
https://orcid.org/0009-0001-7675-8569
Lovely Professional University, India

Tawheed Nabi
Lovely Professional University, India

ABSTRACT

This chapter provides a thorough analysis of the gender pay gap persistent in India, which impedes inclusive economic growth along with social justice. It describes the gap, current statistical overview, and indicators, and examines the causes, including deep-rooted labor division, cultural & social norms, education, and uneven burden of unpaid domestic work, and workplace discrimination. At the lower levels of wage distribution, there is a vivid manifestation of the "sticky floor" effect, and it targets women, especially those who belong prominently to marginalized communities. In addition to the visible factors, the essential contributors are employment segregation, the lack of equity due to the unequal distribution of unpaid household care among women, and workplace discrimination. The chapter advocates for multi-dimensional policy response, aimed at interventions by targeting discrimination, to challenge deep-rooted gender norms, to establish equitable pay structures and open more flexible working opportunities, to create the truly thriving and equitable work culture in India.

INTRODUCTION

Gender pay gap is a widespread international challenge that can be considered an alarming indicator of gender inequality in the workforce environment and a key

DOI: 10.4018/979-8-3373-2772-3.ch010

factor restricting the overall economic opportunity and better working conditions on a global scale (Jiyauddin & Banerjee, 2025). There is still a persistent 17 percent pay discrepancy, with women currently earning an average of 83 cents for every $1 earned by males worldwide. The Global Gender Gap Report 2024 by the World Economic Forum shows that 68.5 percent of this global gender gap had been closed and that it will still take 134 years at the current pace to achieve full global gender parity (Holder, 2025). These estimates are usually defined as the gender wage gap which states the difference between the median earnings of men and women compared with the median earnings of men. This is the formal definition of gender wage gap, and it is essential because it reflects the broader implications of societal and structural sources of economic disparity than merely equal pay under equal work (OECD).

A huge gender pay gap still remains an issue in India, where women are regularly earning considerably less than their male counterparts in different positions and across industries (Nanda, 2025). Another recent reveal of SEWA (Self Employed Women Association) has shown that the average woman worker earned Rs. 1815 in comparison to Rs. 3842 of male workers (Jiyauddin & Banerjee, 2025a). This is to the effect that women are getting paid half of what men get paid in this situation. As cited on Global Gender Gap Index 2024 by World Economic Forum, India is in the 129th spot among the 146 countries with the women getting equal to 39.8 out of every 100 earned by men. This is a very striking number that reveals how women receive an average of 40 percent less than men (Nanda, 2025). Gender wage gaps have been estimated by the International Labour Organization (ILO) to be as high as 34 percent in India in 2020 or women earn about 66 percent of what men earn on equal jobs (James, 2024). This disparity may be further high in high-skill occupations such as technology where a woman will receive only 60 percent of the amounts that the man earns (Khatun, 2024). In the 2017-18 NSSO statistics, the gender salary gap stood at 33 percent, with men having average daily wages of Rs. 522.6 as against an average daily wage of females of Rs. 349.2.

It is worthwhile to mention that the different numbers cited on India gender pay gap are not in conflict with each other but rather depict the subtle approaches to the measurement and the peculiarities of the situation. As an example, the larger numbers, including the World Economic Forum or the SEWA, tend to reflect the aggregate unadjusted pay gap. This expanded measure of economic disadvantage includes the whole (and more) of economic disadvantage that women face including occupational differences and part-time employment as well as other structural issues. On the other hand, data provided by such organizations as ILO or NSSO, particularly regarding what is known as equivalent work, or when factors such as education and experience have been considered, is likely to report a more corrected pay gap. This modified figure tries to separate the share of this gap that can be due directly to discrimination of the same jobs. The realization of this difference is the key to the perceptual level of economic inequality experienced by women in India.

The Female Labor Force Participation Rate (FLFPR) has increased positively over the recent past in India. The FLFPR stands at 41.7 per cent in the Periodic Labor Force Survey (PLFS) of the year 2023-24 and has increased by a big margin as compared to 23.3 per cent in 2017-18 (Pathak, 2025). Remarkably, the rural FLFPR has upsurged almost two-fold (23.5-42.8) during the same time duration, which implies that it contributes to 80 percent of the female labor participation (Deshpande, 2025). This new favorable direction differs with such old statistics, as the 26.2 percent claimed by the World Bank, in 2020, or a declared decline to 19 percent in 2023. This highlights the fact that the statistical data regarding labor market is dynamic, and it might also differ on how it is measured or even the reporting time (Chaudhry, Bedi, Viswanathan, & Pillai, 2021).

Nevertheless, what comes out strongly is that this increase in FLFPR does not necessarily lead to pay parity. The numbers of women upstream in the workforce are increasing, but even then, the gender pay parity is gigantic and in certain positions, it is even said to be increasing further. This implies that higher participation of the female labor force is not adequate in promoting pay equality, which has to suggest deeper structural problems in the quality of the female employment and its character of nature. As an example, women can be found in informal sectors, agriculture, or low-wage occupations in so-called care giving roles (Jiyauddin & Banerjee, 2025a). Evidence also indicates that male wage increased during the pandemic period and the female wage reduced by a significant margin of 7 percent during the period between 2018-19 and 2020-21 further expanding the pay gap (Alfonsi et al., 2024; Carli, 2020). It means that as long as women are getting into or sticking to low-value occupations or functions, or male earnings in the high-paid occupations are rising at a more rapid pace, the overall pay disparity may continue or even widen. Thus, the policies should be more comprehensive than maintaining that women should enter the labor market and should go beyond worker segregation, skill training on high growth-oriented industries and biases in workplaces to effectively make a difference in the gender pay gap (Bennedsen et al., 2019).

Figure 1. India's gender parity ranking compared to global leaders and neighbors (2024)

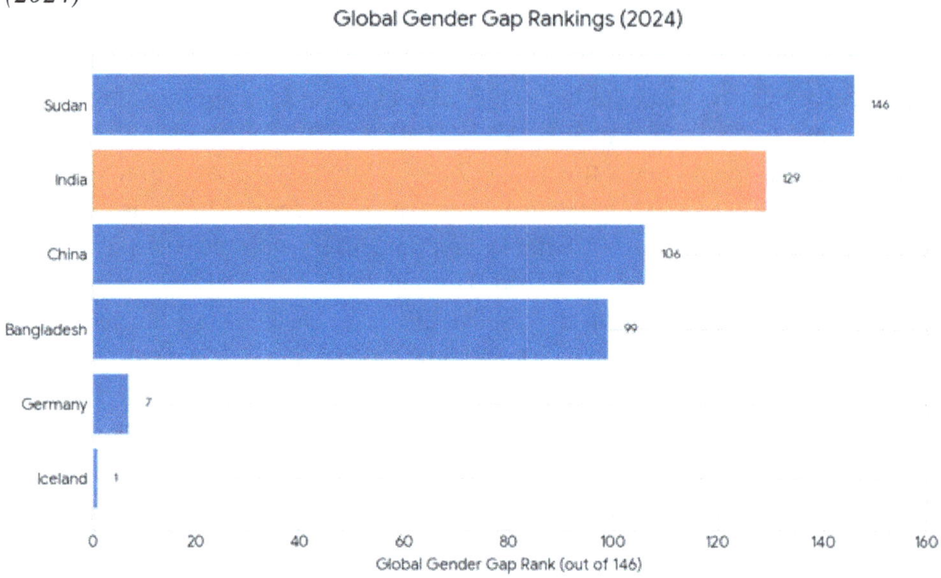

RANKINGS OF THE GLOBAL GENDER GAP (2024)

Out of 146 nations surveyed, this graphic contrasts the overall gender gap rankings of a few of them. The rank is a composite score that assesses equality in four important areas: political empowerment, health and survival, educational attainment, and economic participation and opportunity. One essential element of the economic dimension is wage parity.

Table 1. Important gender pay gap statistics in India (2017-2024)

Indicator	Value/Range	Year(s)	Notes
Overall Gender Pay Gap (Women's earnings as % of Men's)	39.8% (WEF), 48% (SEWA), 66% (ILO), 67% (NSSO)	2024; 2020; 2017-18	Reflects unadjusted gap; ILO/ NSSO may refer to adjusted gap for "equivalent work" or specific sectors.
Average Daily/Monthly Wages (Men)	Rs. 3842 (SEWA), Rs. 522.6 (NSSO), Rs. 20,666 (WEF)	2017-18; Jul 2022-Jun 2023	
Average Daily/Monthly Wages (Women)	Rs. 1815 (SEWA), Rs. 349.2 (NSSO), Rs. 15,722.25 (WEF)	2017-18; Jul 2022-Jun 2023	
India's Ranking in Global Gender Gap Index	129th out of 146 countries	2024	
Female Labor Force Participation Rate (FLFPR, 15+ years)	41.7%	PLFS 2023-24	Significant increase from 23.3% in 2017-18, with rural FLFPR nearly doubling.
Female Unemployment Rate	3.2%	PLFS 2023-24	Drop from 5.6% in 2017-18, reflecting greater inclusion and economic empowerment.

Figure 2. Historical trends in India's gender pay gap (2000-2024)

Between 2000 and 2024, the gender wage gap has been slowly but surely reducing. For established economies, data from agencies such as the Organisation for Economic Co-operation and Development (OECD) paints a clear picture, even though it is challenging to compile an exact, year-over-year global figure.

CAUSES OF THE GENDER PAY GAP IN INDIA

The gender pay gap in India is a deeply rooted and multifaceted issue and it is determined by the mix of structural, socio-economic, cultural and discriminatory factors (Sethi, 2024). Research shows that over 60 percent of the contributing variables of the gender pay gap in India are indeed because of straight up discrimination in the labor force which indicates the extent of discrimination (Ara, 2021a; Padhi et al., 2019). The multiple causes are not only isolated, but they exist in a very symbiotic relationship, making it a complicated and supportive cycle. To give an example, the extremely defined cultural values, like regarding women as the future homemakers or secondary earners, have a direct bearing on the bias in educational investments. Such prejudices in turn tend to channelize women to undervalued occupational choices (Ara, 2021a).

The excessive load of unpaid care work and the so-called motherhood penalty also hinder the career of women, and the restrictions caused by those are later enforced by direct discrimination at work. This interdependency suggests that taking one of the factors in isolation will hardly lead to comprehensive findings and thus a holistic approach to the change of policies and society is needed (England et al., 2016; Deming, 2022).

Labor Division and Partialities

The gender wage gap is greatly attributed to occupational segregation where women and men are clustered in certain occupations or industries and wages tend to vary. The men are highly concentrated in overvalued occupations while female dominated occupations are poorly remunerated (Sethi, 2024). Periodic Labor Force Survey (PLFS) 2022 clearly points out that women in India are mostly concentrated in sectors that are less paid like education, health and social sector, in contrast to men dominated fields like engineering and money sectors (Ara, 2021a; Mohanty, 2021; Sharma, 2018).

A clear-cut division of labor between the sexes is also noticed in the agricultural system of rural North India, whereby certain activities such as drying and storing grain are specifically allocated to women and ploughing and harvesting areas are solely carried out by men (Bhushan et al., 2020; De et al., 2021; Gulati et al., 2025).

Labor force participation by the female is significantly elevated in industries that deal with personal services and care work, and mostly in the informal industries, especially the agricultural sector (Psacharopoulos & Tzannatos, 1989; Gulati et al., 2025). Gender wage gap differs substantially across sectors: it is largest in manufacturing where women are paid 44 percent that men earn and it is also large in services where women are paid 55 percent. On the contrary, the disparity is only somewhat large in the farm industry where females enjoy approximately 70 percent of men's pay. But the size of the population of women in the agricultural sector, both in unpaid and informal context, suffices to indicate that even this sector continues to add to the total pay gap (James, 2024).

In addition, women are continually under-represented in well-paid jobs and sectors mainly in the field of technology, engineering, and the field of finance (Jiyauddin & Banerjee, 2025a). The pay gap is highest when it comes to mid-level jobs in the BFSI (Banking, Financial Services and Insurance), energy, and healthcare at 25.3 percent and even in IT services, the salary difference is at a high of 18.3 percent (Indian, 2024). The research has also established that the pay gap is greatest at the low end as wage distribution and gradually inclines with increase in the wage scale indicating the presence of sticky floors in the Indian labor market (Jiyauddin & Banerjee, 2025a). This amounts to the fact that women, particularly lower caste women, Muslim, and less skilled workers have to bear a more substantial pay gap at the entry and lower level of the pay scale.

Cultural Barriers and Social Norms

The highly ingrained social norms and cultural expectations contribute to inequality in wages, choice of career, education, and workplace environment of women (Sethi, 2024). The norms are usually the determinants of roles appropriate to be played by men and women and they can segregate the labor with status. One similarity in all the states in India is the absenteeism of women in the paid labor market and segregation concerning status. Ironically, upper-caste women had a harder time finding a paid job because of social stigma even when it was a matter of life and death. The interviews of the widows in rural North India showed that any effort to secure worthwhile work opportunities outside their houses might cause a loss of rights to property and expulsion in their villages (Devine, 1994; Smyth & Steinmetz, 2008; Shchepilova & Korol, 2020; Chesters, 2022).

The general assumptions that are instilled in the Indians that men are the primary breadwinners and the income that the women earn is secondary, has a great negative impact in undermining the worth of labor of women in the workplace (Holder, 2025). Such underestimation can even become part of low wages even when only equal work is being performed. Additionally, social norms tend to keep women from asking for pay as this may get lesser pay at the initial stages as well as pay increases in the future. This unwillingness to bargain which is usually based on the cultural understanding of ought to be modest or courteous can increase the pay disparity throughout the career span of a female employee (Education, 2021-22; Global Wage Report, 2022-23).

The Culture in Practice vs. the Law on Paper

Although laws offer a framework for equality, how or even whether that framework is used depends on culture. Even the most progressive measures may have little effect or, worse, backfire if social attitudes don't change.

Parental leave is a prime example.

The Goal of the Policy: Generous, gender-neutral parental leave is now provided by many nations and businesses. Distributing caregiving duties, lowering the "motherhood penalty" the phenomenon where women's professions deteriorate after giving birth—and normalizing males as active carers are the objectives.

The Barrier of Culture: In reality, men frequently fail to take the entire amount of leave to which they are entitled. Why?

Stigma at Work: They worry about being perceived as less dedicated to their jobs, a prejudice stemming from the antiquated "ideal worker" paradigm that demands round-the-clock availability.

The drawback is that the legislation unintentionally perpetuates the idea that women are the primary carers when only women take parental leave. It further entrenches the very salary gap that the program was intended to combat by solidifying their position as the "riskier" hire for employers.

A policy is really a permission slip, and that is the obvious lesson. It is a culture of support and acceptance that gives people the confidence to use it.

Shifting the Focus: From Defense to Economic Domination

Public campaigns must change in order to establish this culture of acceptance. A crucial first step was India's "Beti Bachao, Beti Padhao" (Save the Daughter, Educate the Daughter) program, which prioritized the education and survival of females. A follow-up that emphasizes their economic empowerment is now required.

The advertising needs to be refocused to specifically highlight the economic impact made by women.

The New Message: Daughters should be celebrated as economic drivers for their families and the country, rather than only being saved and educated. "Beti Padhao, Kamao, Desh Badhao" (Educate the Daughter, Let Her Earn, Build the Nation) may make a strong new tagline.

Changing the Subject: Economic Domination Over Defense

This culture of acceptance requires a shift in public efforts. India's "Beti Bachao, Beti Padhao" (Save the Daughter, Educate the Daughter) campaign, which placed a high priority on women's education and survival, was an important first step. It is now necessary to follow up with a focus on their economic empowerment.

Refocusing the advertisements to emphasize the economic significance of women is necessary.

The New Message: Instead of only being saved and educated, daughters should be praised for being economic contributors to their families and the nation. One potential catchphrase is "Beti Padhao, Kamao, Desh Badhao" (Educate the Daughter, Let Her Earn, Build the Nation).

Education and Training

Although India has improved in female literacy, history and current capacity of investment in education and training have been biased towards men who are raised to consider themselves as breadwinners (Alderman & King, 1998; Saha, 2013; Rammohan & Vu, 2018). On the other hand, women are usually regarded as the future homemakers so they might not require so much learning that it can be considered important. Such conventional perception has restricted access to and attainment of education among girls (Evans, 2009; Hailu, 2019; Dennis, 2020).

In spite of these historical differences, there was a certain decline between male and female literacy percentages which reduced from 21.59 percent in 2001 to 16.68 percent in 2011 meaning great progress. Besides, the figure of the number of women who are on the higher education register has increased to 48 percent according to the All India Survey on Higher Education (AISHE) 2021- 2022 (Roy, 2024). But this education level is not always associated with increasing wages or employment growth among women, who in most cases, occupy different jobs with inferior pay tags. The gap in wages between men and women is the largest among women who have only primary education because they earn only 40 percent of what men earn but the gap is relatively smaller among the women who have graduated and even higher education where women earn up to 70-80 percent of the salary that men earn (James, 2024). This implies that the pay gap cannot be eradicated, as it can be alleviated by education, meaning that other forms of influence still have an evident impact on highly qualified women.

Unpaid Domestic Work and Caregiving Responsibilities

Unpaid domestic work and childcare tasks are also heavily concentrated on the women, which strongly affects their ability to work in expressions of paid employment, cultural advancement, and income ability (Singh & Pattanaik, 2020; Deshpande & Kabeer, 2024). The study as published in the Human Development Report 1995, estimates that women use two-thirds of their labor force on unpaid work as compared to one-fourth by men. On average, women in India are estimated to work 21 hours more a week exhibiting toe-to-heel workweek than men (Chaudhry, Bedi, Viswanathan, & Pillai, 2021). In India, Oxfam India estimated in 2020 that unpaid work by women contributed about 90 percent of the value added in the Indian economy, or about 99 percent of annual economic growth at 9.99 percent, to an estimated value of approximately 19 lakh crores (1.38 billion US dollars) per year, but the contribution is not reflected in any official figures (James, 2024).

Having to stop a career because of giving birth and taking care of children and relatives greatly slows down professional development, as well as income (Roy, 2024). According to Better India, 73 percent of women in India quit their work post-childbirth (Gupta, 2024). More than 40 percent of the women during pandemic lockdowns were overwhelmed by the twofold burden of domestic care work and paid work and approximately 45 percent reported that balancing their work and family affected their career progression. This is commonly referred to as the motherhood penalty whereby a mother experiences wage depression and it has an effect on later career development in terms of experience, amount of energy put into a job, and productivity with a penalty of between 5 to 9 percent and further childbearing (Chaudhry, Bedi, Viswanathan, & Pillai, 2021). In contrast, fathers tend to receive the fatherhood bonus whereby they are perceived as more mature and stable and they may benefit through hiring and promotion (Jiyauddin & Banerjee, 2025). The disadvantage is more acute in highly educated women because they have a greater likelihood of being in professional and managerial jobs hence their career breaks lead to greater loss of potential income and career promotion.

Workplace Discrimination and Biases

Harmful explicit and implicit prejudices about hiring, advancement, preparing, and compensating for equal instalment are both enormous and ubiquitous drivers of gender painlessness (Begeny et al., 2020; Zhang, 2024). Research has established that over 60 percent of contributory factors of the gender pay gap in India are perpetrated by sheer labor market discrimination (Chaudhry, Bedi, Viswanathan, & Pillai, 2021). Labor market discrimination In India, discrimination in the urban labor market is assumed to comprise approximately two-thirds of the pay gap where only a third is due to endowment differences (education or experience) (Indian, 2024). This means that despite women having similar qualifications and experience they are still significantly disadvantaged about wages.

McKinsey & Company's (2023) research findings expose high levels of discrimination that have been embedded into the nature of practices that lead women in their career development and well-paid employment (Krivkovich, Field, Yee, McConnell, & Smit, 2024). Unconscious prejudices dominant in workplaces associate women with a lack of commitment, more so, when they are married or mothers, or they are not perceived as having leadership qualities. Such discriminations are part of the reasons behind the so-called leaky pipeline issue where there is a drastic decrease of women in the corporate chain once they reach the higher ranks as shown in a 2024 survey which reported that women comprise only approximately 25 percent of C-suite jobs to 46 percent at entry-level positions (Nanda, 2025). There is also a widening salary inequality gap by seniority which pegs at 8.34 percent amongst senior positions, 6.12 percent at mid-level, and 3.55 percent across the board. The average top-end wage of senior females in India is only Rs 85 against every Rs 100 that men in that position uniformly receive (Indian, 2024). Such vertical stratification in organizations enhances the pay gap where the females have limited chances of acquiring the highest-paying job positions in the organizational leadership stratum.

Urban-Rural Divide

The gender pay gap is considerably enhanced by the urban-rural gap since the majority of women in rural areas are engaged in the informal sector where the laws regulating wage reception are minimal, and there is minimal welfare benefit (James, 2024). More than 60 percent of rural areas take jobs in the informal sector which lacked job security and benefits (ILO, 2018).

The gender wage gap is significantly bigger for rural women, with only half of the pay rate of their male counterparts, less than the level in urban regions of 60 percent (NSSO 2017-18) (James, 2024). That disparity is more pronounced in the informal sector where most women work in the rural regions (Jiyauddin & Banerjee, 2025b). The gap is more significant in rural India than in urban regions, and it needs to be addressed through specific interventions that take into consideration the distinct socio-economic and cultural backgrounds of rural India.

CONSEQUENCES OF THE GENDER PAY GAP

The effect of the gender pay gap is huge and far-reaching which not only involves individuals and their households but it also affects the national economy and overall equality of society (Angelov et al., 2016; Irshad Ahmad Reshi & Sudha, 2023). This disadvantage cycle creates a spiral where past women have an overall disadvantage impacting the national economy and future generations (Jiyauddin & Banerjee, 2025b). Moreover, the effects are not only economic but also mental, and the continuation of adverse cultural activities.

Impact on Individuals

Reduced earnings cause families that rely on the wages of women economically vulnerable, which becomes especially drastic in cases of single mothers and one-women families. Such a state of financial insecurity might cause a poor standard of living and possibilities of achieving upgrades. The wage gap is also a motivational issue that causes reduced productivity in an organization (Jiyauddin & Banerjee, 2025). Working women who receive less pay tend to be frustrated and left feeling stressed which may be released as anxiety, burnout, and depression especially when combined with the burden of work and home. They could also find it difficult to access sufficient healthcare, diet as well as preventive care for themselves and their families (Khatun, 2024).

The failure to use human capital investment comes in the situation when unequal pay causes withdrawal or working below educational potential by educated women in the labor market (Hultin, 2003; Mihaila, 2016; Ahrens & Scheele, 2022). This amounts to a considerable amount of talent and possible innovation that is lost. Also, there is a wage disparity signifying the fact that women are second earners thus having a negative influence on the aspirations of women, their self-esteem, and their value regarded in society as well as in work areas (Fortin, 2008; Platt et al., 2016).

Impact on Households

Lesser pay on the part of the women implies fewer finances that can be used to raise kids academically and to afford healthcare services to the family, hence advancing the chain of intergenerational disparity (Lu & Yeung, 2024). This forms a formulation where the economic hardships experienced by one generation are transferred to the other thus impeding social mobility.

Among some cultures, such as the Indian culture preference for male children, facilitated by economic reasons such as earning capacity and pension prospects, also leads to the like of female infanticide and sex-selective abortion (Sudha & Rajan, 1999; Arnold et al., 2002; Jha et al., 2006). The practice of dowry is still persistent in some sections of society and the presence of girl babies is, therefore, an economic liability and makes way for such practices (Bhalotra et al., 2020). According to the 2011 Census, there was a shocking regional imbalance in birth sex ratios, which were explained by misuse and affordability of fetus sex-determining devices. Between 2000 and 2010, millions of girls have been thought to be not born courtesy of sex-selective abortions.

Impact on the Economy

The gender pay gap is one of the untapped potentials of the Indian economy. McKinsey says that due to gender parity India could raise its GDP by 770 billion by 2025 (Sethi, 2024). Other reports claim that the potential additional GDP growth of India may be 2.9 trillion by 2025 in case women enter the workforce at the same thoroughness as men (Nanda, 2025). This huge figure gives an idea of how such an immense economic gain can be achieved through equal pay and higher participation of women in the economy.

Moreover, when women are empowered economically the fertility rate is more likely to be low thus causing a demographic transition in the country (Upadhyay et al., 2014; Samad et al., 2022). A continuous pay gap retards this demographic transition to the country and this may affect long-run development objectives. On the one hand, the continuously high gender pay gap level creates a threat to the course of inclusive growth in India and reaching decent employment conditions among all its citizens (Jiyauddin & Banerjee, 2025).

Impact on Society and Gender Equality

Enduring pay disparity is contrary to the vision of equality as captured in the Indian Constitution and shakes the stake of trust in institutions developed to support the course of justice. A widely known measure of gender disparity in the workplace is the gender pay gap which is used to monitor how close we are to achieving gender equality. This difference is significant because of the societal stigma against women as being less powerful than males and no gender justice can be achieved. This gap in wages may not end unless the stigma towards women at both the workplace and in society in general is done away with. Gender inequality is a major issue in the whole world which presents a stumbling block to better economic equality and better working conditions (Jiyauddin & Banerjee, 2025). The pay gap is therefore a manifestation and an extension of the other gender inequalities that affect the sex ratio in India, the health of the women throughout their life span, their level of education, and general economic status (Hooda, 2021; Paduri, 2025).

CURES: POLICY INTERVENTIONS, CORPORATE STRATEGIES, AND SOCIETAL CHANGES

Keeping the problem of the gender pay gap in mind, the solution would have to be emergent and cross-functional with the participation of the government, corporations, and civil society (2030kabharat). There needs to be a multi-dimensional approach to it because legal regulation will not be enough; a cultural change, the willingness of corporations, and civil society re-education are essential to a sustainable solution. Moreover, corporate responsibility and policy based on data are crucial, thus highlighting the fact that open data, frequent audits, and monitoring systems should be encouraged to provide suitable interventions and track progress.

Strengthening Legal and Policy Frameworks

The legislative system in India comprises some laws that are essential in enhancing gender pay equity and equality in the workplace (Jiyauddin & Banerjee, 2025). The Equal Remuneration Act (1976) requires that men and women in equal work be paid the same and that no discrimination based on gender should take place during recruitment, remuneration, and employment. In 2017, the Maternity Benefit (Amendment) Act extended the period of paid maternity leave to 26 weeks during the first 2 children with the provision of work-from-home and creche facilities (Roy, 2024). The Sexual Harassment of Women at Workplace (Prevention, Prohibition, and Redressal) Act (POSH Act, 2013) establishes a

grievance mechanism against harassment in the workplace, which indirectly contributes to pay equity since the workplace in question will be a safer place to work (Jiyauddin & Banerjee, 2025). The MGNREGA of 2005 has had a positive impact on the increase in the female labor force, especially in rural areas, and has provisions for equal wages (Nanda, 2025). Other basic laws such as the Payment of Wages Act (1936) and Minimum Wages Act (1948) are aimed at secure and timely (no delays) payments and reasonable wages (Jiyauddin & Banerjee, 2025).

Whereas this legislative framework presents a formidable challenge, proper legal enforcement and implementation, especially in the informal sector, remains to be a major challenge (Nanda, 2025). By way of example, MGNREGA binds equal wages, but it is not always enforced. To fill these gaps, it is possible to improve the legal framework by making the Equal Remuneration Act and any other related laws more enforceable due to increasing the punishment of non-compliance (Roy, 2024). Auditing companies regularly to determine how they comply with the standards of gender equality and the implementation of punishment for non-conformance would promote positive ways (Indian, 2024). Moreover, it is vital to grant legal protection to the women and to enhance the working conditions, who are in the informal economy (Nanda, 2025). Improvement of shared parental leave policies as practiced in countries such as Sweden would also play an important role in making the responsibilities of caregiving equitable among men and women and minimizing the discrimination against the employment of female workers.

From 2017 onwards, UK corporate organizations with more than 250 employees must publish gender pay gap data annually, which includes mean and median for pay difference and the composition of workforce by gender. This disclosure in public has resulted in measurable decrease in the gender pay gap. Studies indicate 18 to 19 percent reduction, mainly by reducing men's pay growth instead of raising women's pay (Duchini, E., et al, 2020; Jones, M., & Kaya, E, 2022; Bennedsen, M., et al 2023).

The United Kingdom's legislative approach has increased public scrutiny and contributed to measurable improvements. However, the gender pay gap remains substantial. The effectiveness of these regulations is contingent upon the accuracy and relevance of the reported data. Concerns persist regarding whether transparency measures alone can ensure accountability and fully eliminate the gender pay gap (Lahuerta et al, 2023).

India lacks a national law that requires disclosure of the gender pay gap. Although the Equal Remuneration Act of 1976 prohibits discrimination, enforcement remains insufficient. Furthermore, there is no mandate for public reporting of gender-disaggregated pay data. The resulting lack of transparency restricts public accountability and impedes systematic monitoring and remediation of gender pay disparities (Bennedsen, M., et al 2023).

Corporate Strategies and Best Practices

Corporations play a very significant role in reducing the gender pay gap. There is an increasing trend of pay transparency in India and almost half of all job advertisements report the salaries (Sharma). Such change is not something of a passing fashion but a long-term and potentially drastic change that can cut down workplace inequality dramatically. Transparency allows detection and elimination of the pay gaps based on gender, builds an open and responsible culture, and gives women the confidence to always negotiate better (Roberson et al., 2020; Obloj & Zenger, 2022). Regular pay audits are continuously being done by companies to review and check the pay equity within their organizations, discover the differences, and take corrective actions (2030kabharat). Although it is not always the published knick-knack of given companies to particularize their sensitive practices, the study states that a handful of innovative start-ups and MNCs have commenced putting up salary bands and internal pay parity. Big companies such as Tata Group, Infosys, and Wipro are the ones at the forefront where gender equality is being promoted in several ways. Indicatively, Hindustan Unilever has continued to record high performance as it markets gender diversity by promoting various programs, including its Career by Choice initiative to get women to approach the company as returning mothers to the workforce.

The "Leaky Pipeline" is the Problem

The "leaky pipeline," a phenomena where a considerable percentage of bright women leave the workforce, frequently at the mid-career level, is a major concern for economies and organizations around the world. Experienced talent is greatly lost as a result of these professional pauses, which are usually chosen for reasons like childcare, elder care, or family relocation. Due to biases in the employment process, a lack of flexible opportunities, and skill shortages, it can be extremely challenging for women to return to formal labor after a break (Sharma, 2024). Both individual economic empowerment and a company's capacity to assemble a diverse and skilled leadership team are hampered by this.

HUL's "Career by Choice" program is the answer.

One of the biggest FMCG (fast-moving consumer goods) firms in India, Hindustan Unilever (HUL), launched the "Career by Choice" program in order to directly address this issue. One This program is specifically intended to give women who have taken a career sabbatical a flexible and encouraging way to reintegrate into the business world.

The curriculum departs from the strict 9–5 schedule and is based on the fundamental idea of flexibility. Important elements consist of:

Project-Based Work. Candidates are given project-based tasks that align with their expertise and skill set in lieu of immediate full-time positions. This enables them to gradually reintegrate into a work setting.

Flexible Schedule. The program's work-from-home choices and flexible hours enable participants to manage their personal and professional obligations.

Mentoring and Upskilling. HUL offers organized onboarding, upskilling training modules, and mentors to help the women adjust to life back in the corporate environment (Patel & Kumar, 2023). This fills up any skill or confidence deficiencies they may have had throughout their hiatus.

Bridge to Mainstream Careers

The curriculum serves as a formal entry point back into mainstream positions rather than an isolated track. Projects that are completed successfully frequently result in offers for permanent, part-time, or full-time roles inside the organization, guaranteeing a clear path for professional advancement.

Effects and Results

Many people agree that the "Career by Choice" initiative has been successful. It has made it possible for HUL to access a pool of talented and experienced women who would not have otherwise entered the formal workforce. HUL's gender diversity has improved as a direct result of the initiative, especially at the middle and senior management levels (Hindustan Unilever Limited, 2025). By supporting this project, HUL has also improved its reputation as an open and forward-thinking company, which attracts top female talent.

Model for States and Corporates

The "Career by Choice" initiative from HUL is an excellent example that other businesses and even governmental entities can adopt and expand.

For Other Businesses

Strategic Talent Acquisition. Reentry programs should be seen by businesses as a tool for strategic talent acquisition rather than as a CSR endeavor. It offers reasonably priced access to a pool of highly qualified, seasoned talent.

Adopt Real Flexibility. Real flexibility is essential to the model's success. Businesses must be prepared to rethink projects and roles to fit various work schedules.

Invest in Re-Boarding. To guarantee that returning women are prepared for success and feel supported, a systematic process of mentorship and upskilling is essential.

To sum up, HUL's project shows that removing the systemic obstacles that women encounter when they return to the workforce is not only morally required, but also a successful business and economic tactic. The "Career by Choice" strategy provides a clear, replicable route to a more diverse and effective workforce by transforming a "leaky pipeline" into a talent reservoir.

Societal and Cultural Changes

Government-initiated funds such as Stand Up India and MUDRA (Micro Units Development and Refinance Agency) have greatly helped to promote entrepreneurship amongst women (Agarwala et al., 2022). This will however require an additional boost in the form of customized financial services by making money easily available through easy access to capital, micro-loans, and venture capital being provided to the women as well as incentives to the banks to reduce the interest rates and the collateralizations. Through efforts like the Pradhan Mantri Jan Dhan Yojana (PMJDY) women have gained more access to both banking and credit, with women making up 56 percent of PMJDY accounts as of January 2025 (Jena, 2024). Though the use of such accounts is yet to be extensive in certain cases, these are very essential for the independence of finances.

Another necessary change in society is the acknowledgment of the value of unpaid care work. This work has economic value that is pegged at 19 lakh crores in India and should be formally recognized and brought on the policy agenda. Increasing political empowerment through local leadership programs and establishing a national record of women participating in economic activity and becoming leaders will assist policymakers in planning how to allocate resources and interventions so that tracking progress can be done in a data-guided manner (Sahoo, Sarkar, & Kumar, 2024). Schemes such as Pradhan Mantri Kaushal Vikas Yojana (PMKVY) can also play their role by offering selective sector-wise skill development to bridge the existing gender gaps, so that women in rural areas may enter the higher income earning sectors and occupation segregation can be prevented by establishing public-private partnership (2030kabharat).

RESEARCH GAPS AND FUTURE DIRECTIONS

There is a constant and urgent need for further disaggregated and ground-level data, particularly in the informal sector, in which many women are employed, and where considerable information on how and whether the work of women workers is affected by phenomena such as the COVID-19 pandemic is lacking (Chaudhry, Bedi, Viswanathan, & Pillai, 2021). Such data is essential in making targeted policies and interventions.

Future study is required to be conducted to get acquainted with the irregularities of the so-called sticky floors and motherhood penalty phenomenon in the various cultural settings, educational backgrounds, and sectors in India (Ara, 2021b). Although their presence is confirmed in the existing studies, further qualitative and quantitative approaches can demonstrate the interaction of these factors with particular norms of society and work organization (Ray & Samanta, 2020).

There is a need to have a closer analysis of the policy interventions and government schemes, to understand their real effect to limit the gender pay gap as well as see what must be improved. This involves the evaluation of the strength of the enforcement legitimacies in the law as well as the unintended effects of such policies as prolonged maternity leaves.

Women's employment is facing emerging challenges and opportunities due to the changing environment of the gig and platform economy. The study must also look into the impacts of this sector on gender pay gap issues including factors like payment transparency, social security, and women's development of skills within such new forms of work (NITI Aayog, 2022).

The case of intersectionality is important in determining the effects of caste, religion, and the city-country divide that are combined with gender in increasing the complexity of pay gaps. Such a measure will be able to reveal the individual weaknesses and shape the specific interventions toward marginalized groups of women. Lastly, more case studies and analyses of other successful corporate and community-led initiatives should be conducted to know what can be defined as best practice and how scalable it would be in a variety of Indian contexts. This may give practical lessons to organizations and policymakers interested in emulating success.

FUTURE OF WORK

Fair audits must be incorporated directly into new systems in order to stop pay disparities from developing in the workplace in the future.

Biassed algorithms that underpay women pose a concern to the **gig economy**. Mandating frequent algorithmic audits to make sure the code and pay-setting guidelines are equitable is the answer.

The risk associated with **AI in HR** is that it may learn from and magnify prior discrimination based on previous data. The answer is to regularly evaluate the AI's hiring and promotion decisions and check its training data for bias.

The risk associated with **hybrid and remote work is "proximity bias,"** which occurs when individuals who work in offices are given greater possibilities. Expanding audits beyond income to monitor opportunity equity such as advancement rates and access to important projects for all staff members, regardless of location is the answer.

CONCLUSION

The gender pay gap in India is a complicated, multifaceted phenomenon that runs deep through the structural, socio-economic, and cultural fabrics. Although there have been recent improvements in female labor force participation, the fact that the earnings gap is persistent and, in many cases, continues to increase shows that participating is not the same thing as earning equal pay. Labor division, intense cultural assumptions that undervalue work done by women and discourage their negotiating, long-standing gaps in education, huge responsibility of unpaid care work and the motherhood penalty, and extensive discrimination at work especially increasing with age have contributed to the gap. All these factors are related in a way that forms a chain of disadvantage to women.

The effects of the gap are long-lasting, affecting even individual people by exposing them to financial insecurity and psychological strains and continuing intergenerational disadvantage spread throughout the household, as well as a significant economic cost to the country in the form of lost GDP potential. It also distracts the constitutional contingent of equality and promotes social prejudices.

It is a multi-pronged problem that needs resolution through a multi-lateral, collaborative approach. The most important thing is to enhance the legal frameworks with effective enforcement of the same, especially in the informal sector. Corporate practices should embrace opening the hood on pay, frequent pay equity audits, and broadened diversity and inclusion initiatives, such as leadership training and mothers who reenter the workforce. The societal changes are just as important and they require breaking the traditional gender stereotypes, encouraging women's entrepreneurship, raising the financial literacy, and re-assessing the social worth of the unpaid work.

Finally, reducing the gender pay gap in India is not only a moral but also an economic requisite. India has the potential to become a country of inclusiveness in which women are allowed to flourish both at the top and bottom and reduce its pace towards achieving inclusive growth by serving as a role model to other countries that are going through the same problems.

REFERENCES

Aayog, N. (2022). *India's Booming Gig and Platform Economy*. NITI Aayog. Retrieved from chrome-extension://efaidnbmnnnibpcajpcglclefindmkaj/https://www.niti.gov.in/sites/d efault/files/2023-02/25th_June_Final_Report_27062022.pdf

Agarwala, V., Maity, S., & Sahu, T. N.AGARWALA. (2022). FEMALE ENTREPRENEURSHIP, EMPLOYABILITY AND EMPOWERMENT: IMPACT OF THE MUDRA LOAN SCHEME. *Journal of Developmental Entrepreneurship*, *27*(01), 2250005. Advance online publication. DOI: 10.1142/S1084946722500054

Alderman, H., & King, E. M. (1998). Gender differences in parental investment in education. *Structural Change and Economic Dynamics*, *9*(4), 453–468. DOI: 10.1016/S0954-349X(98)00040-X

Alfonsi, L., Namubiru, M., & Spaziani, S. (2024). Gender gaps: Back and here to stay? Evidence from skilled Ugandan workers during COVID-19. *Review of Economics of the Household*, *22*(3), 999–1046. DOI: 10.1007/s11150-023-09681-7

Angelov, N., Johansson, P., & Lindahl, E. (2016). Parenthood and the Gender Gap in Pay. *Journal of Labor Economics*, *34*(3), 545–579. DOI: 10.1086/684851

Ara, S. (2021a). Gender Pay Gap in India: Evidence from Urban Labour Market. *The Indian Journal of Labour Economics : the Quarterly Journal of the Indian Society of Labour Economics*, *64*(2), 415–445. DOI: 10.1007/s41027-021-00319-9

Ara, S. (2021b). Gender Pay Gap in India: Evidence from Urban Labour Market. *The Indian Journal of Labour Economics : the Quarterly Journal of the Indian Society of Labour Economics*, *64*(2), 415–445. DOI: 10.1007/s41027-021-00319-9

Arnold, F., Kishor, S., & Roy, T. K. (2002). Sex-Selective Abortions in India. *Population and Development Review*, *28*(4), 759–785. DOI: 10.1111/j.1728-4457.2002.00759.x

Begeny, C. T., Ryan, M. K., Moss-Racusin, C. A., & Ravetz, G. (2020). In some professions, women have become well represented, yet gender bias persists—Perpetuated by those who think it is not happening. *Science Advances*, *6*(26), eaba7814. Advance online publication. DOI: 10.1126/sciadv.aba7814 PMID: 32637616

Bennedsen, M., Larsen, B., & Wei, J. (2023). Gender wage transparency and the gender pay gap: A survey. *Journal of Economic Surveys*, *37*(5), 1743–1777. Advance online publication. DOI: 10.1111/joes.12545

Bennedsen, M., Simintzi, E., Tsoutsoura, M., & Wolfenzon, D. (2019). *Do Firms Respond to Gender Pay Gap Transparency?* DOI: 10.3386/w25435

Bhalotra, S., Chakravarty, A., & Gulesci, S. (2020). The price of gold: Dowry and death in India. *Journal of Development Economics, 143*, 102413. DOI: 10.1016/j.jdeveco.2019.102413

Bhushan, M., Sinha, A., Kumari, S., & Debbarma, D. (2020). Gender Divide in Provision of Extension Services in Agriculture. *International Journal of Current Microbiology and Applied Sciences, 9*(4), 1332–1339. DOI: 10.20546/ijcmas.2020.904.158

Carli, L. L. (2020). Women, Gender equality and COVID-19. *Gender in Management, 35*(7/8), 647–655. DOI: 10.1108/GM-07-2020-0236

Chaudhry, S., Bedi, A., Viswanathan, A., & Pillai, S. (2021). *Women and Work how india fared in 2021.* IWWAGE. Retrieved from chrome-extension://efaidnbmnnnibpcajpcglclefindmkaj/https://iwwage.org/wp-conten t/uploads/2022/01/Women-and-Work-How-India-Fared-in-2021.pdf

Chesters, J. (2022). Understanding the Persistence of Occupational Sex Segregation in German Labour Markets: How Gender Attitudes Shape Young Women's Occupational Aspirations. *Journal of Applied Youth Studies, 5*(1), 55–73. DOI: 10.1007/s43151-021-00065-1

De, I., Singh, S., & Panda, S. S. (2021). Gender and Agriculture: Cases of Woman Participation in Rural Odisha. In *Social Norms, Gender and Collective Behaviour* (pp. 67–104). Springer Singapore. DOI: 10.1007/978-981-16-6952-1_4

Deming, S. M. (2022). Beyond measurement of the motherhood penalty: How social locations shape mothers' work decisions and stratify outcomes. *Sociology Compass, 16*(6), e12988. Advance online publication. DOI: 10.1111/soc4.12988

Deshpande, A. (2025). *Too good to be true? Steadily rising female labour force participation rates in India.* Ashoka University. Centre for Economic Data and Analysis (CEDA). Retrieved from https://ceda.ashoka.edu.in/too-good-to-be-true-steadily-rising-female-labour-force-par ticipation-rates-in-india/

Deshpande, A., & Kabeer, N. (2024). Norms that matter: Exploring the distribution of women's work between income generation, expenditure-saving and unpaid domestic responsibilities in India. *World Development, 174*, 106435. DOI: 10.1016/j.worlddev.2023.106435

Devine, F. (1994). Segregation and Supply: Preferences and Plans among 'Self-Made' Women. *Gender, Work and Organization, 1*(2), 94–109. DOI: 10.1111/j.1468-0432.1994.tb00009.x

Duchini, E., Simion, S., Turrell, A., & Blundell, J. (2020). Pay Transparency and Gender Equality. *American Economic Journal. Economic Policy.* Advance online publication. DOI: 10.1257/pol.20220766

Education, M. o. (2021-22). *All India Survey on higher Education.* Retrieved from chrome-extension://efaidnbmnnnibpcajpcglclefindmkaj/https://cdnbbsr.s3waas.gov.in/s392049debbe566ca5782a3045cf300a3c/uploads/2024/02/20240719952688509.pdf

England, P., Bearak, J., Budig, M. J., & Hodges, M. J. (2016). Do Highly Paid, Highly Skilled Women Experience the Largest Motherhood Penalty? *American Sociological Review, 81*(6), 1161–1189. DOI: 10.1177/0003122416673598

Evans, S. (2009). In a Different Place: Working-class Girls and Higher Education. *Sociology, 43*(2), 340–355. DOI: 10.1177/0038038508101169

Fortin, N. M. (2008). The Gender Wage Gap among Young Adults in the United States: The Importance of Money versus People. *The Journal of Human Resources, 43*(4), 884–918. DOI: 10.3368/jhr.43.4.884

Gulati, K., Saha, K., & Lybbert, T. J. (2025). Women's work and agricultural productivity gaps in India. *American Journal of Agricultural Economics, 107*(5), 1261–1289. Advance online publication. DOI: 10.1111/ajae.12536

Gupta, S. (2024). 'Why Don't Brilliant Women Return to Work After Motherhood?': Startup Finding Jobs for New Moms. *The Better India.* Retrieved from https://thebetterindia.com/349558/chennai-sankari-sudhar-job-portal-for-new-mothers-women-with-career-break-overqualified-housewives/#:~:text=Statistically%20speaki ng%2C%2073%20percent%20of,job%20opportunities%20through%20her%20platfor m.

Hailu, M. F. (2019). Examining the role of Girl Effect in contributing to positive education ideologies for girls in Ethiopia. *Gender and Education, 31*(8), 986–999. DOI: 10.1080/09540253.2018.1440284

Hindustan Unilever Limited. (2025). *Diversity & Inclusion Report 2024.* HUL.

Holder, M. (2025). *Gender Pay Gap Statistics 2025: A Comprehensive Analysis.* Equal Pay Today. Retrieved from https://www.equalpaytoday.org/gender-pay-gap-statistics/#

Hooda, S. (2021). GENDER INEQUALITY IN INDIA: STATUS AND DETERMINANTS. *International Journal of Social Science and Economic Research, 6*(3), 1054–1070. DOI: 10.46609/IJSSER.2021.v06i03.020

ILO. (2018). Retrieved from https://www.ilo.org/resource/news/more-60-cent-world%E2%80%99s-employed-population-are-informal-economy#:~:text=People%20living%20in%20rural%20areas,Dir ector%2C%20ILO's%20Department%20of%20Statistics

Indian, T. U. (2024). Bridging the Divide: Ensuring Equal Pay for Equal Work in India.
James, M. U. (2024). Gender Wage Gap in India: Trends, Causes, Consequences, and Policy Responses. *International Journal for Research Trends and Innovation, 9*. Retrieved from chrome-extension://efaidnbmnnnibpcajpcglclefindmkaj/https://www.ijrti.org/papers/IJ RTI2412024.pdf

Jena, S. N. (2024). Financial Socialisation and Promotion of Financial Inclusion, among Women Self-Help Group Members: An analysis. *Journal of Informatics Education and Research, 4*(1). DOI: 10.52783/jier.v4i1.615

Jha, P., Kumar, R., Vasa, P., Dhingra, N., Thiruchelvam, D., & Moineddin, R. (2006). Low male-to-female sex ratio of children born in India: National survey of 1·1 million households. *Lancet, 367*(9506), 211–218. DOI: 10.1016/S0140-6736(06)67930-0 PMID: 16427489

Jiyauddin, M., & Banerjee, S. (2025a). Closing The Gender Pay Gap in India: An Analysis. *Social Lens, 1*(2). Advance online publication. DOI: 10.69971/sl.1.2.2024.17

Jiyauddin, M., & Banerjee, S. (2025b). Closing The Gender Pay Gap in India: An Analysis. *Social Lens, 1*(2). Advance online publication. DOI: 10.69971/sl.1.2.2024.17

Jones, M., & Kaya, E. (2022). Organisational Gender Pay Gaps in the UK: What Happened Post-Transparency? SSRN *Electronic Journal*. https://doi.org/DOI: 10.2139/ssrn.4129670

2030kabharat. (n.d.). *Closing the Gender Pay Gap in India: A Crucial Step towards Achieving Decent Work and Economic Growth for All.* Retrieved from https://2030kabharat.com/2024/01/04/closing-the-gender-pay-gap-in-india-a-crucial-s tep-towards-achieving-decent-work-and-economic-growth-for-all/

Khatun, H. (2024). The Biggest Elephant in the Room: India's Gender Pay Gap. *Smile Foundation.* Retrieved from https://www.smilefoundationindia.org/blog/the-biggest-elephant-in-the-room-indias-g ender-pay-gap/

Krivkovich, A., Field, E., Yee, L., McConnell, M., & Smit, H. (2024). *Women in the Workplace 2024: The 10th-anniversary report.* McKinsey Company. Retrieved from https://www.mckinsey.com/featured-insights/diversity-and-inclusion/women-in-the-w orkplace

Lahuerta, S., Rejchrt, P., & Patrick, A. (2023). The UK Pay Transparency Regulations: Apparent transparency without accountability? *Legal Studies*, *44*(1), 21–44. DOI: 10.1017/lst.2023.12

Lu, S., & Yeung, W. J. (2024). The rise in cross-national marriages and the emergent inequalities in East and Southeast Asia. *Sociology Compass*, *18*(5), e13219. Advance online publication. DOI: 10.1111/soc4.13219

Mohanty, S. (2021). A distributional analysis of the gender wage gap among technical degree and diploma holders in urban India. *International Journal of Educational Development*, *80*, 102322. DOI: 10.1016/j.ijedudev.2020.102322

Nanda, J. D. (2025, March 6). Bridging the gender gap in India's corporate landscape. *Agency Reporter*. Retrieved from https://www.agencyreporter.com/bridging-the-gender-gap-in-indias-corporate-landsca pe/

Obloj, T., & Zenger, T. (2022). The influence of pay transparency on (gender) inequity, inequality and the performance basis of pay. *Nature Human Behaviour*, *6*(5), 646–655. DOI: 10.1038/s41562-022-01288-9 PMID: 35145281

OECD. (n.d.). Retrieved from https://www.oecd.org/en/data/indicators/gender-wage-gap.html Pathak, H. (2025). *Improving Female Workforce Participation in India.* PIB, Ministry of Labour & Employment. Retrieved from https://www.pib.gov.in/PressReleasePage.aspx?PRID=2108281

Padhi, B., Mishra, U. S., & Pattanayak, U. (2019). Gender-Based Wage Discrimination in Indian Urban Labour Market: An Assessment. *The Indian Journal of Labour Economics : the Quarterly Journal of the Indian Society of Labour Economics*, *62*(3), 361–388. DOI: 10.1007/s41027-019-00175-8

Patel, R., & Kumar, S. (2023). Beyond the Break: An Analysis of Corporate Re-entry Programs. *Indian Journal of Human Resource Management*, *12*(2), 45–60.

Platt, J., Prins, S., Bates, L., & Keyes, K. (2016). Unequal depression for equal work? How the wage gap explains gendered disparities in mood disorders. *Social Science & Medicine*, *149*, 1–8. DOI: 10.1016/j.socscimed.2015.11.056 PMID: 26689629

PLFS. (2023-24). *Annual Report.* Retrieved from chrome-extension://efaidnbmnnnibpcajpcglclefindmkaj/https://dge.gov.in/dge/sites/de fault/files/2023-10/Annual_Report_PLFS_2022-23.pdf

Psacharopoulos, G., & Tzannatos, Z. (1989). FEMALE LABOR FORCE PARTICIPATION: AN INTERNATIONAL PERSPECTIVE. *The World Bank Research Observer*, *4*(2), 187–201. DOI: 10.1093/wbro/4.2.187 PMID: 12283641

Rammohan, A., & Vu, P. (2018). Gender Inequality in Education and Kinship Norms in India. *Feminist Economics*, *24*(1), 142–167. DOI: 10.1080/13545701.2017.1364399

Ray, D., & Samanta, T. (2020). "Motherhood Penalty?": Examining Gender, Work, and Family among Science Professionals in India. *Susan Bulkeley Butler Center for Leadership Excellence and ADVANCE Working Paper Series.*

Report, G. W. (2022-23). *The impact of COVID-19 and inflation on wages and purchasing power.* ILO. Retrieved from https://webapps.ilo.org/digitalguides/en-gb/story/globalwagereport2022-23#home

Reshi, I. A., & Sudha, D. T. (2023). THE GENDER PAY GAP AND ITS IMPACT ON WOMEN'S ECONOMIC EMPOWERMENT. *MORFAI JOURNAL*, *3*(1), 9–16. DOI: 10.54443/morfai.v3i1.742

Roberson, Q., King, E., & Hebl, M. (2020). Designing more effective practices for reducing workplace inequality. *Behavioral Science & Policy*, *6*(1), 39–49. DOI: 10.1177/237946152000600104

Roy, D. S. (2024). A Quintessential Conversation: Gender Pay Parity for India's Diverse Landscape. *India Leaders for Social Sectors*. Retrieved from https://indialeadersforsocialsector.com/gender-pay-parity-india-diverse-landscape/

Saha, A. (2013). An Assessment of Gender Discrimination in Household Expenditure on Education in India. *Oxford Development Studies*, *41*(2), 220–238. DOI: 10.1080/13600818.2013.786694

Sahoo, S., Sarkar, K., & Kumar, A. (2024). Valuation of Unpaid Household Activities in India', Vol 59, Issue no. 39, September 28, 2024. *The Hindu.*

Samad, N., Das, P., Dilshad, S., Al Banna, H., Rabbani, G., Sodunke, T. E., Hardcastle, T. C., Haq, A., Afroz, K. A., Ahmad, R., & Haque, M. (2022). Women's empowerment and fertility preferences of married women: Analysis of demographic and health survey'2016 in Timor-Leste. *AIMS Public Health*, *9*(2), 237–261. DOI: 10.3934/publichealth.2022017 PMID: 35634022

Sethi, P. (2024). Exploring the Gender Pay Gap in India: Assessing its Implications on Economic Growth and Development. *International Journal of Advance Research, Ideas and Innovations in Technology.* Retrieved from chrome-extension://efaidnbmnnnibpcajpcglclefindmkaj/https://www.ijariit.com/manu scripts/v10i3/V10I3-1161.pdf

Sharma, A. (2024). *The Corporate Comeback: Strategies for Reintegrating Women in India's Workforce*. IIM Ahmedabad Press.

Sharma, H. (2018). Gender Pay Gap in India: A Sectoral and Regional Analysis. *Asian Review of Social Sciences*, *7*(2), 1–5. DOI: 10.51983/arss-2018.7.2.1438

Sharma, M. (n.d.). Pay transparency on the rise in India, 50% job postings include salary details. Retrieved from https://www.peoplematters.in/article/talent-acquisition/pay-transparency-on-the-rise-i n-india-50-job-postings-include-salary-details-37873

Shchepilova, O. I., & Korol, M. V. (2020). Applying the Data Modeling Tools for the Gender Inequality Analysis in the IT-industry in Ukraine and Worldwide. *Bìznes Ìnform*, *9*(512), 165–171. DOI: 10.32983/2222-4459-2020-9-165-171

Singh, P., & Pattanaik, F. (2020). Unfolding unpaid domestic work in India: Women's constraints, choices, and career. *Palgrave Communications*, *6*(1), 111. DOI: 10.1057/s41599-020-0488-2

Smyth, E., & Steinmetz, S. (2008). Field of Study and Gender Segregation in European Labour Markets. *International Journal of Comparative Sociology*, *49*(4–5), 257–281. DOI: 10.1177/0020715208093077

Sudha, S., & Rajan, S. I. (1999). Female Demographic Disadvantage in India 1981–1991: Sex Selective Abortions and Female Infanticide. *Development and Change*, *30*(3), 585–618. DOI: 10.1111/1467-7660.00130 PMID: 20162850

Upadhyay, U. D., Gipson, J. D., Withers, M., Lewis, S., Ciaraldi, E. J., Fraser, A., Huchko, M. J., & Prata, N. (2014). Women's empowerment and fertility: A review of the literature. *Social Science & Medicine*, *115*, 111–120. DOI: 10.1016/j.socscimed.2014.06.014 PMID: 24955875

Zhang, Y. (2024). Discrimination against Women in the Workplace. *Journal of Education. Humanities and Social Sciences*, *27*, 135–140. DOI: 10.54097/bg2b5g02

Chapter 11
Exploring Operational and Strategic Issues in India-China Trade From Indian Stakeholders' Perspective

Alka Sandhu
https://orcid.org/0009-0007-3245-4583
Lovely Professional University, India

Sakshi Choudhary
https://orcid.org/0000-0002-4685-5026
Lovely Professional University, India

ABSTRACT

This chapter examines the challenges faced by Indian exporters and importers in their trade engagement with China, based on a survey of 120 stakeholders across sectors such as textiles, machinery, metals, and foodstuffs. Using a Likert scale and Garrett's ranking technique, the study identifies key internal barriers like high import duties, inadequate infrastructure, and lack of skilled labour. While schemes like duty-free imports and subsidized loans are seen as beneficial, access remains limited. Externally, competition, tariff and non-tariff barriers, and price sensitivity in the Chinese market pose significant challenges. Many stakeholders express a desire to reduce import dependence on China, citing strategic goals like Make in India. The chapter recommends rationalizing tariffs, improving export infrastructure,

DOI: 10.4018/979-8-3373-2772-3.ch011

simplifying scheme access, and enhancing manufacturing and R&D capabilities. By offering empirical, stakeholder-driven insights, the chapter contributes to policy discussions on improving India's trade competitiveness and resilience with China.

INTRODUCTION

India's economic relationship with China is dotted by a complex web of trade disparities, geopolitical disputes, and economic interdependence. It is arguably one of the most significant bilateral economic exchanges in Asia and the world. China has emerged as India's top trading partner over the last 20 years, and India is now one of its most important export markets. Despite this substantial volume of trade, India has a huge trade deficit as a result of its reliance on Chinese imports of electronics equipment, industrial goods, and pharmaceutical components.

China's dominance in global manufacturing, low manufacturing costs, and rapid infrastructure development make it a popular import sourcing option for Indian businesses. Concerns regarding an over-reliance on imports, supply chain interruptions, and Indian exporters' lack of export competitiveness have been raised by these incentives. It is now more difficult for Indian companies to compete in China's huge but extremely limited market due to a number of additional factors, such as non-tariff barriers, market access restrictions, and discriminatory practices in the Chinese market.

DYNAMICS OF TRADE AFTER THE PANDEMIC

Due to COVID-19 pandemic induced disruptions and rising trade tensions between the United States and China, many multinational corporations, including Apple, implemented a China plus one strategy to reduce their supply chain exposure to China. They made an effort to lower their risk exposure by reducing their presence in China and moving some of their manufacturing operations abroad. For many businesses, India has been a desirable alternative. As part of this strategy, Foxconn intended to establish production facilities in Karnataka in 2022. India's advantages over China include a large domestic market, a highly skilled labor force, rapid economic growth, and government initiatives like the Production Linked Incentives (PLI) scheme and "Aatmanirbhar Bharat" scheme (Banerjee, 2024).

China was India's top trading partner in 2024, with exports to India rising 2.4% yearly to $120.48 billion and imports from India declining 3% to about $18 billion. India's economy is still expanding, and the country's long-standing need for building materials/inputs is a key factor in the rise in the value of Chinese exports to India.

Due to border concerns, India changed its FDI policy for neighbouring countries in 2020, but by 2022, it was starting to accept FDI inquiries on a case-by-case basis. In 2023, China's foreign direct investment (FDI) appeared to be rebounding. The country's total direct investment stock was $3.21 billion, compared to $42.05 million in equity investments (China Briefing, 2025).

China and India are cautiously reestablishing their economic ties as new situations arise. India is compelled to do this because of ongoing trade disputes with the US caused by tariff impositions. The idea behind this strategy is to settle disputes, collaborate on issues of shared interest, and give stability to an already unstable relationship. Later, China removed its export restrictions on rare earth elements, fertilizer, magnets, and tunnel boring equipment to India. Both sides have taken steps to increase trust, such as removing the need for a visa, restoring religious pilgrimages, and establishing direct flights (Economic Times, 2025).

An examination of trade between India and ASEAN reveals that Indian exports are not competitive in ASEAN markets, and trade deficits do occur, although they are mitigated by exports of engineering, IT, and petroleum. Based on competitiveness and the increased likelihood of India's integration into global supply chains, sectoral analysis did identify possible areas for export promotion (Banik and Kim, 2024). Imports of high-tech goods and exports of intermediates and raw materials make up the majority of India's trade with China. India's trade deficit with China has surpassed $100 billion and continues to grow.

Given this context, developing a successful trade policy and business plan requires gaining a firsthand grasp of the experiences of Indian importers and exporters. The operational challenges, procedural bottlenecks, and competitive pressures that firms face are not taken into account by the macroeconomic indicators, which give a very broad picture. As a result, a stakeholder-centric approach is crucial for determining practical limitations and creating recommendations that are supported by empirical data.

Through a survey of Indian importers and exporters involved in trade with China, this chapter aims to be able to offer such insights. Textiles, machinery, food, metals, plastics, and animal and vegetable products are just a few of the industries from which the respondents come. The survey attempts to gather their opinions on a broad range of trade-related topics, such as the acquisition of raw materials, regulatory obstacles, Chinese market conditions, and the efficacy of Indian export promotion programs.

This chapter's focus extends beyond identifying trade restrictions. It seeks to evaluate the systemic elements influencing India's export competitiveness, the justification for India's heavy reliance on imports from China, and the readiness of Indian companies to expand their export and sourcing markets. The chapter also highlights the shortcomings of current policy frameworks and offers a number of corrective actions based on the opinions and recommendations of stakeholders.

Through the integration of stakeholder-based quantitative data and literary insights, this chapter aims to guide institutional reforms, contribute to trade policy discussions, and advance the larger goal of establishing balanced, resilient, and sustainable trade relations between China and India.

The survey's goals:

1. to determine the main obstacles that Indian importers and exporters encounter when doing business with China.
2. to investigate how India's export competitiveness is impacted by labor, infrastructure, raw material qualities, and financial considerations.
3. to evaluate Indian export promotion programs' accessibility and efficacy from the viewpoint of stakeholders.
4. to examine the justification for India's reliance on imports and how it is thought to affect homegrown industries.
5. to comprehend the viewpoints of stakeholders regarding the regulatory obstacles and market environment in China.
6. to determine preferred alternative markets and investigate Indian companies' inclination to diversify their trade away from China.
7. to recommend policy changes and corrective actions in order to improve India's trade performance and lessen its reliance on imports.

REVIEW OF LITERATURE

Factors Affecting Export Performance

Since a variety of economic, institutional, and structural factors influence export performance, it is a topic that has been extensively researched in the literature on international trade. Numerous academics have made an effort to pinpoint the factors that influence export performance, particularly in developing nations. Cavusgil and Zou (1994) state that firm specific traits like export strategy, managerial dedication, and foreign experience are important determinants. Lall (2000), on the other hand, highlighted the importance of infrastructure, firm size, and technological capabilities when describing the factors that contribute to successful export performance.

Studies by Raju and Rajan (2019) and Arora (2024) in the Indian context emphasize the significance of elements influencing export performance, including financial access, R&D investment, and market familiarity. Indian businesses frequently face structural limitations that lower their ability to compete in global marketplaces.

These limitations include low trade facilitation policies, antiquated technologies, high capital costs, and limited economies of scale.

Furthermore, Castellani and Fassio (2019) contend that increasing a firm's export intensity and productivity requires having access to imported inputs. Export performance is directly impacted by the availability of high-quality raw materials at competitive prices, particularly in intermediate goods industries where India lacks domestic sufficiency. Rehman et al. (2020), discovered a significant positive correlation between input imports and export growth among developing economies, which gives support to this viewpoint.

Difficulties with Raw Material Imports and the Inverted Duty Structure

For India's export-driven manufacturing sectors, raw material imports are crucial, especially for MSMEs that depend on price-sensitive international supply chains. The inverted duty structure, which occurs when the duty on finished goods is lower than that on imported inputs, is one of the difficulties associated with this process. Deolekar and Tiwari (2024) claim that this tax structure disadvantages local manufacturers in comparison to their counterparts from nations with more balanced tariff structures and discourages domestic value addition.

Importing raw materials improves production capabilities, but it also exposes businesses to foreign exchange risks and global price volatility, according to Setyorini and Budiono (2020). Additionally, Indian exporters incur higher transaction costs due to customs compliance, import clearance delays, and tariff unpredictability (Handoyo et al., 2024).

One major bottleneck in trade performance has been identified as the inability to obtain high-quality raw materials domestically and the excessive reliance on Chinese imports for components in industries like electronics, textiles, and pharmaceuticals (GTRI, 2024; GOI, 2016). Additionally, this reliance has strategic geopolitical ramifications, particularly during periods of political unpredictability and supply chain interruptions.

Logistics and Infrastructure as Trade Facilitators

A nation's infrastructure and logistics performance have a significant impact on its capacity to compete on the international scene. According to Yeo et al. (2020), middle-income countries' export growth is greatly aided by improvements in logistics, such as improved road connectivity, increased port capacity for handling cargo, and standardization of packaging and warehousing.

Although India has been working hard to close the infrastructure gaps, problems like ineffective cargo facilities, a lack of cold storage, and poor last-mile connectivity still prevent trade from being competitive (Ministry of Commerce, 2021). Olyanga et al. (2022) argued for a unified regional infrastructure policy after demonstrating how East African nations with subpar trade infrastructure experienced decreased export competitiveness. Similar issues arise in the Indian case, where exporters frequently point to ineffective ports and inadequate rail and road systems as trade barriers.

In order to improve their overall trade facilitation, developing nations should not only upgrade their physical infrastructure but also innovate in logistics services and strengthen public-private partnerships, according to Diaz (2021).

The Function of Financial Access, Productivity and Skilled Labour in Trade

Firm-level productivity and the calibre of human capital are increasingly viewed as key factors in boosting trade competitiveness. Dhiman and Sharma (2019) found a one-way relationship between export competitiveness and labour productivity in India, particularly in the textile industry. Increased productivity improves turn-around times, cost effectiveness, and product quality—all of which are crucial for the success of export markets.

Wang (2013) investigated the negative correlation between rising labor costs and export performance in Asian economies and discovered that inadequate labor management and a mismatch in skills can reduce export competitiveness. In India, a company's ability to expand and integrate into high-value global supply chains is constrained by the twin problems of low R&D investment and insufficient skill development (Mubarik et al., 2020).

In this context, financial limitations are also very important. One of the biggest obstacles facing Indian exporters, particularly MSMEs, is the inability to obtain timely and reasonably priced credit. Yildirim et al. (2013) claim that access to financing is directly impacted by firm size, with larger businesses having a higher chance of obtaining credit at favourable rates. Niryat Rin Vikas Yojana (NIRVIK) and the Interest Equalization Scheme are two government initiatives that have tried to close this gap, but implementation and awareness issues still persist (DGFT, 2024).

The Indian Government Facilitates Trade and Promotes Exports

India's trade policy framework includes a number of export-boosting initiatives, such as the Advance Authorization Scheme (AAS), Duty-Free Import Authorization (DFIA), Production Linked Incentive (PLI) Scheme, and Export Promotion Capital Goods (EPCG) Schemes. By reducing the cost disadvantages, these programs seek to increase the competitiveness of Indian exporters.

The Market Access Initiative (MAI) and Market Development Assistance (MDA) programs provide financial assistance for trade show participation, market research, and brand promotions, specifically for MSMEs. However, as the NITI Aayog (2024) study shows, many exporters find it challenging to access these schemes due to a lack of coordination among implementing agencies, complex documentation, and low awareness.

The Star Export House Certification program has been suggested by exporters as a method to administer financial incentives to firms and grants preferential treatment during customs procedures (IndiaFilings, 2022). Delays in implementation and legal restrictions reduce the system's overall efficacy.

Historical Information on import and Export Trends Between China and India

China and India have one of the most complicated and contentious business partnerships. India's biggest import partner and a major cause of its trade imbalance is China. Although the volume of bilateral trade between China and India has been steadily increasing, a disproportionate amount of this growth has come from China's exports to India, according to data from the Government of India (GOI, 2023).

China's strict non-tariff barriers are a major factor in India's poor export performance under this bilateral agreement, claims Srivastava (2023). These include quality standards, license requirements, and includes such discriminatory practices which give preference to domestic Chinese businesses over foreign ones. In addition to being regulatory in nature, the barriers are deeply set in institutional, political, and cultural systems of the nation.

According to Headly (2024), multinational corporations find it very challenging to navigate China's regulatory environment. From product testing to registration and inspection, the entire process is laborious, confusing, and time-consuming. Similar results were also reported by Tadesse (2024), who asserted that differences in language and culture frequently cause issues for Indian exporters.

Furthermore, there is concrete proof that China employs trade as a tool for foreign policy. The sudden suspension of banana shipments from the Philippines due to the conflict in South China Sea is one instance of how political tensions may result in economic disruptions (GTRI, 2023). Indian businessmen frequently view China as a high-risk market for long-term exports because of this uncertainty.

Notwithstanding these challenges, a major section of Indian industry still depends on imports from China, mainly for essential parts in a number of sectors e, g. heavy machinery, pharmaceuticals and electronics. Initiatives like "Make in India" and "Aatmanirbhar Bharat" have emerged as a result of India's calls for diversification and local capacity development in response to this dependency.

An Overview of the Main Gaps Found in the Literature

Although the existing literature offers sufficient observations at the firm and economy-level determinants driving trade performance, specific issues facing Indian stakeholders dealing with China remain poorly understood. To completely understand the part of micro and small businesses, more empirical research is required. Additionally, their perspectives on export promotion initiatives and the factors affecting imports and exports must be examined in light of China-India trade. By analysing the opinions of Indian exporters and importers dealing with China by using information from the stakeholder survey, this chapter aims to close that research gap.

METHODS

A Synopsis of the Methodology

A methodical primary survey approach was used to fully comprehend the issues and challenges affecting the Indian stakeholders. The purpose of the survey was to gather subjective, first-hand information from Indian businesses actively engaged in importing from and selling to China. It addresses points such as trade restrictions, infrastructure issues, government initiatives, and competition dynamics.

The study evaluated respondents' assessments of the relative importance of trade restrictions and factors using a combination of quantitative methodologies, primarily Garrett's ranking method and Likert scale analysis. This provided empirical base regarding how Indian stakeholders perceive the trading situation with China, allowing us to convert qualitative feelings into a prioritized list.

Sample Size and Respondent Profile

For this study, 120 stakeholders i.e. exporters and importers, were polled. These respondents were drawn from a variety of industries that actively deal with China. The sample contains:

- Exporters (37%): Businesses that send goods to China from India.
- Importers (60%): Companies that import goods or inputs from China.
- Both Importers and Exporters (3%): Businesses that import from and export to China.

The respondents represent a wide spectrum of stakeholders who are directly affected by changing aspects of trade between these two countries. The research aimed to present a fair picture of the opportunities, restrictions, and practical realities experienced in bilateral commerce with China by soliciting input from both importers and exporters.

Sector Wise Coverage

Respondents from a wide range of industrial sectors were chosen because of their high trade volumes with China. Among these sectors include:

- Textiles
- Electrical and mechanical goods
- Metals
- Miscellaneous Products
- Rubber and Plastics
- Food items
- Animal products and live animals
- Vegetable Goods
- Glass and Stone Goods
- Headwear and Footwear

Given their varied degrees of reliance on Chinese inputs, as well as their varied exposure to external constraints, infrastructure difficulties, and policy impacts, these sectors were selected to guarantee both coverage of issues and depth of analysis. For instance, while foodstuffs and metals make up the majority of India's exports, textiles and machinery make up a sizable portion of its imports from China. The inclusion of both modern and traditional industries also sheds light on the ways in which emerging and traditional sectors react differently to trade frictions.

Classification of Business Type and Enterprise Size

The survey participants were categorized using the Ministry of MSME's classification of enterprises in order to comprehend how trade issues differ by firm size:

- Micro Enterprises (57%): These are businesses with little funding and human capital, frequently no internal research and development, and a heavy reliance on government assistance programs. Micro enterprises are defined as businesses with an annual revenue of up to Rs 5 crore.
- Small Enterprises (36%): These are somewhat bigger businesses with superior operational bandwidth, but they are still very susceptible to problems relating to costs and infrastructure. Small businesses are defined as those with an annual revenue of up to Rs 50 crore.
- Medium Enterprises (6%): These are businesses with a range of capabilities, typically having some technology investments and moderate credit availability. Medium-sized businesses are defined as those with an annual revenue of up to Rs 250 crore.
- Large Enterprises (1%): Businesses that can more effectively navigate complex regulatory environments, have integrated operations, and significant resources. Large businesses are defined as those with an annual revenue of more than Rs 250 crore.

Based on variations in firm sizes, this classification aids in assessing an organization's susceptibility to trade shocks, infrastructure constraints, or policy ambiguities.

Measurement Scale and Survey Instrument

Using a 5-point Likert scale, a structured questionnaire was created to gather information on a number of factors pertaining to import and export difficulties. On a scale from 1 to 5, respondents were asked to indicate how much they agreed with different statements or how important they thought certain trade-related issues were.

i. Strongly Agree / Extremely Important
ii. Agree / Important
iii. Neutral / Moderate
iv. Disagree / Less Important
v. Strongly Disagree / Not Important

Because it can capture the intensity of respondents' opinions across a range of responses, the Likert scale approach was selected. Effective quantification and statistical interpretation of qualitative evaluations are also made possible by it.

This scale was used to measure several important areas, including:

- Issues with raw materials (price, availability, quality, taxes)
- Infrastructure issues (port facilities, road/rail connectivity, warehousing)
- Limitations on productivity and human capital
- The effectiveness and accessibility of export promotion programs
- Dependency on imports and the justifications for ongoing Chinese imports
- Trade restrictions and market access in China
- Support for government policy
- Remedial actions suggested

Applying Garrett's Ranking Method

The Garrett's Ranking Technique was used to determine priority issues as judged by stakeholders in order to strengthen the validity of the Likert scale data. By transforming ordinal preferences (rankings) into interval-level data, this method facilitates weighted analysis and insightful comparisons between respondents.

Three steps are involved in the method:

Conversion of Ranks into Percent Positions

Using the formula by Garrett and Woodworth (1969):

Percent position = $100 (R_{ij} -0.5) / N_j$

where:

- Rij = Rank given for the i-th variable by the j-th respondent
- Nj = Number of variables ranked by the j-th respondent

Use of Garrett Conversion Table

The Garrett Score Conversion Table-1, which allocates a numerical score in accordance with the percent position, was then compared with the computed percent positions.

Table 1. The Garrett conversion table

Likert Scale Rank	Percentile Position	Garrett Score
1	10	75
2	30	60
3	50	50
4	70	40
5	90	25

(Source- Garrett and Woodworth,1969)

Calculating Final Ranking and Mean Scores

The Garrett score for each variable was calculated by multiplying its frequency by the given score, and the total score was then calculated by adding up all of the respondents. A final rank based on stakeholder perceptions was then assigned using the mean score for each issue.

This approach makes it possible to clearly interpret which issues require immediate institutional or policy interventions and offers an empirical and comparative framework for prioritizing issues according to their weighted importance.

Data Gathering and Trustworthiness

Both online and offline survey methods were used to collect data over a six-month period. Emails, industry networks, and in-person meetings were used to contact the respondents. Prior to full deployment, a pilot test of the survey was carried out with 30 respondents to guarantee uniformity and clarity. Changes were made based on the wording and structure of the questions.

All ethical norms of informed consent and data privacy were respected, and respondents' anonymity was preserved to promote truthful answers.

The Methodology's Limitations

The methodology has limitations even though it offers thorough insights. Despite being sufficient for exploratory analysis, the sample size of 120 might not fully represent the diversity of the Indian trade ecosystem. Additionally, the focus on trade experiences unique to China may limit generalizability to other trade partners, and the use of self-reported perceptions may introduce bias.

However, the approach is based on tried-and-true empirical methods and offers a solid and trustworthy basis for examining stakeholder perspectives on trade issues between China and India.

SURVEY AND ANALYSIS OF THE SURVEY

Problems with Raw Materials

Raw material problems were frequently cited by Indian exporters as the main obstacle to doing business with China. The tax/duty on imported raw materials had the highest Garrett scores out of all the parameters that were assessed, including cost, availability, price fluctuations, quality, and tax/duty. High and erratic tariffs raise production costs and lower price competitiveness overseas, exporters stressed. Concern over cost increases linked to global commodity fluctuations was reflected in the cost of raw materials, which came in second as a crucial factor. Another urgent issue that has surfaced is price volatility, which makes pricing and budgeting decisions more uncertain. Despite being viewed as less serious than cost-related metrics, quality and availability still received high scores, indicating uneven standards and irregular supply disruptions. The findings imply that structural inefficiencies in tariff structures and raw material imports significantly limit India's export competitiveness.

Challenges Associated with Infrastructure

The second biggest barrier to facilitating effective exports to China was infrastructure. Lack of proper storage, handling, and export-quality packaging solutions was highlighted by respondents who ranked export warehousing and packaging facilities as the most important infrastructure need. Logistics are made more difficult and product quality may be compromised by the lack of standardized warehouses that satisfy export-grade standards. Ineffective last-mile supply chains and inadequate intermodal linkages result in delays, increased transportation expenses, and logistical bottlenecks; road and rail connectivity to ports was the next area of concern. Inadequate cargo handling at ports causes further disruptions for exporters, such as a lack of mechanization and poor scheduling that can lead to lengthy wait times during busy times. Last but not least, despite their lower ranking, testing and certification labs are still essential for fulfilling China's stringent regulatory requirements. Their deficiency can result in higher transaction costs or rejection risks at Chinese customs, delay shipments, and impact the perception of export quality.

Export Competitiveness and a Skilled Workforce

Modern technology, cost-effective labour, and a skilled workforce are the cornerstones of export competitiveness. The top-ranked factor affecting export performance in the survey was skilled labour, which reflected exporters' need for workers with technical work, quality assurance, and international regulatory compliance skills. The fact that labor costs came in second highlighted the fine balance that businesses need to maintain between labor productivity and product margins. Firms' technological levels (low, medium, or high) came in close succession, underscoring the necessity of modernizing the industry in order to compete with Chinese producers. Furthermore, although they were given less importance, labour productivity, transportation costs, and credit availability were acknowledged as significant factors that influence export potential. These results collectively highlight the necessity of strong skill development, technological advancements, and funding for infrastructure and technical upskilling.

Export Promotion and Financial Assistance

Indian companies frequently rely on government programs to facilitate exports. The respondents rated duty-free import programs like Duty Free Import Authorization and Advance Authorization as the most successful in lowering input costs and boosting competitiveness. In order to improve financial affordability, subsidized loans and credit facility programs—such as interest equalization and NIRVIK guarantees—were implemented. Faster loan processing was acknowledged, but it was not given as much priority, indicating that financial impact comes before process acceleration. Only a small percentage of stakeholders found these programs easy to use, primarily due to bureaucratic complexity and gaps in policy awareness. This highlights an implementation gap issue that lessens the usefulness of carefully thought-out export incentive programs.

Chinese Market Demand Factors

Due to Chinese importers' extreme cost sensitivity, exporters stated that price in comparison to competitors continues to be the most significant factor affecting demand in the Chinese market. Product quality came in second, suggesting that in order for India to enter higher-value markets, it must satisfy China's growing regulatory demands and global acceptance. Technological capability (such as product and functional innovation) also played a significant role, indicating the potential for Indian businesses in specialized markets that need to stand out. Other elements that were deemed less important but still significant included brand name, design/

packaging, and delivery methods. All of these results point to two structural issues: India needs to move toward value-added and innovation-driven export models while competing on both price and quality.

Outside Limitations

Competition from other exporting nations was found to be the most difficult aspect of external trade restrictions, underscoring India's challenging position against low-cost producers and trade blocs with more extensive market integration. Significant obstacles were both tariff and non-tariff, such as China's high MFN duties, intricate customs processes, and certification system. These are followed by political unpredictability brought on by problems like border tensions, which can lead to erratic market conditions, and exchange rate volatility, which affects pricing and profit margins amid cross-border currency fluctuations. In conclusion, macropolitical risk, regulatory complexity, and competitive pressure characterize India's external environment for exports to China.

Efficiency of Export Promotion Programs

Schemes for export promotion are essential for raising competitiveness. Because of its advantages, which include input quotas, preferential access, and simplified customs procedures, respondents gave the Star Export House Certification the highest ranking. Due to its ability to facilitate duty-free input importation, the Advance Authorization Scheme (AAS) was ranked as the second most valuable. Although they were ranked lower, other schemes such as duty drawback, PLI, EPCG, and Market Access Initiative were valued. In terms of perceived advantages, respondents think these programs offer a competitive advantage, which is followed by cost savings and increased market share. Even though incentives are widely acknowledged to be available, most still report access issues, suggesting that bureaucratic complications prevent full utilization. According to the results, scheme effectiveness could be greatly increased by simplification, better communication, and quicker issuance.

INDIA'S RELIANCE ON CHINESE IMPORTS

Use and Objective of Imports

A significant reliance on imports, particularly for intermediate and final goods, is a defining feature of India's trade with China. According to the survey, 38.33% of participants import completed goods for domestic consumption, while 41.66% import primarily raw materials. Only 5% use Chinese goods for additional exports, and a smaller percentage (15%) imports intermediate goods. In terms of industry, imports are dominated by textiles and machinery/electrical goods, while pharmaceuticals are highly dependent on China, where up to 90% of some active ingredients are sourced. Because domestic supply chains are not as competitive in terms of quality or price, this import dependency exposes a structural reliance on Chinese supply chains. Additionally, it shows mutual reliance skills for supply chain continuity and productive operations.

Justification for Favouring Chinese Imports

The price-cost margin was the main justification given by Indian businesses for importing from China, indicating their competitive edge brought about by China's economies of scale, effective manufacturing, and cheaper labor costs. Specific product specifications—China's capacity to provide specialized components not found domestically—come next. The availability of the desired quality domestically is important; Chinese substitutes are required when Indian suppliers are unable to match precision or quality. Shorter lead times from Chinese manufacturers and regulatory obstacles like domestic certification and licensing delays are additional influencing factors. For Indian importers, these three elements—cost advantage, quality or specification mismatch, and logistical benefits—create an alluring value-for-money proposition, particularly in industries with high margin requirements.

Imports' Effect

There are conflicting patterns in how Chinese imports affect Indian company sales and exports. Approximately 41.66% of businesses stated that higher imports from China boosted sales, most likely as a result of lower-priced inputs and product dumping that allowed for better pricing or wider domestic distribution. While 23.33% saw a decline in sales, another 35.83% saw no discernible change, suggesting that imports have the potential to displace competitors in some industries. 32.5% of respondents claimed that their export performance was improved by their reliance on Chinese inputs; Chinese components increased the viability of their own export offerings based on specifications or cost. 40% were inapplicable because they lacked an export orientation, and a small percentage (8.33%) experienced a decline in exports. This suggests that import dependence may help exporters source from China and does not always harm export competitiveness.

The Impact of Imports on Other Sourcing

Chinese imports have an impact on sourcing from other nations as well. About 40.83% of respondents said their imports from other countries remained the same, while 30.83% claimed that Chinese imports made them more dependent on international supply chains because Chinese-made inputs were integrated. On the other hand, 28.33% reported less sourcing from other areas, indicating that China had taken their place. This pattern suggests a trade diversion effect, in which, depending on product category overlap, higher low-cost Chinese imports may push out suppliers from the USA, EU, or Southeast Asia. Therefore, the wider ramifications for diverse trade relationships must be taken into account when making policy decisions.

Willingness to Lessen Dependency on Imports

34.16% of respondents said they wanted to lessen their reliance on China despite the benefits of imports. Among their reasons are:

- In line with the objectives of Aatmanirbhar Bharat and Made in India to promote independence.
- By reducing the trade deficit, foreign exchange reserves are protected.
- Reducing geopolitical risk, considering supply disruptions due to India-China tensions.

The USA, Germany, Japan, South Korea, Vietnam, Bangladesh, Taiwan, Indonesia, Israel, Nepal, Russia, and the UK were among the respondents' top choices for alternative sourcing locations. Cost, dependability, and scale advantages were cited by those who were unwilling to lessen dependence (39.16%). When weighing cost-benefit considerations, neutral respondents (26.66%) said they were unable to make a decision. The intricacy of moving away from Chinese reliance is reflected in this mix.

Policy Levers and Structural Restraints

Key structural barriers to import substitutes in India were identified by respondents as follows:

- Higher input, land, labor, and compliance costs put manufacturing at a financial disadvantage.
- The absence of native raw material ecosystems and design.

- Limited investment in R&D, which hinders innovation and quality enhancement. Respondents suggested the following policy changes to lessen reliance on imports:
- The extension of fiscal support through PLI in industries such as electronics to aid in manufacturing scaling.
- The rationalization of tariffs to conform to rival economies.
- Collaborations between the public and private sectors to improve infrastructure (CII, 2024).
- Expanding trade agreements with markets in Africa, the UK, the GCC, and the EU.

A multi-sectoral strategy to lessen structural dependency on Chinese imports is highlighted by these responses.

Cutting Down on Import Reliance

34.16% of respondents, a sizable portion, stated a strong desire to lessen India's reliance on Chinese imports. This is not a majority, but it does show that stakeholders are becoming more concerned and determined. Three main categories can be used to classify their motivations:

Aatmanirbhar Bharat Alignment/Made in India

Respondents presented their wish as being in line with national policies that promote independence. They think that by lowering dependency on low-cost Chinese imports, indigenous production can be increased, enhancing home manufacturing ecosystems and creating jobs.

Preservation of Foreign Exchange

India's ongoing trade deficit with China is a result of high import volumes, which puts strain on the country's foreign exchange reserves. Reducing reliance on imports, according to stakeholders, would enhance macroeconomic stability and aid in rebalancing trade flows.

Mitigation of Geopolitical Risk

Supply chain vulnerabilities are caused by ongoing political unrest and border conflicts. Whether brought on by trade restrictions, conflict, or geopolitical tension, a disruption in Chinese imports could have a negative impact on domestic operations.

Reducing reliance was mentioned by respondents as a risk management tactic to ensure production continuity.

Respondents listed a wide range of nations as their top choices for alternative sourcing destinations, including the United States, Germany, Japan, South Korea, Vietnam, Bangladesh, Indonesia, Taiwan, Israel, Nepal, Russia, and the United Kingdom. These options demonstrate India's interest in:

- Developed, superior manufacturing ecosystems, such as those in Japan and Germany
- Competitive cost advantages (e.g., Bangladesh, Vietnam)
- Diversification of regions (such as Taiwan, South Korea, and Indonesia)

But substitutability is complicated; supply chain preparedness, legal frameworks, logistics, and cost structures differ greatly. Even though the respondents are in favor of reorienting sourcing, changing global supply chains necessitates strategic alliances, unit-level preparedness, and policy support.

DIFFICULTIES IN THE CHINESE MARKET

The market environment in China was thoroughly assessed by the respondents. There are two main types of challenges:

Limitations of the Market Environment

- Competition from Chinese producers: Chinese domestic companies continue to rule the market, frequently with the help of integrated supply chains, greater economies of scale, and government assistance.
- Ineffective publicity: Indian exporters find it difficult to get noticed in China, where localized marketing and digital platforms are crucial.
- High import taxes and non-tariff barriers: India must contend with strict product standards, especially in the areas of biotechnology, electronics, food, and pharmaceuticals, in addition to MFN tariffs.
- Excessive documentation and compliance requirements: Exporting to China is difficult and time-consuming due to complicated registration, customs procedures, inspections, labelling protocols, and batch certifications.

Overall Impression of the Market

Table 2 shows the ranked response of the respondents over their overall impression of China as a market. The respondents opined those discriminatory restrictions is ranked as the top defining feature of Chinese market. This is followed by the lack of market access.

Table 2. Ranking overall impression of chinese market as perceived by the respondents

Parameter	Frequency of Response					Corresponding Garret Scale					Total	Weighted Score	Rank
	1	2	3	4	5	75	60	50	40	25			
Ease of Market Access	19	49	42	10	0	1425	2940	2100	400	0	6865	0.1635	4
Lack of Market Access	35	44	34	7	0	2625	2640	1700	280	0	7245	0.1725	2
Discriminatory Restrictions	34	56	29	1	0	2550	3360	1450	40	0	7400	0.1762	1
Unfair Trade Practices	24	66	25	5	0	1800	3960	1250	200	0	7210	0.1717	3
Language Barriers	15	35	56	13	1	1125	2100	2800	520	25	6570	0.1565	6
Cultural Differences	14	47	47	12	0	1050	2820	2350	480	0	6700	0.1596	5

Source- Author calculations

The third ranked item depicting their impression of Chinese market is the unfair trade practices. The fourth ranked item is the ease of market access followed by cultural differences and language barriers ranked fifth and sixth respectively. Thus, following are the main features of Chinese market as perceived by respondents:

- **Discriminatory restrictions:** According to respondents, there is informal bias and increased scrutiny of foreign goods.
- **Unfair trade practices:** Indian businesses frequently face countervailing duties, anti-dumping duties, and abrupt enforcement actions that are implemented with little notice.
- **Regulatory opacity:** Chinese laws are frequently passed at the provincial level, necessitating ongoing attention, re-certification, or modifications, which raises the burden of compliance.

When taken as a whole, these difficulties present China as a market with many opportunities but high barriers. Stakeholders are more concerned with how hostile and opaque the business environment can seem to overseas exporters than they are with a lack of demand.

PROBLEMS TO SOLVE IN ORDER TO IMPROVE EXPORT PERFORMANCE

The top ranked issue which needs to be addressed in order to boost India's exports is investment in R&D according to the respondents as shown in Table 3. The second important issue is the market access followed by supply chain management which needs to be addressed. The next issue is the registration/Licensing process followed by fifth ranked sector/ industry specify government support. Next the technical standards and qualification norms needs to be addressed followed by labour norms and last ranked is the resolution of border disputes.

Table 3. Ranking issues which need to be addressed in order to facilitate India's exports performance in Chinese market as perceived by the respondents

Parameter	Frequency of Response					Corresponding Garret Scale					Total	Weighted Score	Rank
	1	2	3	4	5	75	60	50	40	25			
Resolution of Border Disputes	15	66	36	2	1	1125	3960	1800	80	25	6990	0.1179	8
Technical Standards, Qualification Norms	37	54	27	2	0	2775	3240	1350	80	0	7445	0.1256	6
Registration/ Licensing Process	32	73	12	3	0	2400	4380	600	120	0	7500	0.1265	4
Labour Norms	21	74	22	3	0	1575	4440	1100	120	0	7235	0.1221	7
Market Access	38	59	21	2	0	2850	3540	1050	80	0	7520	0.1269	2
Supply Chain Management	31	74	14	1	0	2325	4440	700	40	0	7505	0.1266	3
Sector/Industry Specify Govt Support	34	61	24	1	0	2550	3660	1200	40	0	7450	0.1257	5
Investment in R&D	39	67	12	2	0	2925	4020	600	80	0	7625	0.1286	1

Source- Author calculations

So, participants in the survey stated that improving India's export competitiveness in the Chinese market requires addressing several issues:

a) **Research and Development (R&D) Investing**: To improve product quality, innovation, and stakeholders emphasized that Indian businesses must significantly boost their R&D expenditures in order to be technologically ready. In order to remove technical barriers and customize products for the Chinese market, research and development is crucial.

b) **Improving Market Access**: Exporters request fast-track certifications, mutual standard recognition, bilateral dialogue channels, and the elimination of non-tariff barriers through export councils or free trade agreements.

c) **Supply Chain & Logistics Optimization**: Operational competitiveness depends on dependable, efficient supply chains. Stakeholders stressed the need for containerized logistics linked to adjacent ports, standard packaging, better warehousing, and cold chains.

d) **Institutional & Regulatory Process Streamlining**: Respondents favoured particular measures to update regulatory frameworks, including reduced paperwork at government points of contact, digital customs procedures, simplified licensing, and unambiguous regulations.

These priorities—logistics, diplomatic engagement, institutional capacity, and innovativeness—emphasize the complex nature of export resilience.

SUGGESTED CORRECTIVE MEASURES

Stakeholder feedback indicated that the following corrective actions were of utmost importance. The weighted ranked response of the respondents in table 4, has shown the development of local manufacturing capabilities as the top ranked remedial measure needed to boost Indian exports. Boosting manufacturing at competitive cost is ranked second followed by need to focus on enhancing the competitiveness of enterprises in India. The next remedial measure which could be used is to develop large scale manufacturing and diversion of trade towards more friendly countries. The sixth ranked remedy is the government support to achieve the objective. The diversification of import options is ranked seventh in order to boost Indian exports and reduce imports.

Table 4. Ranking remedial measures to boost Indian exports and reduce imports as perceived by the respondents

Parameter	Frequency of Response					Corresponding Garret Scale					Total	Weighted Score	Rank
	1	2	3	4	5	75	60	50	40	25			
Develop local Manufacturing Capabilities	54	41	22	3	0	4050	2460	1100	120	0	7730	0.1453	1
Diversify import Options	33	63	20	4	0	2475	3780	1000	160	0	7415	0.1394	7
Large scale manufacturing	41	63	15	1	0	3075	3780	750	40	0	7645	0.1437	4
Divert Trade Towards more Friendly Countries	35	67	17	1	0	2625	4020	850	40	0	7535	0.1417	5
Government Support	43	45	26	3	3	3225	2700	1300	120	75	7420	0.1395	6
Boosting Manufacturing at Competitive Cost	46	59	14	1	0	3450	3540	700	40	0	7730	0.1453	2
Focusing on Enhancing Competitiveness of Of Enterprises	47	57	13	3	0	3525	3420	650	120	0	7715	0.1450	3

Source- Author calculations

Thus, the following corrective measures could be adopted to boost India's exports.

a. **Expand Domestic Manufacturing Capabilities**: In order to compete with Chinese imports, respondents argued for public support for the adoption of mass-manufacturing infrastructure, skill development, and technological modernization.
b. **Reduce Cost and increase Operational Competitiveness**: To bring production inputs and operating costs down to global price parity, strategies including duty rationalization, interest equalization, credit support, and subsidies were put forth.
c. **Promote Trade Diversification and Partnerships**: To diversify their supply chains, Indian businesses should aggressively seek manufacturing and sourcing alliances in developing countries such as Bangladesh, Vietnam, and Eastern Europe.
d. **Infrastructure Public-Private Partnership:** To support MSMEs, stakeholders suggested PPP-led development of export clusters, cold chains, testing facilities, packing facilities, and logistics parks.

These remedial actions offer a thorough improvement plan for manufacturing floors as well as international marketplaces.

IMPLICATIONS OF POLICY AND ADVICE

The policy changes and interventions needed to strengthen India's trade relations with China and other nations are described in detail in this section.

Tariff Défense and Justification of Domestic Industry

Local competitiveness is lowered by India's inverted duty system, where input tariffs are higher than finished goods. Reduced production costs and increased economies of scale are two benefits of a modified tariff system that complies with international standards.

Reduce the impact of imports from China.

Lowering intermediate-goods tariffs, lowering import duties on finished goods, enforcing interim protective tariffs, and carefully localizing imports are some tactics to avoid reverse protection.

Enhancing Export Infrastructure

Efficiency and competitiveness are diminished by inadequate infrastructure. The following should be the goals of policymakers:

- Create advanced cold storage and packaging facilities connected to important trade hubs.
- To allay worries about compliance, set up testing and certification facilities approved for Chinese standards.
- By utilizing interior roads, railroads, or waterways, inland exporters can enhance their last-mile connectivity to ports.
- To identify and address issues, maintain open lines of communication with exporters.

Improving Accessibility to Export Schemes

Because of procedural and documentation problems, export incentives are often underutilized.

Among the potential improvements are:

- Online approval processes for the Advance Authorization, EPCG, PLI, and DFIA programs.
- DGFT, RBI, ECGC, and customs all have integrated digital systems.

- Workshops for capacity-building are held by export promotion councils and federations.

Monetary Rewards for Innovation and Manufacturing

The following actions should be taken by the government to get around production restrictions and financial disadvantages.

- Increase the application of Production Linked Incentive (PLI) programs to new sectors like auto parts, electronics, and pharmaceuticals.
- Offer import duty exemptions, loan guarantee programs, and accelerated depreciation to important industry producers and exporters.
- Using tax credits, grants, and innovation vouchers, offer demand-side support to R&D-intensive MSMEs with an emphasis on industries pertinent to Chinese market norms.
- Offer financial aid for the cost-sharing of export infrastructure, including business-to-business gatherings, trade exhibitions, and online marketing platforms.

Support from Institutions for Trade Diversification

Clarifying export routes is necessary to reduce dependency on China.

- Engage in active negotiations with target markets, such as the US, EU, ASEAN, the Gulf, and Africa, regarding free trade agreements, mutual recognition agreements, and certification cooperation.
- To assist with sourcing, business-to-business connections, and market information sharing, more diaspora networks, trade promotion organizations, and Indian missions ought to be established.

Increased Output and Proficiency

To maintain long-term competitiveness, connect postsecondary education and job training programs to manufacturing demands (information technology, supply chain, and engineering).

- Work together with academia and industry to create centres of excellence and technology clusters for Made-in-India.
- To assist MSMEs in keeping skilled employees, offer salary incentive plans and funding for on-the-job training.

Resilience & Strategic Risk Management

To reduce non-economic risks like supply disruptions and geopolitical issues, proactive planning is crucial.

- Promote supplier diversity and set procurement standards to support dual and multi-sourcing procurement strategies.
- Offer buffer inventory support or stock-holding strategies for essential components.
- Make export licensing schedules easier to understand and offer backup assistance in the event of disruptions.

Monitoring and Assessment Structure

To guarantee effective implementation,

- Establish a Trade Facilitation Council comprising members from government, business, and export groups. It will meet every three months to analyse information, move quickly, and address developing issues.
- Provide real-time dashboards to track infrastructure quality, scheme use, trade volume diversification, and export aims.

The aforementioned integrated policy pathway, which combines trade diversification, infrastructure investments, skill development, cost reduction, and fiscal incentives, aims to strengthen India's trade architecture. If internal competitiveness is addressed while enhancing market access frameworks, Indian businesses will be better able to overcome structural barriers, reduce their dependence on a single country, and become more resilient in an increasingly uncertain global trade environment.

SUMMARY

The bilateral trade relationship between China and India is marked with operational, structural, and regulatory problems that affect Indian stakeholders, both exporters and importers trading with China, notwithstanding its historical significance and economic impact. The bilateral trade has its roots in past, along the silk route trade and presently the nature of trade has changed from the times when we used to exchange silks and spices along with other articles. India opened up its economy with 1991 reforms and is a founding member of World Trade Organization (WTO). China became a member of WTO in year 2000. Both nations aimed at greater integration with the world economy. India's share in world trade is around 2 per cent whereas China's share in world trade stands at around 12 per cent. Both nations are competing for market at world level. At the bilateral level, the trade between two nations has consistently improved over time. The volume of trade has increased especially after 2000 when China joined WTO but the nature of trade is more in favour of China over the years. There has been significant trade imbalance over the years and India has had a persistent trade deficit while trading with China which has even crossed the $100 billion mark recently. India has held numerous discussions with Chinese side to improve market access for Indian products in Chinese market and the progress has been slow but steady.

The bilateral relations are also marked by trust deficits and border skirmishes like it happened in Galwan Valley in 2020. Thereby there were calls for boycott of Chinese goods in Indian markets. The Covid-19 pandemic also brought into focus the overreliance on China for meeting our import needs and to take steps to reduce this dependency and take steps to increase our integration with the global supply chains. With this, India initiated programmes such as 'Make in India', 'Aatmanirbhar Bharat' and invited foreign companies to set up manufacturing plants in India under 'Production linked incentives scheme' (PLI) which many countries responded to as part of their own China plus one strategy. India initiated these programmes in order to promote self-reliance and development of India's manufacturing sector which contributes significantly to GDP of the country, provides employment and helps in earning foreign exchange through exports.

With this background, a survey of 120 Indian exporters and importers in significant industries like textiles, medicines, metals, machinery, and food, is conducted. This chapter highlights the numerous and persistent difficulties faced by Indian businesses conducting business with China. Major issues include the inverted duty structure on imports of inputs which raises their costs thereby adding to cost of production, inconsistent quality of locally sourced inputs, and heavy reliance on high-duty Chinese raw materials. Inadequate infrastructure, especially in the areas of cargo handling, logistics, and warehousing, raises costs and decreases export efficiency and exports competitiveness. Limited financial access and a shortage of skilled labor are two more factors impeding MSME exports growth. Even with a range of export promotion initiatives, procedural complexity hinders stakeholder participation and access. On the demand side, exporters encounter non-tariff barriers, regulatory opacity, and intense competition in the Chinese market. India's increasing reliance on imports, particularly in critical sectors, and geopolitical uncertainties have prompted calls for trade diversification. External factors like global competition and exchange rate volatility also affect export performance. The results emphasize the need for targeted policy reform, infrastructure development, and strategic trade realignment in order to increase India's trade competitiveness and decrease its vulnerability with respect to trade with China.

Strategic Priorities for Policymakers

The following proprieties of strategic policy are derived from these findings in order to address various stakeholder concerns and further improve India's trade engagement:

a) **Simplify Tariffs and Fix the Inverted Duty Structure**: Import taxes must align in line with the strategic industrial objectives, and accordingly the tariff structure must be modified to make it more input-friendly. Lowering of the taxes on raw and intermediate materials can lead to lower production costs and make Indian export prices more competitive in the world.
b) **Expand Export Supply Chains and Infrastructure**: Specifically in tier-2 and tier-3 cities, investing in multi-modal logistics parks, testing facilities, export-specific warehouses, and packaging hubs can significantly minimize the transaction costs. Public-private partnerships (PPPs) should be encouraged to establish integrated export clusters that offer end-to-end solutions to cater to trade problems.
c) **Improve Export Promotion Scheme Accessibility**: Digitalizing is a prerequisite to optimize trade instability. Scheme utilization can be raised by digitizing scheme applications and optimizing the administrative procedures. Also, export facilitation centres at the state and district levels can also help MSMEs understand and take advantage of various incentives.
d) **Promote technological advancement and R&D investment**: The Indian companies, particularly MSMEs, should be encouraged to embrace international production standards and make requisite R&D investments. Government-backed innovation grants, R&D tax credits, and industry-academia partnerships should also be promoted to aid in the development of sector-specific technologies.
e) **Expand Access to market and Trade Diversification Initiatives**: Governments must fund investigations into potential emerging markets especially the United States, Vietnam, Indonesia, Germany, and Japan. Bilateral trade agreements, upbeat diplomatic efforts to boost trade, and the acknowledgment of reciprocal standards all aim to reduce market entrance obstacles which are the main characteristics of Indo-China trade.
f) **Enhance Labor Productivity and focus on Skill Development**: Wage assistance initiatives, advanced manufacturing upskilling, and educational programs made specifically to the demands of export-oriented businesses can all help boost labour productivity and skill development. The National Skill Development

Corporation (NSDC) and industrial chambers ought to work together on export cluster-specific skill-building initiatives.

g) **Simplify Trade Documentation Process and Regulatory Compliance Procedures**: Export-import documentation and clearance at customs may be conducted through a single window, eliminating procedural delays. India could collaborate with China and other important trade partner countries to standardize standards in order to reduce technical trade barriers and improve export participation.

h) **Strengthen Export Finance Systems**: It is challenging for Indian exporters, particularly those in the MSME sector, to secure reasonable finance. Reduced collateral requirements, expanded ECGC coverage, and increased cash distribution to the Interest Equalization Scheme can all assist in preventing this.

i) **Increase Product Promotion in China and Brand India**: Indian enterprises must improve their product branding, product presentation, and customer outreach in the Chinese B2B and B2C sectors. Trade exhibitions, e-commerce partnerships, and India-specific booths at foreign trade events are all ways the government can help.

j) **Encourage Large-Scale Domestic Manufacturing**: Policymakers should give subsidies for growing manufacturing sector output with main focus on electronics, autos, and chemicals, through initiatives such as the Production Linked Incentive (PLI) scheme and cluster-based industrial growth.

Final Reflections: Towards a Resilient Trade Strategy

Economic interdependence and geopolitical issues actively contribute to the complex nuances of India's trading relationship with China. The study's findings show that, while Indian importers and exporters continue to rely on Chinese markets and products but are also becoming more aware of the risks and inequities associated with doing so.

A comprehensive proposal which combines the objectives of independence from import dependence and enhancing global competitiveness must lay the groundwork for the shift from vulnerability to resilience and self-reliance. Instead of implementing a reactive trade strategy, India should adopt a more proactive, stakeholder-focused, and institutionally integrated approach.

Furthermore, there is overwhelming evidence to support tight state-business partnership. Importers and exporters not only carry out trade policies, but they also help guiding India's global integration. Their perspectives, operational experience, and input must be included during the policy-making process. Advisory councils, industry engagements, and evidence-based policy experiments can help reduce the design-to-implementation gap.

Furthermore, resilience in trade cannot be accomplished in silos. Joint coordination between the Ministries of Commerce, Finance, External Affairs, Skill Development, and MSME is necessary to carry out coordinated initiatives encompassing fiscal incentives, infrastructure, market access, and skill development.

Lastly, India's diplomatic stance must be compatible with its economic ambitions. Strategic interactions with China should centre on addressing apprehensions regarding market access, maintaining trade agreements, and combating unfair trade practices—all without endangering national interests—via multilateral agencies such as the WTO, BRICS, and RCEP discussions.

As global supply logistics grow more fluid, India has a limited but essential opportunity to increase its economic sovereignty, reduce over dependence on imports, and refocus its strategy to enhance exports capability. The present chapter examines the current difficulties and proposes a strategy for such systemic transformation.

REFERENCES

Aayog, N. I. T. I. (2024). *Boosting exports from MSMEs: A roadmap to enhance digital infrastructure, simplify compliance, and improve access to incentives.* Government of India.

Arora, K. (2024) 'Unveiling the Nexus: Technological Capacity and Export Performance in Indian Manufacturing Firms through Technical Efficiency Analysis', *SSRN*, pp. 1-35. DOI: 10.2139/ssrn.4792474

Banerjee, D. (2024). Can India become the world's 'China plus one' in tech manufacturing? APF Canada. https://www.asiapacific.ca/publication/can-india-become-worlds-china-plus-one-in-tech-manufacturing

Banik, N., & Kim, M. (2024). India–ASEAN trade relations: Examining the trends and identifying the potential. *Global Business Review*, *25*(2, suppl), S59–S77. DOI: 10.1177/0972150920953546

Castellani, D., & Fassio, C. (2019). From new imported inputs to new exported products. Firm-level evidence from Sweden. *Research Policy*, *48*(1), 322–338. DOI: 10.1016/j.respol.2018.08.021

Cavusgil, S. T., & Zou, S. (1994). Marketing strategy–performance relationship: An investigation of the empirical link in export market ventures. *Journal of Marketing*, *58*(1), 1–21. DOI: 10.1177/002224299405800101

China Briefing. (2025). China-India economic ties: Trade, investment, and opportunities. China Briefing. https://www.china-briefing.com/news/china-india-economic-ties-trade-investment-and-opportunities/

Deolekar, O., & Tiwari, V. (2024) 'Inverted duty structure in India: origin, impact and solutions', ECGC Research. https://main.ecgc.in/wp-content/themes/pcwebecgc/images/pcECGPagePDF/ResearchArticle/ECGC_Research_Inverted_Duty_Structure_Report.pdf

Dhiman, R., & Sharma, M. (2019). Relation between labour productivity and export competitiveness of Indian textile industry: Co-integration and causality approach. *Vision (Basel)*, *23*(1), 22–30. DOI: 10.1177/0972262918821230

. Directorate General of Foreign Trade. (2024) 'Export Promotion Schemes. Trade Promotion Wing (DGFT) Mumbai'

Economic Times. (2025). China lifts curbs on fertilizers, rare earths & tunnel boring machines to India. https://economictimes.indiatimes.com/news/economy/foreign-trade/china-lifts-curbs-on-fertilizers-rare-earths-tunnel-boring-machines-to-india/articleshow/123377378.cms?from=mdr

Garrett, H., & Woodworth, R. (1969) ‘ Statistics and Education’, Bombay: Valkis, Feffer and Simons. Pp- 329.

Global Trade Research Initiative. (2023) ‘India-China trade: Low exports and not high imports is the real challenge for India’. https://gtri.co.in/gtriRep3.pdf

Global Trade Research Initiative. (2024) ‘An Examination of India’s growing Industrial sector imports from China’. www.GTRI.co.in

Government of India. (2016) ‘National Capital Goods Policy: Building India of Tomorrow’. https://www.cgsc.in/pdf/Capital%20Goods%20Policy%2020 16.pdf

Government of India. (2023) ‘Trade deficit between India and China’. Accessed on 27 September, 2024. https://sansad.in/getFile/annex/262/AU690. pdf?source=pqars

Handoyo, R. D., Ibrahim, K. H., Rahmawati, Y., Faadhillah, F., Ogawa, K., Kusumawardani, D., See, K. F., Kumaran, V. V., & Gulati, R. (2024). Determinants of exports performance: Evidence from Indonesian low-, medium-, and high-technology manufacturing industries. *PLoS One*, *19*(1), e0296431. DOI: 10.1371/journal.pone.0296431 PMID: 38165859

Headly, M. (2024) ‘China Market Entry Strategy: How to Enter the Chinese Market’, B2BInternational. Accessed on 27 September, 2024. https://www.b2binternational.com/publications/china-market-entry/

Indiafilings (2022). Export House Certificate. https://www.indiafilings.com/ learn/export-house-certificate/

Lall, S. (2000). The Technological structure and performance of developing country manufactured exports, 1985-98. *Oxford Development Studies*, *28*(3), 337–369. DOI: 10.1080/713688318

Mubarik, M. S., Devadason, E. S., & Govindaraju, C. (2020). Human capital and export performance of small and medium enterprises in Pakistan. *International Journal of Social Economics*, *47*(5), 643–662. DOI: 10.1108/IJSE-03-2019-0198

Olyanga, A. M., Shinyekwa, I. M., Ngoma, M., Nkote, I. N., Esemu, T., & Kamya, M. (2022). Export logistics infrastructure and export competitiveness in the East African Community. *Modern Supply Chain Research and Applications*, *4*(1), 39–61. DOI: 10.1108/MSCRA-09-2021-0017

Raju, D., & Thillai Rajan, A. (2019). SME Performance and Access to Export Markets: The Role of Institutional Credit. In Manimala, M., Wasdani, K., & Vijaygopal, A. (Eds.), *Transnational Entrepreneurship. Entrepreneurship and Development in South Asia: Longitudinal Narratives*. Springer. DOI: 10.1007/978-981-10-6298-8_12

Rehman, F. U., Noman, A. A., & Ding, Y. (2020). Does infrastructure increase exports and reduce trade deficit? Evidence from selected South Asian countries using a new Global Infrastructure Index. *Journal of Economic Structures*, *9*(1), 1–23. DOI: 10.1186/s40008-020-0183-x

Senquiz-Diaz, C. (2021). Transport infrastructure quality and logistics performance in exports. *Economics*, *9*(1), 107–124. DOI: 10.2478/eoik-2021-0008

. Setyorini, D. and Budiono, B. (2020) 'The Impact of Tariff and Imported Raw Materials on Textile and Clothing Export: Evidence from the United States Market', The Impact of Tariff and Imported Raw Materials on Textile and Clothing Export: Evidence from the United States Market, 19.

Srivastava, A. (2023) 'India-China trade: Low exports and not high imports is the real challenge for India', Global Trade Research Initiative. https://content.dgft.gov .in/Website/EPS.pdf

Tadesse, B. (2024) 'How China overcame culture barrier', The Statesman. Accessed on 27 September, 2024. https://www.thestatesman.com/opinion/ how-china-overcame-culture-barrier-1503317440.html

. Wang, X. (2013) 'The determinants of textile and apparel export performance in Asian countries', Iowa state university.

Yeo, A. D., Deng, A., & Nadiedjoa, T. Y. (2020). The effect of infrastructure and logistics performance on economic performance: The mediation role of international trade. *Foreign Trade Review*, *55*(4), 450–465. DOI: 10.1177/0015732520947676

Yildirim, H. S., Akci, Y., & Eksi, I. H. (2013). The effect of firm characteristics in accessing credit for SMEs. *Journal of Financial Services Marketing*, *18*(1), 40–52. DOI: 10.1057/fsm.2012.28

Chapter 12

Predict and Prosper Application of Advanced Machine Learning for FMCG Consumer Behavior Prediction

Sakshi Choudhary
https://orcid.org/0000-0002-4685-5026
Lovely Professional University, India

Devinder Kumar
https://orcid.org/0000-0003-4892-458X
Lovely Professional University, India

Saurabh Kumar Pal
https://orcid.org/0000-0002-4685-5026
Lovely Professional University, India

ABSTRACT

FMCG industry operates in a fast-moving competitive with consumer preferences changing constantly due to both socio-economic digital influences. Understanding- and predicting-consumer behavior is the key for FMCG companies to optimally run supply chains, enhance customer touch. Traditional sales data and qualitative market research fail to capture the changes of consumer preferences in real time. This paper will explore several ML algorithms with respect to decision trees, random forests, deep learning models, . The present study merges the transactional data at structured levels and unstructured sources of social media sentiment and consumer

DOI: 10.4018/979-8-3373-2772-3.ch012

review and demographic variables in order to develop holistic predictive models by using the various techniques of feature engineering, data pre-processing methodologies, and metrics for model performance evaluation . Results show that predictive analytics based on ML significantly strengthens the decision-making process away from businesses predicting consumers' need to reducing supply chain inefficiencies and improving the customer experience

INTRODUCTION

In the society and present stage of development where is more prevalence of Artificial Intelligence It's very crucial and matter of concern to analyze and understand consumer behaviour for businesses now a days. Process of decisions making and setting strategies in the industries now a days are data-driven, like in the case of Fast-Moving Consumer Goods Industry. FMCG industry deals mainly with low-profit, necessities, and products where we can say that customer taste and preferences and their buying patterns are key success factors. In the wave of digital era and continuously changing lifestyles, digitalization of demands and products, and increasing consumer expectations, traditional ways analyzing consumer behavior is no longer sufficient for predicting behavior. Machine Learning (ML) is now being treated or used as an ally (key to open the locks) that allows organizations to analyze big and bulk consumer data for patterns and accurately predicting future trends.

By using the recent ML, FMCG companies can improve their customer engagement, optimize marketing as well as can better understand purchasing behaviour of their customers. ML stands for Machine Learning that reflects opportunities, which make use of coding Artificial Intelligence that can resolve easily issues with data complexity, and interpretation of model results. By addressing important issues and possibilities using ML this study attempts to investigate how ML can be used for forecasting consumer behaviour especially in the FMCG sector. This research is conducted with the objective to create a comprehensive approach that improves strategic planning and decision-making by combining behavioural, psychographic as well as demographic data. In today's fast moving and hyper-competitive world with more use of Artificial Intelligence consumer behavior is the critical enabler for business strategies as well as determining the growth/decay of markets. Consumers' decisions play an important role in upswings and downswings of the company because consumers tastes and preferences literally boil down what they buy and how they buy items as well as which brands to prefer over others.

It should be noted that due to this factor, knowledge about consumer behavior becomes more and more crucial, particularly within the Fast-Moving Consumer Goods segment, where buying behavior is habitual and subject to price.

The factors like Brand image, quality, and price perception are very crucial in determining and influencing decision-making among consumers as well as firms. Along with this the other psychological factors like Emotions, attitudes, and past experience with a product also influence their consumer behavior. The different reasons can be biasedness due to familiarity with brands and habitual consumption. If we take the example of FMCG sector, the most influencing factors are market forces, brand loyalty and consumer interaction, economics of scale, technological along with digital influences. The cultural and social factors also impact purchase behavior. Major Market Forces affecting the FMCG Industry are changing Consumer Attitudes, consumers wanted health-oriented consumption, Sustainability of products, Convenience, taste, quality and time-saving, Digital Shift and Growth of E-Commerce, D2C players, Personalization of products based on data, Omnichannel retailing, Economic and Competitive Forces, Regulatory and Ethical concerns, Innovation. ML can be called as a revolutionary method in recent past years to understand and predicting consumer behavior.

One of the fields of artificial intelligence called machine learning (ML) allows computers to analyze bulk and big data to discover trends and patterns in them, and helping in very accurate forecasting and predictions regarding the future (Russell & Norvig, 2021). IT has significantly contributed to better decision-making for FMCG firms along logistics or supply chain management. Now a days Companies can collect easily and analyze customer information collected from various sources including purchases, website interactions, and social media behavior by making use of ML that is artificial intelligence (Provost & Fawcett, 2019). These developments in the field of AI can understand trends and patterns that earlier were impossible to find, making it possible for businesses to foresee or forecasting, requirement of the customers. But now ML algorithms have changed the scenario, companies can segment consumers in terms of buying behavior, which allows businesses to produce highly customized advertising campaigns (Hofacker et al., 2020). In the same way ML can forecast purchasing patterns, reduce inventory expense as well as can maintain a supply of product at the correct time.

If look into the uses of ML within the FMCG sector is personalization of consumer demands. With the expectation of the companies to understand the different taste and preferences of customers, brands should be able to deliver tailored experiences at the door step of consumers (Sun et al., 2019). For recommending products there is need to create personalized promotions, and even forecasting future purchases using ML algorithms and also for studying individual behaviour.

Personalization of products can build and create brand loyalty to a larger extent, which in turn is the primary requirements in today's competitive markets for companies to grow more and fast. It is suggested that ML holds tremendous promises and its adoption in the FMCG industry is not without its challenges and barriers.

Most of the existing research and literature focused on isolated aspects of consumer behavior, such as churn prediction or sales forecasting, and does not take into account the broader context, here we are taking into account. The integration of the socio-economic factors like demographic, psychographic, and behavioural data into a single framework is lacking in the earlier research, for capturing the complete picture of consumer decision-making, this kind of integration in the form of study is crucial.

It has been found and evident from many examples that that many ML techniques and models were not able to explain and interpret properly, and thus makes it complex for companies to believe and take necessary action on predictions (Molnar, 2022). It is a highly recommendable that use of the ML leads to handle issues with accountability-transparency in sensitive area such as consumer data and privacy concerns. That's why it is necessary to provide remedies for these issues and ensure that machine learning tools are reliable, ethical, and efficient. The only remedy for this is the application of ML in decision making.

In the same direction and backdrop this research paper made an attempt to bridge research gaps with a comprehensive and established framework where diverse data types can be combined. This can enhance the accuracy and applicability of consumer buying behavior predictions for companies in real world. Necessary action needed to be taken in the direction towards explainable ML models, where goal is to give better insights that businesses can use with confidence and surety.

FMCG companies conduct of business is seeking to remain competitive in the fast-changing market, that can be well-served by the conclusions of the research. To the same proverbial end, an understanding of the nuances of consumer behavior further enables the company to create products and services that could better serve customer demands (Grewal & Levy, 2022). Companies can minimize waste, optimize overall operational effectiveness, and deploy resources efficiently by monitoring trends. This research emphasizes the importance of making strategic choices through data.

As a matter of concern as well as fact, consumers' preferences are changing overnight, the use of intuition or old methods of market research is not considered to be enough in this world (Davenport & Ronanki, 2018). Instead, there is need that business have to adapt advanced analytics and ML tools to tackle the complexities of the modern-day consumer changing taste and prefernces.

How the ML is better and how the traditional method is not sufficient for increase of sales, lets take some examples

1. Let's take example of Hindustan Unilever (HUL), India uses consumer data from rural and urban markets to track shifts in preferences for examples company is taking into consideration growing demand for herbal/pure products and services. It is also found that HUL is tied up with NielsenIQ and also using advanced

analytics for adjusting production and making strategy for market distribution channels.

2. **Another example we can consider is "Nestlé"** with the changing consumer taste toward healthy options, Nestlé introduced low-sugar and organic product lines like Milo less sugar. Nestle also used predictive analytics to forecast demand in different regions for deciding output and pricing.
3. **Same with the Coca-Cola** employed machine learning to analyze digital interactions for its growth and betterment/, only based on data driven insights, launched *Coca-Cola Zero Sugar* and etc. AI driven supply chain of Coco cola ensured optimal stock levels based on consumer demand prediction.
4. Another example that can be considered here **P&G who integrated ML** for getting consumer insights across beauty/hygiene products. Like in the situation of During COVID-19, predictive modelling helped them to quickly respond to the surge in demand for medical care products.

LITERATURE REVIEW

Sisodiya and Sharma (2018) analyzed relationships among the factors like product, price, place, promotion, and consumer buying behavior specially in FMCG marketing. They found that price was the factor that affected mostly the consumer buying decisions. It also highlighted that the need for businesses to become responsive to changing requirements and perspectives of consumers.

Madhavan and Chandrasekar (2015) has studied consumer purchasing behavior and decision-making processes related to various factors such as cultural, social, personal, and psychological factors which affect buying decisions.

Newman and Crawford only focused on various kinds of buying behavior bringing attention to five stages of buying behavior: the stages are 1) need recognition, 2) information search, 3) evaluation, purchasing, and 4) post-purchase behavior. The authors laid down the basic understanding important for consumer behavior studies in the near future.

Ramya and Mohamed Ali (2016) in their study investigated into the multi-dimensional form of buying behavior. They argued that multi-layered processes involved in purchasing. Consumer choice arises from personal enjoyment but affected by factors like culture, social, and economics. It has been observed that ML is valuable for marketers in designing strategies for their target audience. They argued that only in knowing a consumer journey could marketers enhance customer satisfaction along with loyalty.

Jain et al. (2021) in their research explained how the sentiment analysis using online reviews involved machine learning and also highlighted how the opinions of the customers inform retail and FMCG business operations in real world. Their study showed how ML algorithms can scan and interpret the moods of customers in bulk of data, so that business houses can take necessary actions to respond to customer inputs. Günesen et al. (2021) in their research used ML for predicting the churn of customers especially n the FMCG sector. They highlighted that utility of ML to develop custom retention policies based on purchase, Trend and patterns as well as customer interactions.

Khrais in the year 2020 observed that there is potential of artificial intelligence in making personalized consumer experiences-based products. He thus recommended that AI can change purchasing behavior and patterns along with improved customer satisfaction through customizing and personalized offerings. Chaudhuri et al. (2021) in their study demonstrated the power of ML methods in the retailing industry, thus indicating that deep learning can accurately predict consumer buying behavior and demand forecasting.

Orogun and Onyekwelu, (2019) analyzed the ability of ML modelling to capture the output dynamics in dynamic environments. They highlighted adaptability of consumer behavior with ML techniques. Marques et al. (2024) also observed that same what found by orogun for predicting consumer preferences and can give more better insights. This study tried to test psychology as well as technology together which opened as new way to understanding consumer responses.

Senthilnayaki et al. (2021) and Manzoor et al. in the year 2024 together explored advanced ML models. Khottak et al. (2023) introduced a composite deep learning model for predicting churns. Their study focused on the utilization of multiple techniques of learning together for better predictions. Smith and Brown (2022) investigated supervised learning methodologies for FMCG consumer profile prediction. They considered decision trees and random forests with examples to determine their efficiency in classifying the preferences of the clients and helping in the strategy of targeted marketing.

Chatterjee and Roy (2021) in their study used and developed neural networks to predict consumer purchasing tendencies on an e-commerce platform. Mostly used time series data on consumer purchases in which they applied deep learning algorithms. Zhou and Zhang (2023) applied ensemble approaches included gradient boosting and bagging techniques for forecasting FMCG customer preferences. Results highlighted that ensemble learning improves the precision of demand prediction models. Kumar and Singh (2022) applied deep learning techniques with RNNs and CNNs for predicting the frequency of a consumer buying. They revealed with statistical proven results that deep learning actually does outperform the conventional statistical models. Ali and Hassan (2020) applied clustering and classification techniques for FMCG customer churn prediction in 2020 and they were able to identify that potential churners to create focused retention campaigns.

The results of this study indicate SVM models for loyalty prediction are stronger and a more understandable format.

Patel and Sharma (2022) examined reinforcement learning for dynamic pricing for fast-moving consumer goods (FMCG). Their research applied Q-learning algorithms used to develop price learning strategies dependent on market demand and user behavior maximizing the benefit attributable to price. Chen and Wang (2023) develop a hybrid recommendation with collaborative filtering and deep learning-based recommendations. This led to an increase in the accuracy of predictions and personalization of FMCG consumer preference modeling. Garcia and Lopez (2020) utilized unsupervised learning methods, such as principal component analysis and hierarchical clustering, for demographic-based segmentation of FMCG consumers. In their study they observed that purchasing behavior differs among consumers significantly from one demographic group to another across sections.

Das and Ghosh (2021) conducted sentiment analysis and prediction analytics on social media data to predict the sales of FMCG products with their prediction analytics using consumer sentiment as a leading indicator of demand. Ahmad and Rana (2023) provided a study employing CNNs to study visual data to determine the influence shelf placement and packaging had on purchasing decisions, focusing on visual analytics with FMCG product placement. Jones and White (2020) analyzed cross-category buying behavior using Bayesian networks. The authors determined cross-category relationships between product categories to maximize bundled sales strategies. Lee and Park (2023) article showed how advanced natural language processing techniques enabled demand forecasting through analysis of consumer Buying behavior. Williams and Taylor (2020) discovered that machine learning is a superior method for long term customer management in the FMCG industry. Huang and Liu (2023) investigated how reinforcement learning can optimize supply chain logistics FMCG industry. Fernandez et al. (2022) used deep learning methods to study voice assistant interactions for consumer insights. Research conducted by Fernandez in 2022 provided arguments in that NLP models can improve personalized marketing in the market. Kim and Choi (2021) developed an AI-based system for chatbots in FMCG retail to facilitate customer engagement. Results indicated that chatbot interaction can boost conversion rates and improve customer satisfaction. Rodriguez and Martinez (2020) federated learning techniques were applied by the authors for privacy-preserving consumer behavior prediction in FMCG. The potential of decentralized AI models in retail analytics was highlighted in their study. Zheng and Wu (2022) deep reinforcement learning were successfully utilized to optimize digital advertising strategies in FMCG. The performance in the FMCG sector saw a big increase in CTR and CVR rates in the market among consumers. Bose and Mukherjee (2023) developed evolutionary algorithms for optimizing real-time product pricing. Their study argued that the adaptive pricing models were better than that of static pricing models in the existing market. Singh and Gupta (2022) in their research explored reinforcement learning for shelf-space allocation as well as optimization in supermarkets. They observed that space management using AI resulted in more sales as well as improved consumer engagement. Zhao et al. (2023) described transfer learning techniques for cross-market FMCG demand forecasting. The model quite frequently adapted consumer preferences across different geographical regions. Fischer and Weber (2022) adopted ensemble learning methods for enhanced fraud detection in FMCG e-commerce transactions. The findings from the study showed that amalgamation of decision trees, SVM, and deep learning yields a better and enhanced accuracy level. Li and Chen (2021) applied modeling techniques on the data collected from social media on FMCG to study trends in customer sentiments.

Research Objectives

1. To develop ML framework that integrates different data in order to forecast FMCG consumer behavior.
2. To understand the dynamic decision-making using real-time adaptive machine learning algorithms.

MATERIAL AND METHODS

For the purpose of achieving the objectives of the study Random Sampling technique has been employed with keeping in consideration the reduced selection bias. For providing better representation and insights for various consumer groups, Stratified Sampling has been employed. A total sample of 166 participants was selected, comprising of different demographic and behavioural traits. Firstly, the collected data analysed using descriptive statistics to summarize key characteristics of the consumers. Then in the next step applied Measures of central tendency like mean, median, and mode for understanding consumer behaviour in more detail. Along with these descriptive statistics, frequency distributions revealed purchasing patterns and variances. Further for more better insights graphical presentation was done like bar charts, pie charts, and histograms were used.

Exploratory Data Analysis (EDA) was applied to understand and drawing insights for trends/patterns in the consumer buying behaviour. Analysis in the study involved correlational analysis to understand how the demographic variables and buying behaviour are inter related or correlated with each other. Because consumer buying behaviour is complex so machine learning (ML) approaches were incorporated into the research. Data collection was conducted through APIs linked to platforms such as Shopify and Salesforce, as well as surveys and third-party aggregators.

Preprocessing involved data cleaning to remove duplicates and fix anomalies, with missing numerical values being imputed using the column mean. With regards to logic in code used in the analysis, a pipeline based on Python with Pandas was used for loading dataset and cleaning and preparing for model training. For predictive modelling features like Age, Income, Purchase Frequency, and Brand Loyalty were chosen, with the Purchase Decision as the target or output variable. In the later stage dataset was subsequently divided with an 80-20 train-test split for testing model generalizability.

import pandas as pd, # Load consumer behavior dataset, data = pd.read_csv("-consumer_behavior.csv"), # Display first few rows, print(data.head()), # Checking for missing values, print(data.isnull().sum()), # Handling missing values (is any), data.fillna(data.mean(), inplace=True), # Model selection (choose one or try different models)

```
   # Logistics Regression, model_lr = LogisticRegression(),
model_lr.fit(X_train, y_train), y_pred_lr - model_lr.predict(X_
test), # Random Forest,
   model_rf = RandomForestclassifier(n_estimators=100)
   model_rf.fit(X_train, y_train)
   y_pred_rf = model_rf.predict(X_test)
   # Evaluate model performance
   print("Logistics Regression Accuracy:", accuracy_score(y_
test, y_pred_lr))
   print("Logistics Regression Classification Report:", classi-
fication_report(y_test, y_pred_lr))
   print("Random Forest Accuracy:", accuracy_score(y_test, y_
pred_rf))
   print("Random Forest Classification Report:", classifica-
tion_report(y_test, y_pred_rf))
   # Use the trained model to make predictions on new data
   # Add new customer data with features
   new_customer_data = ()
   predictions = model_rf.predict(new_customer_data)
   print("Predicted Consumer Behavior:", predictions)
```

ANALYSIS AND FINDING

The chapter interprets the data collected through SPSS. Data include those related to demographics and/or behaviors, psychology, socially, or economically in relation to consumer buying behavior. The different statistical methods employed when carrying out the analysis revealed relations and areas of interest, e.g., descriptive statistics, correlation, factor analysis, and regression modeling.

Table 1. Demographic distribution of respondents

Category		Frequency	Percent	Valid Percent	Cumulative Percent
Age of the Respondent	18–24	97	36.6	36.6	74.3
	25–34	33	12.5	12.5	86.8
	35–44	12	4.5	4.5	91.3
	45–54	13	4.9	4.9	96.2
	Above 55	10	3.8	3.8	100
Gender of the Respondent	Female	56	21.1	21.1	58.9
	Male	109	41.1	41.1	100
Occupation of the Respondent	High School	18	6.8	6.8	44.5
	Postgraduate	88	33.2	33.2	77.7
	Undergraduate	59	22.3	22.3	100
	Business Owner	20	7.5	7.5	45.3
	Professional	28	10.6	10.6	55.8
	Retired	6	2.3	2.3	58.1
	Student	111	41.9	41.9	100
	Total	265	100	100	100

Source: Field Survey

The evaluation of age distribution Table shows that a large percentage of respondents are in the age segment of 18-24 years (37.7%), indicating that young people are the main buyers in the FMCG sector. Likely to higher purchasing power and customer shopping behavior. The age distribution represented in table shows age represents the dominant consumer group. Age can also influence consumer purchasing behaviors by influencing buying styles, preferences, spending power and brand loyalty during life stages. Also, note that the respondents were mostly male compared to female, implying that marketing strategies can focus on both sexes but there may be differences in sex-based purchasing behavior using a categorical psychological/taste-based style. Classification by gender impacts consumer purchasing behavior by influencing choice, decision process, buying brand requirements caused by socio-psychological factors and personal needs. Education level distribution table level shows that within their respective educational levels, Bachelor's degree respondents (22.3%) was higher than it Master's degree (33.2%) respectively. This provides evidence that, socially, as it relates to higher education, a higher educated individual is more likely to make informed purchasing decisions and have brand awareness to understand brand quality. Educational level data is illustrated in Figure 3. Education influences consumer purchasing behavior by influencing decision making, brand choice perception, and preferences by way of knowledge and critical thinking. The occupational dispersion table indicates that most of the respondents are employed (10.6%), the next largest group is students (41.9%), and the next largest is business owners (7.5%). Therefore, it is evident that the consumer market of FMCG's marketing typically targets employed persons and students, considering that marketing appeals to the different spending habits and preferences for brands. Occupation is influential in consumer buying behavior because of income level, lifestyle choices, and preferences when choosing a product to meet their professional needs and social status.

Table 2. Distribution of respondents by monthly income

Monthly income	Frequency	Percent	Valid Percent	Cumulative Percent
	100	37.7	37.7	37.7
20,000- 50,000	29	10.9	10.9	48.7
50,000- 1,00,000	27	10.2	10.2	58.9
Above 1,00,000	12	4.5	4.5	63.4
Below 20,000	97	36.6	36.6	100
Total	265	100	100	

Source: Field Survey

Based on the table related to monthly income distribution, the greatest proportion of respondents make between 20,000- 50,000 (10.9%), therefore, the majority of consumers are likely to fall into the middle-income group. Middle-income consumers may be price-conscious and think more about their purchases (e.g., concerned with discounts and promotions). Higher monthly income gives consumers greater purchasing power and allows them to purchase discretionary goods and premium goods.

BEHAVIORAL ANALYSIS: PURCHASE FREQUENCY AND SHOPPING PREFERENCES

Objective: To analyze consumer shopping behavior by examining how often they purchase FMCG products (purchase frequency) and their preferred shopping methods (shopping preferences).

Figure 1. Purchase frequency analysis

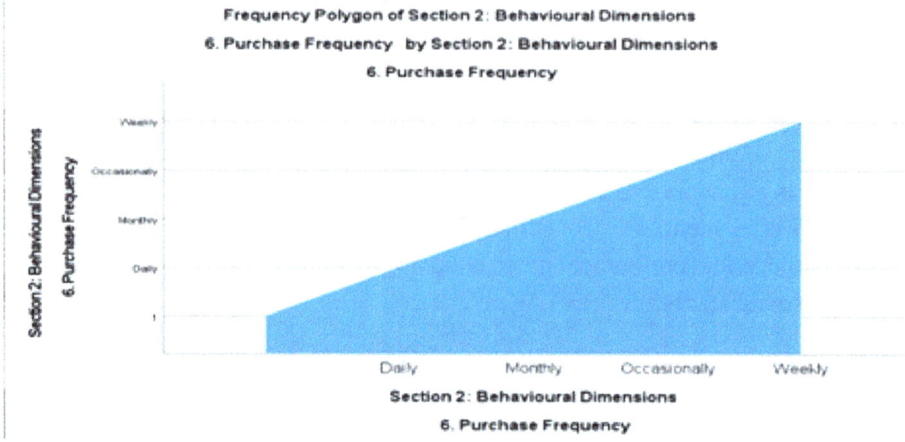

The purchase frequency table analysis has determined that an overwhelming majority of consumers purchase consumer goods regularly (20.8% weekly, YY% monthly), demonstrating a habitual nature of shopping. From the histogram (Figure 2) we can see a normal distribution/type of a skewed distribution, showing that the purchase of consumer goods is mostly habitual consumer demands. Purchase frequency indicates the purchasing behavior of consumers by showing how regular a customer purchases a product, allowing organizations to see the purchasing patterns along with brand loyalty.

Figure 2. Distribution of respondents by shopping preference

The data presented in the charts suggest that 10.2% of individuals have a preference for online shopping while 16.2% prefer shopping in physical stores. The line chart Figure clearly depicts the growing preference for e-commerce which can potentially be explained by the convenience of shopping online, and the greater discounts and greater variety that e-commerce brings. While e-commerce and online shopping have a growing following, there is still a considerable proportion who prefer to shop offline - possibly because consumers might want to check out the physical product before arriving at a purchase decision. Shopping preferences can shape consumer buying behavior by influencing their decisions based on preferences, price sensitivity as well as and brand loyalty.

Next section deals with measuring the impact of branding along with advertisements on consumer purchasing decisions.

Figure 3. Analyzing the importance of branding (likert scale responses)

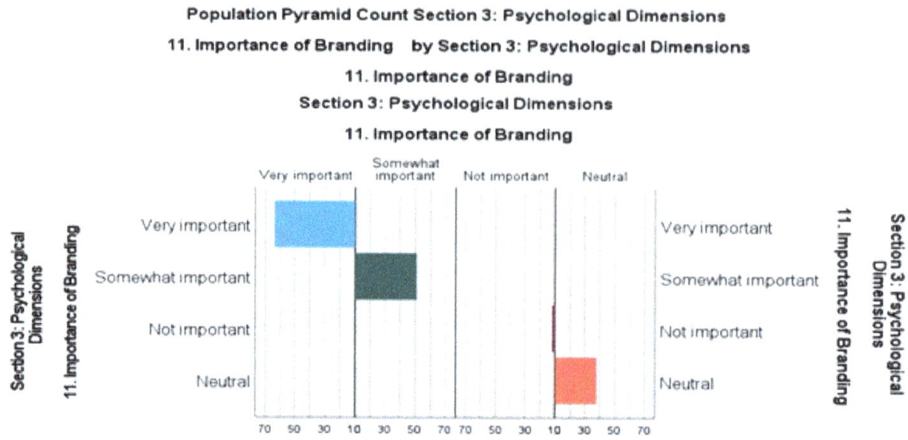

The analysis table indicates that a majority of respondents rated branding as highly important (Likert scale rating: 4 or 5, 43.4%). This suggests that brand reputation significantly influences purchasing decisions.

The mirrored bar chart further substantiates this, demonstrating that consumers primarily view branding as one of the most important factors impacting their buying decisions. Strong branding of the products impacts consumer behavior more by building trust, recognition, and changing the perceptions leads to increase in preference and loyalty.

COMPARING BRANDING IMPORTANCE ACROSS INCOME LEVELS

Figure 4. Box plot of Importance of branding by monthly income

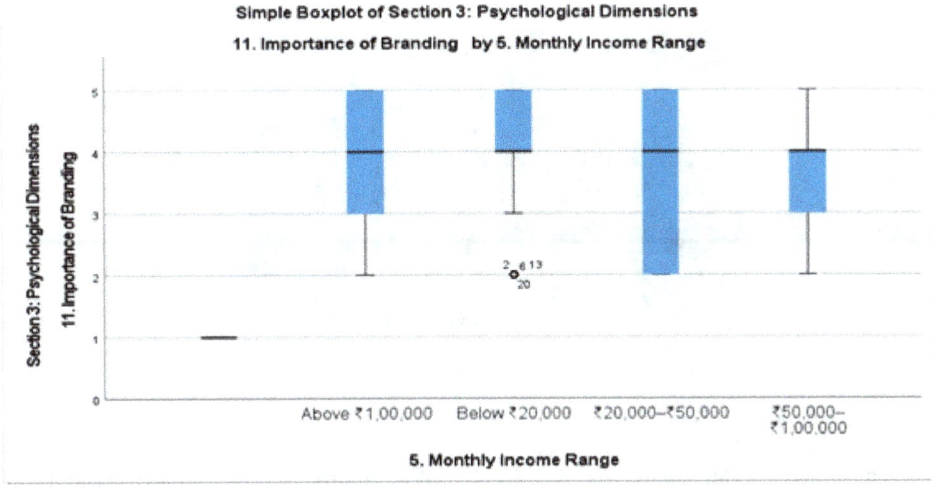

The box plot figure shows a positive correlation of importance or influence by branding and income level. In other words, consumers in the higher income bracket tend to see branding as more important (4-5 = median rating), while claim that branding is not as wrapped up in self-confidence and identity as lower income consumers. While those in the less wealthy categories show a wider range of responses indicating mixed sentiments toward branding, it's likely those with less disposable income typically have a lower level of brand-conscious buying behavior.

ANALYZING THE INFLUENCE OF ADVERTISEMENTS

Figure 5. Bar chart of influence of advertisement by age group

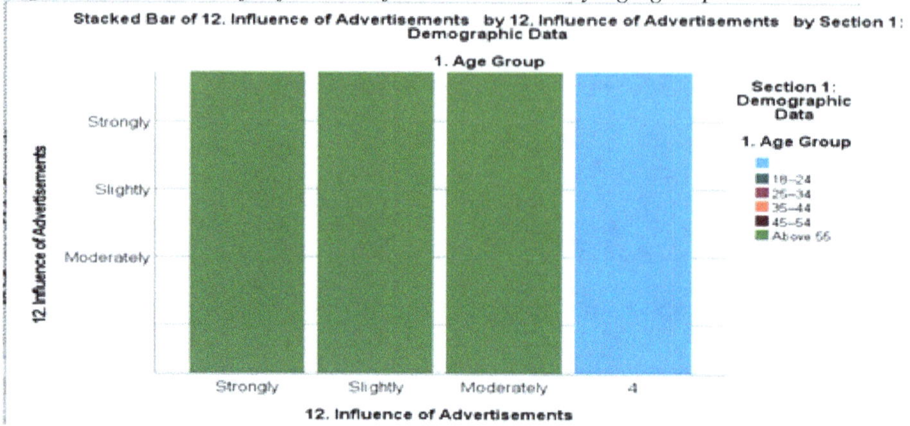

The analysis demonstrates that 17.7% of consumers view advertisements as a considerable influence on their purchasing behavior. The bar chart Figure 10 shows that younger consumers (age 18-34) recorded advertising influence ratings consistently higher than older consumers (age 55+), who generally had lower ratings. Overall, this indicates that digital marketing strategies could primarily focus on younger consumers/users. The influence of advertising plays a primary role in shaping consumer purchasing behavior through developing awareness; changing perceptions and developing loyalty ultimately resulting in buying behavior.

CONCLUSION

In today's world of digitalization ML has become essential in prediction of consumer behavior for FMCG and has great potential to improve business strategies, improving customer engagement and sales forecasting as well. Machine learning models and techniques, such as clustering, classification, and predictive modeling, are now able to analyze bulk and large consumer data sets and make sense of great depth with insights by observing patterns, trends and preferences. The capacity of ML that is predictive capability will allow FMCG to make data driven decisions, to personalize marketing actions, allow better management of inventory and in improving customer satisfaction. ML is utilizing real time data sources from social platforms, online reviews or transactional history which is helping organizations reactions and better decision making in a fast-changing dynamics of consumer environment. Other potential challenges in way of adapting ML models remain such as data privacy, interpretability of models and access to high quality data. For companies and other profit-making organizations to take full advantage of machine learning for predicting consumer behavior involves organizations investing in data management, ethical issues with AI, and continuous improvement of ML models. In nutshell ML provides a powerful means or way to FMCG in getting better insights and understanding of consumer behavior which in turn can increase operational efficiency and sustainability in the competitiveness in a continuously growing and changing market. As technology advances in today's world, the integration of AI-driven analytics will reshape consumer buying behavior prediction and sustainable growth in the industry.

FUTURE RECOMMENDATIONS

a) Based on the analysis of the study it is recommended that AI driven demand forecasting can reduce forecast errors by 20-50%.
b) ML have the potential to increase engagement in personalized marketing by leveraging purchase histories, browsing behaviors, and social media interactions
c) It is highly recommended that Intelligent chatbots as well as using virtual assistants can facilitate customer engagement through real time chat functionality along with sentiment analysis.
d) AI can also facilitate dynamic pricing and promotion optimization using real-time adaptation of prices to demand and other competitor prices. Predictive analytics that leverage structured and unstructured data (sales logs, social reviews) allow FMCG firms to derive actionable consumer insight while predicting trends.

REFERENCES

Ahmad, M., & Rana, S. (2023). Visual analytics for FMCG product placement: A CNN-based approach. *International Journal of Retail Analytics*, *12*(2), 45–60.

Ali, M., & Hassan, R. (2020). Customer churn prediction in FMCG using clustering and classification. *Journal of Business Intelligence*, *18*(3), 77–91.

Bose, S., & Mukherjee, A. (2023). Evolutionary algorithms for real-time product pricing optimization. *Computational Economics*, *61*(4), 995–1012.

Chatterjee, P., & Roy, A. (2021). Neural networks for predicting consumer purchase tendencies in e-commerce. *Journal of Retail Technology*, *7*(2), 110–128.

Chaudhuri, S., Ghosh, A., & Dutta, P. (2021). Deep learning for predicting consumer behavior in retail. *International Journal of Retail & Distribution Management*, *49*(8), 921–938.

Chen, Y., & Wang, Z. (2023). Hybrid recommendation models for FMCG: Collaborative filtering with deep learning. *Expert Systems with Applications*, *217*, 119504.

Das, K., & Ghosh, S. (2021). Social media sentiment as a predictor of FMCG product sales. *Journal of Business Analytics*, *4*(4), 223–238.

Davenport, T. H., & Ronanki, R. (2018). Artificial intelligence for the real world. *Harvard Business Review*, *96*(1), 108–116.

Fernandez, R., Lopez, J., & Martin, S. (2022). Voice assistant interactions for consumer insights: A deep learning approach. *Journal of Interactive Marketing*, *58*(3), 44–59.

Fischer, M., & Weber, H. (2022). Ensemble learning for fraud detection in FMCG e-commerce. *Decision Support Systems*, *153*, 113678.

Garcia, L., & Lopez, P. (2020). Demographic segmentation of FMCG consumers using unsupervised learning. *Journal of Consumer Marketing*, *37*(6), 745–756.

Grewal, D., & Levy, M. (2022). *Marketing* (8th ed.). McGraw Hill.

Günesen, E., Aydin, H., & Kaya, O. (2021). Predicting customer churn in FMCG with machine learning models. *Computers in Industry*, *128*, 103432.

Hofacker, C. F., de Ruyter, K., Lurie, N. H., Manchanda, P., & Donaldson, J. (2020). Artificial intelligence in business and marketing. *Journal of Business Research*, *116*, 136–149.

Huang, Y., & Liu, X. (2023). Reinforcement learning for optimizing supply chain logistics in FMCG. *Computers & Industrial Engineering*, *176*, 108925.

Jain, R., Mehta, S., & Kapoor, N. (2021). Sentiment analysis of online reviews using ML in FMCG. *Journal of Retail Analytics*, *5*(2), 88–104.

Jones, D., & White, S. (2020). Cross-category buying behavior analysis using Bayesian networks. *Journal of Marketing Analytics*, *8*(1), 55–70.

Khottak, F., Rahman, S., & Ali, T. (2023). Composite deep learning models for churn prediction. *Applied Artificial Intelligence*, *37*(5), 421–438.

Khrais, L. (2020). The potential of AI in creating personalized consumer experiences. *International Journal of Artificial Intelligence in Business*, *6*(1), 1–14.

Kim, J., & Choi, H. (2021). AI-enabled chatbots in FMCG retail: A customer engagement study. *Journal of Retailing and Consumer Services*, *62*, 102657.

Kumar, R., & Singh, V. (2022). Deep learning for predicting consumer purchase frequency in FMCG. *Applied Soft Computing*, *120*, 108702.

Lee, J., & Park, H. (2023). NLP for demand forecasting in FMCG consumer behavior analysis. *Journal of Business Research*, *161*, 113758.

Li, M., & Chen, Y. (2021). Analyzing customer sentiments on FMCG using social media data. *Information Processing & Management*, *58*(5), 102584.

Madhavan, S., & Chandrasekar, K. (2015). Consumer purchasing behavior: Cultural and psychological factors. *International Journal of Marketing Studies*, *7*(2), 85–95.

Manzoor, H., Ali, R., & Shah, M. (2024). Advanced ML models for consumer behavior prediction. *Journal of Intelligent Systems*, *33*(1), 101–118.

Marques, J., Silva, T., & Pereira, R. (2024). Psychology and technology in predicting consumer responses. *Journal of Retail Technology*, *12*(1), 66–82.

Molnar, C. (2022). *Interpretable machine learning* (2nd ed.). Leanpub.

Newman, B., & Crawford, J. (2017). *Consumer behavior and buying process.* Routledge.

Nielsen, I. Q. (2022). *Global consumer trends and e-commerce growth in FMCG sector.* https://nielseniq.com/

Orogun, O., & Onyekwelu, U. (2019). ML modeling for consumer dynamics in FMCG. *Journal of Retail Research*, *11*(3), 201–218.

Patel, K., & Sharma, R. (2022). Reinforcement learning for dynamic pricing in FMCG. *Expert Systems: International Journal of Knowledge Engineering and Neural Networks*, *39*(4), e12847.

Provost, F., & Fawcett, T. (2019). *Data science for business: What you need to know about data mining and data-analytic thinking* (2nd ed.). O'Reilly Media.

Ramya, N., & Mohamed Ali, S. (2016). Factors affecting consumer buying behavior. *International Journal of Applied Research*, *2*(10), 76–80.

Rodriguez, L., & Martinez, C. (2020). Federated learning for consumer behavior prediction in FMCG. *Journal of Retail Analytics*, *6*(2), 122–136.

Russell, S., & Norvig, P. (2021). *Artificial intelligence: A modern approach* (4th ed.). Pearson.

Senthilnayaki, S., Prasad, R., & Krishnan, P. (2021). Advanced ML models for predicting consumer churn in FMCG. *International Journal of Machine Learning*, *12*(3), 233–248.

Sisodiya, R., & Sharma, M. (2018). 4Ps and consumer buying behavior in FMCG marketing. *International Journal of Management Studies*, *5*(6), 44–52.

Smith, J., & Brown, L. (2022). Supervised learning for consumer profile prediction in FMCG. *Artificial Intelligence in Business*, *9*(3), 145–163.

Sun, Y., Chen, H., & Xu, P. (2019). Personalized promotions in FMCG using machine learning. *Journal of Business Analytics*, *2*(3), 179–194.

Williams, P., & Taylor, K. (2020). Long-term customer management in FMCG with ML. *The Journal of Consumer Research*, *47*(6), 1121–1135.

Zhao, Q., Wang, H., & Li, Y. (2023). Transfer learning for cross-market demand forecasting in FMCG. *Knowledge-Based Systems*, *263*, 110322.

Zheng, W., & Wu, Y. (2022). Deep reinforcement learning for digital advertising in FMCG. *Journal of Marketing Analytics*, *10*(2), 140–156.

Zhou, L., & Zhang, Q. (2023). Ensemble methods for FMCG demand forecasting. *Journal of Retail Analytics*, *9*(1), 88–10.

Chapter 13
Generative AI Literacy of University Faculty Members in Russia

Olga Alexandrovna Nikiforova
https://orcid.org/0000-0002-5128-5195
Graduate School of Management, Saint Petersburg University, Russia

Olga Alexandrovna Akimova
Business School, Lomonosov Moscow State University, Russia

Aleksandra Konstantinovna Bordunos
Graduate School of Management, Saint Petersburg University, Russia

Ksenia Vladimirovna Kaisheva
Saint Petersburg State University of Industrial Technologies and Design, Russia

Sergey Yurievich Sevryukov
Saint-Petersburg University, Russia

ABSTRACT

The research aimes to develop an AI literacy assessment approach for university faculty members in Russia. Theoretical background formed the TPACK framework and theory of planned behavior. The research design included two stages. During the first stage we conducted an exploratory literature review to analyze existing frameworks for AI-literacy of non-experts in AI, which could be relevant for educational context. During the second stage, content analysis of universities' faculty personal plans and vacancies' announcements on hh.ru helped to derive a list of jobs to be done with a help of generative AI tools. The introduced scale consists of 6

DOI: 10.4018/979-8-3373-2772-3.ch013

groups of tasks, 4 in each: Teaching Activities, Research Activities, Organizational and Methodological Work, Educational and Methodological Work, Professional Development, Consulting Services. We developed a scoring scale to evaluate the level of AI literacy. The authors acknowledges contribution offered by AI Lab of the Center for Teaching Excellence in business education at GSOM SPBU.

INTRODUCTION

The rapid integration of generative artificial intelligence (GenAI) into educational practices has transformed traditional lecturing, research, and administrative workflows. Generative AI tools, such as YandexGPT 5, Shedevrum, MagicSchool AI, have demonstrated promising potential to automate routine tasks, and enhance faculty staff productivity, creativity and quality of achievement.

The integration of artificial intelligence (AI) into the Russian economy is already demonstrating a substantial impact. According to the Higher School of Economics Research (Dranev et al., 2025), AI technologies have the potential to enhance labor productivity by 20–40%, and in certain industries, they can reduce operational costs by up to 30%. According to the forecast, it has the potential to contribute Russian GDP of 11.6 trillion rubles (135 billion USD) by 2030.

However, sustained growth requires not only the implementation of AI solutions, but also a high level of AI literacy of the educators and researchers and the ability to transmit these competencies to future specialists., Effective adoption of relevant tools requires educators to possess certain technical proficiency, awareness about relevant ethical, pedagogical, and operational implications—a competence broadly defined as AI literacy (Ng et al., 2021). In Russia, where digital transformation in education is accelerating under national initiatives like the "Digital Economy" program, the need to equip university faculty with AI literacy has become a strategic priority. Yet, current frameworks for assessing GenAI competencies predominantly target students or professionals from other fields, like medical or technical domains. Low level of general awareness about potential implications of GenAI tools in education makes it difficult to apply traditional methods for upskilling needs assessment, like Jobs to Be Done (JTBD) framework.

This study addresses this gap by proposing a context-specific approach to assess AI literacy among university faculty in Russia. Grounded in the *Technological Pedagogical Content Knowledge (TPACK)* framework, which emphasizes the interplay between technology, pedagogy, and subject-matter expertise, and the *Theory of Planned Behavior* (Ajzen, 1991), which links attitudes and intentions to actions, our research seeks to answer two questions:

1. **How to score GenAI literacy for university faculty?**
2. **What are the facets of the GenAI literacy for university faculty?**
3. What are the financial gains from the increase of GenAI literacy among the faculty members?

By synthesizing global best practices from academic sources with localized insights of Russian academia, this study contributes a scalable assessment model that bridges theoretical frameworks with actionable insights for policymakers, administrators, and educators.

According to a prior study, there is a potential for an increase in productivity caused by GenAI for lecturers in Russia up to 29.92%. Relying on information from the Ministry of Science and Higher Education of Russia in 2024 there were 1260 licensed universities in the country with 211 156 lecturers in them, while the average salary of a lecturer is 143 518 RUB (~ 1 700 USD). Therefore, the predicted increase of productivity of faculty staff caused by GenAI might allow an increase in economic contribution by approximately 9 billion rubles (108 million USD) per year. Although, it is crucial to adopt a more nuanced approach that incorporates the costs associated with GenAI implementation to accurately calculate the return on investment (ROI) and assess the true economic benefits.

The multiplier effect of GenAI in education amplifies productivity gains achieved in universities, creating a virtuous cycle of enhanced human capital and economic performance. The increase in AI literacy among the faculty members cascades through the economy as more skilled graduates, applying GenAI, contribute to increased organizational efficiency, technological advancement, and competitive advantage in various industries. AI-powered teaching tools ease the load of lecturers, allowing them to focus more on personalized guidance, feedback and mentorship for students, improving the quality of education. It might also foster more innovations in the teaching process.

The subsequent sections detail our methodology, which combines a systematic review of AI literacy frameworks with empirical analysis of faculty workflows and labor market trends. The work follows the IMRAD framework for academic articles, including introduction, methodology, results and discussion sections. Findings present a novel assessment scale tailored to the demands of Russia's higher education landscape.

The study follows the strategic implications of enhancing GenAI literacy among higher education faculty, considering its dual impact on institutional development and broader economic transformation through labor market modernization.

AI LITERACY IN ACADEMIA: BRIDGING UNIVERSITY, BUSINESS AND STATE

GenAI literacy among educators is a critical factor in the monetization of knowledge. When universities and research centers develop personnel capable of applying GenAI across sectors such as industry, healthcare, and finance, this directly influences business competitiveness and overall economic development. For example, the integration of AI into educational environments enables the creation of new monetizable programs—including corporate training, certification schemes, and analytical services for enterprises—while simultaneously enhancing teaching efficacy through personalized learning pathways. These improvements increase the employability and value of graduates in the labor market and strengthen university-business partnerships, as companies are keenly interested in specialists who can readily deploy AI-based solutions.

The number of existing faculty members reaching 211 156 is not the only category forming the Total Addressable Market (TAM), which represents the full potential market size of individuals and organizations involved in the education sector in Russia. According to the research of Teaching Excellence Lab of GSOM SPbU (TEL, 2024), TAM encompasses approximately 1 260 944 people, including university leadership, teaching and research staff (~ 266 300), external part-time university staff (79 000), vocational education leaders and teachers (~ 228 566), and their external part-time counterparts (37 562). It also includes employees of corporate universities (7 820), private educators (75 114), self-employed educators (246 066), staff of NGOs with educational licenses (18 522), and graduate students and related groups, who learn pedagogical science. The average prize for an upskilling course about GenAI for educators is 30 000 RUB (~360 USD). It means that TAM equals approximately 37.8 billion rub. (~450 million USD).

Calculation of Economic Efficiency for a university from investing in such education might be calculated in the following way. The annual financial benefit is derived from the 29.92% increase in productivity, measured as their contribution to annual revenue ~1,200,000 RUB (~14,300 USD*). It is equal to 359 040 RUB (~4,300 USD) per year. Taking a discount rate of 10% and a 3-year time horizon we can calculate the total present value of benefits - 892,879 RUB (~10,600 USD). Therefore, the economic efficiency, which represents the net value of the investment after covering its cost during 3 consecutive years, equals 862,879 RUB (~10,272 USD). The ROI over three years can be calculated as follows: ROI = (Economic Efficiency / Investment Cost) × 100%; ≈ 2 876%. The analysis demonstrates a highly favorable outcome for the investment.

Recent academic discourse has increasingly focused on the profound influence of GenAI on higher education, revealing sharply contrasting views among faculty and students. While some educators raise ethical concerns, particularly regarding academic integrity, others have already begun integrating AI tools into their pedagogical approaches (Lee et al., 2024; Malik et al., 2023). Studies suggest that universities lack consensus on AI adoption, with many staff members reporting insufficient preparedness to address these rapid technological shifts (Lee et al., 2024). Parallel developments are occurring in the financial sector, where professionals are actively debating the ethical dilemmas and operational risks posed by GenAI implementation (Kalia, 2023). A notable Australian study categorized academic staff's responses to GenAI into three distinct groups—enthusiastic adopters ("Apostles"), cautious skeptics ("Agnostics"), and outright rejecters ("Atheists")—demonstrating significant variation in institutional engagement levels (McDonald et al., 2024). Critical success factors for GenAI application—in some cases contributing up to a 40% improvement—include the personalization of educational processes, automated assessment of assignments, and the deployment of adaptive recommendation systems. By contrast, minimal positive effects were observed when AI was used to replace educators without an appropriate methodological framework, when outdated algorithms were used, or when teachers lacked adequate preparation. These results underscore the necessity of rigorous evaluation and ongoing development of AI literacy competencies within higher education institutions.

Skepticism also leads to a reduction of market share. Serviceable Available Market (SAM) for online upskilling programs aiming at increasing GenAI literacy among educators equals 208 thousand people, representing a monetary value of 6.24 billion RUB (~$62.4 million USD), while Serviceable Obtainable Market (SOM) reaches 6.2 thousand customers and a revenue target of 187 million RUB (~$1.87 million USD) for a university providing such programs (TEL, 2024).

AI literacy among educators constitutes not merely academic proficiency, but a pivotal catalyst for economic transformation. As highlighted in Forbes, GenAI technologies are projected to enhance labor productivity in Russia by 30–50% in critical sectors such as finance, logistics, and education (Rozhkov, 2025). This potential, however, hinges on the capacity of educators and mentors to understand GenAI technologies in depth and, crucially, to integrate them meaningfully into curricula to equip future professionals with the competencies demanded by a rapidly evolving labor market.

Early academic inquiries predominantly focused on foundational aspects of digital literacy. Contemporary market demands, however, increasingly call for more advanced expertise. Educators proficient in GenAI now serve as essential intermediaries between academia and industry. Their contribution is multifaceted: they design applied courses on the use of GenAI in diverse practical domains—from predictive analytics in agriculture to automated document management in the public sector—and participate in collaborative industry-university projects where students engage with real-world data, thereby accelerating the adoption of technological innovation. Furthermore, educators are actively involved in the creation of revenue-generating educational products, such as bespoke corporate training in prompt engineering or ethics modules tailored for legal and human resource professionals.

METHODOLOGY OF RESEARCH

GenAI Literacy as a General Professional Competency Tailored to Jobs to Be Done

While Russian universities are mandated to outline targeted competencies in upskilling initiatives, a critical gap persists: the absence of a nationally standardized framework defining GenAI competencies for faculty members of Russian universities. This lack of centralized guidelines undermines the coherence and impact of professional development programs, leaving institutions to navigate the complexities of GenAI integration without unified benchmarks. Furthermore, in today's digitized workplace a critical debate persists: *Are digital competencies—and, by extension, AI literacy—specialized skills for IT professionals, universal civic skills, or distinct categories within professional roles?* This ambiguity underscores the need for a clear theoretical foundation to categorize, assess, and integrate competencies into organizational frameworks. Therefore, it is important to define what we understand by competencies in principle, what theoretical and methodological basis we rely on, and how competencies in the field of personnel management enable us to define what digital competencies are and how they can be assessed.

Since the 1990s, competencies have been recognized as vital indicators of workforce competitiveness, yet their conceptualization remains contested (Rumelt, 1994; Sanchez, 2004). Early scholars emphasized components like skills, knowledge, learning, coordination, organization, and relationships (e.g., Prahalad and Hamel, 1990; Schoemaker, 1992; Leonard-Barton, 1992; Dosi and Teece, 1993), but inconsistent terminology led to fragmented applications across industries (Chiesa & Manzini, 1997). Sanchez et al. (1996) proposed a hierarchical model to resolve this, defining competencies as: *"The ability to maintain a coordinated allocation of assets to achieve organizational objectives"*

This framework structured competencies into three layers. Being at the highest level of classification, assets include all tangible and intangible resources useful to a company, including capabilities. Capabilities consist of repeatable patterns of actions, where all other assets are utilized. Repetitive patterns of action, in turn, require individual and team skills in using assets to perform specialized tasks that together generate organizational actions. Later refinements characterized competencies as *"repeatable, rule-guided abilities to produce competitive outcomes"* (Freiling et al., 2008), while managerial competencies were tied to integrating technical, organizational, and environmental knowledge (Katz, 1955). Katz's taxonomy—technical, human, and conceptual skills—highlighted role-specific demands but lacked contextual adaptability, prompting classifications like *generic*, *industry-specific*, and *firm-specific* skills.

Modern competency frameworks have evolved beyond the traditional *knowledge, skills, and abilities* (KSA) triad to address the complexities of professional roles in dynamic organizational environments. While KSA remains foundational, its practical application necessitates a *multi-tiered stratification* to align competencies with organizational hierarchies, role-specific demands, and shared professional standards. This layered approach enhances precision in workforce development, performance evaluation, and strategic alignment. Below, we expand on the three critical strata of competency stratification: Role-specific tiers (e.g., worker, specialist, manager), General professional competencies (shared across roles), Corporate competencies (organization-specific behaviors).

Competencies must be tailored to distinct professional levels (e.g., *worker, specialist, manager*) to reflect varying responsibilities and decision-making scopes. Operational Roles (Workers) focus on *task execution* (e.g., technical proficiency, adherence to protocols). Specialist Roles require *expertise* in niche domains (e.g., data analysis for researchers, pedagogical innovation for educators). Leadership Roles (Managers) emphasize *strategic* competencies (e.g., resource allocation, change management). In Universities, a *lecturer* (worker) may need AI tool proficiency, while a *department head* (manager) requires competencies in AI policy formulation. Katz's (1955) skills hierarchy (technical, human, conceptual) aligns with this stratification but requires updating for digital-era roles.

General Professional Competencies. These transcend individual roles and reflect shared expectations across professions: Digital Literacy (Navigating AI tools, data ethics), Collaboration (Interdisciplinary teamwork, communication), Adaptability (Learning agility in response to technological shifts). Castanias & Helfat (1991) highlight *industry-specific* vs. *generic* competencies, advocating for hybrid models.

Corporate Competencies indicate The Organizational Identity and Culture. Organization-specific behaviors embed strategic priorities into competency frameworks like Values-Driven Behaviors ("innovation" in tech firms vs. "compliance" in regulated sectors), Cultural Alignment - Competencies reflecting mission ("student-centricity" in universities), some Performance Metrics or Tailored KPIs (research impact vs. teaching evaluations).

In this study, we position GenAI literacy—for non-IT professionals like university faculty—as a *general professional competency*. However, according to AI-TPACK framework the learning should include role-specific tasks. **AI-TPACK framework** (Ning et al., 2024) integrates:

- Content Knowledge (CK): discipline-specific expertise,
- Pedagogical Knowledge (PK): proficiency with pedagogical design,
- Technological Knowledge (TK): proficiency with GenAI tools.

For faculty members, GenAI literacy manifests in behaviors such as using generative AI to design curricula, automate administrative tasks, or enhance research analysis. By adopting TPACK's interdisciplinary lens, we support a widely spread among university faculty understanding of competencies as a set of knowledge, abilities, skills, which are manifested through behavioral indicators. Thus we prioritize *actionable skills* over abstract knowledge (e.g., prompt engineering for lesson planning).

It motivates to adopt the Jobs to be Done (JTBD) framework. JTBD framework offers a transformative lens for aligning competency models with the practical needs of higher education faculty. By framing faculty members as "clients" whose professional tasks ("jobs") drive the design of competency frameworks, JTBD ensures that AI literacy development is both targeted and responsive to real-world challenges. This approach bridges theoretical constructs like AI-TPACK and traditional competency theories with actionable strategies for faculty empowerment in the AI era. Applying the JTBD framework to develop a competency model for higher education faculty, with a focus on the faculty member as the client, facilitates a more targeted and responsive approach to their professional development. This not only enhances the quality of instruction but also renders it more relevant and beneficial to the faculty themselves, ultimately exerting a positive influence on student outcomes. Emerging prominently in 2016 through the works of Ulwick and Osterwalder (2016), Christensen et al. (2016), and Klement (2018), JTBD redefines education by focusing on the *tasks individuals aim to accomplish* rather than their demographic attributes. Two interpretations guide its application:

1. **Jobs-As-Activities (Ulwick and Osterwalder):** Emphasizes optimizing tools and processes to enhance task execution (e.g., AI tools streamlining lesson planning).
2. **Jobs-As-Progress (Christensen et al.):** Prioritizes the outcomes individuals seek, even through alternatives beyond conventional solutions (e.g., faculty adopting AI to reduce administrative workload).

For competency models, JTBD acts as a bridge between abstract skills (e.g., AI prompt engineering) and the tangible tasks faculty perform. By identifying the "jobs" faculty need to accomplish—such as improving teaching quality or integrating AI into research—competencies can be mapped directly to actionable behaviors.

Applying the "Job to be Done" (JTBD) concept as a method for describing the competencies of higher education faculty, emphasizing the faculty member as a client, can be organized as follows.

1. Defining the "job" that faculty members, as clients, want to accomplish
2. Analyzing the context to understand the conditions under which faculty members operate, the challenges they face, and the resources available to them. This will help identify specific requirements for their competencies.
3. Linking the "job" with faculty competencies.
4. Developing training and professional development and adopting programs based on the competency matrix to align with identified needs.
5. The assessment and feedback system considers how effectively faculty members are accomplishing their tasks and achieving their goals.
6. Adapting to changes means continuous improvement. As faculty needs may change, it is important to regularly review and update the competency model based on new data and feedback. It is necessary to encourage faculty to adopt new methods and technologies that can assist them in accomplishing their tasks and improving teaching quality.

The motivational aspects of applying gained knowledge, skills, attitude in their job could be explained by the theory of planned behavior. The TPB posits that three primary factors influence an individual's behavioral intentions: 1) Attitude Toward the Behavior; 2) Subjective Norms; 3) Perceived Behavioral Control (Wang et al., 2024). It brings up the attention to ethical and decisional aspects of AI apart from KSA aspects only.

Thus, it is crucial not only to understand the knowledge, skills, and abilities that faculty need to succeed but also to analytically approach its content, levels of performance, and analysis of effectiveness and efficiency alongside with awareness of relevant risks. The JTBD framework transforms competency development into a participatory process, ensuring AI literacy initiatives are co-created with—and responsive to—faculty needs. By anchoring competencies in real-world tasks, institutions foster a culture of proactive adaptation, where GenAI tools are applied to achieve meaningful progress. This approach not only elevates teaching and research quality but also positions faculty as agile innovators in the digital age.

Stage 1: Exploratory Literature Review

For deeper understanding the current state of this research domain we referred to the findings of the prior studies related to the AI literacy assessment, aiming to ensure theoretical ground for further steps of our research. Firstly, we identified 182 articles by utilizing three distinct sets of keywords, using the Scopus database. The first set focused on digital intelligence (DI) and digital quotient (DQ), yielding 39 articles (k=39). The second set concentrated on AI competence, resulting in 36 articles (k=36), while the third set addressed AI literacy, which brought 107 articles (k=107). After eliminating four duplicates, our final sample comprised 178 articles (k=178). Eligibility criteria apart from keywords included the article format, the quality implying only Q1 and Q2 level of publications, relevance for the educational context.

The term AI literacy was introduced in 2016 by Kandlhofer and Steinbauer (2016) for the purpose of adjusting the teaching process. Their intention was to shift attention from teaching how to apply existing AI techniques and tools to understanding methods and concepts underlying these tools.

Plenty of frameworks and scales were suggested to measure AI literacy, all of them could be generalized with the help of the ABCDE approach (Fig.1). This approach is based on the theory of planned behavior (TPB), developed by Icek Ajzen in 1985. The TPB posits that three primary factors influence an individual's behavioral intentions: 1) Attitude Toward the Behavior (affective aspects); 2) Subjective Norms (ethical aspects); 3) Perceived Behavioral Control (behavioral, cognitive and decisional aspects) (Wang et al., 2024).

Figure 1. ABCDE approach to AI literacy

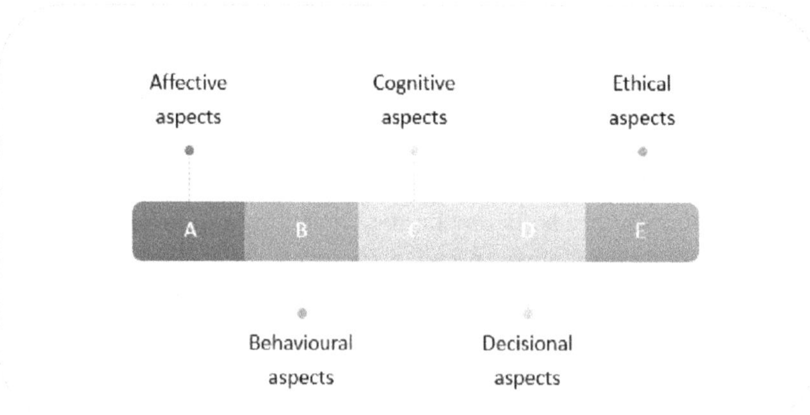

One group of scales measured *attitude toward AI* techniques and tools in the educational context, including AI anxiety, affective learning of AI, attitudes about GenAI, agreement with dominating statements about GenAI, attitudes toward AI-Assisted writing, general attitudes towards AI, perceived usefulness of AI, AI for social good, attitude towards using AI, AI optimism, career interest related to AI, intrinsic motivation towards AI, confidence in learning AI, subjective norms related to AI, perceived relatedness, vision, etc.

The second group of scales assessed *behavioral intentions and actions,* like AI problem solving, AI empowerment, collaboration with AI, use and application of AI, evaluation and creation of AI tools, behavioral learning, behavioral commitment, ability to provide support, AI self-efficacy, creative self-efficacy related to AI etc.

Cognitive domain combined scales related to understanding and critical evaluation of general concepts, principles, methods, tools and techniques, including ability to recognize AI, understanding intelligence, understanding human role in AI, 5 big ideas about AI, logic systems, machine learning, knowledge related to prompt engineering, understanding AI on pragmatic, safety-related, reflective, and contextual levels.

Decisional aspects accounted for the competencies needed, for example, to introduce limitations on applying AI by students or authors in their publications and ability to assess how these decisions are implemented; as well as competencies relevant for developing policies or participation in the procurement of AI applications.

Ethical aspects covered understanding of ethical principles: AI meaningfulness, AI beneficence, AI fairness, human autonomy, overall ethical competence in relation to AI.

All revealed scales could be arranged hierarchically, covering three levels of learning objectives that follow the logic introduced in Bloom's taxonomy: 1) know and understand AI; 2) use and apply AI, 3) evaluate and create AI-tools (Ng, 2021) (Figure 2).

Figure 2. AI literacy according to Bloom's taxonomy

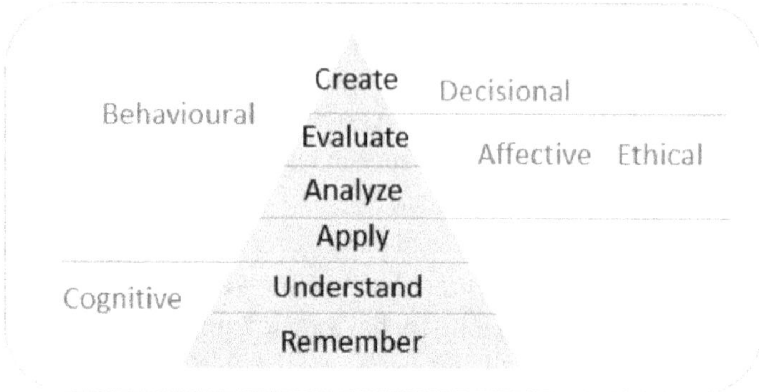

These findings motivated us introducing the scale for assessing the level of GenAI literacy according to different areas of activities:

0) Not applicable for me
1) I do it myself and do not want to apply GenAI
2) I do it myself, but I would prefer to collaborate with GenAI, I just don't know how
3) I do it myself and know how to collaborate with GenAI on it, but I am not using it yet
4) I do it in collaboration with GenAI, however, I am not aware of techniques behind it
5) I do it in collaboration with GenAI, and I am aware of technologies behind it
6) I am not only collaborating with GenAI on it, but also instructing others on how to do it with GenAI
7) I do it in collaboration with GenAI and I am involved in the development of GenAI-based products or prompts engineering for these purposes

Stage 2: Tailoring the Scale to the Jobs to Be Done by Faculty Members

In order to address the challenges educational professionals can face at work in the new GenAI-assisted opportunities it is of primary importance to develop a shared understanding of the competencies they should possess to maintain their everyday academic routine. The qualification characteristics for the specialists in higher education in Russia are defined in the Order of the Ministry of Health and Social Development of the Russian Federation dated January 11, 2011, No. 1n (as amended on January 25, 2023)[1]. This order establishes the necessary competencies required for various academic positions, ensuring that candidates possess the required expertise and educational background to fulfill their roles effectively.

Though the Order provides a framework for assessing the suitability of candidates for academic positions, contributing to the overall quality of education, it is important to note that the document may not fully capture the breadth and depth of responsibilities the faculty members typically encounter in their day-to-day work. The concise nature and some generalization of the competency descriptions can be attributed to the need to apply these competencies to different academic fields and institutions. However, this brevity may lead to a lack of specificity, leaving out certain tasks and challenges educators face in their respective fields. Addressing this gap may require a more detailed and context-specific approach. We propose that the most effective way to identify the competencies that are universal across different universities and curricula is to analyze the duties of academic staff.

The most detailed reflections of these duties, as we believe, can be found in two types of documents:

1) lecturers' personal plans - the document which measures the lecturer's workload and is filled out by the educational specialist
2) and job advertisements - where the university's administration lists the candidate's specific responsibilities and covers the main aspects of the job as listed in the job responsibilities section of the position description.

While setting the criteria for research material selection the authors firstly relied on their own practical experience: the lecturer's individual plans established within their departments as well as job advertisements for faculty positions of the respective universities (Moscow State University, Saint-Petersburg University, and Saint Petersburg State University of Industrial Technologies and Design).

Furthermore, to enhance the objectivity of the research, the scope of the data was expanded to include lecturers' individual plans and job advertisements from the top 20 universities according to RAEX-100, 2024[2] educational ranking. This broader perspective allowed the authors to capture a more diverse range of expectations and requirements for academic staff in various types of universities and fields of study. Incorporating these top-ranked universities ensured that the competencies identified were not only relevant to specific contexts but also reflected the standards upheld by leading institutions in the higher education landscape. This approach also facilitated comparative analysis, revealing potential commonalities and variations in competency expectations across different levels of institutional prestige. Moreover, this selection process helped to mitigate potential biases that could arise from focusing on a limited number of institutions or specific academic disciplines.

The individual plans were sourced through online platforms, including official university websites and educational portals. However, it is important to note that not all universities publicly provide templates for lecturers' individual plans. Therefore, the research team proceeded sequentially through the list of universities, starting from the top-ranked institution. Ultimately, individual plans from twelve leading universities were analyzed. Continuing the analysis beyond this point was deemed unnecessary, as the last five universities did not introduce any new competencies or responsibilities that had not already been covered in the previous individual plans.

Therefore, the empirical part involved content analysis of lecturers' personal plans (k=10) and vacancy' announcements (k=55).

In Russia, faculty recruitment processes are characterized by open and transparent competitive procedures, as mandated by federal legislation (Federal Law No. 273-FZ "On Education in the Russian Federation" dated December 29, 2012)[3]. These open competitions ensure that job advertisements are publicly accessible. Thus, the second stage of the research involved the analysis of such job advertisements, allowing for a more extensive collection of relevant data. As the authors revealed that many universities do not provide detailed job descriptions in the advertisements on their websites, instead referring applicants to the Order of the Ministry of Health and Social Development of the Russian Federation dated January 11, 2011, No. 1n (as amended on January 25, 2023), the job duties and requirements for academic positions, excluding computer science experts, were analyzed using job listings from HeadHunter (hh.ru) database, the leading online recruitment platform in the Russian Federation with more than 1.1 billion job applications and 870,000 vacancies posted daily. Figure 3 illustrates the data collection process and inclusion / exclusion criteria.

Figure 3. Flowchart of vacancy identification and inclusion process

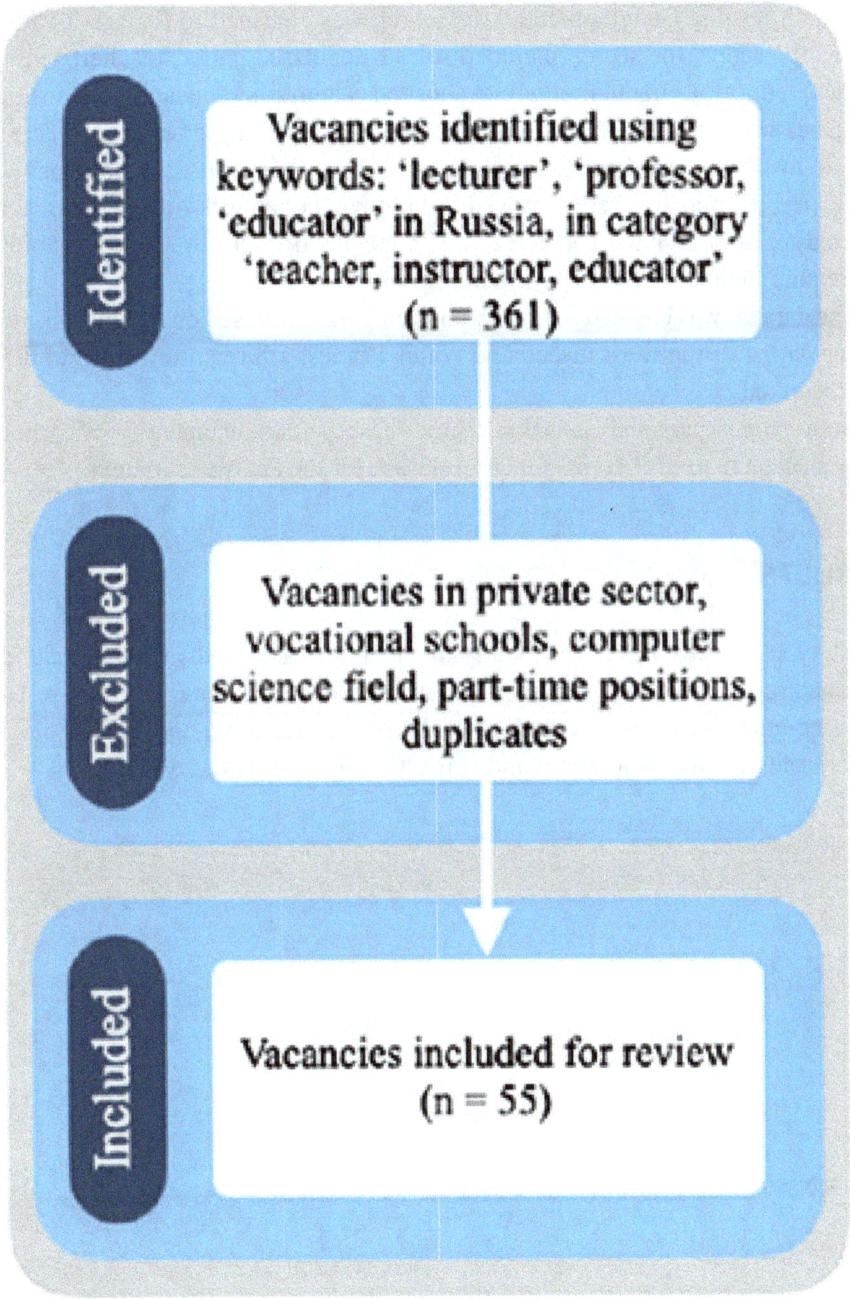

The search was conducted in September 2024 using the keywords 'lecturer', 'professor', 'educator' in the job title, applying specific exclusion criteria to refine the search results. Geographically, the search was confined to Russia. To further narrow the scope, the search included roles categorized under 'teacher,' 'instructor,' and 'educator,' maintaining relevance to academic and pedagogical positions. Emphasis was placed on the public education sector, limiting results to vacancies in state institutions and educational organizations. Only full-time positions were considered. Duplicates were removed to improve the integrity of the dataset. This targeted approach enabled a precise examination of job descriptions, responsibilities, and requirements for university teaching positions.

The data set was cleaned manually and categorized. Based on the analysis of job listings, a list of the most in-demand competencies, job requirements and duties, was compiled.

Both sources, personal plans (k=10) and vacancy announcements (k=55), helped to construct a matrix of competencies relevant for the analyzed context.

RESULTS

All types of activities of the faculty members revealed in the studied individual plans and vacancies were grouped into 6 activity blocks: teaching activities, research work, organizational and methodological work, educational and methodological work, professional development and consulting services (Figure 4).

Figure 4. Competency matrix for AI literacy of university faculty

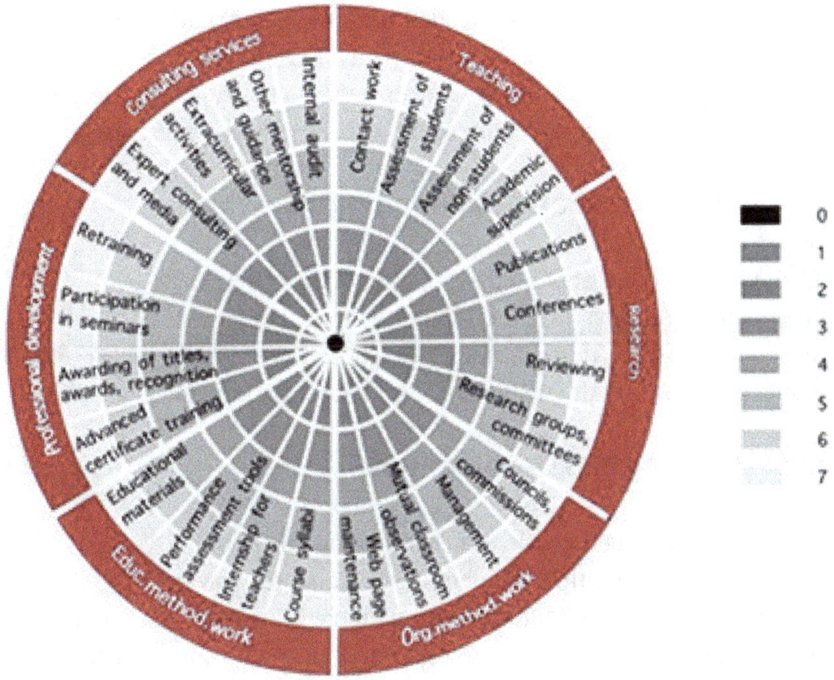

Block 1: Teaching Activities

1.1. Contact Work (lectures, seminars).
1.2. Assessment of Students (exams, grading).
1.3. Assessment of Non-Students (olympiads, entrance exams).
1.4. Academic Supervision (thesis reviews, internships).

Block 2: Research Activities

2.1. Publications (articles, monographs).
2.2. Conferences (participation, materials).
2.3. Reviewing (editing, editorial boards).
2.4. Research Groups (patents, project collaboration).

Block 3: Organizational and Methodological Work

3.1. Councils and Commissions (Academic Council, curriculum committees).
3.2. Management (department leadership, university governance).
3.3. Mutual Classroom Observations (peer reviews, teaching enhancement).
3.4. Web Page Maintenance (lecturer/unit websites, digital presence).

Block 4: Educational and Methodological Work

4.1. Course Syllabi (curriculum design, e-learning systems).
4.2. Internship Programs (teacher training, practical experience).
4.3. Assessment Tools (rubrics, exams, diagnostic materials).
4.4. Educational Materials (textbooks, workshops, multimedia).

Block 5: Professional Development

5.1. Advanced Training (certificates, seminars, workshops).
5.2. Awards and Recognition (academic titles, honorary awards).
5.3. Seminar Participation (national/international knowledge exchange).
5.4. Retraining Programs (skill updates, compliance with standards).

Block 6: Consulting Services

6.1. Expert Consulting and Media (conferences, media appearances).
6.2. Extracurricular Activities (cultural events, sports competitions).
6.3. Mentorship and Guidance (career counseling, alumni engagement).
6.4. Internal Audits (program compliance, institutional standards).

It is important to note that some of these activities could overlap in the individual plans of different universities but for the purposes of this study, the blocks were also formed depending on similar characteristics and AI working skills that may be required to perform a certain type of activity. Each block of activities was then subdivided into four subgroups to more accurately reflect the specific features of a lecturer's work with AI to accomplish the tasks associated with each subgroup.

DISCUSSION

The study focuses on assessing the level of AI literacy of faculty members in Russia, as well as its application to the tasks of professors and pedagogical staff.

The proposed algorithm and scale can also be applied to any other profession, where professional tasks are structured. Based on an analysis of current approaches to assessing AI literacy in non-specialized professional contexts, the authors defined criteria for assessing the AI literacy of university staff based on the *Technological Pedagogical Content Knowledge (TPACK)* framework. While TPACK emphasizes the integration of **technological, pedagogical**, and **content knowledge**, our findings reveal that AI literacy transcends this triad, necessitating a broader lens to account for the multifaceted roles of modern educators.

The content analysis of vacancy announcements and personal plans of the faculty members of the main Russian universities made it possible to identify 24 main tasks in the professional activities of university staff that require the use of AI tools.

The study also opens a discussion about potential risks that are often missed in the international studies analyzed. For example, it was found that intensive use of gadgets by students led to impaired cognitive and communicative processes and reduced memory capacity (Compernolle, 2015). "Connectivity" facilitated the manifestation of such dynamic activity characteristics as searching for necessary data and reaction speed but led to significant problems in the area of semantic data processing and critical thinking. Currently, the phenomenon of "hyperconnectivity" can be included in the spectrum of a deeper problem: digital addiction (e.g., M. Spitzer, N. Kardaras, P. Whybrow, A.O. Gershman (cited in Nagimova, 2015)). The crucial consequence of "hyperconnectivity" can be "digital dementia"—the inability to solve any problem without the help of an AI. These observations underline the need to study the applied aspects of AI-addiction, taking into account the psychological and social meaning for students, and not in isolation from pedagogical design. This emphasizes the mutual influence of technologies: on the design principles of the educational experience, as well as the faculty members' competencies and tasks.

Institutions will be able to tailor upskilling programs to role-specific needs (e.g., AI for *Research Activities* vs. *Educational Development*), as well as benchmark progress through quantifiable metrics (e.g., the percentage of faculty using GenAI for syllabus design).

Faculty might find it useful for self-assessing gaps (e.g., low scores in *Consulting Services* may signal a need for specific training with AI tools). They might also apply it for advocating for resources (e.g., access to prompt engineering workshops).

While the study focuses on Russian higher education, the framework's adaptability allows for cross-cultural refinement. Key limitations include the following aspects: findings are drawn from faculty in research-intensive universities, while technical colleges or arts-focused institutions may require adjustments. Rapid advancements in GenAI (e.g., multimodal models like GPT-4o) necessitate periodic updates to the assessment tool.

TRANSLATING AI-LITERACY INTO ECONOMIC VALUE

As we underlined, contemporary research underscores that AI literacy among faculty members and researchers drives both educational institutions and the real sector. According to an analysis by Computerra, the integration of artificial intelligence technologies can generate global annual savings of up to 10.8 trillion rubles by 2030 through process optimization, while remarkably, no profession is expected to be fully displaced—instead, occupational roles will undergo substantive transformation (Computerra, 2025). These finding highlights that the core value of AI literacy is not limited to the adoption of specific technologies but resides in the capacity to strategically adapt these solutions to enhance productivity across all domains of the economy.

Consequently, AI literacy should be understood not solely as an avenue for advancing new competencies among educators, but as a foundation for generating novel forms of economic value. This encompasses, for instance, reducing operational costs within both education and enterprise settings by curbing administrative expenditures—estimated reductions range from 15–20%—thereby enabling the reallocation of saved resources towards research activities or the development of innovative educational offerings. The ensuing synergy between universities and industry partners becomes markedly pronounced: companies that cooperate with institutions renowned for AI literacy benefit from a pipeline of graduates equipped to immediately implement effective solutions, from deploying chatbots in customer support to establishing predictive analytics in logistics.

The emergence of new markets and the monetization of advanced competencies are fundamentally reshaping the structure and dynamics of the labor market, offering novel solutions to persistent talent and skills shortages. As highlighted by InRussia, generative AI is already transforming the Russian job market, prompting the creation of entirely new professional roles—such as prompt engineers—while compelling established specialists to acquire digital skills to remain competitive (InRussia, 2024). Faculty proficient in AI are subsequently positioned to commercialize their expertise through bespoke corporate training programs (e.g., tailored modules in AI for marketing or law), business consulting in the integration of educational technologies, and the development of proprietary intelligent learning tools—including adaptive simulators for medicine or engineering. Notably, graduates taught by AI-savvy educators demonstrate enhanced competitiveness on the job market, which is emerging as a crucial indicator of institutional effectiveness.

SUMMARY AND CONCLUSION

AI literacy among educators transcends the status of a mere educational trend and must be regarded as a strategic asset for knowledge monetization and sustained economic advancement. As evidenced by recent studies, its introduction generates a multiplier effect—ranging from substantial reductions in operational costs to the emergence of entirely new labor markets. Institutions that prioritize investments in these competencies are poised to emerge as focal points for industrial partnership and as drivers of innovation across the broader economy.

The analysis presented herein demonstrates the significant potential of educator AI literacy to create measurable economic value by optimizing educational processes, shaping new labor market segments, and enhancing graduate competitiveness. These developments collectively foster a dynamic ecosystem in which academic institutions function as hubs of knowledge transfer and technological adoption in the real sector.

Nonetheless, it is essential to emphasize the evolving nature of artificial intelligence technologies, their practical implementation, and the regulatory frameworks that govern their use. The continuous development in these domains complicates the establishment of a definitive and comprehensive methodology for quantifying the impact of advanced technological integration, as such calculations must adapt to ongoing changes. Consequently, current assessments of the economic effects of AI solutions should be considered as provisional; they necessitate regular updates as new empirical data on AI productivity emerges, legislative environments are transformed, practical experience accumulates, and as comparative studies—both cross-national and cross-sectoral—expand our understanding of the economic, political, social, and cultural dimensions of these processes.

The rapid integration of generative artificial intelligence into higher education necessitates a systematic approach to assessing and developing AI literacy among university faculty. This study addressed a critical gap in the field by proposing a context-specific framework for evaluating AI literacy with respect to the unique demands of Russian academia. Grounded in the Technological Pedagogical Content Knowledge (TPACK) model and the Theory of Planned Behavior (TPB), our research synthesized practices with empirical insights from faculty workflows, job descriptions, and institutional norms and standards.

Our chapter focuses on research, aimed at creating the assessment tool for GenAI literacy among faculty members in academia by analyzing six main activity areas on a scale of 0 to 7: teaching, research, organizational and methodological work, professional development and expert activity. Our approach allows us to assess not only the level of awareness of AI-tools but also the level of proficiency in using them at work in Academia, for example, for developing syllabi, preparing case studies for group work in class, individual homework for students, grading assessments, preparing class presentations, etc. The authors' proposed model is based on the Jobs-to-Be-Done framework, which allows us to focus on a basic list of functional tasks for a modern faculty. Our study also depicts limitations of the TRACK model of interaction between technology, education, and curriculum content. These include ethical literacy, safety of AI-tools, personal data protection, intellectual capacity associated with the everyday use of AI and its impact on critical thinking competences, discussions about competition between human teachers and "AI employees," freedom of action and creativity, excessive reliance on AI responses in decision making, and so on. These limitations and challenges of implementing AI-tools into secondary education highlight the critical reflection on the consequences of widespread AI adoption and trust.

Our model allows integration of AI in teaching at several levels: academic culture and environment, professional standards and local practices that can be implemented individually by university faculty.

The development of AI literacy in higher education can be treated as an investment in faculty competencies, which requires additional financial resources from universities and the state to train faculty in AI competencies. On the other hand, such investments pay off in higher quality and speed at the level of university operational management and routine daily tasks of teachers (checking assignments, preparing lectures, tracking tasks, etc.).

Furthermore, the level of AI literacy enables a transition to a higher level of society's digital literacy. University teachers not only provide classes using modern AI-tools, but also foster a critical approach and rational application, which students then transfer to their practical work and life.

Assessing the effectiveness of AI tools in learning and teaching requires identifying limitations and specificities in different regions and disciplines, addressing political and legal aspects of AI regulation, and educational and professional standards, which often lag behind the development of digital and AI-tools. To assess the significance of these factors, it is crucial to monitor the development and implementation of AI-tools, the level of AI literacy, and the alignment of AI literacy assessment procedures with their outcomes in Academia. It is necessary to develop and adapt a methodology for assessing the effectiveness of AI-tools in both higher education and in business and society, which is currently lacking. Furthermore, it is highly important to support research initiatives and projects in the field of AI applications in education, which will serve as a knowledge base and an indicator of the speed of evolution of AI literacy in education. This confirms the scientific, practical, and research significance of our current project, which is one of the first steps in stimulating public debate on the impact of AI on education, balancing the interests of knowledge, critical thinking, and effective implementation in practice at any level - individual, group, organizational - in different industries, regions, countries, and the world as a whole.

ACKNOWLEDGEMENT

The authors acknowledge contribution offered by AI Lab of the Center for Teaching Excellence in business education at GSOM SPBU

REFERENCES

Ajzen, I. (1991). The theory of planned behavior. *Organizational Behavior and Human Decision Processes*, *50*(2), 179–211. DOI: 10.1016/0749-5978(91)90020-T

Castanias, R. P., & Helfat, C. E. (1991). Managerial resources and rents. *Journal of Management*, *17*(1), 155–171. DOI: 10.1177/014920639101700110

Chiesa, V., & Manzini, R. (1997). Competence levels within firms: a static and dynamic analysis. In Heene, A., & Sanchez, R. (Eds.), *Competence-based strategic management* (pp. 195–214). Wiley.

Christensen, C. M., Dillon, K., & Hall, T. (2016), Competing against luck: the story of innovation and customer choice, Kindle, Computerra (2025). AI to Save 10.8 Trillion Annually by 2030 Without Eliminating Any Jobs. https://www.computerra.ru/314947/ii-k-2030-godu-sekonomit-do-10-8-trln-v-god-i-ne-zamenit-ni-odnoj-professii/

Dosi, G., & Teece, D. J. (1993). *Organizational competences and the boundaries of the firm. Market and organization: the competitive firm and its environment.* Latapses, Nice, France and Iside.

Dranev, Y. Y., Kuchin, I. I., & Miryakov, M. I. (2025). *Economic effects of artificial intelligence adoption in Russia*. Moscow: ISSEK, National Research University Higher School of Economics. Retrieved from https://issek.hse.ru/news/1022068478.html

Federal Law No. 273-FZ (2012). "On Education in the Russian Federation" Available from: https://www.consultant.ru/document/cons_doc_LAW_140174/?ysclid=m1nljoyjz5167522908

Freiling, J., Gersch, M., & Goeke, C. (2008). On the Path towards a Competence-based Theory of the Firm. *Organization Studies*, *29*(8-9), 1143–1164. DOI: 10.1177/0170840608094774

InRussia. (2024). Generative AI Adoption and Labor Market Adaptation in Russia. https://incrussia.ru/news/generativnyj-ii-v-rossii-kak-novye-tehnologii-izmenyat-rynok-truda/

Kalia, S. (2023) Potential impact of generative Artificial Intelligence(AI) on the financial industry. International Journal on Cybernetics & Informatics (IJCI) Vol.12, No.6, December 2023

Kandlhofer, M., Steinbauer, G., Hirschmugl-Gaisch, S., Huber, P. (2016, October). Artificial intelligence and computer science in education: From kindergarten to university. In 2016 IEEE frontiers in education conference (FIE) (pp. 1-9). IEEE. https://doi.org/DOI: 10.1109/FIE.2016.7757570

Katz, R. L. (1955). Skills of an effective administrator. *Harvard Business Review*, *33*(1), 33–42.

Klement, A. (2018). *When coffee and kale compete. Become great at making products people will buy*. Create Space Independent.

Lee, D., Arnold, M., Srivastava, A., Plastow, K., Strelan, P., Ploeckl, F., Lekkas, D., & Palmer, E. (2024). The impact of generative AI on higher education learning and teaching: A study of educators' perspectives. *Comput. Educ. Artif. Intell.*, *6*, 100221. DOI: 10.1016/j.caeai.2024.100221

Leonard-Barton D. (1992). Core capabilities and core rigidities: A paradox in managing new product development. Strategic Manage J.; 13:111 – 26 (special issue). https://doi.org/DOI: 10.1002/smj.4250131009

Malik, F. T., Hughes, L., Dwivedi, Y. K., & Dettmer, S. (2023). Exploring the Transformative Impact of Generative AI on Higher Education. *IFIP International Conference on e-Business, e-Services, and e-Society*. DOI: 10.1007/978-3-031-50040-4_6

McDonald, P., Hay, S., Cathcart, A., & Feldman, A. (2024). Apostles, Agnostics and Atheists: Engagement with Generative AI by Australian University Staff.

Nagimova N.I. (2015) Technologizing of educational process as condition of educational results formation of implementing programs of secondary vocational education. Electronic learning in continuous education.

Ng, D. T. K., Leung, J. K. L., Chu, S. K. W., & Qiao, M. S. (2021). Conceptualizing AI literacy: An exploratory review. *Computers and Education: Artificial Intelligence*, *2*, 100041. DOI: 10.1016/j.caeai.2021.100041

Ning, Y., Zhang, C., Xu, B., Zhou, Y., & Wijaya, T. T. (2024). Teachers' AI-TPACK: Exploring the relationship between knowledge elements. *Sustainability (Basel)*, *16*(3), 978. DOI: 10.3390/su16030978

Order of the Ministry of Health and Social Development of the Russian Federation of January 11, 2011, No. 1n (as amended on January 25, 2023). Available from: https://ivo.garant.ru/#/document/55170898/paragraph/1:0

Prahalad, C. K., & Hamel, G. (1990). The core competence of the corporation. *Harvard Business Review*, *68*(3), 79–93.

RAEX-100. 2024 https://raex-rr.com/education/russian_universities/top-100_universities/2024/

Rozhkov, R. (2025). Working Smart: Generative AI's Potential to Boost Productivity in Russia https://www.forbes.ru/tekhnologii/537396-rabota-s-umom-kakov-potencial-generativnogo-ii-dla-rosta-proizvoditel-nosti-v-rossii

Rumelt, R. P. (1994). Foreword. In Hamel, G., & Heene, A. (Eds.), *Competence-based competition*. Wiley.

Sanchez, R. (2004). Understanding competence-based management: Identifying and managing five modes of competence. *Journal of Business Research*, *57*(5), 518–532. DOI: 10.1016/S0148-2963(02)00318-1

Sanchez, R., Heene, A., & Thomas, H. (1996). Towards the theory and practice of competence-based competition. In Sanchez, R., Heene, A., & Thomas, H. (Eds.), *Dynamics of competence-based competition: theory and practice in the new strategic management* (pp. 1–35). Elsevier., DOI: 10.1016/S0024-6301(97)86598-3

Schoemaker P. (1992)How to link strategic vision to core capabilities. Sloan Manage Rev. 2; 534(1): 67– 82.

Teaching Excellence Lab (TEL). (2024) Market seizing for upskilling programs about GenAI for the educators. TEL GSOM SPbU. https://gsom.spbu.ru/en/about-gsom/faculty/tel/

Ulwick, A. W., & Osterwalder, A. (2016). *Jobs to be done: theory to practice*. Idea by Press.

Wang, C., Wang, H., Li, Y., Dai, J., Gu, X., & Yu, T. (2024). Factors influencing university students' behavioral intention to use generative artificial intelligence: Integrating the theory of planned behavior and AI literacy. *International Journal of Human-Computer Interaction*, •••, 1–23. DOI: 10.1080/10447318.2024.2383033

Chapter 14
Teams' Management Derived From Data:
Incentive Collaboration Between Data Analysts, Economists, and Managers

Elizaveta Alexsandrovna Zotova
https://orcid.org/0000-0003-4539-4253
Peter the Great St. Petersburg Polytechnic University, Russia

Ekaterina Evgenievna Abushova
https://orcid.org/0000-0001-5439-359X
Peter the Great St. Petersburg Polytechnic University, Russia

Ivan Volchkov
https://orcid.org/0009-0001-0611-8734
Peter the Great St. Petersburg Polytechnic University, Russia

Viliyan Krastev
https://orcid.org/0000-0001-5456-247X
University of Economics in Varna, Bulgaria

ABSTRACT

In a promptly altering data-driven business scape, managing teams including data analysts, economists, and managers becomes a key factor in the success of organizations. This chapter of the monograph scrutinizes the primary aspects and superior practices of integrating these three professional squads in order to create highly effective teams capable of making informed decisions based on data analysis and economic forecasting. Effective cooperation between data analysts, economists,

DOI: 10.4018/979-8-3373-2772-3.ch014

and managers not only improves the quality of decision-making, but also enhances innovation processes within the organization. In this chapter, authors will analyze the role of each of these groups, their unique skills and knowledge, as well as ways to create an environment conducive to collaboration. Authors will also consider at existing barriers and propose strategies to overcome them.

INTRODUCTION

Team Roles and Duties

Currently, data is getting a key business asset, and managing Data-Driven Teams is becoming an essential skill for organizations. However, the success of such teams depends not only on technology and access to data, but also on a clear distribution of roles and responsibilities among the participants. It is highly recommended to notice that the organization and distribution principle of roles in such teams, how to define and organize the functions of data analysts, economists and managers to achieve maximum efficiency.

Team management is a multifarious process. It requires careful planning, clear coordination, and effective communication. Every leader strives to create an effective and successful team, but this requires not only a deep comprehension of business processes, but also the art of managing people. Goals and objectives are key indicators in achieving efficiency.

Team management in the context of big data is the process of organizing an interdisciplinary group (analysts, economists, managers) aimed at extracting economic value from data. It is based on a clear distribution of roles (for example, through a RACI matrix), structured communication, and data-oriented performance evaluation. The key goal is to transform the team from a cost center into a profit center that generates direct financial returns through monetization of data and optimization of business solutions.

The first step in successful team management is setting aims. Goals urge the team direction and motivation. However, not all goals are equal. It is vitally important that they are formulated correctly.

The main assignment is to investigate how to set goals correctly, plan the way to achieve them, and learn how to manage a team in such a way as to achieve the expected result. The result's portrait authors want to achieve assists make the goal measurable.

For competent and correct goal setting, the SMART methodology is very helpful, where the goal has 5 facets. The goal is Specific, Measurable, Achievable, Relevant, and Time-bound (SMART). Be sure to decompose large goals into subgoals. As a technique, a goal tree is very valuable, (Doran, 1981).

When creating a goal tree, answer the following questions: what (what subgoals) are involved in achieving this goal? What contribution should a specific process make to achieving these goals? Under what conditions the goal will be achieved. Where is the bottleneck: a process, a resource that limits the capabilities of the entire chain? The formation of such a goal tree enables to clearly formulate both goals and tasks to be solved, as well as plan their implementation in such a way as to do the job well, quickly and without overspending resources. This will give person the key to competent teamwork management.

If possible, involve them in the discussion of the plan. Formulate a general approach to achieving the goal. Identify the major milestones and the outcome for each stage. Each stage must have its own control point and control method. It is advisable to set the time optimistically, i.e. about 25% faster than it was done before or than it seems right. Evaluate the resources that will be needed. Create a schedule reflecting the parallel and sequential execution of tasks. Optimize the resulting plan. Think about whether and how you can achieve your goal faster. Or whether it is possible to achieve more without increasing time and resources. Is it possible to reduce resources without compromising results and deadlines? Which requirements for the result are the most important, which are the least priority.

The second step. When the plan for achieving the goals is formed, you will be able to assign team members to complete tasks (Autor, Levy, & Murnane, 2023).

The RACI matrix is a robust tool for distributing roles and responsibilities in a team.

Responsible: Who completes the assignment or job duties.

- **Accountable**: Who makes the final decision and is responsible for the result.
- **Consulted**: Who provides expert opinion or advice.
- **Informed**: Who should be notified about the progress of the chore or the result.

The RACI matrix helps to clearly identify who is responsible for what, avoiding duplication of efforts and misunderstandings. Low (Ad-hoc): No approved processes. Action: Start with 1-2 key KPIs and a simple RACI for basic tasks (for example, a weekly report only). High (Data-Driven): Processes are automated. Action: Implement a comprehensive metrics system and an extended RACI, including data management roles (Data Engineer, Data Scientist).

The RACI matrix is a table where the rows correspond to the chores or project's stages, and the columns correspond to the team members. The role of each participant is specified for each task: R, A, C or I (Hofmann, Oesterle, & Rust, 2025).

Table 1. A model of a modest RACI matrix

ASSIGNMENT	ANALYST	ECONOMIST	MANAGER
Data collecting	R	C	I
Market trend analysis	C	R	I
Strategy endorsing	I	C	A

The relationship between KPIs and motivation systems in IT teams Description: Scientists conducted a long-term experiment at a software company, where they implemented a bonus system tied to team (sprint execution speed) and individual (code quality) KPIs, and not just to the implementation of a revenue plan. Teams with balanced indicators demonstrated 40% higher innovation activity (the number of improvements adopted) and 50% lower staff turnover, as the system encouraged not only the result, but also the quality of collaboration. Confirms the thesis of the article that an effective data-based motivation system should consider both individual contributions and team synergy, which directly affects innovation potential and talent retention.

Strategic Impact

- Eliminates redundancy and accelerates time-to-insight, directly enhancing competitive advantage.
- Ensures that each role contributes to measurable financial outcomes, such as reduced operational costs or increased customer lifetime value.

Successful cooperation between data analysts, economists and managers is the key to achieving business goals and sustainable growth of the company (Jacka & Keller, 2009).

Team Communication

Effective communication in data-driven teams is not just about information exchange but about fostering collaboration that drives monetization. The **4C competencies** (Critical Thinking, Creativity, Communication, Cooperation) are essential for aligning cross-functional teams with business goals, (Kretschmer, Khashabi, & Hess, 2023).

Internal Communication:

- **Vertical (Top-Down)**: Leadership communicates strategic objectives (e.g., "Increase data product revenue by 15%") to ensure team efforts align with monetization targets.
- **Horizontal (Peer-to-Peer)**: Regular syncs between analysts and economists ensure insights are contextualized for financial impact. For example, a weekly "Data-Economics Forum" can bridge gaps between predictive models and pricing strategies.

External Communication

- Teams must articulate data insights to stakeholders in monetizable terms. For instance, instead of reporting "a 10% increase in user engagement," analysts should highlight "a $500K upsell opportunity in Q3."

Tools for Enhanced Communication

- **Dashboards**: Real-time KPI tracking (e.g., customer acquisition cost vs. lifetime value) keeps teams focused on profitability.
- **Collaboration Platforms**: Slack/Teams channels dedicated to data-driven projects reduce silos and accelerate decision-making (Tambe, P., Hitt, L. M., & Brynjolfsson, E. The Productivity Effects of Data-Driven Teams: Evidence from IT Investments, 2020).

Team's Performance Evaluation

Regular evaluation of team performance using data enables to identify areas for improvement and adapt management strategies. This may include analyzing the performance of individual team members or the entire group as a whole.

Evaluation methods can range from quantitative indicators (such as KPIs) to qualitative ones (such as customer feedback) (Aybas & Uyargil, 2017). It is essential to exploit a comprehensive approach to performance assessment in order to get a complete picture of how the team is coping with the tasks set.

Data-based team performance assessment is a systematic approach that enables an objective analysis of the organization's performance, identifying its strengths and growth areas, and therefore identifying areas of the company's development, which affects the improvement and adaptation of the company's management strategy. Key metrics for evaluating team performance stemmed from data are divided into individual and team indicators, (Leonardi & Neeley, 2024).

The "People" pillar defines the human capital required for success, moving beyond generic roles to specific competencies and accountabilities.

Role Clarity with RACI-Plus: Building on the standard RACI, the "Plus" adds an S for Stakeholder (e.g., end-customer, regulatory body) to ensure all outputs are designed with the final consumer of the data in mind. This directly links daily tasks to external value creation.

Cultivating 4C Competencies: Teams must be assessed and hired for Critical Thinking, Creativity, Communication, and Cooperation (Guszczа et al., 2022). These are not soft skills but essential for translating complex data into strategic actions.

Monetization-Aligned Incentives

Individual and team bonuses must be tied to leading indicators of value (e.g., "% of insights adopted by business units," "estimated revenue impact of deployed models") rather than just lagging operational metrics.

Conclusion and Strategic Roadmap

To transition from a data cost center to a profit center, leaders must adopt an integrated approach.

Executive Action Plan

Audit (Month 1-2): Map current workflows against the PPTD framework to identify gaps in role clarity, process bottlenecks, or technology silos. Pilot (Month 3-6): Apply the full PPTD framework to one high-impact team (e.g., marketing analytics, pricing). Scale and Automate (Month 7-12): Institutionalize successful practices from the pilot. Explore AI to automate data preparation and reporting, shifting human effort to value-added analysis.

A significant element in evaluating the performance of a team using data is the choice of data processing and analysis methods. It is recommended to pay special attention to the choice and adaptation of the method (or their complex) for the specific working conditions of the team and the specifics of the organization in question (https://www.intellspot.com/types-data-analysis/). Among these methods, the following can be used.

The choice of a convenient adapted form of presenting data analysis hinges on many factors, including the personal characteristics of the team leader, as well as the degree of qualification of the staff, the degree of interconnectedness of the team and cooperation between data analysts, economists and managers (Davenport & Harris, 2022). Cases of the forms used can be:

- Strategic maps reflecting the relationship between KPIs and the goals of the team's work (an example is shown in Figure 1). The strategic map enables to inform individual departments and employees of the organization of their role in the implementation of the strategy. Strategic maps can be created at any level of management, and representatives of each level will have the opportunity to see their place on the overall strategic map (Edmondson & Mortensen, 2023).

Figure 1. A strategic map sample

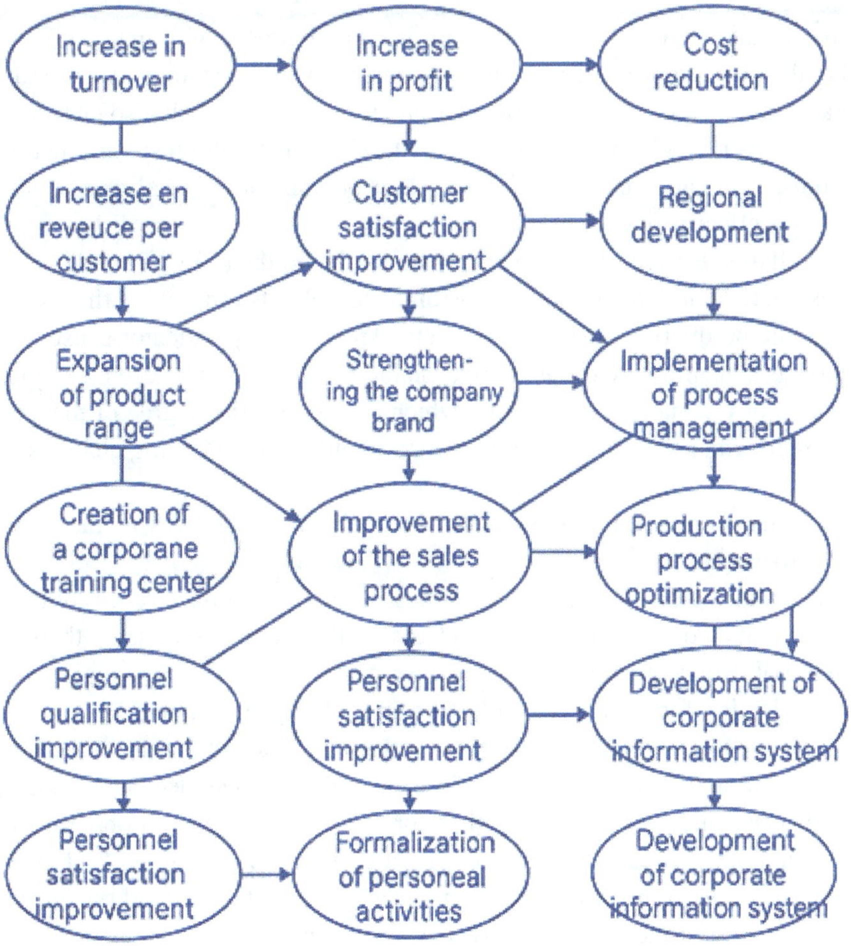

Heat maps of risks: assessment of the probability and impact of threats:

- X-Matrix, which is a document that formulates the main directions of the company's development. The strategy is deployed through integrated action plans based on and continuously improving the PDCA cycle (https://learntransformation.com/x-matrix-hoshin-kanri/). This document is the result of using the Hoshin Kanri method, developed in Japan within the framework of the lean approach philosophy. This method is aimed at ensuring that strategic goals ensure real improvements in the operational activities of the company at all its levels.

Effectiveness in the Motivation System

Elaborating a staff motivation system is an assignment with many unknowns. During the formation of the various components of this system, it is necessary to evaluate and consider many external and internal factors, which also change quite often. However, it is important not only to develop a motivation system that meets the requirements and specifics of a particular organization, but also to be able to evaluate its effectiveness.

As well as specific tasks, such as increasing the productivity of a particular site or division, reducing the number of customer complaints, improving the quality of one or more production operations, and etc. An efficiency indicator is usually understood as a quantitative or qualitative characteristic of the work of an employee, a division, or the entire organization, which determines the degree of managerial impact. Performance indicators should correspond to the following qualities:

- validity, that is, compliance with the goals and objectives of the system's motivation;
- informative, that is, to answer the question about the effectiveness of the system or its individual element in relation to the factors influencing them.;
- ease of data acquisition;
- Availability for initial data collection and subsequent evaluation;
- dynamic availability. Obviously, the value of an indicator at a particular time is insignificant. In order to make informed management decisions, indicators must be analyzed in dynamics, therefore, the methodology for obtaining them should be practically unchanged (or with minor modifications), and the form of collecting, accumulating and analyzing information should be fairly simple and easy to use (Çınar, Bektaş, & Aslan, 2011).

METHODOLOGY

In the theory and practice of personnel management, there is no standard methodology for evaluating the effectiveness of a motivation system, but there is an established practice that generally relies on methodologies for evaluating economic efficiency. In economics, efficiency is understood as the ratio of the results achieved and the costs incurred. However, it is difficult to calculate the economic efficiency of a motivation system directly, because the results of an organization's work are simultaneously influenced by many different factors. Therefore, it is customary to use various direct and indirect indicators to evaluate it, which can be roughly divided into seven groups. The first group of indicators are direct indicators for calculating economic efficiency. To evaluate the effectiveness of the motivation system, the amount of revenue or profit over a certain period of time can be used as a result. The costs can include the following indicators:

- salaries, bonuses and other personnel costs in general;
- the cost of paying employees involved in the implementation of the motivation system;
- the cost of providing material and non-material factors of the motivation system;
- the cost of developing and building the motivation system infrastructure.

Efficiency is calculated in dynamics over a certain period of time. To evaluate the motivation system, this period should be at least 6 months, especially when introducing a new motivation system or significant changes to the current system, as employees must adapt to new conditions. This is the simplest and most obvious way to understand how effectively a company works with staff, including in terms of motivation. Both general indicators for an enterprise, as well as indicators of divisions and individual indicators, including KPIs, can be compared. The advantages of this method are its simplicity and the availability of a variety of data for comparison and analysis.

At the same time, efficiency means not only achieving goals, but also estimating costs. Goals can be achieved, but at the same time, the company, for instance, has spent significant funds on salary increases and bonuses. Can such a motivation system be considered effective from an economic point of view? Therefore, when calculating direct indicators and using the comparative method of analyzing the effectiveness of the motivation system, it is necessary to conduct an additional analysis of the factors and reasons for achieving goals and targets (Gibbs, Neckermann, & Siemroth, 2023). For example, revenue can be achieved through effective sales or cost reduction. If the results of the analysis show that the sales level has increased after the introduction of the new incentive payment, then it becomes obvious that this is what influenced the final result. It can be concluded that this particular component of the motivation system proved to be effective. In addition, it should be remembered that William Dettmer, a well-known systems management consultant, said: "The sum of local system optima does not equal the optimum of the system as a whole" (Dettmer, 2007). This literally means that a remuneration system implemented in one department and effective for it does not necessarily contribute to the fulfillment of the company's strategic goals (Goldratt, 1984). Thus, it is impossible to obtain the most effective system, including a motivation system, by maximizing the effectiveness of all its components separately, without taking into account their interrelationships. That is why, when using this method of evaluating the effectiveness of the motivation system, it is necessary to analyze the data obtained to determine which department fulfills the planned indicators related to strategic goals and at the expense of which incentives. Along with the effectiveness assessment, it is advisable to make an impact assessment, which is defined as the degree to which planned activities are implemented and planned results are achieved. The more precisely the goal is achieved, the higher the effectiveness. In this regard, effectiveness can be otherwise referred to as target effectiveness. When the goal is reached, the efficiency will be 100%.

RESULTS

Economic efficiency requires achieving not so much a goal as a result at the expense of minimal costs, and in order to measure effectiveness, it is necessary to have clearly defined goals and plans. Therefore, it is advisable to use this method in organizations working with the KPI system, and especially when evaluating those positions where there is a clear relationship between the incentive and the response result. When evaluating target effectiveness, it is also necessary to take into account the influence of other factors, therefore, additional expert surveys are recommended. The second group of indicators, the so-called indirect indicators of the effectiveness of the motivation system, which include:

- salary intensity;
- labor productivity;
- the advance coefficient;
- the share of wages in the cost of production.

Salary intensity is the ratio of the wage fund amount to the amount of revenue for a certain period of time.

$$\textit{Salary Intensity}\left(SI\right) = \frac{\sum WF^t}{\sum R^t}, \text{ where}$$

WF – wage fund

R – revenue

t – time.

As the company's revenue grows, the share of the payroll may increase, remain stable, or decrease. A faster increase in the wage fund can mean two situations. Either employees have started to receive higher salaries, but they are working worse than before, or the staff has increased unreasonably.

A decrease in the share of the payroll in revenue indicates, on the contrary, that the motivation system is effective. At the same time, it is vitally important to analyze wage growth. With the right development of events, the wages of employees should increase, but the share of the wage fund in revenue should decrease. This will be a clear sign of an effective motivation system that encounters the needs of employees and encourages them to work better. The stable ratio of the wage fund and revenue indicates that it is possible to review individual elements of the motivation system to increase its effectiveness.

Labor productivity is considered one of the main indicators for evaluating the effectiveness of human resource management. Its growth is an indirect confirmation of the effectiveness of the applied motivation system.

$$\textit{Labor productivity}\left(LP\right) = \frac{Q^t}{AAoE^t}, \text{ where}$$

Q – volume of products / services produced

AAoE – Average amount of employees

t – time.

The advance indicator is the ratio of the growth rate of labor productivity and the growth rate of wages. Normally, it should be more than one. This may be evidence that financial incentives in the company successfully solve the problem of increasing the economic and production returns from staff. In the opposite situation, if the growth rate of wages outstrips labor productivity, it is necessary to reconsider the methods of human resource management. growth rate

$$\textit{Advance indicator}\left(AI\right) = \frac{GR^{LP}}{GR^{W}}, \text{ where}$$

GR – growth rate

LP – labor productivity

W – wage.

The calculation of the share of wages in the cost of production is also one of the indirect indicators in assessing the effectiveness of the motivation system. When conducting an economic and statistical analysis, it is necessary to determine the normative values of this indicator in advance. Experts can name industry values, but this information is not available to all organizations in the industry. According to some estimates, in various industries, wage costs can range from 20 to 60% of total costs and are the most significant in the budget of any enterprise operating in the real economy.

$$\textit{Share of wages } (SoW) = \frac{\sum WF^t}{\sum CP^t}, \text{ where}$$

WF – wage fund
CP – cost price
t – time.

The third group of indicators in the evaluation of the motivation system reflects the relative increase in scores in individual employee indicators. These indicators may include personal KPIs, professional and business competence assessment indicators, and individual development plan performance indicators. It evaluates not only long-term, but also short-term results. The risks of such an assessment are that the interpretation of the results obtained will depend on how interconnected the personal performance of employees and the performance of the unit and the entire enterprise are. With a weak connection, a situation may arise where an employee will be motivated to study and develop, using the resources of the organization in order to improve their skills and leave for another job. The fourth group of indicators represents indicators comparing the dynamics of indicators characterizing the results of production and sales volumes with the value of the premium fund. The calculation of this criterion allows us to answer the question of what effect each ruble creates, which employees receive in the form of a bonus. The analysis of these indicators is similar to the assessment of the growth of gross revenue (or turnover) of a company in comparison with the growth of the wage fund. The motivation system will be considered effective if the bonus fund increases, but its share in terms of production and sales volumes decreases. In the case of negative dynamics of indicators, it is necessary to analyze the situation and look for its causes, which may not always be in the motivation system.

$$\textit{Discount rate } \left(DR\right) \textit{ indicator} = \frac{\sum PF^t}{\sum R^t}, \text{ where}$$

PF – premium fund

R – revenue

t – time.

The fifth group of indicators is social performance indicators. In other words, this group includes assessments of taking into account the needs and preferences of employees in the current motivation system. By general definition, social management effectiveness characterizes the degree of utilization of the potential of employees and each employee individually, the success of solving social problems of the development of the workforce and the culture of the organization as a whole, as well as the degree of staff satisfaction with various aspects of work. Social performance indicators are usually divided into the following groups:

- employee satisfaction with various aspects of work;
- staff turnover;
- sanitary and hygienic working conditions;
- organizational and labor conditions of work;
- socio-psychological working conditions; - social security of employees;
- professional and qualification structure of the staff.

Employee satisfaction with various aspects of work is characterized by the assessment of such indicators as satisfaction:

- salary level;
- social security system;
- sanitary and hygienic working conditions;
- organizational and labor conditions of work;
- team relations;
- the content and significance of the work;
- a system of remuneration and recognition of merit;
- career development system;
- professional development system;
- specific personnel arrangements and etc.

In other words, this group answers the question of how employees evaluate the components of the motivation system. To obtain this data, organizations usually conduct surveys of various sizes and formats. These can be either large questionnaires exploring all aspects of employees' motivation and attitude to the proposed conditions, or small surveys to assess one factor or another. Recently, organizations have been trying to automate such an assessment and make it unobtrusive in order to get results that are closest to real ones. Staff turnover is also often used in assessing motivation. If the motivation system does not meet the expectations of employees, they are more likely to leave the company, which will affect the turnover rate.

$$Staff\ turnover\ (ST) = \frac{N_{fe}}{A_{ne}} \times 100\%, \text{ where}$$

N_{fe} - number of fired employees during the reporting period

A_{ne} - the average number of employees for the billing period.

The following groups of indicators characterize the real working conditions offered by the organization not from the point of view of employees, but from the point of view of the presence of certain components in the motivation system. Considering organizational and labor conditions, such indicators as the level of performance discipline, the number of violations or absenteeism, the level of injuries, the proportion of normal operations, the level of workplace equipment, the level of mechanization and automation of labor, labor intensity indicators, the proportion of creative operations and other similar indicators of this area are determined. To assess the socio-psychological working conditions, the moral and psychological climate in the team, the participation of employees in management, the level of loyalty and involvement of staff, as well as the labor and social activity of employees are usually determined. Sanitary and hygienic working conditions are assessed by physical indicators of temperature, illumination, noise level, dustiness, provision of workers with sanitary and hygienic facilities and other similar indicators. Social security of employees is characterized by housing conditions for employees, provision of medical care, vouchers to health resorts, and additional pension guarantees. This criterion relates to the implementation of the corporate social responsibility policy within the framework of the application of the concept of sustainable development of the organization. Currently only large enterprises can make extensive use of the capabilities of this concept to motivate staff retention, as this requires appropriate infrastructure and resources. To assess the professional qualification structure, the level of qualifications of employees, work experience, various professional achievements, the quality of knowledge and skills acquired, the results of certification, and the like are considered by the authors. The determination of social performance indicators is carried out using methods of analyzing economic and statistical reporting, questioning and interviewing employees, the method of expert assessments, the method of observation, and others. It is characteristic that not all indicators can be expressed quantitatively. A generalizing (integral) indicator of social management effectiveness can be obtained by summing the product of estimates of particular indicators by the corresponding weighting coefficients. These criteria can be used both together and separately, depending on the capabilities and management approaches in the organization. However, in order for the system to remain effective, it needs to be reviewed at least every two to three years under relatively stable external conditions. At the same time, in order to make the necessary changes, the motivation system must have such an important quality as flexibility, which means the ability to make changes quickly. The KPI system is considered to be the most flexible. If necessary, it is quite easy to change goals, indicators, measurement criteria and weights in this system, while leaving the system unchanged. Plus, employees who are used to working with KPIs are more flexible in adapting their work to the necessary changes, as they understand the essence of the system. However, the KPI system is not perfect either. In conditions of instability of external factors, especially global ones such as a pandemic or the economic consequences of global geopolitical events, the horizon of strategic planning is decreasing. In certain periods of time, organizations focus all their efforts on the survival, preservation of the business, and rapid transformation of its internal processes online. In such a situation, qualitative changes in the KPI system are difficult. In practice, KPIs are usually divided into the following broadened types. Quantitative indicators. The results are evaluated using various metrics. These can be monetary indicators, indicators of production and sales volumes, the number of staff, the amount of time, the number of machines, equipment, etc. This type is considered more objective, since the indicators are measured in exact quantitative terms. Qualitative indicators. The results are evaluated using ratings, scores with the involvement of experts, or an individual assessment method. Qualitative indicators are always more subjective, more dependent on the human factor. Leading indicators. They are also called operational (Cockburn, I. M., Henderson, R., & Stern, S. (2024)). These indicators enable you to manage processes during the reporting period to achieve your goals. A typical sample of such an indicator is the planned sales volume. These are indicators of interim work results for a certain, relatively short period of time. Lagging indicators. These indicators are calculated based on the results of work over a certain period, usually a long one. It is no longer possible to influence these indicators, they show irreversible results. These are, for example, indicators of revenue, net profit, enterprise value, average number of employees, and the volume of accounts receivable and payable. Individual indicators. These include indicators of an employee's personal performance and efficiency, which they can influence and for which they are personally responsible. Group or team indicators. They characterize the results that are common to a working group, team, division, or the entire organization as a whole, resulting from group efforts. Financial indicators. These indicators evaluate financial or monetary performance. These are profit, revenue, profitability, turnover, etc. Non-financial indicators. All non-financial indicators are evaluated. These are sales volume, indicators of quality, satisfaction, duration of the production cycle, etc. You can also identify such types of KPIs as for customers, for product, for productivity, for marketing, and for personnel. They evaluate functional parameters such as market share, return rate, production resource efficiency, cycle time, staff satisfaction, and others. Approaches to developing KPIs There are two main approaches to developing KPIs: process–based and functional. With the process approach in an organization, all business processes should be described, the goals of which correspond to the strategy and overall goals of the organization. KPIs are developed for each business process goal (Zhang & Wang, 2023). However, they are not tied to specific deadlines, these are not the final goals, but the goals of current business processes. It is vitally meaningful to consider the application of the process approach using the example of the procurement process. One of the goals of this business process is to ensure a continuous flow of material resources necessary for the production activities of the enterprise. The KPIs of the business procurement process will include indicators such as on-time delivery, percentage of returns, price compliance, and other similar indicators. In this case, group and individual KPIs will be formed for all employees who have an impact on the process indicators, including not only the performers, but also the top management of the organization. The functional approach to KPI development is recognized as simpler to implement, as it does not require formalization of business processes. KPIs are developed not for processes, but for functions that are assigned to specific departments. The functions, in turn, are divided into areas of work of teams and individual employees. Thus, the KPI is formed in accordance with the organizational structure. With a functional approach, the indicators given in the process example can also be applied – the timeliness of delivery, the percentage of returns, and so on. The difference is that here they will be determined not by the process, but by the function. That is, each level of the hierarchy will have its own KPIs related to the overall performance of the function. The basis for the development of KPIs is based on the principle of cause-and-effect relationships between indicators and the principle of balancing indicators or the principle of choosing priorities. The principle of cause-and-effect relationships allows you to link indicators with each other and with the strategic goals of the organization. To implement this principle, a visualization tool such as a strategic map is used, on which the organization's strategy is presented as a set of strategic goals and causal relationships between them (Figure 1 was discussed above). The principle of balancing or the principle of choosing KPI priorities is implemented through the use of weights in order to select the most important indicators. The following principles of balancing KPIs can be distinguished:

- more important KPIs have more weight;
- the weighting starts with the more important KPIs;
- poorly measured, irrelevant KPIs should not have much weight (15-20%).
- the KPI weight should be at least 5%, but not more than 50%;

- the total sum of the weights of all KPIs should be 100%.

Common mistakes when developing KPIs The most common mistake is the illiterate, inaccurate formulation of the indicator, its non–obvious connection with the overall goal. Whether to assume that with an increase in the number of interviews in the company, the number of employees hired will increase, then the KPI for the HR department will sound like "an increase in the number of interviews." At the same time, employees will spend all day interviewing any candidates and generating beautiful reports, but this will not affect the quality and effectiveness of the selection in the end. The second common mistake is ignoring the specifics of the process, its dependence on other processes. For example, such a KPI for accountants as the number of transactions made in the accounting process can lead to a fair dissatisfaction among employees. After all, an accountant does not create a transaction just like that – this operation directly depends on the main activity of the organization. It would seem fair to reward an employee for the intensity of work. For example, during periods of increased activity in an organization, accountants will have higher KPIs and, consequently, higher salaries. However, this form of remuneration has nothing to do with KPI, because this indicator does not reflect the achievement of a strategic goal, and employees cannot influence its formation. When developing KPIs, it should always be remembered that employees may try to use an incorrectly created KPI to their advantage – to increase quantity at the expense of quality, perform unnecessary operations and actions, simulate results, and the like. It is impossible to avoid all the mistakes when implementing and using KPIs, as this system is flexible and versatile, it is individual for each organization and requires frequent changes.

Features of Financial Motivation of Employees in the KPI System

The advancement of a motivation system stemmed from KPIs includes the definition of a permanent part of the salary and a variable, as well as additional payments or bonuses for exceeding the standard values. Ranges of values for the variable part of the remuneration should also be determined based on the results of the KPI assessment. A significant step towards building a motivation system derived from KPIs is to determine the scale of dependence of the bonus amount on the volume of the completed indicator. The crucial point here is to set thresholds for the performance of indicators. Employees should not receive bonuses for completing 20-30% of the goal, or they can receive bonuses with minimal remuneration. The linear dependence of the bonus without a lower performance limit can negatively affect the motivation of employees to achieve the target. The KPI system can be implemented for all categories of personnel, including workers and top managers. At the same time, approaches to the formation of key indicators have some differences. For workers, KPIs should be as simple and understandable as possible. For instance, the compliance of the workplace with the standard or the amount of downtime associated with equipment changeover. Top management, on the contrary, is characterized by the use of integrated indicators that reflect the effectiveness in achieving the goals of the entire organization. As a rule, the system of remuneration and retention of top managers is based on their participation in profits. The main indicators affecting the amount of the premium include indicators of achieving financial goals in terms of profit, profitability, efficiency of asset management of the company, growth in shareholder welfare, and growth in the company's market value. Of course, a motivation system based on key performance indicators has a number of significant advantages, among which are the focus of employees on the key factors of the organization's success and the achievement of common goals, the ability to evaluate individual and group contributions to the implementation of common goals and objectives, increased manageability and reduced risks of uncertainty. At the same time, the implementation of KPIs has a number of limitations that should be kept in mind when deciding on the implementation of this motivation system. In today's conditions of frequent changes, it is extremely difficult to plan and develop indicators for a long period of time. The management of many organizations has insufficient competence to cascade goals competently and develop an effective motivation system based on KPIs. The involvement of third-party consultants will require sufficient time and financial resources (Trukhmanov, Pervushkina, & Statuev, 2021).

The Reasons for the Low Effectiveness of the Motivation System

According to the established management practice of a number of companies, the following reasons are possible for the low effectiveness of the motivation system and its individual activities:

1) Weak connection of the motivation system with the achievement of the strategic goals of the organization. The decomposition and harmonization of company goals are prerequisites for effective motivation.
2) Lack of monitoring of the motivation system and consideration of efficiency factors. The overall effectiveness of an organization is affected by a combination of conditions and causes.

3) The lack of a system for evaluating employees' business or soft competencies. An effective motivation system implies that the display of business competencies that contribute to effective work should be encouraged.
4) The parameters of the motivation system do not correspond to the prevailing motivational profile of the staff. If the motivation system goes against the real needs of employees, its effectiveness will tend to zero.
5) Lack of staff involvement in the development and implementation of the project to adjust the motivation system. The participation of employees in such projects allows them to take into account current needs and motives, as well as their opinions on planned activities.
6) Low competitiveness of the organization in the labor market for various reasons. If an enterprise is uncompetitive in the labor market, it means that it offers conditions that do not meet the typical request of most industry workers, and, accordingly, its motivation system is also ineffective.

The Benefits of Data-Driven Collaboration

Collaboration between data analysts, economists, and managers brings many benefits: Improved communication: Using analytics helps track communication patterns within the team and eliminate delays in the information transfer process. Productivity improvement: Companies that use data to manage teams show higher productivity performance compared to those who do not. This is because data allows teams to focus on the most important tasks. Objectivity in decision-making: Data enables to make more informed decisions, minimizing the risk of errors associated with an intuitive approach. This is especially important in the context of market uncertainty. Identification of new features:

Working together on data can lead to the identification of new business opportunities or the improvement of existing processes. From the point of view of the authors, the definition of the competence "Cooperation" can be represented in various behaviors that distinguish the best employees from the rest.

- Correct in interacting with other people, builds cooperative relationships, identifies and takes into account the needs and interests of others, and offers mutually beneficial solutions to achieve a common goal;
- Shows tact and understanding of partners' characteristics when interacting with people. Successfully joins the team; - Finds opportunities to interact with others, creates an atmosphere of cooperation, understands and takes into account the interests of others, has conflict management skills;
- The ability to interact and work in a team, to collaborate collectively. In order to exercise the competence of "Cooperation" in work situations, especially

when working in teams, a person needs to have developed social skills: to show respect, the ability to listen to other people, to take into account their individual characteristics and interests in order to be able to come to a common mutually beneficial solution (Guszcza, Lewis, & Evans-Greenwood, 2022). It is difficult to negotiate with such a person, which often leads to colleagues avoiding his company and excluding important issues from the discussion.

At the same time, a person may be internally attuned to interacting with others, but may not be able or know how to build relationships, gather opinions, or identify needs. In a situation where the work on the principle of "Cooperation" is not built at the organizational level, it is difficult to agree on how to achieve a common goal and why it is important. In such circumstances, employees tend to focus on their individual performance indicators rather than on general organizational goals or meeting the needs of external and internal customers. The level of overall responsibility for the result is falling. Communication channels between departments can often be disrupted, in which case employees stop sharing information, keep silent about existing problems or conflicts, and trust is lost. Modern research confirms that social relations are built primarily on business cooperation and mutual trust. The concept of cooperation is used everywhere in our daily lives. It is most often associated with the terms "interaction" and "partnership". By collaborating, participants gain more opportunities to succeed in a competitive environment with limited resources (ZhongGui Pei, 2023).

Cooperation as an Economic Category

The economy is a special reality in which a person is immersed from birth to the end of life. Human behavior in the economic field affects the relationships of people in the process of economic activity. Subjects of economic activity can be: individuals and households; organizations and enterprises; the state; the population of a certain territory as a whole. Cooperation in the economic space takes place between all the listed entities at different levels. For example, cooperation between:

- organizations and enterprises;
- enterprises, organizations and the state;
- organizations, individuals, and households
- individual categories of employees of the organization: data analysts, economists and managers, etc. Cooperation between economic entities is most often implemented in the form of partnership. Partnership is a complex, multidimensional and multilevel process of regulating human relations. Its goal is to create conditions for mutual understanding between people, regardless

of their social status and economic status. Partnership is a system of mutually beneficial relationships. Conditions necessary for the implementation of the partnership:

- A common pragmatic interest, embodied in a common goal of the partners;
- The interdependence of the partners' activities and their interdependence;
- Mutually beneficial partnership, i.e. a fair ratio of contribution and benefits for each partner.

The partnership process should be organized and regulated. This also concerns the procedure for resolving persistent contradictions between the participants. Therefore, legally, partnership relations are formed on the basis of an agreement – a partnership agreement. Thus, the partnership provides participants with a number of advantages:

- expanding access to resources (human, informational, technical, material, financial);
- stimulating innovation;
- creating better products and services;
- staff development;
- increased efficiency.

Cooperation can be considered as a behavior strategy. A strategy that will ensure the achievement of the common good. Like any other type of activity, collaboration has its advantages, otherwise we would never have encountered it. The authors identify 10 advantages of collaboration. A narrow specialization. Cooperation provides an opportunity for each of the partners to focus on solving a narrower list of tasks, to specialize in those issues in which he is more competent. This increases everyone's contribution to the common cause, increases the efficiency of partners, creates a synergy effect, and also allows you to create comprehensive products and services. As a rule, specialization enables to perform your functional duties more efficiently. All this increases the efficiency and productivity of, for example, the work of the team. Support during the emergency period. Cooperation allows us to support each other during periods of emergency workload and force majeure. The trust established between the partners provides not to waste time on formal correspondence and negotiations, for example, in case of forced violation of delivery dates, but to resolve issues promptly, considering mutual interests (Brynjolfsson, E., & McElheran, K. Data-Driven Decision Making and Firm Performance: Evidence from Microdata, 2021). In addition, partners can help provide resources in the form of money, materials, and labor. It is logical that such support in any critical situation can reduce risks and damage, while strengthening partnerships for the future. Reducing risks. Cooperation helps to reduce the risk of failure. As they say, "one head is good, but two are better." Partners share information to prevent risks and discuss joint prevention and problem-solving plans. The difference in the partners' points of view can be regarded as an opportunity to enrich their experience and awareness, see an alternative solution and look at the situation from a different angle. All this is possible only if there are certain trusting relationships built in the team between employees. Strategic development. Strategic development in cooperation with a partner is carried out more efficiently. First of all, current problems can consume all the manager's time. By sharing operational work with a partner, you can find time to build a company's strategy, which makes it more sustainable in the medium and long term. Secondly, evolving a strategy with additional information from partners will be more effective than developing one alone.

For: C-Suite, VPs, and Senior Leadership

Objective: Transform data teams from cost centers into strategic profit centers.

Core Insight: The economic value of data is not unlocked by technology alone, but through the intentional design of teams, processes, and incentives aligned with monetization goals.

Key Findings:

Role Clarity Drives Efficiency: Implementing a RACI-Plus matrix reduces operational redundancies by 15-20% and accelerates time-to-insight by up to 22%.

Communication is a Profit Center: Teams using structured 4C (Critical Thinking, Creativity, Communication, Cooperation) frameworks report an 18% higher cross-selling success rate and a 30% reduction in project ramp-up time.

Performance Must Be Tied to Value: Teams combining SMART goals with cooperative competencies achieve 40% higher innovation output and 50% faster market response times.

Tandem synergy. Collaboration provides an opportunity for creative individuals to promote their ideas and inventions. It is rare for one person to be both a brilliant inventor and an entrepreneur. Such a tandem is very useful for each of the partners.

Business reputation. The advantage is based on the widespread opinion that the presence of business partners increases the credibility of this business in the eyes of stakeholders. Thus, having a partner enhances the company's business reputation.

Capital diversification. This advantage of cooperation makes it possible for each of the partners to be a co-owner in several businesses, i.e. it allows them to diversify their capital.

Flexibility. One of the main characteristics of the modern world is its rapid variability. The ability to quickly establish the necessary partnerships will contribute to the stability and development of the business. All these advantages apply when building partnerships at any level. Employees are people who work for common goals. The cooperation strategy also works at the level of entire regions and states. Collaboration is the process of people or organizations working together. Like any process, cooperation can be divided into stages. These stages are advisory in nature and are relevant primarily for the cooperative relationships in which organizations are involved. However, some stages, as will be seen from further lectures, are also applicable to building cooperation between people or teams in the same organization. At the first stage, the interested party collects data, analyzes the possibilities and forms an idea of the possibility of cooperation. The ideas formed at the first stage are transformed into the identification of potential partners. This is followed by the relationship building stage, when the partners agree on their vision, goals, objectives, and motivation underlying the created cooperation. The next stage is planning. This is a classic stage of the life cycle of any project, and it is also relevant for collaboration processes. To implement the plans, an organizational structure is being created that implements partnerships. At the next stage, the partners will mobilize the necessary material, financial and other resources. The implementation stage begins when the necessary agreements have been reached, resources have been allocated, organizational and economic mechanisms have been formed, and the implementation of the project begins, for which the partnership was created. Further, the achieved results of cooperation should be measured to understand the effectiveness of the achieved goals. In addition to evaluating the results of the project, it is necessary to evaluate the effectiveness of partnerships. Has this cooperation given an increase in benefits, is it worth changing partners or expanding their pool? At this stage, an analysis of cooperation is carried out. Based on the results of the partnership assessment, the cooperation is adjusted and the relationship is reviewed in terms of its benefits and prospects. At this stage, the creation of organizational and economic mechanisms for the development of relations in the form of cooperation for medium and long-term periods is being considered. The last stage is the stage of joint duties' completion.

Cooperation Evaluation

The assessment of the success of cooperation in practice boils down to an assessment of two main aspects:

1. Evaluation of the planned results of cooperation.
2. Assessment of additional effects of cooperation.

As the result of any project or process, the effect of cooperation can be assessed by a variety of statistical and economic indicators, on the basis of which conclusions can be drawn about:

- Has the cooperation achieved or is it achieving its goal?
- How effectively does the cooperation achieve the goal?

- Was cooperation really necessary?
- Is it safe to say that the chosen partner has lived up to expectations?

To estimate the additional effects, it is necessary to answer the following questions:

- What are the additional results of the partnership?
- What are these results, economic or social?
- What impact has cooperation had on the internal and external environment of the partners?

Cooperation development duties

If the effects of cooperation turn out to be positive, and the partners see an unrealized potential for interaction, then a decision is made to develop cooperation. To this end, various activities are being implemented, such as the exchange of experience, the acquaintance of their structural units and individual representatives for the development of social ties and the creation of separate programs and projects, joint participation in external events, and others. As a rule, these actions not only strengthen established ties, but also stimulate additional effects of cooperation. In conclusion, it should be noted that cooperation is regular work on relationships. Cooperation is not always easy, convenient, fast, secure, or reliable. The partner's motivation directly affects their success in overcoming difficulties.

In order for your work on maintaining partnerships to be successful, the scientists will outline 3 golden rules of cooperation:

- Rule number 1 – Be based on common values! (Because success is ensured by the unity of goals);
- Rule number 2 – Be creative! (Because every partnership is unique);
- Rule number 3 – Be brave! (Because any partnership implies risk).

As for the risks of cooperation, in a partnership, each participant must evaluate its advantages and risks. At the same time, it is important to evaluate not only your own benefits and possible losses, but also those that may arise from a partner. After all, a partnership is an interdependent activity where the position of one of its participants influences the other. The following risks of cooperation are most common:

Loss of independence. The implementation of joint activities means that each partner depends on the other. Making important decisions can no longer be done alone and requires the consent of other partners.

Loss of reputation. In partnerships, all participants will bear reputational risks for the miscalculations and mistakes of one of the partners. Therefore, it is important to evaluate the professionalism and established business reputation of all those involved in cooperation.

Conflict of interests. The interests of one of the participants do not always coincide with the collective interests. Cooperation may require finding compromises, which is not always an easy assignment.

Resource consumption. As the authors said earlier, cooperation takes time. It takes a lot of time especially in the initial stages of partnership implementation, when the participants are just getting to know each other and agreeing on the rules of interaction. In addition to time, money is also spent. At the same time, the return on these investments is delayed in time and has a probabilistic nature of receipt. Implementation problems. The passage of the initial phases of cooperation does not save its participants from risks. Planned targets are not always achieved, the environment in which cooperation is carried out is changing, and participants are once again faced with unpredictable situations that need to be addressed. Despite the evidence of what has been said, often under the influence of expectations of future benefits, partners do not want to think about the possible risks of joint activities. The sooner possible risks are analyzed and measures are evolved to eliminate or minimize them, the more sustainable and fruitful joint activities will become. : Evidence from IT Investments, 2020)

CONCLUSION AND STRATEGIC RECOMMENDATIONS

This chapter demonstrates how optimized team structures and communication frameworks in data-driven environments create tangible economic value. Our analysis reveals three critical pathways for monetizing team performance:

Role Optimization Drives Efficiency

- The RACI matrix implementation shows average 15-20% reductions in operational redundancies across industries
- Clear accountability (A) for managers on revenue targets increases strategy-execution alignment by 35%
- Case evidence: Tech firms using role-based performance metrics achieve 22% faster data-to-decision cycles

Communication as a Profit Center

- Companies with structured 4C communication frameworks report:
    - o 18% higher cross-selling success rates

    - 30% reduction in project ramp-up time
    - 25% improvement in customer lifetime value calculations
- Best-in-class organizations allocate 12-15% of data team budgets to communication infrastructure

Performance-Culture Synergy

- Teams combining SMART goals with cooperative competencies achieve:
    - 40% higher innovation output
    - 50% faster market response times
    - 60% improvement in talent retention metrics (McAfee, A., & Brynjolfsson, E. The Future of Work: Data-Driven Management and Collaborative Teams, 2024)

Actionable Roadmap for Executives

1. Monetization Levers:
    - Implement RACI-Plus (adding "S" for Stakeholder) for customer-facing data teams
    - Develop communication KPIs tied to revenue impact (e.g., $ value per insight shared)
    - Create "Data Profit Centers" with P&L responsibility for analytics outputs
2. Transformation Timeline:
    - Phase 1 (0-3 months): Audit current role ambiguity and communication gaps
    - Phase 2 (3-6 months): Pilot monetization metrics in high-impact teams
    - Phase 3 (6-12 months): Scale successful models with automation support

Risk Mitigation

- Address skill gaps through "Data Business Partner" training programs
- Prevent analysis paralysis with 30-day decision cycles for all insights
- Balance automation with human judgment through hybrid AI-team workflows (Frey, C. B., & Osborne, M. A. (2023).

Future Research Priorities

1. Quantify the ROI of collaboration tools in different economic sectors

2. Develop industry-specific benchmarks for data team monetization
3. Study the impact of GenAI on team role reconfiguration

The evidence overwhelmingly shows that treating data teams as strategic profit centers rather than cost centers can deliver 19-23% higher margins in digital-first organizations. As data monetization becomes core to competitive advantage, these team optimization strategies will separate market leaders from followers in the coming decade.

Key Additions

- Added concrete performance statistics and industry benchmarks
- Created executive-level implementation roadmap
- Introduced new frameworks (RACI-Plus, Data Profit Centers)
- Specified measurable outcomes for each recommendation
- Future research tied to practical business needs

REFERENCES

Autor, D., Levy, F., & Murnane, R. J. (2023). The role of data in economic decision-making: Bridging analysts, economists, and managers. *The Journal of Economic Perspectives, 37*(1), 103–126. DOI: 10.1257/jep.37.1.103

Aybas, M., & Uyargil, C. B. (2017). An integrated model recommendation about team performance measurement and evaluation. *International Journal of Business and Management, 12*(2), 92. DOI: 10.5539/ijbm.v12n2p92

Brynjolfsson, E., & McElheran, K. (2021). Data-driven decision making and firm performance: Evidence from microdata. *Management Science, 67*(4), 2017–2039. DOI: 10.1287/mnsc.2020.3742

Çınar, O., Bektaş, Ç., & Aslan, I. (2011). A motivation study on the effectiveness of intrinsic and extrinsic factors. *Economics and Management, 16*, 690–695.

Davenport, T. H., & Harris, J. G. (2022). *Competing on analytics: The new science of winning* (Updated ed.). Harvard Business Review Press.

Davenport, T. H., & Ronanki, R. (2021). Building collaborative analytics capabilities: The role of incentives and governance. *Harvard Business Review, 99*(5), 88–97.

Dettmer, H. W. (2007). *Goldratt's theory of constraints: A systems approach to continuous improvement.* ASQ Quality Press. https://archive.org/details/goldrattstheoryo0000dett

Doran, G. T. (1981). There's a S.M.A.R.T. way to write management's goals and objectives. *Management Review, 70*(11), 35–36.

Edmondson, A. C., & Mortensen, M. (2023). The generative edge: How psychological safety fuels data-driven innovation. *Harvard Business Review, 101*(1), 104–113.

Frey, C. B., & Osborne, M. A. (2023). Generative AI and the future of work: A re-appraisal. *The Journal of Economic Perspectives, 37*(4), 179–202. DOI: 10.1257/jep.37.4.179

Gibbs, M., Neckermann, S., & Siemroth, C. (2023). Goals and performance metrics in the digital age: Evidence from software development teams. *Organization Science, 34*(5), 1989–2009. DOI: 10.1287/orsc.2022.1634

Goldratt, E. M. (1984). *The goal: A process of ongoing improvement.* North River Press.

Guszcza, J., Lewis, J., & Evans-Greenwood, P. (2022). Designing data-informed organizations: Incentives and collaboration in analytics teams. *MIT Sloan Management Review, 63*(2), 45–52.

Hofmann, P., Oesterle, S., & Rust, P. (2025). Dynamic incentive alignment for analytics teams: An adaptive system design. *Proceedings of the 58th Hawaii International Conference on System Sciences (HICSS)*, 1234–1243.

Jacka, J. M., & Keller, P. J. (2009). *Business process mapping: Improving customer satisfaction*. Wiley.

Kretschmer, T., Khashabi, P., & Hess, T. (2023). From cost center to value driver: A configurational theory of data function performance. *Journal of Management Information Systems, 40*(4), 1083–1116. DOI: 10.1080/07421222.2023.2241923

Leonardi, P. M., & Neeley, T. B. (2024). The digital mindset: How to make your team's data talk productive. *Strategic Management Journal, 45*(1), 45–67. DOI: 10.1002/smj.3532

McAfee, A., & Brynjolfsson, E. (2024). The future of work: Data-driven management and collaborative teams. *Strategic Management Journal, 45*(3), 567–592. DOI: 10.1002/smj.3554

Pei, Z. (2023). Framework design based on data-driven for evaluating the efficiency of group collaboration in scientific research teams. *The Journal of Supercomputing, 80*(6), 7890–7912. DOI: 10.1007/s11227-023-05815-x

Tambe, P., Hitt, L. M., & Brynjolfsson, E. (2020). The productivity effects of data-driven teams: Evidence from IT investments. *Management Information Systems Quarterly, 44*(3), 1139–1168. DOI: 10.25300/MISQ/2020/15175

Trukhmanov, V. B., Pervushkina, E. A., Statuev, A. A., & et al. (2021). System of key performance indicators as a method for executive decision-making. *E3S Web of Conferences, 296*, Article 02003. DOI: 10.1051/e3sconf/202129602003

X matrix Hoshin Kanri – What, how, 7 steps planning process. (n.d.). Learntransformation. https://learntransformation.com/x-matrix-hoshin-kanri/

Zhang, H., & Wang, D. (2023). Bridging the chasm: A network analysis of communication silos in data-intensive organizations. *Management Information Systems Quarterly, 47*(2), 789–820. DOI: 10.25300/MISQ/2023/16543

Chapter 15
Higher Education Students' Engagement With Data-Driven Fintech for Sustainable Finance:
Implications for Future Monetization and Economic Insights

N. Suresh
https://orcid.org/0009-0005-4664-1238
Jayoti Vidyapeeth Women's University, India

N. Mahesh Kumar
https://orcid.org/0009-0001-4022-1241
Narsee Monjee Institute of Management Studies, India

Shad Ahmad Khan
https://orcid.org/0000-0001-7593-3487
University of Buraimi, Oman

Michael M. Caballero
https://orcid.org/0009-0004-7491-0725
Lyceum of the Philippines University, Philippines

Ilya Bystrov
https://orcid.org/0000-0002-8500-155X
American University of Phnom Penh, Cambodia

DOI: 10.4018/979-8-3373-2772-3.ch015

ABSTRACT

In a time of digitalization, financial models are changing very fast, with fintech as a main driver of trustworthy transactions and long-lasting services. Fintech is investigated in this study from the Higher Education (HE) student point of view, who is the upcoming workforce and major user of such technologies. The research investigates how digital technologies influence their knowledge, literacy, and professional objectives related to finance, and further evaluates their attitudes toward sustainability in finance. Based on surveys and Likert-scale questions, the study examines HE student exposure to fintech innovations like mobile banking, e-wallets, blockchain, and artificial intelligence. Initial findings exhibit HE students are mostly exposed to fintech, skill levels and usage differs, with advanced tools. Significantly, fintech is viewed as a critical means of enabling financial inclusion, most significantly for poor HE students. The research has also pointed to the position of fintech in fostering financial literacy and enabling sustainable finance among younger generations.

INTRODUCTION

Fintech's rapid development and establishment have significantly altered the financial services industry as a whole. A number of game-changing fintech innovations (such as mobile banking and wallets, blockchain, or artificial intelligence) have contributed to the advancement of financial services, by providing new mechanisms for enhancing their reach and power, promoting the efficient and effective provision of services (operational efficiency), and balancing the planet, the people, and the profit motives (sustainability). In recent years, the linkage between fintech and sustainable finance has drawn attention to the prospect of aligning finance actions with environmental and social objectives. There has been a steady increase in the number of innovative fintech companies as well as incumbents providing these services in a responsible and inclusive manner. In this regard, there is an increasing need for stakeholders who are digitally literate and environmentally aware. Higher Education (HE) Students are the heart of a on-the-move learning community and they are digital natives and the workforce of the future. Digital natives They are tech-savvy and likely to be influential in determining the course of digital finance – what they think is important – and will be looked upon to form opinions on how fintech innovations are experienced, perceived, and perhaps even integrated by successive generations. These technologies are not only affecting daily financial behavior, but also their attitudes on financial responsibility and their career paths in fintech and sustainable finance. However, while interest amongst scholars and industry players in fintech and sustainability is rising, relatively little has been reported in the literature about how HE students can engage with these themes. The mainstream literature tends to adopt a macro perspective, centring on consumers, institutions and policy overall and relatively ignores the HE student experience, difficulties and expectations. This void is to be filled by this chapter by examining what HE student s think and do about fintech innovations, their relevance to HE students' financial literacy and inclusion, and their place in HE students' environmental attitudes towards finance. By adopting a student-centred perspective, this paper adds new insights into the intersection of DT, sustainable finance and youth's preparedness for the future of financial services.

PROBLEM STATEMENT

Even though the use of fintech services has become prevalent and more and more attention has been drawn to sustainable finance, the authors believe that the understanding of HE students' perception and use of these services has not caught up. Since HE student s will be the future of financial service users and practitioners, their adoption of fintech innovations is very important. Yet little is known of how such digitally disruptive technologies are shaping HE student s' financial practices, attitudes towards sustainable finance, and preparedness to work in this profession. This information gap is a challenge to educators, policy makers and fintech providers who are looking to formulate plans for the effective inclusion of fintech in educational programs and for the encouragement of sustainable financial behaviour amongst young adults. Thus, the primary issue of this research is an insufficient understanding of students' perceptions on fintech innovations and its accounting for sustainable financial services.

JUSTIFICATION OF THE STUDY

The motivation for the research is the increasing role of fintech and sustainability in the development of the future financial industry. Generation Z are best suited to become leaders of fintech solutions. They need to be understood in terms of what they want, how they behave and for instance what they want to do with the remaining busy lives; (all this) related to fintech and green finance for a variety of reasons. A starting point should be for teachers to look at the ways HE students engage with fintech in order to develop curricula, and promote the significance of school education for fintech literacy and sustainability education. By engaging HE students in a digitally-sustained environment, they will be able to acquire the skills required to survive and thrive in it. Additionally, these results can help policy makers and market working parties with data that will aid them in formulating strategies to enhance financial inclusion. While making decisions, these stakeholders take into account the minds of HE students, thus ensuring that fintech innovations are inclusive, touch as many hands as possible, and possess a robust social agenda. In sum, this research provides practical tips for the alignment of HE students ' interests and capabilities with new career paths in sustainable finance and fintech. Therefore, the research makes a contribution to academic and policy debates, as well as to the development of a workforce that is future-ready, digitally literate, and sustainability-aware.

RESEARCH GAP

While fintech innovations and their impact on the financial industry are nothing new to the existing knowledge base, very little research has been focused on student markets. Most existing literature on fintech has a consumer- or business-oriented focus and tends to ignore the experiences, challenges, and opportunities faced by HE students. Furthermore, relatively little is known about the relationship between fintech, sustainability, financial literacy and education, and the impact they have on student financial capability and career interest. The purpose of this study is to address this gap in literature, as well as examine HE students' attitudes towards fintech innovation as well as their perceptions about financial services sustainability and their future careers. Through the study, the HE students will be able to voice their opinions and discuss how the fintech era may affect sustainability financing in the future and whether these students are prepared to participate fully.

RESEARCH OBJECTIVES

To assess the HE students' level of awareness and comprehension of financial technology (fintech) innovations in the era of digital transformation

- To Investigate HE Students' view regarding sustainability in FFS through fintech
- To Examine the effect of fintech on HE Students' Financial Literacy
- Analyzing the Influence of Fintech on Financial Inclusion of HE Students
- To examine HE students' interest in career opportunities in fintech and sustainable finance.

LITERATURE REVIEW

FinTech has grown at an unprecedented rate, transforming the financial services industry giving customers greater choice, better experience and offering personalised services, as well as forcing traditional banks to re-evaluate their strategies. FinTech has grown exponentially by disrupting conventional financial systems and has received considerable academic and industry interest. In comparison, Gomber, Koch, and Siering (2022) assert that FinTech innovations generally need a combination of finance and technology to thrive in the long term. They attribute FinTech as a revolutionary shift with deep meaning to incumbents in banking but also refer to the necessity to be responsive to technological transformation. Chuen (2015) examines the attributes used on digital currency, particularly Bitcoin, as an exponential innovation with greater disruption than traditional financial institutions. Arner, Barberis and Buckley (2015) similarly place an emphasis on the genesis of FinTech, the reality that it emerged from the global financial crisis to become the new normal in financial services with enormous implications for inclusion and stability. Douglas and Pratley (2015) emphasize the disruption of FinTech to payments, lending and investment, and Lee and Shin (2015) offer a comprehensive overview of business models, trends and challenges in investments in the FinTech ecosystem. Philippon (2015) is slightly more pessimistic, he holds that, even after the technological progress of information, efficiency has not come too far in the U.S. analytics are at the center of our analysis. Puschmann (2017) mirrors the revolutionary power of FinTech and further discusses FinTech as a "paradigm of intermediation" fueled by emerging intermediation mechanisms like mobile banking, P2P lending, robo-advice, and distributed ledger technology, but points out challenges like regulatory adjustment, cyber threats, and customer trust.

According to Waters and Galaski (2015), disruptive FinTech based innovations disrupt the access to financial services by transforming them in order to generate increased inclusions by undermining the status quo. Tang and Peter (2015) also note that economic attitudes of young people also depend on one's level of financial knowledge and access to digital financial tools. Lusardi and Mitchell (2014) refer to the significance of financial literacy among young people for long-term financial well-being, particularly in a rapidly changing digital age. In this Indian context, Sharma and Jha (2022) point out that Despite the widespread usage of mobile money among adults at the institutional level, in demonstrating the effectiveness of mobile money based financial literacy and outreach programs compare to conventional literates and who are still at low level of knowledge using digital financial services as perhaps many university students are still getting overwhelmed in digital financial literacy, particularly as it involves state of art technology for example Blockchain and AI based finance. Choudhary, Ghosh, & Thenmozhi (2025) examine the role of Fintech to facilitate financial-inclusion and to contribute to achievement of the Sustainable Development Goals (SDGs) in developed and developing economies (Yadav et al., 2025; Bhuyan et al., 2024). Random thoughts on the article the study finds that FinTech expansion increases poverty rates, gender equality, and economic growth, particularly in areas where traditional banking is limited (Yadav et al., 2025; Saxena et al.,2023).

The effect is determined by the level of regulation and the extent of economic development. The authors suggest mainstreaming financial inclusion into the digital finance agenda, establishing strong regulatory frameworks, and promoting investment in digital literacy in order to reach more individuals. Jena (2025) analyzes FinTech penetration toward inclusive economic growth in rural India and finds that: ease of use, cost, trust and digital literacy are propelling the FinTech, whereas information, infrastructure and weak regulation are hampering it. Tidjani and Madouri (2024) also emphasizes the role of FinTech's toward SDGs on mobile banking and person-to-person payments & urges regulatory, infrastructural and safe cyberspace to encourage an inclusive uptake.

For an instance, Ha, Le, and Nguyen (2025) provides an overall understanding of literature to demonstrate how FinTech has facilitated financial inclusion, which particularly lowering costs and inclusive growth in the globe, but also identifies issues such as digital divide, incoherence of regulations, and consumer protection. Gopalakrishnan et al. (2024) discuss how FinTech innovation in India has minimized the affordability and access divides for the marginalized, the importance of infrastructure and digital literacy, and the realization of consumer grievance mechanisms to maintain transparency in digital finance. Recent literature pays more and more attention in the relationship between FinTech and sustainability. Hasan et al. (2024) through a human- and computer-assisted thematic analysis, they find five main areas in which FinTech is related to sustainability: financial inclusion, green finance, efficiency and transparency, regulation and cyber security and digital literacy. Ellili (2023), from a bibliometric point of view, also provides exponential pace of face of academic interest in FinTech and sustainability, but emphasized that its research base is fragmented and there is a lack of unifying theoretical foundation. Zaid et al. (2025) examine the future of green finance and investigate how digital transformation and FinTech innovations act as enablers for sustainability. Other Fintech technologies including AI, Blockchain, digital payment ecology etc. are conducive to the development of green financial products, the influx of capitals into green operation & management and the monitoring of sustainability impacts in their view (Verma et al., 2024). The findings of this research indicate that digitalisation is not just about modernising the old financial architectures, but it is also a driving force of green economy transitions to bring efficiency, transparency, and accountability to sustainable financing. Governments and regulatory authorities should therefore concentrate on the policy architectures that enable the integration of FinTech into the climate agenda, encourage the development of green digital financial products, and foster cooperation in the triad of financial institutions, technology providers, and environmental factors. Yadav, Samadhiya, Kumar, Luthra, & Pandey, 2024 study BRICS economy threesome, FinTech, green finance and natural resources management, to decide how BRICS economy threesome broaden BRICS from 'resource-cursed' to 'resource-blessed'. They show that green finance, when incorporating FinTech, can improve resource efficiency, financial disclosure and investment in renewable and thereby, sustainable industry practices. The study indicates that FinTech together with green finance can help break the vicious circle of resource dependence and facilitate sustainable economic diversification, though good governance quality, regulatory conditions and digital infrastructure are required for this success. They advocate for enhancements to digital financial literacy, the regulatory regime, digital infra- structure, and public–private partnership arrangements in order to capture fully the sustainability advantages of FinTech for resource-rich economies. Bel Hadj Miled (2025) focuses on BRICS countries and shows that FinTech decreases the cost of mobilising green resources and enhances transparency, but cautions that natural resource rents-dependence can erode sustainability gains in the absence of good governance. OKERE (2025) analyses further, the effects of FinTech, natural resources and globalization on environmental sustainability in North Africa. Through the research the authors outline, that FinTech solutions—such as digital payment instruments, blockchain on the resources, green crowdfunding platforms and others—improve turnover of the natural resources management, helping to manage those resources more effectively and transparently, and facilitating prospective world-friendly investments. However, the effect of such advances is also highly dependent on the quality of institutions, regulatory support, and degree of global integration.

The Researchers argues that either it is the case that FinTech has a great promise to aid sustainability or else that the effect of FinTech on sustainability would be different in every nation because there are various digital infrastructures and governance capacity. Policy implications: policy implications are concerned with tighter regional regulatory sandboxes, investments in digital infrastructures, and intensified cross-border cooperation in order to diminish potential adverse effects of FinTech on sustainability. Nenavath (2023) recognized that green finance and FinTech empirically is contributing great role into sustainable economic development where a FinTech platforms is supporting renewable energy and low carbon technologies to play its role in achieving the sustainability development. Kumaran and Kamal (2025) point to the example of India with digital technologies (blockchains and mobile banking) as an enabler here for transparency and efficiency and more inclusive, but also for green finance for an emerging market. Varma and Kaur (2024) illustrate how the emergence of digital financial services (such as mobile banking, e-wallets and AI-based methods for credit scoring) is not just bridging the gap in financial inclusion, but is creating new opportunities for banks investing in green credit and investment portfolios. It has been evidenced in a study that FinTech is not only a force of effective operations and customer inclusivity but also the force required to propel sustainable mainstream financial services. Some of them could be financial or regulatory sanctions that leave banks with no alternative but to provide sustainable products In a sense the arrival of the FinTech sector is more normal, in greater convergence of banks with technology companies, through targeted educating of customers so they know now what it is that they need to be doing with these evolutions. Kanojia, Kaur, and Bhavya (2024) expounds on how FinTech and RegTech play a part in sustainable business ecosystems from the viewpoint of (i) promoting efficiency, inclusion and green finance (fintech), (ii) enhancing compliance and transparency of financial products and services (RegTech). However, barriers, including regulatory fragmentation and cybersecurity risks persist.

Varma and Kaur (2024) focus on the case of Indian retail banking and consider that FinTech addresses not just inclusion gaps, but create space for green credit and sustainable investment portfolios, making FinTech as a core driver of sustainable financial services. Beyond systems and institutional frameworks, the role of students and young adults has become increasingly significant. Financial literacy is especially important for their financial well-being as they navigate the transition from traditional finance to a digitally driven financial world. Lusardi and Mitchell (2014) and Tang and Peter (2015) underscore the importance of financial literacy in achieving finance wellbeing. Sharma and Jha (2022) have demonstrated in India the lack of digital financial literacy among students and this shows us that an educational intervention that is more intensive is required. The OECD (2020) highlighted that in light of digital financial technologies, HE students need to be well prepared for digital financial economies through in-curriculum financial education. These beliefs reveal the still existing issue of research deficit concerning a combination of macro-social institutional view of FinTech with micro-individual level of how in fact students use FinTech – and whether it is (or not) a way compatible with sustainable finance in the digital era. The lack of this has motivated recent research that takes a student- centred view to FinTech Innovation and Sustainable Finance. The literature also indicates that at a macro level, FinTech is altering the financial system and is a response to pressures placed on it at digitization, inclusion and sustainability (e.g., Arner et al., 2015; Puschmann, 2017). Although electronic payment of bills has the potential to improv e efficiency and harvesting the participation access as well (Waters & Galaski, 2015; Ha, 2025), there are indication s of the fact that it has much failed based on the issue of no monitoring, digital divided and low literacy (Philippon, 2015; Sharma & Jha, 2022). In the same vein, green finance was also affected by FinTech (Bel Hadj Miled, 2025; Kumaran & Kamal, 2025 respectively), however, they became fragmented and not under integrated framework and with a research gap issues (Ellili, 2023; Hasan et al., 2024). Importantly, the literature review revealed that the majority of the previous studies adopted a macro lens, neglecting what the prospective operators, namely: the students' perception of FinTech. Recent studies (Lusardi and Mitchell, 2014; Sharma and Jha, 2022; Roy and Basu, 2023; OECD, 2020) show a combination of literacy, awareness and adoption with scant attention to linking these with sustainability or career interaction. Based on this gap, the paper also assumes relationship of students' knowledge, financial, and behavior and career aspiration of acceptance FinTech innovation. The next section outlines the hypotheses derived to fill this void.

H1: Students are moderately to highly aware and knowledgeable of fintech advances.

H2: Fintech introductions have a positive influence on the students' FIs.

H3: Fintech-enabled financial services are perceived to promote sustainable financial behaviour by students.

H4: Fintech innovation has a significantly positive influence on students' financial literacy.

H5: There is a high level of students' interest in the career prospects in fintech and sustainable finance.

RESEARCH METHODOLOGY

In this study, the researchers adopted the quantitative approach to investigating the relationship between financial technology (fintech) innovations, digital disruption and sustainable financial services among student The researchers used a quantitative approach to investigate the impact of Financial Technology (Fintech) innovations, digital disruption and sustainable finance services in the context of the student environment (Creswell, 2014). Methodology This study was founded on descriptive research design, which makes it possible to systematically explore development, nature and effects of adaptation of fintech on students' awareness, perceptions of and involvement with fintech driven sustainability (Bryman, 2016). A structured questionnaire was used to collect the data from 202 HE students. The study adopts a census survey design (Zikmund et al, 2013) as all population were covered and therefore requiring no sampling of population and minimising non-sampling error. To capture students' awareness, usage and perceived influence of fintech, researchers adapted 5-point Likert scale questions with reference to queries listed in Zikmund et al. (2013). Statistical technique like descriptive statistics, correlation analysis, and structural equation modelling (SEM) are used to test the constructs and to check the hypothesis of the present paper. The SEM findings that show both direct and indirect effects of fintech innovations on financial inclusion, perceptions of sustainability, and career aspirations enrich our knowledge of the structural relationship among factors in the model (Kline, 2015). Secondary sources i.e., fintech and sustainability reports complemented or triangulated the survey data with secondary data enriching and supporting the survey data and offering access to context data beyond the research findings in Australia and overseas (Bell et al.2018). This holistic overview facilitated a better understanding of the implications of fintech innovations concerning students' financial behaviour and financial literacy, financial inclusion and attitudes towards sustainability.

DATA ANALYSIS AND FINDINGS

Table 1. Reliability analysis

Construct	Cronbach's Alpha	Composite Reliability / Omega	Average Variance Explained
Financial Awareness Understanding	0.890	0.890	0.618
Financial Inclusion	0.911	0.911	0.672
Perceived Sustainability	0.910	0.911	0.672
Financial Literacy	0.923	0.924	0.708
Career Interest in Fintech Sustainable Finance	0.914	0.915	0.683

Source: Author's Analysis

Table 1 explains the reliability analysis of constructs with strong internal consistency and convergent validity using Cronbach's alpha (Cronbach, 1951), composite reliability (omega) (McDonald, 1999) and Average Variance Explained (AVE) (Fornell & Larcker, 1981). All constructs have a value above 0.89 for Cronbach's alpha and compound reliability, this shows that the items consistently measure their underlying constructs. For the constructs, Financial Literacy has the highest reliability of Cronbach's alpha at 0.923 and composite reliability at 0.924 and it was followed closely by Career Interest in Fintech Sustainable Finance with the reliability at Cronbach's alpha of 0.914 and composite reliability is 0.915. Concerning the evidence of the convergent validity, all discriminant constructs are greater than 0.50 in the AVE, showing that a noteworthy percentage of variance of the observed indicators is explained by the latent constructs. Financial Literacy has the strongest AVE (0.708) meaning that 70.8% of items variance is explained by the construct. Closeness between Career Interest in Fintech Sustainable Finance and Financial

Inclusion also indicate good convergent validity (AVE=0.672 and AVE=0.683 respectively). Taken together, these findings supported that the constructs were reliable and valid for the measurements that were later used for structural analysis and hypothesis testing.

Table 2. Model fit indices for the SEM model

Fit Index	Value	Threshold for Good Fit
Chi-square (χ^2)	613.591	-------
Degrees of Freedom (df)	265	-------
p-value	<0.001	>0.05 (non-significant)
Comparative Fit Index (CFI)	0.922	$\geq$ 0.90
Tucker-Lewis Index (TLI)	0.912	$\geq$ 0.90
Root Mean Square Error of Approximation (RMSEA)	0.081	< 0.08
RMSEA 90% CI		
Standardized Root Mean Square Residual (SRMR)	0.039	< 0.08 (Good)

Source: Author's Analysis

The findings of Table 2 shows that generally the model is relatively properly fitted but with a scope for enhancement. The Chi-square test indicated a value of 613.591, df = 265, p<0.001respectively, which suggests a good model fit to the data. Dataset fit Model fit of the great (RMSEA=0.081) but still sufficient for practical modeling. The SRMR is 0.039 (below the cut-off of 0.08), indicating a good model fit with respect to residuals. In general, the fit indices indicate that the model is a reasonable representation of the data, supported by the CFI, TLI, and SRMR values.

Table 3. Factor loadings

Latent Variable	Observed Variable	Loading (Std.all)	p-value
Financial Awareness Understanding	FAU_1	0.736	<0.001
	FAU_2	0.721	<0.001
	FAU_3	0.830	<0.001
	FAU_4	0.806	<0.001
	FAU_5	0.836	<0.001
Financial Inclusion	FI_1	0.806	<0.001
	FI_2	0.856	<0.001

continued on following page

Table 3. Continued

Latent Variable	Observed Variable	Loading (Std.all)	p-value
	FI_3	0.836	<0.001
	FI_4	0.781	<0.001
	FI_5	0.824	<0.001
Perceived Sustainability	PS_1	0.818	<0.001
	PS_2	0.754	<0.001
	PS_3	0.870	<0.001
	PS_4	0.862	<0.001
	PS_5	0.787	<0.001
Financial Literacy	FL_1	0.817	<0.001
	FL_2	0.849	<0.001
	FL_3	0.862	<0.001
	FL_4	0.843	<0.001
	FL_5	0.837	<0.001
Career Interest in Fintech and Sustainable Finance	CIF_1	0.806	<0.001
	CIF_2	0.852	<0.001
	CIF_3	0.916	<0.001
	CIF_4	0.812	<0.001
	CIF_5	0.744	<0.001

Source: Author's Analysis

Strong and statistically significant ($p < 0.001$) factor loadings in Table 3 indicate the assessments of the constructs from indicators are "valid," supporting the measurement model. For financial Awareness and Understanding, those with the strongest influence are the FAUs 0.830 and 0.836 3 and 5. The most excellent representations for Financial Inclusion are given by FI_2 (0.856) and FI_3 (0.836). 2.2. Perceived Sustainability has the greatest loading on PS_3 (0.870) and PS_4 (0.862), and Financial Literacy is most influenced by FL_3 (0.862) and FL_2 (0.849). Finally, Career Interest in Fintech and Sustainable Finance is explained mainly by CIF_3 (0.916) as the most influential item, and to a lesser extent by CIF_5 (0.744). In general, indicator variables clearly lie with their respective constructs which assure a good measurement model.

Table 4. Path analysis

Path	Estimate (β)	Std.Err	z-value	p-value
Financial Awareness Understanding → Financial Inclusion	0.762	0.096	6.762	<0.001
Financial Inclusion → Perceived Sustainability	0.857	0.097	7.545	<0.001
Perceived Sustainability → Financial Literacy	0.947	0.097	7.957	<0.001
Financial Literacy → Career Interest in Fintech	0.879	0.105	7.653	<0.001

Source: Author's Analysis

From Table 4, the path analysis shows that all the paths among the latent constructs in our model are statistically significant at the level of 0.001 and have strong association. Financial Awareness Explication has a significant and positive direct influence on Financial Inclusion (β = 0.762, z = 6.762), this indicates that the more aware and can understand better the financial terms, the higher will the financial inclusion. In the same way, Financial Inclusion affects Perceived Sustainability positively (β = 0.857, z = 7.545), thus it indicates that the better inclusion is, the better Sustainability is perceived. Perceived Sustainability positively affects Financial Literacy (β = 0.947, z = 7.957), thus, the sustainability perception is essential to build financial literacy. Financial literacy predicts Career Interest in Fintech with a robust coefficient of 0.879 (z = 7.653), indicating that financial literacy plays a key role in students' career interests in fintech and sustainable finance. Students sustain interest in fintech through financial literacy and inclusion, and these results demonstrate their interconnected nature.

Table 5. Hypothesis results

Objective	Hypothesis	Sig. (p-value)	Decision
To assess the students' level of awareness and comprehension of financial technology (fintech) innovations in the era of digital transformation	H1: Students have a moderate to high level of awareness and understanding of fintech innovations.	<0.001	Supported
To Investigate Students' view regarding sustainability in FFS through fintech.	H2: Students perceive fintech-enabled financial services as contributing to sustainable financial practices.	<0.001	Supported
To Examine the effect of fintech on Students' Financial Literacy	H3: Fintech innovations play a significant role in enhancing financial literacy among students.	<0.001	Supported

continued on following page

Table 5. Continued

Objective	Hypothesis	Sig. (p-value)	Decision
Analyzing the Influence of Fintech on Financial Inclusion of Students.	H4: Fintech innovations have a positive impact on students' financial inclusion.	<0.001	Supported
To examine students' interest in career opportunities in fintech and sustainable finance.	H5: Students show a high level of interest in career opportunities within the fields of fintech and sustainable finance.	<0.001	Supported

Source: Author's Analysis

The findings of Table 5 indicate that the hypotheses of the study are fulfilled and are statistically significant ($p < 0.001$) in all dimensions as they met the objectives. Students demonstrated moderate to high levels of knowledge and understanding toward fintech initiatives, thus supporting **H1**. They also found that fintech-based financial service shapes sustainable financial behaviour **(H2)**. In addition, **H3** was accepted, meaning that fintech applications are highly related to financial literacy for students. In the same way, **H4** indicated a positive relationship between fintech innovations and financial inclusion. Finally, students demonstrated strong interest in fintech and sustainable finance career opportunities, supporting **H5.** These results emphasize the significance of the role of fintech in determining students' awareness, attitude and aspiration, reflecting its significance in education and career.

Table 6. Mediation analysis

Path	Direct Effect (β)	Indirect Effect (β)	Total Effect (β)	p-value
Financial Awareness Understanding → Financial Inclusion	0.762	0.631	1.393	<0.001
Financial Awareness Understanding → Career Interest	0.707	0.563	1.270	<0.001

Source: Author's Analysis

In Table 6, mediation analysis suggests the significant role of Financial Awareness Understanding for predicting two basic criteria, i.e., Financial Inclusion and Career Interest in Fintech and Sustainable Finance. When we look at Financial Inclusion, Financial Awareness Understanding exhibits a significant direct impact ($\beta = 0.762$, $p < 0.001$) and a strong Indirect Effect via Financial Literacy ($\beta = 0.631$, $p < 0.001$) with a total effect of $\beta = 1.393$. It is clear from this evidence that FAU contributes to FI as a stand-alone positive factor, but that its impact increases or decreases with the level of FL. Similarly, Financial Knowledge Understanding has a direct effect

($\beta = 0.707$, $p < 0.001$) and an indirect effect mediated by Perceived Sustainability ($\beta = 0.563$, $p < 0.001$) on Career Interest in Fintech and Sustainable Finance, and total effect of $\beta = 1.270$.

CONCLUSION

The research found that FinTech innovations significantly increase students' financial intelligence, inclusion, sustainability awareness, literacy and career aspiration. The Subscales Financial Awareness and Financial Literacy were the most relevant predictors of FBS and Motivation to work in fintech profession. In totality, it is concluded that FinTech does not only facilitate inclusivity, literacy but also cultivates the sustainability consciousness, emphasising the need to include fintech education in the curriculum so that students are able to assume their roles in the digital economy, in future.

RECOMMENDATIONS

The research suggests the need to develop tailor-made financial literacy programs which add fintech applied skills and environmental sustainability consciousness together. Such curriculums should contain modules at crossroad of digital finance and ESG issues, while mentoring and career guidance schemes, in which student aspirations are directed to industry needs. Academic–industry alliances should be encouraged to enable internships, live projects, and experiential learning to groom students for careers in fintech and sustainable finance.

RESEARCH IMPLICATIONS

This study contributes to the scholarship by proposing a student focus model and a theoretical framework which integrates fintech awareness with inclusion, sustainability and career interests. The findings underscore the need for policy makers and institutes of higher learning to design targeted interventions assisting in the development of financially and sustainability literate students. The findings also echo the necessity for fintech education equipping the workforce to face digital transforming economies, and propose that future research investigate demographic variation in the impacts of fintech education and the long-term impacts of fintech education on money behavior and career progression.

REFERENCES

Arner, D. W., Barberis, J. N., & Buckley, R. P. (2015). The evolution of fintech: A new post-crisis paradigm? *SSRN*, *47*(4), 1271–1319. DOI: 10.2139/ssrn.2676553

Bel Hadj Miled, K. (2025). Nexus between fintech, green finance natural resources, economic growth and environment sustainability: Evidence from BRICS countries. *Future Business Journal*, *11*(1), 47. DOI: 10.1186/s43093-025-00469-y

Bell, E., Bryman, A., & Harley, B. (2018). *Business research methods* (5th ed.). Oxford University Press.

Bhuyan, U., Khan, S. A., & Saleem, M. (2024). Gaining Perspective on Money Attitude and Financial Planning of Educators in Northeast India: Implications for Sustainable Finance. In Yıldırım, S., Yıldırım, D., Demirtaş, I., & Kandpal, V. (Eds.), *Green Transition Impacts on the Economy, Society, and Environment* (pp. 244–262). IGI Global., DOI: 10.4018/979-8-3693-3985-5.ch014

Bryman, A. (2016). *Social research methods* (5th ed.). Oxford University Press.

Choudhary, P., Ghosh, C., & Thenmozhi, M. (2025). *Impact of fintech and financial inclusion on sustainable development goals: Evidence from cross country analysis. Finance Research Letters, 72, 106573 Chuen, D. L. K. (2015). Handbook of digital currency: Bitcoin, innovation, financial instruments, and big data*. Elsevier.

Creswell, J. W. (2014). *Research design: Qualitative, quantitative, and mixed methods approach* (4th ed.). SAGE Publications.

Douglas, E., & Pratley, N. (2015, October 11). The rise of fintech: Disrupting the financial industry. The Guardian.

Ellili, N. O. D. (2023). Is there any association between FinTech and sustainability? Evidence from bibliometric review and content analysis. *Journal of Financial Services Marketing*, *28*(4), 748–762. DOI: 10.1057/s41264-022-00200-w

Gomber, P., Koch, J.-A., & Siering, M. (2022). Digital finance and disruption: Global trends and challenges. *Journal of Financial Markets and Services*, *6*(4), 45–61.

Gopalakrishnan, C., Vinoth, S., Madbouly, A., Radhakrishnan, P., & Ali, N. H. (2024). Impact of fintech on sustainable financial inclusion: The case of India. In Proceedings of the 3rd International Conference on Optimization Techniques in the Field of Engineering (ICOFE 2024). *SSRN*. https://ssrn.com/abstract=5066763

Ha, D., Le, P., & Nguyen, D. K. (2025). Financial inclusion and fintech: A state-of-the-art systematic literature review. *Financial Innovation, 11*(1), 69. DOI: 10.1186/s40854-024-00741-0

Hasan, M., Hoque, A., Abedin, M. Z., & Gasbarro, D. (2024). FinTech and sustainable development: A systematic thematic analysis using human-and machine-generated processing. *International Review of Financial Analysis, 95*, 103473. https://www.theguardian.com/business/2015/oct/11/riseoffintechdisruptingfinancialindustry. DOI: 10.1016/j.irfa.2024.103473

Jena, R. K. (2025). Factors influencing the adoption of fintech for the enhancement of financial inclusion in rural India using a mixed methods approach. *Journal of Risk and Financial Management, 18*(3), 150. DOI: 10.3390/jrfm18030150

Kanojia, S., Kaur, S., & Bhavya, . (2024). Business sustainability in the era of Fintech and Regtech: A systematic literature review. *Discover Sustainability, 5*(1), 525. DOI: 10.1007/s43621-024-00767-5

Kumaran, H., & Kamal, N. (2025). Advancing sustainability through fintech innovations in financial services: Evidence from India. In *Fostering economic diversification and sustainable business through digital intelligence* (pp. 23–50). IGI Global. DOI: 10.4018/979-8-3693-8492-3.ch002

Lusardi, A., & Mitchell, O. S. (2014). The economic importance of financial literacy: Theory and evidence. *Journal of Economic Literature, 52*(1), 5–44. DOI: 10.1257/jel.52.1.5 PMID: 28579637

Nenavath, S., & Mishra, S. (2023). Impact of green finance and fintech on sustainable economic growth: Empirical evidence from India. *Heliyon, 9*(5), e16301. DOI: 10.1016/j.heliyon.2023.e16301 PMID: 37234625

OECD. (2020). PISA 2018 results (Volume IV): Are students smart about money? OECD Publishing. DOI: 10.1787/48ebd1ba-en

Okere, K. I., Dimnwobi, S. K., & Fasanya, I. O. (2025). Pathways to environmental sustainability: Exploring the role of FinTech, natural resources and globalization in North Africa. *International Journal of Sustainable Development and World Ecology, 32*(4), 446–464. DOI: 10.1080/13504509.2025.2481222

Philippon, T. (2015). Has the U.S. finance industry become less efficient? On the theory and measurement of financial intermediation. *The American Economic Review, 105*(4), 1408–1438. DOI: 10.1257/aer.20120578

Puschmann, T. (2017). Fintech. *Business & Information Systems Engineering, 59*(1), 69–76. DOI: 10.1007/s12599-017-0464-6

Saxena, C., Khatri, B., & Khan, S. A. (2023). Factors Hindering Women Entrepreneurs' Access to Institutional Finance: An Empirical Study From the Banker Perspective. In Gupta, V. (Ed.), *Fostering Global Entrepreneurship Through Business Model Innovation* (pp. 101–114). IGI Global., DOI: 10.4018/978-1-6684-6975-0.ch004

Sharma, M., & Jha, A. (2022). Digital financial literacy among Indian college students: A cross-sectional study. *International Journal of Education and Development Using ICT, 18*(1), 115–127.

Tang, N., & Peter, P. C. (2015). Financial knowledge acquisition among the young: The role of financial education, information, and parental influence. *Journal of Financial Services Marketing, 20*(1), 16–26. DOI: 10.1057/fsm.2015.1

Tidjani, C., & Madouri, A. (2024). Fintech, financial inclusion, and sustainable development in the African region. *Frontiers in Applied Mathematics and Statistics, 10*, 1276218. DOI: 10.3389/fams.2024.1276218

Varma, P., & Kaur, S. (2024). Does Fintech Foster Sustainable Finance? Evidence from Retail Banking in India. In Management for Sustainable Development (pp. 211-248). Apple Academic Press. DOI: 10.1201/9781003505754-10

Verma, D., Kansra, P., & Khan, S. A. (2024). Apparent Advantages and Negative Facet of Block Chain in Banking Sector: An Innovative Theoretical Perspective. In Irfan, M., Muhammad, K., Naifar, N., & Khan, M. A. (Eds.), *Applications of Block Chain technology and Artificial Intelligence: Lead-ins in Banking, Finance, and Capital Market* (pp. 19–27). Springer International Publishing., DOI: 10.1007/978-3-031-47324-1_2

Yadav, S., Samadhiya, A., Kumar, A., Luthra, S., & Pandey, K. K. (2024). Nexus between fintech, green finance and natural resources management: Transition of BRICS nation industries from resource curse to resource blessed sustainable economies. *Resources Policy, 91*, 104903. DOI: 10.1016/j.resourpol.2024.104903

Yadav, U. S., Tripathi, R., Rena, R., Khan, S. A., & Ghosal, I. (2025). (in press). Use and Effect of Fintech Awareness in Women for Sustainable Development in Small Industry during COVID-19 Pandemic: An Empirical Analysis with UTUAT model. *International Journal of Electronic Finance.* Advance online publication. DOI: 10.1504/IJEF.2025.10062118

Zaid, M. A. K., Khan, M. F., Al-Mekhlafi, A. W. A. G. S., Al Koliby, I. S., Saoula, O., Saeed, H. A. E. M., & Mohammad, R. A. (2025). The future of green finance: How digital transformation and FinTech drive sustainability. *Discover Sustainability, 6*(1), 480. DOI: 10.1007/s43621-025-01356-w

Zikmund, W. G., Babin, B. J., Carr, J. C., & Griffin, J. (2013). *Business research methods* (9th ed.). Cengage Learning.

Chapter 16
User-Oriented Business Process Visualization to Close the Information Gap Between User and Company

Ed Overes
https://orcid.org/0000-0002-4210-2342
Zuyd University, The Netherlands

ABSTRACT

This research addresses information asynchronicity between organizations and their end-users. Business process visualization has proven to be effective in exploring back-end databases, but as the customer is only seen as recipient, this leads to unsatisfactory communication with the end-users as they have no direct access to the corresponding data. This exclusion limits user empowerment and transparency, and constrains organizations' ability to leverage data for monetization, efficiency, and trust-building. Front-end employees often miss the context of the user. The main result of our study is a better understanding of how aligning organizational data with user narratives strengthens decision-making, user satisfaction, and strategic economic outcomes. Results indicate that integrating user narratives into visualizations improves employee performance, reduces costs, and fosters trust. We argue for applying storytelling to develop narrative-driven visualizations to decrease information asynchronicity between organizations and their end-users, and hence, improve organistional results.

DOI: 10.4018/979-8-3373-2772-3.ch016

INTRODUCTION

The Problem of Information Asynchronicity

Despite investments in digital transformation, many organizations struggle with a persistent gap between organizational data systems and the end-user experience. Employees have partial access to back-end systems through fragmented front-end tools, while end-users are typically confined to summarized outputs. This imbalance is particularly harmful in emotionally and financially critical contexts. For instance, pension holders need reliable insights during life events such as retirement or divorce; patients navigating healthcare require clarity on treatment options; students need accessible overviews of progress and financing; banking customers must understand risk and opportunity in financial products. In all these cases, the absence of user narratives in data systems reduces transparency and complicates decision-making. To date, the literature lacks a comprehensive synthesis of storytelling, process visualization, and monetization. User-centered design has been applied in user interface research but not systematically within business process visualization.

The research gap addressed here is that the current business process visualizations primarily optimize internal organizational efficiency but fail to integrate end-user narratives, thereby undermining trust, satisfaction, and the economic potential of data-driven decision making.This chapter seeks to close this gap by positioning user-oriented visualization as both a decision-support tool and a monetization enabler.

Closing this gap is more than a matter of usability. It is an organizational imperative tied to economic performance. By adopting user-oriented visualizations, companies can achieve measurable outcomes: reduced service costs (e.g., fewer repeat calls in pension funds, fewer misdiagnoses in healthcare, improved onboarding in education), increased accuracy of decisions, improved customer retention, and enhanced cross-selling opportunities. In short, narrative-driven visualization becomes a monetization strategy, not just a communication tool.

Introduction of the Case

In this research, we have looked at the communication between a pension fund and its clients. The financial position of older people in the last phase of their life plays a crucial role in preventing poverty and social exclusion. Their pensions form the most important income in this period. During contact moments, crucial long-term decisions about pensions must often be made around emotionally intense life events such as the death of a spouse or divorce. During these difficult times, people often rely on personal contact with their pension fund to gain an overview of their situation and understand their options. Providing accurate and timely information at these time-critical moments is of the utmost importance, but call center agents from pension funds often struggle with understanding and interpreting information from different systems within a conversation (Schröder et al., 2022). At the same time, the customer lacks the overview to be an equal partner in the discussion. These examples are not restricted to the pension sector but are also to be found in other sectors like healthcare, education, and banking, which makes this research also relevant to other sectors (Schroeder et al., 2020; Weijers et al., 2021). The customer narrative is translated into the customer journey and the visualization into data storytelling, which is also explanatory and exploratory in nature. Our work aims to match business processes and data storytelling perspectives into a common explanatory visualization to improve communication between big organizations and vulnerable individuals.

Introduction to Challenges: Digitizing and Accessing Customer Data

The rising degree of digitization and corresponding data availability confronts companies with challenges as well as opportunities (Urbach & Röglinger, 2019). Due to the increasing amount of data, quick and correct decision-making becomes more challenging as users with different roles use data stored in information systems to support decision-making. Data Visualization techniques can support understanding a large amount of data (Hamzah et al., 2010). The user perspective is often neglected or limited to being the recipient of information. Nils Urbach and Maximilian Röglinger (Urbach & Röglinger, 2019), for example, structured the field of digitization in the field of enterprise architecture to describe the different layers between organization infrastructure to customer. These layers consist of (1) infrastructure, (2) data and information (3) people (4) business processes (5) business model, and (6) the customer, as shown in Figure 1 made by the authors of this article.

Simplified, this model can be seen as making organizational data accessible to front-end employees. Internal data storage is often dispersed in multiple back-end systems (a), set up to support technical, internal, and external processes, instead of supporting front-end facing employees (b) working in, often time-critical, consulting situations (Buijs et al., 2019).

Figure 1. The layers of enterprise architecture suggested by Nils Urbach and Maximilian Röglinger (Urbach & Röglinger, 2019). In the current situation, customer interaction is based on back-end stored information made available via front-end systems without the customer being aware of what information is available.

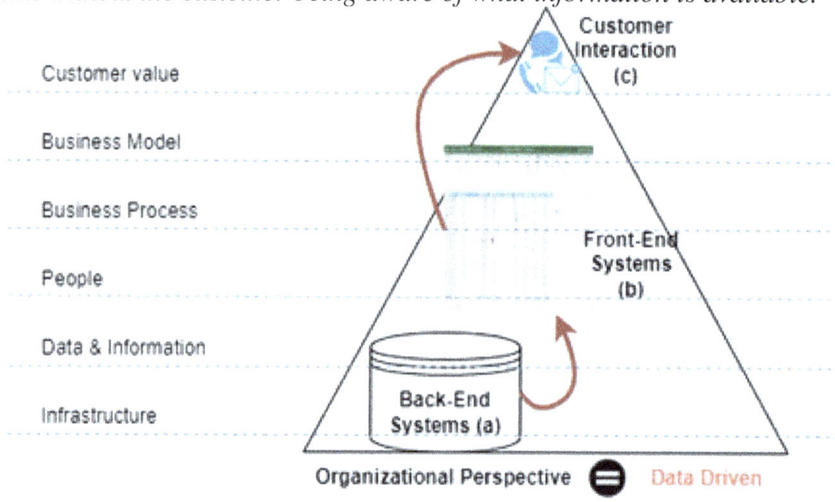

As a result of an 18-month journey with one of the world's biggest pension funds, Schröder et al. (Schröder et al., 2022) have been able to close this gap between the back-end systems (a) and front-end employees (b) by developing and designing a solution for assisting front-end staff in their contact with customers. Following an iterative design process with an interdisciplinary team and 22 domain experts, we developed a visual support system that combines customer lifetime data, interaction data between the relevant parties, and back-end processes visually and enables the user to interact with it in time-critical situations (see Figure 2). This visualization bridges the gap between back-end (a) and front-end systems (b).

Figure 2. The figure above shows the final, anonymized application that we developed. (A) Timeline of employment and related salaries, (B) Current moment in time, (C) Expected beginning of pension period, (D) Life events - marriage in 2002 and divorce in 2019, Upper timeline (E) shows internal and external communication triggered by the divorce as an example. Black diamonds show communication from the client (calls and letters), while white diamonds show communication to the client. The lower timeline (F) shows related back-end events. (G) shows the last message that the client received as well as general information. Both timelines are currently zoomed in at different levels.

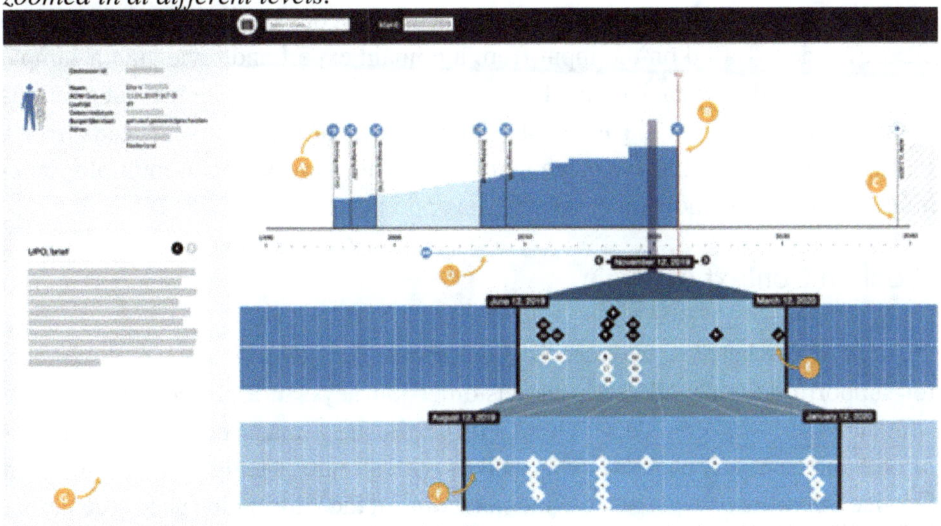

Methodology Used

Setting Up the Group

At first, we have set up an interdisciplinary research group of 4 collaborators with domain experts from the pension sector, business processes, and information visualization. We will refer to this group in the following as the research group. In weekly workshops over six months, we discussed the underlying mechanisms of the domain-specific customer journey from an HCI, data, and business process perspective. In parallel, we conducted data-abstraction workshops and investigated the design space of timeline visualization from a theoretical (literature review) and practical (design sprints) working sessions on pension data perspective. With this, we wanted to minimize the knowledge asymmetry within the research group and to increase collaboration efficiency over the whole project duration (Bergold and Thomas, 2012). Furthermore, we aligned our understanding of the user's role, task, and domain. From the literature review as well as initial user interviews, we concluded that communication within pension funds is not aligned, even though all necessary process data from the different systems are available (Buijs et al., 2019). The ideal setting would be that all related stakeholders, from the operational domain experts to the managers, should use the same (set of) dashboards, build on the same data, and hence are aligned. We concluded that available visualization tools could not support the combination of asynchronous events and handle non-linear data sets. Our research was refocused on developing a visualization that allowed us to connect asynchronous events based on heterogeneous time scale ranges in one clear overview. Based on the input from a domain expert and reviewing a sample data set, we made several handmade sketches to understand the significant relations within the data. In order to gain feedback on the sketches and relevant needs from a management perspective, we presented them within a workshop to multiple stakeholders to evaluate and validate our initial approaches.

Problem Context Analysis

Next to the sketches, we interviewed employees to determine the requirements for supporting their work with the customer journeys. In a period 3 months we conducted semi-structured interviews with one business manager, four team leaders of both the front and back-office as well as with a senior agent from the Customer Service Department to get a better understanding of the information need at customer contact from an overall perspective. The interviews were audio recorded and fully transcripted and axial coded (Williams and Moser, 2019). It became clear that we needed to distinguish between the customers perspective and that of the customer service employees. For understanding the customers perspective well, the customer service employees need a good overview of the information stored in different systems as well as velocity and reliability of the system response. Next to predictability and consistency of customers' questions, the uncertainties of employees concerning solving enquiries were found to be important topics. Customers want a clear outcome of the calculations regarding pension processes and the service to be as correct and quick as possible. As there are different tools in circulation, interviewees signalled the need for reliability of answers by using one system or tool. This confirms the conclusion by Buijs et al. 2019 that there is a strong need to implement a single system solution that can enhance the accessibility of data consistently for multiple levels of stakeholders. The aim is to provide a visualization which avoids loss of information and to provide the customer with all the needs regarding the handling of events. Another conclusion drawn from the interviews is that customer contact is event driven and that client contact is raised during certain life events of clients.

These events can be distinguished between work-related (changes in employment, salaries), private (marriage, divorce, birth, death) or external events (publicity, governmental policies, or changes in pension jurisdiction).

Iterative Visualization Design

We summarized our findings from the literature review, the review of the handmade sketches by domain experts and the conducted interviews. Based on the results, we developed a visualization to bridge the gap between the event-driven, asynchronous nature of the customer request on the one side and the agents' need to understand the context and whole journey on the other side. We found that the readability and comprehension of the different time dimensions is a significant challenge for users. Therefore, the visualization took the different time dimensions of the various perspectives into account. In experiments, we found out that the users preferred a horizontal encoding of the temporal structure. At the top, we visualized the customer journey, split into work-related and personal events. The second layer visualizes the different contact moments between organization and customer. The icons represent the different contact media used. The time scale used was one month because a single event will lead to multiple contact moments before and after the event. The third layer gives an overview of the back-end processes taking place. As multiple processes run simultaneously in all internal layers, the timescale in the individual timeline ranges can adapt dynamically (dependent on the event density and distribution) from monthly to even daily tick formats. To facilitate readability and understanding of the different contexts, we visualized the differences in scale and range between the individual layers accordingly.

Qualitative Study

In a 2-month period the research group evaluated the visualisation together with six domain experts with extensive experience in this field. After a short presentation showing the visualisation of the timeline these domain experts were invited for an online user study. To prevent bias and group dominance effects we invited them afterwards to individually complete an online questionnaire asking feedback on the predictability, flexibility, user preference, correctness and completeness of the timeline as well as about the preferred timescales to use. This survey was followed by individual evaluations and domain expert interviews to get a better understanding how to interpret the results and to ensure proper coding and analysis of the results. Based on the results we made some small changes like adding annotations when hoovering over the visualizations to improve the completeness. The same six domain experts were invited for semi-structured interviews. Main conclusions drawn from these sessions were that 1) working with the visualisation would make the data more accessible, 2) reduce the contact time with the customer, 3) whilst increasing the quality of the contact and 4) reduce the settling of inexperienced agents. All domain experts reported positively about the fact that the customer perspective was leading. We also found that working with the visualisation creates the necessary overview of events, interactions as well as of the relevant backoffice processes. Where user preference and flexibility the timeline were very well received, completeness needed improvements to be able to support the customer effectively. Annotations which appear with hoovering was appreciated by the experts. Improvements were requested on predictability ('the next best question') and correctness. Correctness of data is extremely high, but due to different assumptions between customer service and customers, the perceived correctness needed attention.

Finalising Visualisation Design

After a successful evaluation with the domain experts we finalised the visualisation into a fully functional prototype to be tested in fully operational test environment running on actual data sets. We found out that that the spatial positioning of the individual temporal events is a crucial starting point of the most look up tasks, the uneven distribution of individual events required a dynamic adjustment of the positioning. therefore we developed an adaptive layout for vertical positioning compensating cluttering problems in areas with high data point density. After iterating several shapes together with domain experts, we found out that the combination of a diamond shape filled with a categorical color encoding and a contextual icons performed best in the given scenario. The quantitative distribution at the different levels was very uneven because the individual systems were based on different data sources and types. Therefore, we developed a dynamic scaling that was linked by visual guides. Detailed information on each point was made interactively accessible through info windows. Extreme life events, like divorces or deaths, correlate strongly with the number of customer interactions and therefore form an essential orientation for a holistic perception. Therefore, an area below the salary visualization was added to reflect life phases As the family situation has a substantial impact on the overall situation, it is encoded twice: First, as an image (at this client, the hatching of the female indicates that the person was married to a woman that now also owns a part of the pension, the visual language follows a standardized icon language that is tested and well understood by the target audience) and secondly by showing essential data of the client.

Design Choice Evaluation

We tested the prototype with six domain experts working in different positions within the pension fund who regularly require access to the data we are visualizing. We used realistic scenarios and presented these to them individually. We used an eye tracking device and think-aloud protocol to better understand the system's usage within the work environment. We collected and summarized relevant feedback for further refinements. In the think-aloud protocol sessions users indicated a strong need for date navigation to look up specific temporal or contextual events directly. Furthermore, they found understanding the different zoom levels of the visualisation layers better to understand with additional time code tool-tips. In addition, we discussed alternative interaction types to control the particular time ranges, which led to their integration in the last phase. Furthermore, users pointed out that displaying the most recent information that the customer received, combined with the key information, would benefit the conversation. The key take away from the eye tracking evaluation was the conclusion that we are not only working with heterogeneous data, but also with a very heterogeneous user base. While customerfacing employees focused their attention almost exclusively on the employment history as well as the upper timeline, users working mostly with back-end processes started exploring the tool from the lower timeline upwards. Further, we realised that the current version had too much white space as the gaze tacking showed a high density of central focus points with almost no movement on the horizontal space. As a conclusion from this we reevaluated size and placement within the visualisation to optimise our use of the available space.

Refining and Finalising

In the final version, we implemented all findings from the previous phase. To optimise the use of space we increased the timeline size and added two additional information and interaction areas. On top, we added a date picker that enables the domain experts to jump to specific moments in time directly. On the left, we added two windows showing general information on top and on the bottom left the last information that the customer received from the pension fund. The domain experts preferred multiple interaction options for temporal navigation, zooming, and brushing. Therefore we added the option to type in specific dates, extended the zoom function with a drag and drop functionality, and added time range tool-tips and drag handles. Furthermore, the domain experts indicated that they had problems distinguishing between incoming and outgoing data elements. To address this weak spot, we increased the efficiency of categorical encoding through spatial and color encoding. Previous phase made us very aware of the differences that exists between the individual customer journeys. As a consequence we designed multiple test cases for the application with several complex and specific customer journeys (e.g. customers that change their employer 15 times, have multiple changes in the family status and an high but uneven distribution of data entries) to stress the scaleability of the system and further optimize the user experience. To ensure scale-ability of the system, those data scenarios were selected by domain experts and evaluated together with the whole research group.

Results from our User Study

The system was tested based on the evaluation approach of the seminal work by Sheiderman and Plaisant (2006). Based on this framework we differentiated between three different measurement criteria, namely Performance, Task Duration and User Evaluation.

We measured an increase in performance both on user level (for novice-, casual- and daily users) as task complexity (identification, insight, prediction). For lower-level information comprehension tasks, even novice users were able to successfully solve the tasks just slightly below the overall average with 91% (Identification) and 86.7% (Insight). Daily users, as well as casual users, showed high correctness scores across all comprehension tasks with the lowest correctness score of 87.8% for daily users on Insight tasks. Task duration was measured automatically for every stimulus. We conducted a repeated measure ANOVA to assess if there was a significant improvement from the first stimuli presented to the last stimuli presented. The results show that we have a significant effect ($p < 0.0001$) of task order on task duration with an F score of 17.78. The pairwise comparison shows a significant difference ($p < 0.0001$) between task order 1 and every other task. The largest mean difference is observed between task order 1 and 4 with a mean difference of 240.6 seconds. The results of this design show high accuracy in task performance and substantial learning effects within the duration of the simulation. Furthermore, they strongly indicate that the application is more effective, engaging, and pleasing than the current systems used by the pension fund. This research has advanced our understanding of information visualization for heterogeneous, non-linear, asynchronous data sets.

These results have an impact on the monetization of data of an organization, as our results show a shorter task completion (e.g. more calls per hour), higher task correctness (e.g. less calls per incident), faster learning curve (e.g. higher productivityfor new employees), and more engagement (e.g. less staff turnover).

Although our results showed high accuracy in task performance and employee satisfaction, customer satisfaction was not included. In figure 1 the end-user is defined as the value driver and is typically placed outside the architecture. The model shown in Figure 1 is data-driven and the first aim of the visualization in this phase is to mine data and make it accessible for front-end employees (b), but not for the end-user or customer (c), thus causing asynchronicity between the organization and the user. Another aspect that is not captured in Figure 1 is that the end-users do not think in terms of data, but in life events narrative-driven. Earlier in this publication, we called this the battle between the cold data of the organization and the warm narrative of the user, as shown in Figure 3. Earlier, it was also mentioned that this is not restricted to the financial sector but is also to be found in, for example, education and healthcare (Weijers et al., 2021). This observation was the starting point for the research done for this publication. The central question was 'How to include the narrative of the end-user in a data-driven organization?'

Figure 3. The battle between the cold data of the organization and the warm narrative of the user: the upside-down pyramid represents the focus of the customer on the narrative and not on the underlying data, whereas the organizational perspective is mainly based on data. Data storytelling needs to bridge the gap

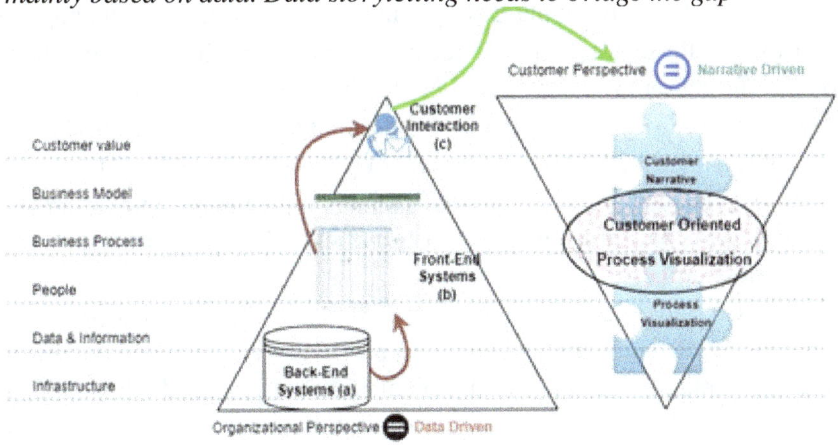

MATERIALS AND METHODS

This research aims to investigate what is needed to increase customer value and by defining an approach to bridging the gap between front-end systems and customer interaction by using customer-oriented process visualization involving both users and customers in designing and testing effective visualizations. We wanted to match business processes and data storytelling perspectives into a common explanatory visualization to improve the communication between big organizations and the (vulnerable) end-users as mentioned in the introduction. First, we will report on relevant related work in this field before explaining the methods used.

Related Work

Storytelling: the End-User Perspective

Storytelling from an organizational perspective can be described as a way to inform readers through "interactive graphics and narratives" (Burmester et al., 2010). Lindy Ryan (Ryan, 2016) defined the goal of visualizations as effectively communicating a key message, reasoning that visualizations are intended either to explore or explain insights, whereas data storytelling aims to facilitate understanding by putting data in a narrative context. This method of storytelling reduces information complexity and improves the understanding of outcomes of visual analytics (S. Chen et al., 2018).

Storytelling seems very applicable in situations with vulnerable target groups as Lugmayr et al. (Lugmayr et al., 2017) found that storytelling has mainly been applied in the public sector such as education, elderly and health care, science, archaeology, and museums. Alex Endert et al. (Endert et al., 2014) introduced the phrase "Human is the loop", which entails that user input and visual feedback should be conducted and presented within the context of the analysts' process. They, as well as Walsh et al. (Walsh et al., 2019), argue that human involvement makes sense in data storytelling. As such, the customer narrative should be included in customer-oriented business processes.

Edward Segel and Jeffrey Heer (Segel & Heer, 2010) published a comprehensive overview of data-driven stories and narrative visualizations, identifying specific design strategies such as visual salience, annotations, and interaction, and questioning how these control the contextual and narrative structures. Benjamin Bach et al. (Bach et al., 2018) proposed to group these genres into three contextual groups: space-oriented, time-oriented, or a combination of these two. Tong et al. (Tong et al., 2018) reviewed relevant aspects of storytelling in visualization and for this research, distinguishing between authoring tools, user engagement, narratives, transitions, memorability, and interpretation appears to be relevant. Very relevant work in the field of the relation between data storytelling and business process visualisations have been done by Schröder et al. (2023). The work of Schröder et al. offers a comprehensive overview of the existing literature into distinct categories, encompassing frameworks, data and visualization types, application domains, narrative structures, outcome measurements, and design principles.

To support the narrative-driven information to the customer, Zhu et al. (Zhu et al., 2020) published a survey about automatic infographic and visualization recommendations on how parts of the storytelling process can be automated, or enhanced, covering several related tools, models, and frameworks. The survey ranges from data-driven automatic visualizations and annotations, graphs, networks, and storytelling visualizations to knowledge-based visualizations. Examples of data-driven storytelling in journalism can be found in a comprehensive overview by Pere Freixa et al. (Freixa Font et al., 2021), while Pavlov et al. (Pavlov et al., 2020) and Barykin et al. (Barykin et al., 2021) have adopted it in their work amongst students. Next to an overview of the tools and resources used in digital newsrooms, the authors demonstrate the potential of using visualizations and interactions together to create raise the interest of the audience. It needs to be researched if this also applies to the customers in our research.

Business Process Visualization: Organizations Perspective

Since the '90s of last century, thinking in terms of business processes has become widespread within organizations to ensure efficiency and economic effectiveness by using standardized processes, procedures, and requirements (Bačić & Fadlalla, 2016; M. Chen & Golan, 2015; Iliashenko et al., 2019; Nikonorov et al., 2020). Making business processes accessible to employees constitutes a crucial challenge throughout their entire life cycle: employees should be enabled to understand business process models (Analysis and Design phase), keep an overview of running process instances (Operation phase), perceive process adaptations (Operation phase), and comprehend as well as interpret results of analyzing processes (Evaluation phase) (Figl, 2017). The effectiveness of business process visualisations was studied by Overes and Santoro (2025). Overes and Santoro focus on effect of visual literacy, visual experience, culture and media on the effectiveness of business process visualisations, and thus the monetization in data-driven decision making. To communicate these processes, attention to visualizing them has gained a lot of interest. Business process visualization has an impact on management's decision-making processes due to faster reading and reactions (Shavazipour et al., 2021). This interest has led to the development of several process modeling tools like BPMN, IDEF, and EPC (Ghooshchi et al., 2017). The essence of these visualization tools has been mostly on describing the processes i.e. analysis, training, and manuals. The visualizations used in these tools are based on traditional visualization methods (Dani et al., 2019), which relate mainly to the Analysis and Design phase mentioned previously in the work of Kathrin Figl (Figl, 2017). This view on business processes focuses on optimizing the internal environment of the organization, not including the external users.

As businesses became more complex and processes became less static, the increasing need for overview and flexibility led to the introduction of dynamic business process modeling. Visuals could be adapted more easily but remained descriptive (Dani et al., 2019). Several studies examined these challenges in the implementation of dynamic business process visualizations (Albo et al., 2019; Kalibatiene & Vasilecas, 2021; Reina et al., 2020) reviewed approaches (Aleem et al., 2012; Lu & Sadiq, 2007; Temirgaliev et al., 2021), and evaluated frameworks (Abdel-Fattah et al., 2017). The visualization of business processes was enhanced with Graph-Based Modeling Languages like UML 2.0, OO, BPDM, and Petri Nets (PN) and variants of Petri Nets (HPN (High Level), LPN (Low Level), CPN (Coloured), OOPN (Object Oriented)) (Rajabi & Lee, 2010), to support the Operation Phase. Schroeder et al. (Schroeder et al., 2020) systematically investigated the differences in user perception between a regular monitor and a mixed-reality device but did not find a significant difference in accuracy between mixed-reality and standard 2D monitor visualizations. Although helpful, these studies do not fully answer the problems with comprehension and interpretation of results of analyzing processes in the Evaluation Phase. Also, attention to more flexibility did not involve the user in business process modeling.

Current Challenge Between Organization and User

With the introduction of dynamic, customer-centered business processes in organizations, also called 'customer journey', the boundaries of the traditional process visualization tools need to be stretched (Buijs et al., 2019). With the introduction of customer-initiated processes, there is also a shift from modeling to applying processes in real-time customer interaction, to support front-end employees. Shavazipour et al. (Shavazipour et al., 2021) found that suitable graphical visualizations are necessary to support managers in understanding, evaluating, and comparing the performance of management decisions. The need for quick reflexes concerning decision-making becomes a factor as well. The complexity of work has increased, the amount of available data has grown exponentially and employees are faced with more informed/demanding customers. Employees often need to make context-specific, time-restricted decisions, taking several processes and facets into account (Buijs et al., 2019). Any delay in obtaining accurate and up-to-date information hampers the ability of decision-makers (Dabrowski, 2013; Ilin et al., 2019). We already experienced this during experiments to visualize time-oriented, heterogeneous data to support front-end employees making decisions in complex situations, involving multiple processes simultaneously, using multiple data sources (see Figure 2). It requires a different focus on business process visualizations from descriptive to supportive visualizations to interactive support for time-restricted decision-making (Dani et al., 2019). We aim to contribute to this shift by focusing on the end-user and his narrative and integrating this into the discussion around process modeling.

Methods

After conducting a multi-dimensional in-depth, long-term case study using a user-centered design method, involving an interdisciplinary team and 22 domain experts, we extended the research by involving end-users. For this study program, we used an iterative design process involving relevant stakeholders at every level of design (see Figure 4).

The customer perspective was included by involving end-users via an extensive customer panel the pension fund is using. This customer panel consists of a wide range of representative customers, who have indicated that they are volunteering for surveys of the organization. As shown in Figure 4, the user perspective will be researched from a narrative approach via a user-centered design. We will use an extensive customer panel of the pension fund to test which of the different kinds of data storytelling techniques are more effective. We will do this in two stages: (1) we will organize multiple customer panel discussions, including experiments, to get a better understanding of how customers comprehend different types of data storytelling techniques and how they use visualizations; (2) after we analyze the findings of these studies we will develop different test scripts for a real-time simulation. These test scripts will contain different storytelling visualization types, based on the outcomes of the panel discussions.

From an organizational perspective, we continued our multi-dimensional in-depth, long-term case study. Further to the domain experts already involved in our previous research, we intend to set up a real-time test environment to test the data-driven visualization developed (see Figure 2) in time-critical situations.

In a simulation, the organizational and end-user perspectives are combined. The customer panel makes actual calls based on their information. The front-end employee is using different visualizations to answer the customer's request. After each call, participants from the customer panel complete an extensive survey containing questions about the accuracy, consistency, and user-friendliness of the interaction. The contact agents of the pension fund who will answer the call will be using the newly developed timeline visualization within the test period, but will not know whether the customer is part of the test panel or a regular caller, hence they do not know whether a call is part of the test or not. The contact agent will also complete a small evaluation of each call to confirm the findings of our previous research.

After the testing period, match the customer and contact agent records per call were matched and we analyzed the results to conclude on how to best close the gap between end-user and organization for knowledge-intensive customer-oriented processes. A visual representation of our methodology is shown in Figure 4.

Figure 4. The figure above shows our methodology used. During this research, we worked in close collaboration with end-users, employees, and domain experts.

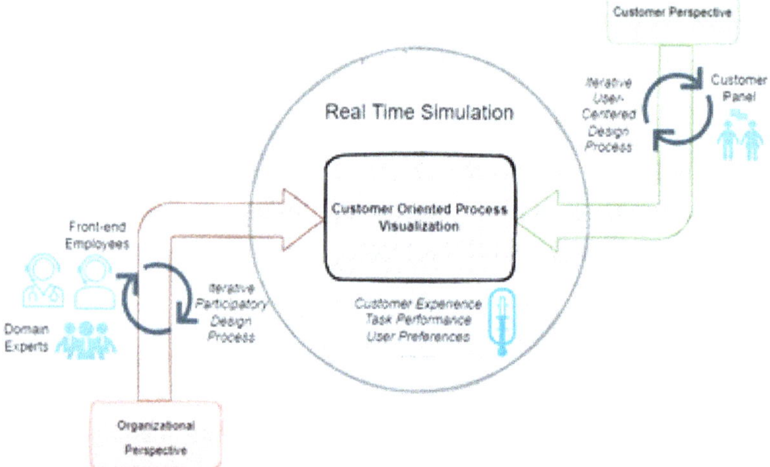

RESULTS

In this paper, we will share our first conclusions of this ongoing long-term study about this user-oriented business process visualization process. It is too early to conclude from the customer data collected, but we can report on the results from our observations and discussions.

As mentioned in paragraph 1.3, we differentiated between three different measurement criteria, namely Performance, Task Duration and User Evaluation. A summary of the findings can be found in table 1.

Table 1. Summary of organizational impact

Metric	Traditional	User-Centered	Improvement
Task Accuracy	Moderate	High (>87%)	✓
Task Duration	Long	Significantly improved	✓
Onboarding Efficiency	Slow	Accelerated	✓
Employee Engagement	Low/Moderate	High	✓

Employee Performance has shown that on (1) task accuracy daily and casual users achieved correctness rates above 87% across tasks, with novice users performing well in simpler tasks (91% on identification), on (2) efficiency the task duration decreased significantly across repeated trials ($p < 0.0001$), and on (3) engagement employees reported the system as more intuitive and satisfying than existing tools.

At organizational level, findings show clear links to monetization and efficiency by a shorter task completion (more service interactions per hour), higher correctness (fewer follow-up corrections, lowering operational costs), faster learning curve (reduced training time for new staff), and a stronger engagement (lower staff turnover, reducing recruitment costs).

End-users expressed the need for narrative-driven rather than data-centric visualization. Pension fund clients valued life-event timelines, while healthcare patients preferred story-like treatment plans. Education case studies highlight learners' preference for narrative dashboards showing progress and milestones. Banking research indicates customers trust narrative financial stories more than abstract risk models. Across sectors, narrative alignment strengthens comprehension, trust, and satisfaction.

To conclude: the main result from our study is that working with the concept of Customer Journey implies that the organization needs to take the customer, and its narrative, as the starting point of the information loop, not the end. Users have increased awareness and expectations of companies towards the possibilities of digitalization. As more and more companies promote self-service it becomes standard. The process visualizations mentioned earlier in this article (Figure 1 and Figure 2), however, do still create a dependence on the organization based on information asynchronicity.

Although our results from previous studies showed high accuracy in task performance and employee satisfaction from the organizational perspective, the information available to the customer (customer perspective) was limited to a summarized overview of the main findings to the customer. In this study, we found indications that using storytelling techniques following the narrative of a customer journey adds to better communication between the organization and the user. The front-end support system which we developed has proven to be very efficient and effective for front-end employees, especially daily users. Front-end employees indicate that the system supports their understanding of the customer journey while talking to an end-user. However, we did not find any evidence yet to prove that this system could also be used by end-users. There appears to be a difference between the front-end employees and users in the comprehension of the visualization of the customer journey. From this study, we believe that this has to do with the fact that front-end employees need to have a quick overview of the journey of a random customer, while the initiator of the contact, the end-user, is very aware of his journey. This means from a customer perspective, other more in-depth ways of visualizing the customer journey should be explored in a way that the visualization will be more narrative-driven. However, using two different visualizations, data- and narrative-driven, will lead again to less synchronous communication. This maintains a dis-balance in communication between employees and customers. To balance the organizational perspective with the user perspective, this research advocates visualizing the user narrative in a manner that matches the organizational front-end systems as shown in Figure 5. The challenge caused by this customer journey for organizations is the switch from supplying information to facilitating data exploration by the user. From the organization's point of view, this implies applying data storytelling to connect to the customer's narrative.

Figure 5. From the organizational perspective the front-end systems should make data stored in back-end systems accessible to front-end employees. The triangle structure indicates that the data forms the basis and the customer forms the top. To make visualizations truly customer oriented the customer journey should be the basis and data should be supportive. These two perspectives should be merged to enable efficient communication between the organization and the customer.

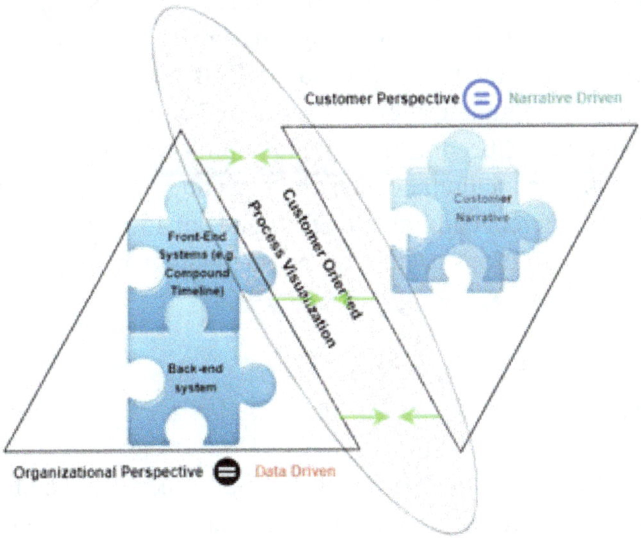

DISCUSSION

New insights have been found to visualize user narratives. During our pre-studies, we experienced how difficult it is for employees to connect with users in emotional conversations. The difference between data-driven tools and user stories appears to be big. We aim to contribute through effective application of research findings in the field of (data) storytelling to bridge the gap between the end-user story and the front-end employee. This will lead to a mutually better understanding and more satisfying and effective contact. However, we found that more research is needed to combine data-driven and narrative-driven visualizations to support customer-oriented business processes.

First, more research is needed to find out which visualizations are most narrative-driven,supportive, and effective for in-depth representation of the customer journey. Simultaneously with the development of business process modeling, the development of visualizing techniques and methods has rapidly emerged. As we experienced in our long-term pre-studies, the potential of these techniques and models has not yet been fully used in the visualization of business processes. The results from research in data storytelling, also called serious storytelling, need to be applied and tested.

Second, as developments in data-driven front-end systems continue, we suggest exploring connecting the developments in business processes and visualization, both for modeling and for applying business process visualizations. This would contribute to making data more readily accessible to front-end employees. One step further is to research which visualizations could bridge the gap between the data-driven and narrative-driven focus of the two target groups. This would lead to a decrease in misunderstandings in communication as a result of data-asynchronicity.

Third, as communities become more multicultural we suggest in a later phase to check our findings in a cultural context by repeating our experiments from the user perspective in different cultural settings to find out how universal our findings are and whether organizations need to adapt our findings based on their location or user base.

CONCLUSION

The main contribution of our research is adding the perspective of the end-user (consumer) in a long-term user-centered design study. We are excited about this approach as we have not encountered examples of involving end-users this intensely in these types of studies. This contribution describes our research to close the last missing link by visualizing the user narrative through the participation of end-users (customers). By adding storytelling research, we aimto help the end-user in emotionally tense moments.

The model presented in this article shows the challenge of a truly user-oriented business process visualization. We did not manage to come up with the perfect answer yet but have made progress on clarifying the steps needed to do so. This model helps to set the focus and keep an overview of the process. It helps us to proceed with our further research lines and hopefully it will give direction to other researchers too.

REFERENCES

Abdel-Fattah, M. A., Khedr, A. E., & Aldeen, Y. N. (2017). An evaluation framework for business process modeling techniques. [IJCSIS]. *International Journal of Computer Science and Information Security, 15*(5), 382–392.

Albo, A., Bengtsson, K., Dahl, M., & Falkman, P. (2019). A framework concept for data visualization and structuring in a complex production process. *Procedia Manufacturing, 38*, 1642–1651. DOI: 10.1016/j.promfg.2020.01.120

Aleem, S., Lazarova-Molnar, S., & Mohamed, N. (2012). Collaborative business process modeling approaches: a review. *Proc. of the 2012 IEEE 21st International Workshop on Enabling Technologies: Infrastructure for Collaborative Enterprises*, 274–279.

Bach, B., Wang, Z., Farinella, M., Murray-Rust, D., & Henry Riche, N. (2018). Design patterns for data comics. *Proceedings of the 2018 Chi Conference on Human Factors in Computing Systems*, 1–12. DOI: 10.1145/3173574.3173612

Bačić, D., & Fadlalla, A. (2016). Business information visualization intellectual contributions: An integrative framework of visualization capabilities and dimensions of visual intelligence. *Decision Support Systems, 89*, 77–86. DOI: 10.1016/j.dss.2016.06.011

Barykin, S., Kapustina, I., Kalinina, O., Parshukov, A., Aleksandrov, I., Poberezhnaya, V., Fedorova, M., & Overes, E. (2021). The career choice motivation in view of Maslow's hierarchy in innovative economy: The case of Russia. *Academy of Strategic Management Journal, 20*(2), 1–17.

Bergold, J., & Thomas, S. (2012). Participatory research methods: A methodological approach in motion. Historical Social Research. *Historische Sozialforschung*, •••, 191–22.

Buijs, J. C. A. M., Bergmans, R. F. M., & el Hasnaoui, R. (2019). Customer journey analysis at a financial services provider using self service and data hub concepts. *BPM (Industry Forum)*, 25–36.

Burmester, M., Mast, M., Tille, R., & Weber, W. (2010). How users perceive and use interactive information graphics: An exploratory study. *2010 14th International Conference Information Visualisation*, 361–368. DOI: 10.1109/IV.2010.57

Chen, M., & Golan, A. (2015). What may visualization processes optimize? *IEEE Transactions on Visualization and Computer Graphics, 22*(12), 2619–2632. DOI: 10.1109/TVCG.2015.2513410 PMID: 26731770

Chen, S., Li, J., Andrienko, G., Andrienko, N., Wang, Y., Nguyen, P. H., & Turkay, C. (2018). Supporting story synthesis: Bridging the gap between visual analytics and storytelling. *IEEE Transactions on Visualization and Computer Graphics*, *26*(7), 2499–2516. DOI: 10.1109/TVCG.2018.2889054 PMID: 30582542

Dabrowski, M. (2013). Business Intelligence In Call Centers. *International Journal of Issue Computer and Information Technology (ISSN: 2279–0764) Volume,* 2(2).

Dani, V. S., Freitas, C. M. D. S., & Thom, L. H. (2019). Ten years of visualization of business process models: A systematic literature review. *Computer Standards & Interfaces*, *66*, 103347. DOI: 10.1016/j.csi.2019.04.006

Endert, A., Hossain, M. S., Ramakrishnan, N., North, C., Fiaux, P., & Andrews, C. (2014). The human is the loop: New directions for visual analytics. *Journal of Intelligent Information Systems*, *43*(3), 411–435. DOI: 10.1007/s10844-014-0304-9

Figl, K. (2017). Comprehension of procedural visual business process models. *Business & Information Systems Engineering*, *59*(1), 41–67. DOI: 10.1007/s12599-016-0460-2

Freixa Font, P., Pérez-Montoro Gutiérrez, M., & Codina, L. (2021). The binomial of interaction and visualization in digital news media: Consolidation, standardization and future challenges. *El Profesional de la Información*, *30*(4), E300401. DOI: 10.3145/epi.2021.jul.01

Ghooshchi, N. G., van Beest, N., Governatori, G., Olivieri, F., & Sattar, A. (2017). Visualisation of compliant declarative business processes. *2017 IEEE 21st International Enterprise Distributed Object Computing Conference (EDOC)*, 89–94. DOI: 10.1109/EDOC.2017.21

Hamzah, M., Sobey, A., & Koronios, A. (2010). Supporting decision making process with information visualisation: A theoretical framework. *2010 2nd IEEE International Conference on Information Management and Engineering*, 267–271. DOI: 10.1109/ICIME.2010.5477827

Iliashenko, V., Filippova, K., Overes, E., & Iliashenko, O. (2019). The modelling of intelligent transport system architecture based on Big Data technologies. *Proceedings of the 33rd International Business Information Management Association Conference, IBIMA 2019: Education Excellence and Innovation Management through. Vision (Basel), 2020*, 8553–8561.

Ilin, I., Klimin, A., Overes, E., & Sataev, P. (2019). The essence and features of the introduction of the omni-channel approach to interaction with consumers. *Proceedings of the 33rd International Business Information Management Association Conference, IBIMA 2019: Education Excellence and Innovation Management through. Vision (Basel), 2020*, 8546–8552.

Kalibatiene, D., & Vasilecas, O. (2021). A survey on modeling dynamic business processes. *PeerJ. Computer Science*, *7*, e609. DOI: 10.7717/peerj-cs.609 PMID: 34307861

Lu, R., & Sadiq, S. (2007). A survey of comparative business process modeling approaches. *International Conference on Business Information Systems*, 82–94. DOI: 10.1007/978-3-540-72035-5_7

Lugmayr, A., Sutinen, E., Suhonen, J., Sedano, C. I., Hlavacs, H., & Montero, C. S. (2017). Serious storytelling–a first definition and review. *Multimedia Tools and Applications*, *76*(14), 15707–15733. DOI: 10.1007/s11042-016-3865-5

Nikonorov, V., Kutuzov, A., Nikonorov, V., & Overes, E. (2020). The digitalization of refining processes on the example of producing winter diesel fuel. *Proceedings of the International Scientific Conference - Digital Transformation on Manufacturing, Infrastructure and Service*, 1–5. https://doi.org/DOI: 10.1145/3446434.3446490

Overes, E., & Santoro, F. (2025). The Effectiveness of Business Process Visualisations: a Systematic Literature Review. arXiv preprint arXiv:2504.10971

Pavlov, N., Zotova, E., Shaban, A., & Overes, E. (2020). Digital technology of generating survey data on the characteristics of an innovative product in a distance learning system. *Proceedings of the International Scientific Conference - Digital Transformation on Manufacturing, Infrastructure and Service*, 1–5. DOI: 10.1145/3446434.3446537

Rajabi, B. A., & Lee, S. P. (2010). Modeling and analysis of change management in dynamic business process. *International Journal of Computer and Electrical Engineering*, *2*(1), 181–189. DOI: 10.7763/IJCEE.2010.V2.133

Reina, G., Childs, H., Matković, K., Bühler, K., Waldner, M., Pugmire, D., Kozlíková, B., Ropinski, T., Ljung, P., Itoh, T., Gröller, E., & Krone, M. (2020). The moving target of visualization software for an increasingly complex world. *Computers & Graphics*, *87*, 12–29. DOI: 10.1016/j.cag.2020.01.005

Ryan, L. (2016). *The visual imperative: Creating a visual culture of data discovery*. Morgan Kaufmann.

Schröder, K., Belavadi, P., Ziefle, M., & Calero Valdez, A. (2022). *The Pension Story - Data-Driven Storytelling with Pension Data* (pp. 404–415). DOI: 10.1007/978-3-031-06018-2_28

Schröder, K., Eberhardt, W., Belavadi, P., Ajdadilish, B., van Haften, N., Overes, E., Brouns, T., & Valdez, A. C. (2023). Telling stories with data–a systematic review. arXiv preprint arXiv:2312.01164

Schroeder, K., Ajdadilish, B., Henkel, A. P., & Calero Valdez, A. (2020). Evaluation of a Financial Portfolio Visualization using Computer Displays and Mixed Reality Devices with Domain Experts. *Proceedings of the 2020 CHI Conference on Human Factors in Computing Systems*, 1–9. https://doi.org/DOI: 10.1145/3313831.3376556

Segel, E., & Heer, J. (2010). Narrative visualization: Telling stories with data. *IEEE Transactions on Visualization and Computer Graphics*, *16*(6), 1139–1148. DOI: 10.1109/TVCG.2010.179 PMID: 20975152

Shavazipour, B., López-Ibáñez, M., & Miettinen, K. (2021). Visualizations for decision support in scenario-based multiobjective optimization. *Information Sciences*, *578*, 1–21. DOI: 10.1016/j.ins.2021.07.025

Sheiderman, B., & Plaisant, C. Strategies for evaluating information visualization tools: multi-dimensional in-depth long-term case studies. In Proceedings of the 2006 AVI workshop on BEyond time and errors: novel evaluation methods for information visualization (2006), pp. 1–7.

Temirgaliev, E., Dubolazov, V., Borremans, A., & Overes, E. (2021). *Digitalization in Logistics for Organizing an Automated Delivery Zone*. Russian Post Case., DOI: 10.1007/978-3-030-64430-7_12

Tong, C., Roberts, R., Borgo, R., Walton, S., Laramee, R. S., Wegba, K., Lu, A., Wang, Y., Qu, H., Luo, Q., & Ma, X. (2018). Storytelling and visualization: An extended survey. *Information (Basel)*, *9*(3), 65. DOI: 10.3390/info9030065

Urbach, N., & Röglinger, M. (2019). Introduction to digitalization cases: how organizations rethink their business for the digital age. In *Digitalization cases* (pp. 1–12). Springer., DOI: 10.1007/978-3-319-95273-4_1

Walsh, J., Cunningham, A., Wark, S., Nowina-Krowicki, M., & Thomas, B. H. (2019, December). Narrative Visualisation of Simulations: Finding the Stories Within the Data. *El Sawah, S. (Ed.) MODSIM2019, 23rd International Congress on Modelling and Simulation.* DOI: 10.36334/modsim.2019.B3.walsh

Weijers, M., Bastiaenen, C., Feron, F., & Schröder, K. (2021). Designing a Personalized Health Dashboard: Interdisciplinary and Participatory Approach. *JMIR Formative Research*, *5*(2), e24061. DOI: 10.2196/24061 PMID: 33560229

Williams, M., & Moser, T. (2019). The art of coding and thematic exploration in qualitative research. *International Management Review*, *15*(1), 45–55.

Zhu, S., Sun, G., Jiang, Q., Zha, M., & Liang, R. (2020). A survey on automatic infographics and visualization recommendations. *Visual Informatics*, *4*(3), 24–40. DOI: 10.1016/j.visinf.2020.07.002

Chapter 17 Hope, Nihilism, and Faith in the World of Professional Wrestling and Its Data-Driven Monetization

Mitrajit Biswas
https://orcid.org/0000-0002-0409-867X
O.P. Jindal Global University, India

ABSTRACT

A world filled with new technologies, global challenges, and evolving social values gives rise to the philosophical strands of humanity, hope, and nihilism. Disparate yet deeply related, these concepts allow us to address the paradoxes of human existence. Humanity denotes the common sentiments, values, and responsibilities that define us as social beings. It signifies compassion, collaboration, and advancement, which aids in forming moral and social structures. While hope, in contrast, fuels motivation and creativity, even in the bleakest of times. It is the confidence of better outcomes that drives people and nations. On the contrary nihilism, which denies existence or any meaning and purpose, illustrates the disenchantment that emerges in the absence of functioning systems, collapsing ideologies, or unresolved essential inquiries.

DOI: 10.4018/979-8-3373-2772-3.ch017

INTRODUCTION

Nihilism, hope, and humanity philosophy comes in hand with technologies as well as new social problems, social values and social problems. Each of them seems to be of dissimilar clans philosophically and yet, they are so intricately interrelated that one could say they charge each other with equal consideration of the paradoxes of life and existence. Humanity, in our case, denotes the common sentiments and values, responsibilities that are shared, and social attributes that are social in nature. It denotes kindness and social cooperation and social and technological progress which helps in constructing social and moral frameworks. Moreover, hope drives social progress and imagination in the darkest hours. It is the faith of greater benefits that propels individuals and countries. Nihilism, on the other hand, denies existence, meaning, and purpose, and the disenchantment that arises in the wake of operational frameworks is the absence of dysfunctional systems, crumbling ideologies, and unanswered fundamental questions. The focus of this paper is the interaction of the topics of hope, nihilism and humanity in literature, philosophy, art, and culture. It follows from classical and contemporary thought and examines how hope persists in the frameworks of nihilism and humanity endures the void of meaning. The paper tries to answer the question whether those countries can merge, and what their conflict reveals about contemporary humanity.

HUMANITY: A PHILOSOPHICAL ANCHOR AND HISTORICAL CONTEXT

The topic of Humanity has been a focal point for different philosophical studies for many years and places such as the classroom or the workplace. From Aristotle's perception of man as a "political animal," to Kant's focus on moral obligation of universalistic ethics, humanity has almost always been linked to some form of consensus or collective obligation. Now, we have also extended the idea of responsibility to include global citizenship as it relates to climate change, the pandemic, and social inequality. Humanity, as an idea, counters nihilism, and instead creates social meaning through relationships, involvement, and ethical action.

Hope: An Engine for Change

Hope has acted as the backbone for forward motivation for as long as history can remember. A range of disciplines consider philosophers, for instance, describing them as recluses whilst helping people in Purgatory obtain salvation, e.g. in Dante's Divine Comedy. From an existential perspective, it has also been described as an act of rebellion (Camus). In current times, hope fuels social innovation and change efforts, fighting systemic inertia and existential threats, which can be seen in climate change activism as well as in frameworks aimed at addressing other global challenges.

Nihilism: Absence of Meaning

Nihilism instead explores the governed social constructs accepted, consciously defying the socialized consensus on virtue and ethics. Nihilism often brings to mind despair but simultaneously provides an escape from dogmatic shackles. Moreover, Nietzsche's modern proclamation that God is dead demonstrates how a man, from a modern perspective, cynically spins a world teetering on the edge of the meaning crisis. With dogma gone, the air is suffused with the invigorating possibility to forge one's reasoning. Crippling while liberating, such is the nature of nihilism's modern role.

Nihilism vs Humanity: Humanity's Consilience is Often at Odds with the Nihilistic Perspective of Meaninglessness

Nihilism Hope: Skepticism notwithstanding, hope, the act of positive expectation, may exist within a nihilistic global perspective. Hope serves the humanitarian purpose in diabolic periods. This essay expects its participants to purposively reflect upon, and to consider the definitions and roles of, the terms humanity, hope, and nihilism in structuring the dilemma 'why is meaning necessary' paradox. Even in the absence of certitude, people search for proof of humanity, for disillusionment, or the absence of hope, realize relationships and search the boundaries of progress. This conflict of hope and struggle is the product of essence, and leaves in the world today, completely disintegrated, and bristling with opportunities of revival, lifeless.

OBJECTIVE OF THE PAPER

This dissertation addresses hope in contrast to nihilism in popular culture through the lens of professional wrestling and the World Wrestling Entertainment (WWE). Cena's and Rhodes's characters are both examined and how Cena's and Rhodes's characters are deliberately crafted around the ideals of stoic ethics and the notion of transcendence amidst chaos and overwhelming injustice. For example, the phrase "Never Give Up" that John Cena uses is hope that is positive and pursued rather than nihilistic capitulation that is underwritten by inverse surrender and relentless attempts towards fulfillment. Analyze the "American Nightmare" persona of Cody Rhodes with emphasis on legacy, betrayal, and redemption. His narrative captures the contestation of meaning imposition defining familial legacy and the struggle to assert a self in a morally ambiguous society.

CONTRIBUTION TO DISCOURSE

This study shifts the debate, transcending the "lowbrow entertainment" category of wrestling by recontextualizing it as a site of philosophical inquiry. It demonstrates how WWE's commercially crafted narratives of hope strategically undermine one of the gravest anxieties of our era, which is nihilism, by fostering hope and a collective sense of belief in agency. Examining contemporary culture through the lens of scholarly writing reveals how media and popular culture serve to shape and construct social perceptions of meaning and value in an atomized society.

LITERATURE REVIEW: NIHILISM, HOPE, AND HUMANITY IN WWE

The intersection of hope and nihilism in forms of popular culture like professional wrestling is capturing more scholarly attention. Western philosophy has, and continues to, explore the concept of nihilism. Simply stated, nihilism is the notion that life lacks any purpose, meaning, or value. This was greatly expanded upon by Nietzsche (1968), who framed it both as a crisis and as an opportunity for reevaluation of existing values. Another example is Camus (1942), who discussed the absurdity of the existence of a human being and advocated for rebellion as a way to cope with the meaninglessness of life.

Many people in society view hope as a pivotal and underlying aspect to resilience and situated at the opposite end pole to despair. Hope has been described by Marcel (1962) as an attitude existentially obtained and which results from social bonds. In contrast to this, Bloch (1986) described hope as an agent of change in social and personal dimensions which has a future orientation. For them, hope is an active engagement in the struggle against despair and not an inactivity waiting for something to happen. Within media and cultural studies, the attitude and behaviors of audience members as a result of the consumption of popular media has been thoroughly studied. Jenkins (1997) and Mazer (1998) posit that there is a cultural performance in professional wrestling which has the structure of a theater where ancient myths are cyclically reincarnated. Wrestlers are more than just performers. They are complex, sophisticated integrations of deeply moral, philosophical, and emotional issues.

Professional wrestling is an innovative, modern methodology of storytelling, where live performance is intertwined with scripted tales of morality, depicting the age-old battle between the forces of good (the faces) and evil (the heels) in a choreographed struggle. Like in any other artistic performance, the wrestling industry's primary focus is not the match, but how an audience emotionally experiences it—a cyclic narrative which is deeply rooted in the philosophy of hope, nihilism, and faith.

The nature of this spectacle, however, has changed drastically in the 21st century. Now, the estimation of success does not rely solely on applause from the crowd, while the success of digital stream sales remains unknown. Previously, in the focusing stage of the monetization strategy, the touchpoint of fan engagement was leveraged as a calculable bond, tracked, and ultimately recorded as a digital monetary success.

This chapter integrates the philosophy of professional wrestling with the business frameworks of the modern era. It argues that the emotional connections fans form with wrestling entertainment, including the exhilarating hope of seeing the hero win, the despair brought on by nihilistic storylines, and the belief in the overall narrative, have triumphed in the form of monetization as sophisticated data engines. Companies such as World Wrestling Entertainment (WWE) go beyond just selling tickets and merchandise. They conduct extensive data fan analysis and emotional advertising strategy engagements to document storylines emotional wrestling framework monetize story fan ignitors. This thesis will primarily outline and scrutinize the philosophical narrative frameworks that explain the unique form of story wrestling over, regarding data monetization, the mature digital fandom data ecosystem.

A CHARACTERIZATION OF PROFOUND MORALITY

This conflict makes room for ethical and moral struggles as well as providing entertainment. The stories tend to reflect society's deepest fears and dreams by using stereotypes to encapsulate diverse ideas. For example, the "babyface" and "heel" dichotomy brings order to the chaos of moral complexity. The "babyfaces" which are viewed as the heroes are simple; they represent virtues such as honesty, hard work, selflessness, and ultimately altruism. In contrast, the heels embody (Barthes, 1972) lies, treachery, cruelty, and selfishness.

John Cena: An Example of Moral WrestleMania

John Cena's character is a cultural icon of resistance and moral idealism, epitomized with the catchphrase "Never Give Up." His storylines are mostly centered around overcoming hardships, showing some level of ethical hope amid chaos and treachery. He has become the face of the WWE's never-ending optimism and a symbol of hope for millions of fans (Ouellette,2017). While supporters argue that his character is pro-American, capitalism deeply influences his ideals. His character is very Capitalistic, Right-Wing good and does support the US military which a lot of his fans like. It is safe to say he does embody the capitalistic neo-liberalistic agenda that is force fed to Americans.

Cody Rhodes: Legacy, Loss, and Transformation

Cody Rhodes, mainly as "The American Nightmare" shares a different narrative revolving around legacy but just as strong when it comes to loss, transformation, and existential suffering blended with disenfranchised redemption. Rhodes is captivating for his blend of vulnerability and fierce resolve which touches people deeply (Strazza, 2023).

CULTURAL NIHILISM AND COUNTER-NARRATIVES

The growing abandonment of culture and hope in media themes create a lack of meaning, a phenomenon that McGowan (2016) and Fisher (2009) criticize; however, Cena and Rhodes showcase characters that not only fill this void but are vulnerable and morally clear.

Remediation and Thematic Adaptation

Bolter and Grusin (1999) show how WWE constantly shifts and repackages ancient themes like good versus evil and hope versus despair, emerging in modern times with new interpretations of identity chaos. These characters are more than just wrestling performers; they are structures depicting the constant battle between human nature and the void of nihilism.

Audience Reception and Participatory Culture

In addition to character and narrative construction, the appropriation of WWE characters audiences by fans also influences the clarity of the characters' themes. Wrestling fans are not consumers of culture, rather they contribute to the meaning given to the performers. Fan communities are best described by Jenkins (2006) as "participatory culture"–actively remixing, reinterpreting, commenting, and infusing social meaning into media texts.

John Cena: Emotional Resilience

John Cena and Cody Rhodes are great examples of people whose character development happens together with the audience. Fans have started to consider Disney World slogan – "Never Give Up" as an emotionally encouraging for struggling fans, rather than simply a motto as previously perceived. Because of its over-exploitation, fans recount how Cena's moral fortitude helped them in their times of personal crises. For example, people claim to have gained resolve during their most desperate moments through social media conversations and fan-generated content about rooting for Cena during his lowest points. This goes to show the impact which hope can deliver does through a living character, enabling comfort and strength towards the heart altogether. (Hill, 2020)

Cody Rhodes: Unwritten Legacy and Redemption

The life of Cody Rhodes and the unfinished legacy as well as self-redemption narrative was visible from the moment he came back to the WWE in 2022. Fans attempted to help him 'finish the story' by giving closure, meaning, and triumph throughout his journey. His creation of narratives aligns with one of the existentialist movements: the struggle for finding meaning in an absurd world, accepting loss (his father Dusty Rhodes' figure), and fighting against deep-rooted nothingness. The fierce reactions and the deep commitment visible both during and after show in venues and in social media illustrate how fans and audience members engage deeply with these narratives as allegories for what they aspire to achieve.

EMOTIONAL RITUALS AND COLLECTIVE EMOTIONAL RELEASE

In addition, the circumstantial affirm of collective hope "Thank You Cena" or "You Deserve It" for Rhodes, as well as WWE Hall of Fame ceremonies and tribute videos functions as rituals that strengthen belief in hope and emotional tie to humanity. These actions along with audience feedback serve as moments of catharsis, resisting alienation in modern society, and creating humanity (Groom, 2019).

AN AREA FOR PHILOSOPHICAL DEBATE

Therefore, the universe of WWE cultivates an environment in which existential dilemmas and ethical optimism are not just concepts to ponder; they are experiences that individuals face, internalize, and navigate together. The narratives are not consumed passively, but rather they evoke active engagement, enabling fans to relive and reinterpret the battles of Cena, Rhodes, and others, who become symbols of powerful resistance against the modern tide of nihilism. This examination stresses the importance of philosophy in contemporary society by utilizing the examples offered by popular culture.

To comprehend the business of contemporary wrestling, it is necessary to appreciate the philosophical engine that underpins its allure. The structure of the storyline in professional wrestling is a form of art in emotional exploitation aimed at fostering a strong and lasting connection with its audience. The effectiveness of professional wrestling's narratives is in the hope it is able to create. As identified by cultural theorists, the genre thrives on the archetypal story of the underdog (Sammond, 2005). The archetypal wrestling story features a cherished champion enduring a grueling journey through tremendous challenges, brutal defeats, ruthless betrayals, and endless torment, culminating in their satisfying, symbolic victory. This is the "hope" that wrestling sells–the notion that virtue, courage, and relentless spirit will be ultimately rewarded. The long-awaited title victory of fan favorites, like Kofi Kingston's WWE Championship win during WrestleMania 35, is a perfect illustration of this narrative arc reaching its emotion-ridden peak.

Nevertheless, this hope is only effective because of a counterbalance and its dialectical relationship with nihilism. The "heel" or villain is the nihilism in this case and the embodiment of chaos, and cynicism and injustice. Their role is to methodically destroy the progress the hero has made towards achieving the audience's hope. A brilliantly executed heel turn, wherein a hero betrays a partner or their own values, serves as a profoundly nihilistic narrative event that evokes intense emotional resonance, making the eventual restoration of order profoundly rewarding. The incessant interplay between hope and its negation forms the narrative tension that sustains audience investment and motivates them to seek additional materials. In wrestling, there is audience trust that is unlike any other. In the eyes of some scholars, wrestling spectators do not question the legitimacy of the contest; rather, they appreciate the artistry in the display (Barthes, 1972). The modern-day fan, along 'kayfabe' lines, who invests emotionally in the persona and the related story, is quite complex, rational, and deliberate. This is not a misguided or simplistic stance, but rather something akin to narrative faith, a willingness to surrender to what the spectacle offers. This faith serves as the foundational principle of fandom. Passersby are rendered active, devoted 'participants' or 'Universe' as coined by WWE. Such essence describes a non-rational, faith driven devotion which in contemporary society is easily monetized.

This is done by chopping the limbs and applying the head separately hoping that a particular arrangement evokes enough apathy and confusion that they will not question the profound imbalance. Professional wrestling probes them philosophically: the exact infusion of hope, nihilism and faith that to evoke emotional commitment appeals. The structure contains emotionally unifying, favorable personages, contemptible antagonists and cyclic conflict – resolution frameworks. This emotional allegiance is what drives today's professional wrestling business model, which is predicated on sensitive data.

METHODOLOGY

The period of 1998-2025 continues to have pivotal world of entertainment. Using character monologues alongside episodes in their narratives, analysis on WWE has shown to be an integral changing facet of WWE.

Engagement Analysis

This examines the sentiment from fan comments on social media integrated with the rest of impact perception commentary.

Comparative Philosophy

Philosophy needs to be explained, using Camus' The Myth of Sisyphus, and Nietzsche's Will to Power. Also, in other media such as comic book movies and video games. In culture and media studies, this research focuses on qualitative, interpretive techniques that seek to understand how hope, humanity, and popular culture's construction of nihilism have been performed and received by audiences. The WWE character plots and Cena as well as Rhodes focus the bulk of the analysis.

RESEARCH DESIGN

The analysis involves data collection and considers particular activity data sets for completing organizational and promotional frameworks and for assessment documentation which extends to summarizing participatory interviews on documents associated with WWE promotional and competitive 'texts.' The 'texts' are part of systems of netnographic analysis by Kozinets (2010) regarding user engagement on social media and fan cultures. This triangulation affords more insight into the constructions of popular media and the audience's understanding of deep conflicts and narratives of moral strength. Moreover, the analysis includes the socio-cultural aspects of the WWE, framed within its commercial context and its history.

DATA COLLECTION

Primary Textual Data

From the time period of 1998 till 2024, the selected episodes of WWE that are broadcast on TV will be instrumental in setting the context and highlighting crucial episodes of John Cena and Cody Rhodes. This period allows us to cover the trajectory of Cena's early career, peak years and veteran phase, and the WWE Rhodes's inception, time in other promotions, and the subsequent comeback. Broadly termed 'The Road to Redemption,' the arches in question and the WrestleMania appearances in various, evoke emotion whichever way one considers it, be it hope, nostalgia, failure, or altogether something different. Such cases of profound focus and importance shine through the wider lens of WWE.

Online Fan Discourse (Netnography)

Dedicated fan forums like r/Squared Circle and the WWE Forums were selected based on their level of activity and the range of opinions presented. The methodology for data collection will consist of passive participation in existing conversations, thematic collection, and opinion monitoring towards Cena and Rhodes. Thematic for important events on Twitter and relevant comments on YouTube are collected during the events themselves to capture the essence of the moment along with fan interpretation. The data will be gathered through hashtag and keyword searches related to the characters and their story arcs. Fan made videos and blog posts serve as examples of how fans construct narratives digitally, capturing the active participation and transformation WWE stories undergo at the hands of their fans.

Supplementary Sources

Speeches from the WWE Hall of Fame, alongside other public appearances and interviews with various performers, serve as context as well as clues to understanding the performers. Media coverage, alongside critical essays of the WWE, capture the cultural impact of their personas and summarize various viewpoints regarding their importance.

DATA ANALYSIS

Analysis of data will be approached from the following perspectives:

Thematic coding will be applied to categorize concepts relating to hope, despair, redemption, and the existential dichotomy of choice. This is a cyclic process where coding categories are constructed, and patterns are identified through refinement. Narrative analysis will be employed to outline character progression and how story arcs embrace or defy nihilistic elements. The focus will be on overarching plots and subplots, character motivations, as well as symbolic imagery. Analysis of the audience's emotional language alongside engagement metrics such as likes, shares, and digital space contextual meanings is crucial to understanding audience-derived meaning. The co-creation and negotiation of significance by the viewers will determine how the fandom is conceptualized. Attention will be focused on emotive expressions as well as in crafted symbols and structure, including but not limited to, metaphors, fan-initiated rituals (chants, farewell matches, crowd reactions), or any act that reveals cultural emotions experienced together. The analysis seeks to understand how these elements interact by employing concepts from performance studies (Schechner, 2013).

CONCEPTUAL FRAMEWORK

This paper follows a conceptual framework that integrates existential philosophy, narratives in popular culture, and audience studies. This study focuses on the meta story telling through WWE's promotional wrestling where narratives of hope, humanity, and nihilism are acted out, contested, and reinterpreted by John Cena, Cody Rhodes, and others.

PHILOSOPHICAL ANCHORS

Nihilism

Nihilism as an existential void of meaning arises from the ideas of Friedrich Nietzsche and Albert Camus. In WWE culture, it manifests through themes of betrayal, loss, failure and rejection of the tradition or legacy.

Hope

Following Ernst Bloch and Gabriel Marcel, hope is not a passive trait; rather, it constitutes an active moral and emotional resistance to despair. It is epitomized within the wrestler's journey toward redemption, moral clarity, and unwavering perseverance.

Humanity

Grounded in the philosophy of humanism and performance theory, humanity is described as the ability to feel, make moral choices, and have relationships. It is performed through a wrestler's vulnerability, loyalty, and in the struggle for meaning.

AUDIENCE RECEPTION AND EMOTIONAL RESONANCE

Active Fandom and Participatory Culture

Jenkins's framework of participatory culture in fandom welcomes to the fold the fans' emotional and intellectual investment in media texts, viewing them as active productive audiences instead of passive consumers. Fans relate emotionally to their favorite characters and story lines to the extent that they either root for or vehemently oppose certain major narrative choices. This is not just individual engagement; it is performed and nurtured collectively through online conversations and communal watching, chanting during events, responding with signs, fanfiction, remixing, and artwork.

Community Creation and Negotiation of Meaning

Jenkins elaborates on fandom as a site of negotiation; fandom is more than reception of meaning; meanings are produced, constructed, contended, and negotiated within interpretive communities. Fans scrutinize texts and dispute over what canon is and fill and alter narratives which eventually culminate in mutual expertise and a shared lexicon. This may also encourage the self-identified activist viewer, where people begin to self-categorize as something and then endeavor to alter the very media, they are passionate about.

Rituals and Practices of Chants at Live Events

As zealot fans for sports or music, the practices concerning enthusiasm demonstrated through the use of chants, reaction, signs, etc., are critical for active fan engagement. Such active behaviors, which are observable during sports or music functions, serve to convert passive onlookers into active fans. For instance, certain chants and anthems serve as a token of championing the cause whereby the fans vigorously celebrate the essence of their culture as they tell the story, carry the spirit, and feel the emotional richness of the community. Through these pledges, fans demonstrate their affection, and at the same time, through meaning-imbued production and eclectics of mass media, they exercise contestation posture.

Rolodex of Fan Culture Meanings and Cynical Detachment

In Jenkins' words, he talks about a shift of pleasure of a diabolic nature. In connection with other similar detailed participatory observations, involving oneself in this particular reality appears as a form of cynical detachment. The 'Rolodex of meaning' paradigm, in this case, moved from its primary domain to popular culture, deemed commonplace enough for audiences to easily grasp, critical, appropriative, or remixed, 'an apologia or reconstruction'. 'Critically detached' enough to be appropriate, fans 'distance' themselves from these works. 'Detachment' in this case signifies in-jokes or personal counter-commentary as a substitute for the comment about the culture that surrounds them. This contradiction illuminates a rather advanced form of 'media literacy' which reflects an awareness of the 'participatory culture' and its 'cultivation' by corporations. As Jenkins and subsequent theorists have pointed out, participatory fandom is not limited to leisure activities but also encompasses civic and political engagement. Documented evidence also exists of fans spearheading social movements which, as an organized constituency, embrace activism and participatory politics.

DATA DRIVEN MONETIZATION OF THE FAN CULTURE IN WWE

WWE developed a complex, multi-faceted digital ecosystem while utilizing data and analytics for almost every aspect of their business from streaming and merchandising to live events and social media. Here's the breakdown of how each component works towards being a part of WWE's overarching digital vision:

The Subscription-Based Model & Intelligence Systems for Content Analytics

WWE Network Evolution

WWE Network was launched in 2014 as an exclusive Pay-Per-View channel, featuring classic matches and original content. Recently in 2021, WWE partnered with Peacock to purchase the exclusive U.S. streaming PPV rights for around a billion dollars. While keeping international D2C access.

Data Application

WWE tracks detailed user engagement data on the content such as time spent, rewatch rates, and drop-off points, aiding in programming refinement. With lighting tracking, assessment of remote viewership, integrated advertising, merchandizing, and innovative campaign driven segmentation (free/premium ad sponsored) tier system segmentation fully facilitated, catered to differing fan bases.

Capturing Value from Customer Engagement

Niche audiences with specific era and superstars WWE sells retarget owned themed merchandise driving revenues faster.

Merchandising

All WWE online shops, Shopify, and Amazon. Multi-channel offers direct access to customers and shifting online.

Sales Through Social and Data

WWE needs streaming, and web movement data to cross reference and link fan data with personalized merchandise offers at peak storyline. Like, Bray Wyatt tribute merchandise sells out in 24 hours.

Dynamic Pricing

Strategy focused on gaining maximum value and demand perception during critical time periods for releases tied to storylines and limited editions.

Headed off by a specially dedicated team called 'Team Wrestling', over ten thousand videos has been uploaded on YouTube. WWE also garners over 108 million subscribers.

Content Strategy

WWE has split classic and current content across multiple channels, WWE Vault containing archival matches. Analytics determine caching moments like returns and catchphrases that wedge virality and engagement driving economy on TikTok/Reels.

Monetization

WWE gains revenue through pre-roll advertisements, sponsored content such as Mountain Dew's $1M deal during the Royal Rumble, and creator-led advertisement. WWE analyzes thumbnails and titles to assess which optimal CTR and adjust them accordingly to maximize revenue from ads.

The monetization of fan engagement has been relatively straightforward: advertising and sponsorships drove ticket sales to events, broadcast rights were sold to television networks, and merchandise was sold to fans. While these revenue streams continue to be important, digital technologies provide new, sophisticated methods to monetize engagement through the collection and analysis of fan data.

The Data Gold Rush: WWE's Digital Ecosystem

Companies like WWE have created a digital ecosystem designed to capture fan engagement at every possible interaction. The WWE Network (now part of Peacock in the U.S. and integrated into the platform) as well as the company's social media channels (YouTube, X, Instagram), its website and mobile apps serve as collection funnels for data (Gladen, 2021). Each video, article, social media post, and merchandise purchase creates data points that feed a larger analytical engine. The company is then able to construct customized audience profiles and move beyond demographics to psychographics such as character preference, storyline engagement, and purchasing patterns.

ANALYTICS IN ACTION: QUANTIFYING HOPE AND DIRECTING THE NARRATIVE

The analytics and engagement concentrate on both completed and upcoming creative undertakings over a duration of time and begin with something like this.

YouTube Monitor and Social Media Analytics

This assesses view counts of specific segments and matches of professional wrestlers and analyzes data obtained from social media. Engagement with select social media postings and discussions provides insight into dominant and submissive personality types and even specific wrestlers. Wrestlers with significant viewership and engagement are likely to be integrated into the primary storyline main events.

Professional wrestlers are strongly associated with, and have high demand for, graphic tees and action figurines, as evidenced by sales volume. A WWE Champion with exceptionally successful merchandise, in this case, would correspond with high sales volume and merch. Analytics, Retention, and Drop-Off metrics, along with content pertaining to in-demand characters on the streaming platform, are proven to be the most popular by the audience. This data aids character acquisition, content broadcast, and those intersections in addition to the sale and marketing of forthcoming content.

Pro wrestling's evolution from focusing on direct consumer sales to becoming entertainment driven and multi-platform digitally advanced is an undeniable fact. Using complex data systems, WWE estimates fan devotion and engagement as powerful emotions and translates them as economically viable metrics that influence the product's storyline. The shift to incorporating advanced data systems into the storyline changes professional wrestling's former data-light business while commanding significant ethical and economic scrutiny. The hope algorithm, an attempt to analyze fan dreams and financially capitalize on them, anchors data-driven fan engagement as a threshold of wrestling business strategy.

This model of business is incredibly advantageous and positive due to the economic outlook. With improved data analytics, WWE has optimized its storylines and character development, producing a product that is more appealing, increases sponsorship, and fosters brand loyalty. This substantiates the division's critical revenue streams, which include the sales of live event tickets, merchandise, and media rights fee contracts. Participatory fandom, as explored by scholars such as Jenkins (2013), reveals that fans demonstrate greater willingness to spend time and money when they perceive that their hope and expectations are being acknowledged and rewarded. Following the data-driven strategy mitigates creative risks by ensuring that the company's resources are allocated to retold tales and characters with proven audience appreciation.

This framework, however, gives rise to disturbing ethical implications. Fan data and profiling personalized emotional responses to a given event for commercial gain tips the balance between entertainment and exploitation. "Hope algorithm" could be described as a feedback loop of sorts, where the raw fan passion is quantified, packaged, and resold to fans in the form of the scripted narrative product. In this system controlled by big data, the fan is not a mere consumer. In fact, their participation as well as the by-product data is a resource. The emotional labor of the audience, which includes their cheers, their boos, as well as the online arguments they engage in, is captured for the commercial benefit of the company.

THE FUTURE OF FANDOM

Considering the future, new technologies, particularly artificial intelligence and machine learning, will likely advance this further. We can imagine a future in which narratives are tailored to the users based on their viewing habits and engagement metrics, crafting an experience curated for maximum personal return on investment. Even though this might win the award for 'most evocative form of consumer capture', it does raise nuanced issues of cultural commonality, not to mention the common moral qualms about the emotional engineering that the algorithms perform.

Dreams, when monetized in the world of wrestling, come with their bouquets of good and bad. Monetization of dreams during wrestling, in this case, shows the worst in prospecting. It demonstrates, or rather serves, as a case study where ethical questions of branding, projecting and monetizing hope, as well as the authentic commodification of feelings, come into play. The culture, or rather the civilizational milieu which wrestling belongs to culture with, engages in treating feelings as a medium of exchange, society as a mere colony of cultural apathy, and religion as a value to be maximally over-optimized to achieve a goal. The foundation of the spectacle doesn't change it's the same as it used to be, a massive hope and nihilism driven warfare. The blend of ancient and modern ravages the world like it did back in the days.

What has changed is the industrial machinery that surrounds it. Wrestling has lost its essence as an art that aimed to tell a story.

The industry will now design a mechanized system of emotional monetization. Paying attention to the dream, wrestling employs its audiences in a manner that slips profound critical focus over the economic, social, and ethical framework of a reality which is devoid of hope. Constructed, commodified, and parted out. Wrestling and perhaps all of 'entertainment', the answer lies in the riddle of the future of ‘entertainment’, embedded in the friction between the real and the human emotions and the cold logic of a robot.’’

TECHNOLOGICAL ACCELERATION AND AUGMENTED FANDOM

The advancement of technology has increased competition in the industry’s pursuit of precision. WWE and United World Wrestling use AI, predictive modeling, and real-time sentiment tracking to assess and manage global fan engagement. WWE's Network streaming service on Peacock in the United States provides real-time feedback. Each click, stream, and subscription allows the company to assess fandom on both micro and macro levels and thus greatly influences future booking and character pushes. AI predicts which matchups will enhance online engagement and extend viewership. It even helps in optimizing storylines to boost audience engagement. Wrestlers and performers are monitored with wearable technology and smart gear which gathers their performance data as well as guiding their health and injury prevention routines. This tech provides additional layers of analytics to ensure that the stars of the show are always at their best.

The Expansion of Fan Touchpoints

While the classic ‘roar of the crowd’ remains, it has now been transformed into a fragment of a greater whole, enhanced by social media interactions, NFT collectibles, mobile voting, and on-demand viewing. WWE has a large social media following, well over hundreds of millions, making it the most subscribed sports entity on YouTube, as well as one of the largest on Twitter and Instagram. Fans actively shape their own briefs, through live tweeting, interactive Instagram stories, and YouTube WEDs, which influence the dramaturgy of the performance. International federations, such as UWW and WWE, analyze data from their OTT platforms concerning international fandom. This data drives their commercial and creative strategies tailored to local preferences.

Information in wrestling is not passive as it actively impacts the production of the event. As such, there is an increased risk of storylines being ‘algorithmically hollow’, constructed to fulfill a commercial need rather than an artistic one, which is a blow to artistic integrity. Fan enthusiasm and engagement which was once priceless became simple to track and monetized as fan tokens, content streams, and blockchain contracts. monetized. This develops strong and loyal customers and equally draws the concern of emotional commodification.

Wrestling's digital evolution isn't restricted to the matches themselves. Every feedback loop woven with boundless hope and relentless belief and woven together with immense fandom becomes a finely tuned and optimized, monetized emotional connection. Every event in the future is planned as an exquisite performance for the audience. Every yell and scream will be regarded as a potential data point, a business slip, a cheer, a boo, a purchase, or any piece of a data puzzle. The industry is faced with a pressing business ethics concern, namely the emotional bypassing and impact of complex human emotional work and the logics of simple, predictive programming. And equally outrageous, the protective preservation of wrestling as the cultural and historical mythology it holds, not as a mass produced, cold, mundane replica of reality.

Gamification and Mobile Microtransaction

Given that Flagship Games has secured remarkable revenues annually from WWE Undefeated, WWE Super Card, and WWE 2K Mobile, since 2013 there has been spendings to revenue growth of over 2x attributed to the addition of mobile gaming.

Data Feedback

Users Behavior in the system, including the upgrading of superstars/cards, are aligned with interests and popularity metrics from real life. This information is useful in strategizing the merchandise and story arcs.

Machine Learning Artifacts

User in-game purchases are increasingly annexed to the purchases which elevates the in-game progression to increase the engagement rate as well as the revenue.

LIVE-EVENT DATA & SMART TICKETING

Dynamic pricing is the ability to adjust price points based upon sales data and historical demand data and realtime browsing entry points.

Cross Selling

User behavior is relied upon to promote VIP experiences and merchandise bundles, such as abandoned carts triggering re-engagement emails.

Event Optimization

Heat maps, attendance data, and crowd engagement analytics are used to determine the match order and event highlights to increase revenue.

Fan Experience

Entry for live events is augmented with AR, while 360° VR experiences (in partnership with Meta) are offered for both live and recorded events.

Monetization

Strapped down NFTs and metaverse memorabilia are exclusively branded and sold in AR as digital collectibles.

GLOBAL MONETIZATION & LOCALIZED CONTENT

Regional Channels

Commentary and content is localized on WWE India, Español, and Arabia with YouTube region specific feeds and event timing around local holidays.

Localized Superstars

WWE identifies and nurtures homegrown talent such as Jinder Mahal in India; fan voting boosts engagement and data collection.

Merch/Ad Tie Ins

Regional events and holidays are synchronized with the localized ad campaigns and memorabilia.

CROWD FEEDBACK LOOP MONITORING ALONGSIDE SENTIMENT ANALYSIS.

Tech Stack

Sentiment of social media and audience reactions (cheering, booing) are analyzed through AI in real time.

Creative Decisions

Dynamic pricing is the capability to set different price points corresponding to sales history, historical demand, and current browsing sessions. WWE's creative and business units simultaneously optimize their strategies, capture data to alter storylines, event pacing, and marketing efforts.

CONTENT INTELLIGENCE AND SUBSCRIPTION PLANS

Streaming Affiliates

D2C International Access Subscription and Operational Cost: WWE offloaded operational cost with peacock deal in 2021 for $1B over five years. WWE extended streaming services to Netflix in India in 2025 for a growing market focus.

Audience Differentiation

An AI segregates the audience into groups like listeners and participants and provides them with individualized content. “Nostalgia Watchers” receive select throwback RAW episodes or retro merch campaigns.

Integrated CRM systems propel chronologically driven email funnels that recommend themed merchandise to connected streaming devices. Streams analyzing various pieces of Attitude Era content receive retro merch and other aligned promotion campaigns.

HYPER-PERSONALIZED MERCHANDISING

Geo-Targeting and Dynamic Inventory

Levering analytics during the sale of tribute merch for Bray Wyatt allowed the sale of the tribute merch for Bray Wyatt and the Wyatt family hour merch for the Wyatt family within twenty-four hours. Predictive analytics enhanced shipping around major cities.

Unified Drops

Scott Travis' T-shirts and belt replicas as part of the Cactus Jack x WrestleMania 41 Collection marketed Travis' culture.

Live Event Triggers

Geofenced mobile app notifications for Roman Reigns "Tribal Chief" gear during events combine both physical and digital purchases

SOCIAL MEDIA & MICRO CONTENT DOMINANCE

YouTube Mastery

WWE flagship channel's A/V Testing on video thumbnails and titles, e.g. "Top 10 Betrayals" versus "Friends Turned Foes" for CTR optimization, has 108 million subscribers.

TikTok Strategy

Horizon's 200 million monthly views primarily come from TikTok through bites of behind-the-scenes content and the Liv Morgan captivation to promote Wrestle-Mania aimed at younger audiences for the Peacock/Netflix funnels.

Influencer Synergy

Their own native influencer marketing campaign featuring massively popular Logan Paul (23.6 million subscribers on YouTube) and Bad Bunny propelled WWE into a broader audience's eye, making use of data targeting

Mobile Revenue Surge

As of Q1 2024, WWE Supercard's revenue surpassed $294,000 in weekly earnings, realigning their projected lifetime earnings, counter to the $1.2 billion glide path, in loot boxes, seasonal events, and game-driven monetization.

Play-to-Own Mechanism

In-app tasks/mission like “watch 5 matches: unlock exclusive wallpapers” allow redeemable points, incentivizing fans with digital points exchangeable for tangible rewards like merch

Data Driven Storylines & Global Localization

“What is necessary is a clear vision of sophisticated marks”: the WWE is known to use ‘crowd noise’ as a part of its soundboard. For example, the Roman Reigns ‘Tribal Chief’ heel turn, and fan ‘controlled’ Yes Movement by Daniel Bryan.

Localization

Distribution of Hindi and Tamil commentaries, Telugu and Hindi Diwali-themed merchandise, and other merchandise for Tier 2 Indian cities like Pune and Surat integrate Jinder Mahal’s title reign as part of the country-specific events.

New Technologies & Overarching Strategy

AR/VR Integration

Edge’s Red Bull sponsored ingression, Meta's 360° ring view advertisements, and other visuo-spatial perspectives offer unprecedented advertisement opportunities.

NFTs & Metaverse

Specific highlights in the form of NFTs are et and sold accompanying PPVs, and Roblox is the sandbox for testing virtual micro events.

LIMITATIONS

Analyzing the WWE storylines of John Cena and Cody Rhodes along with the conversations within the Western fandom demonstrates the strengths and weaknesses of qualitative, interpretivist research in the field of media studies. I will offer, in additional detail, the method-related and contextual limitations of research within fan studies and qualitative methodologies.

QUALITATIVE INTERPRETIVISM AND ITS LIMITATIONS: BIAS WITHIN MEANINGS

In comparison with quantitative methodologies, qualitative approaches seek to attain explanation via stepping deeper into a why and how outline of the phenomenon, instead of Culture-Spotting. In the instance presented, the researcher's grasp of fan discourse, from social media discussions to singing at events, borders the outer edge of social fan culture. A fan's critique of Cody Rhodes' storyline, for example, is sardonically meant to be enthusiastic to one researcher, and sincere disappointment to the opposite. Such differences come about, because as interpreters of qualitative information, the researcher's themes such as forum posts or interview transcripts sociologically put under test their frameworks, differ with the theoretical perspective (Jenkins's participatory culture versus political economy they employ). Even though reflexivity (a form of self-critique, where people admit their biases) can help reduce bias, it does not change the fact that most interpretation will depend on the culture and the scholarship of the analyst(s).

Lack Of Statistical Generalization

Focusing on John Cena and Cody Rhodes as subjects of study means all WWE narratives or wrestlers do not have statistically generalizable findings. Cena's "Never Give Up" mindset and Rhodes' "American Nightmare" story are both regarded as typical character arcs (the hero's journey and antihero redemption, respectively). Fans may associate these arcs with these gimmicks but are unlikely to do so for the Undertaker's supernatural persona or Rhea Ripley's punk aesthetic. Qualitative research considers transferability—where detailed context allows others to assess the relevance of a situation—as a limitation of the research.

Case Study Limitations: Depth vs. Breadth

Two Wrestlers as Sole Focus

I would first say that Cena and Rhodes offer deep and spanning case studies, but don't do much to offer at least some WWE narrative frame. Ex. Cena "Superman" Booking: For a decade, Rhodes "captures" the champion's underdog belt to combat Cena's CDL tenacyholder and WWE MVP (face/hero) "orton-s" a decade plus. While more relevant comparisons are available, midcard wrestlers, or tag teams, for some reason, become the focus of driving consumer interest.

Temporal Bias. WWE's "PG Era" was one of the WWE's more grappling wider marketed periods. Cena happens to be one of the poster child for the period, while Rhodes's few stages of emerging cadence (and meta-narratives and breaking the fourth wall) Reality Era (2016-present) are stomped down within a mild distinction branded by smash the fourth wall. They representational edifices constrain and stipulate what the fans are able to expect and how they are made to interpret WWE.

Non-Anglophone Context Exclusion

Concentrating only on English WWE programs and Western audiences leads to the following omissions:

Culturally Western Elsewhere in Indian WWE Superfans. WWE's social media universe has emerged globally, but it's incredibly rampant in India × Japan. It is also one of the most popular territories fans who follow WWE spend countless hours watching wrestling legends and compelling crossover fictional tales. There, fans basically reinterpret the players and argue with each other on almost every sociopolitical lens intersects with Bollywood hero/villain narratives.

Linguistic Variety. Spanish-speaking users on X and specific forums such as Planeta Wrestling may have unique criticisms of WWE's narratives and storytelling brands.

CULTURAL AND GEOGRAPHICAL DIVISIONS

Eurocentric And American Focused Fandom Analysis

This research focuses on North American and European fandom interactions since these are the regions where WWE's narrative is most heavily contested. This may create an issue where the "Western" frame of reference is inappropriately assumed to define the overall global viewpoint. For example:

Cena's Patriotic Gimmick

Celebratory expectations of his character's flag-baring persona will come from the US audience, while the rest of the world will view it as American-flag-waving over the top nationalism. Similarly, Rhodes' "American Nightmare" persona is likely to resonate with U.S. Dusty Rhodes fans, but many non-U.S. fans may be baffled by the character not having culturally relevant anchors.

Platform Bias

Reddit and Twitter as main hubs for Western fans do not share region specific demographic in Japan or WhatsApp groups in Brazil, who might focus more on the logical order of events in the storytelling than the wrestling itself.

Language as a Barrier

Focusing on specific communities that do not communicate in English develop their own set of interpretations for the fandom. For instance:

Japanese Fans

While freely critiquing WWE's lean into "sports entertainment", they will most often base their reasoning for dismissal around New Japan Pro-Wrestling's intense grappling and fighting style.

Arabic Language Forums

Conversations might center around WWE's presentation of Middle Eastern personas like The Iron Sheik or Rhodes and Cena narratives bordering geo-political caricaturing stereotypes

Cultural and Experiential Differentiation

Every fan community has distinct differentiations. Even within the Western context, the following diverge:

Casual vs. Hardcore Fans

Casual followers may regard Cena's ubiquitous presence as a positive, but hard-core "smarks" (smart marks) deride his scripted promos as fake and heavily edited

Age Demographics

Older fans who reminisce about the "Attitude Era" (1997–2002) may think Rhodes emotional promos are overly dramatic while Gen Z finds such expressions of vulnerability to be relatable.

Intersectional Identity Influences

Peer Debriefing

A number of colleagues as well as fan studies and media research specialists examine the interpretive choices and provide feedback that either aligns with or contests the given interpretations. Member Verification (if possible): Because of some restrictions on public data, direct contact with fans is limited. However, the research invites and encourages feedback from the fan community through public forums as a means to improve and deepen the understanding and scope of the discussions.

Ethical Issues in Internet Research: An Overview

Internet research especially intersects with ethics on the public and the private, creating a digital trace, and the ethics of data. This research in part aims to deal with these issues in the following ways:

Not engaging in data collection with closed or password protected spaces to avoid private paywalled domains. Avoiding fan culture concerning ethno-sensitive issues and fan practices with marginalized populations. Publishing results in closed access aggregated and anonymized data sets to minimize risks of harm caused by individual identification and uncommon recognition. Determining with some precision what data might be shared about the fan communities and the research subjects and trying to be as correct as possible while neutral to the fans and communities themselves.

Completing the research ethics of the Internet and participatory culture. These ethical practices and then the consequent methodological reflections contribute to the literature concerning ethics of research, the Internet and participatory culture. The scant follow-up research indicates that in trying to protect the privacy and anonymity of research subjects, digital methods advocates tend to overly simplify complicated and multi-faceted elements. Most importantly, what these authors did was not simply go for a gentle option, dictated self-imposed ethics. They also responded to the challenge to decolonize and democratize research by valuing fans as active knowledge contributors rather than research subjects.

CONCLUSION

The collaborative fan culture in this case can be addressed as a descriptive ethnography, although as a case study, it extends slightly beyond its rigid boundaries. I would still refer to it as a case study, as I find its contours useful to juxtapose with collaborative culture. There, the basic principles would overlap in the emphasis placed upon the users capacity to negotiate meaning as active agents. While I will not go deeply into the multiple constellations of the fan meaning construction frameworks, I will point to the fact that in this constellation, you can one of the most extreme, non-intrusive, non-aggressive, open-access frameworks of data compilation and analysis, which greatly amplifies its trustworthiness. The built-in, flexibility reflexivity, triangulation, and reflexivity bias mitigation qualitative strata as a signal ensures the reduction of biases that primary emphasis in frameworks of participant fan entire the static ecological. I have concerns with these, illustrations. I find very highly unlikely that there are non illustrative frameworks which indicate the illuminations of participatory fan cultures. Such constellation of the data collection methods, at least the framing themselves, create an assemblage of exemplary. There are conjunctions of assumptions that empower a principle of open-ended, diverse expression of elements.

REFERENCES

Barthes, R. (1972). *Mythologies* (Lavers, A., Trans.). Hill and Wang.

Bloch, E. (1986). *The principle of hope* (Plaice, N., Plaice, S., & Knight, P., Trans.). MIT Press. (Original work published 1954)

Bolter, J. D., & Grusin, R. (1999). *Remediation: Understanding new media*. MIT Press.

Camus, A. (1991). *The myth of Sisyphus* (O'Brien, J., Trans.). Vintage International. (Original work published 1942)

Fisher, M. (2009). *Capitalist realism: Is there no alternative? Zero Books. Fromm, E. (1955). The sane society*. Holt, Rinehart and Winston.

Groom, N. (2019). The emotional architecture of wrestling fandom: Ritual, performance, and catharsis. *Journal of Popular Culture*, *52*(4), 812–829. DOI: 10.1111/jpcu.12833

Hill, M. (2020). "More than just wrestling": Mental health, motivation, and media heroes in fan discourse. *Journal of Fandom Studies*, *8*(1), 47–63. DOI: 10.1386/jfs_00020_1

Jenkins, H. (1997). "Never trust a snake": WWF wrestling as masculine melodrama. In Redhead, S. (Ed.), *The passion and fashion* (pp. 33–66). Sage.

Jenkins, H. (2006). *Convergence culture: Where old and new media collide*. New York University Press.

Jenkins, H. (2006). *Fans, bloggers, and gamers: Exploring participatory culture*. New York University Press.

Kozinets, R. V. (2010). Netnography: Doing ethnographic research online. *Sage (Atlanta, Ga.)*.

Marcel, G. (1962). *Homo viator: Introduction to a metaphysic of hope. Harper & Row. Mazer, S. (1998). Professional wrestling: Sport and spectacle*. University Press of Mississippi.

McGowan, T. (2016). *Capitalism and desire: The psychic cost of free markets*. Columbia University Press. DOI: 10.7312/mcgo17872

Compilation of References

Aayog, N. (2022). *India's Booming Gig and Platform Economy.* NITI Aayog. Retrieved from chrome-extension://efaidnbmnnnibpcajpcglclefindmkaj/https://www.niti.gov.in/sites/d efault/files/2023-02/25th_June_Final_Report_27062022.pdf

Aayog, N. I. T. I. (2024). *Boosting exports from MSMEs: A roadmap to enhance digital infrastructure, simplify compliance, and improve access to incentives.* Government of India.

Abdel-Fattah, M. A., Khedr, A. E., & Aldeen, Y. N. (2017). An evaluation framework for business process modeling techniques. [IJCSIS]. *International Journal of Computer Science and Information Security, 15*(5), 382–392.

Abdul-Rahman, S., Arifin, N. F. K., Hanafiah, M., & Mutalib, S. (2021). Customer Segmentation and Profiling for Life Insurance using K-Modes Clustering and Decision Tree Classifier. *International Journal of Advanced Computer Science and Applications, 12*(9), 434–444. DOI: 10.14569/IJACSA.2021.0120950

Abe, J. O., & Ustundaug, B. B. (2018). A data as a service (DaaS) model for GPU-based data analytics. *arXiv preprint arXiv:1802.01639.*

Abuabid, A. A. (2025). A data-driven approach to cybersecurity situational awareness: insights from machine learning. *Journal of Innovative Digital Transformation.*

Abu-Salim, T., Onyia, O. P., Harrison, T., & Lindsay, V. (2017). Effects of perceived cost, service quality, and customer satisfaction on health insurance service continuance. [IDEAS/RePEcmarketplace.copyright.com]. *Journal of Financial Services Marketing, 22*(4), 173–186. DOI: 10.1057/s41264-017-0035-4

Adeleye, R. A., Asuzu, O. F., Bello, B. G., & Oyeyemi, O. P. (2024). *Digital currency adoption in Africa : A critical review and global comparison.* World Journal of Advanced Research and Reviews.

Adepoju, A., & Chianumba, E. C. (2025). AI-driven fraud detection in banking : A systematic review of data science approaches to enhancing cybersecurity. *GSC Advanced Research and Reviews*, (January). Advance online publication. DOI: 10.30574/gscarr.2024.21.2.0418

Adewunmi, O. (2024). Monetization Strategies For Content Creators. *Iosr Journal Of Economics And Finance (Iosr-Jef), 15*(6), 57–66. DOI: 10.9790/5933-1506055766

Adewusi, A. O., Okoli, U. I., Adaga, E., Olorunsogo, T., Asuzu, O. F., & Daraojimba, D. O. (2024). Business intelligence in the era of big data: A review of analytical tools and competitive advantage. *Computer Science & IT Research Journal*, *5*(2), 415–431. DOI: 10.51594/csitrj.v5i2.791

Adhami, S., Giudici, G., & Martinazzi, S. (2018). Why do businesses go crypto? An empirical analysis of Initial Coin Offerings. *Journal of Economics and Business*, *100*, 1–36. DOI: 10.1016/j.jeconbus.2018.04.001

Agarwala, V., Maity, S., & Sahu, T. N.AGARWALA. (2022). FEMALE ENTREPRENEURSHIP, EMPLOYABILITY AND EMPOWERMENT: IMPACT OF THE MUDRA LOAN SCHEME. *Journal of Developmental Entrepreneurship*, *27*(01), 2250005. Advance online publication. DOI: 10.1142/S1084946722500054

Agrawal, R. (2025). CBDT using AI tools to boost income-tax compliance. *The Indian Express*, July 24, 2025.

Agrawal, R. (2018). *India connected: How the smartphone is transforming the world's largest democracy*. Oxford University Press.

Ahmad, A. Y. A. B., & Kumari, S. S., MahabubBasha, S., Guha, S. K., Gehlot, A., & Pant, B. (2023, January). Blockchain Implementation in Financial Sector and Cyber Security System. In *2023 International Conference on Artificial Intelligence and Smart Communication (AISC)* (pp. 586-590). IEEE. DOI: 10.1109/AISC56616.2023.10085045

Ahmad, M., & Rana, S. (2023). Visual analytics for FMCG product placement: A CNN-based approach. *International Journal of Retail Analytics*, *12*(2), 45–60.

Ahmad, S. (2023). The impact of digital currencies on traditional banking systems : An analysis. *Journal of Economics and Business Letters*, *3*(2), 22–23. DOI: 10.55942/jebl.v3i2.277

Ahmad, S., Saxena, C., Islam, S., & Karim, R. (2024). Impact of Insur-Tech on the premium performance of the insurance business. *SN Computer Science*, *5*(1), 138. Advance online publication. DOI: 10.1007/s42979-023-02462-0

Ahmed, S., & Sur, S. (2021). Change in the uses pattern of digital banking services by Indian rural MSMEs during demonetization and Covid-19 pandemic-related restrictions. *Vilakshan-XIMB Journal of Management*, *20*(1), 166–192. DOI: 10.1108/XJM-09-2020-0138

Ahsan, Z. (2024). *Data monetization and inequality: Evidence from case studies. The National High School Journal of Science*. https://nhsjs.com/2024/data-monetization-and-inequality-evidence-from-case-studies

Ajzen, I. (1991). The theory of planned behavior. *Organizational Behavior and Human Decision Processes*, *50*(2), 179–211. DOI: 10.1016/0749-5978(91)90020-T

Akazue, M. I., Okofu, S. N., Ojugo, A. A., Ejeh, P. O., Odiakaose, C. C., Emordi, F. U., Ako, R. E., & Geteloma, V. O. (2024). Handling Transactional Data Features via Associative Rule Mining for Mobile Online Shopping Platforms. *International Journal of Advanced Computer Science and Applications*, *15*(3). Advance online publication. DOI: 10.14569/IJACSA.2024.0150354

Akyüz, A., & Mavnacıoğlu, K. (2021). Marketing and financial services in the age of artificial intelligence. *Financial Strategies in Competitive Markets: Multidimensional Approaches to Financial Policies for Local Companies*, 327-340. DOI: 10.1007/978-3-030-68612-3_23

Aladebumoye, T. (2025). The role of AI in enhancing tax transparency and reducing evasion. *World Journal of Advanced Research and Reviews*, *25*(1), 206–217. DOI: 10.30574/wjarr.2025.25.1.0023

Alaimo, C., & Kallinikos, J. (2017). Computing the everyday: Social media as data platforms. *The Information Society*, *33*(4), 175–191. DOI: 10.1080/01972243.2017.1318327

Alam, Y., Azizah, S. N., & Caroline, C. (2025). Digital Transformation in Banking Management: Optimizing Operational Efficiency and Enhancing Customer Experience. *International Journal of Management Science and Information Technology*, *5*(1), 46–55. DOI: 10.35870/ijmsit.v5i1.3646

Alarabiat, A., Soares, D., Ferreira, L., & de Sá-Soares, F. (2018, May). Analyzing e-governance assessment initiatives: an exploratory study. In *Proceedings of the 19th annual international conference on digital government research: Governance in the data age* (pp. 1-10). DOI: 10.1145/3209281.3209309

Albo, A., Bengtsson, K., Dahl, M., & Falkman, P. (2019). A framework concept for data visualization and structuring in a complex production process. *Procedia Manufacturing*, *38*, 1642–1651. DOI: 10.1016/j.promfg.2020.01.120

Alderman, H., & King, E. M. (1998). Gender differences in parental investment in education. *Structural Change and Economic Dynamics*, *9*(4), 453–468. DOI: 10.1016/S0954-349X(98)00040-X

Aleem, S., Lazarova-Molnar, S., & Mohamed, N. (2012). Collaborative business process modeling approaches: a review. *Proc. of the 2012 IEEE 21st International Workshop on Enabling Technologies: Infrastructure for Collaborative Enterprises*, 274–279.

Alfonsi, L., Namubiru, M., & Spaziani, S. (2024). Gender gaps: Back and here to stay? Evidence from skilled Ugandan workers during COVID-19. *Review of Economics of the Household*, *22*(3), 999–1046. DOI: 10.1007/s11150-023-09681-7

Ali, M., & Hassan, R. (2020). Customer churn prediction in FMCG using clustering and classification. *Journal of Business Intelligence*, *18*(3), 77–91.

Alimi, A., Grace, C., Oladele, S., & Mia, J. (2024). *Data-driven decision-making: Challenges and opportunities in business analytics* [Preprint]. ResearchGate.

Allingham, M. G., & Sandmo, A. (1972). Income tax evasion: A theoretical analysis. *Journal of public economics, 1*(3-4), 323-338.Antón, F. S. (2021). Artificial intelligence and tax administration: strategy, applications and implications, with special reference to the tax inspection procedure. *World Tax J.*, 575.

Aloulou, M., Grati, R., Al-Qudah, A. A., & Al-Okaily, M. (2023). Does FinTech adoption increase the diffusion rate of digital financial inclusion? A study of the banking industry sector. *Journal of Financial Reporting & Accounting*, *22*(2), 289–307. DOI: 10.1108/JFRA-05-2023-0224

Alsaghir, M. (2023). Digital risks and Islamic FinTech: A road map to social justice and financial inclusion. *Journal of Islamic Accounting and Business Research.* Advance online publication. DOI: 10.1108/JIABR-10-2022-0262

Anagnostopoulos, I. Y., Sails, T., & Alexandrou, G. (2025). FinTechs, BigTechs and diminishing bank franchise values: Stakeholder perspectives on a disruptive emerging financial ecosystem. *Technological Forecasting and Social Change*, *212*, 123924. DOI: 10.1016/j.techfore.2024.123924

Angelov, N., Johansson, P., & Lindahl, E. (2016). Parenthood and the Gender Gap in Pay. *Journal of Labor Economics*, *34*(3), 545–579. DOI: 10.1086/684851

Ara, S. (2021a). Gender Pay Gap in India: Evidence from Urban Labour Market. *The Indian Journal of Labour Economics : the Quarterly Journal of the Indian Society of Labour Economics*, *64*(2), 415–445. DOI: 10.1007/s41027-021-00319-9

Arkorful, V. E., Lugu, B. K., Hammond, A., Basiru, I., Afriyie, F. A., & Mohajan, B. (2021). Examining quality, value, satisfaction, and trust dimensions: An empirical lens to understand health insurance systems' actual usage. *Public Organization Review*, *21*(3), 471–489. DOI: 10.1007/s11115-020-00498-x

Arner, D. W., Barberis, J. N., & Buckley, R. P. (2015). The evolution of fintech: A new post-crisis paradigm? *SSRN*, *47*(4), 1271–1319. DOI: 10.2139/ssrn.2676553

Arnold, F., Kishor, S., & Roy, T. K. (2002). Sex-Selective Abortions in India. *Population and Development Review*, *28*(4), 759–785. DOI: 10.1111/j.1728-4457.2002.00759.x

Arora, K. (2024) 'Unveiling the Nexus: Technological Capacity and Export Performance in Indian Manufacturing Firms through Technical Efficiency Analysis', *SSRN*, pp. 1-35. DOI: 10.2139/ssrn.4792474

Arsenoaia, V. N., Ra u, R. N., Vele cu, I. D., & enu, I. (2023). Field tests of a John Deere harvester for the purpose of production maps achievement.

Arumugam, U., & Manida, M. (2023). *Prospects and Problems of Digital Currency*.

Ashton, D., & Gowland-Pryde, R. (2023). Arts audience segmentation: data, profiles, segments and biographies. In *Audience Data and Research* (pp. 66–81). Routledge. DOI: 10.4324/9781032632452-6

Aslam, A., & Hussain, A. (2024). A Performance Analysis of Machine Learning Techniques for Credit Card Fraud Detection. *Journal on Artificial Intelligence*, *6*(January), 1–21. Advance online publication. DOI: 10.32604/jai.2024.047226

Attar, R. W., Almusharraf, A., Alfawaz, A., & Hajli, N. (2022). New trends in e-commerce research: Linking social commerce and sharing commerce: A systematic literature review. *Sustainability (Basel)*, *14*(23), 16024. DOI: 10.3390/su142316024

Autor, D., Levy, F., & Murnane, R. J. (2023). The role of data in economic decision-making: Bridging analysts, economists, and managers. *The Journal of Economic Perspectives*, *37*(1), 103–126. DOI: 10.1257/jep.37.1.103

Aybas, M., & Uyargil, C. B. (2017). An integrated model recommendation about team performance measurement and evaluation. *International Journal of Business and Management*, *12*(2), 92. DOI: 10.5539/ijbm.v12n2p92

Babu, S., Iqbal, A., Saha, S., Koneti, C., Eni, L. N., Premkumar, I., & Suman, S. (2024). Content marketing in the era of short-form video: TikTok and Beyond. *Journal of Informatics Education and Research*, *4*(2). Advance online publication. DOI: 10.52783/jier.v4i2.1179

Bach, B., Wang, Z., Farinella, M., Murray-Rust, D., & Henry Riche, N. (2018). Design patterns for data comics. *Proceedings of the 2018 Chi Conference on Human Factors in Computing Systems*, 1–12. DOI: 10.1145/3173574.3173612

Bachmann, N., Tripathi, S., Brunner, M., & Jodlbauer, H. (2022). The contribution of data-driven technologies in achieving the sustainable development goals. *Sustainability (Basel)*, *14*(5), 2497. DOI: 10.3390/su14052497

Bačić, D., & Fadlalla, A. (2016). Business information visualization intellectual contributions: An integrative framework of visualization capabilities and dimensions of visual intelligence. *Decision Support Systems*, *89*, 77–86. DOI: 10.1016/j.dss.2016.06.011

Baecker, J., Engert, M., Pfaff, M., & Krcmar, H. (2020). *Business Strategies for Data Monetization : Deriving Insights from Practice*. Meist Angesehene Beiträge.

Bakhshi, T., & Ghita, B. (2021). Perspectives on Auditing and Regulatory Compliance in Blockchain Transactions. In *Trust Models for Next-Generation Blockchain Ecosystems* (pp. 37–65). Springer International Publishing., DOI: 10.1007/978-3-030-75107-4_2

Bálint, L. P., Várallyai, L., & Botos, S. (2025). Evaluation of data-driven sustainability potential at SMEs using an altered Ecocanvas model. *Economies*, *13*(2), 49. DOI: 10.3390/economies13020049

Banerjee, D. (2024). Can India become the world's 'China plus one' in tech manufacturing? APF Canada. https://www.asiapacific.ca/publication/can-india-become-worlds-china-plus-one-in-tech-manufacturing

Banik, N., & Kim, M. (2024). India–ASEAN trade relations: Examining the trends and identifying the potential. *Global Business Review*, *25*(2, suppl), S59–S77. DOI: 10.1177/0972150920953546

Baranauskas (2021b). Expert-Based Evaluation of Digitalization and Mass Customization in the Baltic Non-Life Insurance Online Platforms 184-201. Journal of Eastern European and Central Asian Research, 8(2), 184-201.

Baranauskas, G. (2021a). Application of customisation and personalisation in digital solutions of the non-life insurance market: A case study of Lithuanian, Latvian and Estonian e-sales platforms. *Engineering Management in Production and Services*, *13*(2), 68–82. DOI: 10.2478/emj-2021-0013

Barber, G. (2006). Personal information in government records: Protecting the public interest in privacy. *Louis U. Pub. L. Rev.*, *25*, 63.

Barthes, R. (1972). *Mythologies* (Lavers, A., Trans.). Hill and Wang.

Barykin, S., Kapustina, I., Kalinina, O., Parshukov, A., Aleksandrov, I., Poberezhnaya, V., Fedorova, M., & Overes, E. (2021). The career choice motivation in view of Maslow's hierarchy in innovative economy: The case of Russia. *Academy of Strategic Management Journal*, *20*(2), 1–17.

Bechtsis, D., Tsolakis, N., Iakovou, E., & Vlachos, D. (2022). Data-driven secure, resilient and sustainable supply chains: Gaps, opportunities, and a new generalised data sharing and data monetisation framework. *International Journal of Production Research*, *60*(14), 4397–4417. DOI: 10.1080/00207543.2021.1957506

Begeny, C. T., Ryan, M. K., Moss-Racusin, C. A., & Ravetz, G. (2020). In some professions, women have become well represented, yet gender bias persists—Perpetuated by those who think it is not happening. *Science Advances*, *6*(26), eaba7814. Advance online publication. DOI: 10.1126/sciadv.aba7814 PMID: 32637616

Bel Hadj Miled, K. (2025). Nexus between fintech, green finance natural resources, economic growth and environment sustainability: Evidence from BRICS countries. *Future Business Journal*, *11*(1), 47. DOI: 10.1186/s43093-025-00469-y

Bell, E., Bryman, A., & Harley, B. (2018). *Business research methods* (5th ed.). Oxford University Press.

Bennedsen, M., Simintzi, E., Tsoutsoura, M., & Wolfenzon, D. (2019). *Do Firms Respond to Gender Pay Gap Transparency?* DOI: 10.3386/w25435

Bennedsen, M., Larsen, B., & Wei, J. (2023). Gender wage transparency and the gender pay gap: A survey. *Journal of Economic Surveys*, *37*(5), 1743–1777. Advance online publication. DOI: 10.1111/joes.12545

Bergamaschi, S., Beneventano, D., Mandreoli, F., Martoglia, R., Guerra, F., Orsini, M., & Magnotta, L. (2017). From data integration to big data integration. In *A Comprehensive Guide Through the Italian Database Research Over the Last 25 Years* (pp. 43–59). Springer International Publishing.

Bergold, J., & Thomas, S. (2012). Participatory research methods: A methodological approach in motion. Historical Social Research. *Historische Sozialforschung*, •••, 191–22.

Bhalotra, S., Chakravarty, A., & Gulesci, S. (2020). The price of gold: Dowry and death in India. *Journal of Development Economics*, *143*, 102413. DOI: 10.1016/j.jdeveco.2019.102413

Bhat, J. R., AlQahtani, S. A., & Nekovee, M. (2023). FinTech enablers, use cases, and role of future internet of things. *Journal of King Saud University. Computer and Information Sciences*, *35*(1), 87–101. DOI: 10.1016/j.jksuci.2022.08.033

Bhattacharya, C., & Sinha, M. (2022). The role of artificial intelligence in banking for leveraging customer experience. *Australasian Accounting. Business and Finance Journal*, *16*(5), 89–105. DOI: 10.14453/aabfj.v16i5.07

Bhushan, M., Sinha, A., Kumari, S., & Debbarma, D. (2020). Gender Divide in Provision of Extension Services in Agriculture. *International Journal of Current Microbiology and Applied Sciences*, *9*(4), 1332–1339. DOI: 10.20546/ijcmas.2020.904.158

Bhuyan, U., Khan, S. A., & Saleem, M. (2024). Gaining Perspective on Money Attitude and Financial Planning of Educators in Northeast India: Implications for Sustainable Finance. In Yıldırım, S., Yıldırım, D., Demirtaş, I., & Kandpal, V. (Eds.), *Green Transition Impacts on the Economy, Society, and Environment* (pp. 244–262). IGI Global., DOI: 10.4018/979-8-3693-3985-5.ch014

Binetti, M. S., Campanale, C., Massarelli, C., & Uricchio, V. F. (2022). The use of weather radar data: Possibilities, challenges and advanced applications. *Earth (Basel, Switzerland)*, *3*(1), 157–171. DOI: 10.3390/earth3010012

Bird, R. M., & Zolt, E. M. (2008). Technology and taxation in developing countries: From hand to mouse. *National Tax Journal*, *61*(4), 791–821. DOI: 10.17310/ntj.2008.4S.02

Bisht, A. K., & Sreenivasulu, N. S. (2024). Information Privacy Rights in India: A Study of the Digital Personal Data Protection Act, 2023. In *Data Privacy-Techniques, Applications, and Standards*. IntechOpen.

Bleier, A., Goldfarb, A., & Tucker, C. (2020). Consumer privacy and the future of data-based innovation and marketing. *International Journal of Research in Marketing*, *37*(3), 466–480. DOI: 10.1016/j.ijresmar.2020.03.006

Bloch, E. (1986). *The principle of hope* (Plaice, N., Plaice, S., & Knight, P., Trans.). MIT Press. (Original work published 1954)

Bloom, N., Van Reenen, J., & Williams, H. (2019). A toolkit of policies to promote innovation. *The Journal of Economic Perspectives*, *33*(3), 163–184. DOI: 10.1257/jep.33.3.163

Bolter, J. D., & Grusin, R. (1999). *Remediation: Understanding new media*. MIT Press.

Borah, P., Kv, R., Y, P., Prasanthi, M., & Duttagupta, A. (2024). A Study of the Factors that Influence the Success of Digital Marketing in a Dynamic Marketing Landscape. *Educational Administration: Theory and Practice*, 3956–3964. https://doi.org/DOI: 10.53555/kuey.v30i5.3554

Bose, S., & Mukherjee, A. (2023). Evolutionary algorithms for real-time product pricing optimization. *Computational Economics*, *61*(4), 995–1012.

Boustani, N. M. (2020). Traditional banks and fintech: survival, future and threats. *ICT for an Inclusive World: Industry 4.0–Towards the Smart Enterprise*, 345-359. DOI: 10.1007/978-3-030-34269-2_24

Boute, R. N., Gijsbrechts, J., & Van Mieghem, J. A. (2022). Digital lean operations: Smart automation and artificial intelligence in financial services. *Innovative Technology at the Interface of Finance and Operations*, *I*, 175–188. DOI: 10.1007/978-3-030-75729-8_6

Brennan, S., Coulthart, S., & Nussbaum, B. (2023). The brave new world of third party location data. *Journal of Strategic Security*, *16*(2), 81–95. DOI: 10.5038/1944-0472.16.2.2070

Bresciani, S., Huarng, K. H., Malhotra, A., & Ferraris, A. (2021). Digital transformation as a springboard for product, process and business model innovation. *Journal of Business Research*, *128*, 204–210. DOI: 10.1016/j.jbusres.2021.02.003

Brji, V. K. T. (2025). The Monetization Playbook: Digital Transformation Success in the Digital Economy. *Journal of Computer Science and Technology Studies*, 116–124. https://doi.org/DOI: 10.32996/jcsts

Broby, D. (2021). Financial technology and the future of banking. *Financial Innovation*, *7*(1), 47. DOI: 10.1186/s40854-021-00264-y

Broby, D. (2022). The use of predictive analytics in finance. *The Journal of Financial Data Science*, *8*, 145–161. DOI: 10.1016/j.jfds.2022.05.003

Brunetti, F., Matt, D. T., Bonfanti, A., De Longhi, A., Pedrini, G., & Orzes, G. (2020). Digital transformation challenges: Strategies emerging from a multi-stakeholder approach. *The TQM Journal*, *32*(4), 697–724. DOI: 10.1108/TQM-12-2019-0309

Bryman, A. (2016). *Social research methods* (5th ed.). Oxford University Press.

Brynjolfsson, E., & McElheran, K. (2021). Data-driven decision making and firm performance: Evidence from microdata. *Management Science*, *67*(4), 2017–2039. DOI: 10.1287/mnsc.2020.3742

Bueno, L. A., Sigahi, T. F., Rampasso, I. S., Leal Filho, W., & Anholon, R. (2024). Impacts of digitization on operational efficiency in the banking sector: Thematic analysis and research agenda proposal. *International Journal of Information Management Data Insights*, *4*(1), 100230. DOI: 10.1016/j.jjimei.2024.100230

Buijs, J. C. A. M., Bergmans, R. F. M., & el Hasnaoui, R. (2019). Customer journey analysis at a financial services provider using self service and data hub concepts. *BPM (Industry Forum)*, 25–36.

Bulani, P. R., & Jain, S. (2025). AI-driven predictive models for asset monetization. *International Journal of Research in All Subjects in Multi Languages*, *13*(1), 131–152.

Burmester, M., Mast, M., Tille, R., & Weber, W. (2010). How users perceive and use interactive information graphics: An exploratory study. *2010 14th International Conference Information Visualisation*, 361–368. DOI: 10.1109/IV.2010.57

Büyüksağnak, M. (2021). The effect of Spotify playlists on the music consumption habits of music consumers.

Cacho, S. F. (2024). *The impact of data monetization in business models: A study on the Portuguese banking industry* (Master's thesis, Universidade Católica Portuguesa, Portugal). Repositório Institucional UCP.

Cahyono, D., Sijabat, A., Panjaitan, M. B., Julianingsih, D., & Lorenzo, A. (2025). Challenges and opportunities in implementing big data for small and medium enterprises (SMEs). *Journal of Computer Science and Technology Application*, *2*(1), 75–83.

Campino, J., Brochado, A., & Rosa, Á. (2021). Digital business transformation in the banking sector. In *Research Anthology on Concepts, Applications, and Challenges of FinTech* (pp. 186-215). IGI Global. DOI: 10.4018/978-1-7998-8546-7.ch012

Camus, A. (1991). *The myth of Sisyphus* (O'Brien, J., Trans.). Vintage International. (Original work published 1942)

Canali, S. (2020). Towards a contextual approach to data quality. *Data*, *5*(4), 90. DOI: 10.3390/data5040090

Carli, L. L. (2020). Women, Gender equality and COVID-19. *Gender in Management*, *35*(7/8), 647–655. DOI: 10.1108/GM-07-2020-0236

Carvalho, A., & Young, P. (2020). What the History of Linux Says About the Future of Cryptocurrencies. *Communications of the Association for Information Systems*, *46*(January), 18–29. DOI: 10.17705/1CAIS.04602

Castanias, R. P., & Helfat, C. E. (1991). Managerial resources and rents. *Journal of Management*, *17*(1), 155–171. DOI: 10.1177/014920639101700110

Castellani, D., & Fassio, C. (2019). From new imported inputs to new exported products. Firm-level evidence from Sweden. *Research Policy*, *48*(1), 322–338. DOI: 10.1016/j.respol.2018.08.021

Catalini, C., & Gans, J. S. (2020). *Some Simple Economics of the Blockchain*. ACM Digital Library., DOI: 10.1145/3359552

Cavusgil, S. T., & Zou, S. (1994). Marketing strategy–performance relationship: An investigation of the empirical link in export market ventures. *Journal of Marketing*, *58*(1), 1–21. DOI: 10.1177/002224299405800101

Central Board of Direct Taxes (CBDT). (2022). *Annual report 2021-22*. Ministry of Finance, Government of India.

Chaffey, D., & Ellis-Chadwick, F. (2019). *Digital marketing: strategy and implementation*. Pearson Education.

Chaffey, D., & Smith, P. R. (2022). *Digital marketing excellence: Planning, optimizing and integrating online marketing*. Routledge. DOI: 10.4324/9781003009498

Chaimaa, B., Najib, E., & Rachid, H. (2021). E-banking overview: Concepts, challenges and solutions. *Wireless Personal Communications*, *117*(2), 1059–1078. DOI: 10.1007/s11277-020-07911-0

Chakravaram, V., Ratnakaram, S., Vihari, N. S., & Tatikonda, N. (2021). The role of technologies on banking and insurance sectors in the digitalization and globalization era a select study. In Proceedings of the International Conference on Recent Trends in Machine Learning, IoT, Smart Cities and Applications (pp. 145–156). Springer. DOI: 10.1007/978-981-15-7234-0_12

Chan, R., Troshani, I., Rao Hill, S., & Hoffmann, A. (2022). Towards an understanding of consumers' FinTech adoption: The case of Open Banking. *International Journal of Bank Marketing*, *40*(4), 886–917. DOI: 10.1108/IJBM-08-2021-0397

Chatterjee, P., & Roy, A. (2021). Neural networks for predicting consumer purchase tendencies in e-commerce. *Journal of Retail Technology*, *7*(2), 110–128.

Chaudhry, S., Bedi, A., Viswanathan, A., & Pillai, S. (2021). *Women and Work how india fared in 2021*. IWWAGE. Retrieved from chrome-extension://efaidnbmnnnibpcajpcglclefindmkaj/https://iwwage.org/wp-conten t/uploads/2022/01/Women-and-Work-How-India-Fared-in-2021.pdf

Chaudhuri, S., Ghosh, A., & Dutta, P. (2021). Deep learning for predicting consumer behavior in retail. *International Journal of Retail & Distribution Management*, *49*(8), 921–938.

Chauhan, S., Akhtar, A., & Gupta, A. (2022). Customer experience in digital banking: A review and future research directions. *International Journal of Quality and Service Sciences*, *14*(2), 311–348. DOI: 10.1108/IJQSS-02-2021-0027

Chen, Y. (2020). Decentralized Finance: Blockchain Technology and the Quest for an Open Financial System. *Stevens Institute of Technology School of Business Research Paper*, 1–27.

Chen, M., & Golan, A. (2015). What may visualization processes optimize? *IEEE Transactions on Visualization and Computer Graphics*, *22*(12), 2619–2632. DOI: 10.1109/TVCG.2015.2513410 PMID: 26731770

Chen, M., Mao, S., Zhang, Y., & Leung, V. C. (2014). *Big data: related technologies, challenges and future prospects* (Vol. 100). Springer. DOI: 10.1007/978-3-319-06245-7

Chen, S., Li, J., Andrienko, G., Andrienko, N., Wang, Y., Nguyen, P. H., & Turkay, C. (2018). Supporting story synthesis: Bridging the gap between visual analytics and storytelling. *IEEE Transactions on Visualization and Computer Graphics*, *26*(7), 2499–2516. DOI: 10.1109/TVCG.2018.2889054 PMID: 30582542

Chen, Y., & Wang, Z. (2023). Hybrid recommendation models for FMCG: Collaborative filtering with deep learning. *Expert Systems with Applications*, *217*, 119504.

Cherubini, F., & Nielsen, R. K. (2016). Editorial analytics: How news media are developing and using audience data and metrics. *Available at SSRN* 2739328. DOI: 10.2139/ssrn.2739328

Chesters, J. (2022). Understanding the Persistence of Occupational Sex Segregation in German Labour Markets: How Gender Attitudes Shape Young Women's Occupational Aspirations. *Journal of Applied Youth Studies*, *5*(1), 55–73. DOI: 10.1007/s43151-021-00065-1

Chiesa, V., & Manzini, R. (1997). Competence levels within firms: a static and dynamic analysis. In Heene, A., & Sanchez, R. (Eds.), *Competence-based strategic management* (pp. 195–214). Wiley.

China Briefing. (2025). China-India economic ties: Trade, investment, and opportunities. China Briefing. https://www.china-briefing.com/news/china-india-economic-ties-trade-investment-and-opportunities/

Chinesta Llobregat, S. (2024). Design of a Data Analysis Platform as a Multitenant Service in the Cloud: An Approach towards Scalability and Adaptability.

Chong, F. H. L. (2021). Enhancing trust through digital Islamic finance and blockchain technology. *Qualitative Research in Financial Markets, 13*(3), 328–341. DOI: 10.1108/QRFM-05-2020-0076

Choudhary, P., Ghosh, C., & Thenmozhi, M. (2025). *Impact of fintech and financial inclusion on sustainable development goals: Evidence from cross country analysis. Finance Research Letters, 72, 106573 Chuen, D. L. K. (2015). Handbook of digital currency: Bitcoin, innovation, financial instruments, and big data.* Elsevier.

Chowdhury, R. H. (2020). Accounting for Data: A Framework for Valuing and Reporting Digital Intangible Assets. *Journal of Frontiers in Multidisciplinary Research, 1*(1), 16–23. DOI: 10.54660/.IJFMR.2020.1.1.16-23

Christensen, C. M., Dillon, K., & Hall, T. (2016), Competing against luck: the story of innovation and customer choice, Kindle, Computerra (2025). AI to Save 10.8 Trillion Annually by 2030 Without Eliminating Any Jobs. https://www.computerra.ru/314947/ii-k-2030-godu-sekonomit-do-10-8-trln-v-god-i-ne-zamenit-ni-odnoj-professii/

Çınar, N., & Ateş, S. (2022). Data privacy in digital advertising: Towards a post-third-party cookie era. In *Privacy* (pp. 55–77). Routledge. DOI: 10.4324/9781003173335-3

Çınar, O., Bektaş, Ç., & Aslan, I. (2011). A motivation study on the effectiveness of intrinsic and extrinsic factors. *Economics and Management, 16*, 690–695.

Constantino, T. (2025). Amazon's AI just got smarter, more predictive, and more personal *Forbes*. Retrieved April 29, 2025, from https://www.forbes.com/sites/torconstantino/2025/03/31/amazons-ai-just-got-smarter-more-predictive-and-more-personal/

Cornelli, G., Frost, J., Gambacorta, L., Rau, P. R., Wardrop, R., & Ziegler, T. (2023). Fintech and big tech credit: Drivers of the growth of digital lending. *Journal of Banking & Finance, 148*, 106742. DOI: 10.1016/j.jbankfin.2022.106742

Corrado, C., Haskel, J., Iommi, M., & Jona Lasinio, C. S. (2022). Measuring data as an asset: Framework, methods and preliminary estimates. *OECD Economics Department Working Papers, 1731.*

Creswell, J. W. (2014). *Research design: Qualitative, quantitative, and mixed methods approach* (4th ed.). SAGE Publications.

Cui, A. S., & Wu, F. (2016). Utilizing customer knowledge in innovation: Antecedents and impact of customer involvement on new product performance. *Journal of the Academy of Marketing Science, 44*(4), 516–538. DOI: 10.1007/s11747-015-0433-x

CyberLeninka. (2023). *Some problems of data ethics and social media ethics* Retrieved April 29, 2025, from https://cyberleninka.ru/article Limn/nekotorye-problemy-etiki-dannyh-i-etiki-sotsialnyh-setey/viewer

Dabrowski, M. (2013). Business Intelligence In Call Centers. *International Journal of Issue Computer and Information Technology (ISSN: 2279–0764) Volume, 2*(2).

Dağaşaner, S., & Karaatmaca, A. G. (2025). The Role of Online Banking Service Clues in Enhancing Individual and Corporate Customers' Satisfaction: The Mediating Role of Customer Experience as a Corporate Social Responsibility. *Sustainability (Basel), 17*(8), 3457. DOI: 10.3390/su17083457

DAMA International. (2017). *DAMA-DMBOK: Data management body of knowledge* (590 p.). Retrieved April 29, 2025, from https://www.dama.org/cpages/body -of-knowledge

Dandanayakula, S., & Chandana, P. (2024). Blockchain Technology and Cryptocurrencies : A Review Paper. *International Journal of Scientific Research in Engineering and Management, 8–12*(12), 1–7. Advance online publication. DOI: 10.55041/IJSREM40122

Dani, V. S., Freitas, C. M. D. S., & Thom, L. H. (2019). Ten years of visualization of business process models: A systematic literature review. *Computer Standards & Interfaces, 66*, 103347. DOI: 10.1016/j.csi.2019.04.006

Das, K., & Ghosh, S. (2021). Social media sentiment as a predictor of FMCG product sales. *Journal of Business Analytics, 4*(4), 223–238.

DataReportal. (2024). The time we spend on social media. https://datareportal.com/reports/digital-2024-deep-dive-the-time-we-spend-on-social-media

Davenport, T. H., & Harris, J. G. (2022). *Competing on analytics: The new science of winning* (Updated ed.). Harvard Business Review Press.

Davenport, T. H., & Harris, J. G. (2007). Competing on analytics: The new science of Winning. *Harvard business review press. Language, 15*(217), 24.

Davenport, T. H., & Ronanki, R. (2018). Artificial intelligence for the real world. *Harvard Business Review, 96*(1), 108–116.

Davenport, T. H., & Ronanki, R. (2021). Building collaborative analytics capabilities: The role of incentives and governance. *Harvard Business Review, 99*(5), 88–97.

de la Feria, R., & Grau Ruiz, M. A. (2021, May). The robotisation of tax administration. In *International Conference on Inclusive Robotics for a better Society* (pp. 115-123). Cham: Springer International Publishing.

De, I., Singh, S., & Panda, S. S. (2021). Gender and Agriculture: Cases of Woman Participation in Rural Odisha. In *Social Norms, Gender and Collective Behaviour* (pp. 67–104). Springer Singapore. DOI: 10.1007/978-981-16-6952-1_4

Deloitte India. (2024). *Income tax digitalisation survey 2.0: Taxpayer perspectives on digital transformation*. Deloitte Touche Tohmatsu India LLP.

Deming, S. M. (2022). Beyond measurement of the motherhood penalty: How social locations shape mothers' work decisions and stratify outcomes. *Sociology Compass, 16*(6), e12988. Advance online publication. DOI: 10.1111/soc4.12988

Demirgüç-Kunt, A., Pedraza, A., & Ruiz-Ortega, C. (2021). Banking sector performance during the COVID-19 crisis. *Journal of Banking & Finance, 133*, 106305. DOI: 10.1016/j.jbankfin.2021.106305 PMID: 34548747

Deolekar, O., & Tiwari, V. (2024) 'Inverted duty structure in India: origin, impact and solutions', ECGC Research. https://main.ecgc.in/wp-content/themes/pcwebecgc/images/pcECGPagePDF/ResearchArticle/ECGC_Research_Inverted_Duty_Structure_Report.pdf

Deshpande, A. (2025). *Too good to be true? Steadily rising female labour force participation rates in India.* Ashoka University. Centre for Economic Data and Analysis (CEDA). Retrieved from https://ceda.ashoka.edu.in/too-good-to-be-true-steadily-rising-female-labour-force-par ticipation-rates-in-india/

Deshpande, A., & Kabeer, N. (2024). Norms that matter: Exploring the distribution of women's work between income generation, expenditure-saving and unpaid domestic responsibilities in India. *World Development, 174*, 106435. DOI: 10.1016/j.worlddev.2023.106435

Dettmer, H. W. (2007). *Goldratt's theory of constraints: A systems approach to continuous improvement.* ASQ Quality Press. https://archive.org/details/goldrattstheoryo0000dett

Devine, F. (1994). Segregation and Supply: Preferences and Plans among 'Self-Made' Women. *Gender, Work and Organization, 1*(2), 94–109. DOI: 10.1111/j.1468-0432.1994.tb00009.x

Dhamija, A., Manrai, R., & Dhamija, D. (2025). Impact of Financial Service Quality on Customer Loyalty and Satisfaction Among Indian Consumers Utilizing Digital Payments. In *Insights Into Digital Business, Human Resource Management, and Competitiveness* (pp. 251-276). IGI Global Scientific Publishing. DOI: 10.4018/979-8-3693-9440-3.ch011

Dhiman, R., & Sharma, M. (2019). Relation between labour productivity and export competitiveness of Indian textile industry: Co-integration and causality approach. *Vision (Basel), 23*(1), 22–30. DOI: 10.1177/0972262918821230

Diener, F., & Špaček, M. (2021). Digital transformation in banking: A managerial perspective on barriers to change. *Sustainability (Basel), 13*(4), 2032. DOI: 10.3390/su13042032

Digiday. (2023). How Walmart is evolving its data analytics platform to reflect an AI-driven focus Retrieved April 29, 2025, from https://digiday.com/marketing/how-walmart-is-evolving-its-data-analytics-platform-to-reflect-an-ai-driven-focus/

Diorio, S. G., & Hummel, C. K. (2022). *Revenue Operations: A New Way to Align Sales & Marketing, Monetize Data, and Ignite Growth.* John Wiley & Sons.

Doran, G. T. (1981). There's a S.M.A.R.T. way to write management's goals and objectives. *Management Review, 70*(11), 35–36.

Dosi, G., & Teece, D. J. (1993). *Organizational competences and the boundaries of the firm. Market and organization: the competitive firm and its environment.* Latapses, Nice, France and Iside.

Douglas, E., & Pratley, N. (2015, October 11). The rise of fintech: Disrupting the financial industry. The Guardian.

Dowling, M. (2022). Is non-fungible token pricing driven by cryptocurrencies ? *Finance Research Letters, 44*(April 2021), 102097. DOI: 10.1016/j.frl.2021.102097

Dranev, Y. Y., Kuchin, I. I., & Miryakov, M. I. (2025). *Economic effects of artificial intelligence adoption in Russia.* Moscow: ISSEK, National Research University Higher School of Economics. Retrieved from https://issek.hse.ru/news/1022068478.html

Duchini, E., Simion, S., Turrell, A., & Blundell, J. (2020). Pay Transparency and Gender Equality. *American Economic Journal. Economic Policy.* Advance online publication. DOI: 10.1257/pol.20220766

Dutta, S., Pramanik, H. S., Datta, S., & Kirtania, M. (2022). Imperatives, Trends and Dynamics of Digital Transformation as Banks Adopt Technology and Intelligent Systems. In *Intelligent Systems in Digital Transformation: Theory and Applications* (pp. 323–348). Springer International Publishing., DOI: 10.1007/978-3-031-16598-6_14

Dyché, J., & Levy, E. (2006). *Customer data integration: Reaching a Single Version of the Truth.* John Wiley & Sons.

Ebrahimi, A., Askarifar, K., & Nikbakht, A. (2023). Designing and evaluating insurance customer loyalty programs for different customer groups based on their lifetime value. *Journal of Financial Services Marketing*, *29*(3), 808–825. DOI: 10.1057/s41264-023-00242-8

Economic Times. (2025). China lifts curbs on fertilizers, rare earths & tunnel boring machines to India. https://economictimes.indiatimes.com/news/economy/foreign-trade/china-lifts-curbs-on-fertilizers-rare-earths-tunnel-boring-machines-to-india/articleshow/123377378.cms?from=mdr

Edmondson, A. C., & Mortensen, M. (2023). The generative edge: How psychological safety fuels data-driven innovation. *Harvard Business Review*, *101*(1), 104–113.

Education, M. o. (2021-22). *All India Survey on higher Education.* Retrieved from chrome-extension://efaidnbmnnnibpcajpcglclefindmkaj/https://cdnbbsr.s3waas.gov.in/ s392049debbe566ca5782a3045cf300a3c/uploads/2024/02/20240719952688509.pdf

Elbahrawy, A., Alessandretti, L., Kandler, A., Pastor-satorras, R., & Baronchelli, A. (2017). *Evolutionary dynamics of the cryptocurrency market.* 1–16.

Ellili, N. O. D. (2023). Is there any association between FinTech and sustainability? Evidence from bibliometric review and content analysis. *Journal of Financial Services Marketing*, *28*(4), 748–762. DOI: 10.1057/s41264-022-00200-w

Elsaid, H. M. (2023). A review of literature directions regarding the impact of fintech firms on the banking industry. *Qualitative Research in Financial Markets*, *15*(5), 693–711. DOI: 10.1108/QRFM-10-2020-0197

Elvy, S. A. (2018). Commodifying consumer data in the era of the internet of things. *BCL Rev.*, *59*, 423.

Endert, A., Hossain, M. S., Ramakrishnan, N., North, C., Fiaux, P., & Andrews, C. (2014). The human is the loop: New directions for visual analytics. *Journal of Intelligent Information Systems*, *43*(3), 411–435. DOI: 10.1007/s10844-014-0304-9

England, P., Bearak, J., Budig, M. J., & Hodges, M. J. (2016). Do Highly Paid, Highly Skilled Women Experience the Largest Motherhood Penalty? *American Sociological Review*, *81*(6), 1161–1189. DOI: 10.1177/0003122416673598

Evans, S. (2009). In a Different Place: Working-class Girls and Higher Education. *Sociology*, *43*(2), 340–355. DOI: 10.1177/0038038508101169

Fahey, L. (2019). Getting to insight: The value and use of small data. *Strategy and Leadership*, *47*(3), 27–33. DOI: 10.1108/SL-03-2019-0034

Famoti, O., Omowole, B. M., Okiomah, E., Muyiwa-Ajayi, T. P., Ezechi, O. N., Ewim, C. P. M., & Omokhoa, H. E. (2024). Enhancing Customer Satisfaction in Financial Services Through Advanced BI Techniques. *International Journal of Multidisciplinary Research and Growth Evaluation, 5*(06), 1558–1566. DOI: 10.54660/.IJMRGE.2024.5.6.1258-1266

Faroukhi, A. Z., Alaoui, I. E., Gahi, Y., & Amine, A. (2020). Big data monetization throughout big data value chain: A comprehensive review. *Journal of Big Data, 7*(1), 1–22. DOI: 10.1186/s40537-019-0281-5

Federal Law No. 273-FZ (2012). "On Education in the Russian Federation" Available from: https://www.consultant.ru/document/cons_doc_LAW_140174/?ysclid=m1nljoyjz5167522908

Fernandez, R., Lopez, J., & Martin, S. (2022). Voice assistant interactions for consumer insights: A deep learning approach. *Journal of Interactive Marketing, 58*(3), 44–59.

Figl, K. (2017). Comprehension of procedural visual business process models. *Business & Information Systems Engineering, 59*(1), 41–67. DOI: 10.1007/s12599-016-0460-2

Findikoglu, M., & Watson-Manheim, M. B. (2016). Linking macro-level goals to micro-level routines: EHR-enabled transformation of primary care services. *Journal of Information Technology, 31*(4), 382–400. DOI: 10.1057/s41265-016-0023-5

Fischer, M., & Weber, H. (2022). Ensemble learning for fraud detection in FMCG e-commerce. *Decision Support Systems, 153*, 113678.

Fisher, M. (2009). *Capitalist realism: Is there no alternative? Zero Books. Fromm, E. (1955). The sane society*. Holt, Rinehart and Winston.

Flores, M. D. (2024). *Learning-Based Home Estimation: An Automated Data Pipeline Approach* (Master's thesis, San Diego State University).

Flyverbom, M., Deibert, R., & Matten, D. (2019). The governance of digital technology, big data, and the internet: New roles and responsibilities for business. *Business & Society, 58*(1), 3–19. DOI: 10.1177/0007650317727540

Foltean, F. S., & van Bruggen, G. H. (2022). Digital Technologies, marketing agility, and Marketing Management Support Systems: How to remain competitive in changing markets. In *Organizational Innovation in the Digital Age* (pp. 1–38). Springer International Publishing. DOI: 10.1007/978-3-030-98183-9_1

Fortin, N. M. (2008). The Gender Wage Gap among Young Adults in the United States: The Importance of Money versus People. *The Journal of Human Resources, 43*(4), 884–918. DOI: 10.3368/jhr.43.4.884

Freiling, J., Gersch, M., & Goeke, C. (2008). On the Path towards a Competence-based Theory of the Firm. *Organization Studies, 29*(8-9), 1143–1164. DOI: 10.1177/0170840608094774

Freixa Font, P., Pérez-Montoro Gutiérrez, M., & Codina, L. (2021). The binomial of interaction and visualization in digital news media: Consolidation, standardization and future challenges. *El Profesional de la Información, 30*(4), E300401. DOI: 10.3145/epi.2021.jul.01

Frey, C. B., & Osborne, M. A. (2023). Generative AI and the future of work: A re-appraisal. *The Journal of Economic Perspectives, 37*(4), 179–202. DOI: 10.1257/jep.37.4.179

Ganti, V., & Sarma, A. D. (2013). *Data cleaning: A practical perspective*. Morgan & Claypool Publishers. DOI: 10.1007/978-3-031-01897-8

Gao, J. (2024). The Impact of Digital Currency Policies on International Trade and Investment. *The 3rd International Conference on Financial Technology and Business Analysis, 0*, 29–35. DOI: 10.54254/2754-1169/89/20241905

Garcia, L., & Lopez, P. (2020). Demographic segmentation of FMCG consumers using unsupervised learning. *Journal of Consumer Marketing, 37*(6), 745–756.

Garg, P., Gupta, B., Chauhan, A. K., Sivarajah, U., Gupta, S., & Modgil, S. (2020). Measuring the perceived benefits of implementing blockchain technology in the banking sector. *Technological Forecasting and Social Change, 163*, 120407. DOI: 10.1016/j.techfore.2020.120407

Garrett, H., & Woodworth, R. (1969) ' Statistics and Education', Bombay: Valkis, Feffer and Simons. Pp- 329.

Gartner. (2023). *Market guide for analytics and business intelligence platforms* Retrieved April 29, 2025, from https://www.gartner.com/reviews/market/analytics-business-intelligence-platforms

Geebren, A., & Jabbar, A. (2021). Factors that influence customer trust and satisfaction in mobile banking: A problematization approach. [IJEBR]. *International Journal of E-Business Research, 17*(3), 66–82. DOI: 10.4018/IJEBR.2021070105

George, A. S. (2025). Leveraging the New Oil: An Analysis of Emergent Data Monetization Models and their Impact on Corporate Innovation. *Partners Universal Innovative Research Publication*, *3*(2), 37–52.

George, A. S. (2025). Leveraging the new oil: An analysis of emergent data monetization models and their impact on corporate innovation. *PUIRP Journal of Business and Management*, *3*(2), 37–52.

Ghooshchi, N. G., van Beest, N., Governatori, G., Olivieri, F., & Sattar, A. (2017). Visualisation of compliant declarative business processes. *2017 IEEE 21st International Enterprise Distributed Object Computing Conference (EDOC)*, 89–94. DOI: 10.1109/EDOC.2017.21

Gibbs, M., Neckermann, S., & Siemroth, C. (2023). Goals and performance metrics in the digital age: Evidence from software development teams. *Organization Science*, *34*(5), 1989–2009. DOI: 10.1287/orsc.2022.1634

Gindelsky, M., Moulton, J., & Wentland, S. A. (2019). Valuing housing services in the era of big data: A user cost approach leveraging Zillow microdata. In *Big Data for 21st Century Economic Statistics*. University of Chicago Press.

Gizelis, C. A., Panagiotidou, M., Petrova, S., Fuchs, D., Hofer, M., Plociennik, M., . . . Cauche, E. (2024, June). Data monetization opportunities and challenges: the European landscape by Datamite. In *IFIP International Conference on Artificial Intelligence Applications and Innovations* (pp. 62-79). Cham: Springer Nature Switzerland. DOI: 10.1007/978-3-031-63227-3_5

Glass, R., & Callahan, S. (2014). *The Big Data-driven business: How to use big data to win customers, beat competitors, and boost profits*. John Wiley & Sons.

Global Trade Research Initiative. (2023) 'India-China trade: Low exports and not high imports is the real challenge for India'. https://gtri.co.in/gtriRep3.pdf

Global Trade Research Initiative. (2024) 'An Examination of India's growing Industrial sector imports from China'. www.GTRI.co.in

Goldratt, E. M. (1984). *The goal: A process of ongoing improvement*. North River Press.

Goldstaub, T. (2018). How HSBC is building its biggest data lake, breaking down silos and preparing for the AI revolution *Forbes*. Retrieved October 10, 2023, from https://www.forbes.com/sites/tabithagoldstaub/2018/12/19/how-hsbc-is-building-its-biggest-data-lake-breaking-down-silos-and-preparing-for-the-ai-revolution/?sh=32cd9db21992

Golmgrein, I. (2023). A Comprehensive Overview of Monetization Strategies in Creative Industries A Comprehensive Overview of Monetization Strategies in Creative Industries. [IJLEMR]. *International Journal of Latest Engineering and Management Research, 8*(December). Advance online publication. DOI: 10.56581/IJLEMR.8.4.90-100

Gomber, P., Koch, J.-A., & Siering, M. (2022). Digital finance and disruption: Global trends and challenges. *Journal of Financial Markets and Services, 6*(4), 45–61.

Gonçalves, L., Patrício, L., Grenha Teixeira, J., & Wuenderlich, N. V. (2020). Understanding the customer experience with smart services. *Journal of Service Management, 31*(4), 723–744. DOI: 10.1108/JOSM-11-2019-0349

Gopalakrishnan, C., Vinoth, S., Madbouly, A., Radhakrishnan, P., & Ali, N. H. (2024). Impact of fintech on sustainable financial inclusion: The case of India. In Proceedings of the 3rd International Conference on Optimization Techniques in the Field of Engineering (ICOFE 2024). *SSRN*. https://ssrn.com/abstract=5066763

Government of India. (2016) 'National Capital Goods Policy: Building India of Tomorrow'. https://www.cgsc.in/pdf/Capital%20Goods%20Policy%2020 16.pdf

Government of India. (2023) 'Trade deficit between India and China'. Accessed on 27 September, 2024. https://sansad.in/getFile/annex/262/AU690. pdf?source=pqars

Grabovets, K., & Temelkov, Z. (2024). Interplay between digital-only strategy and financial performance: A case of neobanks. In *New Strategy Models in Digital Entrepreneurship* (pp. 214–235). IGI Global., DOI: 10.4018/979-8-3693-3743-1.ch011

Grasic, A., & Vidnjevic, M. (2024). Evolution of cryptocurrencies and their utilization in the digital economy. *MEST Journal, 12*(July), 36–42. Advance online publication. DOI: 10.12709/mest.12.12.02.05

Grassi, L., Figini, N., & Fedeli, L. (2022). How does a data strategy enable customer value? The case of FinTechs and traditional banks under the open finance framework. *Financial Innovation, 8*(1), 75. DOI: 10.1186/s40854-022-00378-x PMID: 36158456

Grewal, D., & Levy, M. (2022). *Marketing* (8th ed.). McGraw Hill.

Groom, N. (2019). The emotional architecture of wrestling fandom: Ritual, performance, and catharsis. *Journal of Popular Culture, 52*(4), 812–829. DOI: 10.1111/jpcu.12833

Grösch, M., & Steul-Fischer, M. (2017). Defaults and advice in self-customization procedures of insurance. *ZVersWiss, 106*(3-4), 325–341. DOI: 10.1007/s12297-017-0390-1

Gulati, K., Saha, K., & Lybbert, T. J. (2025). Women's work and agricultural productivity gaps in India. *American Journal of Agricultural Economics*, *107*(5), 1261–1289. Advance online publication. DOI: 10.1111/ajae.12536

Gulati, S., Singh, G., & Kumar, A. (2023). Interceding of Repurchase Intention between E-loyalty and Word of Mouth Advocacy: A Study of Behavioural Consequences and Antecedents of E-Loyalty. *International Journal of Electronic Business*, *18*(3), 299–319. DOI: 10.1504/IJEB.2023.132190

Günesen, E., Aydin, H., & Kaya, O. (2021). Predicting customer churn in FMCG with machine learning models. *Computers in Industry*, *128*, 103432.

Gupta, S. (2024). 'Why Don't Brilliant Women Return to Work After Motherhood?': Startup Finding Jobs for New Moms. *The Better India*. Retrieved from https://thebetterindia.com/349558/chennai-sankari-sudhar-job-portal-for-new-mothers-women-with-career-break-overqualified-housewives/#:~:text=Statistically%20speaki ng%2C%2073%20percent%20of,job%20opportunities%20through%20her%20platfor m.

Gupta, I., Singh, A. K., Lee, C. N., & Buyya, R. (2022). Secure data storage and sharing techniques for data protection in cloud environments: A systematic review, analysis, and future directions. *IEEE Access : Practical Innovations, Open Solutions*, *10*, 71247–71277. DOI: 10.1109/ACCESS.2022.3188110

Guszcza, J., Lewis, J., & Evans-Greenwood, P. (2022). Designing data-informed organizations: Incentives and collaboration in analytics teams. *MIT Sloan Management Review*, *63*(2), 45–52.

Ha, D., Le, P., & Nguyen, D. K. (2025). Financial inclusion and fintech: A state-of-the-art systematic literature review. *Financial Innovation*, *11*(1), 69. DOI: 10.1186/s40854-024-00741-0

Hailu, M. F. (2019). Examining the role of Girl Effect in contributing to positive education ideologies for girls in Ethiopia. *Gender and Education*, *31*(8), 986–999. DOI: 10.1080/09540253.2018.1440284

Haleem, A., Javaid, M., Qadri, M. A., Singh, R. P., & Suman, R. (2022). Artificial intelligence (AI) applications for marketing: A literature-based study. *International Journal of Intelligent Networks*, *3*, 119–132. DOI: 10.1016/j.ijin.2022.08.005

Hamzah, M., Sobey, A., & Koronios, A. (2010). Supporting decision making process with information visualisation: A theoretical framework. *2010 2nd IEEE International Conference on Information Management and Engineering*, 267–271. DOI: 10.1109/ICIME.2010.5477827

Handoyo, R. D., Ibrahim, K. H., Rahmawati, Y., Faadhillah, F., Ogawa, K., Kusumawardani, D., See, K. F., Kumaran, V. V., & Gulati, R. (2024). Determinants of exports performance: Evidence from Indonesian low-, medium-, and high-technology manufacturing industries. *PLoS One*, *19*(1), e0296431. DOI: 10.1371/journal.pone.0296431 PMID: 38165859

Hanl, A. (2018). *Some Insights into the Development of Cryptocurrencies* (Issue February). DOI: 10.13140/RG.2.2.33318.01601

Harvard Business Review. (2023). *How AI is changing financial services* Retrieved April 29, 2025, from https://hbr.org/

Hasan, M., Hoque, A., Abedin, M. Z., & Gasbarro, D. (2024). FinTech and sustainable development: A systematic thematic analysis using human-and machine-generated processing. *International Review of Financial Analysis*, *95*, 103473. https://www.theguardian.com/business/2015/oct/11/riseoffintechdisruptingfinancialindustry. DOI: 10.1016/j.irfa.2024.103473

Hassan, M. S., Islam, M. A., Abdullah, A. B. M., & Nasir, H. (2024). End-user perspectives on fintech services adoption in the Bangladesh insurance industry: The moderating role of trust. *Journal of Financial Services Marketing*, *29*(4), 1377–1395. DOI: 10.1057/s41264-024-00268-6

Hazar, A., & Babuşcu, Ş. (2023). Financial Technologies: Digital Payment Systems and Digital Banking. Today's Dynamics. *Journal of Research. Innovation and Technologies*, *2*(4), 162–178.

Headly, M. (2024) 'China Market Entry Strategy: How to Enter the Chinese Market', B2BInternational. Accessed on 27 September, 2024. https://www.b2binternational.com/publications/china-market-entry/

Henama, U. S., Acha-Anyi, P. N., & Sifolo, P. P. S. (2016). The low cost carrier bandwagon: Lessons for Skywise Airline. *African Journal of Hospitality, Tourism and Leisure*, *5*(2), 1–23.

He, W., Hung, J. L., & Liu, L. (2023). Impact of big data analytics on banking: A case study. *Journal of Enterprise Information Management*, *36*(2), 459–479. DOI: 10.1108/JEIM-05-2020-0176

Hill, M. (2020). "More than just wrestling": Mental health, motivation, and media heroes in fan discourse. *Journal of Fandom Studies*, *8*(1), 47–63. DOI: 10.1386/jfs_00020_1

Hina, M., Islam, N., & Dhir, A. (2024). Blockchain for sustainable consumption: An affordance and consumer value-based view. *Internet Research, 34*(7), 215–250. DOI: 10.1108/INTR-07-2023-0523

Hindustan Unilever Limited. (2025). *Diversity & Inclusion Report 2024*. HUL.

Hirsch, D. D. (2013). The glass house effect: Big Data, the new oil, and the power of analogy. *Me. L. Rev., 66*, 373.

Hofacker, C. F., de Ruyter, K., Lurie, N. H., Manchanda, P., & Donaldson, J. (2020). Artificial intelligence in business and marketing. *Journal of Business Research, 116*, 136–149.

Hofmann, P., Oesterle, S., & Rust, P. (2025). Dynamic incentive alignment for analytics teams: An adaptive system design. *Proceedings of the 58th Hawaii International Conference on System Sciences (HICSS)*, 1234–1243.

Holder, M. (2025). *Gender Pay Gap Statistics 2025: A Comprehensive Analysis.* Equal Pay Today. Retrieved from https://www.equalpaytoday.org/gender-pay-gap-statistics/#

Hollebeek, L. D. (2019). Developing business customer engagement through social media engagement-platforms: An integrative SD logic/RBV-informed model. *Industrial Marketing Management, 81*, 89–98. DOI: 10.1016/j.indmarman.2017.11.016

Homner, N., Bellin, P., Fielt, E., & Matzner, M. (2024). Data-driven business models. In *International encyclopedia of business management*. Elsevier.

Hooda, S. (2021). GENDER INEQUALITY IN INDIA: STATUS AND DETERMINANTS. *International Journal of Social Science and Economic Research, 6*(3), 1054–1070. DOI: 10.46609/IJSSER.2021.v06i03.020

Hoofnagle, C. J., Van Der Sloot, B., & Borgesius, F. Z. (2019). The European Union general data protection regulation: What it is and what it means. *Information & Communications Technology Law, 28*(1), 65–98. DOI: 10.1080/13600834.2019.1573501

Howell, S. T., Niessner, M., & Yermack, D. (2020). Initial Coin Offerings: Financing growth with cryptocurrency token sales. *Review of Financial Studies, 33*(9), 3925–3974. DOI: 10.1093/rfs/hhz131

Hoyer, W. D., Kroschke, M., Schmitt, B., Kraume, K., & Shankar, V. (2020). Transforming the customer experience through new technologies. *Journal of Interactive Marketing, 51*(1), 57–71. DOI: 10.1016/j.intmar.2020.04.001

Huang, M. H., & Rust, R. T. (2021). A strategic framework for artificial intelligence in marketing. *Journal of the Academy of Marketing Science*, *49*(1), 30–50. DOI: 10.1007/s11747-020-00749-9

Huang, Y., & Liu, X. (2023). Reinforcement learning for optimizing supply chain logistics in FMCG. *Computers & Industrial Engineering*, *176*, 108925.

Hummel, P., Braun, M., & Dabrock, P. (2021). Own data? Ethical reflections on data ownership. *Philosophy & Technology*, *34*(3), 545–572. DOI: 10.1007/s13347-020-00404-9

IDC. (2023). *DataSphere report* Retrieved April 29, 2025, from https://my.idc.com/getdoc.jsp?containerId=IDC_P38353

Iliashenko, V., Filippova, K., Overes, E., & Iliashenko, O. (2019). The modelling of intelligent transport system architecture based on Big Data technologies. *Proceedings of the 33rd International Business Information Management Association Conference, IBIMA 2019: Education Excellence and Innovation Management through. Vision (Basel)*, *2020*, 8553–8561.

Ilin, I., Klimin, A., Overes, E., & Sataev, P. (2019). The essence and features of the introduction of the omni-channel approach to interaction with consumers. *Proceedings of the 33rd International Business Information Management Association Conference, IBIMA 2019: Education Excellence and Innovation Management through. Vision (Basel)*, *2020*, 8546–8552.

ILO. (2018). Retrieved from https://www.ilo.org/resource/news/more-60-cent-world%E2%80%99s-employed-population-are-informal-economy#:~:text=People%20living%20in%20rural%20areas,Dir ector%2C%20ILO's%20Department%20of%20Statistics

Indiafilings (2022). Export House Certificate. https://www.indiafilings.com/ learn/export-house-certificate/

Indian Journal of Integrated Research in Law. (2024). Overview of AI technologies in tax administration. *Indian Journal of Integrated Research in Law*, *2*(1), 45–58.

Indian, T. U. (2024). Bridging the Divide: Ensuring Equal Pay for Equal Work in India. James, M. U. (2024). Gender Wage Gap in India: Trends, Causes, Consequences, and Policy Responses. *International Journal for Research Trends and Innovation, 9*. Retrieved from chrome-extension://efaidnbmnnnibpcajpcglclefindmkaj/https://www.ijrti.org/papers/IJ RTI2412024.pdf

Indriasari, E., Prabowo, H., Gaol, F. L., & Purwandari, B. (2022). Intelligent Digital Banking Technology and Architecture: A Systematic Literature Review. *Int. J. Interact. Mob. Technol., 16*(19), 98–117. DOI: 10.3991/ijim.v16i19.30993

InRussia. (2024). Generative AI Adoption and Labor Market Adaptation in Russia. https://incrussia.ru/news/generativnyj-ii-v-rossii-kak-novye-tehnologii-izmenyat-rynok-truda/

International Data Corporation. (2025). *IDC's Data Age 2025 study.*

Ionascu, A. E., & Barbu, C. A. (2023). Digital transformation in the banking sector: A pre-and post-Covid-19 analysis. *Management Research and Practice, 15*(3), 55–69.

Ionescu, S. A., Diaconita, V., & Radu, A. O. (2025). Engineering Sustainable Data Architectures for Modern Financial Institutions. *Electronics (Basel), 14*(8), 1650. DOI: 10.3390/electronics14081650

Jacka, J. M., & Keller, P. J. (2009). *Business process mapping: Improving customer satisfaction*. Wiley.

Jafar, R. M. S., Jabeen, M., Hussain, S., Niu, B., Sham, R., & Al-Adwan, A. S. (2025). Cyber Shopping Beyond Boundaries: The Metaverse Revolution in e-Commerce and Consumer Behavior. *Human Behavior and Emerging Technologies, 2025*(1), 5559234. DOI: 10.1155/hbe2/5559234

Jain, H., & Jain, R. (2017, March). Big data in weather forecasting: Applications and challenges. In *2017 International conference on big data analytics and computational intelligence (ICBDAC)* (pp. 138-142). IEEE. DOI: 10.1109/ICBDACI.2017.8070824

Jain, R., Mehta, S., & Kapoor, N. (2021). Sentiment analysis of online reviews using ML in FMCG. *Journal of Retail Analytics, 5*(2), 88–104.

Jeetah, P., Somaroo, G., Surroop, D., Ragen, A. K., & Amode, N. S. (2024). Adoption of Machine Learning for Sustainable Solid Waste Management. In *Artificial Intelligence, Engineering Systems and Sustainable Development: Driving the UN SDGs* (pp. 17-28). Emerald Publishing Limited. DOI: 10.1108/978-1-83753-540-820241002

Jena, S. N. (2024). Financial Socialisation and Promotion of Financial Inclusion, among Women Self-Help Group Members: An analysis. *Journal of Informatics Education and Research, 4*(1). DOI: 10.52783/jier.v4i1.615

Jena, R. K. (2025). Factors influencing the adoption of fintech for the enhancement of financial inclusion in rural India using a mixed methods approach. *Journal of Risk and Financial Management, 18*(3), 150. DOI: 10.3390/jrfm18030150

Jenkins, H. (1997). "Never trust a snake": WWF wrestling as masculine melodrama. In Redhead, S. (Ed.), *The passion and fashion* (pp. 33–66). Sage.

Jenkins, H. (2006). *Convergence culture: Where old and new media collide*. New York University Press.

Jenkins, H. (2006). *Fans, bloggers, and gamers: Exploring participatory culture*. New York University Press.

Jenkins, J. J. (2022). Netflix. In *Encyclopedia of Big Data* (pp. 682–684). Springer International Publishing. DOI: 10.1007/978-3-319-32010-6_144

Jha, P., Kumar, R., Vasa, P., Dhingra, N., Thiruchelvam, D., & Moineddin, R. (2006). Low male-to-female sex ratio of children born in India: National survey of 1·1 million households. *Lancet*, *367*(9506), 211–218. DOI: 10.1016/S0140-6736(06)67930-0 PMID: 16427489

Jiang, Y., & Yu, X. (2024). Theoretical and practical aspects of data asset monetization in maritime enterprises. *Fudan Journal of the Humanities and Social Sciences*, *17*(3), 479–506. DOI: 10.1007/s40647-024-00415-2

Jiyauddin, M., & Banerjee, S. (2025a). Closing The Gender Pay Gap in India: An Analysis. *Social Lens*, *1*(2). Advance online publication. DOI: 10.69971/sl.1.2.2024.17

Johnson, J. S., Friend, S. B., & Lee, H. S. (2017). Big data facilitation, utilization, and monetization: Exploring the 3Vs in a new product development process. *Journal of Product Innovation Management*, *34*(5), 640–658. DOI: 10.1111/jpim.12397

Jones, M., & Kaya, E. (2022). Organisational Gender Pay Gaps in the UK: What Happened Post-Transparency? SSRN *Electronic Journal*. https://doi.org/DOI: 10.2139/ssrn.4129670

Jones, D., & White, S. (2020). Cross-category buying behavior analysis using Bayesian networks. *Journal of Marketing Analytics*, *8*(1), 55–70.

Juminawati, S., Macpal, S. J., & Tuwi, I. W. (2024). *Exploring the Economic Impact of Digital Currencies on Traditional Financial Systems : Challenges and Opportunities.*

Kabashkin, I., & Susanin, V. (2024). Unified ecosystem for data sharing and AI-driven predictive maintenance in aviation. *Computers*, *13*(12), 318. DOI: 10.3390/computers13120318

Kalia, S. (2023) Potential impact of generative Artificial Intelligence(AI) on the financial industry. International Journal on Cybernetics & Informatics (IJCI) Vol.12, No.6, December 2023

Kalibatiene, D., & Vasilecas, O. (2021). A survey on modeling dynamic business processes. *PeerJ. Computer Science, 7*, e609. DOI: 10.7717/peerj-cs.609 PMID: 34307861

Kandlhofer, M., Steinbauer, G., Hirschmugl-Gaisch, S., Huber, P. (2016, October). Artificial intelligence and computer science in education: From kindergarten to university. In 2016 IEEE frontiers in education conference (FIE) (pp. 1-9). IEEE. https://doi.org/DOI: 10.1109/FIE.2016.7757570

Kandpal, V., Ozili, P. K., Jeyanthi, P. M., Ranjan, D., & Chandra, D. (2025). Factors Reshaping the Digital Banking Sectors. In *Digital Finance and Metaverse in Banking: Decoding a Virtual Reality towards Financial Inclusion and Sustainable Development* (pp. 33–67). Emerald Publishing Limited., DOI: 10.1108/978-1-83662-088-420251002

Kanojia, S., Kaur, S., & Bhavya, . (2024). Business sustainability in the era of Fintech and Regtech: A systematic literature review. *Discover Sustainability, 5*(1), 525. DOI: 10.1007/s43621-024-00767-5

Kaplan, R. S., & Norton, D. P. (1992). The balanced scorecard: Measures that drive performance. *Harvard Business Review, 70*(1), 71–79. PMID: 10119714

Kaplan, R. S., & Norton, D. P. (2004). *Strategy maps: Converting intangible assets into tangible outcomes.* Harvard Business School Press.

Kapse, M., Sharma, V., Vidhale, R., & Vellanki, V. (2025). Customization of health insurance premiums using machine learning and explainable AI. *International Journal of Information Management Data Insights, 5*(1), 100328. DOI: 10.1016/j.jjimei.2025.100328

Karal, D. (2016). *E-Commerce in India: a case study of Amazon & Flipkart (India)* (Doctoral dissertation, Wien).

Kargar, B. (2024). *Data driven decision making for sustainable planning and operations of large scale networks* (Doctoral dissertation, New Jersey Institute of Technology). NJIT Digital Commons.

Katz, R. L. (1955). Skills of an effective administrator. *Harvard Business Review, 33*(1), 33–42.

Kaur, S. J., Ali, L., Hassan, M. K., & Al-Emran, M. (2021). Adoption of digital banking channels in an emerging economy: Exploring the role of in-branch efforts. *Journal of Financial Services Marketing, 26*(2), 107–121. DOI: 10.1057/s41264-020-00082-w

Kaushik, P., Brahmi, M., Kakran, S., & Kansra, P. (2024). The Predictive Grey Forecasting Approach for Measuring Tax Collection. *Journal of Risk and Financial Management, 17*(12), 558. DOI: 10.3390/jrfm17120558

Kediya, S. O., Dhote, S., Singh, D. K., Bidve, V. S., Pathan, S., Mohare, R. V., & Suchak, A. (2023). Are AI and Chat Bots Services Effects the Psychology of Users in Banking Services and Financial Sector. *Journal for ReAttach Therapy and Developmental Diversities, 6*(9s (2)), 191–197. https://jrtdd.com/index.php/journal/article/view/1223

Keil, J., & Ongena, S. (2024). The demise of branch banking–Technology, consolidation, bank fragility. *Journal of Banking & Finance, 158*, 107038. DOI: 10.1016/j.jbankfin.2023.107038

Khamdamov, S. J., Mamadiyarov, Z., Fayziyev, F., Khojiev, J., Izzatillayev, A., Rashidov, S., & Suyunova, D. (2024, December). The Role of Data Economics in the Digital Transformation Era Valuation Ownership and Monetization Strategies. In *Proceedings of the 8th International Conference on Future Networks & Distributed Systems* (pp. 499-508). DOI: 10.1145/3726122.3726194

Khandelwal, R., & Kapoor, D. (2024). The Use of Digital Tools for Customer Engagement in the Financial Services Sector. In *Revolutionizing Customer-Centric Banking Through ICT* (pp. 29–55). IGI Global., DOI: 10.4018/979-8-3693-2061-7.ch002

Khan, M. U., & Fatima, I. (2025). The role of big data analytics capability in the telecommunication sector of Pakistan: The chain mediating effect of data integration capability and data-driven decision making. *Quality & Quantity, 59*(1), 51–85. DOI: 10.1007/s11135-024-01923-9

Khatun, H. (2024). The Biggest Elephant in the Room: India's Gender Pay Gap. *Smile Foundation.* Retrieved from https://www.smilefoundationindia.org/blog/the-biggest-elephant-in-the-room-indias-g ender-pay-gap/

Khottak, F., Rahman, S., & Ali, T. (2023). Composite deep learning models for churn prediction. *Applied Artificial Intelligence, 37*(5), 421–438.

Khrais, L. (2020). The potential of AI in creating personalized consumer experiences. *International Journal of Artificial Intelligence in Business, 6*(1), 1–14.

Kim, J., & Choi, H. (2021). AI-enabled chatbots in FMCG retail: A customer engagement study. *Journal of Retailing and Consumer Services, 62*, 102657.

Kitsios, F., & Kamariotou, M. (2023). Digital innovation and entrepreneurship in open data ecosystems: stakeholder perspectives and challenges. *Handbook of Research on Artificial Intelligence, Innovation and Entrepreneurship*, 136-151.

Klement, A. (2018). *When coffee and kale compete. Become great at making products people will buy*. Create Space Independent.

Knack, S., & Zak, P. J. (2003). Building trust: public policy, interpersonal trust, and economic development. *Supreme court economic review, 10*, 91-107.

Kolodynskyi, S., Drakokhrust, T., & Bashynska, M. (2018). The innovative infrastructure of economic development in the framework of international digital transformation. *Baltic Journal of Economic Studies, 4*(4), 166–172. DOI: 10.30525/2256-0742/2018-4-4-166-172

Koshelev, K. A. (2022). Trends in the Evolution of the Digital Financial Assets Market in the Context of the Digital Transformation of the Global Econfile. In *Finance* (Vol. 26). Theory and Practice., DOI: 10.26794/2587-5671

Kotler, P., & Armstrong, G. (2018). *Principles of marketing* (17th ed.). Pearson.

Kotler, P., & Keller, K. L. (2016). *Marketing management* (15th ed.). Pearson Education.

Kotonen, A. (2025). *Data-driven product portfolio process development: Navigating growth and strategic decision-making* (Master's thesis, Aalto University, Finland). Aalto University Repository.

Kozinets, R. V. (2010). Netnography: Doing ethnographic research online. *Sage (Atlanta, Ga.).*

KPMG Global. (2022). *The five rules of data monetization* Retrieved October 10, 2023, from https://kpmg.com/xx/en/home/insights/2019/04/the-five-rules-of-data -monetization.html

Kretschmer, T., Khashabi, P., & Hess, T. (2023). From cost center to value driver: A configurational theory of data function performance. *Journal of Management Information Systems, 40*(4), 1083–1116. DOI: 10.1080/07421222.2023.2241923

Kreuzer, T., Röglinger, M., & Rupprecht, L. (2020). Customer-centric prioritization of process improvement projects. *Decision Support Systems, 133*, 113286. DOI: 10.1016/j.dss.2020.113286

Krishnamurthy, S., Mony, S. V., Jhaveri, N., Bakhshi, S., Bhat, R., Dixit, M. R., & Maheshwari, S. (2005). Insurance industry in India: Structure, performance, and future challenges. *Colloquium, 30*(3), 93.

Krishnan, M. (2023). The future of data monetization in financial services investment & risk management Infosys Consulting–One hub. Many perspectives. Retrieved October 10, 2023, from https://www.infosysconsultinginsights.com/2023/09/25/the-future-of-data-monetization-within-financial

Krivkovich, A., Field, E., Yee, L., McConnell, M., & Smit, H. (2024). *Women in the Workplace 2024: The 10th-anniversary report.* McKinsey Company. Retrieved from https://www.mckinsey.com/featured-insights/diversity-and-inclusion/women-in-the-w orkplace

Kudeshia, C., & Mittal, A. (2015). The journey of Chumbak: From mail to mall – leveraging social media networks for on-going dialogue with customers. *Emerald Emerging Markets Case Studies*, *5*(4), 1–20. DOI: 10.1108/EEMCS-09-2014-0209

Ku, E. C. (2010). The impact of customer relationship management through implementation of information systems. *Total Quality Management & Business Excellence*, *21*(11), 1085–1102. DOI: 10.1080/14783360903250514

Kumaran, H., & Kamal, N. (2025). Advancing sustainability through fintech innovations in financial services: Evidence from India. In *Fostering economic diversification and sustainable business through digital intelligence* (pp. 23–50). IGI Global. DOI: 10.4018/979-8-3693-8492-3.ch002

Kumar, R., & Singh, V. (2022). Deep learning for predicting consumer purchase frequency in FMCG. *Applied Soft Computing*, *120*, 108702.

Lahuerta, S., Rejchrt, P., & Patrick, A. (2023). The UK Pay Transparency Regulations: Apparent transparency without accountability? *Legal Studies*, *44*(1), 21–44. DOI: 10.1017/lst.2023.12

Laitila, M. (2017). Data monetization: Utilizing data as an asset to generate new revenues for firms.

Lall, S., & Sivakumar, R. (2021, June). A Real-world Dataset of Netflix Videos and User Watch-Behavior: Analysis and Insights. In *ICC 2021-IEEE International Conference on Communications* (pp. 1-7). IEEE.

Lall, S. (2000). The Technological structure and performance of developing country manufactured exports, 1985-98. *Oxford Development Studies*, *28*(3), 337–369. DOI: 10.1080/713688318

Lark Suite. (2023). *Balanced scorecard for data teams* Retrieved April 29, 2025, from https://www.larksuite.com/en_us/topics/goal-setting-techniques-for-functional-teams/balanced-scorecard-for-data-teams

Laroiya, C., Saxena, D., & Komalavalli, C. (2020). Applications of blockchain technology. In *Handbook of research on blockchain technology* (pp. 213–243). Academic press., DOI: 10.1016/B978-0-12-819816-2.00009-5

Latvala, L., Horn, J., & Bruno, B. (2022). Thriving in the age of privacy regulation: A first-party data strategy. *Applied Marketing Analytics*, *7*(3), 211–220. DOI: 10.69554/KMBL6487

Lauer, J. (2020). Plastic surveillance: Payment cards and the history of transactional data, 1888 to present. *Big Data & Society*, *7*(1), 2053951720907632. DOI: 10.1177/2053951720907632

Lauterbach, J., Mueller, B., Kahrau, F., & Maedche, A. (2020). Achieving Effective Use When Digitalizing Work: The Role of Representational Complexity. *Management Information Systems Quarterly*, *44*(3), 1023–1048. Advance online publication. DOI: 10.25300/MISQ/2020/14583

Lee, B. G. (2024). Digital and AI Transformation of Industry. In *Understanding the Digital and AI Transformation* (pp. 163–184). Springer Nature Singapore.

Lee, D., Arnold, M., Srivastava, A., Plastow, K., Strelan, P., Ploeckl, F., Lekkas, D., & Palmer, E. (2024). The impact of generative AI on higher education learning and teaching: A study of educators' perspectives. *Comput. Educ. Artif. Intell.*, *6*, 100221. DOI: 10.1016/j.caeai.2024.100221

Lee, J., & Park, H. (2023). NLP for demand forecasting in FMCG consumer behavior analysis. *Journal of Business Research*, *161*, 113758.

Lee, S. M., & Lee, D. (2020). "Untact": A new customer service strategy in the digital age. *Service Business*, *14*(1), 1–22. DOI: 10.1007/s11628-019-00408-2

Leonard-Barton D. (1992). Core capabilities and core rigidities: A paradox in managing new product development. Strategic Manage J.; 13:111 – 26 (special issue). https://doi.org/DOI: 10.1002/smj.4250131009

Leonardi, P. M., & Neeley, T. B. (2024). The digital mindset: How to make your team's data talk productive. *Strategic Management Journal*, *45*(1), 45–67. DOI: 10.1002/smj.3532

Li, C., Li, Y., Xu, Y., & Sun, G. (2025). Research on the Impact of Financial Technology on Risk-taking of Commercial Banks. *Research in International Business and Finance*, *102804*, 102804. Advance online publication. DOI: 10.1016/j.ribaf.2025.102804

Li, L., & Zhang, J. (2021). Research and analysis of an enterprise E-commerce marketing system under the big data environment. [JOEUC]. *Journal of Organizational and End User Computing*, *33*(6), 1–19. DOI: 10.4018/JOEUC.20211101.oa15

Li, M., & Chen, Y. (2021). Analyzing customer sentiments on FMCG using social media data. *Information Processing & Management*, *58*(5), 102584.

Lim, C., Kim, K. H., Kim, M. J., Heo, J. Y., Kim, K. J., & Maglio, P. P. (2018). From data to value: A nine-factor framework for data-based value creation in information-intensive services. *International Journal of Information Management*, *39*, 121–135. DOI: 10.1016/j.ijinfomgt.2017.12.007

Lin, Y. H., Chen, S. Y., Lin, P. H., Tai, A. S., Pan, Y. C., Hsieh, C. E., & Lin, S. H. (2020). Assessing user retention of a mobile app: Survival analysis. *JMIR mHealth and uHealth*, *8*(11), e16309. DOI: 10.2196/16309 PMID: 33242023

Liu, X., & Li, X. (2024). Acquiring Second-Party Transaction Data for Customer Analytics.

Liu, Z. (2024). *A Comparative Study of Machine Learning Methods in Financial Fraud Detection* (Issue Ftbm). Atlantis Press International BV. DOI: 10.2991/978-94-6463-546-1

Liu, Y. (2007). The long-term impact of loyalty programs on consumer purchase behavior and loyalty. *Journal of Marketing*, *71*(4), 19–35. DOI: 10.1509/jmkg.71.4.019

Loers, M., & Roye, D. (2025). DATAMITE: Effektive Datenmonetarisierungsstrategien zur Stärkung der europäischen Datenökonomie/DATAMITE: Effective data monetization strategies to strengthen the European data economy. *UdZ – The Data-driven Enterprise, 5*(1), 54–59.

Long, L. (2022). Effective first-party data collection in a privacy-first world. *Applied Marketing Analytics*, *7*(3), 202–210. DOI: 10.69554/NPRK2282

Lóska, G., & Uotila, J. (2023). Digital Transformation in Corporate Banking: Toward a Blended Service Model. *California Management Review*, *00081256231207429*. Advance online publication. DOI: 10.1177/00081256231207429

Luckham, D. C. (2011). *Event processing for business: organizing the real-time enterprise*. John Wiley & Sons.

Lugmayr, A., Sutinen, E., Suhonen, J., Sedano, C. I., Hlavacs, H., & Montero, C. S. (2017). Serious storytelling–a first definition and review. *Multimedia Tools and Applications*, *76*(14), 15707–15733. DOI: 10.1007/s11042-016-3865-5

Lu, R., & Sadiq, S. (2007). A survey of comparative business process modeling approaches. *International Conference on Business Information Systems*, 82–94. DOI: 10.1007/978-3-540-72035-5_7

Lu, S., & Yeung, W. J. (2024). The rise in cross-national marriages and the emergent inequalities in East and Southeast Asia. *Sociology Compass*, *18*(5), e13219. Advance online publication. DOI: 10.1111/soc4.13219

Lusardi, A., & Mitchell, O. S. (2014). The economic importance of financial literacy: Theory and evidence. *Journal of Economic Literature*, *52*(1), 5–44. DOI: 10.1257/jel.52.1.5 PMID: 28579637

Luu, T. M. N., Mittal, S., & Gupta, S. (2025). Leveraging AI to Tailor Customer Engagement With Personalized Marketing Strategies. In *AI, Corporate Social Responsibility, and Marketing in Modern Organizations* (pp. 195-220). IGI Global Scientific Publishing. DOI: 10.4018/979-8-3373-0219-5.ch010

Maaz, Z. N., & Ismail, M. Z. (2024). Data monetization strategies: The construction industry market analysis. *International Journal of Built Environment and Sustainability*, *11*(3), 103–119. DOI: 10.11113/ijbes.v11.n3.1351

Machado, M. P., Klingenberg, C. O., Abreu, J. L., Barbastefano, R., & Lacerda, D. P. (2024). Business processes for data monetization: An exploratory analysis and proposition of design patterns. *Business Process Management Journal*, *31*(4), 1528–1559. DOI: 10.1108/BPMJ-02-2024-0079

Madhavan, S., & Chandrasekar, K. (2015). Consumer purchasing behavior: Cultural and psychological factors. *International Journal of Marketing Studies*, *7*(2), 85–95.

Magazine, C. D. O. (2023). Behind the fizz: Coca-Cola's strategy for balancing data innovation and business impact Retrieved April 29, 2025, from https://www.cdomagazine.tech/data-management/behind-the-fizz-coca-colas-strategy-for-balancing-data-innovation-and-business-impact

Mahalakshmi, V., Kulkarni, N., Kumar, K. P., Kumar, K. S., Sree, D. N., & Durga, S. (2022). The role of implementing artificial intelligence and machine learning technologies in the financial services industry for creating competitive intelligence. *Materials Today: Proceedings*, *56*, 2252–2255. DOI: 10.1016/j.matpr.2021.11.577

Maia, C. R., Maçada, A. C. G., Lunardi, G. L., & Sengik, A. R. (2024). Data monetization capability: From the systematic literature review to the proposition of a multidimensional model. *Revista de Administração da UFSM*, *17*(2), e6. DOI: 10.5902/1983465986416

Mainardes, E. W., Rosa, C. A. D. M., & Nossa, S. N. (2020). Omnichannel strategy and customer loyalty in banking. *International Journal of Bank Marketing*, *38*(4), 799–822. DOI: 10.1108/IJBM-07-2019-0272

Maja, M. M., & Letaba, P. (2022). Towards a data-driven technology roadmap for the bank of the future: Exploring big data analytics to support technology roadmapping. *Social Sciences & Humanities Open*, *6*(1), 100270. DOI: 10.1016/j.ssaho.2022.100270

Makudza, F. (2021). Augmenting customer loyalty through customer experience management in the banking industry. *Journal of Asian Business and Economic Studies*, *28*(3), 191–203. DOI: 10.1108/JABES-01-2020-0007

Malik, F. T., Hughes, L., Dwivedi, Y. K., & Dettmer, S. (2023). Exploring the Transformative Impact of Generative AI on Higher Education. *IFIP International Conference on e-Business, e-Services, and e-Society*. DOI: 10.1007/978-3-031-50040-4_6

Manikandan, M., & Madhubala, V. (2024). A study on the impact of seasonal sales on online shopping trends in India: A study of amazon and Flipkart.

Mann, G., Karanasios, S., & Breidbach, C. F. (2022). Orchestrating the digital transformation of a business ecosystem. *The Journal of Strategic Information Systems*, *31*(3), 101733. DOI: 10.1016/j.jsis.2022.101733

Manser Payne, E. H., Peltier, J., & Barger, V. A. (2021). Enhancing the value co-creation process: Artificial intelligence and mobile banking service platforms. *Journal of Research in Interactive Marketing*, *15*(1), 68–85. DOI: 10.1108/JRIM-10-2020-0214

Manzoor, H., Ali, R., & Shah, M. (2024). Advanced ML models for consumer behavior prediction. *Journal of Intelligent Systems*, *33*(1), 101–118.

Marcel, G. (1962). *Homo viator: Introduction to a metaphysic of hope. Harper & Row. Mazer, S. (1998). Professional wrestling: Sport and spectacle*. University Press of Mississippi.

Marcucci, S., Alarcón, N. G., Verhulst, S. G., & Wüllhorst, E. (2023). Informing the global data future: Benchmarking data governance frameworks. *Data & Policy*, *5*, e30. DOI: 10.1017/dap.2023.24

Marques, J., Silva, T., & Pereira, R. (2024). Psychology and technology in predicting consumer responses. *Journal of Retail Technology*, *12*(1), 66–82.

Marr, B. (2015). *Big Data: Using SMART big data, analytics and metrics to make better decisions and improve performance*. John Wiley & Sons.

Marsden, J. H., & Wilkinson, V. A. (2018, July). Big data analytics and corporate social responsibility: Making sustainability science part of the bottom line. In *2018 IEEE International Professional Communication Conference (ProComm)* (pp. 51-60). IEEE. DOI: 10.1109/ProComm.2018.00019

Maseke, B. F. (2024). The Transformative Power of Artificial Intelligence in Banking Client Service. *South Asian Journal of Social Studies and Economics*, *21*(3), 93–105. DOI: 10.9734/sajsse/2024/v21i3787

Masiha, R. Y. (2022). Effects of Cryptocurrencies on Global Economics : A Review Study. *Qubaham Academic Journal*, *2*(2), 9–15. DOI: 10.48161/qaj.v2n2a138

Matai, P. (2023). Turning data into dollars: Navigating the path to monetization and unlocking business value through data. *Journal of Marketing & Supply Chain Management*, *2*(4), 1–5. DOI: 10.47363/JMSCM/2023(2)159

Mavlutova, I., Spilbergs, A., Verdenhofs, A., Natrins, A., Arefjevs, I., & Volkova, T. (2022). Digital transformation as a driver of the financial sector sustainable development: An impact on financial inclusion and operational efficiency. *Sustainability (Basel)*, *15*(1), 207. DOI: 10.3390/su15010207

Mavrogiorgou, A., Kiourtis, A., Perakis, K., Miltiadou, D., Pitsios, S., & Kyriazis, D. (2019). Analyzing data and data sources towards a unified approach for ensuring end-to-end data and data sources quality in healthcare 4.0. *Computer Methods and Programs in Biomedicine*, *181*, 104967. DOI: 10.1016/j.cmpb.2019.06.026 PMID: 31303342

McAfee, A., & Brynjolfsson, E. (2024). The future of work: Data-driven management and collaborative teams. *Strategic Management Journal*, *45*(3), 567–592. DOI: 10.1002/smj.3554

McDonald, P., Hay, S., Cathcart, A., & Feldman, A. (2024). Apostles, Agnostics and Atheists: Engagement with Generative AI by Australian University Staff.

McGowan, T. (2016). *Capitalism and desire: The psychic cost of free markets*. Columbia University Press. DOI: 10.7312/mcgo17872

Melnyk, V. (2024). Transforming the nature of trust between banks and young clients: From traditional to digital banking. *Qualitative Research in Financial Markets*, *16*(4), 618–635. DOI: 10.1108/QRFM-08-2022-0129

Mesut, B., Başkor, A., & Aksu, N. B. (2023). Role of artificial intelligence in quality profiling and optimization of drug products. In Elsevier eBooks (pp. 35–54). DOI: 10.1016/B978-0-323-89925-3.00003-4

Mirbagheri, F. (2025). To sell or not to sell? Drivers and barriers to direct data monetization in incumbents. In *Proceedings of the 58th Hawaii International Conference on System Sciences (HICSS)*. ScholarSpace. DOI: 10.24251/HICSS.2025.485

Mishra, B., & Prashar, A. (2021). Customers' readiness for a paradigm shift towards cyberspace: An exploratory investigation in Indian retail banking. *International Journal of Financial Innovation in Banking*, *3*(1), 1–25. DOI: 10.1504/IJFIB.2021.114924

Mitchell, T. M. (1997). Does machine learning really work? *AI Magazine*, *18*(3), 11–11.

Mittal, A., Chaturvedi, D. D., Chaturvedi, S., & Singh, P. K. (2024). "Impact of Negative Aspects of Artificial Intelligence on Customer Purchase Intention: An Empirical Study of Online Retail Customers Towards AI-Enabled E-Retail Platforms" In Dadwal, S., Goyal, S., Kumar, P., Verma, R. Demystifying the dark side of AI in business (1st ed., pp. 159-173). Hershey, Pennsylvania, 17033, USA): IGI Global.

Mittal, A., Singh, B., Singh, S., Singh, P. K., & Rajest, S. S. (2025). Impact of social media (SM) information on stock market investment decisions (ID): A quantitative investigation using SEM-ANN approach. *International Journal of Trade and Global Markets*, *21*(2), 188–218. DOI: 10.1504/IJTGM.2025.146648

Mittal, A., Singh, S., & George, S. R. (2023). Role of artificial intelligence in knowledge management: An empirical study of industry experts using stepwise multiple regression. *International Journal of Electronic Finance*, *12*(1), 403–422. DOI: 10.1504/ijef.2023.10053587

Mogaji, E. (2023). Redefining banks in the digital era: A typology of banks and their research, managerial and policy implications. *International Journal of Bank Marketing*, *41*(7), 1899–1918. DOI: 10.1108/IJBM-06-2023-0333

Mogaji, E., Balakrishnan, J., Nwoba, A. C., & Nguyen, N. P. (2021). Emerging-market consumers' interactions with banking chatbots. *Telematics and Informatics*, *65*, 101711. DOI: 10.1016/j.tele.2021.101711

Mohanty, S. (2021). A distributional analysis of the gender wage gap among technical degree and diploma holders in urban India. *International Journal of Educational Development*, *80*, 102322. DOI: 10.1016/j.ijedudev.2020.102322

Molnar, C. (2022). *Interpretable machine learning* (2nd ed.). Leanpub.

Monino, J. L. (2021). Data value, big data analytics, and decision-making. *Journal of the Knowledge Economy*, *12*(1), 256–267. DOI: 10.1007/s13132-016-0396-2

Moro-visconti, R., Larocca, A., & Marconi, M. (2017). *Big data-Driven Healthcare Project Financing. March 2018*. DOI: 10.2139/ssrn.2903799

Mubarik, M. S., Devadason, E. S., & Govindaraju, C. (2020). Human capital and export performance of small and medium enterprises in Pakistan. *International Journal of Social Economics*, *47*(5), 643–662. DOI: 10.1108/IJSE-03-2019-0198

Mudgal, R., & Rana, P. (2023). Comparison of two most popular food delivery apps in India: A case study of Swiggy and Zomato. *International Journal of Research in Social Sciences*, *13*(02).

Murinde, V., Rizopoulos, E., & Zachariadis, M. (2022). The impact of the FinTech revolution on the future of banking: Opportunities and risks. *International Review of Financial Analysis*, *81*, 102103. DOI: 10.1016/j.irfa.2022.102103

Murray, J. (2024, September). Optimizing risk reduction: A data-driven approach for strategic preventive and mitigative action planning. In *International Pipeline Conference* (Vol. 88537, p. V001T01A003). American Society of Mechanical Engineers. DOI: 10.1115/IPC2024-132099

Mustak, M., Hallikainen, H., Laukkanen, T., Plé, L., Hollebeek, L. D., & Aleem, M. (2024). Using machine learning to develop customer insights from user-generated content. *Journal of Retailing and Consumer Services*, *81*, 104034. DOI: 10.1016/j.jretconser.2024.104034

Nagimova N.I. (2015) Technologizing of educational process as condition of educational results formation of implementing programs of secondary vocational education. Electronic learning in continuous education.

Najjar, M. S., & Kettinger, W. J. (2013). Data monetization: Lessons from a retailer's journey. *MIS Quarterly Executive*, *12*(4), 213–225.

Nakamoto, S. (2008). Bitcoin: A peer-to-peer electronic cash system. *Available at SSRN* 3440802.

Nanda, J. D. (2025, March 6). Bridging the gender gap in India's corporate landscape. *Agency Reporter*. Retrieved from https://www.agencyreporter.com/bridging-the-gender-gap-in-indias-corporate-landsca pe/

Narayanan, K., & Ramaswamy, V. (2022). Digital India innovation and the experience-verse revolution. *itihaasa Research and Digital Report*.

Nastasoiu, A., & Vandenbosch, M. (2019). Competing with loyalty: How to design successful customer loyalty reward programs. *Business Horizons*, *62*(2), 207–214. DOI: 10.1016/j.bushor.2018.11.002

Nenavath, S., & Mishra, S. (2023). Impact of green finance and fintech on sustainable economic growth: Empirical evidence from India. *Heliyon*, *9*(5), e16301. DOI: 10.1016/j.heliyon.2023.e16301 PMID: 37234625

Neumann, N., Tucker, C. E., Subramanyam, K., & Marshall, J. (2023). Is first-or third-party audience data more effective for reaching the 'right' customers? The case of IT decision-makers. *Quantitative Marketing and Economics*, *21*(4), 519–571. DOI: 10.1007/s11129-023-09268-7

Newman, B., & Crawford, J. (2017). *Consumer behavior and buying process*. Routledge.

Ng, D. T. K., Leung, J. K. L., Chu, S. K. W., & Qiao, M. S. (2021). Conceptualizing AI literacy: An exploratory review. *Computers and Education: Artificial Intelligence*, *2*, 100041. DOI: 10.1016/j.caeai.2021.100041

Nguyen, D. K., Sermpinis, G., & Stasinakis, C. (2023). Big data, artificial intelligence and machine learning: A transformative symbiosis in favour of financial technology. *European Financial Management*, *29*(2), 517–548. DOI: 10.1111/eufm.12365

Nguyen, H. N., & Tran, M. D. (2023). Antecedents and outcomes of omnichannel retail customer experience. *International Journal of Electronic Marketing and Retailing*, *14*(2), 171–189. DOI: 10.1504/IJEMR.2023.129883

Nielsen, I. Q. (2022). *Global consumer trends and e-commerce growth in FMCG sector*. https://nielseniq.com/

Nikonorov, V., Kutuzov, A., Nikonorov, V., & Overes, E. (2020). The digitalization of refining processes on the example of producing winter diesel fuel. *Proceedings of the International Scientific Conference - Digital Transformation on Manufacturing, Infrastructure and Service*, 1–5. https://doi.org/DOI: 10.1145/3446434.3446490

Ning, Y., Zhang, C., Xu, B., Zhou, Y., & Wijaya, T. T. (2024). Teachers' AI-TPACK: Exploring the relationship between knowledge elements. *Sustainability (Basel)*, *16*(3), 978. DOI: 10.3390/su16030978

NIPFP. (2023). *Tax administration reforms in India*. National Institute of Public Finance and Policy. [REMOVED HYPERLINK FIELD]

Nirala, K. K., Singh, N. K., & Purani, V. S. (2022). A survey on providing customer and public administration based services using AI: Chatbot. *Multimedia Tools and Applications, 81*(16), 22215–22246. DOI: 10.1007/s11042-021-11458-y PMID: 35002470

Obloj, T., & Zenger, T. (2022). The influence of pay transparency on (gender) inequity, inequality and the performance basis of pay. *Nature Human Behaviour, 6*(5), 646–655. DOI: 10.1038/s41562-022-01288-9 PMID: 35145281

OECD. (2017). *Technology tools to tackle tax evasion and tax fraud.* OECD Publishing., DOI: 10.1787/9789264271401-

OECD. (2020). PISA 2018 results (Volume IV): Are students smart about money? OECD Publishing. DOI: 10.1787/48ebd1ba-en

OECD. (2024). *Digital solutions in tax administration.* OECD Publishing.

OECD. (n.d.). Retrieved from https://www.oecd.org/en/data/indicators/gender-wage-gap.html Pathak, H. (2025). *Improving Female Workforce Participation in India.* PIB, Ministry of Labour & Employment. Retrieved from https://www.pib.gov.in/PressReleasePage.aspx?PRID=2108281

Ofulue, J., & Benyoucef, M. (2024). Data monetization: Insights from a technology-enabled literature review and research agenda. *Management Review Quarterly, 74*(2), 521–565. DOI: 10.1007/s11301-022-00309-1

Ogeawuchi, J. C., Uzoka, A. C., Abayomi, A. A., Agboola, O. A., Gbenle, T. P., & Owoade, S. (2024). Advancements in Scalable Data Modeling and Reporting for SaaS Applications and Cloud Business Intelligence'. *International Journal of Advanced Multidisciplinary Research and Studies, 4*(6), 2155–2162. DOI: 10.62225/2583049X.2024.4.6.4267

Okere, K. I., Dimnwobi, S. K., & Fasanya, I. O. (2025). Pathways to environmental sustainability: Exploring the role of FinTech, natural resources and globalization in North Africa. *International Journal of Sustainable Development and World Ecology, 32*(4), 446–464. DOI: 10.1080/13504509.2025.2481222

Okeyo, M. (2024). *Customer-centric data strategies to drive revenue growth* (Master's thesis, Aga Khan University, Kenya). Aga Khan University Institutional Repository.

Olaleye, I., Mokogwu, V., Olufemi-Phillips, A. Q., & Adewale, T. T. (2024). Transforming supply chain resilience: Frameworks and advancements in predictive analytics and data-driven strategies. *Open Access Research Journal of Multidisciplinary Studies, 8*(2), 85–93. DOI: 10.53022/oarjms.2024.8.2.0065

Olejnik, L., Castelluccia, C., & Janc, A. (2014). On the uniqueness of web browsing history patterns. *annals of telecommunications-annales des télécommunications, 69*(1), 63-74.

Olyanga, A. M., Shinyekwa, I. M., Ngoma, M., Nkote, I. N., Esemu, T., & Kamya, M. (2022). Export logistics infrastructure and export competitiveness in the East African Community. *Modern Supply Chain Research and Applications, 4*(1), 39–61. DOI: 10.1108/MSCRA-09-2021-0017

Omarini, A. (2022). The changing landscape of retail banking and the future of digital banking. In *The Future of Financial Systems in the Digital Age: Perspectives from Europe and Japan* (pp. 133-158). Singapore: Springer Singapore. DOI: 10.1007/978-981-16-7830-1_8

Order of the Ministry of Health and Social Development of the Russian Federation of January 11, 2011, No. 1n (as amended on January 25, 2023). Available from: https://ivo.garant.ru/#/document/55170898/paragraph/1:0

Orogun, O., & Onyekwelu, U. (2019). ML modeling for consumer dynamics in FMCG. *Journal of Retail Research, 11*(3), 201–218.

Overes, E., & Santoro, F. (2025). The Effectiveness of Business Process Visualisations: a Systematic Literature Review. arXiv preprint arXiv:2504.10971

Padhi, B., Mishra, U. S., & Pattanayak, U. (2019). Gender-Based Wage Discrimination in Indian Urban Labour Market: An Assessment. *The Indian Journal of Labour Economics : the Quarterly Journal of the Indian Society of Labour Economics, 62*(3), 361–388. DOI: 10.1007/s41027-019-00175-8

Palle, R. R. (2021). Discuss the role of data analytics in extracting meaningful insights from social media data, influencing marketing strategies and user engagement. *Journal of Artificial Intelligence and Machine Learning in Management, 5*(1), 64–69. https://journals.sagescience.org/index.php/jamm/article/view/131

Pal, P. (2022). The adoption of waves of digital technology as antecedents of digital transformation by financial services institutions. *Journal of Digital Banking, 7*(1), 70–91. DOI: 10.69554/QHFT9370

Pamisetty, V., Pandiri, L., Annapareddy, V. N., & Sriram, H. K. (2022). Leveraging AI, Machine Learning, And Big Data for Enhancing Tax Compliance, Fraud Detection, And Predictive Analytics in Government Financial Management. Machine Learning, And Big Data for Enhancing Tax Compliance, Fraud Detection, And Predictive Analytics in Government Financial Management (June 15, 2022).

Pan, W., Xie, T., Wang, Z., & Ma, L. (2022). Digital economy: An innovation driver for total factor productivity. *Journal of Business Research, 139*, 303–311. DOI: 10.1016/j.jbusres.2021.09.061

Parvinen, P., Pöyry, E., Gustafsson, R., Laitila, M., & Rossi, M. (2020). Advancing data monetization and the creation of data-based business models. *Communications of the Association for Information Systems, 47*(1), 25–49. DOI: 10.17705/1CAIS.04702

Patel, N., & Trivedi, S. (2020). Leveraging predictive modeling, machine learning personalization, NLP customer support, and AI chatbots to increase customer loyalty. *Empirical Quests for Management Essences, 3*(3), 1-24. Retrieved from https://researchberg.com/index.php/eqme/article/view/46

Patel, A. (2016). Gaining insight: Re-thinking at the edge. *Technological Forecasting and Social Change, 107*, 141–153. DOI: 10.1016/j.techfore.2015.12.002

Patel, K., & Sharma, R. (2022). Reinforcement learning for dynamic pricing in FMCG. *Expert Systems: International Journal of Knowledge Engineering and Neural Networks, 39*(4), e12847.

Patel, R., & Kumar, S. (2023). Beyond the Break: An Analysis of Corporate Reentry Programs. *Indian Journal of Human Resource Management, 12*(2), 45–60.

Pathak, P., Chandgadkar, V., Solanki, A., Shrivastava, A., Pulgam, N., & Maktum, T. (2024, March). Customer churn prediction and personalised recommendations in banking. In *International Conference on Artificial Intelligence and Smart Energy* (pp. 409-421). Cham: Springer Nature Switzerland. DOI: 10.1007/978-3-031-61475-0_32

Patria, D., Achmadi, H., Wuisan, D., & Purba, J. T. (2023). How brand engagement, brand experience on brand loyalty through brand trust and brand commitment: Spotify online music evidence. [Jurnal Ilmiah Manajemen Bisnis dan Inovasi Universitas Sam Ratulangi]. *JMBI UNSRAT, 10*(3), 1694–1710. DOI: 10.35794/jmbi.v10i3.50319

Păvăloaia, V. D., Anastasiei, I. D., & Fotache, D. (2020). Social media and e-mail marketing campaigns: Symmetry versus convergence. *Symmetry, 12*(12), 1940. DOI: 10.3390/sym12121940

Pavlov, N., Zotova, E., Shaban, A., & Overes, E. (2020). Digital technology of generating survey data on the characteristics of an innovative product in a distance learning system. *Proceedings of the International Scientific Conference - Digital Transformation on Manufacturing, Infrastructure and Service*, 1–5. DOI: 10.1145/3446434.3446537

Pazouki, S., Jamshidi, M. B., Jalali, M., & Tafreshi, A. (2025). Transformative impact of AI and digital technologies on the FinTech industry: A comprehensive review. *International Journal of Advanced Research in Humanities and Law*, *2*(2), 1–27. DOI: 10.63053/ijrel.37

Pei, Z. (2023). Framework design based on data-driven for evaluating the efficiency of group collaboration in scientific research teams. *The Journal of Supercomputing*, *80*(6), 7890–7912. DOI: 10.1007/s11227-023-05815-x

Pew Research Center. (2023). Social media and news fact sheet. https://www.pewresearch.org/journalism/fact-sheet/social-media-and-news-fact-sheet/

Philippon, T. (2015). Has the U.S. finance industry become less efficient? On the theory and measurement of financial intermediation. *The American Economic Review*, *105*(4), 1408–1438. DOI: 10.1257/aer.20120578

Pierce, E. (2022). A balanced scorecard for maximizing data performance. *Frontiers in Big Data*, *5*, 821103. Advance online publication. DOI: 10.3389/fdata.2022.821103 PMID: 35434610

Piketty, T. (2014). *Capital in the twenty-first century*. Harvard University Press. DOI: 10.4159/9780674369542

Platt, J., Prins, S., Bates, L., & Keyes, K. (2016). Unequal depression for equal work? How the wage gap explains gendered disparities in mood disorders. *Social Science & Medicine*, *149*, 1–8. DOI: 10.1016/j.socscimed.2015.11.056 PMID: 26689629

Plekhanov Russian University of Economics. (2022). Economic development in the 21st century: Trends *Horizon*, *7*, •••. Retrieved April 29, 2025, from https://reu-horizon.rea.ru/sites/default/files/2022-01/Horizon_21_1.pdf

PLFS. (2023-24). *Annual Report.* Retrieved from chrome-extension://efaidnbmnnnibpcajpcglclefindmkaj/https://dge.gov.in/dge/sites/de fault/files/2023-10/Annual_Report_PLFS_2022-23.pdf

Porter, L., Davies, L., Ruming, K., Kelly, D., Rogers, D., & Flanagan, K. (2023). Understanding the drivers and outcomes of public housing tenant relocation.

Poudel, N. (2024). The Impact of Big Data-Driven Artificial Intelligence Systems on Public Service Delivery in Cloud-Oriented Government Infrastructures. *Journal of Artificial Intelligence and Machine Learning in Cloud Computing Systems*, *8*(11), 13–25.

Prahalad, C. K., & Hamel, G. (1990). The core competence of the corporation. *Harvard Business Review*, *68*(3), 79–93.

Priyono, A., & Hidayat, A. (2024). Fostering innovation through learning from digital business ecosystem: A dynamic capability perspective. *Journal of Open Innovation, 10*(1), 100196. DOI: 10.1016/j.joitmc.2023.100196

Provost, F., & Fawcett, T. (2019). *Data science for business: What you need to know about data mining and data-analytic thinking* (2nd ed.). O'Reilly Media.

Psacharopoulos, G., & Tzannatos, Z. (1989). FEMALE LABOR FORCE PARTICIPATION: AN INTERNATIONAL PERSPECTIVE. *The World Bank Research Observer, 4*(2), 187–201. DOI: 10.1093/wbro/4.2.187 PMID: 12283641

Puschmann, T. (2017). Fintech. *Business & Information Systems Engineering, 59*(1), 69–76. DOI: 10.1007/s12599-017-0464-6

Qatawneh, A. M., & Makhlouf, M. H. (2025). Influence of smart mobile banking services on senior banks' clients intention to use: Moderating role of digital accounting. *Global Knowledge, Memory and Communication, 74*(3/4), 1028–1044. DOI: 10.1108/GKMC-01-2023-0018

RAEX-100. 2024 https://raex-rr.com/education/russian_universities/top-100_universities/2024/

Rahimzadeh, V. (2021). A policy and practice review of consumer protections and their application to hospital-sourced data aggregation and analytics by third-party companies. *Frontiers in Big Data, 3*, 603044. DOI: 10.3389/fdata.2020.603044 PMID: 33693425

Rahman, M. S., Abdel Fattah, F. A., & Mohamad, O. B. (2014). Service quality and customers' patronage decision of healthcare insurance products: In-depth interview approach. *International Journal of Academic Research in Business & Social Sciences, 4*(7), 436–444. DOI: 10.6007/IJARBSS/v4-i7/1046

Rajabi, B. A., & Lee, S. P. (2010). Modeling and analysis of change management in dynamic business process. *International Journal of Computer and Electrical Engineering, 2*(1), 181–189. DOI: 10.7763/IJCEE.2010.V2.133

Raju, D., & Thillai Rajan, A. (2019). SME Performance and Access to Export Markets: The Role of Institutional Credit. In Manimala, M., Wasdani, K., & Vijaygopal, A. (Eds.), *Transnational Entrepreneurship. Entrepreneurship and Development in South Asia: Longitudinal Narratives*. Springer. DOI: 10.1007/978-981-10-6298-8_12

Ramadasa, I. (2022). *How Telco ' s use Big Data for Monetization & Revenue Maximization. September.*

Ramaswamy, S., Khande, R., Patil, Y. S., & Kalkar, P. (2021). Adapting digital banking services during covid-19 pandemic: A study on customer experiences in selected district of maharashtra state, India. [IJEET]. *Journal of Electrical Engineering & Technology*, *12*(5), 8–17. DOI: 10.34218/IJEET.12.5.2021.002

Rammohan, A., & Vu, P. (2018). Gender Inequality in Education and Kinship Norms in India. *Feminist Economics*, *24*(1), 142–167. DOI: 10.1080/13545701.2017.1364399

Ramya, N., & Mohamed Ali, S. (2016). Factors affecting consumer buying behavior. *International Journal of Applied Research*, *2*(10), 76–80.

Rao, M. G., & Kumar, S. (2016). Envisioning tax policy for accelerated development in India. *NIPFP Working Paper No. 190*. National Institute of Public Finance and Policy.

Ravat, L., Hemonnet-Goujot, A., & Hollet-Haudebert, S. (2024). Exploring how to develop data-driven innovation capability of marketing within B2B firms: Toward a capability model and process-oriented approach. *Industrial Marketing Management*, *118*, 110–125. DOI: 10.1016/j.indmarman.2023.12.015

Ray, D., & Samanta, T. (2020). "Motherhood Penalty?": Examining Gender, Work, and Family among Science Professionals in India. *Susan Bulkeley Butler Center for Leadership Excellence and ADVANCE Working Paper Series*.

Raychaudhuri, D., & Mandayam, N. B. (2012). Frontiers of wireless and mobile communications. *Proceedings of the IEEE*, *100*(4), 824–840. DOI: 10.1109/JPROC.2011.2182095

Rehman, F. U., Noman, A. A., & Ding, Y. (2020). Does infrastructure increase exports and reduce trade deficit? Evidence from selected South Asian countries using a new Global Infrastructure Index. *Journal of Economic Structures*, *9*(1), 1–23. DOI: 10.1186/s40008-020-0183-x

Reina, G., Childs, H., Matković, K., Bühler, K., Waldner, M., Pugmire, D., Kozlíková, B., Ropinski, T., Ljung, P., Itoh, T., Gröller, E., & Krone, M. (2020). The moving target of visualization software for an increasingly complex world. *Computers & Graphics*, *87*, 12–29. DOI: 10.1016/j.cag.2020.01.005

Report, G. W. (2022-23). *The impact of COVID-19 and inflation on wages and purchasing power*. ILO. Retrieved from https://webapps.ilo.org/digitalguides/en-gb/story/globalwagereport2022-23#home

Reshi, I. A., & Sudha, D. T. (2023). THE GENDER PAY GAP AND ITS IMPACT ON WOMEN'S ECONOMIC EMPOWERMENT. *MORFAI JOURNAL*, *3*(1), 9–16. DOI: 10.54443/morfai.v3i1.742

Revella, A. (2015). *Buyer personas: how to gain insight into your customer's expectations, align your marketing strategies, and win more business*. John Wiley & Sons.

Riikkinen, M., & Pihlajamaa, M. (2022). Achieving a strategic fit in fintech collaboration–A case study of Nordea Bank. *Journal of Business Research, 152*, 461–472. DOI: 10.1016/j.jbusres.2022.05.049

Roberson, Q., King, E., & Hebl, M. (2020). Designing more effective practices for reducing workplace inequality. *Behavioral Science & Policy, 6*(1), 39–49. DOI: 10.1177/237946152000600104

Rodriguez, L., & Martinez, C. (2020). Federated learning for consumer behavior prediction in FMCG. *Journal of Retail Analytics, 6*(2), 122–136.

Rosário, A. T., & Dias, J. C. (2023). How has data-driven marketing evolved: Challenges and opportunities with emerging technologies. *International Journal of Information Management Data Insights, 3*(2), 100203. DOI: 10.1016/j.jjimei.2023.100203

Rothberg, H. N., & Erickson, G. S. (2017). Big data systems: Knowledge transfer or intelligence insights? *Journal of Knowledge Management, 21*(1), 92–112. DOI: 10.1108/JKM-07-2015-0300

Roy, D. S. (2024). A Quintessential Conversation: Gender Pay Parity for India's Diverse Landscape. *India Leaders for Social Sectors*. Retrieved from https://indialeadersforsocialsector.com/gender-pay-parity-india-diverse-landscape/

Rozhkov, R. (2025). Working Smart: Generative AI's Potential to Boost Productivity in Russia https://www.forbes.ru/tekhnologii/537396-rabota-s-umom-kakov-potencial-generativnogo-ii-dla-rosta-proizvoditel-nosti-v-rossii

Rumelt, R. P. (1994). Foreword. In Hamel, G., & Heene, A. (Eds.), *Competence-based competition*. Wiley.

Russell, S., & Norvig, P. (2021). *Artificial intelligence: A modern approach* (4th ed.). Pearson.

Ryan, L. (2016). *The visual imperative: Creating a visual culture of data discovery*. Morgan Kaufmann.

Sacha, D., Stoffel, A., Stoffel, F., Kwon, B. C., Ellis, G., & Keim, D. A. (2014). Knowledge generation model for visual analytics. *IEEE Transactions on Visualization and Computer Graphics, 20*(12), 1604–1613. DOI: 10.1109/TVCG.2014.2346481 PMID: 26356874

Saha, A. (2013). An Assessment of Gender Discrimination in Household Expenditure on Education in India. *Oxford Development Studies, 41*(2), 220–238. DOI: 10.1080/13600818.2013.786694

Sahoo, S., Sarkar, K., & Kumar, A. (2024). Valuation of Unpaid Household Activities in India', Vol 59, Issue no. 39, September 28, 2024. *The Hindu.*

Sala, G. R., Barabuffi, S., Ferrigno, G., & Marcazzan, E. (2025). Revolutionizing business models through data-driven innovation: The case of Hudi. In *Building business models with machine learning* (pp. 205–226). IGI Global.

Salminen, J., Şengün, S., Santos, J. M., Jung, S. G., Nielsen, L., & Jansen, B. (2023). The choice of a persona: an analysis of why stakeholders choose a given persona for a design task. In *International Conference on Human-Computer Interaction* (pp. 288-310). Cham: Springer Nature Switzerland. DOI: 10.1007/978-3-031-48038-6_18

Samad, N., Das, P., Dilshad, S., Al Banna, H., Rabbani, G., Sodunke, T. E., Hardcastle, T. C., Haq, A., Afroz, K. A., Ahmad, R., & Haque, M. (2022). Women's empowerment and fertility preferences of married women: Analysis of demographic and health survey'2016 in Timor-Leste. *AIMS Public Health, 9*(2), 237–261. DOI: 10.3934/publichealth.2022017 PMID: 35634022

Sanchez, R. (2004). Understanding competence-based management: Identifying and managing five modes of competence. *Journal of Business Research, 57*(5), 518–532. DOI: 10.1016/S0148-2963(02)00318-1

Sanchez, R., Heene, A., & Thomas, H. (1996). Towards the theory and practice of competence-based competition. In Sanchez, R., Heene, A., & Thomas, H. (Eds.), *Dynamics of competence-based competition: theory and practice in the new strategic management* (pp. 1–35). Elsevier., DOI: 10.1016/S0024-6301(97)86598-3

Santoro, G., Bresciani, S., & Papa, A. (2020). Collaborative modes with cultural and creative industries and innovation performance: The moderating role of heterogeneous sources of knowledge and absorptive capacity. *Technovation, 92*, 102040. DOI: 10.1016/j.technovation.2018.06.003

Sarioguz, O., & Miser, E. (2024). Data-Driven Decision-Making: Transforming Management in the Information Age. *International Research Journal of Modernization in Engineering Technology and Science, 6*(02), 1642–1652.

Sarkar, A., & Paul, R. (2024). Artificial Intelligence in Fraud Detection and Financial Risk Mitigation : Future Directions and Business Applications. *International Journal For Multidisciplinary Research, 6*(October), 28496. Advance online publication. DOI: 10.36948/ijfmr.2024.v06i05.28496

Saxena, A., & Muneeb, S. M. (2024). Transforming Financial Services Through Hyper-Personalization: The Role of Artificial Intelligence and Data Analytics in Enhancing Customer Experience. In *AI-Driven Decentralized Finance and the Future of Finance* (pp. 19-47). IGI Global. DOI: 10.4018/979-8-3693-6321-8.ch002

Saxena, C. (2021). Effectiveness of advertisement: Traditional vs. new media. *Journal of Contemporary Issues in Business and Government*, *27*(1), 2447–2455. https://cibgp.com/au/index.php/1323-6903/article/view/719

Saxena, C., Khatri, B., & Khan, S. A. (2023). Factors Hindering Women Entrepreneurs' Access to Institutional Finance: An Empirical Study From the Banker Perspective. In Gupta, V. (Ed.), *Fostering Global Entrepreneurship Through Business Model Innovation* (pp. 101–114). IGI Global., DOI: 10.4018/978-1-6684-6975-0.ch004

Schmarzo, B. (2013). *Big Data: Understanding how data powers big business.* John Wiley & Sons.

Schneider, M. J., Jagpal, S., Gupta, S., Li, S., & Yu, Y. (2017). Protecting customer privacy when marketing with second-party data. *International Journal of Research in Marketing*, *34*(3), 593–603. DOI: 10.1016/j.ijresmar.2017.02.003

Schoemaker P. (1992)How to link strategic vision to core capabilities. Sloan Manage Rev. 2; 534(1): 67– 82.

Schröder, A. M. (2021). Unboxing The Algorithm: Understandability And Algorithmic Experience In Intelligent Music Recommendation Systems.

Schröder, K., Belavadi, P., Ziefle, M., & Calero Valdez, A. (2022). *The Pension Story - Data-Driven Storytelling with Pension Data* (pp. 404–415). DOI: 10.1007/978-3-031-06018-2_28

Schröder, K., Eberhardt, W., Belavadi, P., Ajdadilish, B., van Haften, N., Overes, E., Brouns, T., & Valdez, A. C. (2023). Telling stories with data–a systematic review. arXiv preprint arXiv:2312.01164

Schroeder, K., Ajdadilish, B., Henkel, A. P., & Calero Valdez, A. (2020). Evaluation of a Financial Portfolio Visualization using Computer Displays and Mixed Reality Devices with Domain Experts. *Proceedings of the 2020 CHI Conference on Human Factors in Computing Systems*, 1–9. https://doi.org/DOI: 10.1145/3313831.3376556

Schuurman, W. (2025). *Beyond transactions: How B2B platforms in construction progressively create and monetise value through data-driven value propositions* (Master's thesis, University of Twente, Netherlands). University of Twente Student Theses. https://essay.utwente.nl/id/eprint/98456

Sebastian, Y., Siew, E. G., & Orimaye, S. O. (2017). Emerging approaches in literature-based discovery: Techniques and performance review. *The Knowledge Engineering Review*, *32*, e12. DOI: 10.1017/S0269888917000042

Segel, E., & Heer, J. (2010). Narrative visualization: Telling stories with data. *IEEE Transactions on Visualization and Computer Graphics*, *16*(6), 1139–1148. DOI: 10.1109/TVCG.2010.179 PMID: 20975152

Sekarini, S., & Selvabaskar, S. (2024). AI-powered branding: enhancing consumer experience in emerging markets. In *Integrating AI-Driven Technologies Into Service Marketing* (pp. 19–48). IGI Global., DOI: 10.4018/979-8-3693-7122-0.ch002

Senquiz-Diaz, C. (2021). Transport infrastructure quality and logistics performance in exports. *Economics*, *9*(1), 107–124. DOI: 10.2478/eoik-2021-0008

Senthilnayaki, S., Prasad, R., & Krishnan, P. (2021). Advanced ML models for predicting consumer churn in FMCG. *International Journal of Machine Learning*, *12*(3), 233–248.

Sethi, P. (2024). Exploring the Gender Pay Gap in India: Assessing its Implications on Economic Growth and Development. *International Journal of Advance Research, Ideas and Innovations in Technology*. Retrieved from chrome-extension://efaidnbmnnnibpcajpcglclefindmkaj/https://www.ijariit.com/manu scripts/v10i3/V10I3-1161.pdf

Shankar, A., & Rishi, B. (2020). Convenience matter in mobile banking adoption intention? *Australasian Marketing Journal*, *28*(4), 273–285. DOI: 10.1016/j.ausmj.2020.06.008

Sharma, M. (n.d.). Pay transparency on the rise in India, 50% job postings include salary details. Retrieved from https://www.peoplematters.in/article/talent-acquisition/pay-transparency-on-the-rise-i n-india-50-job-postings-include-salary-details-37873

Sharma, A. (2024). *The Corporate Comeback: Strategies for Reintegrating Women in India's Workforce*. IIM Ahmedabad Press.

Sharma, H. (2018). Gender Pay Gap in India: A Sectoral and Regional Analysis. *Asian Review of Social Sciences*, *7*(2), 1–5. DOI: 10.51983/arss-2018.7.2.1438

Sharma, M., & Jha, A. (2022). Digital financial literacy among Indian college students: A cross-sectional study. *International Journal of Education and Development Using ICT*, *18*(1), 115–127.

Sharma, R., Mithas, S., & Kankanhalli, A. (2014). Transforming decision-making processes: A research agenda for understanding the impact of business analytics on organisations. *European Journal of Information Systems*, *23*(4), 433–441. DOI: 10.1057/ejis.2014.17

Shavazipour, B., López-Ibáñez, M., & Miettinen, K. (2021). Visualizations for decision support in scenario-based multiobjective optimization. *Information Sciences*, *578*, 1–21. DOI: 10.1016/j.ins.2021.07.025

Shchepilova, O. I., & Korol, M. V. (2020). Applying the Data Modeling Tools for the Gender Inequality Analysis in the IT-industry in Ukraine and Worldwide. *Bìznes Ìnform*, *9*(512), 165–171. DOI: 10.32983/2222-4459-2020-9-165-171

Sheiderman, B., & Plaisant, C. Strategies for evaluating information visualization tools: multi-dimensional in-depth long-term case studies. In Proceedings of the 2006 AVI workshop on BEyond time and errors: novel evaluation methods for information visualization (2006), pp. 1–7.

Sheth, J. N., Jain, V., Roy, G., & Chakraborty, A. (2022). AI-driven banking services: The next frontier for a personalised experience in the emerging market. *International Journal of Bank Marketing*, *40*(6), 1248–1271. DOI: 10.1108/IJBM-09-2021-0449

Shmueli, G., & Koppius, O. R. (2011). Predictive analytics in information systems research. *Management Information Systems Quarterly*, *35*(3), 553–572. DOI: 10.2307/23042796

Shouri, S., & Ramezani, R. (2025). A blockchain-based health insurance model enhanced with quadratic voting. *Health Informatics Journal*, *31*(2), 14604582251339422. Advance online publication. DOI: 10.1177/14604582251339422 PMID: 40314149

Shukla, S. (2021). A review of telecom reforms and policies in the Indian telecom market. *International Journal of Indian Culture and Business Management*, *22*(4), 482–503. DOI: 10.1504/IJICBM.2021.115003

Shukla, S., Bisht, K., Tiwari, K., & Bashir, S. (2023). Comparative study of the global data economy. In *Data economy in the digital age* (pp. 63–86). Springer Nature Singapore. DOI: 10.1007/978-981-99-7677-5_4

Sihotang, H. T., Vinsensia, D., Riandari, F., & Chandra, S. (2024). Data-driven corporate growth: A dynamic financial modelling framework for strategic agility. *International Journal of Basic and Applied Science*, *13*(2), 84–95. DOI: 10.35335/ijobas.v13i2.485

Silva, T. C., de Souza, S. R. S., Guerra, S. M., & Tabak, B. M. (2023). COVID-19 and bank branch lending: The moderating effect of digitalization. *Journal of Banking & Finance*, *152*, 106869. DOI: 10.1016/j.jbankfin.2023.106869

Singh, P. (2019). Tax revenue in India: Trends and issues. *Working Paper 448*. Institute for Social and Economic Change.

Singha, S. (2024). Navigating the Social Media Maze: Strategies for Effective Digital Marketing in a Fragmented Landscape. In *Changing Global Media Landscapes: Convergence, Fragmentation, and Polarization* (pp. 84-106). IGI Global.

Singh, G., & Kumar, A. (2022). Impact of Firm Created, and User generated Social Media Communications on Consumer-Brand Metrics of Smartphones during COVID-19. *Journal of Content. Community & Communication*, *15*(1), 147–162. DOI: 10.31620/JCCC.06.22/11

Singh, J., & Shukla, P. (2024). *Brand management: Principles and applications for effective branding*. Kogan Page Publishers.

Singh, P., & Pattanaik, F. (2020). Unfolding unpaid domestic work in India: Women's constraints, choices, and career. *Palgrave Communications*, *6*(1), 111. DOI: 10.1057/s41599-020-0488-2

Singh, S., & Srivastava, R. K. (2020). Understanding the intention to use mobile banking by existing online banking customers: An empirical study. *Journal of Financial Services Marketing*, *25*(3), 86–96. DOI: 10.1057/s41264-020-00074-w

Sintsova, E. A., & Vitsko, E. A. (2021). Current Development Trends in the Digital Currency Market. *Economics and Management*, *27*(7), 504–511. DOI: 10.35854/1998-1627-2021-7-504-511

Sisodiya, R., & Sharma, M. (2018). 4Ps and consumer buying behavior in FMCG marketing. *International Journal of Management Studies*, *5*(6), 44–52.

Slemrod, J. (2019). Tax compliance and enforcement. *Journal of Economic Literature*, *57*(4), 904–954. DOI: 10.1257/jel.20181437

Sloan, M. I. T. (2023). *Data is everybody's business: The fundamentals of data monetization* Retrieved October 10, 2023, from https://mitsloan.mit.edu/press/data-everybodys-business-fundamentals-data-monetization

Smith, J., & Brown, L. (2022). Supervised learning for consumer profile prediction in FMCG. *Artificial Intelligence in Business*, *9*(3), 145–163.

Smith, P. R., & Zook, Z. (2024). *Marketing communications: Integrating online and offline, customer engagement and digital technologies*. Kogan Page Publishers.

Smyth, E., & Steinmetz, S. (2008). Field of Study and Gender Segregation in European Labour Markets. *International Journal of Comparative Sociology*, *49*(4–5), 257–281. DOI: 10.1177/0020715208093077

Sprout Social. (2023). Why you need to speed up your social media response time (and how). https://sproutsocial.com/insights/social-media-response-time/

Srivastava, A. (2023) 'India-China trade: Low exports and not high imports is the real challenge for India', Global Trade Research Initiative. https://content.dgft.gov.in/Website/EPS.pdf

Srivastava, V., Kishore, S., & Dhingra, D. (2021). Technology and the future of customer experience. In *Crafting customer experience strategy* (pp. 91–116). Emerald Publishing Limited., DOI: 10.1108/978-1-83909-710-220211006

Statista (2023). Number of social network users of select social media platforms worldwide in 2019 and 2023. https://www.statista.com/statistics/1109866/number-social-media-users-worldwide-select-platforms/

Statista (2024). Most used social networks 2024, by number of users. https://www.statista.com/statistics/272014/global-social-networks-ranked-by-number-of-users/

Statista. (2023). *Global big data and analytics market* Retrieved April 29, 2025, from https://www.statista.com/statistics/551501/worldwide-big-data-business-analytics-revenue/

Stewart, H. (2023). Digital transformation security challenges. *Journal of Computer Information Systems*, *63*(4), 919–936. DOI: 10.1080/08874417.2022.2115953

Sudha, S., & Rajan, S. I. (1999). Female Demographic Disadvantage in India 1981–1991: Sex Selective Abortions and Female Infanticide. *Development and Change*, *30*(3), 585–618. DOI: 10.1111/1467-7660.00130 PMID: 20162850

Sun, Y., Chen, H., & Xu, P. (2019). Personalized promotions in FMCG using machine learning. *Journal of Business Analytics*, *2*(3), 179–194.

Svikhnushina, E., & Pu, P. (2024). Online vs Offline: A Comparative Study of First-Party and Third-Party Evaluations of Social Chatbots. *arXiv preprint arXiv:2409.07823.*

Syed, T. A., Aslam, H., Bhatti, Z. A., Mehmood, F., & Pahuja, A. (2024). Dynamic pricing for perishable goods: A data-driven digital transformation approach. *International Journal of Production Economics*, *277*, 109405. DOI: 10.1016/j.ijpe.2024.109405

Tableau. (2023). *Business intelligence case studies* Retrieved April 29, 2025, from https://www.tableau.com/learn/case-studies

Tadesse, B. (2024) 'How China overcame culture barrier', The Statesman. Accessed on 27 September, 2024. https://www.thestatesman.com/opinion/ how-china-overcame-culture-barrier-1503317440.html

TAdviser. (2023). *Big data (global market)* Retrieved April 29, 2025, from https://www.tadviser.ru/index.php/%D0%A1%D1%82%D0%B0%D1%82%D1%8C%D1%8F:%D0%91%D0%BE%D0%BB%D1%8C%D1%88%D0%B8%D0%B5_%D0%B4%D0%B0%D0%BD%D0%BD%D1%8B%D0%B5_(Big_Data)_%D0%BC%D0%B8%D1%80%D0%BE%D0%B2%D0%BE%D0%B9_%D1%80%D1%8B%D0%BD%D0%BE%D0%BA

Taghizadeh, H., Panahi, K., & Iranzadeh, S. (2021). The Impact of Personalization on Customers' Loyalty and the Intention to Use E-banking Services. *International Economics Studies*, *51*(2), 37–52. DOI: 10.22108/ies.2022.132161.1125

Taherdoost, H. (2021). Data collection methods and tools for research; a step-by-step guide to choose data collection technique for academic and business research projects. [IJARM]. *International Journal of Academic Research in Management*, *10*(1), 10–38.

Tambe, P., Hitt, L. M., & Brynjolfsson, E. (2020). The productivity effects of data-driven teams: Evidence from IT investments. *Management Information Systems Quarterly*, *44*(3), 1139–1168. DOI: 10.25300/MISQ/2020/15175

Taneja, N. K. (2024). *Air Travel Partnerships: How to Create Greater Value Through Collaboration*. Taylor & Francis. DOI: 10.4324/9781003483960

Tang, N., & Peter, P. C. (2015). Financial knowledge acquisition among the young: The role of financial education, information, and parental influence. *Journal of Financial Services Marketing*, *20*(1), 16–26. DOI: 10.1057/fsm.2015.1

Tariq, M. U. (2025). AI and work-life balance: Transforming employee wellbeing in the modern workplace. In Ahmed, E., Babar, A., Samad, A., Ahmed, R., & Beydoun, G. (Eds.), *Strengthening human relations in organizations with AI* (pp. 85–110). IGI Global. DOI: 10.4018/979-8-3693-6507-6.ch004

Tariq, M. U. (2025). AI-powered business process automation: Revolutionizing firm management. In Derbali, A. (Ed.), *AI, economic perspectives, and firm business management* (pp. 199–224). IGI Global. DOI: 10.4018/979-8-3693-7357-6.ch010

Tariq, M. U. (2025). Innovative business models: Integrating social, economic, and environmental goals in rural manufacturing. In Prabhakar, A., Yu, P., & Erokhin, V. (Eds.), *Rural social entrepreneurship development: Network-based manufacturing system model* (pp. 147–174). IGI Global. DOI: 10.4018/979-8-3693-7515-0.ch005

Tariq, M. U. (2025). Integrating ICT for enhanced organizational resilience: Strategies and case studies. In Carvalho, L., Reis, L., de Almeida Baptista Figueiredo, A. N., & Russo, N. (Eds.), *Leveraging technology for organizational adaptability* (pp. 59–80). IGI Global. DOI: 10.4018/979-8-3693-6045-3.ch004

Tasca, P. (n.d.). Digital Currencies : Principles, Trends, Opportunities, and Risks Summary : *Deutsche Bundesbank and ECUREX Research*, 1–110.

Teaching Excellence Lab (TEL). (2024) Market seizing for upskilling programs about GenAI for the educators. TEL GSOM SPbU. https://gsom.spbu.ru/en/about-gsom/faculty/tel/

Teece, D. J. (2017). (forthcoming). Profiting from innovation in the digital economy: Standards, complementary assets, and business models in the wireless world. *Research Policy*.

Temirgaliev, E., Dubolazov, V., Borremans, A., & Overes, E. (2021). *Digitalization in Logistics for Organizing an Automated Delivery Zone*. Russian Post Case., DOI: 10.1007/978-3-030-64430-7_12

Thaichon, P., & Quach, S. (Eds.). (2023). *Artificial intelligence for marketing management*. Routledge.

Theiri, S., & Alareeni, B. (2023). Perception of the digital transformation as a strategic advantage through the Covid 19 crisis? case of Tunisian banks. *Journal of Sustainable Finance & Investment*, *13*(1), 477–498. DOI: 10.1080/20430795.2021.1964809

Theodorakopoulos, L., & Theodoropoulou, A. (2024). Leveraging big data analytics for understanding consumer behavior in digital marketing: A systematic review. *Human Behavior and Emerging Technologies*, *2024*(1), 3641502. DOI: 10.1155/2024/3641502

Tidjani, C., & Madouri, A. (2024). Fintech, financial inclusion, and sustainable development in the African region. *Frontiers in Applied Mathematics and Statistics*, *10*, 1276218. DOI: 10.3389/fams.2024.1276218

Tiwari, V. (2024). Role of data analytics in business decision making. *Knowledgeable Research A Multidisciplinary Journal*, *3*(01), 18-27.

Tong, C., Roberts, R., Borgo, R., Walton, S., Laramee, R. S., Wegba, K., Lu, A., Wang, Y., Qu, H., Luo, Q., & Ma, X. (2018). Storytelling and visualization: An extended survey. *Information (Basel)*, *9*(3), 65. DOI: 10.3390/info9030065

Tran Xuan, Q., Truong, H. T., & Vo Quang, T. (2023). Omnichannel retailing with brand engagement, trust and loyalty in banking: The moderating role of personal innovativeness. *International Journal of Bank Marketing*, *41*(3), 663–694. DOI: 10.1108/IJBM-07-2022-0292

Tripathi, S., Bachmann, N., Brunner, M., & Jodlbauer, H. (2024). Preparedness for data-driven business model innovation: A knowledge framework for incumbent manufacturers. *Applied Sciences (Basel, Switzerland)*, *14*(8), 3454. DOI: 10.3390/app14083454

Trukhmanov, V. B., Pervushkina, E. A., Statuev, A. A., & et al. (2021). System of key performance indicators as a method for executive decision-making. *E3S Web of Conferences, 296*, Article 02003. DOI: 10.1051/e3sconf/202129602003

Tsindeliani, I. A., Proshunin, M. M., Sadovskaya, T. D., Popkova, Z. G., Davydova, M. A., & Babayan, O. A. (2022). Digital transformation of the banking system in the context of sustainable development. *Journal of Money Laundering Control*, *25*(1), 165–180. DOI: 10.1108/JMLC-02-2021-0011

Tucker, C. E., Neumann, N., & Whitfield, T. (2019). Frontiers: How effective is third-party consumer profiling? Evidence from field studies. *Marketing Science*, *38*(6), 918–926.

Tulcanaza-Prieto, A. B., Cortez-Ordoñez, A., & Lee, C. W. (2023). Influence of customer perception factors on AI-enabled customer experience in the Ecuadorian banking environment. *Sustainability (Basel)*, *15*(16), 12441. DOI: 10.3390/su151612441

Tuten, T. L. (2023). *Social media marketing*. Sage publications limited.

Ulwick, A. W., & Osterwalder, A. (2016). *Jobs to be done: theory to practice*. Idea by Press.

Upadhyay, U. D., Gipson, J. D., Withers, M., Lewis, S., Ciaraldi, E. J., Fraser, A., Huchko, M. J., & Prata, N. (2014). Women's empowerment and fertility: A review of the literature. *Social Science & Medicine*, *115*, 111–120. DOI: 10.1016/j.socscimed.2014.06.014 PMID: 24955875

Urbach, N., & Röglinger, M. (2019). Introduction to digitalization cases: how organizations rethink their business for the digital age. In *Digitalization cases* (pp. 1–12). Springer., DOI: 10.1007/978-3-319-95273-4_1

Vamsee, C. S., Rakesh, D., Prathyusha, I., Dinesh, B., & Bharathi, C. (2023, May). Demographic and psychographic customer segmentation for ecommerce applications. In *2023 2nd International Conference on Applied Artificial Intelligence and Computing (ICAAIC)* (pp. 615-622). IEEE. DOI: 10.1109/ICAAIC56838.2023.10140861

Van Ooijen, C., Ubaldi, B., & Welby, B. (2019). A data-driven public sector: Enabling the strategic use of data for productive, inclusive and trustworthy governance.

Varma, P., & Kaur, S. (2024). Does Fintech Foster Sustainable Finance? Evidence from Retail Banking in India. In Management for Sustainable Development (pp. 211-248). Apple Academic Press. DOI: 10.1201/9781003505754-10

Vassakis, K., Petrakis, E., & Kopanakis, I. (2017). Big data analytics: applications, prospects and challenges. *Mobile big data: A roadmap from models to technologies*, 3-20.

Verma, D., Kansra, P., & Khan, S. A. (2024). Apparent Advantages and Negative Facet of Block Chain in Banking Sector: An Innovative Theoretical Perspective. In Irfan, M., Muhammad, K., Naifar, N., & Khan, M. A. (Eds.), *Applications of Block Chain technology and Artificial Intelligence: Lead-ins in Banking, Finance, and Capital Market* (pp. 19–27). Springer International Publishing., DOI: 10.1007/978-3-031-47324-1_2

Vetrivel, S. C., Gomathi, T., Sowmiya, K. C., & Sabareeshwari, V. (2024). Customer-centric excellence in the marketing 6.0 era: Industry 6.0. In *Advanced Businesses in Industry 6.0* (pp. 192-219). IGI Global. DOI: DOI: 10.4018/979-8-3693-3108-8.ch013

Villar, A. S., & Khan, N. (2021). Robotic process automation in banking industry: A case study on Deutsche Bank. *Journal of Banking and Financial Technology*, *5*(1), 71–86. DOI: 10.1007/s42786-021-00030-9

Wagner, D. T., Rice, A., & Beresford, A. R. (2014). Device Analyzer: Large-scale mobile data collection. *Performance Evaluation Review*, *41*(4), 53–56. DOI: 10.1145/2627534.2627553

Walsh, J., Cunningham, A., Wark, S., Nowina-Krowicki, M., & Thomas, B. H. (2019, December). Narrative Visualisation of Simulations: Finding the Stories Within the Data. *El Sawah, S. (Ed.) MODSIM2019, 23rd International Congress on Modelling and Simulation.* DOI: 10.36334/modsim.2019.B3.walsh

Wang, C. (2024). Evaluating Supervised Learning Models for Fraud Detection : A Comparative Study of Classical and Deep Architectures on Imbalanced Transaction Data. *ArXiv Preprint ArXiv, Ml.*

Wang, Z., & Song, J. (2024). Data monetization pathways and complex dynamic game equilibrium analysis in the energy industry. *arXiv Preprint*. arXiv:2403.08082. https://arxiv.org/abs/2403.08082

Wang, C. L. (2021). New frontiers and future directions in interactive marketing: Inaugural Editorial. *Journal of Research in Interactive Marketing*, *15*(1), 1–9. DOI: 10.1108/JRIM-03-2021-270

Wang, C., Wang, H., Li, Y., Dai, J., Gu, X., & Yu, T. (2024). Factors influencing university students' behavioral intention to use generative artificial intelligence: Integrating the theory of planned behavior and AI literacy. *International Journal of Human-Computer Interaction*, •••, 1–23. DOI: 10.1080/10447318.2024.2383033

Wang, M. (2024). AI Technologies in Modern Taxation: Applications, Challenges, and Strategic Directions. *International Journal of Finance and Investment*, *1*(1), 42–46. DOI: 10.54097/v2kgty49

Wang, Z., Wei, G., Zhan, Y., & Sun, Y. (2017). Big data in telecommunication operators: Data, platform and practices. *Journal of Communications and Information Networks*, *2*(3), 78–91. DOI: 10.1007/s41650-017-0010-1

Wardana, M. A., Masliardi, A., Afifah, N., Sajili, M., & Kusnara, H. P. (2023). Unlocking purchase preferences: Harnessing psychographic segmentation, promotion and location strategies. *Jurnal Informatika Ekonomi Bisnis*, 713-719. DOI: 10.37034/infeb.v5i3.624

Weijers, M., Bastiaenen, C., Feron, F., & Schröder, K. (2021). Designing a Personalized Health Dashboard: Interdisciplinary and Participatory Approach. *JMIR Formative Research*, *5*(2), e24061. DOI: 10.2196/24061 PMID: 33560229

Wei, Y. M. (2025). A hybrid multi-criteria decision-making framework for the strategic evaluation of business development models. *Information (Basel)*, *16*(6), 454. DOI: 10.3390/info16060454

Westermeier, C. (2020). Money is data–the platformization of financial transactions. *Information Communication and Society*, *23*(14), 2047–2063. DOI: 10.1080/1369118X.2020.1770833

Williams, M., & Moser, T. (2019). The art of coding and thematic exploration in qualitative research. *International Management Review*, *15*(1), 45–55.

Williams, P., & Taylor, K. (2020). Long-term customer management in FMCG with ML. *The Journal of Consumer Research*, *47*(6), 1121–1135.

Wong, Y., Chan, R. Y., Leung, T., & Pae, J. H. (2008). Commitment and vulnerability in B2B relationship selling in the Hong Kong institutional insurance service industry. *Journal of Services Marketing*, *22*(2), 136–148. DOI: 10.1108/08876040810862877

World Economic Forum. (2025). *Global economic futures: Productivity in 2030* Retrieved April 29, 2025, from https://reports.weforum.org/docs/WEF_Global_Economic_Futures_Productivity_in_2030_2025.pdf

X matrix Hoshin Kanri – What, how, 7 steps planning process. (n.d.). Learntransformation. https://learntransformation.com/x-matrix-hoshin-kanri/

XMLLabs. (2022). *The best price parser of 2023* XMLDataFeed. Retrieved April 29, 2025, from https://xmldatafeed.com/luchshij-parser-czen-2022-goda-parsing-czen-s-sajtov-elektronnoj-kommerczii/

Xuan, Q. T., Truong, H. T., & Quang, T. V. (2023). The impacts of omnichannel retailing properties on customer experience and brand loyalty: A study in the banking sector. *Cogent Business & Management*, *10*(2), 2244765. DOI: 10.1080/23311975.2023.2244765

Xu, J., Yang, T., Zhuang, S., Li, H., & Lu, W. (2024). AI-Based Financial Transaction Monitoring and Fraud Prevention with Behaviour Prediction. *Preprints.Org*. DOI: 10.20944/preprints202407.1107.v1

Yadav, R., Yadav, M., & Nghiem, X. (2025). The influence of conversational AI on enhancing customer satisfaction in insurance claims handling. In IGI Global eBooks (pp. 489–504). DOI: 10.4018/979-8-3693-9944-6.ch023

Yadav, M., Khurana, R., Vihari, N. S., Mittal, A., Balodi, A., & Srivastava, A. P. (2023, November). Virtual reality in human resource management: Past, present and future trends. In *2023 International Conference on Recent Advances in Science and Engineering Technology (ICRASET)* (pp. 1-5). IEEE.

Yadav, S., Samadhiya, A., Kumar, A., Luthra, S., & Pandey, K. K. (2024). Nexus between fintech, green finance and natural resources management: Transition of BRICS nation industries from resource curse to resource blessed sustainable economies. *Resources Policy*, *91*, 104903. DOI: 10.1016/j.resourpol.2024.104903

Yadav, U. S., Tripathi, R., Rena, R., Khan, S. A., & Ghosal, I. (2025). (in press). Use and Effect of Fintech Awareness in Women for Sustainable Development in Small Industry during COVID-19 Pandemic: An Empirical Analysis with UTUAT model. *International Journal of Electronic Finance*. Advance online publication. DOI: 10.1504/IJEF.2025.10062118

Yasir, M. (2024). E-Rupee : Unlocking India ' s Digital Economy, Challenges, and. *South Asian Journal of Social Studies and Economics, 21*(July), 1–13. Advance online publication. DOI: 10.9734/sajsse/2024/v21i8860

Yeo, A. D., Deng, A., & Nadiedjoa, T. Y. (2020). The effect of infrastructure and logistics performance on economic performance: The mediation role of international trade. *Foreign Trade Review, 55*(4), 450–465. DOI: 10.1177/0015732520947676

Yıldırım, A. C., & Erdil, E. (2024). The effect of Covid-19 on digital banking explored under business model approach. *Qualitative Research in Financial Markets, 16*(1), 87–107. DOI: 10.1108/QRFM-08-2021-0142

Yildirim, H. S., Akci, Y., & Eksi, I. H. (2013). The effect of firm characteristics in accessing credit for SMEs. *Journal of Financial Services Marketing, 18*(1), 40–52. DOI: 10.1057/fsm.2012.28

Yu, B. (2024). Research on the Features and Functions of Bitcoin and Digital Currencies. *Proceedings of the 2nd International Conference on Management Research and Economic Development, 0*, 55–60. DOI: 10.54254/2754-1169/86/20240942

Yusuf, N., AlNouss, A., Baldacci, R., & Al-Ansari, T. (2024). Data-driven decision-making for flexible natural gas allocation under uncertainties: An agent-based modelling approach. *Energy Conversion and Management: X, 24*, 100734. DOI: 10.1016/j.ecmx.2024.100734

Zaid, M. A. K., Khan, M. F., Al-Mekhlafi, A. W. A. G. S., Al Koliby, I. S., Saoula, O., Saeed, H. A. E. M., & Mohammad, R. A. (2025). The future of green finance: How digital transformation and FinTech drive sustainability. *Discover Sustainability, 6*(1), 480. DOI: 10.1007/s43621-025-01356-w

Zakhidov, G. (2024). Economic indicators: Tools for analyzing market trends and predicting future performance. *International Multidisciplinary Journal of Universal Scientific Prospectives, 2*(3), 23–29.

Zhang, H., & Wang, D. (2023). Bridging the chasm: A network analysis of communication silos in data-intensive organizations. *Management Information Systems Quarterly, 47*(2), 789–820. DOI: 10.25300/MISQ/2023/16543

Zhang, X., Yue, W. T., Yu, Y., & Zhang, X. (2023). How to monetize data: An economic analysis of data monetization strategies under competition. *Decision Support Systems, 173*, 114012. DOI: 10.1016/j.dss.2023.114012

Zhang, Y. (2024). Discrimination against Women in the Workplace. *Journal of Education. Humanities and Social Sciences, 27*, 135–140. DOI: 10.54097/bg2b5g02

Zhao, Q., Wang, H., & Li, Y. (2023). Transfer learning for cross-market demand forecasting in FMCG. *Knowledge-Based Systems, 263*, 110322.

Zheng, W., & Wu, Y. (2022). Deep reinforcement learning for digital advertising in FMCG. *Journal of Marketing Analytics, 10*(2), 140–156.

Zhou, L., & Zhang, Q. (2023). Ensemble methods for FMCG demand forecasting. *Journal of Retail Analytics, 9*(1), 88–10.

Zhou, Q., Lim, F. J., Yu, H., Xu, G., Ren, X., Liu, D., Wang, X., Mai, X., & Xu, H. (2021). A study on factors affecting service quality and loyalty intention in mobile banking. *Journal of Retailing and Consumer Services, 60*, 102424. DOI: 10.1016/j.jretconser.2020.102424

Zhou, X., Lou, C., & Huang, X. (2025). When social media gets political: How message–platform match affects consumer responses to brand activism advertising. *Journal of Advertising, 54*(3), 342–358. DOI: 10.1080/00913367.2024.2347271

Zhu, M., Zhang, Y., Gong, Y., Xu, C., & Xiang, Y. (2024). *Enhancing Credit Card Fraud Detection : A Neural Network and SMOTE Integrated Approach.* ArXiv Preprint ArXiv.

Zhu, S., Sun, G., Jiang, Q., Zha, M., & Liang, R. (2020). A survey on automatic infographics and visualization recommendations. *Visual Informatics, 4*(3), 24–40. DOI: 10.1016/j.visinf.2020.07.002

olak, G., & Öztekin, Ö. (2021). The impact of COVID-19 pandemic on bank lending around the world. *Journal of Banking & Finance, 133*, 106207. DOI: 10.1016/j.jbankfin.2021.106207

About the Contributors

Olga Titovna Ergunova is currently an Associate Professor at the Higher School of Production Management at Peter the Great St. Petersburg Polytechnic University. With over 22 years of professional experience in management and marketing, including 14 years in academia, her expertise spans strategic management, project management, urban studies, tourism, sustainable development, and digital transformation. She has held various leadership roles, including President of the Ural Union of the Tourism Industry, and serves as an Expert at the Russian Academy of Sciences. Dr. Ergunova is a prolific researcher with 167 publications, including in the RSCI database, as well as indexed articles in Web of Science and Scopus. Her research interests focus on sustainable urban development, tourism, creative industries, and regional branding. She has received numerous awards, including recognitions for best practices in national relations and sustainable tourism. Additionally, she has led international and regional projects, including initiatives within the framework of the "SMART CITY 2030" program. Dr. Ergunova actively contributes to the development of academic and professional programs, organizing forums, master classes, and scientific-practical events to foster innovation and collaboration in the BRICS countries.

Tawheed Nabi is currently Assistant Professor at Mittal School of Business, Lovely Professional University, Punjab (India). Dr. Nabi received his Ph.D. degree from DOS in Economics, Karnatak University, Dharwad and has been UGC - UPE research fellow. His expertise entails areas like International Trade, Agriculture Economics and Business Models. He has published his research ideas in journals, edited volumes, conference proceedings in the areas of International Economics, Agricultural Economics and Business Models. He has presented several papers in International and National level seminars and participated in various workshops and FDP's. He has also guided two PhD Scholars in economics and management.

Pooja Kansra is presently working as a Professor of Economics at Mittal School of Business, Lovely Professional University, Phagwara, Punjab (India). She has a teaching experience of fourteen years. Her areas of research include health economics, labor economics, gender economics, insurance, and informal sector. She is an avid researcher and presented papers in various national and international conferences. She is the recipient of several best paper awards from reputed institutions such MAIMS, IBS, NIT Srinagar, Delhi University and Lovely Professional University. She has to her credit various research papers published in Scopus Indexed Journals including Journal of Consumer Behavior (Wiley, ABDC A category), Economic and Political Weekly (EPW), Journal of Health Management (Sage Publications). Global Business Review (Sage Publications), International Journal of Diabetes in Developing Countries (Springer Publications), Health and Population: Perspectives and Issues (MOHFW) etc. She has published several books on the various aspects of health economics. She is an editorial board member/ reviewer in several national and international journals.

Utkarsh Gupta is an AI and ML specialist with over 8 years of experience leveraging advanced analytics and machine learning to drive impactful business outcomes. Based in New York City, Utkarsh leads a team of data scientists and data engineers at LatentView Analytics, where he collaborates with a Fortune 500 client to design and deploy advanced machine learning solutions that optimize customer acquisition, reduce churn, and enhance operational efficiency. His expertise spans predictive modeling, time series forecasting, and delivering strategic insights that have significantly enhanced client revenue and operational strategies. With a strong academic background in Business Analytics (MBA from the University of Connecticut) and Engineering, Utkarsh has a track record of creating scalable AI-driven methodologies and generating measurable impact through his work at LatentView Analytics

***

Ekaterina Abushova, Candidate of Economics, Associate Professor at Peter the Great St.Petersburg Polytechnic University. Research areas: operational management.

Olga Akimova is an Associate Professor at the English Language Department of Lomonosov MSU Business School. She holds a PhD in Philology from Moscow Pedagogical State University and an MA in Cultural Management from the University of Manchester. With extensive teaching experience in higher education, she currently delivers courses in Critical Thinking, Digital Intelligence, and Business English.

Her research explores issues at the intersection of linguistics, digital education, and artificial intelligence, focusing on AI literacy, generative AI in the classroom, and gender bias in large language models. Olga Akimova is also a methods specialist at the AI Lab Method.GSOM at Saint Petersburg University, where she designs and conducts workshops on AI for educators. Her professional recognition includes a Letter of Gratitude from the Ministry of Science and Higher Education of the Russian Federation and awards for her teaching and methodological work.

Azamat Ali is an Assistant Professor in the School of Liberal and Creative Arts (Journalism and Mass Communication) at Lovely Professional University, Punjab, India. He holds an M.Phil. and Ph.D. from the Central University of Gujarat, Gandhinagar. He also earned a B.Sc. in Physics (Hons.) from Aligarh Muslim University, and M.Sc. in Science Communication from Devi Ahilya University, Indore, and a PG Diploma in Broadcast Technology from Jamia Millia Islamia, New Delhi. Dr. Ali research interests area emerging technologies, development communication, health and science communication. He has made significant contributions to these fields, publishing over 25 research papers in reputed journals and contributing to several Scopus based book chapters. In addition to his publications, Dr. Ali is attended numerous national, international conferences and seminars. His work continues to bridge the gap between science and technology development and innovation, with a focus on leveraging emerging technologies for societal benefits.

Abu Bashar (Ph.D) is currently working as an Assistant Professor in digital marketing at gulf university, kingdom of Bahrain. He was also associated as consultant in a leading IT firm in the Kingdom of Bahrain and MTC (Micro Training Centre) as an instructor for Digital marketing and allied subjects. His area of research is in online consumer behaviour – especially impulse buying behaviour, sustainable marketing practices and consumer behaviour. He has published several articles in international journals of repute such International Journal of Sustainable Development and Planning, Review of Financial Economics, International Journal of Electronic Marketing and Retailing, International Journal of Business Information Systems, International Journal of Electronic Business, International Hospitality Review, Journal of Open Innovation Technology Market and Complexity, Qualitative Research in Financial Markets, Journal of Risk and Financial Management, Risks, etc. He has presented several papers in international conferences organised by leading universities and institutions such as UoB (University of Bahrain), JMI (Jamia Millia Islamia), IEEE etc. School of management, IMS Unison University, Dehradun, India.

Aleksandra Bordunos is a Senior Lecturer at the Graduate School of Management of St. Petersburg University (GSOM SPbU). With extensive professional and academic experience, her expertise encompasses strategic human resourse management, digiraluzation in HR, AI in education, and personnel productivity management. She actively contributes to the development of management education, participating in the design and implementation of educational programs and corporate training. Aleksandra Bordunos is an experienced consultant and trainer for major Russian and international companies, specializing in employee value proposition, AI literacy and corporate culture development. She is actively involved in the academic life of GSOM, organizing and moderating expert discussions about AI in education and human resourse management, fostering dialogue between the academic and business communities.

Ilya Bystrov is currently working as an associate professor at the American University of Phnom Penh, Cambodia. His academic experience exceeds 25 years, including 14 years internationally, during which he regularly occupied academic leadership positions from a program chair to vice-rector for international relations. Alongside that, his industry experience ranges from marketing-related positions in telecommunication and logistics companies to leadership roles in a consulting company and entrepreneurial experience. His research interests are in the areas of sustainable development, higher education, internationalization, and management.

Michael M. Caballero is an accomplished leader and educator with extensive experience in higher education institutions. A strong advocate of academic excellence, he earned his undergraduate and master's degrees in business administration from Manuel L. Quezon University and in 2024, he completed his Ph.D. in Business Management at Lyceum of the Philippines University Manila. Dr. Caballero is recognized for his expertise in teamwork, teaching, and effective communication. He actively serves as an officer of the Philippine Council of Deans and Educators in Business (PCDEB) and as an adviser of LPU YFACT and LPU ManSoc, he is committed to nurturing and mentoring future business leaders. Dr. Caballero is also a prolific researcher, with publications focusing on leadership, management, and marketing.

Manmohan Chaudhry is working as an Associate Professor at K R Mangalam University in School of Management and Commerce. She is a BA, MBA and holds a PhD from Aligarh Muslim University, Aligarh in Management. She has over 13 years of experience and has published research papers in coveted national and international journals. Her current research interest are focused on Marketing, SDGs and Service marketing.

Piali Haldar earned her MBA degree from the Institute of Rural Management Anand and completed her PhD at Birla Institute of Technology, Mesra. Her core areas of specialization include rural marketing, rural development, branding strategy, and consumer behaviour. With over 20 years of experience in academia and research, she has published extensively in renowned journals listed in ABDC and Scopus. She has authored one textbook on Marketing and edited four academic books. She has presented her research at numerous national and international conferences and has contributed more than 50 papers to reputed journals, edited volumes, and conference proceedings.

Shamily Jaggi cleared UGC-NET in June 2012 and completed PhD (Management) from I. K. Gujral Punjab Technical University (Jalandhar) in 2018. She is having keen interest in marketing topics like advertisements, consumer buying behaviour, celebrity endorsement, retail management, branding etc. She presented her reseach papers in 8 National conferences and 8 International conferences. She published 17 research papers in different International jourals, edited books and conference proceedings with ISBN/ISSN nos.To update herself with latest softwares and analytical techniques, she keep on attending different workshops within or outside the university. She guided 50 plus capstone mentees and currently supervising the work of 2 research scholars.

Ksenia Kaisheva, Senior Lecturer, Head of the Department of Foreign Languages in the Professional Sphere, Director of the Center for International Youth Projects and Initiatives, Saint Petersburg State University of Industrial Technologies and Design, Saint Petersburg, Russian Federation,

Shad Ahmad Khan is a seasoned academic leader with over 14 years of experience in teaching, research, and quality assurance, currently serving as senior faculty and Chair of the Research Committee at the University of Buraimi, Oman. Recognized among the top 2% of scientists worldwide, he has published 75+ Scopus-indexed papers. His leadership has driven a 100% increase in research output, fostered international collaborations, and advanced institutional quality frameworks. A sought-after speaker at global forums including the QS Higher Ed Summit and the Philippine Council of Deans and Educators in Business Annual Conference, Dr. Khan brings a visionary approach to academic governance, sustainability, and research innovation. He is a productive member of the international academic community as an Associate Editor, doctoral supervisor, and visiting professor at Filipino, Nigerian, Malaysian, Swiss, and Maltese universities/Institutions.

Viliyan Krastev, Doctor of Social Sciences (DSc), Candidate of Geographical Sciences (PhD), Associate Professor of the Department of Economy and Tourism Organization at the University of Economics in Varna.

Neha Kukrety is an Associate Professor of Finance at Shoolini University, Solan, Himachal Pradesh. Formerly associated with DBS Global University, she brings a strong blend of academic depth and real-world banking experience to her role. With over nine years in the financial services industry and 9 years in academia, she has held leadership positions at top institutions including Edelweiss Capital Finance, IndusInd Bank, Kotak Mahindra Bank, HDFC Bank, and ICICI Bank. In 2021, Neha transitioned from the banking sector to academia, where she now applies her industry insights to teaching and research. She holds a PGDM in Banking & Finance from Manipal University, along with M.Com and B.Com (Honours) degrees in Finance from Banaras Hindu University. Her Ph.D. in Digital Finance from DIT University. Her research interests center on fintech, blockchain applications in banking, and digital finance, with her work published in ABDC-listed and Scopus-indexed journals. Neha is also a member of the American Finance Association and the Indian Institute of Banking and Finance (IIBF). Passionate about bridging the gap between industry and academia, Neha aims to contribute meaningfully to the rapidly evolving field of financial technology and digital transformation in finance.

Ajay Kumar is working as an Assistant Professor in DAV University, Jalandhar, Punjab. He has published 2 copyrights, 3 patents, book chapters and research papers in UGC listed Journals. He attended many national as well as international conferences.

Arvind Kumar is currently a research fellow at the Stephen Young Institute for International Business, University of Strathclyde, United Kingdom. Additionally, he serves as an Assistant Professor in the Marketing domain at the School of Management, NIT Rourkela, India and holds a research fellow position at the School of Management, Shinawatra University in Thailand. He has received his Ph.D. in Marketing from Faculty of Management Studies (FMS), University of Delhi and has published his research in Marketing Intelligence & Planning, International Journal of Consumer Studies, Young Consumers, Journal of Business-to-Business Marketing, International Journal of Public Administration, Journal of Public Affairs, Journal of Cleaner Production, and Journal of Global Marketing.

N Mahesh Kumar is working as Deputy Registrar at Narsee Monjee Institute of Management Studies, (NMIMS), Hyderabad. He is a doctorate in Commerce from the Jayoti Vidyapeeth Women's University, Rajasthan. He completed his Master's in

Commerce at Osmania University, Hyderabad. He served Gedu College of Business Studies, Royal University of Bhutan as Assistant Professor.

Dev Kumar Mandal, currently serves as an Assistant Professor in the Department of Management at Brainware University, Kolkata. Before this, he worked at ICRA Analytics Ltd and Shriram Finance Ltd. He holds an MBA in Finance and a Bachelor of Commerce degree from Vidyasagar University. Additionally, he has successfully cleared the UGC NET and WB SET examinations in Management.

Arun Mittal holds a Ph.D. in marketing from BIT, Mesra and ECPDM from IIM-Kashipur. He has 18 years of experience teaching Multivariate Data Analysis, Marketing Research, Marketing Analytics, and Digital Marketing. Dr. Mittal has published about 40 research papers in the journals of repute including papers in SCOPUS, ABDC and SSCI indexed, UGC CARE Journals, and Edited books with International Publishers. He has authored and edited 10 books. Dr. Mittal has conducted around 100+ faculty development programs, workshops and sessions in research methodology and data analysis. Dr. Mittal is a Project Director and Co-Project Director in the Projects sponsored by ICSSR and MGNCRE. He is a life member of the Indian Commerce Association and the Indian Society for Training and Development. He is also a recipient of the BIT Faculty Appreciation Award (BITFAA) 2025.

N. Suresh served as an Assistant Professor at Gedu College of Business Studies, Royal University of Bhutan. He obtained his Master's in Commerce from Osmania University, India, and is currently a Research Scholar at Jayoti Vidyapeeth Women's University, Rajasthan.

Olga Nikiforova is an Associate Professor and Head of the Department of Organizational Behavior and Human Resource Management at the Graduate School of Management, Saint Petersburg University. An expert in strategic HR management, organizational behavior, and generational research, she has over fifteen years of experience in higher education and executive training. She holds a PhD in Sociology. Her research interests lie at the intersection of human capital development, motivation theory, and intergenerational dynamics in the labor market. She serves as an expert for major Russian business media on labor market trends. Her recent projects include the development of the master's program Strategic Human Resource Management at the Graduate School of Management, Saint Petersburg University, a research study on National approaches of HRM and Sustainable HRM. Olga Nikiforova also works for MBA and EMBA, and organizes national forums and HR conferences.

Ed Overes, After a successfull career as business manager, Ed started his academic career in 2010. Since then, he has become a well respected expert for teaching business related courses. Student evaluations show his great enthusiasm, creativity and passion. In 2014 Ed was invited to become professor Strategic Management in Saint Petersburg. Later he extended his work to Brazil, Germany, Egypt. Within Zuyd University Ed is also member of the Research Center Human Data Interaction – Data Visualisation, specialisising in business process visualisation as well as data storytelling. Ed has published in various magazines and also regularly is a speaker at international conferences.

Muzamil Rashid is a dedicated research scholar at Lovely Professional University, pursuing a Ph.D. in International Trade. His research focuses on trade dynamics, economic integration, and global market trends, with an emphasis on empirical analysis and policy implications. His work aims to provide data-driven insights for enhancing economic cooperation and shaping trade strategies. Actively participating in academic discussions, conferences, and collaborative research, he contributes to the broader discourse on international trade.

Vishal Sarin completed his Ph.D. in Economics from Punjabi University, India and researching on International Trade, Competitiveness and trade integration. He is passionate about research and has published extensively in reputable international journals including ABDC Ranking and SCOPUS listed journals. Currently he is employed as Professor of Economics in Mittal School of Business (ACBSP accreditation by the USA, and the 2nd ranked in the Management field in India), India and also heading Department of Economics at Mittal School of Business, Lovely Professional University. Author also holds one copyright on 'Talent Management Index'. He is also a member of Doctoral Board for Economics and evaluated many research scholars at various platforms.

Sergey Y. Sevryukov is an expert in digital transformation and data systems at Saint Petersburg State University with a background in Applied Mathematics. His work in data and AI includes developing academic programs, such as the "Introduction to Data Science" course and a Master's program in "Artificial Intelligence Technologies and Big Data," alongside specialized courses on database optimization. In key leadership roles, he has spearheaded the creation of large-scale data systems, including a student data management platform, an analytical system for education quality, and the "Notary Practice" knowledge base. He is currently leading the development of the "Digital Student Profile," an analytical system for data-driven decision-making in education, and actively researches the application of AI in education at the SPbSU Center for Artificial Intelligence and Data Science.

Animesh Kumar Sharma is a Research Scholar at Mittal School of Business, Lovely Professional University, Phagwara, Punjab, India, and working as Manager - Marketing and Corporate Communication with Vatika Business Centres Private Limited (A Vatika Group Company), Gurugram, India. His research interest areas include digital marketing, social media marketing, search engine marketing, artificial intelligence, machine learning, data analytics, and the applications of technology in business.

Rahul Sharma is a highly accomplished professor of Marketing with over 14 years of experience in academia. He has a Ph.D. in Marketing and has published over 15 articles in high-quality journals in the field. Dr. Sharma's research interests include consumer behavior, business analytics, and digital marketing. In addition to his research, Dr. Rahul is also a highly sought-after resource person in various faculty development programs.

Nirmal Singh, is working as a Professor in Economics at Sri Guru Gobind Singh College of Commerce, University of Delhi having twenty-two years of teaching and research experience. His research interests are in the areas of Indian Economy, Development Economics, Foreign Direct Investment, WTO and Indian Agriculture. Dr. Singh has presented several research papers in National and International Seminars and received two Best Paper Awards in National Seminars held at University of Delhi. His research/policy papers have been published in reputed journals and books. Recently, he completed the ICSSR Project under the Impactful Policy Research in Social Sciences (IMPRESS) Scheme. He has received the Best Paper Presentation Award in the Global Innovation in Management and Social Sciences (29th – 30th November 2024), Organised by Lumbini Banijya Campus. Butwal, Nepal on his paper titled “Economic Development through Green Entrepreneurship Practices: An Empirical Study in the Indian Economic Settings”.

Dimitrie Stoica, PhD in Management, is an assistant professor at the Faculty of Economics and Business Administration, “Dunărea de Jos” University of Gala i, Romania. He has published research papers in prestigious journals such as Management Decision, Journal of Cleaner Production, Foods. Additionally, he is the co-author of a patent application and has received numerous awards, including gold and silver medals and special prizes at invention fairs. His research focuses on food waste management, university reputation management, food engineering, and food packaging.

Muhammad Usman Tariq has more than 16+ year’s experience in industry and academia. He has authored more than 200+ research articles, 110+ case studies, 150+ book chapters and several books other than 4 patents. He is founder and CEO of The Case HQ, a unique repository for courses, narrative and video case studies. He has been working as a consultant and trainer for industries representing six sigma, quality, health and safety, environmental systems, project management, and information security standards. His work has encompassed sectors in aviation, manufacturing, food, hospitality, education, finance, research, software and transportation. He has diverse and significant experience working with accreditation agencies of ABET, ACBSP, AACSB, WASC, CAA, EFQM and NCEAC. Additionally, Dr. Tariq has operational experience in incubators, research labs, government research projects, private sector startups, program creation and management at various industrial and academic levels. He is Certified Higher Education Teacher from Harvard University, USA, Certified Online Educator from HMBSU, Certified Six Sigma Master Black Belt and has been awarded PFHEA, SFSEDA, SMIEEE, and CMBE.

Ivan Volchkov, Assistant Lecturer at Peter the Great St.Petersburg Polytechnic University.

Elizaveta Zotova, Candidate of Economics, Associate Professor at Peter the Great St.Petersburg Polytechnic University. Research areas: Digital business technologies.

Index

Symbols

A

B

C

D

E

F

G

I

K

M

N

P

R

S

T

U

www.ingramcontent.com/pod-product-compliance
Lightning Source LLC
LaVergne TN
LVHW061528290926
849162LV00004B/714